FINDING THE FOURTH BEATLE - CD 1

To help further understand the various drummers who played with The Quarrymen through to The Beatles, we decided to produce an optional double CD featuring as many of the 23 drummers as possible, whether the recordings were with John, Paul and George, or with another band. Some of these tracks have been analysed within the book, so you can read the analysis by our experts, and decide whether you agree with them, or not.

More information from www.thefourthbeatle.com

CD 1

TRACK	ARTIST	DRUMMER
1. In Spite of all the Danger	The Quarrymen	Colin Hanton
2. Tommy Moore interview (BBC)		Tommy Moore
3. It Ain't Necessarily So	Ian and the Zodiacs	Cliff Roberts
4. St. Louis Blues	Ernie Mack's Band	Norman Chapman
5. My Bonnie	Tony Sheridan and the Beat Brothers	Pete Best
6. Who Do You Think You Are	Candlewick Green	Alan Leyland
7. Like Dreamers Do	The Beatles	Pete Best
8. Money (That's What I Want)	The Beatles	Pete Best
9. To Know Her Is To Love Her	The Beatles	Pete Best
10. Memphis Tennessee (1)	The Beatles	Pete Best
11. Till There Was You	The Beatles	Pete Best
12. Sure To Fall (In Love With You)	The Beatles	Pete Best
13. Besame Mucho (1)	The Beatles	Pete Best
14. The Love of The Loved	The Beatles	Pete Best
15. Hello Little Girl	The Beatles	Pete Best
16. Three Cool Cats	The Beatles	Pete Best
17. September in The Rain	The Beatles	Pete Best
18. Take Good Care of My Baby	The Beatles	Pete Best
19. Crying, Waitin', Hoping	The Beatles	Pete Best
20. The Sheik of Araby	The Beatles	Pete Best
21. Searchin'	The Beatles	Pete Best

FINDING THE FOURTH BEATLE

Written by: David Bedford and Garry Popper

Edited by Mark Naboshek

Designed and assembled by Paul Skellett

Produced by: Garry Popper

Printed by Prime Group in the UK

Published 2018 by GBF

ISBN No: 978-3-7323-9842-3

This book is dedicated:

By David: to Alix Bedford; Philippa, Ryan and Noah Kilroe; Lauren, and Ashleigh Bedford, and to the memory of Colin Bedford, Judy Place and Alexander Dowbiggin

And

By Garry: to my wife, Linda, my brother, Gordon, and my daughters, Marisa, Rosalyn and Anita for keeping me going after my stroke. Much love and kisses
xxx

ACKNOWLEDGEMENTS

No author works in isolation. To do justice to a work on this scale requires a good researchers and the input of reliable witnesses, so it is fitting to acknowledge the friendships and associations that David and Garry share with some of
Liverpool's legends of the Merseybeat and Beatles era.

During their rise to fame, The Beatles didn't always give due credit to the many contributors who helped shape their success either, mostly due to Brian Epstein's efforts to re-invent their story, with himself at the 'Eppycentre' of it all. So we feel it's only right to mention some here, because without them, there might not have been a Mersey scene at all, or The Beatles – or this work!

People like Johnny Hutchinson, Bill Harry, Sam Leach, Dave Forshaw, Billy Hatton, Wally Hill, Beryl Marsden, Faron, Arty Davies, Joe Ankrah, Dave Jamieson, Freda Kelly, Michael Hill, Billy Kinsley, Ted "Kingsize" Taylor, Lee Curtis, Billy Butler, Alistair Taylor, Allan Williams, The Quarrymen, Howie Casey, Chas Newby, Andy White, Tony Barrow and not forgetting the late Geoff Nugent and Harry Prytherch, to name just a few. These are the old guard: the musicians, Beatles friends, promoters and publicists; the 'other guys' so often ignored or airbrushed out of Brian Epstein's carefully stage-managed Beatles story. We were privileged to talk privately and record most of them over many years. Their personal insights have added so much to the making of this book.

We also could not have written this book without the research skills of Ed Jackson, who has been working with David since 2010 after Liddypool was published to solve the mystery of the sacking of Pete Best, and Henrik Enevoldsen for his research for the Jimmie Nicol Story. Also a thank you to Jim Berkenstadt for his assistance, as well as the many family and friends of those people featured in this book, too numerous to mention here. Our expert drummers and those providing legal advice, especially David Harris and Peter Bounds, have also contributed greatly to the book.

Last, but by no means least, the two people without whom we could not have produced this book. Firstly, we owe a great debt of thanks to Mark Naboshek, whose tireless work in editing this book has been invaluable in producing Finding the Fourth Beatle. We couldn't have done it without him. And secondly, to Paul Skellett, for his unique art and design skills in putting the book together. Thank you both.

David Bedford

Garry Popper

ABOUT THE AUTHORS

Liverpool runs through David Bedford and Garry Popper's veins like the River Mersey itself. Coming from the birthplace of The Beatles also gives them big advantages over other writers in their understanding of the nature of the city, its people and its music history, hence Finding The Fourth Beatle brings with it an unrivalled wealth of 'insider' knowledge from first hand sources, local contacts and friends in the music community.

David Bedford missed the longest party in music history by a whisker, but since 2000, his life's great mission has been to record it honestly, filling in the missing parts, and in the process demolishing some of the many myths and half-truths that abound. Born in 1965 just after the golden Merseybeat era, he grew up in the heart of Liverpool's Dingle district where his family lived within a drum beat of Ringo's home in Madryn Street. They were both as close to the river as it gets without falling in. It was this closeness and familiarity that drew David into the successful campaign to save Ringo's birthplace from demolition.

The Dingle was also where he met and married his wife, Alix. She was just 17... well, you know what I mean? Today, she's the boss and they live in Mossley Hill near Penny Lane not far from Dovedale School where his three daughters attended. It was also where John Lennon and George Harrison began their education many years earlier.

At the age of 35, serious illness forced David to retire early. The alternative was to join a band, go to jail, or take up writing to keep idle hands busy. But write about what? This was the question. So began what has since become a lifetime's quest to discover as much as he could about The Beatles, Merseybeat and Liverpool.

It's been a long and winding road since then, starting when he began writing for the London Beatles Fan Club (now the British Beatles Fan Club) in 2000. The experience opened up a new career as a dedicated researcher and writer, resulting in the publication of his much applauded book, *Liddypool – Birthplace of The Beatles* in 2009. Its success triggered David's passion to uncover even more about The Beatles early history, and four more years of diligent research resulted in his second mighty book, *The Fab One Hundred and Four* in 2013. He also co-authored *The Beatles Book* with Hunter Davies, Spencer Leigh and Keith Badman in 2016.

Since then, David's passion has turned him into a well-respected guest speaker at Beatles events in the U.S.A, the U.K and Europe. He has also been appointed as an official cultural ambassador for The Beatles Story Museum in Liverpool, as well as being a highly valued historical researcher for Get Back Films and producer Garry Popper. It was this collaboration which led to a eureka moment when Garry realized that David had highlighted one of the most defining aspects of Beatle history that had never been fully documented in a unified account: the struggle to find and keep a steady drummer in The Beatles. A flurry of research confirmed they had stumbled on a totally unique story and *Finding the Fourth Beatle* was born.

Garry Popper was born in 1948 in Liverpool's quiet district of Knotty Ash. Famous for its jam butty mines and comedian Ken Dodd, Knotty Ash nestles between West Derby village and the outlands of Page Moss and Huyton. It also played host to a vast tented transit camp for American and British Empire troops in both world wars.

Some of Garry's fondest memories are of the mid 1950s, with Saturday afternoons filled with the sound of music echoing from his sister's blue Dansette record player, plus the battery powered wireless (radio) which became a family focal point in the evenings when the Jack Jackson show and Radio Luxembourg whined to life as the tuner homed in. Weeoo.. weeooooo!. Wonderful!

Garry was also a frequent visitor to his Uncle Ed's café, which was a haven for Rockers and Teddy Boys alike in the late 1950s, thanks to a Wurlitzer jukebox stacked with the latest chart hits from, mostly from America. The jukebox attracted teenagers like bees to honey and gave Garry his first real insight into how music unites different tribes.

Music was still only a pastime, because his growing artistic talent was to take him to the legendary Liverpool Art High School. Located in the grand Victorian terraces of Gambier Terrace, directly opposite the Anglican Cathedral, the Art High School became a launch pad for many artists and musicians in the 1960s, including Stuart Sutcliffe, Cynthia Lennon and Bill Harry. A few doors away John Lennon and Stuart shared a flat, which quickly became a student hangout for Rod Murray, John Lennon, Bill Harry, Cynthia, and many others.

Garry's journey into the world of art and design led to Liverpool College of Art across the road in Hope Street, next door to the Liverpool Institute where Paul, George and Neil Aspinall were students. He studied graphic design and photography, and also developed an interest in writing, inspired by his poet tutor, Roger McGough (of Scaffold fame) and Adrian Henri. His career eventually took him away from Liverpool in the 1970s, beginning as a graphic designer and progressing in turn as a Creative Director, Head of corporate film, Marketing Manager and Marketing Director before going it alone as a design consultant. During this time he also indulged in staging dance events and bought two hospitality coaches, playing host to George Harrison, Grand Prix legend Jackie Stewart, Paul McCartney's band Wings and many others in what he fondly remembers was his own magical mystery tour!

The journey came full circle in 2010 when he returned to Liverpool to set up Get Back Films with partners John Adams and Roger Appleton, to produce the music documentary, *Get Back – The Story of The City That Rocked the World* in 2012. He has just produced Looking for Lennon and in addition to co-writing and producing this book, he is busy preparing the next documentary – something called *Finding the Fourth Beatle*.

FINDING THE FOURTH BEATLE

CONTENTS

FOREWORD

by Sam Leach

Sam Leach was a legendary promoter on the Merseybeat scene, and a great friend to The Beatles. Anyone who takes a critical look back on the formative years of The Beatles will discover Sam at the very epicentre of the story. This savvy promoter was among the very first to see their potential, taking them from the smaller Liverpool clubs and booking them into the larger venues like the Tower Ballroom where their unique style of rock 'n' roll could be heard by a greater number of locals. Sam worked with a lot of the drummers featured in this book, and he offered us his thoughts on them in his last interview, given shortly before his death at the end of 2016. He was a dear friend, and an essential part of Beatles, and Merseybeat, history. David Bedford and Garry Popper

"I remember when Lonnie Donegan came to Liverpool, and I was up on the stage by the drums, so Lonnie said, 'Can you give me a drum roll?' So I picked up the snare drum, and rolled it along the floor towards him. We had a good laugh at it, and that was as close as I got to playing a drum roll!

"I loved rock 'n' roll, and was one of the first promoters working with the Liverpool bands in clubs like the Cassanova Club, the Iron Door, and of course at New Brighton's Tower Ballroom. They told me I was mad to try and promote groups at the Tower, but I knew it could work. I laid on buses so that everyone could stay to the end, and those Operation Big Beats became the best concerts ever on Merseyside, with all the top groups.

"I got to work with the top drummers. Johnny Hutch had amazing power in his beat, and the quality of the sound from The Big Three was incredible. He was the best drummer in Liverpool. There was nobody like him, and he could sing, too. He had perfect timing and was so powerful that they had to nail his drums to the floor. Nobody messed with Johnny! When I set up the Cassanova Club, The Big Three were the best band in Liverpool. Cass had left The Cassanovas and, now as The Big Three, they honed their sound, and there was probably only Rory Storm and The Hurricanes who came close. Rory was a great showman, performer, and had a big personality. With them all in suits, dancing in time like The Shadows, they always drew a big crowd.

"Gerry and The Pacemakers, by the end of 1961, were right up there with The Beatles. Gerry was very versatile, and could include show tunes, like 'You'll Never Walk Alone' and, as a group, they were tight, and top performers. They were running neck and neck with The Beatles, and I promised them, once I had secured a deal for The Beatles, they would be next. Freddie Marsden was a really good drummer, and helped develop the sound of the Pacemakers, though the group was really about Gerry as the front man.

"Pete Best put the beat in The Beatles when he joined. When they returned from Hamburg at the end of 1960, they were pure rock 'n' roll. Pete was a great drummer, and versatile, which a lot of people don't realise, and the group had learned together in Hamburg, and had a great sound. Pete, though, didn't socialise with the others, and was more of an introvert. I started promoting them in early 1961, and they were incredible.

THE
IRON
DOOR
CLUB

13 TEMPLE ST.
(off Dale Street)

Membership only
2/6

The newest and brightest entertainment centre in the heart of the city

Meet old friends and new . . . Watch the "Echo" or 'atest details of top attractions now being booked

Don't Miss SATURDAY NEXT

LEW HIRD'S JAZZBAND

with PAM on trumpet

No Weirdies, Batniks or Teddy Boys admitted

Host Compere — KEN LAURIE

Original painting by Paul Skellett (www.skellett.com)

"Ringo, on the other hand, was a more experienced drummer, and I think a better drummer. He had more versatility than Pete, because of the songs Rory Storm and The Hurricanes were doing, and he had been drumming for a few years by then. He was a good professional, too, and that experience helped him. He was also a decent enough singer, who had his own 'Starr Time' with Rory.

I remember Ringo singing three songs: 'Hit the Road, Jack', 'Boys' and 'What'd I Say', which I remember on one occasion going on for nearly 20 minutes, before Rory grabbed the microphone off him! Ringo also had a really good driving beat, like Pete did, though not as dominant.

"At the end of 1961, I made plans with The Beatles to become their manager, and make a record. I hired a car to impress them, and tried to get them to London, though ended up in Aldershot. At the same time, Eppy had come on the scene, and was also offering to be their manager. They approached me, and told me what Brian was offering, and even though it meant me missing out, I knew I couldn't offer them what Brian could.

"At the time, The Beatles were the best rock 'n' roll group anyone had ever seen, but Brian took their raw talent, and cleaned them up. I didn't like it at the time, but it worked, and you can't deny that. Brian was the only one who could have done that, and he deserves the recognition for what he achieved."

Sam Leach
Beatles Friend and Promoter

Sam with David Bedford at Sam's book launch for The Rocking City

Ringo's famous Ludwig kit

BEHIND THE FOURTH BEATLE

It's been nearly fifty years since the breakup of the most famous band in the world. Many books and many stories about those four fab lads have emerged since then. Incredibly, in all that time, no one has fully revealed the conflicts and clashes of personality that shaped one of the most crucial periods of The Beatles history – their 'dubious origins' as Lennon put it.

'Crucial' is not an exaggeration, for as you'll see, the real Beatles story was defined by a series of critical make-or-break crises where virtually everything hung in the balance – all for want of a drummer! The Larry Parnes' Wyvern Club audition, the coming-of-age trip to Hamburg, the EMI recording tests, the later Abbey Road sessions and the 1964 world tour are just a few of those crucial moments when The Beatles' success or failure depended on finding a drummer! Indeed, it's tempting to think that if anyone had dared to ask John Lennon, "Where are we going now, Johnny?" in these tense moments his reply might well easily have been, "Nowhere fast without a bloody drummer!"

In the end, the Fabs made it to the toppermost of the poppermost. But, as is so often forgotten by writers and fans taking the magical music history tour, they made it literally by the skin of a drum. For that reason alone, *Finding The Fourth Beatle* is an important reminder about how essential to the story the crises were – far more in fact than has previously been acknowledged or written about.

TESTING BEATLES HISTORY: JUST GIMME SOME CON**FAB**ULATION

I'm sick and tired of hearing things...... I've had enough of reading things......
All I want is the truth, Just gimme some truth.
John Lennon

Confabulation is a memory problem in which the individual produces false memories. When people confabulate, they either report remembering events that never occurred, or remember events as having occurred at an incorrect time or place. For example, a person who is confabulating may report a conversation that never occurred, or may report a conversation that occurred three years ago as having happened today.

When it comes to chronicling Beatles history, writers have several problems to overcome, especially those of us who are die-hard Beatles fans with unbridled passion for the subject. Because of the subject matter, it is almost impossible for authors to stay impartial. An author who has taken a similar approach to us is Erin Torkelson Weber in her book, The Beatles and the Historians: An Analysis of Writings About the Fab Four. Her use of "historiography", the study of the way history has been and is written, "is necessary to understanding any major historical event or cultural phenomenon." That is the approach we have followed.

The first official Beatles history appeared in Parlophone's press release to promote *"Love Me Do"*, which is reproduced in this book. It started the pattern of telling The Beatles' story in their own way, and as they want you to know it.

It is full of errors. There was only one official biography, **The Beatles: The Authorised Biography**, written by Hunter Davies. Based on extensive interviews with The Beatles and their families, friends and colleagues over a two-year period, it gives the boys' own spin on Beatles history. Still, it remains a unique, valuable resource because Davies was the first author to be granted exclusive, close contact with the group members. Often overlooked sources from the 1960s are Michael Braun's *Love Me Do! The Beatles' Progress*, and the *The Beatles Book Monthly*, an incredible resource rife with interviews with key, and lesser-known, eyewitnesses to the events.

In the 1970s, John Lennon gave several lengthy interviews, including the legendary ones with *Rolling Stone* and *Playboy*, as well as lesser-known accounts like the Red Mole interviews where he went into greater detail about his political opinions. In 1980, there was a series of new interviews as he prepared to return to the public arena with his new album, *Double Fantasy*. You have to study them all to see and understand what John was feeling, as his opinions changed more often than he changed his socks! Sadly, those final interviews saw a man, full of life and optimism as he was just "Starting Over", only to be robbed of his life in such a tragic way.

In the 1980s, we had Philip Norman's *Shout!*, which was the most comprehensive biography published since the '60s, and is still a popular book. However, when examined, there was a clear bias towards Lennon and against McCartney. Geoff Emerick did the opposite, praising McCartney over Lennon in *Here, There and Everywhere: My Life Recording the Music of The Beatles*.

Many more memoirs and personal recollections have given us the story from other personal viewpoints, which often means that there is a bias. McCartney worked with Barry Miles on a biography, Many Years From Now, as he sought to put over his story, and George published I Me Mine to tell his version of Beatles history.

Ringo, the subject of surprisingly few biographies, would tell his story through the songs he recorded from 2008 onward.

Unfortunately, the facts woven into many Beatles books have seldom been challenged. "They were repeated in biography after biography and from narrative to narrative until they became accepted wisdom. Numerous Beatles authors also apply a blatant moral double standard: absolving or omitting the character and musical flaws of their favourite Beatle while emphasizing or inventing those of the group's other members."*(The Beatles and the Historians: An Analysis of Writings About the Fab Four)*

In an effort to reclaim their history, the "Threetles" (Paul, George and Ringo) gave us *Anthology* in the 1990s, including archival interviews from John.
The documentary and book were promoted as The Beatles' own story, told in their own words. But as historian and author Erin Torkelson Weber wrote: "With four voices offering their own personal view of The Beatles' story, different memories of events emerged, most often between McCartney and Harrison. Both men's accounts are self-serving." *(The Beatles and the Historians: An Analysis of Writings About the Fab Four)*

A new breed of Beatles author emerged in Mark Lewisohn, who had been heavily involved in the *Anthology* project. His outstanding books – *The Beatles Live!, A Day In The Life, The Beatles Chronicles* and *The Complete Beatles Recording Sessions* – should be in every serious Beatle fan's collection. However, *Tune In*, his first volume in a trilogy meant to create the best, and most complete, history of The Beatles, is different to his earlier works as it is a biography, not a reference book, and should be tested in the same way as other books. "Those Beatles writers who dispute Lewisohn's interpretations will be faced with two choices. In order to establish a counter-narrative, they can either use Lewisohn's sources and interpret them in different ways, or discover new, equally credible sources which contradict Lewisohn's." *(The Beatles and the Historians: An Analysis of Writings About the Fab Four)*

We have therefore decided to examine every aspect of the Fourth Beatle story as scholars and historians, especially that polarizing period in 1962 when Ringo replaced Pete, without bias to either, and giving credit where it is due. We have applied standard tests used by historians to examine the evidence and every account of these events, and have shown at each relevant stage what tests we have applied, as well as our conclusions based on the evidence. If there is not enough evidence available and we can only offer an opinion or an assumption, then we have also made that clear. We have also included the relevant source in the text, whether author interview or other source.

Eyewitnesses

In any legal hearing or trial, there is the case for the defence and the case for the prosecution. Both sides will attempt to provide proof, beyond reasonable doubt, that the accused is either innocent or guilty.

Documentary evidence is not open to speculation, though it can be misinterpreted, but the most crucial part of either the defence or prosecution is the summoning of their eyewitnesses. These people can swing a case either way, depending on their reliability, honesty and objectivity. However, neither side in the court will rely solely on what the eyewitness says; they also have the chance to cross-examine them and scrutinize their testimony. Only then will the jury be satisfied that they are telling the truth, or lying under oath. What we have done is examine not only the eyewitness testimony of those who were intimately involved in The Beatles' story, but the findings of authors, including ourselves, who have written about The Beatles. Of course, we know that none of us authors is infallible!

Where possible, we have interviewed those key eyewitnesses again. However, because so many of those first-hand observers are no longer with us, we have to also apply similar tests to the authors.

We present the case for the prosecution and defence; you are the jury who will examine the evidence.

The Tests

Can the eyewitness testimony be trusted? Since it is the most vital of evidence, and can be compelling and convincing, we have used these tests:

1. Intention. Was the intention of the writer or eyewitness to accurately preserve history, or did they have an ulterior motive in presenting their testimony in this way? "Hearsay and unverified testimony is often misrepresented as fact." *(The Beatles and the Historians: An Analysis of Writings About the Fab Four)*

2. Bias. Is there a bias by the author or eyewitness to make either themselves or those around them look better than they really were? Is it objective, honest and fair? "Many authors of Beatles books use technically factual evidence in misleading ways – for example, by quoting a source who supports the author's point of view while ignoring countervailing evidence... when in fact it was just one source's perspective on a given event." *(A Day in the Life - Mark Hertsgaard)*

3. Timing. How close to the event is the testimony given? The closer the eyewitness testimony is to the date of the event, the less likely the possibility for legendary embellishment or development. We take into account faulty memories and wishful thinking, as well as deliberate revisionism.

4. Is there multiple, corroborative, independent attestation? What other eyewitness accounts or physical evidence is there that can corroborate the testimony, or contradict it? The more accounts that can confirm the story, the more reliable it is, and the more likely it is to be accurate. It doesn't mean that a single source should be discounted, but a higher level of scrutiny is required.

"Eyewitness testimony that lacks verification from other, independent sources will be regarded as valuable but not unquestionable. However, eyewitness testimony will be granted more weight than secondhand accounts or hearsay." *(The Beatles and the Historians: An Analysis of Writings About the Fab Four)*

5. Oral History. Have the accounts been passed down so many times that errors creep in, resulting in an accidental "truth" being perpetuated? It has been

Original painting by Paul Skellett (www.skellett.com)

said that if you tell a lie often enough and loud enough, people believe it is true. That is why we have approached this book with an open mind, accepting nothing and challenging everything.

6. Consistency. Do all the accounts concur, or are there discrepancies? Have eyewitnesses changed their stories over the years? What can be considered the truth? As historians, the truth is often unattainable, but we must gather as much evidence as possible, and get as close as we can to the truth.

Documentary Evidence

There are many documents available for inspection. Printed materials like letters, contracts, posters, tickets and programs help us clearly corroborate the events and support, or refute, eyewitness testimonies.

Experts

Weber says that when analysing The Beatles' music and musicianship, we should consider "the subjectivity of music, and the tenuous authority of writers, particularly those with no musical training, to bestow or withhold the title of genius on musicians." *(The Beatles and the Historians: An Analysis of Writings About the Fab Four)*

Our knowledge as historians and writers is not always sufficient for the topic being analysed. For the task of scrutinizing and dissecting the drumming abilities of Pete Best and Ringo Starr, we have consulted independent experts in their field – professional drummers. We feel this has far more merit than our humble opinion as uninformed authors. When combined with the musical evidence and opinion of these experts, we will present the case and leave it to you to make your judgment.

For parts of The Beatles story, we have had to take independent legal advice as to the status of various contracts and agreements that underpin the relationship the group had with record companies and manager Brian Epstein. This has helped us to understand the events more clearly.

Evidence and Proof

What is the difference between evidence and proof? Author and historian J. Warner Wallace – *Cold Case Christianity* – says that "while evidence is a matter of objective truth, proof is in the mind of the evaluator, and many of us resist the truth in spite of the evidence." How can authors come to such different conclusions when they are often examining the same evidence? We can offer evidence like eyewitness testimony and documents all day long, but you have to have an open mind to examine it, and decide if the evidence supports the facts that we have stated, and whether you feel we have given you sufficient proof.

Evidence: The facts we offer to support our claims of truth
Proof: What we infer from the facts offered

Abductive Reasoning

When examining testimony and evidence, we sometimes have to consider the implications of what has been revealed. There are several ways of doing this,

and one of the most dangerous is speculation, which can be constructed to suit the agenda of the writer. However, what is more appropriate is the adductive reasoning approach, which is a form of logical conclusion, which starts with the available evidence, and then seeks to find the simplest and most likely explanation. It is important, therefore, to keep away from supposition, speculation and presumption where no evidence exists, and we have endeavoured to follow the evidence. We have therefore ensured that we have shown our sources within the text, to save flicking between footnotes.

You Decide

Don't just take our word, or the words of any author, based solely on who we are, our reputations, or previous works, but on the facts and evidence put before you. The truth is what you make of it, based on the evidence, not the writer. To counter an argument made with evidence, you need to provide rebuttal evidence.

To quote Daniel Patrick Moynihan;

"Everyone is entitled to his own opinion, but not his own facts."

As John Lennon said:

"Gimme Some Truth".

CAVERN IN THE TOWN

AT THE CAVERN is the LP that puts the original Liverpool sound on record. Sixteen titles and every one a winner. They line up like this : **Dr. Feelgood; Keep On Rolling** (THE MARAUDERS) **Sure, The Girl I Love; You Really Got A Hold On Me** (THE FORTUNES) **Everybody Loves A Lover** (BERYL MARSDEN) **Devoted To You; You Better Move On** (THE DENNISONS) **Somebody To Love; I Got A Woman** (HEINZ) **Little Queenie; Diddley Diddley Daddy** (DAVE BERRY AND THE CRUISERS) **If You Ever Chang Your Mind** (THE BIG THREE) **Skin Minny; Jezebel** (LEE CURTIS AN THE ALL-STARS) **Talking Abo You; Little Egypt** (BERN ELLIOTT AND THE FENMEI

Lee Curtis—his singing raises the screams, (and the roof.)

set for the session, and what a session !

Maraccas and 'mood' music from Dave Berry.

The Merseyside miss scores a hit—Beryl Marsden.

ns have girls frenzied.

Testing time for Heinz, Noel (left) and Terry.

Heinz brings out the screamers at The Cavern. Hundreds of them!

is in Liverpool with the lowdown...

MEET THE BEATLES

When "Love Me Do" was issued in October 1962, Parlophone released a press release that for the first time, told the story of The Beatles.

As you will read, even with The Beatles themselves providing the information, the myths have begun, and have been repeated so many times. It is because of this that we have examined every account of The Beatles' history, from this press release, through *Beatles Book Monthly*, Hunter Davies' authorised biography *The Beatles*, their own *Anthology* and up to and including *Tune In*.

On page three of the press release, we are told of the ***"background story of Britain's most exciting new vocal and instrumental R & B quartet."***

This is their version of Beatles history: how many errors can you spot?

CHURCH HALL HOPS AND A CHINATOWN STRIP JOINT

Way back in '56 when the grind and scratch of skiffle was just starting to graze the pop horizon, the three founder members of THE BEATLES - John, Paul and George - were busily experimenting with washboard 'n' banjo sounds at every out-of-school opportunity. Their '62 breakthrough is backed by six years of maturing musical notions and solid practical experience which has taken them from Liverpool ballrooms to Hamburg night clubs, from church hall hops to colourful strip club stints in Liverpool's Chinatown.

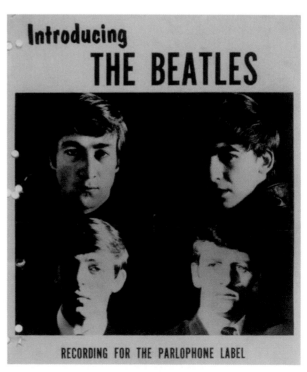

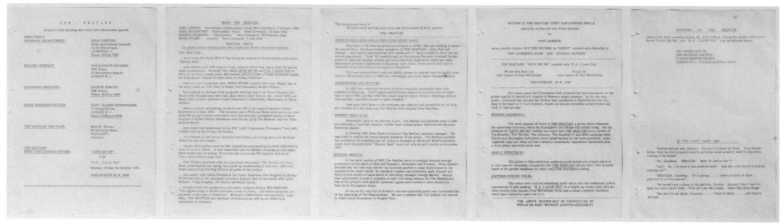

The "Meet The Beatles" promo leaflet, 1962

The boys outgrew their rock and skiffle phases to explode onto the highly competitive Merseyside scene in 1960 as a thoroughly grounded, super-charged quartet.

Hamburgers and Beatles

In 1960 they undertook the first of three unusually successful night club seasons in Hamburg. Their impact upon German audiences carried such strength that in April 1961 and May 1962 they made lengthy return visits to Hamburg, playing increasingly important venues on each occasion.

Last year their fame on the continent was swollen and intensified by the Polydor release of a disc featuring The Beatles with vocalist Tony Sheridan.

Mersey BEAT -ALLS

Meanwhile, back at the Mersey ranch, The Beatles had gathered such a faithful following of fans that capacity crowds were commonplace wherever the dynamic foursome played.

In October 1961 Brian Epstein became The Beatles' personal manager. He was swift to realise the extraordinary potential of the group. The Beatles justified his confidence by smashing past all rivals to triumph as the North West's favourite outfit when the publication '*Mersey Beat*' came out with its poll results in November 1961.

DIGGING MOGULS

In the early months of 1962 The Beatles were in constant demand among promoters as far apart as Hull and Nuneaton, Doncaster and Preston. Brian Epstein decided that the time was ripe for his talented quartet to make itself known to the moguls of the music world. He planed to London and eventually made himself and his precious bundle of tapes heard to recording manager George Martin. George was enthusiastic enough to schedule a swift

recording session for The Beatles and two of the group's most popular personal-appearance numbers were chosen for their first Parlophone single.

So far as the majority of Britain's record-collecting public are concerned this is the beginning of The Beatles' story. We are confident that The Beatles will sprout chart-sized dimensions in Chapter One!

OUR DRUM EXPERTS

In a book about drummers, as neither author is a drummer himself, we felt that it was appropriate to bring in experts to analyse the drummers being discussed.

Analysing Pete Best

When analysing the early Beatles, especially the various recording sessions with Pete Best in Hamburg, and with Decca and EMI, we asked Mike Rice, Derek Hinton and Andrew Hinton – three drummers from different generations – to listen to the recordings and give us their objective feedback. None of them had listened to these studio recordings before. When analysing the Decca audition, we also enlisted the help of experienced record producer Steve Levine, whose unique insight helps us understand what Decca was likely looking for, what he would have been looking for, and how The Beatles would have fared with other record companies.

Analysing Ringo

To analyse Ringo's recordings, we recruited two experienced drummers who have been studying his recording career for their book, Ringo Starr and The Beatles Beat. Alex Cain and Terry McCusker have 80 years drumming experience between them and, in their book, have critically analysed every song The Beatles recorded. We also enlisted the help of two drummers who work closely with Ringo: Gary Astridge and Rob Shanahan. Producer Steve Levine was also asked for his observations on Ringo, having worked with him when producing The Beach Boys.

Finally, we wanted to have the input of drummers who have been trying to play like Ringo in Beatles tribute bands. Mitch Kozera and Phil Kelly have studied Ringo's drumming for years, and provide unique insight into the often complex drum patterns that Ringo created, and the challenges they faced trying to get that "Ringo sound".

Our drummers are:

Gary Astridge
A drummer and collector of replicas of Ringo's drum kits, Gary has now assumed the role of "Curator of Ringo's Kits", working with Ringo on several projects.

Alex Cain
Like John Lennon a quarter-century before him, Alex was born at Oxford Road Maternity Hospital, Liverpool, as The Beatles' latest single "Eleanor Rigby"/"Yellow Submarine" sat atop the UK charts. He has been a drummer for many years, and has enjoyed a career in TV sound, most notably working on Channel 4's *Brookside* and *Hollyoaks*, plus numerous productions for BBC, ITV and independents. He is particularly proud of his contribution to the BBC documentary of another of his heroes, *Dennis Wilson – The Real Beach Boy*.

Derek Hinton
An accomplished drummer, Derek has been performing in bands for over 30 years, also playing guitar and bass. He is a fan of rock music in particular, and is a Beatles fan.

Andrew Hinton
Andrew, Derek's son, is an excellent drummer, bassist and lead guitarist. He recently gained a music degree at Liverpool University. He has an eclectic taste in music of all decades.

Clockwise (from top left): Gary Astridge (with Ringo); Phil Kelly; Alex Cain, Terry McCusker; Rob Shanahan (with Ringo); Derek Hinton; Andrew Hinton; Lou Longobardi; Mike Rice, Mitch Kozera.

Phil Kelly

Phil has been playing drums in various Beatles tribute bands for many years now, and has spent many hours studying Ringo's drum style and performances so that he can recreate them as closely as possible when he plays.

Mitch Kozera

Mitch Kozera is a classic rock drummer and vocalist from Detroit, Michigan, USA. He has nearly four decades of drumming experience and has performed in bands in Michigan since the 1980s.

Lou Longobardi

A lifelong Beatles fan who saw The Beatles at Shea, Lou is also a drummer and multi-instrumentalist who has tried to reproduce Ringo's drum patterns, and studied the music of The Beatles for many years.

Terry McCusker

Terry worked in the same building as the Cavern and became a regular at the legendary club. He witnessed Merseybeat and, after watching Pete Best play with The Beatles, decided to become a drummer. He was playing the same clubs as the bands he had watched, and became a freelancer, performing all over Europe, America and the Middle East. Terry has been studying the drumming of Ringo Starr and has shared that knowledge in the book he co-wrote with Alex Cain.

Mike Rice

Mike was a drummer with The Senators, a 1960s Merseybeat band, and also drummed for other groups from the '60s until recently. He is a fan of both Pete Best and Ringo Starr, and saw both drum with The Beatles.

Rob Shanahan

Rob has been photographing Ringo – and most of the top rock stars on the planet – while playing in a Rolling Stones tribute band. However, because he and Ringo are both left-handed drummers playing right-handed kits, they share the same drumming technique.

Drummers? You Can't Beat Them

Hopefully, this will give you an insight into the role of the drummer, which non-drummers rarely understand. As with most things musical, everything is subjective and you may or may not agree with these drummers. That is why we have created the *Finding the Fourth Beatle Album* with over 40 tracks featuring as many of the drummers covered in this book as we could find. This includes the Tony Sheridan recording, Decca audition, Parlophone audition and the two September sessions at EMI Studios. Read the opinions of the drummers, listen to the tracks, and see whether or not you agree.

LIVERPOOL: THE FIFTH BEATLE?

It's clichéd, but yes, The Beatles phenomenon really did change everything, especially in Liverpool. More than being the most famous band in music history, The Beatles triggered a revolution in modern music and social thinking that changed western society forever. However, to fully appreciate the impact of that revolution, we owe it to the memory of many people who also played their part to put an end to the myths and deliberate misinformation.
Liverpool's musical tidal wave didn't begin or end with The Beatles alone.

Where do we begin? Liverpool - in the town, where they were born!

They were only one of hundreds of bands in the city, and this is still the case today! For serious music lovers and Beatles fans to fully appreciate the essence of the group and the role it played as a catalyst for change in the 1960s, we believe it is essential to understand how their birthplace shaped and affected their outlook. Here we show how Liverpool, with its unique cultural and musical heritage provided the essential seed bed for their characters to develop and grow.

Just as important is the need to appreciate that, despite revisionist nonsense, London wasn't, and still isn't, at the epicentre of everything that happens in Britain. Apart from two particular events that took place in the 1960's in London's now legendary 2i's Café, the capital made no direct contribution to the birth of the Merseybeat revolution – a true teenage phenomenon which developed in splendid isolation. More to the point, "Swinging London" was nonexistent until the cream of Liverpool talent was forced to head south to the record label's studios

Scouse, Not English

Historically, Liverpool has long been socially, culturally, politically and geographically disconnected from London. It's as much a state of mind as anything else – a state within a state fueled by north/south rivalries and a large influx of Irish settlers whose long-held anti-establishment grievances are a legacy of their ancestor's struggle for independence.

It's not surprising that Liverpool is referred to as the capital of Ireland. The cry of "Scouse not English!" is regularly heard among local left-wing champions of republicanism. Of course, these are only expressions of a sense of difference and are far removed from the long seafaring history that has influenced Liverpool's underlying nature.

Like many northern towns, the port has always had a strong sense of close community spirit. Fiercely communal in outlook, the port has a powerful matriarchal heartbeat at its core, borne from centuries of developed inner strength, self-reliance and the need to survive when the menfolk were at sea for weeks or months at a time. There's an old saying in Liverpool that men rule the roost but it's the women who decide what they think – and when! An example can be seen in John Lennon's close maternal family, the Stanleys, where attitudes to the menfolk had such a dramatic effect on his development.

Maritime Influences

Until recent times, Liverpool was Britain's second biggest maritime gateway to the world. After the ending of the American war of independence in 1783, the port profited from its strategic location by becoming Britain's main import and export link to the Americas. This led the newly independent American

Government to establish a permanent trade and cultural Consulate in Paradise Street in Liverpool and, soon enough, other international consular offices did likewise.

As international trade grew, the port expanded along both sides of the River Mersey's shoreline. The city became the number one port of entry and departure for goods and people alike, first to the British Empire, then the British Commonwealth and, later, for travellers to and from America and Canada. Eventually it accounted for over 9 million migrants on the regular trans-Atlantic passenger service.

Not everyone made that final journey. Many European migrants opted to stay in the city, adding to a rapidly rising population, among them the entrepreneurs who established new trades and businesses during the 1800s. Sadly, those with lesser fortunes or skills, particularly Irish migrants, found themselves trapped in the inner city's squalid, overcrowded court tenements. The net result was that by the end of the 19th century, Liverpool's population tripled. So did the port's booming export and import trade. However, it was the poorest social classes – the large families of dockers and unskilled men – who saw little benefit. Daily life had become a vicious circle of hardship and uncertainty as their men headed off at dawn each morning, hoping to be picked for the most poorly paid work of the day.

Daydream Believers

By the 1960s, a hundred years later, another cyclic boom had gone bust. Once again, the city's unemployed youth faced the same old problem, with over 33 applicants for every vacancy. It was no accident that the eventual rise of teenage pop groups found a new momentum. Faced with a choice between unemployment or national service, many a male teenager looked at the latest idea of becoming an entertainer with fresh eyes at the prospect of a good time, paid gigs, respect and girls galore. It wasn't a difficult decision, because for those with little money, the idea of fame and fortune surely appealed! The dream of being part of *The Big Beat* scene beat the hell out of working hard for a living, or queuing at the labour exchange, or worse still, being called up for the armed services, as every member of a Liverpool group would vouch for.

Recording the First International Hit

For centuries, countless sailors acknowledged the port as a lively place where leisure and pleasure went hand in hand, a fact made known to millions of others later on when The Beatles alluded to their salty heritage in an impromptu recording of Liverpool's often raunchy anthem, "Maggie May". Known to sailors across the seven oceans as an old sea shanty about a notorious Liverpool prostitute, the original version of "Maggie May" was first written down in a leather-bound diary in 1830 by Charles Picknel, an able seaman serving on The Kains, which carried convicts to Van Diemens Land (Tasmania). In it is a special mention to heavily-chained female prisoners from Liverpool, suggesting they were far tougher than usual and, although the song was meant as a moral warning to unwary sailors about the dangers of prostitutes in foreign ports, we don't know if it really worked. However, Maggie was soon widely lamented (or feted) as one of Liverpool's best-known attractions, until her night time work earned her a long, sunny vacation in an Australian convict colony.

Whether Maggie was real or imagined is a mystery to this day, but Maggie and the salty sea shanty had the honour of becoming Liverpool's first international celebrity. It was also a regular chart topper, most notably recorded by The Vipers and produced by George Martin, until The Beatles eventually took both crowns when they stopped the world in 1964.

Cultural Tidal Waves

Being second in importance only to London as an international port also meant that every new tide brought in something or someone different. And with each wave of migrants and seamen there came another precious cargo – their music. Always eager to be entertained, and served by a nightlife that could burst into song at the drop of a hat, Liverpolitans quickly learned to soak up, recycle and remake other people's music to suit their own tastes.

In 1839, Herman Melville, the American author of Moby Dick, stayed in the city and gave an excellent account of the social scene.

"In the evening, especially when sailors are gathered in great numbers, these streets present a most singular spectacle, the entire population of the vicinity being seemingly turned into them. Hand-organs, fiddles and cymbals, plied by strolling musicians, mix with the songs of the seamen, the babble of women and children, and the whining of beggars. From the various boarding houses… proceeds the noise and revelry and dancing."

It could so easily describe the social atmosphere of the Merseybeat years – or even today.

By the 1860s, Liverpool had developed a thirst for more refined quality venues offering music, culture and the arts. The rising demand led to a rapid expansion in the number of public palaces offering entertainment. Playhouses offered nothing new to the city, with some dating back to the mid-1700s. But, by the late 19th century, the demand for low-brow variety or novelty acts led to the rise of music halls and multi-function theatres – a feature ranked only second to the pubs and ale houses across the city.

The following list of venues gives a good idea of how popular music halls and theatres were, not only for local audiences, but also for the American and Allied troops encamped in Liverpool through two world wars:

Alexandra Theatre
Cambridge Music Hall
Constellation Music Hall
Empire Theatre - Still in Use
Everyman Theatre – Still in Use
Garston Britannia
Garston Empire
Garston Palace
Grand Theatre and Opera House
Haymarket Music Hall
Hengler's Cirques
Kelly's Theatre
Liver Theatre, Church Street
Liver Music Hall, Whitechapel
Liver Music Hall, Mersey Street
Lyric Theatre
Metropole Theatre, Bootle
Neptune / Crane Theatre (Now the Epstein)
Olympia Theatre – Now restored as a Theatre
Pantheon Theatre, Church Street
Park Palace
Paddington Palace
Pavilion Theatre
Philharmonic Hall - Still in Use
Playhouse Theatre - Still in Use
Prince of Wales Theatre
Queen's Theatre, Paradise Street
Queen's Theatre, Charlotte Street
Queen's Music Hall / Bijou Theatre
Rotunda Theatre
Royal Adelphi Theatre
Royal Colosseum Theatre
Royal Court Theatre - Still in Use
Royal Hippodrome
Royal Liver Theatre, Church Street
Royal Muncaster Theatre, Bootle
New Prince's Theatre, Bootle
Shakespeare Theatre
Star Music Hall
St. George's Hall - Still in Use
The Grafton Rooms
Theatre Royal, Breck Road
Theatre Royal, Williamson Square
Theatre of Varieties
Tivoli Palace of Varieties

In the post-war years, Merseyside-born entertainers and comedians cut their teeth in such places, notably Arthur Askey, Ted Ray, Tommy Handley and Tommy Trinder in the 1940s and '50s, and Ken Dodd and Jimmy Tarbuck in the 1960s. Other attractions had a lasting influence on budding musicians like George Harrison, Paul McCartney and John Lennon who were among the thousands who went to the Empire Theatre to see George Formby playing the ukulele. It was an experience they wouldn't forget, because the same three teenagers appeared at the Empire themselves, first as The Quarrymen in a talent show fronted by Carroll Levis and, finally, when they appeared again as The Beatles in 1963, on the brink of international fame and fortune.

Never Mind the Bombs: Save the Piano

During WWII, Liverpool's vital location in Britain made it a major destination for Allied and Empire forces and a vital supply line for trans-Atlantic shipping. It was also a busy transit camp for millions of troops from Canada, America, and the British Empire, with districts like Mossley Hill, Knotty Ash, Dovecot, Page Moss and Huyton soon becoming vast tented encampments.

The city's strategic importance also made it a prime target for Nazi air raids. Hitler was determined to destroy the port's ability to function as a hub for Britain's import of food, armaments and troops. So too was his need to destroy the secret Allied command headquarters that controlled the entire Atlantic naval and maritime operations. Buried deep underground in the city centre, these secret bunkers survived every attempt to destroy them. However, it was the existence of these twin targets that would finally make Liverpool the most bombed city in Britain after the capital itself and, by the end of the war, the city had witnessed over 68 massed air raids, including the infamous May Blitz of 1941 when Liverpool was subjected to two weeks of constant air raids.

As one old wit mused rather wistfully years later: "My family lost the roof over their heads when our neighbourhood was flattened by bombs. We lost all our possessions… like everyone else, we didn't have much to start with, and now we didn't have a pot to piss in, either. We lived day by day 'cos no one knew if we'd live to see tomorrow, but you know what us Scousers are like – everyone got stuck in and helped each other. At least we could still have a good 'ole laugh and a sing-song around the piano in our pub, thank God. Somehow the Jerrys (Germans) missed that. Pity, really. It was a dump anyway!"

Here, in photos and facts, is a sobering reflection of what was at stake.

From 1939 to 1945, the city and its people paid a very high price for their war effort:
- The port of Liverpool handled over 75 million tons of cargo (31% of all British imports)
- It received 74,000 airplanes and gliders and 4.7 million troops of which 1.2 million were American.
- Britain's merchant navy engaged 195,000 seamen. 130,000 were British, 50,000 were Indian and Chinese and 10,000 were Liverpool men. John Lennon's father was just one!
- During the bombing raids, 4,000 people were killed and up to 5,000 injured in Liverpool.
- 10,000 city homes and properties were destroyed. Over 184,000 were damaged.

Liverpool was the second most bombed city in Britain after London during the war. The city centre (above) was devastated in the May 1941 blitz

For many years afterward, the terrible scale of destruction was a major factor in the city's physical appearance. Unlike other cities in Europe, Britain wasn't a beneficiary of America's Marshall Aid Plan. Liverpool had no financial help or means to rebuild quickly from the ashes, and it took several decades to recover from the widespread devastation. The only good news is that the inner city was left with a lot of unused commercial cellars that escaped the bombs. Someone was bound to find a new use for them sooner or later...

Play it again, Uncle Sam – a very American Affair

Throughout the war, the U.S. Air Force operated the largest military airbase in Europe at Burtonwood on the outskirts of Liverpool. Home to thousands of American air force crews and army personnel up until the end of the cold war, their presence brought many popular perks for Liverpolitans, too. Not only did the base offer locals a regular supply of all the latest American records brought in by U.S. servicemen, it also provided the city with frequent weekend parties of off-duty "Yanks" eager to enjoy the lively dance halls and pubs.

Chocolate, cigarettes, chewing gum and silk stockings were a bonus for local girls – and quite a few Anglo-American marriages followed. Liverpool musician Mike Kinney traces his love for country music back to his father Kenneth Edward Kinney's deep southern American roots, while legendary Toxteth singer Joe Ankrah and The Chants have a natural affinity with black American music, probably thanks to their uncle who was one of many black U.S. airmen at Burtonwood Air Base. These are just two examples, but both have made untold contributions to Liverpool's music heritage.

Growing up with Post-War Blues – a very personal reflection

Nostalgia always clouds our view of the past, especially the so-called good old days we thought would last forever. They didn't, thank heavens, because life was Spartan indeed. Food and raw materials were scarce, rationing was enforced and luxuries were non-existent. Is it any wonder that young people growing up in post-war Britain must have felt it had fallen into a deep hole?

As for the national media and popular entertainment, a 'stiff upper lip' mentality clung on to the power in every public sphere while, unlike America, British television, still in its flickering black and white infancy, closed down far too early, and even earlier on Sunday! Fortunately, after fifteen years of hard grind, 1954 saw an end to rationing as the amount of consumer goods accelerated. Okay, washing machines and cars still looked like they were made from scrap Panzer tanks, and probably were, but happily, "they don't make 'em like that anymore." Amen to that!

With only 4% of the population owning a TV in 1953, the radio was the main source of news and entertainment. The media generally was regulated by strict broadcasting regulations, which censored everything morally and culturally unsuitable for the nation, while Aunty BBC and its founding Director General, Lord John Reith, added further to the public straight-jacket with their own brand of self-righteous nonsense.

Reith was outwardly a zealot, driven by a strong sense of moral superiority that became a tyrannical doctrine. As his daughter, Marista, remarked many years later, Reith often displayed the manic traits of two wartime leaders he had admired so much – Hitler and Mussolini! "My father shared many characteristics with Mussolini," she revealed. "He was dictatorial, ruthless and exploitative. He could elevate someone, or ruin them in seconds, which was terrifying. And you never knew when one of his rages was coming. He was most impatient with those who feared him." Given Reith's omnipresence at the BBC, it's not surprising that many a liberal-minded producer's attempts to try out new ideas were perpetually stifled for fear that one wrong move could end their career.

The biggest victim in all of this was the long-suffering nation as Britain endured years of bland shows posing as light entertainment. *The Billy Cotton Band Show, Workers' Playtime, Music While You Work and Variety Bandbox were typical offerings. Other oddities included The Black and White Minstrel Show and Friday Night at The Blackpool Tower* (an interminable hour listening to someone droning on and on with a Wurlitzer organ). I know it seems quaint now, even funny for some, but it was horrid at the time.

Neither should we forget the dross churned out by whole armies of orchestras led by the saccharin sweet charms of Mantovani, Victor Sylvester and Semprini – guaranteed to send grandparents into a comatose state on Sunday afternoons. With all this excitement going on, was it any surprise that church youth coffee clubs did so well? A soft drink, the latest sounds and the local vicar trying hard to be cool was far more entertaining than staying home with Mantovani, Sylvester or Semprini.

Sadly, few of us managed to escape the dreaded rendition of "God Save Queen" either. It was mandatory to play it in every theatre and cinema as well as on radio and TV, and there seemed no escape, unless you were a good runner. Usherettes often risked being trampled to death in the stampede to get out before the drum roll kicked in. In fact, "Queen Lizzies' boring song was played everywhere – day and night without a tea break– for the entire decade, making it the most played long-playing record in music history! So much for the good old days!

Echoing the times, the same 'we-know-what's-best-for-you' attitude also held sway in London's record industry. Stuck in a complacent groove, many a chief executive seemed reticent to upset the status quo. Accordingly, while America had already waved goodbye to Glenn Miller's big band swing era and was now dominating charts on both sides of the Atlantic with fresher faces like Frank Sinatra, the London music moguls were happy to offer only a token resistance in the 1950s. Paler offerings like Johnny Ray, Matt Monroe, David Whitfield and Frank Ifield led Britain's popular choice of easy listening – popular being a euphemism for what the record industry thought was best for their bank accounts rather than us.

Fortunately, the tide began to turn. Leading the way was American Forces Network radio broadcasting daily across Europe under the banner of Radio Luxembourg. It was here that the first stirrings of rock 'n' roll hit the airwaves in between the station's mix of popular easy listening, chart hits and the evergreen country and western music. Programs such as Jack Jackson's innovative DJ-style show also broke new ground, attracting teenage audiences in Britain eager to tune in and turn on to whatever was coming out of America.

The eventual appearance of youth acts (the word 'teenager' was still emerging) like Tommy Steele, Joe Brown and His Bruvvers and Cliff Richard and the Shadows was just about as risqué as it got to U.S. rivals Bill Haley, Elvis, Eddie Cochran or Little Richard. More importantly, they owed much to the role played by the 2i's Café as we will see below.

Admittedly Liverpool added its fair share to the rather timid offerings hitting the charts and Michael Holliday, Lita Roza and Frankie Vaughan all achieved UK chart success. "(How Much Is) That Doggie In The Window?" by Liverpool singer Lita Roza was a massive chart hit. It may have seemed like sugary nonsense, but it was pure gold for record label sales. Unfortunately, it hung around the lovely Lita's career like a wet sandbag for the rest of her life, so much so that she refused to sing it later on. Then came Billy Fury, Liverpool's answer to Elvis. Billy's arrival really sexed up the British music scene when he mimicked Elvis Presley's lip curling, hip-swiveling act well into the 1960s. Unlike his fellow artists, Billy preceded The Beatles' writing talents with several self-penned chart hits, a feat almost unheard of at the time.

2i's are better than one

In 1953, a strange fad took hold in London, not in politics or theatre, but in its seedier back streets – the Coffee Bar. Cafés were nothing new, but the big innovation came with stripped back walk-in shops where customers could experience real coffee made to order from a Gaggia Espresso coffee machine. Out went drab and dreary post-war tea rooms with tired old waitresses in stained aprons, and in came the shiny Formica laminate look.

The brains behind this Italian look was actress Gina Lollobrigida, who'd set up a shop in London's Soho.

Its success spawned a rash of similar cafés all over that district before spreading through the entire country like a rash. The revolution was completed when the café owners went one step further by adding jukeboxes and soft drinks, specifically Pepsi and Coke – a surefire combination that attracted both teenagers and higher profits. It was a variation of this blueprint that inspired a gruff young Liverpudlian named Allan Williams to open the Jacaranda in a bohemian backwater of Slater

Street, Liverpool.

The same idea had been taken up in 1955 by two brothers in Soho. Using the initial "I" from their surname, Freddie and Sammy Irani opened the "2i's Coffee Bar" in Compton Street. They ran it for a year until April 1956 when they sold the bar to two former Australian wrestlers – Paul "Dr. Death" Lincoln and Ray "Rebel" Hunter and moved into the nightclub business (as Allan Williams would later do).

With stiff competition from other cafés, the 2i's takings struggled at first, until one day in July a local Skiffle group turned up and, without warning, broke into a live set in the café. Far from being annoyed, Lincoln invited The Vipers to come back and sing there any time. The Vipers gladly accepted, and were soon performing regularly as the resident act, helping to put the 2i's on the local map as the place to go to hear live music.

A few months later, a budding young singer named Tony Hicks was 'talent spotted' by impresario John Kennedy during a session with The Vipers and, in turn, Kennedy invited Decca's A&R man, Hugh Mendl, to come along and check Hicks out. Mendl promptly signed the singer to the label and Hicks, now rebranded as Tommy Steele, became Britain's first acknowledged rock 'n' roll star, with his debut record released barely a month later.

This event sealed the 2i's reputation as the place to be for Rock 'n' Rollers and Skifflers in addition to being a local shop window for visiting impresarios, agents and A&R men. Decca's A&R men were regulars, as were Jack Good, Larry Parnes, Don Arden, and a certain George Martin. But it was a chance meeting by two day-tripping businessmen, Allan Williams (who was trying to get a gig for Derry and the Seniors) and Herr Bruno Koschmider from Hamburg (who was trying to get an act for his club) that changed music history forever.

The 2i's became a revolving door for fame and fortune seekers, or those simply trying to land a gig. Others came in search of backing artists, nearly all of whom would emerge as household names in the 1960s: Hank Marvin, Joe Moretti, Ritchie Blackmore, Albert Lee, Vince Taylor (and the Playboys), Cliff Richard, the Drifters (soon to join Cliff as the Shadows), Wee Willie Harris, Gene Vincent and Jerry Lee Lewis, Joe Brown, Bruce Welch, Brian Bennett, Tony Meehan, Jet Harris, Brian 'Licorice' Locking, Vince Eager, Terry Dene, Wee Willie Harris, Adam Faith, Carlo Little, Clem Cattini (The Tornados), Eden Kane, Screaming Lord Sutch, Keith Kelly, Tim Fitzpatrick, Lance Fortune, Jay Chance, Johnny Kidd, Ritchie Blackmore, Alex Wharton, Mickie Most – and a certain young Tony Sheridan who took advantage of Herr Koschmider's invitation to play in Hamburg and never came back.

Despite the small beacons of light emerging from 1956, for the British record labels, the watchword throughout the decade seemed to be to play it safe, or not at all. With only one or two exceptions, a quick look at the No.1 chart hits shows how American sounds totally dominated the British music scene in the 1950s. It says a lot about our home grown music in those times...

Original painting by Paul Skellett

Al Martino	"Here In My Heart"	14 November 1952
Jo Stafford	"You Belong To Me"	16 January 1953
Kay Starr	"Comes A-Long-A-Love"	23 January 1953
Eddie Fisher	"Outside Of Heaven"	30 January 1953
Perry Como	"Don't Let The Stars Get In Your Eyes"	6 February 1953
Guy Mitchell	"She Wears Red Feathers"	13 March 1953
The Stargazers	"Broken Wings"	10 April 1953
Lita Roza	"How Much Is That Doggie In The Window?"	17 April 1953
Frankie Laine	"I Believe"	24 April 1953
Eddie Fisher	"I'm Walking Behind You"	26 June 1953
Frankie Laine	"I Believe"	3 July 1953
Mantovani	"The Song From Moulin Rouge"	14 August 1953
Frankie Laine	"I Believe"	21 August 1953
Guy Mitchell	"Look At That Girl"	11 September 1953
Frankie Laine	"Hey Joe"	23 October 1953
David Whitfield	"Answer Me"	6 November 1953
Frankie Laine	"Answer Me"	13 November 1953
David Whitfield	"Answer Me"	11 December 1953
Eddie Calvert	"Oh Mein Papa"	8 January 1954
The Stargazers	"I See The Moon"	12 March 1954
Doris Day	"Secret Love"	16 April 1954
The Stargazers	"I See The Moon"	23 April 1954
Johnnie Ray	"Such A Night"	30 April 1954
Doris Day	"Secret Love"	7 May 1954
David Whitfield	"Cara Mia"	2 July 1954
Kitty Kallen	"Little Things Mean A Lot"	10 September 1954
Frank Sinatra	"Three Coins In The Fountain"	17 September 1954
Don Cornell	"Hold My Hand"	8 October 1954
Vera Lynn	"My Son, My Son"	5 November 1954
Don Cornell	"Hold My Hand"	19 November 1954
Rosemary Clooney	"This Ole House"	26 November 1954
Winifred Atwell	"Let's Have Another Party"	3 December 1954
Dickie Valentine	"The Finger Of Suspicion"	7 January 1955
Rosemary Clooney	"Mambo Italiano"	14 January 1955
Dickie Valentine	"The Finger Of Suspicion"	21 January 1955
Rosemary Clooney	"Mambo Italiano"	4 February 1955
Ruby Murray	"Softly, Softly"	18 February 1955
Tennessee Ernie Ford	"Give Me Your Word"	11 March 1955
Perez Prado & His Orchestra	"Cherry Pink (And Apple Blossom White)"	29 April 1955
Tony Bennett	"Stranger In Paradise"	13 May 1955
Eddie Calvert	"Cherry Pink (and Apple Blossom White)"	27 May 1955
Jimmy Young	"Unchained Melody"	24 June 1955
Alma Cogan	"Dreamboat"	15 July 1955
Slim Whitman	"Rose Marie"	29 July 1955
Jimmy Young	"The Man From Laramie"	14 October 1955
Johnston Brothers	"Hernando's Hideaway"	11 November 1955
Bill Haley & His Comets	"Rock Around The Clock"	25 November 1955
Dickie Valentine	"Christmas Alphabet"	16 December 1955
Bill Haley & His Comets	"Rock Around The Clock"	6 January 1956
Tennessee Ernie Ford	"Sixteen Tons"	20 January 1956
Dean Martin	"Memories Are Made Of This"	17 February 1956
The Dream Weavers	"It's Almost Tomorrow"	16 March 1956
Kay Starr	"Rock And Roll Waltz"	30 March 1956
The Dream Weavers	"It's Almost Tomorrow"	6 April 1956

Winifred Atwell	"The Poor People of Paris"	13 April 1956
Ronnie Hilton	"No Other Love"	4 May 1956
Pat Boone	"I'll Be Home"	15 June 1956
Frankie Lymon and The Teenagers	"Why Do Fools Fall in Love"	20 July 1956
Doris Day	"Whatever Will Be, Will Be"	10 August 1956
Anne Shelton	"Lay Down Your Arms"	21 September 1956
Frankie Laine	"A Woman In Love"	19 October 1956
Johnnie Ray	"Just Walking In The Rain"	16 November 1956
Guy Mitchell	"Singing The Blues"	4 January 1957
Tommy Steele	"Singing The Blues"	11 January 1957
Guy Mitchell	"Singing The Blues"	18 January 1957
Frankie Vaughan	"The Garden Of Eden"	25 January 1957
Guy Mitchell	"Singing The Blues"	1 February 1957
Tab Hunter	"Young Love"	22 February 1957
Lonnie Donegan	"Cumberland Gap"	12 April 1957
Guy Mitchell	"Rock-A-Billy"	17 May 1957
Andy Williams	"Butterfly"	24 May 1957
Johnnie Ray	"Yes Tonight Josephine"	7 June 1957
Lonnie Donegan	"Puttin' On The Style"/"Gamblin' Man"	28 June 1957
Elvis Presley	"All Shook Up"	12 July 1957
Paul Anka	"Diana"	30 August 1957
The Crickets	"That'll Be The Day"	1 November 1957
Harry Belafonte	"Mary's Boy Child"	22 November 1957
Jerry Lee Lewis	"Great Balls Of Fire"	10 January 1958
Elvis Presley	"Jailhouse Rock"	24 January 1958
Michael Holliday	"The Story of My Life"	14 February 1958
Perry Como	"Magic Moments"	28 February 1958
Marvin Rainwater	"Whole Lotta Woman"	25 April 1958
Connie Francis	"Who's Sorry Now"	16 May 1958
Vic Damone	"On The Street Where You Live"	27 June 1958
The Everly Brothers	"All I Have To Do Is Dream"/"Claudette"	4 July 1958
The Kalin Twins	"When"	22 August 1958
Connie Francis	"Carolina Moon"/"Stupid Cupid"	26 September 1958
Tommy Edwards	"It's All In The Game"	7 November 1958
Lord Rockingham's XI	"Hoots Mon"	28 November 1958
Conway Twitty	"It's Only Make Believe"	19 December 1958
Jane Morgan	"The Day The Rains Came"	23 January 1959
Elvis Presley	"I Got Stung"/"One Night"	30 January 1959
Shirley Bassey	"As I Love You"	20 February 1959
The Platters	"Smoke Gets In Your Eyes"	20 March 1959
Russ Conway	"Side Saddle"	27 March 1959
Buddy Holly	"It Doesn't Matter Anymore"	24 April 1959
Elvis Presley	"A Fool Such As I"/"I Need Your Love Tonight"	15 May 1959
Russ Conway	"Roulette"	19 June 1959
Bobby Darin	"Dream Lover"	3 July 1959
Cliff Richard & The Shadows	"Living Doll"	31 July 1959
Craig Douglas	"Only Sixteen"	11 September 1959
Jerry Keller	"Here Comes Summer"	9 October 1959
Bobby Darin	"Mack the Knife"	16 October 1959
Cliff Richard & The Shadows	"Travellin' Light"	30 October 1959
Adam Faith	"What Do You Want?"	4 December 1959
Emile Ford & The Checkmates	"What Do You Want To Make Those Eyes At Me For"	18 Dec 1959

The record labels added even more clutter to the music charts with their steady output of so-called novelty records alongside other officially safe genres such as the classics, jazz, and melody-lite ballads. It's worth remembering that Parlophone was EMI's bargain basement label, known as 'joke' records, the staple fair of newly-promoted producer, George Martin, until he was 'persuaded' to audition The Beatles!

Unknown to Martin at the time, Brian Epstein was struggling to get The Beatles a record deal and was so desperate to secure a contract that he resorted to leaning on EMI's management with veiled threats that if he didn't get a record deal soon, he'd pull the plug on the sale of EMI records at his NEMS stores. The irony is that George Martin was just as eager to find something or someone to help him break out of the 'joke' record department groove he was in. Although Martin drew a short straw when it came to auditioning The Beatles, it was to prove both a historical turning point and a blessing when the cheeky lads from Liverpool strolled into Abbey Road Studios in 1962.

Breaking out of the Groove

Before then, it's fair to say that Ingerlund (and London in particular) simply didn't swing 'like a Penduuluumm Doooooo' as American popster Roger Miller once drawled. Doh! In fact, apart from passing fads like the Skiffle craze, there had been no identifiably "teenage" music in Britain at all.

Skiffle swept the country like chicken pox, but it was only after Lonnie Donegan wowed the crowd at Liverpool's Empire Theatre that something special happened in the city. It was as if Lonnie had reached out and, at a stroke, converted every young man in the theatre, including George Harrison, who later tracked him to a private house to get his autograph. Suddenly, Liverpool lads rushed to Rushworth & Dreapers and Hessy's Music Stores to buy acoustic guitars on the 'never-never' (the newly-relaxed hire purchase laws) then rushed back home to master Lonnie's magical 'three chords' in their bedrooms, back sheds or alleyways. One such convert was a young Liverpool man called Faron Ruffley (of Faron's Flamingos fame). Faron fondly remembers trying to electrify his guitar by plugging the wires straight into an electric socket. Fortunately, his DIY attempt to become Britain's hottest burnt cinder was foiled when his dad came home and stopped him just in the nick of time.

Meantime, Skiffle groups sprang up overnight like mushrooms and, although the world is now familiar with the legendary Quarrymen, very few realize they were only one of hundreds of Skiffle and country music groups on Merseyside.

In our Liverpool home

Skiffle proved to be a relatively short-lived craze and the shift to sexier rock 'n' roll soon followed, with Liverpool adding its distinctly gritty nasal catarrh sound to the mix. Not everyone appreciated the new wave however. Deep in the city's underground dungeons, the die-hard trad jazz beatniks held a firm grip on local club owners until the dam was breached forever when Rory Storm and The Hurricanes staged an open rebellion one night and broke into a rock 'n' roll set in a smelly cellar called The Cavern Jazz club. The purists in the audience were so outraged that they pelted the band with a hail of old brass pennies. Rory toughed it out and collected the pennies later on. It was far more than the club fee they'd been paid and, more importantly, Rory's act of defiance is remembered for kick-

starting the Liverpool stampede to rock and pop with a vengeance.

A new counter-culture was born that night – an exclusive teenage underground movement that spread slowly but surely to every city district. Each area already had its fair share of local clubs, promoters and bands that were now being followed by an increasing number of dedicated fans – girls especially. One of the biggest factors in the development of the city's territorial venues was the problem of public transport. In those days the bus services finished early across the entire city (11pm latest) and rather than risk a very long walk home late at night (and face the anger of their strict fathers), many girl clubbers chose to stay local.

Gangs were also a big problem for any youth silly or brave enough to venture out of his or her own district alone and, generally, personal safety played a big part in deciding where to go and what club to attend. Rather perversely, some venues, such as Garston's notorious 'Blood Baths', attracted regular gangs of so-called Teddy Boys like wasps to a honey pot. For them, Friday night was fight night, when even local police preferred to round up the broken bodies after they flew out through the club doors, rather than go inside. Today, we view it all with misty-eyed nostalgia. It may not have been a widespread issue, but few can deny there were times when fight nights were a real danger for bands and clubbers alike as Rory Storm, John Lennon, Stu Sutcliffe and many other groups found out to their cost.

Even before the beat wave swept over the rest of the country, Liverpool had over 300 live acts, most of them performing seven nights a week in just as many jive hives, night clubs, coffee clubs and pubs – not to mention the church halls, ice rinks, swimming baths, and the Mersey ferry boats. In contrast to London's cabaret and theatre scene around Soho and the West End, Liverpool's music venues were firmly embedded in every community across the city, Merseyside and the Wirral. One only has to read the following list to appreciate the scale and diversity of venues and acts available at the time.

THE CLUBS

Aintree Institute
All Hallows, Allerton
All Saints, Stoneycroft
Angers House, Netherton
Blair Hall
Bootle Town Hall
Brighton Rd Methodist Church, Southport
Childwall Labour Club
Columba Hall
Congregational Church, Speke
David Lewis Theatre
Deacon Road Labour Club
Dovecot Mission Hall
Emmanuel Church, Fazakerley
Emmanuel Hall, West Derby Rd.
Empress Club
Garston Parish Church
Garston Swimming Baths
Grosvenor Ballroom
Hambleton Hall
Hartington Road Congregational
Holy Trinity, Formby
Holy Trinity, Walton
Holyoake Hall
Hoylake Evangelical Church
Huyton Congregational
Kensington Ice Rink
Knotty Ash Village Hall
La Mystere
La Scala
Lathom Hall (now a living museum and club)
Litherland Town Hall
Little Neston Methodist Hall
Liverpool Dockers Club
Liverpool Seamen's Mission
Liverpool Stadium
Merrifield
Merseyside Civil Service Club
Methodist Church, Netherton
Methodist Church, St. Helens
Methodist Youth Club, Aigburth
Mossway Hall
MPTE Social Club Dovecot
MPTE Social Club Speke
N.U.R.
Neston Institute
New Brighton Tower Ballroom
New Clubmoor Hall
Norgreen Social
O.D.V.A. Social Club
Orrel Park Ballroom
Orrel Park Baptist Church
Ozzie Wade's
Page Moss Baptist Church
Palm Grove Methodist Church, Birkenhead
Quaintways
Royal Navy Club
Salvation Army Hall, Clubmoor
Skelmersdale Christian Fellowship
Skelmersdale Town Hall
Southport Floral Hall
St. Ambrose, Everton

St. Andrew's, Bebington
St. Andrew's, Clubmoor
St. Anne's, Aigburth
St. Benedict's, Everton
St. Catherine's, Birkenhead
St. Cuthbert's, Everton
St. Cyprian's, Edge Hill
St. David & St. Mark, St. Helens
St. George's Hall
St. Helens Parish Church
St. John & St. James, Bootle
St. John's Hall
St. John's, Ainsdale
St. John's, Waterloo
St. John's, Widnes
St. Leonard's, Bootle
St. Luke's, Cantril Farm
St. Mark's, Newtown
St. Mary's Church School, Bootle
St. Mary's, Upton
St. Mathew's, St Helens
St. Paul's, Hatton Hill
St. Philemon's, Toxteth
St. Phillip's, Litherland
St. Simon and St Jude, Southport
Stanley Abattoir Social Club
Stanley Rd. Baptist Church, Bootle
The 5 Club
The Black Cat
The Blue Angel
The Cabaret Club
The Caribbean Club
The Casbah Club
The Cassanova
The Cavern
The City Mission
The Downbeat Club
The Empire Theatre
The Gordon Smith Institute
The Grafton Rooms
The Iron Door
The Jacaranda
The Jive Hive
The Lowlands Club
The Mardi Gras
The Odd Spot
The Peoples Church, Everton
The Peppermint Lounge
The Pink Parrot
The Rialto (burned out in the Toxteth Riots)
The Sink
The Temple Club
Valentine Rock Club
Warrington Independent Methodist Hall
Wavertree Town Hall
West Kirby Methodist Church
Willow Club
Wilson Hall
York Street Mission, St. Helens

NB. It's been widely claimed that Liverpool City Council has now done more damage to the city's music club heritage than the bombing of 1940 and who are we to argue? Our apologies if we have omitted or misspelled any club names.

As competition to obtain regular bookings began to grow, so did the rivalry. Competition forced groups to improve their acts, visually and musically, or risk being jettisoned by promoters and fans alike. Nevertheless, the local gold fever soon turned into a stampede as eager young men rushed to grab their share of the girls!

Following is probably the most complete list ever published of known groups or artists (over 700 here) who were active on Merseyside from 1956 to 1964. There were probably many more, but their names and fates are now lost in the dust of time. For this reason we apologise here for any misspelt or omitted any names in advance.

A

Aarons, The
Abraham & His Lot
Adam & The Sinners
Agents, The
Alamos, The
Alaskans, The
Alby & The Sorrals
Aldo, Steve
Alfie Diamond & The Skiffle Kings
Alibis, The
Allen, Tony
Alley Cats, The
Almost Blues, The
Alphas, The
Ambassadors, The
Amos & The TTs
Amos, Bonny
Anzacs, The
Aristocrats, The
Arrow & The Archers
Arrows, The
Atlantas, The
Aztecs, The

B

Babs and Joan
Bachelors, The
Backbeats, The
Bags Blue Beats
Banshees, The
Barbara Grounds
Barmen Skiffle Group, The
Beat Boys, The
Beatcombers, The
Beathovens, The
Beatles, The
Beatwoods, The
Bertie Collins & The Sundowners
Big Lox Blues Band, The
Big Three, The
Billy Forde & The Phantoms
Billy J. (added period) Kramer & The Dakotas
Black Cats, The
Black Diamonds, The
Black Knights, The
Black Velvets, The
Black, Cilla
Blackjacks, The
Blackwells, The
Blak Katz, The
Blue Beats, The
Blue Chips, The
Blue Country Boys, The
Blue Diamonds, The
Blue Four, The
Blue Mountain Boys, The
Blue Notes, The
Blues System, The

Bob Evans & The Five Shillings
Bobby & The Bachelors
Bobby & The Halers
Bobby Bell Rockers, The
Bob's Vegas Five
Boleros, The
Boot Hill Billies, The
Boys, The
Breakaways, The
Brokers, The
Brown, Irene
Bruce & The Cavaliers
Buddy Dean & The Teachers
Buffaloes, The
Bumblies, The

C

Cadillac & The Playboys
Cadillacs, The
Calderstones, The
Caribbeans, The
Carl Vincent & The Counts
Carol & The Corvettes
Carroll, Irene
Carrolls, The
Cass & The Cassanovas
Casuals, The
Cavaliers, The
Cavemen, The
Caverners, The
Centaurs, The
Centremen, The
Chain Gang, The
Challengers, The
Champions, The
Chants, The
Cheaters, The
Cheetahs, The
Cheetham, Vicki
Chelseas, The
Chessmen, The
Chick Graham & The Coasters
Ching, Christine
Chris & The Diamonds
Christian, Tony
Chuckles, The
Cimarrons, The
Cirques, The
Citadels, The
Citrons, The
City Beats, The
Clansmen, The
Classics, The
Clay Ellis & The Raiders
Clayton Squares, The
Cliff Roberts' Rockers
Climbers, The
Coins, The

Collage
Collegians, The
Columbians, The
Comets, The
Concords, The
Coney Island Skiffle Group, The
Connoisseurs, The
Conquests, The
Conspirators, The
Contenders, The
Contrasts, The
Corals, The
Cordelles, The
Cordes, The
Corsairs, The
Corvettes, The
Countdowns, The
Country Comfort
Country Cousins
Country Five, The
Coupiers, The
Creoles, The
Crescendos, The
Crestas, The
Crossbeats, The
Cruisers, The
Crusaders, The
Cryin' Shames, The
Cy & The Cimmarons
Cy Tucker's Friars

D

Dale Roberts & The Jaywalkers
Daleks, The
Danny & The Asteroids
Danny & The Escorts
Danny & The Hi-Cats
Danny Havoc & The Secrets
Danny Havoc & The Ventures
Danny Lee & The Stalkers
Darktown Skiffle Group, The
Dateliners, The
Dave & Corvettes
Dave & The Rave-Ons
Dave Bell & The Bell Boys
David Garick
Daybreakers, The
Dealers, The
Dean Fleming & The Flamingos
Dean Stacey & The Dominators
Deans, The
Debutones, The
Dee & The Dynamites
Dee Beats, The
Dee Fenton's Silhouettes
Dee Young & The Pontiacs
Dee, Barbara
Deepbeats, The
Deerstalkers, The

Deesiders, The
Defenders, The
Defiants, The
Del Renas, The
Delameres, The
Delcardoes, The
Delltones, The
Delmont Four, The
Delmonts, The
Demoiselles, The
Demon Five, The
Denems, The
Denis & The Newtowns
Dennisons, The
Denny Seyton & The Sabres
Deputies, The
Derry Wilkie & The Others
Derry Wilkie & The Pressmen
Detonators, The
Detours, The
Diablos, The
Diamonds, The
Dimensions, The
Dino & The Wild Fires
Diplomats, The
Dixie & The Daredevils
Dominant Four, The
Downbeats, The
Drifting Cowboys, The
Dynachords, The
Dynamic Daybreakers, The
Dynamos, The

E

Earl Preston & The Realms
Earl Preston & The TTs
Earl Royce & The Olympics
Earls, The
Earthlings Blues Band, The
Easybeats, The
Eddie Clayton Skiffle Group
Eddie Dean & The Onlookers
Eddie Lee Five, The
Eddy Falcon & The Vampires
Electrons, The
Elektones, The
Epics, The
Escorts, The
Everests, The
Everglades, The
Excelles, The
Excheckers, The
Executioners, The
Explorers, The
Expressions, The
Eyes, The

F

Factotums, The
Falcons, The
Fallons, The
Faron & The Burnettes
Faron & The Crossfires
Faron & The Tempest

Faron's Flamingos
Fast Cats, The
FBI, The
Federal Five, The
Feelgoods, The
Few, The
Fire-Flites, The
Fix, The
Flames, The
Flintstones, The
Flyaways, The
Flyovers, The
Foggy Mountain Ramblers, The
Fontanas, The
Four Aces, The
Four Aristokats, The
Four Clefs, The
Four Dimensions, The
Four Gents, The
Four Hits & A Miss
Four Jays, The
Four Just Men, The
Four Musketeers, The
Four Originals, The
Fourmost, The
Frank Knight & The Barons
Freddie Starr & The Delmonts
Freddie Starr & The Midnighters
Freddie Starr & The Ventures
Fruit Eating Bears, The
Fury, Billy
Futurists, The

G

Galaxies with Doreen, The
Galvanizers, The
Gary B. Goode & The Hot Rods
Gay Tones, The
Gee Gee & The Go Men
Gems, The
Gene Day & The Django Beats
Geoff Stacey & The Wanderers
George Nield Trio, The
Georgians, The
Gerry & The Pacemakers
Gerry Bach & The Beathovens
Gerry De Ville & The City Kings
Ghost Riders, The
Gibsons, The
Gin Mill Skiffle Group, The
Globetrotters, The
Griff Parry Five, The
Group One
Groups Inc.
Gus & The Thundercaps
Gus Travis & The Midnighters

H

Halliday, Michael
Hailers, The
Hammers, The
Hank & The Drifters
Hank Walters & The Dusty Road
Ramblers

Harlems, The
Hartford West
Heartbeats, The
Hellions, The
Heralds, The
Hi-Cats, The
Hideaways, The
Hi-Fi Three, The
Hi-Hats, The
Hillsiders, The
Hi-Spots, The
Hi-Spots, The
Howie Casey & The Seniors
Hughes, Rita
Huntsmen, The
Hustlers, The
Hylites, The

I

Ian & The Zodiacs
Ice Blues, The
Idle Hours
Illusions, The
Impacts, The
Incas, The
Inmates, The
Invaders, The
Irene & The Sante Fès

J

J.C. & The Strollers
J.J. & The Hi-Lites
Jackie & Bridie
Jackobeats, The
Jaguars, The
James Boys, The
Jaybeats, The
Jaywalkers, The
Jenny & The Tallboys
Jensons, The
Jet & The Valiants
Jets, The
Jimmy & The Jokers
Jimmy & The Midnighters
Joan & The Demons
Johnny Apollo & The Spartans
Johnny Gold & The Country
Johnny Gus Set, The
Johnny Marlowe & The WhipChords
Johnny Martin & The Martinis
Johnny Paul & The Dee Jays
Johnny President & The Senators
Johnny Ringo & The Colts
Johnny Rocco & The Jets
Johnny Saint & The Travellers
Johnny Sandon & The RemoFour
Johnny Sandon & The Searchers
Johnny Tempest & The Tornadoes
Jokers, The
Jordan, Tommy

K

Kandies, The
Kansas City Five, The
Karacters, The
Karina
Karl Terry & The Cruisers
Ken Dallas & The Silhouettes
Kenny Johnson & Northwind
Kentuckians, The
Keoki & The Hawaiianeers
Kingpins, The
Kingsize Taylor & The Dominoes
Kingstrums, The
Kinsleys, The
Kirkbys, The
Kliff Hilton & The Merseys
Knutrockers, The
Kobras, The
Koobas, The
Kordas, The
Kruzads, The

L

Landslides, The
Lawmen, The
Lee Castle & The Barons
Lee Crombie & The Sundowners
Lee Curtis & The All Stars
Lee Curtis & The Detours
Lee Eddie & The Chevrons
Lee Eddie Five, The
Lee Shondell & The Boys
Lee Shondell & The Capitols
Leesiders, The
Legends, The
Lenny & The Team Mates
Les Stewart Quartet, The
Liam & The Invaders
L'il Three, The
Lilli Leyton
Lincolns, The
Little Ginny Band
Liverbirds, The
Lonely Ones, The
Lonesome Travellers
Long & The Short, The
Louie & The Weimars
L'Ringo's

M

M.I.5. The
Mafia, The
Mailman, The
Mal Craig Three, The
Malloy, Joan
Managers, The
Maracas, The
Marescas, The
Mark Peters & The Method
Mark Peters & The Silhouettes
Mark Swain & The Tornadoes
Markfour, The
Marlins, The
Marsden, Beryl

Martin, Jackie
Martin, Jill
Martinis, The
Masqueraders, The
Masterminds, The
Mastersounds, The
Mavericks, The
Megatones, The
Memphis R&B Combo, The
Memphis Three, The
Merchants, The
Mersey Bluebeats, The
Mersey Five, The
Mersey Four, The
Mersey Gamblers, The
Mersey Men, The
Mersey Monsters, The
Mersey Sounds, The
Merseybeats, The
Meteors, The
Method, The
MGs, The
Michael Allen Group, The
Mikados, The
Mike & The Explorers
Mike Byrne & The Thunderbirds
Mike Savage & The Wildcats
Mike See & The Detours
Miller Brothers, The
Minibeats, The
Minutes, The
Missouri Drifters, The
Mojos, The
Moments, The
Morockans, The
Mosquitos, The
Motives, The
Mr. Lee & Co.
Music Students, The
Musicians, The
Mustangs, The
Mystery Men, The
Mystics, The

N

Nameless Ones, The
Nashpool Four, The
Night Boppers, The
Nightriders, The
Nocturnes, The
Nomads, The
Notions, The

O

Obsession, The
Ogi & The Flintstones
Onlookers, The
Others, The
Outkasts, The
Outlaws, The

P

Pacifics, The
Paddy Kelly Band, The

Page Boys, The
Paladins, The
Panthers, The
Paragons, The
Pathfinders, The
Paul & The Diamonds
Paul Francis & The Wanderers
Paul Valance & The Tremors
Pawns, The
Pegasus Four, The
Pete Picasso & The Rock
Peter Demos & His Demons
Phantoms, The
Phil Brady & The Ranchers
Phil's Feelgoods
Pikkins, The
Pilgrims, The
Plebs, The
Plims, The
Pontiacs, The
Poppies, The
Premiers, The
Press Gang, The
Principles, The
Profiles, The
Prowlers, The
Pulsators, The
Pyramids, The

Q

Quarrymen, The
Quickly, Tommy
Quiet Ones, The
Quintones, The

R

Rainchecks, The
Rainmakers, The
Ramrods, The
Ranchers, The
Ravens, The
Ray Satan & The Devils
Rebel Rousers, The
Rebels, The
Reds Incorporated
Remo Four, The
Renegades, The
Renicks, The
Rent Collectors, The
Rhythm & Blues Incorporated
Rhythm Amalgamated
Rhythm Quintet, The
Rhythm Rockers, The
Richmond Group, The
Rick & The Delmonts
Ricky & The Dominant Four
Ricky Gleason & The Top Spots
Rikki & The Red Streaks
Riot Squad, The
Rip Van Winkle & The Rip-It-Ups
Rivals, The
Road Ramblers
Roadrunners, The
Robettes, The

Robin & The Ravens
Rockerfellers, The
Rockin' Climbers, The
Rockin' Rivals, The
Rocky Stone & The Pebbles
Rogers, Rita
Rogues Gallery
Ron Pickard Combo, The
Rondex, The
Rontons, The
Rory & The Globe Trotters
Rory Storm & The Hurricanes
Rory Storm & The Wild Ones
Rosa, Lita
Roy & The Dions
Roy Montrose & The Midnighters
Runaways, The

S
Saddlers, The
Sandgrounders, The
Sandstorms, The
Santones, The
Sapphires, The
Savva & The Democrats
Schatz, The
Screaming Skulls, The
Scorpians, The
Sculptors
Searchers, The
Secrets, The
Seftons, The
Senators, The
Seniors, The
Sensations, The
Sepias, The
Set Up, The
Shades, The
Shakers, The
Shimmy Shimmy Queens
Silvertones, The
Sinners, The
Skeletons, The
Skylarks, The
Skyliners, The
Sneakers, The
Sobells, The
Some People
Sonnets, The
Sonny Kaye & The Reds
Sorrals, The
Soul Agents, The
Soul Seekers, The
Sounds Plus One
Spectres, The
Spidermen, The
Spinners, The
Sportsmen, The
Squad with Rita, The
St. Louis Checks
St. Louis Checks, The
Statesmen, The
Stereos, The
Steve & The Syndicate

Steve Day & The Drifters
Strangers, The
Strettons, The
String Dusters, The
Subterranes, The
Sundowners, The
Swaydes, The
Swinging Blue Jeans, The
Syndicate, The

T
Tabs, The
Take Five
Talismen, The
Team-mates, The
Teen Tones, The
Teenage Rebels, The
Teenbeats, The
Templars, The
Tempos, The
Tenabeats, The
Tennessee Five, The
Terry Hines Sextet, The
Texans, The
That Group
Them Grimbles
Thoughts, The
Three Bells, The
Three Deuces, The
Three of Diamonds, The
Thrillers, The
Thunderbeats, The
Thunderbirds, The
Tiffany's Dimensions
Tiffany's Thoughts
TJs, The
TL's Bluesicians
Tokens, The
Tom and Bernie
Tommy & The Metronomes
Tommy & The Olympics
Tommy & The Satellites
Tony & The Checkers
Tony & The Quandros
Tony Carlton & The MerseyFour
Topics, The
Tornadoes, The
Traders, The
Travellers, The
Tremas, The
Trends, The
Trents, The
Tributes, The
Triffids, The
Triumphs, The
Troubles, The
Tudor Four, The
Tudors, The
Tuxedos, The
Two Tones, The
U
Undertakers, The
V

V.I.C.'s, The
V.I.P.'s, The
Vaders, The
Valentinos, The
Valkyries, The
Vampires, The
Vance Williams Rhythm Four
Vaughan, Franky
Vegas Five, The
Ventures, The
Verbs, The
Vernon Girls, The
Vic & The TTs
Vic Takes Four
Vigilantes, The
Vikings, The
Vikki Lane & The Moonlighters
Vince Earl & The Talismen
Vince Earl & The Zeroes
Vince Reno & The Sabres
Vinny & The Dukes

W
Walter Corless Combo, The
Washington Band, The
Wayne Calvert & The Cimmarons
Wayne Stevens & The Vikings
Weeverbeats, The
Wells Fargo
Western Union
Westerners, The
West Virginia
Wheels, The
White, Lorraine
Wild Harkes, The
Willows, The
Wolfgang Combo
Wranglers, The
Wump & His Werbles

Y
Young Ones, The

Z
Zenith Six, The
Zephyrs, The

It was Merseyside's myriad of clubs that hundreds of groups vied with each other to be the best group, have the best new songs, and the best routines. Standing out from the crowd would never be easy, and finding the right mix of musicians to make the perfect group would also take a lot of tinkering, experimenting, and dumping of musicians.

Once John, Paul and George got together in The Quarrymen by the end of 1957, the nucleus of The Beatles was formed. All they needed was the right drummer, a task that proved to be more difficult than they would have imagined.

The search for the Fourth Beatle had begun.

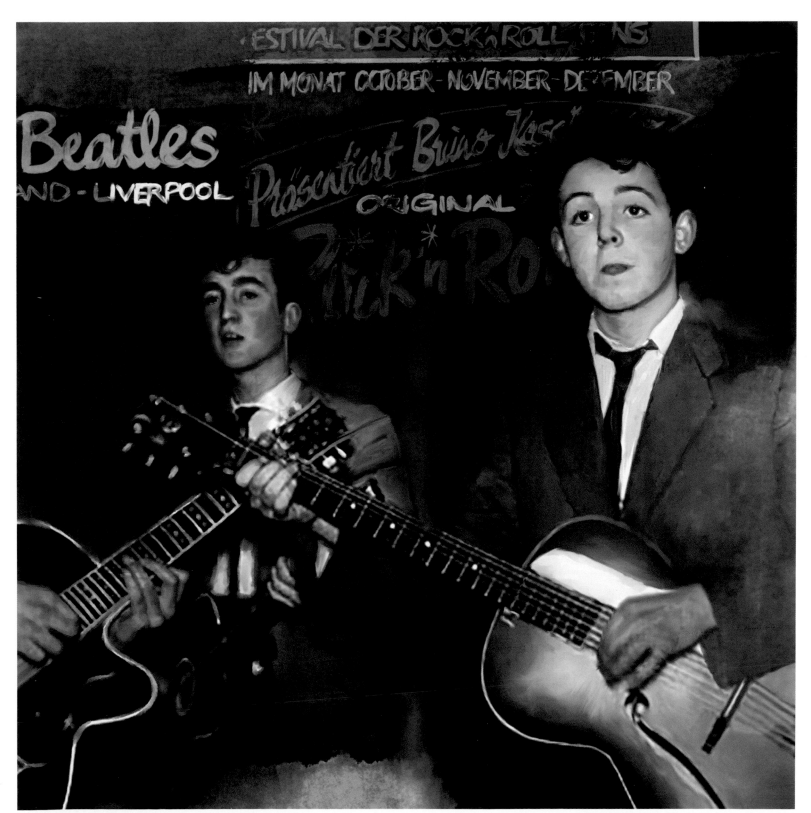

Original painting by Paul Skellett (www.skellett.com)

35

A BRIEF HISTORY OF THE DRUM

The playing of drums can be traced back to ancient China around 5500 BC, where archaeology has shown that they were used in religious or ritual ceremonies - Cymbals date to 1100 BC, and were mainly found in Turkey and China, though also in Israel and Egypt. In addition to their use in places of worship, the drum was also prevalent in times of war as early as 680 BC, providing encouragement and also setting the marching beat. Existing evidence indicates that a battle between the Qi and Lu was significantly changed because of the use of the drums. Around 500 BC, the instruments were used in Sri Lanka as a form of communication, and this has been replicated in many ancient civilisations.

The modern drum set is comprised mainly of the snare drum and bass drum, with associated tom-toms and cymbals. The earliest snare drum, known as Tabors, appeared in medieval Europe around 1300 AD and would have been beaten with an early form of drumstick. The Timpani appeared in Europe in the 1400s, though regular use isn't found for another two hundred years. The bass drum, which is the driving beat of any modern day band, appeared in the 1400s and has its origins in Turkey and is therefore often referred to as the Turkish drum. In the 1700s, the drumstick started to evolve, and a variety of woods were used, with ebony the most popular.

With the snare drum and bass drum established, the modern tom-toms have their roots in the bongo drums from the tribes in the Savanna of North Africa, and were often played as a twin set. Through the slave trade, these instruments accompanied the two million slaves who travelled from Africa to the Caribbean and then the southern states of the U.S. As typified by the American Civil War, the marching snare drum became popular, as did marching bands centred in New Orleans.

The concept of double-drumming – the playing of two drums by one drummer – originated around 1865 as percussionists experimented with sound. In the 1890s, photographs were taken that show bass drums being played with pedals. Also, the massive influx of immigrants into the United States saw many of these newcomers bringing with them various musical instruments which were then incorporated into the musical evolution taking place.

The musicians therefore needed to assemble these separate drums into a drum set, the earliest of which appeared in the early 1900s. Kits became a staple of modern music groups as marching bands gave way to ragtime, jazz, blues, gospel and, of course, rock 'n' roll. Ragtime greats like Buddy Gilmore made records that featured a drummer and, in 1909, one the greatest names in drumming, Ludwig, patented the bass drum pedal that is still being used. The pure wooden drum sticks weren't lasting long and, in 1913, the retractable flyswatter was patented and used by many drummers as the first style of drum brushes.

The first jazz records made were by the The Original Dixieland Jazz Band in 1917, and drummers like New Orleans-based Baby Dodds become well known. Two years later, as prohibition was enforced, Chicago became the hub of jazz music, which reached its peak in the Roaring Twenties. Musicians were in demand to help provide the backing for silent movies, but as the "talkies" started to appear at the end of the 1920s, many musicians were put out of a job. As swing music came to the fore at the end of the decade, the drum kit was enhanced by the use of hi-hat cymbals, a feature that became a permanent fixture.

By 1935, this new style of swing music evolved into the big band sound and, with it, the first drummer to make a name for himself – Gene Krupa, a virtuoso who would influence a whole generation of drummers. Krupa provided the rhythm for the Benny Goodman Orchestra, one of many big bands that would define the era.

The 1940s saw the development of the be-bop style of music in Harlem – and the continuing evolution of the music scene as a new genre was born in the small-band heavy shuffle of pioneers like Louis Jordan. By 1949, this new sound was dubbed "rhythm and blues", which featured the heavy use of the snare drum for the first time. In 1955, rock 'n' roll was first featured in a movie as "Rock Around The Clock" by Bill Haley brought this exciting new music form to the world, especially to a small town on the west coast of England: Liverpool.

The last drum revolution involved drum sticks. In 1958, with rock 'n' roll on the rise and the wooden sticks and brushes not up to the task, Joe Calato invented a nylon-tipped drum stick, which is now the norm for drummers the world over. In 1963, Vic Firth patented, designed and commercially sold pairs of drum sticks based on their weight and pitch, which revolutionised how sticks were made.

The following year, Buddy Rich, one of the greatest drummers of all time, put together his band, influencing countless drummers. Then in 1965, when The Beatles' televised concert at Shea Stadium was broadcast, Ringo's "matched grip", as opposed to the "traditional grip", became popular.

Ringo would go on to redefine the role of the drummer in popular music, impacting a new generation of drummers who cite him as their greatest influence.

THE 23 DRUMMERS

Who are the 23 featured drummers in Finding the Fourth Beatle?

Colin Hanton
1956-1958

Pete Shotton
24th August 1957

Mike McCartney
November 1958

Tommy Moore
10th May - 13th June 1960

Johnny Hutchinson
10th May 1960
and 16th August 1962

Cliff Roberts
14th May 1960

Paul McCartney
16th - 20th June 1960
and 22nd - 23rd August 1968

Ronnie the "Ted"
11th June 1960

Jackie Lomax
11th/ 18th June 1960

Norman Chapman
June - August 1960

Pete Best
15th August 1960
15th August 1962

Ringo Starr
15th October 1960,
27th December 1961,
5th February 1962,
26th March 1962,
then 18th August 1962 - 1970

Alan Leyland
Spring 1961 - one night

Terry McCann
9th December 1961

Andy White
11th September 1962

Bobby Graham
24th March 1963

Norman Smith
16th April 1964

Jimmie Nicol
4th - 15th June 1964

Anil Bhagwat
11th April 1966

Mal Evans
1st June 1966

Natwar Soni
15th March 1967

Keith Moon
25th June 1967

Mahapurush Misra
13th January 1968

Others Who Played With Some Of Them

Aneurin Thomas

(The Vikings with Paul and George)
July 1958

Ray Skinner

(George with the Les Stewart Quartet)
February 1959

Jeff Wallington

(Derry & The Seniors and The Beatles jam)
4th October 1960

Freddie Marsden

(The Beatmakers - Gerry and the
Pacemakers and The Beatles together)
19th October 1961

Rudiger Neber

(The Bats with Stuart Sutcliffe)
February 1962

Dave Lovelady

(The Four Jays and The Beatles)
5th April 1962

Almost The Fourth Beatle But Didn't Play With The Group

Terry Hymans

August 1960

Gerry Winstanley

August 1960

Trevor Morais

August 1962

Ritchie Galvin

August 1962

Bill Buck

August 1962

Claimed To - But Didn't Play

Bernard Purdie

Dave Rowe

1956 - 1958

COLIN HANTON - THE FIRST FOURTH BEATLE

The very first drummer who played with The Fab Three was Colin Hanton, the teen who kept the beat for John Lennon's first group, The Quarrymen.

Colin's family, who had lived in Bootle, then moved to Woolton and lived at 4, Heyscroft Road, halfway between the houses of Quarrymen Eric Griffiths and Rod Davis. Colin met Eric on the bus, and when Eric discovered that Colin had a set of drums, he recruited him into the Quarrymen, though the exact date is unknown.

"I used to listen to jazz records and play the beat on the furniture," explained Colin. "My parents said that if I bought the drums, I could play them in the house." Hanton did what many Liverpool lads were doing, and headed down to Hessy's – Frank Hessy's Music Centre – where he bought a drum kit in installments of ten shillings a week. "It was £34 in total," Colin recalled. This was a sizeable sum, though, unlike his future Quarrymen friends, Colin was already earning a living. "Eric asked if he could hear me play," he recalled. "I set up the drums, put on a record and played along to it." That was all Eric needed to hear. "So Eric said, 'Come and meet the lads'. That was it. I was a Quarryman."

(David Bedford Interview 2008)

The first engagements that Colin remembered playing with The Quarrymen were at St. Peter's Church Hall, where John and his friends were members. It was just for fun, not for money, and good experience for the fledgling group. They then progressed to a real booking at Lee Park Golf Club, arranged by their friend and manager Nigel Walley. Colin remembers them being stuck in a corner, with people "sitting around two sides of the room" as they played. It was here that Colin attracted his first "groupie". A young girl pulled up a chair alongside him

The Quarrymen, 6th July 1957

while he was trying to play. "She kept on grabbing hold of my left arm, so I couldn't play. Then she started asking me questions about drumming."

(Hunter Davies. The Quarrymen)

Not quite the mania that would grab The Beatles a few years later! The admiring young lady then offered the group a lift, and dropped them all off in Woolton Village. Although they hadn't been paid a fee, food and drink had been provided. The obligatory hat had also been passed round for tips, so they did earn "a few bob".

Colin at that time had developed an interest in wearing rings; he was a trendsetter among drummers. The group's repertoire was largely based on the songs of Lonnie Donegan and American folk and railroad songs. It was Donegan's popular version of "Rock Island Line" that kick-started the skiffle craze that swept Britain between 1956 and 1958. Other songs the group played were "Cumberland Gap", "Midnight Special", "Railroad Bill", "Worried Man Blues", "Freight Train", "Blue Moon of Kentucky", "Lost John", "Don't You Rock Me Daddy-O", "Putting On The Style" and the Liverpool favourite, "Maggie May".

The Empire Theatre

Although the first recorded appearance of The Quarrymen was at Quarry Bank school in October 1956, the first advertised performance of The Quarrymen was at the Liverpool Empire on 9th June 1957 at a Carroll Levis Discoveries TV Show, one of the leading talent spotters. "For the Carroll Levis audition," recalled Colin, "we had to go to the Empire on the Sunday afternoon. We queued up outside with a lot of people to get in this very small door. Forms were given out which we had to fill in. John filled them in on behalf of The Quarrymen. All the acts not playing sat in the stalls while the ones about to play went backstage to get ready.

"Carroll Levis sat at a small writing desk at the side of the stage," said Colin. The group successfully progressed through the heat and made it to the next round, which was held on the Wednesday. By this heat, progress was measured with a "clapometer", which determined your success by audience reaction. Now at a dead heat with another group, they were both asked to play again. "It was all running late," he said, "so we didn't get much time, but the other group got three minutes more – and they won. Carroll Levis did say afterwards it had been a bit unfair, so we shouldn't give up." *(Hunter Davies. The Quarrymen)* The group was obviously starting to gel, just in time for two important dates.

Rosebery Street: 22nd June 1957

Hanton was a rarity in most skiffle groups because he was a drummer. Most groups relied on the washboard and tea-chest bass for rhythm, so The Quarrymen had an advantage over other bands. Through Hanton's friend Charlie Roberts, The Quarrymen were booked to appear at a street party celebrating Liverpool's 750th birthday in Rosebery Street, Liverpool 8. At this party on 22nd June 1957, Roberts took the very first photographs ever of John Lennon and The Quarrymen.

Colin remembered the event. "Charlie Roberts was one of my friends, and it was the 750th Anniversary of Liverpool, though we didn't know it at the time. I didn't hang around with John and the other Quarrymen members. I knew Eric

well, but I was a bit older than the others, so I was off drinking in town with my friends. Unless we were rehearsing, I was drinking with Charlie and Kevin Hansen, who was my closest mate for a long time." *(David Bedford Interview 2008))*

"At that time," remarked Charlie, "The Quarrymen would play anywhere for free, because they were doing it for fun. They became more serious after Paul joined, and maybe John was taking it seriously, but it was really just friends having some fun. They all turned up, and set themselves up on the back of a wagon that Fred Tyler had brought along. He also wired up a speaker system so that they had something for the microphones, so they made quite a loud noise, which was good." *(David Bedford Interview 2008)*

Colin's drums proudly displayed the name "Quarry Men" in the centre of the bass drum and "Colin Hanton" printed at the top. Charlie Roberts enjoyed the Quarrymen's performance. "I thought they were great, playing good music and entertaining. When you compare them to other bands, I suppose they weren't that good, but I enjoyed listening to them, and so did the crowd." *(David Bedford Interview 2008)*

Colin remembered them playing in the afternoon "on the back of a coal wagon and then I went to the pub." The Quarrymen actually played twice that afternoon. At the second performance, a famous event took place: John Lennon caused trouble and the police were involved, though the story has grown in legend over the years. Colin remembered what happened. "I knew some of the other lads in the crowd, and heard that they were planning to grab John as he got off the wagon, because he had been making eyes at the girls in the crowd, and the lads weren't happy. I was on the end of the wagon with my drums, so I called John over and told him, so we jumped off quickly, and headed for Charlie Robert's house, which was the only one we could get into. The lads chased us, but we just made it into the house in time." *(David Bedford Interview 2008)*

Hanton also confirmed what part the police had to play in the story. "We had to finish early because of the trouble, so the police were called and this bobby (local policeman) came and walked the other band members down to the bus stop." Colin was exempt from the police escort though, because "I had met this girl in the pub earlier, so I walked her to her house, which was in Rosebery Street." And what did the Quarrymen's romeo drummer put it down to? "I think it was the drums that did it!" *(David Bedford Interview 2008)*

St. Peter's Church: 6th July 1957

Colin was also present just a couple of weeks later at St. Peter's Church in Woolton when Ivan Vaughan brought his schoolmate Paul McCartney to meet John Lennon. It was Colin who first witnessed an introduction in the afternoon. "At some time in the afternoon after playing," he said, "we had stored our equipment in the big Scout hut. We went in, and I was messing with my drums and there was a lad on his trumpet and then there was John and Ivan and this other lad, who of course turned out to be Paul McCartney.

"Now, everyone says that the meeting of John and Paul took place in the church hall later on that day, but I wasn't in the hall then, so it must have been in the Scout hut. I couldn't confuse the two. I reckon the first introduction happened in the Scout hut in the afternoon. I am adamant that the introduction took place in

Original painting by Paul Skellett (www.skellett.com)

the afternoon in that hut. Paul suggested John was drunk, but you couldn't get hold of booze, there were no off-licences (shops where you could purchase alcohol to be consumed elsewhere) or places to buy booze, and if you looked under eighteen there was no chance at all, so he couldn't have been drunk. He maybe had obtained a bottle off someone, but that would have been all." *(David Bedford Interview 2008)*

The most important part of the meeting between Lennon and McCartney took place in the church hall before the evening performance, though Colin said, "For the meeting with Paul in the evening I wasn't there, as the hall was on my side of the village. I had probably gone home for some tea, while the others hung around until the evening performance." Shortly after, Pete Shotton and Rod Davis left the group, but Colin was still there when Paul McCartney joined the group. By the time Paul's friend George Harrison joined the group, Colin was the only remaining original member other than John. The Fab Three were together by the end of 1957.

Paul McCartney's Debut

Most books will tell you that Paul McCartney made his debut with The Quarrymen on 18th October 1957 at New Clubmoor Hall. But that wasn't the case.

"We were just desperate to get onstage. We got on at the Cavern – Paul wasn't there because he was away with the scouts. It was Open Mic night, which was how we got down there, and then we got paid for it, so there was no way Paul joined in July and did not play until October at Clubmoor. We rehearsed and played in St. Peter's Hall, and then appeared at the contest at Wilson Hall." (David Bedford Interview 2008)

Colin explained how that happened. "After the summer fete in July '57," he said, "we used to play a lot at St. Peter's Church Hall on a Saturday night, and the guy had no microphone for us, and we kept asking for one. The Saturday dance became very big and they were getting all of their friends from school to come." Colin recalled that Paul was present. "Paul was there – saying to John there was no mic and he had been promised there would be a microphone. We got there late afternoon to set up, and John was looking round and there was no mic. The guy said he couldn't get one. John argued with the guy who said he hadn't been able to get a microphone. Paul said, 'He's rattled now because he's whistling' and so that was that: John decided we were not playing and we walked out, which was a bit of a mistake.

"I went home with my drums, and then back to the hall to look for the others. I got to the door and asked if John and the lads were there, and the guy said 'no, and he'll never get back in here!' This was soon after the fete and we used to rehearse there, too. They had a dance evening with a record player there by the stage, which was cranked up to full volume and then they danced the usual three waltzes and three quick steps and then as a musical interlude The Quarrymen would play." *(David Bedford Interview 2008)* By now, Rod Davis and Pete Shotton had quit the group, and there were more changes on the way soon.

Wilson Hall

It was these appearances at St. Peter's Church Hall on Saturday nights where Paul made his debut with The Quarrymen. This then lead to an appearance at Wilson Hall in Garston, at dances run by promoter Charlie McBain. "McBain had a good system whereby he had a 6-piece dance band/ orchestra who would play and then want a 45-minute break to go to the pub," explained Colin. "In the past he put the record player on, but he decided to have a skiffle contest. All he needed were five or six groups. You needed to pay two shillings and sixpence to get in, which at four or five people a group, and five or six groups, it was a great idea and he was quids in. John said, 'I'm not paying that, we're here for the competition', but Paul said the prize is £1 so just pay the money then we'll split the winnings." And how did they get on? "We didn't win!" said Colin emphatically. But all was not lost.

"McBain must have seen something," he said. "Even though we didn't win, that's how we got our bookings with him. Nigel Walley was a bit of a manager and he got us five ten-shilling notes – £2.50 – for playing. We definitely did Wilson Hall before Clubmoor, and that's how we got it, from the competition." *(David Bedford Interview 2008)* Charlie McBain ran promotions at both Wilson Hall and New Clubmoor Hall. The latter club was in north Liverpool, so there was no logical reason why they would have been picked to play there. McBain was the common denominator.

New Clubmoor Hall: 18th October 1957

And so it was that on 18th October 1957, Paul McCartney made his paid debut with The Quarrymen at New Clubmoor in North Liverpool. By this time, Paul was already starting to influence The Quarrymen. "Paul never challenged John's authority," Colin said, "but he was very diplomatic, very subtle. He always got his own way, but with subtle means. I remember at the start Paul wanted to smarten The Quarrymen up, but he never said let's get jackets, he just said to John, 'I'm going to wear a jacket'. He didn't say that we should wear one – it was sort of oatmeal colour, so of course John went out and got one too. So Paul got John dressed up without having a row or telling him to do it," as can be seen in the famous photograph, taken at Wilson Hall. *(David Bedford Interview 2008)*

When Paul made a mess of a guitar solo that night, he confessed to John that he wasn't a lead guitarist, but he knew one: George Harrison. Over the next few weeks, there would be more changes in personnel, with Len Garry leaving and Eric Griffiths being replaced by George. In 1958, bolstered occasionally by pianist John Duff Lowe, the bookings became more frequent, and so they decided to make a record.

Percy Phillips' Studio

Colin became the first drummer to record with John, Paul and George. The five Quarrymen – John, Paul, George, Colin and John Duff Lowe – turned up at Percy Phillips' studio at 38, Kensington, Liverpool, on 12th July 1958. They each paid seventeen shillings and sixpence (equivalent to 87.5 pence) to make a straight-to-disk double-sided shellac record. They recorded Buddy Holly's "That'll Be The Day" and the McCartney/ Harrison-credited song, "In Spite of All The Danger".

"We met at a theatre and walked up there," recalled Hanton. He remembered this so-called studio as a "back room with electronic equipment in the corner." They set up the equipment "with me in the corner and the lads with their guitars; there were no amps, it was all-acoustic." Poor John Duff Lowe was stuck over by the wall on the piano. "I was hitting the drums and he said that they were too loud, so I tried again but there was still the same problem, which was finally fixed by putting a scarf over the snare to soften it and keep it as quiet as possible." *(David Bedford Interview 2008)*

John Duff Lowe recalled that there was only one microphone hanging down from the ceiling, which picked everything up. Lowe suggested that they should pay the extra three shillings and sixpence (17.5 pence) and have it recorded to tape first, but that suggestion was dismissed. "John and Paul went white at the thought of a pound," said Hanton.

"Percy was fed up because we were taking too much time, and starting to look at the clock." One of the problems was that "In Spite Of All The Danger" was "quite long, and he said to chop a verse off," said Hanton. "John said 'no'. John Lowe could see Phillips from where he was sitting and he was apparently telling John to finish. We kept going, so the record ended with the song going almost to the centre of the disc, right to the hole in the middle." *(David Bedford Interview 2008)*

"He gave us the disc and it was a big thing. How many people had records like popular crooner, Matt Monro?"

Sadly, just three days later, John's mother Julia was knocked down and killed by an off-duty policeman on Menlove Avenue. The future of The Quarrymen hung in the balance. Colin's days were also numbered and he became the last of the original Quarrymen, apart from John, to leave.

The End

The Quarrymen were auditioning at the Finch Lane Busmen's Sports & Social Club. "We all turned up and George's dad was there," recalled Hanton. Colin was outside of the friend group: "I didn't spend much time with John and Paul, I just received a call to say we were playing somewhere."

They were performing with the hope of being booked to play for thirty minutes in between houses at the Pavilion Theatre in Lodge Lane. "As the curtains opened, John started straight into the songs, and then he would introduce us. After our last song – we did about five songs – the curtains were due to close, but they were stuck, so John joked, 'While they get the curtains fixed, we'll play another song'. We did 'Lost John' and then the curtains did close this time."

John's quick thinking impressed the manager, who mistakenly gave them all a pint of beer at the bar. "We didn't just stop at one, and then me, Paul and John were drunk, and there was only poor George who wasn't drunk," said Colin. They went back on stage for the second half, and at one point, "I said to John, 'What are we doing?' and Paul laughed and John said, 'See, he doesn't even know what we're doing,' – if you weren't drunk you'd be embarrassed." They finished playing and headed to the dressing room.

The man from the Pivvy then came in; he had obviously just come off stage as he still wore heavy theatrical makeup on his face and around his eyes. That was easy picking for a sober Lennon, but to a drunk Lennon? "He ribbed the poor man unmercifully, as only John could." The man gave them a lecture about being professional and how to treat your audience, and suddenly, Colin sobered up quickly, not realising how important the audition was. "Things didn't seem that funny anymore."

The Quarrymen headed home on the bus, and an argument broke out between Colin and Paul. "Paul had started to do this funny voice," said Colin. "I had some deaf friends, and you know how a deaf person speaks, well he was doing this voice. I'm sure he wasn't insulting deaf people, as that wasn't his way, but I was in this drunken state, sobering up.

"Paul kept making these noises and talking in this stupid voice, and I just rounded on him and verbally attacked him. I don't think it would have come to anything. We just had the row, I told Paul to shut up and I think he was shocked. Pete Shotton was with us and he shouted, 'This is our stop, Colin'. So we ran down the stairs, I grabbed my drums and we jumped off." It wasn't their stop, but Shotton found a way to diffuse the situation.

That was the end of Colin's membership in The Quarrymen. "We had to get the bus back to Woolton. I just went back to my house and put my drums away and that was me, finished." He never said the words, I quit, "but they never contacted me again. I thought, 'I don't need this'. They probably didn't want me and I didn't want them, so that was it." Once the drums were put away on top of the wardrobe, that really was that, and he never joined another group or was ever interested in pursuing a musical career. Instead, he completed his apprenticeship at Guy Rogers as an upholsterer.

As Colin wasn't in the same social circles as the rest of The Quarrymen, he didn't see anyone else for a long time after he quit. Just after Pete Best joined the group, Colin bumped into John on the bus and they said a quick hello. However, the next time Colin saw them was on the television, as The Beatles, with John, Paul and George along with their new drummer, Ringo Starr.

"I could see they had improved and they sounded better."

(Hunter Davies. The Quarrymen)

Colin has no regrets about it: "You just have the life you've been given." After celebrating the 40th anniversary of the meeting of Lennon and McCartney, Colin began playing again with The Quarrymen, and is still playing today. He has travelled the world with his fellow musicians, recreating those exciting moments from The Beatles' earliest days when he was the first drummer on John's road to becoming a Beatle. Could he have been the Fourth Beatle? Colin remembers people saying:

"Here's Colin, he could have been a Beatle. I hated all that."

(Hunter Davies. The Quarrymen)

A career in music wasn't for him.

PETE SHOTTON - THE FIRST PETE IS SACKED

The first Pete to become surplus to requirements in John Lennon's band was Pete Shotton, whose role in John's life and the history of The Quarrymen, makes him one of the central characters of those early days in Woolton Village. At Quarry Bank School, John and Pete were the Butch Cassidy and Sundance Kid of the area, terrorizing parents, property and schoolmasters. Lennon and Shotton were also known as "Shennon and Lotton", a phrase coined by John, while local parents adopted another widely used phase to warn their children to stay away from "that Lennon". The two were inseparable from the age of five, and would remain lifelong friends

Rock 'n' Washboard

Shotton was only in the group because he was John's best friend. He never professed to be a great musician, hence the reason he played the washboard. But John discussed everything with him, especially the biggest decision of The Quarrymen's career so far: should Paul McCartney be allowed into the group? Pete agreed with John that he would make the group better, and, although John claimed in some later interviews that he made the offer to Paul to join the group on 6th July 1957, the truth is that it was Shotton who actually made the approach. A couple of weeks after the Woolton fete, Shotton spotted McCartney on Vale Road and asked him to join the group.

However, with the addition of McCartney to the group, it was clear that the direction of The Quarrymen was changing from a group of friends having fun with skiffle, toward a rock 'n' roll group.

And there was no place for a washboard player in a rock 'n' roll group, so

Pete's role in the The Quarrymen was drawing to an end, much sooner than he expected. That was not going to be a discussion either Shennon or Lotton wanted to have.

In His Life

Not long after John met Paul at St. Peter's Church, The Quarrymen were booked to appear at a wedding reception. The date was on or around 24th August 1957 and it was for the sister of a girl Colin Hanton had met when the group played in Rosebery Street in June. This time they would be playing in a small venue in Upper Parliament Street, about half a mile from Rosebery Street in Toxteth.

Although Paul had been invited to join The Quarrymen, he had not played with them yet, and wasn't with them on this particular night. "We were invited to play and did our first set early in the evening," recalled Hanton, the group's drummer, who then disappeared with some of the bride's family to the local pub. "I soon found myself, pint in hand, sat at a table with Mum, Dad, bride and groom and other members of the immediate family, having a great time," he said. In fact, Colin was enjoying himself so much that, even when prompted to return to the venue to join his bandmates for the next part of the performance, he politely declined.

However, when Hanton did return, due to the need to have to begin playing again without him, the empty drum stool had been filled by the most unlikely of people: Pete Shotton. Colin Hanton recalled that "as I hadn't come back from the pub in time, he'd sat in for me on drums. He was very wary and apologetic, because he knew I didn't like anyone touching my drums." However, Hanton had imbibed just enough beer so as to be calm and relaxed about the situation, and didn't react when learning that Pete Shotton had broken one of his drumsticks. "Normally, I would have been angry, but not on this occasion." *(Pre:Fab!)*

Pete Was Framed

For Shotton, the move from washboard to drums was only temporary, because this was the night that would mark the end of his career with the group. Lennon didn't want to sack his best friend, and Shotton didn't really want to quit, but both knew it had to happen. After downing several more beers, the matter was settled once and for all when Lennon smashed the washboard over Shotton's head. With the wooden frame of the washboard hanging around his neck, his time with The Quarrymen was clearly over. Lennon quipped, "That takes care of that, then," and both friends broke into spontaneous laughter.

As Shotton later recalled: "The washboard frame slid neatly round my neck and tears of laughter rolled down my face, not only was I feeling any pain: I knew the destruction of my washboard (which I certainly wasn't about to repair or replace) had effectively released me from all further obligations as a Quarry Man." *(John Lennon, In My Life)*

For Pete Shotton, his first and only public appearance as a drummer marked his musical departure from The Quarrymen. However, it didn't mark the end of his friendship with John, since Shennon and Lotton would ride again for many years to come, even if Pete was not in the group. Whenever Pete needed a friend, John would be there. When he had a business idea, or needed money, John backed Pete to the hilt, even buying him a supermarket on Hayling Island. During The Beatles years, Shotton was a regular visitor to Lennon's home and even accompanied him to several Abbey Road sessions. John remained loyal to his childhood friend.

Apple

When The Beatles formed Apple, Lennon turned to Shotton, making him manager of the short-lived Apple Boutique, and also the first managing director of Apple Corps. The two drifted apart when Yoko Ono entered the scene, and Shotton eventually returned to his Hayling Island supermarket. But Shennon and Lotton would be forever parted in December 1980, which, naturally, was a devastating blow for Pete.

Pete Shotton was reunited with his fellow Quarrymen in 1997 when, to celebrate the 40th Anniversary of the meeting of John and Paul, the group reformed for a one-off concert. However, that one-off reunion continues today, with the remaining Quarrymen still performing. Pete only appeared a few times with the group, before retiring once and for all.

Business success did eventually come to Shotton when he set up a new restaurant chain, called Fatty Arbuckle's in the 1980s. He later sold it for a huge, undisclosed sum, at which time he retired to Dublin, Ireland. He died at the age of 75 in 2017.

While he was never destined to be a drummer, most importantly, John Lennon could rightly say that Pete Shotton was 'in my life'.

Pete Shotton with The Quarrymen

NOVEMBER 1958

MIKE MCCARTNEY - THE FIRST BEATLES' DRUMMER?

On 17th April 2014, *The Daily Mail* in the UK carried the headline:

"I should have been a Beatle, too: Macca's little brother reveals HE was the band's first drummer".

Although the story appeared to be new, Mike has made no secret of the fact that he had played with The Beatles very early on in the band's evolution. He certainly wasn't the first drummer, as we know that was Colin Hanton in The Quarrymen. So when did he drum for them?
"It was when John (Lennon) used to come to the house in Forthlin Road with The Quarrymen, before George (Harrison) was even there."

John, Paul, George and Mike

The occasion was at the end of November 1958, after Hanton had quit the group, and they were down to just John, Paul and George. A friend of John's from Art College, Derek Hodkin, had purchased a tape recorder, and was invited to visit Paul's house at 20, Forthlin Road for a recording session. To add to the fun, Paul's brother Mike was asked to be the drummer for the evening. Not much is known about the makeup of the drum kit, which was probably cobbled together from loose bits of kit that had been left behind in venues and subsequently "acquired" by Paul. They spent a fun evening in what would almost be a prequel to Mike's career with The Scaffold, as they recorded "repartee, jokes, laughs, practice, songs, and quite a few ribald remarks about my French girlfriend," *(TuneIn)* recalled Hodkin.

They then played the tape back and enjoyed listening to themselves, with Hodkin being asked to be their manager, not of The Quarrymen, but of Japage 3, the same group with a new name. It seemed clear from this newly-adopted moniker that Mike would not be joining them permanently; the name was inspired by its limited membership – J (for John), Pa (for Paul), Ge (for George) and "3" as in a trio.

John, Paul and George

Mike McCartney with Geoff Nugent

With George's brother Harry set to be married on 20th December 1958, his kid brother and his mates were asked to play at the reception. John, Paul and George found themselves in the front bar of the Childwall Abbey Hotel performing as Japage 3 for the first time, though without Hodkin's knowledge. (*Tune In*)

There is a photograph of John, Paul and George standing in the window of the Childwall Abbey Hotel. John is singing, with no guitar, while appearing to either stroke his eyebrow or brush his impressive quiff from his eyes. Paul is on John's right, also singing and sporting a quiff that is not quite as outrageous as his bandmate's. George, sporting a quiff that he loved, is on John's left, curling his lip like Elvis while playing his guitar and looking the most natural musician of the three.

Harry Harrison recalled that night well. "Our wedding was one of those occasions where they thought they would practice on people and see what happened. They were not exactly what the majority of people there expected. They had a tea break, and an elderly lady who was one of the guests came along to play the piano, who was a real pub player. She could really hammer out tunes that you could really sing along to. Three lads reappeared from the bar, pints in hand, and John just poured the pint over this lady's head and said;

'I anoint thee David,' and just walked away. This lady surprised me. There was no reaction. She just smiled and got off and went away and got dry again." (*Film: Living in the Material World*)

Take A Break

Mike did not play that night, and sadly, his chances of being the permanent drummer had already ended. While at Scout camp in Derbyshire the previous year, Mike had an accident. The lads strung up some rope with a piece of pipe attached and Mike was volunteered to test it over the edge of a cliff.

He fell from the rope and landed in a heap at the bottom of the cliff, suffering multiple fractures in his left arm and serious nerve damage. Mike spent the next four weeks with his arm in plaster, stranded on the wrong side of the Pennines in Sheffield, Yorkshire, with occasional visits from Liverpool by his dad. Even though the plaster came off at the end of August 1957, the injury was to leave him with permanent nerve damage. As Mike recalled: *"I had to have electric shocks and hot stuff put on my arm to get the nerves back. For a couple of years, I had to wear a support strap with a wire. If I hadn't broken my arm, I'd have been a Beatle. But I did break my arm and I'm not a Beatle. You always have to deal in reality, not dreams."*

Using the stage name Mike McGear, he went on to have hit records with The Scaffold, the Liverpool group known for its mixture of comedy, poetry and music. The Scaffold had a Top 5 record in the UK with "Thank U Very Much", but surpassed that with a number 1 hit, "Lily The Pink". In 1974, he recorded an album, McGear, with his brother Paul. He currently serves as ambassador for the Wirral where he lives across the Mersey from Liverpool. He is as famous for his photography as he is for his music career. Unfortunately for Mike, he never got the breaks to be the Fourth Beatle.

Lee Curtis and the All Stars, Billy Kramer with the Coasters, Group One.

SUNDAY, 18th NOV.
Vic and the Spidermen, Alby and the Sorrels.

MONDAY, 19th NOV.
Ian and the Zodiacs The Beat-Cats.

WEDNESDAY, 21st NOV.
Under 16's Disc Club.

THURSDAY, 22nd NOV.
Parlaphone recording Stars
THE BEATLES

SATURDAY, 24th NOV.
Lee Curtis and the All Stars, Billy Kramer with the Coasters, The Four Most.

SUNDAY, 25th NOV.
THE DAKOTAS

MONDAY, 26th NOV.
Gus Travis and The nighters. The 4 Clefs.

THURSDAY, 19th NOV.
THE BEATLES

50

10th May 1960

TOMMY MOORE

THE SILVER BEATLES DRUMMER

Inspired by watching one of their heroes, Gene Vincent, take to the stage with local bands at Liverpool Stadium on 3rd May 1960, John, Paul, George and Stuart decided to press promoter Allan Williams to give them gigs at the Jacaranda.

However, as Williams reminded them, they lacked one essential group member: a drummer. Following the success of the Stadium event, manager and promoter Larry Parnes decided to bring to town his latest star, Liverpool-born Billy Fury, to seek and secure a backing group for Fury's forthcoming tour. They agreed to meet up at Williams' new venue, the Wyvern Club, on 10th May 1960. Having agreed to manage The Silver Beatles, Allan Williams added his new group to the list of those auditioning, but first, he had to get them a drummer.

There are two versions of how Tommy Moore was recruited. Williams said he spoke to Brian Casser of Cass and the Cassanovas, and he suggested Tommy Moore. Tommy was considered a very good drummer and, although he was a few years older than the others, he was just what they needed. He had played with a modern jazz band at the Temple in Dale Street and was technically-gifted, probably more so than any of the drummers who played for The Beatles. However, in an interview in 1970 for a Portuguese magazine, Moore said: "I went to work for The Beatles through an advertisement I saw in a newspaper where Paul (McCartney) and George (Harrison) were looking for a drummer," he recalled. "I joined the group but it was a tough living in the beginning." It seems that Moore remembered being recruited in the same way that another drummer would, a few months later, miss his chance to join the group – through a newspaper advert. However, no evidence of the advert has been found.

Cass appears to have been involved as he even suggested a new group name, though the exact name is unclear. It was a variation on Long John and The Silver Beetles. Although the band members felt obliged to Cass, they settled on The Silver Beetles, but were never truly happy with it. For a few months in 1960, they called themselves The Quarrymen and The Beatals, but were now The Silver Beetles, or Silver Beatles. For a short time, they even adopted the name The Silver Beats.

Paul remembered the discussion about the name. "Brian Casser said, 'What's your name?' We had just thought of 'The Beatles' so we thought we would try this out at the audition. Cass said, 'Beatles - what's that? It doesn't mean anything.' (Everyone hated the name, fans and promoters alike.) He asked John's name. John, who at that time was pretty much the lead singer, said, 'John Lennon'. 'Right, Big John... Long John... okay, Long John Silver.' So we compromised and had Long John and the Silver Beetles. We would do anything for a job, so that's what we became." *(Anthology)* Tommy Moore was now a member of the group, whatever they were called.

Tommy Moore

Thomas Henry Moore was born on 12th September 1931 and lived in the Dingle, not far from where another drummer, Richard Starkey, was born in 1940.

Original painting by Paul Skellett

In 1953, Tommy married Veronica "Vera" Hughes, who was a few years younger than him, being born on 8th June 1936. They had two daughters, Veronica Helen Hughes and Angela, and lived at 49, Fern Grove, off Lodge Lane in Liverpool 8.

(David Bedford Interview with Michelle Lawson)

Tommy worked at the Garston Bottle Works as a forklift truck driver, where he stayed for the next thirty years. Whenever possible, he drummed in the evenings with a variety of groups. Anthony "Ant" Hogan knew Tommy well, as his father, Bernie Hogan, worked with Tommy at the Bottle Works and was a good friend of his.

"Tommy used to come round to our house, and if he started talking about John, Paul and George, I wasn't interested, because I wanted to know about Rory Storm and the Hurricanes," he recalled. "He was like an uncle, always at our house. He'd take us out, or come over telling stories, not always about bands; always a good bloke to be around and I loved the bones of him." (David Bedford Interview 2015)

Tommy had never settled in one group, and like many musicians in Liverpool, was available at short notice to sit in with any group that needed him. "He played in the Hurricanes," said Ant, which is evidenced by the fact that he appears in Johnny Guitar's diary: "Tom Moore *(R. Leas brother)* 49 Fern Court, 8 *(Comment 'Good')*". He was obviously an able deputy for Ringo. As Ant recalled, "He played in lots of other groups all the time, not set in one group. He loved jazz, not so much rock 'n' roll, but he'd played in jazz bands. He had a huge collection of jazz records." *(David Bedford Interview 2015)*

The age difference between Tommy and the other members of The Silver Beetles was a point of contention and led to several arguments among the boys, especially with John, who was nine years younger than Tommy and maybe intimidated by the older man. Moore had been a musician for several years, and was a working man providing for his family, so there was a difference in maturity, not just in age.

Allan Williams considered Tommy to be a great drummer and recalled that George was also positive about him. "Tommy Moore was the best drummer we ever had at any time," Williams recalled George saying in Ringo's presence, though this quote has also been attributed to John Lennon! *(The Man Who Gave The Beatles Away)* However, George seemed to suggest that Moore was unreliable. "We had a drummer, Tommy Moore," he recalled, "who had come with us to Scotland. He was a funny kind of guy who played with a lot of different bands. He used to show up for a while and then not show up again, so we'd get someone else." *(Anthology)* It wasn't quite as straightforward as that, and his tenure with the group did not start well.

Tommy's debut with The Silver Beetles would be the audition at the Wyvern Club. It is not known if they managed to rehearse beforehand, as this was only one week after the Stadium concert. As if the group wasn't nervous enough on audition day, they had another problem on their hands: Tommy hadn't turned up

Tommy Moore with The Silver Beatles

yet! This didn't impress the band, but even worse, it didn't impress promoter Larry Parnes. In a panic, Williams grabbed Johnny Hutchinson from Cass and the Cassanovas. He stood in until Tommy finally arrived and finished the audition. Parnes noticed that Moore was older and did not seem to fit in, but this did not stop him from booking The Silver Beetles as Johnny Gentle's backing band for a tour of Scotland. Paul McCartney was impressed with Tommy's drumming skills, in particular his ability to reproduce the tricky drumming on the Everly Brothers' number "Cathy's Clown". *(The Man Who Gave The Beatles Away)*

Larry Parnes attached one condition to his plans to use the group on the Gentle tour. He allegedly told them that he would book them, but not with their bass player (Stu). John rejected the proposition. However, Parnes later told *Mersey Beat* editor Bill Harry that he thought "he (Stuart) could play the instrument quite well" *(Beatles Appreciation Society Magazine 1979)* and that it was Tommy turning up late that was a problem, though obviously not too much of a problem as Parnes booked them anyway. If he was prepared to book them, even with Tommy turning up late, then they must have impressed him.

Following the audition, Tommy rehearsed with the group in The Jacaranda for several hours before they began playing anything resembling good rock 'n' roll. From that point on, the band vastly improved. "You could detect a day-to-day improvement," Williams observed. *(The Man Who Gave The Beatles Away)*

"Tommy played music for fun," said Bob Cepican, who interviewed Tommy, "and never saw himself turning full-time professional. He played in a variety of trad (traditional) jazz bands and some beat groups, just for fun, and to make a few bob (some money). He was happy for The Beatles' success, and never lamented on 'what could have been'; never kicked himself for not staying with the group. So he had no regrets. I found that remarkable." Those sessions in The Jacaranda obviously stayed with him, as Tommy did have some fond memories. "I lost a lot of sweat in The Jac," said Tommy. "We used to play from midnight to about four in the morning for cups of coffee and a jam buttie (sandwich). I don't remember getting paid. The only time we got paid was when we played outside of The Jac, and Allan was more interested in keeping us in The Jac because we were bringing in the people." *(Yesterday Came Suddenly)*

The Silver Beetles' repertoire consisted of mainly rock 'n' roll standards at that time, including songs by Little Richard, Gene Vincent, and the Everly Brothers. "It was just a matter of rattling songs off, one after the other, just to make the night go by," recalled Tommy. "We played one Everly Brother *Tune In* particular, 'Cathy's Clown'. I remember that the drum part was difficult for me at the time. We did a couple of good blues numbers, too. All that mattered to us was that it rocked. I used to do my own bit on the drums," continued Tommy. "A solo to keep the crowd happy on the floor while the others were off and had a bit of a break behind stage. So I'd be playing for some time and I'd turn around every so often to see where they were and when they were coming out, and all I'd see is John Lennon pulling faces at me from behind the curtain." *(Yesterday Came Suddenly)*

Moore wasn't impressed by the lack of professionalism of his colleagues. "I was getting a bit fed up with things," he said. "No one was telling me how much we were supposed to get paid for a gig or what job was down the line. Everything was so secretive. So I said to John one day outside The Jac, as we were getting our equipment into the van, 'You know what John? I'm getting a bit cheesed off with all this business here.' John said, like a typical Scouser, 'Why? You're getting paid, aren't you?' I said, 'Well, yes, but what are we getting paid? Buttons!' He said, 'What else do you want, then?' I said, 'There's nothing happening, nothing is materializing. In the near future, I'm bailing out and going back to me old job in the factory.' He said to me, very seriously, 'I'd sooner die first, mate, than go to work.'" It seems that even back in 1960, John looked on the drummer as just the hired hand, and not really part of the group.
(Yesterday Came Suddenly)

The Tour of Scotland - 20th May 1960

In the meantime, Tommy had a tour of Scotland to play with the group, beginning in Alloa on 20th May, and it was certainly eventful, especially his relationship with Lennon. "I did not like Lennon," Tommy recalled in Allan's book. "I couldn't stand him. He had some awful ways. He was a very aggressive boy. When we went up to Scotland, we didn't have any money at all. It was Allan's idea that the money would be sent to us in advance from Larry Parnes in London. All I was interested in was getting on with the tour; I wasn't interested in who was doing the business. It was our understanding that Allan was looking after the financial part of it and that the money would be sent to us from London to hold us over." *(The Man Who Gave The Beatles Away)*

The deal was that each of the musicians would receive £15 per week. Even before the tour started, John famously rang Larry Parnes, screaming "where's the bloody money?" It didn't arrive, so the penniless Silver Beetles arrived in

Scotland and often went without food and drink during that tour. Billed alongside Johnny Gentle as simply "His Group", they had decided, apart from Moore, to assume stage names as Johnny Gentle – who was born John Askew – had done. John Lennon stuck with simply Johnny Lennon, but Paul went for Paul Ramon, George chose Carl Harrison and Stu selected Stuart de Stael.

"On the way up there, it was fairly exciting," said Tommy. "The idea of just travelling was exciting. After the first few dates, things got a bit sticky and I started getting funny feelings about the tour, particularly about Allan. I told the others in a hotel, 'I don't like the looks of this at all.' We literally had to scrounge for food. In the hotel we were staying at, I felt like a tramp. We kept getting telephone calls saying that the money was on its way, but it never came." They took smuggled food from the restaurants where they ate – saltines, bits of cheese wrapped in paper, slices of bread and dinner rolls – back to their hotel rooms and divided their haul. Once, John was so hungry that he ordered a huge meal and walked out of the restaurant without paying. "We walked in front of him and he sort of used us as a shield," Tommy said. *(Yesterday Came Suddenly)*

There was no time to rehearse before the tour started so, with twenty minutes to go before curtain-up, Johnny Gentle and His Group had their first meeting and first practise. They quickly discussed what songs they would perform. Gentle was less than impressed at this initial meeting. "I did wonder what Larry Parnes had sent me," recalled Gentle. "They were dressed in jeans and sweaters and were the roughest bunch of lads I had seen in my life. John and Stu were at Art College and they looked it. Their hair fell over their collars and Stu had a beard. George was serving an apprenticeship and looked like it, as did Paul who was studying for his A-Levels. John told me excitedly, 'This is our big break'". *(Johnny Gentle and The Beatles)*

Their opening night repertoire consisted of Ricky Nelson's "Poor Little Fool", Jim Reeves' "He'll Have To Go", Elvis Presley's "I Need Your Love Tonight" and Clarence Frogman Henry's "I Don't Know Why I Love You But I Do". Johnny would then hand the show over to The Silver Beatles, whose set was more rock 'n' roll. In addition to playing a couple of their own songs,

"Hello Little Girl" and **"One After 909",** they performed The Everly Brothers' **"Bye Bye Love"**, Little Richard's **"Tutti Frutti"**, **"Lucille"** and **"Long Tall Sally"**, Eddie Cochran's **"Twenty Flight Rock"** and **"Hallelujah I Love Her So",** Buddy Holly's **"That'll Be The Day",** Gene Vincent's **"Wild Cat"** and **"Be Bop A Lula",** Elvis' **"Stuck On You",** Ray Charles' **"What'd I Say",** Chuck Berry's **"Little Queenie"** and The Olympics' **"Hully Gully".**

Their performance the first night was lackluster and the promoter, Duncan McKinnon, made sure that they knew it. They also didn't dress the same, so Johnny gave George a black shirt that matched those worn by John and Paul. Johnny was less than impressed by McKinnon, whom he described as "more like a farmer than a man who put on shows in dance halls". (Johnny Gentle and The Beatles) Johnny and The Silver Beatles spent the night having a few – and, in George and Paul's case, illegal – beers in the lounge of their hotel. After a long night, the lads lay in bed until late morning, but had to be up for rehearsals in the afternoon. They wanted to try out a few new songs, among them Buddy Holly's "Words of Love" and Little Richard's "Kansas City", and also to work on their own composition, "One After 909". *(Johnny Gentle and The Beatles)*

Johnny Gentle was certainly impressed, noticing that George Harrison's guitar playing "had greatly improved" and "the close harmonies of Lennon and McCartney were near perfect." Gentle also saw that the backing band was stepping out of his shadow, and that they "simply stunned the audience. Their own songs were cheered as loudly as the others, but the most successful song of the night was 'Kansas City' and it remained a part of their repertoire for many years to come." *(Johnny Gentle and The Beatles)*

On the journey towards Fraserburgh, Tommy ended up in hospital in the aftermath of an accident in their van. "Johnny Gentle could never go on stage unless he had a few drinks," remarked Tommy. "He was just starting out on his first tour, and whenever we were with him, he was always under the influence. One night, Johnny had a few drinks and, after the show, he suddenly got it into his head that he would drive the minibus. Well, he got behind the wheel and took a wrong turn and – bang!" In the crash, one of the guitar cases had been thrown forward and hit Tommy in the face. He told Ant Hogan what happened in the hospital. According to Ant: "John came in with someone and John told Tommy to get out of the f'in bed and Tommy said 'no way', because he was still dizzy and concussed and on very strong painkillers. John started screaming at Tommy on an open ward and everyone was looking at them, so Tommy got embarrassed because the nurses were coming up to him and complaining, so he got dressed and went with them. He said, 'I've no idea how I played as I was stoned on painkillers'. He decided there and then that it was the end. Tommy told them when they came back, 'I'm off', but they said they had two or three bookings already, so he agreed to play the last few gigs and then he was off."*(David Bedford Interview 2015)*

In Stitches

Tommy arrived at the theatre, drowsy from the effects of the drugs and with stitches in his upper lip, two teeth missing, and a bandage around his head. John thought this was hilarious and mocked him during the performance, making faces, and trying to stretch the stitches in Tommy's lip by making him laugh. Occasionally, John would turn around while performing, look at Tommy, and burst out laughing. "Lennon must have thought, 'This is it, this time I'm gonna have a go at him," Tommy surmised. *(Yesterday Came Suddenly)*

All he remembered was Lennon laughing at the state of his bruised and battered face. It's no surprise that on his return from the tour, Tommy's thoughts turned to quitting the group. "I'd had a belly full of that Scottish tour when we got back," he recalled. "And I'd had my belly full of Lennon. You know, I think he was sick. He seemed to love watching the fights that broke out in the dance halls between the rival gangs. He'd say, 'Hey look at that guy putting the boot in there'.

He got a sadistic delight out of it all. At least his conduct indicated this. When our train got into Liverpool, the rest of the lads went to the tea van that used to be sited just across the road in Lime Street. I said, 'Goodnight lads,' and took a cab home. I was pissed off with Lennon. I had had enough of him." *(The Man Who Gave The Beatles Away)* Bob Wooler knew who was to blame. "Tommy Moore came in for the Lennon treatment. Moore was a very working class lad and he

was not able to cope with the Lennon attitude and, taking his lead from Lennon, McCartney would be similar. At times, they reminded me of those well-to-do Chicago lads, Leopold and Loeb, who killed someone because they felt superior to him." *(Best of Fellas)*

Just as it would be for many people over the years, the relationship with John Lennon was the deal-breaker. Ant remembered what Tommy told him about his relationship with John: "John picked on people who were weaker than him, and that used to wind Tommy up. Paul used to go along with John, trying to impress him, because he said 'I don't think Paul was like that'. They were in the Jacaranda one day, and Stu was sitting there at the table with them all and John was picking on him, and then John told him to go and sit on his own on another table, and Stu did." John admitted that he did this: "We were terrible. We'd tell Stu he couldn't sit with us, or eat with us. We'd tell him to go away, and he did – that was how he learnt to be with us. It was all stupid, but that was what we were like." *(Anthology)*

"So Tommy went and sat with him," Ant continued, "and John stood up and told Tommy to sit down again, but Tommy refused. So John told him to f**king sit down, and Tommy refused, so they fronted up and got pulled apart before a fight broke out. Stuart wasn't an idiot and could stand up for himself, but he allowed John to talk to him like that, and Tommy couldn't understand why." *(David Bedford Interview 2015)*

After the last appearance, one of Tommy's friends arrived with his van and took most of the drummer's kit. "Tommy went back in and said goodbye to Stu, Paul and George and then he went over to John," Ant said. "Tommy had a stick hidden up his sleeve and then hit John over the head and knocked him down. Lennon didn't get up, and that was that. Tommy said he 'wanted to jump all over him, but I didn't and I'm not like that' because Tommy was a gentle man, so it must have taken something to make him that angry." *(David Bedford Interview 2015)*

For Johnny Gentle, drumming for Moore was "never going to amount to anything more than a sideline, whilst having a bit of fun." Gentle also observed that Moore "despised the acerbic put-down wit of middle class college boy Lennon" and the arty conversation "went straight over his head", though "according to John Lennon, he was the best drummer they ever had." *(Johnny Gentle and The Beatles)*

It Is Me, Or The Group!

Tommy made a few appearances with them during May and June 1960, but when he failed to turn up at a gig at the Grosvenor Ballroom in Wallasey on 11th June 1960, he left the group in an awkward position. Williams drove the boys to Tommy's house where they were greeted by the drummer's wife Vera. Tommy had quit the band, she told them. It was either her or The Silver Beatles. Tommy had returned to work full-time at the Bottle Works, so they jumped into the car and drove to Garston, where they summoned him. Tommy refused to come with them, leaving no doubt that his time with the group was at an end. "I've got mouths to feed," explained Moore. "I'm not like the rest of you. I'm a working lad who has to make some money to feed the people who depend on me. I can't go on living like this anymore. Honest I can't, she'd kill me," he said, referring to his wife. "Sorry lads, I need more than a measly fiver a week to keep me and mine. You ought to know that. I don't mind going on a diet, but starving is a different kettle of fish. Sorry boys." *(The Man Who Gave The Beatles Away)*

Despite Tommy's insistence that it was over, his bandmates wouldn't take no for an answer. At this point, Ant Hogan's father, Bernie, stepped in. "Paul, George and Stuart were pleading with Tommy," recalled Ant, "but John Lennon was standing away from them, and not getting involved; he was obviously told to stay quiet. 'Come on Tommy' they kept begging, so my dad came over and he asked Tommy what they wanted and if he wanted to play with them, and he said 'No'. So my dad told them to F-off, and my dad was a big fella, quite scary, and so off they went. Tommy always said in jest, 'it was your dad's fault I wasn't a Beatle!' My dad told him, 'you are better off without them', because he never liked them, even when they were famous. If it wasn't Hank Williams, 'they were not worth talking about' he said." Tommy didn't hate John; he liked him and once said that "if I was in a fight I'd rather have him on my side, but he just had these times when he changed moods and he was not nice."
He just didn't like that part of Lennon. *(David Bedford Interview 2015)*

Bob Wooler, the legendary Cavern deejay, knew Tommy "from my days on Garston docks" and had respect for him. Tommy was a messenger there. "He told me that he was crazy about drums," said Wooler. "He took drum lessons and he held the drumsticks in the correct position – that is, the conventional dance band way, which has gone out of fashion now." Wooler remembered how Tommy had gone to Scotland backing Johnny Gentle, but Tommy's wife was "contemptuous of the beat groups as she never thought they would lead to success. In the end, she told him to stick to his job driving a fork-lift truck at Garston Bottle Works." *(Record Collector 227 July 1998)* Everyone who encountered Tommy Moore seems to have the same opinion of him as a decent drummer who was torn between work and music. No matter, his experience with Lennon would not have encouraged him to stay with the group.

Lovely Rita

By the end of 1960, Tommy's stormy marriage to Vera was ending and they eventually divorced. The following year, he met Rita and the couple married and had three daughters: Lorraine (born in 1963), Colette (born in 1966) and Louise (born in 1972). "I met Tommy after he had left The Silver Beatles, and he didn't talk very much about those days," Rita said. She confirmed that his first wife had threatened him with that infamous choice – either her or the group. "If it had been me, I would have told him to go for it, because he was a fantastic drummer. But he chose her and his job at the Garston Bottle Works. To be fair, it was a good steady job and he was a grafter."

Tommy certainly worked hard for his family, and Rita remembered how he would sometimes call to tell her he was working a double or even triple shift at the Bottle Works. "Sometimes I would say goodbye to him at 7am and not see him until 7am the next day or even the day after." Tommy wasn't one for going out at night to pubs or clubs and would much sooner stay home with his wife and children. "He was a devoted family man, and worked so hard for us. A great husband and father." *(David Bedford Interview 2015)*

After leaving The Silver Beatles, Tommy's drums were stolen, so he didn't play for a while. He never played in another group. He did eventually get another

drum kit. The couple first lived in Princes Road, then in Lark Lane off Aigburth Road, but, as Rita recalled, "we got thrown out of the flat (in Lark Lane) because of complaints about his drumming making too much noise!" They then moved to a house in 41, Hartington Road, not far from the Fern Grove home he had shared with his first wife. They remained there for about four years, before moving to the house next door, 39, Hartington Road, where they lived for the next five years.

Lorraine has fond memories of her father. "I remember he was very much into DIY (do-it-yourself), which is probably where I get it from," she said. "He was very practical. One thing that sticks in my mind when we lived in Hartington Road was I remember him building me some furniture, and he painted it green. It was just a desk and a cupboard in the corner, with green or brown velvet curtains. I remember him putting 'Pippi Longstocking' wallpaper on the walls. When I was a bit older, he bought me a David Essex poster to put on the wall because I wasn't well." *(David Bedford Interview 2015)*

Long-Haired Lover From Liverpool

Rita and Lorraine both remember that Tommy was always smartly dressed, very neat, often with a jacket on if not the full suit. But the thing he prized the most was his long hair. "He wouldn't change his hair," said Rita. "He always wore it long, so maybe that put some potential employers off, but that was how he liked it. Always reminded me of Peter Wyngarde who played Jason King on television." Rita believes that some of this neatness and discipline came from his time in the army during National Service – something that would deprive The Beatles of Tommy's replacement, Norman Chapman. Quite bizarrely, Tommy told Rita about a pet he had acquired on National Service in Africa. "He said it was the most beautiful creature," Rita recalled, "and I was shocked when he told me it was a praying mantis! He thought it was amazing."

Long hair may very well have been the extent of Tommy's rebellious nature. His attention to detail in the clothing he wore would make sense given two years of army life, but the long hair was the polar opposite of what the army allowed.

Tommy (left) with a fan

Lorraine always pictures him being "very smart, with a scarf like a cravat, and his hair was long in a feather cut." Tommy was a smoker, and every now and then when Lorraine smells a whiff of smoke in her smokeless house, she thinks of him.

The accident in Scotland left Tommy with one lasting reminder of his time with The Silver Beatles: his false teeth. Lorraine remembered "he used to play around with them in his mouth and I told him to stop it!" Tommy had a thing about teeth, and would tease Lorraine about hers. "Because I had what he thought were big teeth," she said, "he thought there was something wrong with them. So he made me go to the dentist, and there was nothing wrong with them – I just had to grow into them. He also had this thing, our private joke, about the way I spoke on the phone. I, like many scousers, speak very fast, so he used to say, 'calm down, slow down, you're like a typewriter', so I would have to speak slower!" *(David Bedford Interview 2015)*

Tommy had his drums set up in the house, as Rita remembered: "Our house in Hartington Road was huge, and Tommy had his drums in the living room, where he would sit and play." He didn't play along to records, just practised on his own. "He was a fantastic drummer," she said with pride. "I remember him playing there, saying, this is 'marry-your-daddy, marry-your-daddy' which must have been a drum technique or something." It is actually a form of "paradiddle" that drummers use, which is "mammy - daddy" repeated over and over with alternate hands, learning a drum roll.

Musicians came and went, and many times Tommy looked at starting a new group, but it never happened. Lorraine has a few memories of her dad playing drums, and she was especially fascinated with his drummers' brushes. Music was always important to him, and his first love was jazz. He had a grand radiogram in the living room at home and enjoyed listening to music. "Music was important to him," Rita recalled, "and I always associate 'Take Five' by Dave Brubeck with him, every time I hear it. It was one of his favourites. He would have been playing music till the day he died if he had joined a group, because he loved it so much. But he would have become too frustrated playing with The Beatles, as they weren't that good musically and he had very high standards.
I think Lennon would have got rid of Tommy because of the image. He was a lot older with a family and working, and Lennon was only 19. It wouldn't have worked." *(David Bedford Interview 2015)*

Moore, a technically-gifted jazz drummer, would have just been bored playing basic rock 'n' roll with The Silver Beatles. Even so, he wasn't just interested in jazz, and was a fan of The Beatles' records. Lorraine's husband Mick only met Tommy once, but they got on very well. "He learned some of the Police tracks and copied them," Mick said, "learning the drum parts from the records. He also liked Lou Reed and Velvet Underground, which were groups I liked. He, of course, was a big jazz fan, and he mentioned John Coltrane was a favourite of his. He also liked bluegrass which, of course, has some jazz roots, too. Tommy told me he had a Lambretta scooter, the same as mine, though when he was riding his, the wheels got stuck in the tram tracks so he had to dive off before the tram hit him. I felt we had a lot in common." *(David Bedford Interview 2015)*)

Colette Moore, Tommy's middle daughter, remembered her father as a wonderful man, "albeit obsessed with drums! Drumming was a big part of his life, and I remember when we lived in the house in Belle Vale, he had his drum kit in the living room. I don't know how he got away with the volume. The neighbours must have enjoyed it." She also confirmed that Tommy "played on his own. Sometimes he had a friend round but it was usually me, always singing and dancing around to The Beatles' music. I still love them now; they hold so many memories for me." *(David Bedford Interview 2015)*

Making it in the music business sometimes requires, even demands, a ruthless streak, and this is something that, unlike Lennon, McCartney and Harrison, Tommy never had. For him, providing for his family was more important. "He was a very proud man, a good family man, a good provider and a good husband," said Rita. "He never liked to go out to the pubs or clubs, and was happy staying at home watching the children, which was a job in itself. A brilliant dad. He was also a good cook, and tried to get a job as a chef, but not with that hair!" Unfortunately, when times were hard in the 1970s, Tommy was made redundant from the Bottle Works and never found another job, despite putting in numerous applications over the years. Liverpool, in the late '60s and all through the '70s, had a very high unemployment rate and jobs were scarce. Like many working men – and much like Lennon did by choice in the late 1970s – Tommy became a house-husband, bringing up the children while Rita went out to work in the pubs and clubs behind the bar, including places like the Blue Dolphin.

Although he was good at DIY, he kept his skills indoors. "He wasn't much of a gardener," said Lorraine, "but in Hartington Road, my dad built a ranch-style fence around a portion of the grass, and the rest was crazy paving. I always remember the grass was high; it was okay to play in, but that was all. No flowers, just long grass and crazy paving." *(David Bedford Interview 2015)* Ironically, one of Rita's jobs was working with Freda Kelly in The Beatles Fan Club in Liverpool between 1968 and 1970, where she stuffed envelopes with Beatles photos to be sent all over the world. She never met The Beatles, but has always been a fan, as was Tommy.

Tommy in Portugal?

In March 1970, Tommy and his family were photographed by the Daily Express for an article that was only published in Portugal. Rita recalled with a smile: "We were living in Vronhill Street," which was situated off High Park Street in the Dingle. "It was like being a film star; all these people wanting to take our picture, just for a day or two." The photographs portray Tommy with Rita, Lorraine and Colette in what looks like a poor house, with Tommy drumming on an old biscuit tin. The article said:

This Beatle lives in poverty. Sadder than trying to be a Beatle and not to achieve it, is to have been a Beatle only once and never again. Tommy Moore is a slim, pale, poorly dressed guy from Liverpool. He is 36 years old and he works in a bottle factory and he lives, repenting for the mistake he made 10 years ago. In 1960, he was the drummer for John, Paul and George. The band "with no name" (Silver Beatles) played at the Grosvenor Ballroom in Wallasey for £20 per night.

Tommy thought that it was a bad job and he found a steady job, so he started to work in a factory driving carts (fork-lift trucks). It is the same place where he suffers the hurt of the past. "I remember I went to work with The Beatles *when I read an advertisement in the newspaper because they were looking for a*

Êste beatle vive

éria ié-ié

"Muito mais triste do que pretendser um beatle na vida e não conseguir é ter sido um beatle uma vez e nunca mais poder ser." O ditado é de um homem magro, pálido e mal vestido de Liverpool, Tommy Moore. Ele tem 36 anos, trabalha como carregador de peso numa fábrica de garrafas e vive arrependido pelo êrro que cometeu dez anos atrás. Em 1960, Tommy era o baterista de três rapazes chamados John Lennon, Paul McCartney e George Harrison. O conjunto nem tinha nome e tocava na boate Grosvenor Ballroom, em Wallasey, por NCr$ 20,00 à noite. Tommy achou que aquilo era apenas um biscate e resolveu "arranjar um emprêgo mais seguro". Passou a dirigir as carretas da mesma fábrica onde hoje curte a mágoa do passado.

"Lembro que fui trabalhar com os Beatles através de um anúncio no jornal em que John, Paul e George procuravam baterista", diz Tommy. "Uni-me ao grupo e passamos a ganhar a vida com dificuldades. Basta dizer que recebemos, aím, um convite para uma turnê na Escócia, uma turnê muito cansativa, mas imaginem que cada um de nós só ganhou 25 libras pela brincadeira. Eu precisava me garantir, afinal. Abandonei aquêle hobby de tocar bateria. Os três rapazes depois foram me procurar. Já se chamavam The Beatles e apareceram num Jaguar branco. Voltei a tocar bateria mais duas noites. Não via, porém, futuro na coisa. Desisti definitivamente."

Tommy Moore, segundo o empresário Alan Williams, que trabalhava com os Beatles naquela época, "era um bom baterista, mas talvez um tanto idoso para o grupo. Era dez anos mais velho e, além disso, andava sempre insatisfeito com o negócio. Achava aquilo um simples quebra-galhos". Agora Tommy mora num modesto apartamento alugado em Vronhill Street, Liverpool. Trabalha 10 horas por dia "para ganhar uma miséria" e só tem uma vontade: retornar ao show business e "começar de onde os Beatles começaram, isto é, do nada". Enquanto John Lennon dirige o seu Mercedes-Benz 600 de luxo, superequipado (ver FeF n.º 476), o ex-Beatle Tommy Moore guia a sua carrêta de garrafas, assoviando Get Back e outros hits dos velhos companheiros, que só se lembram dêle como "a única pessoa no mundo que não deu um tostão por nós".

22

Casado, dois filhos, Tommy Moore hoje se lembra do tempo em que era o baterista dos Beatles (vistos à esquerda, em 1960, logo depois que Pete Best substituiu Tommy no conjunto). O máximo que faz agora é batucar numa lata de biscoitos (abaixo)

Tommy's article in the Portuguses magazine

58

drummer. I joined the band but it wasn't an easy life. We were invited for a tour in Scotland, which very hard and the salary was only 25 pounds. I needed another job. So I left this hobby, but they sought me out. By then, their name was The Beatles and they came in a white Jaguar car.

So I played twice more with them, but I didn't see any future in it and I gave it up. According to Allan Williams, he was a good drummer, but maybe too old for the band. He was 10 years older and he was unhappy. Tommy now lives in a modest house in Vronhill St, Liverpool 8. He works 10 hours per day for very little. He has only one desire: to be in show business again and to start from scratch. While John is driving his own luxury Mercedes-Benz 600 car, Tommy drives his fork-lift truck with bottles, whistling "Get Back" or other Beatle songs.

He is married. He has two children. All he can do now is to play on a biscuit tin.
(Translation by Carmen Villoria)

Interestingly, this 1970 interview shows that Tommy still looked back on his time with The Silver Beatles with some regret, as he realised what he had given up, even though it may not have worked out. It is testament to Tommy's ability that the other Silver Beatles were desperate to retain his services, and also clear that his only desire was "to be back in show business again". He was one of many musicians who came and went with The Beatles, and spent years realising what he had lost.

Tommy on TV

The following year, 1971, Bob Wooler, Allan Williams and Bill Harry tried to resurrect the Merseybeat scene in Liverpool with an event featuring musicians and Beatles people, like promoter Dave Forshaw and Beatles Fan Club Secretary Freda Kelly. When the resulting documentary aired on BBC Television, one of those interviewed was Tommy.

He was asked about his time with The Beatles and how he felt now: "Same as it was for me back then," said Moore, "a bit downhearted, and still making a couple of pounds a night. We weren't making any headway at the time, so we made this contract with a guy and did a tour of Scotland, where we started to make some money – to earn a few shillings. It was about £2 10 shillings a night." Tommy was then asked by interviewer Bernard Falk if he had any regrets when he sees what became of The Beatles. "Wouldn't anybody?", he answered honestly. "They are millionaires and so popular." When asked why he left the group, he replied that "because of a car accident, I ended up in hospital for three weeks, and when we came back to Liverpool, I did not play, and then someone walked off with my drums from Allan's club – I mean, stole them – it left me a bit puzzled as to what to do about it. So I considered it was no use to me, and went back to my job at the Garston Bottle Works as a forklift truck driver." *(BBC TV)*

Tommy's daughter Colette also confirmed that her dad had talked about his regrets. "He talked about his dreams and what could have been."
(David Bedford Interview 2015)

Tommy told his friend Ant Hogan that he had regrets, and still felt sad for missing out on fame. It was clear where the problems lay, as Ant remembered: "Tommy did have all kinds of trouble with his first wife. This led to him missing gigs as she never wanted him to play in a band. Tommy told me she suffered depression and was violent. He said she once met The Beatles and told them to f*** off!"
(David Bedford Interview 2015)

Allan Williams, Again

Tommy and Rita's third daughter, Louise, was born in 1972, but by the end of the decade, their marriage had broken down and they divorced, though amicably. Tommy stayed in Belle Vale and, for a time, his daughter Colette lived with him while Rita and Lorraine lived in Hartington Road. Rita met Ernie Greenhalgh, a friend of Tommy's, who remembered him fondly: "He worked for me occasionally, doing the odd bit of handiwork, as he was good with his hands." Ernie also encouraged Tommy with his music, took him around several venues looking at groups, and bought a drum kit for him. Ernie continued: "Tommy was such a talented drummer, but every group we went to see, he would say the same thing: they're not good enough. He had such high standards that even when he tried to get a group together, he couldn't find the right musicians. Tommy told me that he had sat in with a big band at some point, but I don't know where or when. It was only once or twice." The plan was to get Tommy into a group again, and Ernie would be his road manager and help support him.

Ant Hogan got to know Tommy well when he moved to the Belle Vale area of Liverpool, by which time Tommy had moved on and dealt with most of those regrets that had dogged him for years. "He was never bitter about leaving the band," said Ant. "He had all the albums and would tell me tales about them. He took me to my first Beatles convention and got me really hooked on them. I lived over the road from him, only a short walk away, and I'd go round with my friend Chris, and Tommy would get his drums out and play a bit for us. He taught me a few things on the drums, but I couldn't really play, so I played my guitar. It was great to watch him, because he was a fantastic drummer – unbelievable! He was really good, technically, and had his drums set up in the house.
He was teaching all of us to play. He took me to the Cavern Mecca and one time Tommy turned up with Bob Wooler at a Beatles convention and people pointed him out – 'There's Tommy Moore who played drums with The Beatles' – but he didn't like the attention; he was quite shy. Tommy was the one who got me into The Beatles." *(David Bedford Interview 2015)*

Neighbours

Tommy settled well into the Belle Vale area, and would often stop in for "last orders" at the Highwayman Pub on Belle Vale Road before heading home. Anthony Steinmetz was a neighbour of Tommy's and became a good friend. "I would have first encountered him around and about in 1975," he said. "My main knowledge of Tommy for the first couple of years after meeting him was simply that he was a jazz enthusiast. He later told me that he'd been a drummer – however did not mention The Beatles. When I eventually found out Tommy had played with The Beatles, it seemed a bit incongruous, as his background was so strongly rooted in jazz." Tommy told Anthony about the drummers he listened to, including Gene Krupa, Buddy Rich, Elvin Jones and, more recently, a young Jon Hiseman. "A favourite record of Tommy's was 'Solid Bond' by the Graham Bond Organisation, which I remember was frequently on his turntable."
(David Bedford Interview 2015)

Anthony and Tommy found a shared interest in "a broad range of music, although he was less keen on what he felt was derivative, or unoriginal. Musical debates often took place in the Coronation pub, Tommy's local, on Childwall Valley Road. A couple of years previously, The Tony Williams Lifetime had played at St. George's Hall and made a big impression in the city. Jazz itself had moved on from what was heard during the Cavern's early days, and Tommy loved the wide gamut of musical experience that jazz provided." Anthony also got to know Tommy, the man. "He had great sincerity and kindness, and a comradely, gentle nature. This may have been played upon by John Lennon," observed Anthony, "and at some point, John decided he was going to have a field day with Tommy. The tour of Scotland must have been a miserable experience for Tommy. He said that they had no money, and were living on biscuits."

As well as knowing Tommy the man, Anthony also observed Tommy playing his drums. "I heard him play quite a bit, and his interest in playing had been rekindled toward the end of his life. He had raised a family, and music became more of a focus again. Tommy was very comfortable playing in a fluent and unscripted way, and was an excellent drummer by any standards. He didn't seek to cultivate a flamboyant style that you sometimes see with jazz drummers, but his playing was very effective for each musical situation. I think he would have been bored playing in a lot of pop bands, having to sit there thumping the snare on beats 2 and 4." *(David Bedford Interview 2015)*

Tommy introduced Anthony to what was happening at the Hunts Cross Hotel, just outside Woolton, which used to have a great little jazz club upstairs. "It was run by a jazz aficionado who was an ex-boxer, with trophies and related memorabilia on the walls. There was a house band, playing jazz standards, who were enjoyable. Eventually, when Tommy and I turned up, they would let us sit in with them, mainly just free-jamming. This would have been around 1979. Tommy seemed liberated and happy when he was playing and it seemed a shame that, for whatever reasons, he had not spent more of his life behind a drum kit."

No Kick Against Modern Jazz

Tommy told Anthony that when The Silver Beatles were singing the Chuck Berry song "Rock and Roll Music", John Lennon would sing the line 'I've got no kick against modern jazz' and nod to him. So Lennon wasn't being horrible to Tommy the whole time, just most of the time.

Anthony recalled: "Tommy enjoyed some of his time with The Beatles, but probably not the Scotland tour, for all of the well publicised reasons. He said that John, Paul and George were quite driven and close knit, but that the whole band managed to adapt well to situations where they had to perform with little or no rehearsal time." This also reflects what Johnny Gentle had said – that although at the first concert they were disjointed, by the end of the tour the group had learned quickly how to perform together and were even out-performing him, the "star" of the tour. Would Tommy have stayed with The Beatles? As Anthony observed: "The extraordinary story about Tommy's girlfriend (wife - sic) successfully persuading him to leave The Beatles because 'they had no prospects' is not as history-changing as it sounds. Tommy knew that he and The Beatles would have parted ways eventually; there were too many differences and incompatibilities." *(David Bedford Interview 2015)*

Tommy died at the relatively young age of 50. "On 29th September 1981, we couldn't get an answer from Tommy's house, and the light had been on in his bedroom, so we called the police," said Ant Hogan. "Tommy had not been seen for three days, and we had seen him through an upstairs window. The police knocked the door down and found Tommy on the floor. He had suffered a brain haemorrhage. I remember the day well. I was standing outside his house when they got in. I was 16 and it was horrible. I remember my father running up the road from work and going into Tommy's house. I could see the hurt on his face. Tommy was a special man to me and my father."

Rita also remembered the day well. "It was so sad when he died," she said. "I was working at Ford's in the canteen the day Tommy died, and the strangest thing was that I had a funny turn that day. I don't know what it was, but I went dizzy and everything was weird. Then when I got home I was told the news. I was due to get married in a couple of weeks and I thought of calling it off. Tommy had an aneurysm which he'd had for years, and he died from a brain haemorrhage. When Colette was living with Tommy, the next door neighbour's kid had an argument with Colette and the father came round and butted Tommy. I can never prove it, but that is what I think killed him, in my heart of hearts." Lorraine says she had one particular regret when her dad died. "I used to write to him a lot, every couple of months, and I had a letter ready to send to him which I never got to send to him before he died."

"Sadly, only 11 people came to his funeral. Bob Wooler was there and spoke highly of Tommy, but Allan Williams wasn't there," said Ant. "Tommy was a great bloke who did so much for me." *(David Bedford Interview 2015)*

Would Tommy have become the Fourth Beatle? Technically, as a drummer, he was very talented and could have performed the role quite comfortably, though his first love was jazz. However, Tommy didn't fit in with the others, due to age, family circumstances and his shy personality, which meant that, even if he had stayed with them, it would most likely have only been for a short time. He was probably too good for them.

He made his name in Cass and the Casanovas, the group that evolved into The

"Now then . . . what's all this about a new gimmick . . . ?"

10th May 1960

JOHHNY HUTCHINSON

THE BIG ONE

***Johnny "Hutch" Hutchinson was the undisputed best drummer in Liverpool
in the early 1960s, according to the musicians in his own city.***

Big Three. He sat in with the Silver Beatles and was asked to join The Beatles to replace Pete Best, which he turned down. Who is this enigmatic, straight-talking drummer?

Hutchinson was born in Malta, the son of a Regimental Sergeant Major. Johnny's father, Howard, played rugby for Wales. Johnny was also a keen sportsman, though cricket was his game. He even played for England schoolboys against Wales, but it was music, not sport, that would become his life.

Cass and the Casanovas was formed in December 1959 by Brian Casser, who also performed under the names of Casey Valance and Casey Jones. Cass had completed his National Service in the army and formed a skiffle group with Bill Wyman, who became a founding member of The Rolling Stones. After he left the army, Cass turned down Wyman's offer to join a group with him and teamed up instead with Adrian Barber, a Yorkshire musician who had arrived in Liverpool. For a short time, they had a drummer called Brian Hudson, but Johnny Hutch soon replaced him. Adrian said of Johnny, "He could do all the patterns that Brian couldn't. He was a rock 'n' roll man." *(Mersey Beat)*

Johnny made his debut with them at the age of eighteen at the Corinthian Club in Slater Street, Liverpool. As he recalled: "I remember being in the Corinthian Club with my girlfriend and I was about 17, she was 16. Cass and the Casanovas were playing. At the interval, Cass passed me by and asked me what I thought, so I told him his drummer was crap. So he said, 'Could you do any better?'

So I told him 'yes', and he told me to get up with the group in the second half, so I did. I'd never played drums before, but I was obviously better than the one they had, so I became their drummer." *(David Bedford Interview 2015)*

Hutch never had any drumming lessons. "I had clarinet lessons and learned to read music – something I had over all the other musicians, that I could read music and they couldn't," he observed. "Music is an international language. You can talk music to anybody." He didn't purchase sheet music for the group though. "No, we didn't even practice. I'd say to Johnny Gus, 'Have you heard this song?' and he'd say 'Yes' so I said 'We'll do it tonight.' That is how it was." *(David Bedford Interview 2015)*

Hutch even pioneered the heavy snare sound by reversing his drum sticks and hitting the drum with the thicker end of the stick, as opposed to the drum tip. Many others copied his style.

As with all Liverpool groups, getting hold of songs was key to success. "We used to get them from Stanley House," Hutch said, talking about the club on Upper Parliament Street in Liverpool 8. This club was frequented by the mainly black population of the area, as well as the visiting American servicemen from the nearby air force base at Burtonwood. At Stanley House, they discovered many records that they could learn quickly and introduce to their set. Getting the song before the competition was the aim of every group. "We were the first group to bring 'What'd I Say' into the country," he said proudly. "Ray Charles was one of

the greatest performers ever.

There was nobody like him; when he was stoned in concert and singing, he put his heart and soul on stage. Fats Domino was another great performer, who'd never leave the stage." *(David Bedford Interview 2015)*

Ask almost any drummer of the period who they considered their greatest drumming influence and they will give the same answer. "Gene Krupa," Hutch

Gene Krupa

Krupa has often been considered to be the first drum "soloist". Krupa worked well with other musicians and introduced the extended drum solo into jazz. He is also considered the father of the modern drum set, as he convinced H.H. Slingerland, of Slingerland Drums, to make tunable tom-toms. Up to that point, tom-toms had "tacked" heads, which left little ability to change the sound.

The new drum design was introduced in 1936 and was termed "Separate Tension Tunable Tom-Toms". Krupa was also called on by Avedis Zildjian to help develop the modern hi-hat cymbals. Krupa's first recording session was a historic one. It occurred in December 1927 when he became the first drummer to record with a bass drum. Krupa, along with rest of the McKenzie-Condon Chicagoans were scheduled to record at OKeh Records in Chicago. OKeh's Tommy Rockwell was apprehensive about recording Gene's drums but relented. Rockwell said, "All right, but I'm afraid the bass drum and those tom-toms will knock the needle off the wax and into the street." *(drummerman.net)*

replied immediately, responding for himself and his drumming contemporaries. It is no surprise then that the two hardest hitting drummers in Liverpool, Pete Best and Johnny Hutch, cite Krupa as their biggest influence. One other aspect of Krupa's drumming impressed Hutch. "He drummed with two matchsticks on a matchbox. He would play a rhythm on the side of the matchbox with the matchsticks without striking a light." *(David Bedford Interview 2015)*

Krupa wasn't Hutch's only influence. "Louie Bellson was a great drummer, too." Luigi Paulino Alfredo Francesco Antonio Balassoni, known by the stage name Louie Bellson, was an American jazz drummer. He was a composer, arranger, bandleader, and jazz educator, and is credited with pioneering the use of two bass drums. "I loved that big band sound," continued Johnny, "and some of those drummers, like Dave Black, who played with the Duke Ellington Band. Pete Appleby was another great jazz drummer who played with Lonnie Donegan." He, of course, also mentioned the most legendary drummer of the 20th century: "Buddy Rich was a brilliant drummer." *(David Bedford Interview 2015)*

The first time Johnny Hutch arrives in The Beatles story is on 3rd May 1960 when Cass and the Casanovas appeared on the bill at Liverpool Stadium supporting Gene Vincent in the wake of the death of his co-headliner, Eddie Cochran. In the audience were John, Paul, George and Stuart who still didn't have a formal group. After that concert, the four approached Allan Williams about getting them some bookings and a drummer. It was Brian Casser, the leader of Cass and the Casanovas, who recommended drummer Tommy Moore to them. He also suggested that The Beatals was not a great name and they should change it to something like Long John and the Silver Beatles – there are variations on what the suggestion was – so, out of respect for Casser, they went with The Silver Beatles. Johnny Hutch was soon to perform with this new group. Larry Parnes, the top music promoter in the country, was looking for a group to back his Liverpool-born star Billy Fury, and Allan Williams had convinced.

Parnes to use a Liverpool outfit for the tour. Using the Wyvern Club, Williams' new venue soon to be known as the Blue Angel, the auditions for Parnes took place on 10th May 1960. The Silver Beatles were one of the groups asked to audition, though not on merit, but because Allan Williams had agreed to manage them. At that stage, nobody had heard of them and they hadn't been performing anywhere to build a reputation. Their new drummer Tommy Moore was late, and Larry Parnes wasn't a man to be kept waiting. They had no option but to find a drummer to sit in with them. Again, Brian Casser would provide them with a drummer, if only on a temporary basis. They turned to Johnny Hutch who, in Cheniston Roland's photographs, appears none too pleased to play for a group whose name he'd never heard. "We turned up for the audition and then I was told this group needed a drummer. They said, 'Can you do us a favour and play drums with us?' I didn't know who they were and didn't care, so I just played the drums with them until their drummer turned up. The Beatles were crap at that point and nobody had heard of them." *(David Bedford Interview 2015*

Moore eventually turned up and sat in with his new group, using Hutch's drums. They weren't particularly good but Parnes took a chance and booked them to support Johnny Gentle on a short tour of Scotland. Johnny Hutch's group did much better; they were the group selected to support Billy Fury. Cass and the Casanovas later ended up heading to Scotland too, and also supported Gentle. "We ended up touring Scotland for 18 months," he said, "including with Johnny Gentle. I've been to just about every town in Scotland, so we didn't know what was going on in Liverpool." Like Rory Storm and the Hurricanes, Johnny's group was away from Liverpool and out of touch with what was happening in their hometown. Those Silver Beatles, after not making much of an impression in front of Parnes, would be on a quick learning curve during their tour of Scotland, in preparation for their trip to Hamburg.

On one memorable occasion while on tour in Scotland, Johnny Hutch was on the same bill as Joe Brown and the Bruvvers, and each group was only given a few minutes before the curtain went up. "There were around two thousand people in Dundee, and there were only three minutes between groups, so I was busy setting my drums up and my bass pedal fell off. But the curtains started going up, and I was shouting 'no not yet', but it was too late, and the curtains went up and it was quiet. It could have been awkward, so I just fixed my pedal, and said to the crowd: 'I see you won eh?' That day Scotland had played England at football, and Scotland had won. The noise was incredible and the crowd wouldn't let us off stage! They couldn't get Joe Brown on. That saved us."
(David Bedford Interview 2015)

At the end of 1960, Brian Casser left the Casanovas and the remaining members decided to become a trio called The Big Three. They became one of the best groups in Liverpool. Hutch felt that his group was the best, especially compared to The Beatles. "We were on a different level to them and because we were away from Liverpool for so long, in Scotland and Hamburg, we then didn't know many of the other bands or musicians at the time. I did like Ian and the Zodiacs and Derry Wilkie was a great performer. I liked the underdog, too. I used to walk downtown in Liverpool and get to the top of Church Street and think, 'I own this town!' When The Beatles would see me coming, they crossed the road!" *(David Bedford Interview 2015)*

When The Beatles began conquering Liverpool and Hamburg, Hutch didn't see too much of them. Although his later business relationship with Brian Epstein did not work out, when the Big Three were managed for a short time by Epstein, Hutch still respects him. "They would have been nowhere without Eppy. I don't care what anyone says; they wouldn't have done it without him, any of them, The Beatles, Gerry, Billy Kramer or any of them. And it was Germany that made them (The Beatles) and made all of us." *(David Bedford Interview 2015)*

Working those long hours in the Hamburg clubs would prove essential to the success of the Liverpool bands, as John Lennon concurred.

"We grew up in Hamburg."

In the summer of 1962, having recently signed to Epstein's NEMS stable, Johnny came into close contact with The Beatles when Brian approached him about joining the band as Pete Best's replacement. Johnny declined, and has never regretted it. Johnny Hutchinson was almost the Fourth Beatle; twice.

Johnny Hutchinson with the Big Three

Johnny Hutchinson with the Silver Beatles

14th May 1960

CLIFF ROBERTS

As their period of transition from a group of friends with musical ambitions to becoming a rock 'n' roll group was finally underway – and having secured the Johnny Gentle tour for Larry Parnes – the group still hadn't settled on a name. They had already experimented with the name The Beatals and were now playing around with variations on Silver Beatles, though they never liked it.

Two Cliff Roberts

On 14th May 1960, two men by the name of Cliff Roberts would have an effect on their career. The Silver Beatles had turned up at the Casanova Club where Cliff Roberts and the Rockers were appearing. "We first encountered the Silver Beatles at the Billy Fury audition at the Wyvern Club on 10th May," remembered Allan Schroeder, drummer with Cliff Roberts and the Rockers. "We were regulars at Lathom Hall and were booked there a few days after the Wyvern Club. Cliff Roberts also accepted a booking from Cass (Brian Casser) to do the Casanova Club in Temple Street. We were now double booked.

"We went to the Cassanova Club and were setting up. Cass & the Cassanovas were also on, with Cass running things. The Silver Beetles came in and said to Cliff; 'We are on here tonight.' Cliff said, 'I don't think so', and asked Cass, who confirmed that it was Cliff Roberts and the Rockers who were on. Cliff then said to the Silver Beatles; 'we are supposed to be on Lathom Hall tonight. Would you like to go and fill in for us and tell Brian Kelly I am ill? They were very happy with this and went on their way. When we next went to the Lathom again, the feed back was that they weren't very good!" *(David Bedford Interview 2017)*

The Silver Beatles took advantage of the offer and turned up to play at Lathom Hall, Seaforth, in the north of Liverpool.

The Moore Not Merrier

Their lineup now consisted of John, Paul, George, Stuart and new drummer Tommy Moore. As they weren't expecting to play that night, Moore didn't have his kit, so he asked one of the other drummers in the club if he could use theirs. The drummer he approached was another Cliff Roberts, who played with Kingsize Taylor and the Dominoes, and not the singer who recommended them to go to the Lathom that night. Not knowing Tommy or wanting anyone else near his kit, Roberts refused the request. If they were to perform, the only solution was for Roberts to play drums with The Silver Beatles.

Cliff Roberts, having assembled a drum kit, had started a group with friends Sam Hardie, a great pianist, and singer Arthur Baker, after they left school in 1957. Following the recruitment of other musicians, they added Ted Taylor in 1958 and changed their name to The Dominoes. Ted "Kingsize" Taylor, so-called for his 6' 5" height, joined as lead vocalist and guitarist. Bobby Thompson, with whom Taylor had played in another skiffle group, the James Boys, joined on bass guitar and vocals.

The group was completed with John Kennedy on guitar and Geoff Bethell, who often stood in for Hardie on piano. Taylor, known for his vivid checkered jackets, developed a burgeoning reputation as one of the best rock 'n' roll singers in Liverpool, establishing the group as one of the greatest to emerge in the

Merseybeat era.

Taylor recalled the night he witnessed Cliff Roberts playing with this early incarnation of The Beatles. "My recollection of this night was that they did have a drummer with them," he recalled, "but Cliff would not allow him to use his drums, so he said that he would drum for them, as it was only an audition. They played a maximum of four or five numbers then (promoter) Brian Kelly closed the curtains on them. When we went back on stage, they all sat with pen and paper in hand and attempted to write down the lyrics to the numbers that we were doing, each taking down a line each. This was observed by Sam Leach, and is well-documented." *(David Bedford Interview 2015)*

And what did Taylor think of The Silver Beatles? "In spite of what was supposedly written in the Crosby Herald, they were crap, but obviously had the potential." *(David Bedford Interview 2015)*

Crosby Herald reporter Alan Walsh, wrote the first concert review of "The Beatles". He said that there was a "stunned silence when The Beatles came on, like 'What's this lot doing here?' and compared to everybody else, they were very loud." His quote was "The Beatles closed the show with their own brand of feet-tapping rock." *(TuneIn)* It is interesting to note that the article refers to them as The Beatles.

Roberts recalled The Silver Beatles' appearance that first night: "They were a scruffy bunch whose drummer hadn't brought his kit and asked if he could borrow mine. I had a brand new Olympic kit that I hadn't even used on stage myself, so I naturally refused." Together with The Beatles, they performed six numbers which were, as Roberts later recalled, "four rock 'n' roll standards that all the groups played, and two originals that they had to teach me." *(Mersey Beat)* It is interesting to note that even though they hadn't been performing for long, they still felt confident enough to perform two of their own songs.

By the summer of 1960, Cliff Roberts' group was being billed as Kingsize Taylor and the Dominoes. They were top of the bill and playing at some of the best clubs in Liverpool. "By now," recalled Roberts, "we were playing interval spots at Litherland Town Hall, the most prestigious venue in North Liverpool. We were local celebrities now. We'd made it!" *(Mersey Beat)*

Taylor was impressed with Cliff Roberts as a drummer. "Cliff was a good steady all-round drummer," Taylor said, "ideal for the changing face of music, i.e. from skiffle to rock, which in our case was very rapid. The fact that he was a local lad, and we all knew him personally made it easy for us to build up the band the way we wanted it. Later, he left The Dominoes and we acquired Dave Lovelady, very similar in style, and also a local lad to us. Dave was the drummer that we took to Hamburg first. But in late 1964, when my group disbanded, I put together another, which did include Cliff Roberts again, and we played the Star Club Circuit, and other venues around Germany and Denmark. A good solid drummer."
(David Bedford Interview 2015)

Promoter Brian Kelly booked The Beatles for the following week, Saturday 21st May 1960, publicizing them as The Silver Beats alongside the Dominoes and the Deltones. This was the first time the group had officially appeared in an advertisement. Even so, they did not turn up for the gig as they had already departed for a tour of Scotland as Johnny Gentle's backing band. As they had failed to inform Kelly of their other engagement, he consequently did not book them again for several months – until Bob Wooler talked him into putting them on the bill at Litherland Town Hall on their return from Hamburg in December 1960.

Cliff Roberts did not see The Beatles again until 19th January 1961 at Alexandra Hall, Crosby. He recalled the evening clearly: "They wore black leather, had brand new instruments and played brilliantly." *(Mersey Beat)* Of course, by then, Tommy Moore had been replaced by Norman Chapman, who in turn had been replaced by Pete Best, and The Beatles were firmly established as the premier rock 'n' roll group in Liverpool.

For one night only, Cliff Roberts was the Fourth Beatle.

Cliff Roberts with Kingsize Taylor and the Dominoes

11th June 1960

RONNIE "THE TED" (aka Ronnie "the Cosh")

After Tommy Moore quit the group to return to his job at the Garston Bottle Works, The Silver Beatles still had to fulfil a performance that had already been booked for 11th June 1960 at The Grosvenor Ballroom, Wallasey.

Paul remembered the venue quite clearly: "The Grosvenor Ballroom in Wallasey was one of the worst places; there would be a hundred lads from Wallasey squaring up to a hundred lads from Seacombe and all hell would break loose. I remember one night a rumble had started before I realised what was happening. I ran to the stage to save my Elpico amp, my pride and joy at the time. There were fists flying everywhere. One Ted grabbed me and said, 'Don't move, or you're bloody dead!' I was scared for my life, but I had to get that amp." *(Anthology)*

It was at this nightmare venue that a strange incident occurred – one which has almost passed into legend. Playing without a drummer one night, John tried to make a joke about their absent band member, asking if there were any drummers in the room. Not expecting a response, he was shocked when Ronnie 'The Ted' (Teddy Boy) stepped up, took a seat behind Moore's drum kit and bashed away at the skins for the evening. It turned out that Lennon and The Silver Beatles were too intimidated to challenge this hulking figure of a man.

Allan Williams remembered the incident: "When The Beatles went on stage, there was the usual mob of kids determined on mischief." As The Silver Beatles set up, Williams saw the gang leader, who "had a mass of red hair and was about six feet two inches tall, and around seventeen years old. He had hands like anchors, shoulders like a brick outhouse and piggy eyes which gleamed out uncertainly, madly, at a highly suspect world." *(The Man Who Gave The Beatles Away)*

Ronnie had a reputation for hospitalising people who crossed him, supported by his gang. Williams recalled that Lennon "joked that they could play without a drummer, but it would be better if they had one and then stupidly asked for volunteers". Not expecting a response, just a laugh, Lennon was struck dumb when the menacing Ronnie stepped forward. Lennon looked at him and realised what he had done. They had seen Ronnie in action at the Grosvenor, so what could they do but let him bash away on the drums? At the end of the night, Ronnie asked John if he could join them permanently.

In a panic, they phoned Williams, who by this time was back at the Jacaranda. "John brought me up to speed with what had happened, and sounded really afraid, which was not often the case with John. I drove over there as fast as I could and, by the time I arrived, the lads had finished and were in the band room with Ronnie and some of his gang." Williams introduced himself as their manager, and chatted away with Ronnie. "I was thinking on my feet, because I'm only five feet small!" said Williams.

As he had no bouncer with him, Williams had to find a way out of this situation without a fight, because it was one they couldn't win. "As we finished packing up, Ronnie approached me. 'Well, you're the manager, what about it?' obviously wanting me to appoint him as the group's new drummer. I tactfully explained that Tommy was still our drummer, and he was just busy this night.

And then I left him with a promise. 'The lads are playing here again next week.

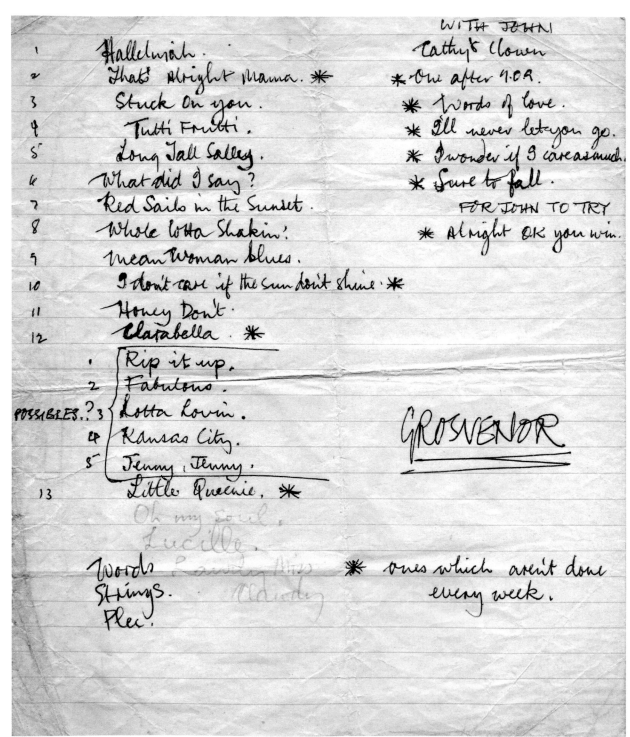

Set list from the Grosvenor Ballroom for the Silver Beatles, June 1960

If we haven't got another drummer by then, you can sit in with the boys. How about that?' Ronnie was happy with that compromise, and we escaped."
(The Man Who Gave The Beatles Away)

Williams managed to negotiate his way out of the situation, and returned to Liverpool to try and convince Tommy Moore to play one more time. It wasn't to be.

Who Was He?

After many local appeals on Merseyside, Ronnie 'The Ted' may have been identefied at last. Geoff Nugent, who had a successful career with Merseybeat group The Undertakers, was there that night, and told his friend Peter Hodgson that he knew who Ronnie was. Geoff recalled that he frightened the life out of everyone over the water one night. "He got up on the drums and was bashing away, and they (The Silver Beatles) were too scared to say anything to him," said Geoff. Known locally as a bully, his name was Ronald Hoolihan, and and everyone was terrified of him and his mates. "He carried a cudgel," also known as a cosh, a popular weapon of choice for gangs back then. "Everyone called him 'Ronnie the Cosh'," although he has become better known as Ronnie "the Ted".

For one night only, Ronnie "the Cosh" was the Fourth Beatle, and definitely not for another single night.

THE TED

Ronnie is referred to as "the Ted" as he was the leader of a gang of Teddy Boys, the name given to a subculture of young men who adopted the style associated with the type of clothing worn in the Edwardian era – named after King Edward V11 who reigned between 1901 and 1910. The style of clothing was briefly reintroduced after the Second World War, but was adopted by youths initially in London in the 1950s. The term "Teddy Boy" was coined by the Daily Express newspaper which shortened Edwardian to Teddy. These Teddy Boys were the first identifiable group of teenagers in Britain. When the American film Blackboard Jungle was shown in London in 1956, Teddy Boys tore the cinema apart, leading to riots across the country in cinemas that showed the film. The clothes were typified by a long, drape jacket, often with a velvet collar, high-waisted drainpipe trousers, shirts with a "Billy Eckstine" collar (named after the jazz musician) and bright coloured socks, all accompanied by 'brothel creepers', those chunky-soled suede shoes. The hair was worn in a "DA" (Duck's Arse) style, which was greased to the back of the head and with a huge quiff at the front. It was this style that John and the others aspired to, though they were never real "Teddy Boys".

Jackie Lomax with David Bedford

11th June 1960

JACKIE LOMAX: THE UNDERTAKER WHO DIED ON STAGE WITH THE BEATLES

Jackie Lomax made his name in Liverpool as the frontman of one of the most popular Merseybeat groups, The Undertakers, playing rhythm guitar or bass, as well as being a vocalist.

In April 1964, The Undertakers had a Top 40 UK hit with "Just A Little Bit", and in 1967, following the group's split, Lomax and his new band were briefly managed by Brian Epstein. After Brian's death, The Beatles' newly-formed Apple organization took responsibility for his recording career.

In 1968, after John Lennon advised him to go solo, Lomax was signed by Apple, and his debut album for the label, Is This What You Want? *(produced by George Harrison)*, was released in March of the following year. For the recording of the album, George enlisted the help of other musicians, including his fellow Beatles, and also played guitar with Lomax. The lineup on "Sour Milk Sea" included Paul McCartney *(bass)*, Ringo Starr *(drums)*, Nicky Hopkins *(keyboards)* and Eric Clapton *(lead guitar)*. Klaus Voormann *(bass)*, Bishop O'Brien *(James Taylor's drummer)*, and Clapton played on some of the other London sessions. For the completion of the album in Los Angeles, Wrecking Crew members Larry Knechtel *(keyboards)*, Joe Osborn *(bass)* and Hal Blaine *(drums)* were recruited.

Just One Song

However, nearly a decade before his involvement with Apple, a 16-year-old Lomax played with The Beatles, then known as The Silver Beatles. The group consisted of John, Paul, George, Stuart and drummer Tommy Moore, though after Moore quit, the group had yet another drummer issue to resolve. Lomax recalled the event years later: "I even played drums for them *(The Silver Beatles)* one night when they didn't have a drummer," he said. "Just one song, that was enough.

I was terrible. It was at the Grosvenor Ballroom, Wallasey, which is where I come from. It was 1960. They were great. They sounded like a record, even then."
Most probably on the same evening that Ronnie 'the Ted' play with them, Jackie Lomax played drums on only one song, so there was no way he was ever going to be the "Fourth Beatle". Thankfully, he stuck to what he did best and became one of the best frontmen of the Merseybeat scene, and an Apple recording artist.

The Beatles at Shea

After The Undertakers called it a day, Brian Epstein became Jackie's manager, with the deal agreed upon in New York, where the musician was based. "I went with The Beatles to Shea Stadium in 1966," he recalled, "and it was then that Brian asked me to become a solo singer. I said, 'Well, I've just got a new band together, do you want to hear us?' So he came to a rehearsal and was impressed, and he brought us back to England (in 1967). We were called the Lomax Alliance – two American guys, two English. We started an album, but Brian died in the middle of it, so it all ended in confusion."

Without Brian, Lomax had to form a new group. "The rest of the band went back to New York, but I stayed in London," he said. "I met up with Chris Curtis, the drummer from The Searchers, and we went to NEMS to see if The Beatles would help us out." John Lennon reiterated Epstein's suggestion to go solo. "John took me aside and said, 'Hey Jackie, Brian told me you write songs?' I said, 'Well, I'm just starting out, but yeah'. He said, 'We want songwriters, so go and see Terry Doran at Apple Publishing'.

The Undertakers

So I did, and I got signed as a writer." This was before they'd launched the Apple record label. "I'd tape my demos on a two-track in the attic in Baker Street, above the Apple Boutique," he said.

"I thought I was writing songs for other artists, but then George Harrison heard them, and he said, 'I'm going to India, but when I come back, do you want to do an album, and I'll produce it?'"

Jackie Lomax never really achieved the success he deserved with The Undertakers, at Apple, and most certainly not through his one-song gig as The Beatles' drummer, but he was always grateful to George Harrison for his support. "George was a champion," he said. "He made time for me and was protective even, inviting me to his home. I felt really privileged. It was incredible. To have my name associated with The Beatles – what better thing could happen to a budding artist?"

(www.applerecords.com/albums/is_this_what_you_want)

June 1960

PAUL MCCARTNEY: THE SECOND BEATLE BECOMES THE FOURTH BEATLE

Even before Pete Best joined the group in August 1960, Paul was a strong contender for the position of permanent drummer.

After his kid brother Mike badly injured his arm in an accident, Paul spent the entire time Mike was in hospital learning to play his incapacitated sibling's drum kit. "I have a kit which is based on Ringo's. I figure I can't go far wrong with a kit like his," McCartney said. "So it's lovely, I love it. I always like a chance to get on the kit. I've done it since the early days of The Beatles."

Stripped Down Drummer

This skill was put to the test on numerous occasions over the years, especially in the summer of 1960 when The Silver Beatles were struggling to find a permanent drummer. Between Tommy Moore and Norman Chapman, Allan Williams secured a booking for them backing Janice the Stripper at the New Cabaret Artistes Club in Upper Parliament Street. Paul became their temporary drummer. "At that point it was just the three of us—just John, George and me. That was nucleus of the band. But that meant there were three guitars and no drums." McCartney sat behind the kit, but had to be creative with the microphone. "They didn't really have any good mic-ing, so I got a brush, an old broom, and just tied the microphone to the end of it and just stuck it in between my legs. Believe me, trying to hold that broom and drum at the same time was not that easy, but we made it through. It was a gig backing this stripper called Janine (or Janice). She was a girl from London, and we got an eyeful at the end. Those were the days, my friend."

Although his bandmates may have considered him for the permanent job when they went to Hamburg in August 1960, it wasn't possible. Bruno Koschmider wanted a five-piece group, so Paul was disqualified, much to his relief. However,

he did get the chance to play drums in Hamburg, though not with The Beatles, who had Pete Best. "There'd be these kits lying around from the other bands," he recalled." I'd occasionally get down and practice on 'em and see if I could figure 'em out. But one of the nights, one of the guys we used to work with, Tony Sheridan, his drummer hadn't turned up. So I drummed with him.

It was terrifying, but it gave me a love of drumming." *(People Music 31 March 2017)*

A Twist of Drummers

Paul was to sit in with other musicians, especially in the early days. On 5th April 1962, while at the Cavern Club, The Beatles joined forces with The Four Jays on stage and performed their original song "Pinwheel Twist". Pete Best emerged from behind his drums to dance with his girlfriend – and future wife – Kathy. Paul replaced Pete on drums for the first time.

Paul is a Stranger

A few weeks later, on 20th June 1962, The Beatles shared the bill at The Cavern with The Strangers. When the Strangers' drummer, Brian Johnson, developed cramp in his leg, it became clear that he wouldn't be able to play.

Paul McCartney quickly volunteered and they gratefully accepted his offer. So for one night only, Paul McCartney became The Strangers' drummer.

Curiosity

On a visit to Liverpool on 25 October 1968, Paul made an "unannounced" visit to the Cavern Club with his new girlfriend, Linda Eastman.
The current owner of The Cavern, Alf Geoghegan, dashed out to buy a camera, which he gave to Linda, who took several photographs that day. There was a band, Curiosity Shop, who were rehearsing on stage, so Paul couldn't resist the chance to join the group and get behind the drums. He also got behind the piano in the lounge and treated his small audience to a solo performance of *"Hey Jude"*.

Original painting by Paul Skellett (www.skellett.com)

74

16

June 1960

NORMAN CHAPMAN

John, Paul, George, Stuart and Norman? Yes, for a short time in 1960, the group that would soon become known as The Beatles had the strangely sounding lineup of John, Paul, George, Stuart Sutcliffe and Norman Chapman.

The Silver Beetles had failed to convince Tommy Moore that drumming was better than driving a fork-lift truck at Garston Bottle Works, so they had to find a replacement quickly. With Allan Williams now managing them, the bookings had started to flow in.

One evening in June 1960, Williams was standing with his group outside of the Jacaranda when the sound of drumming caught their attention. They looked around to try and determine its source and realised it was coming from a warehouse at the corner of Slater Street and Seel Street. They ventured across the road and tried their best to get the attention of the solitary drummer.

They eventually did, and from the door came Norman Chapman, a picture framer from the art shop R. Jackson & Son, opposite the Jac. Allan Williams recalled what happened: "One night, we heard the sound of drums coming from the street, so we went outside to find out where it was coming from. There was a drummer rehearsing across the road from The Jac – in what became the Bamboo Club – and the company repaired old cash registers."

(The Man Who Gave The Beatles Away)

In one of his only known interviews, with author Spencer Leigh in 1980, Chapman recalled how he joined the group: "I worked in a shop in Slater Street originally, Jackson's Art Shop, and I was practicing in a place further down from there with my drum kit… in a workshop I used to work in, in Slater Street.

Allan and Beryl Williams with Lord Woodbine

I think the drum kit cost about £20, and I was dead keen on playing, but never had any thoughts of playing with a group. One afternoon in Jackson's, my boss Mr. Brewer said somebody wants to see you downstairs at the front of the shop. When I went down to see who it was, it was Paul McCartney, and he had heard me practicing and he asked me if I would like to sit in with the band that night, which I did."

Though McCartney tried not to appear desperate, they hastily invited Norman to join the group. "It was just sit in and play," Norman said, "and just one of those nights where you just go down and do your thing. There were no rehearsals or band calls; it just happened you know, the twelve-bar blues and general music like that."

The Boy's Brigade

Norman's daughter Ann-Marie revealed how her father became a drummer. "He learned to play the drums in the Boy's Brigade," she said, "and was given his first set of cymbals by a drum tutor called Red Carter. He went down to Hessy's to get his first set of drums on finance." Chapman fit in with the group immediately. "Dad spent a lot of time rehearsing with them," explained Ann-Marie, "and soon showed that he was a talented drummer. We know that he did rehearse with the lads at John's Aunt Mimi's home, 'Mendips', among other places, and they quickly became friends." *(David Bedford Interview 2013)*

Norman drummed with them for three consecutive Saturday night performances at the Grosvenor Ballroom in Wallasey – on 18th June, 25th June, and 2nd July 1960.

Allan Williams remembers Norman fondly. "He was a big guy, about six feet two, and spoke in a very quiet, gentle voice. His drumming was a hobby and he hadn't even sat in with a band before. I told him about the band, and that they were playing around Merseyside, earning about ten pounds a night, and asked him if he was interested. 'I sure am,' he told me, 'I could do with the money because drum kits are so expensive. That'll help me pay for the money for the kit.' The others liked him, too." *(The Man Who Gave The Beatles Away)*

Williams met up with Norman many years later and the drummer talked about his time with the group. "Those guys really loved the game," Norman told Williams. "You could tell even then that they had something special going for them. Everything they did and said was directed at making their sound better and better, day by day. I remember Paul as the dominant one, not John, although everyone nominated John as the leader. One night when we were playing at the Grosvenor Ballroom in Wallasey, a fight broke out. Fights were always breaking out. There were chairs flying through the air, bottles whizzing about and bodies hurling in every direction. The police charged in and they were carting bodies out and stacking them on the lawns outside. What a scene. We kept playing the music all the way through. John was hiding behind the curtain and laughing his head off and Paul was somehow crouched under the piano. The music never stopped. What a night."

London?

At this point, when John met beat poet Royston Ellis, The Beatles as a group could have split. "John and Stuart were on a poetry kick at the time" Norman

Norman's drums in the Jacaranda, Liverpool

recalled, "and they asked me to go down to London with them to play while some guy read his poetry out. I was married at the time so I did not go with them. John's flat in Gambier Terrace was a scream of a place. It was so dirty and untidy. They never cleaned the ashes out of the fireplace and things got so bad the ashes stretched from the fireplace to the middle of the floor." *(The Man Who Gave The Beatles Away)*

In a Record & Show Mirror article, Ellis even mentioned that he had this great group called The Beetles, who would be coming to back him, playing the music behind his poetry. A year later, Ellis was immortalised by John as the "Man on the Flaming Pie" because he suggested to John the spelling change in the group name. By replacing the double "ee" in "Beetles" with "ea", the new name "Beatles" would signify beat music and beat poetry. The flaming pie was the pie that Ellis burnt in the Gambier Terrace bedsit when he overcooked it. Thankfully for Beatles history, the move to London never happened. There was another city that was soon calling them.

With the group coming together and the trip to Hamburg on the horizon, a cruel twist of fate changed Norman Chapman's destiny and abruptly ended any chance he had to remain The Beatles' drummer. "Being slightly older than the others, Dad was called up for National Service," recalled Ann-Marie, "and was conscripted into the army, joining the Liverpool Scottish Guards for two years. He was soon heading for Kenya and Kuwait to complete his two years of active service." *(David Bedford Interview 2013)*

Suddenly, Norman's brief tenure in the group was over. It was cruel, as he was so close to not having to join. The last man to be called up for National Service was 22-year-old Richard Vaughan on 17 November 1960, just three months after Chapman was summoned. Thankfully, the other Beatles escaped National Service, but just barely, or history could have been so different.

that, with the advent of superior weapons, manual fighting would not be as necessary. It was thought that banishing conscription was one reason that Harold MacMillan's Conservative party won the 1959 election in such big numbers. They decreed that anyone born on or after 1st October 1939 would not be called up, thus saving The Beatles from conscription. Unfortunately, Norman Chapman wouldn't be able to accompany his bandmates on a trip to the country that National Service was founded to fight: Germany. *(BBC News Magazine May 2015)*

Norman was typically philosophical about his time with the group. "It was just one of those things, me being called up for the army," he said. "I never rose above private, and when I came back to Liverpool, The Beatles were getting really big so there was no opportunity for me to go back with them. I sometimes think that maybe I should be rich by now, but I had no control over the situation at the time so it doesn't really worry me. It's not as though I parted with The Beatles voluntarily." *(Spencer Leigh Interview)*

On his return home from the service, Norman opened a picture-framing business in Southport. "Dad did work with some of the famous local footballers," explained Ann-Marie, "but he never tried to make a lot of money. He was not interested in making money, just enjoying what he did. For many years, he played drums in groups, including one called Ernie Mack's Saturated Seven, a name that parodied the more famous Temperance Seven, whose number one hit in 1961, "You're Driving Me Crazy", was produced by future Beatles producer George Martin. His longest lasting friendship was with 'Old' Joe Royle, father of the former Everton Football Club manager, Joe Royle. They enjoyed playing gigs together for many years until Joe passed away.

Sadly, Norman Chapman died young. "Dad contracted lung cancer and ended up in hospital," Ann-Marie said. "We were travelling up from Brighton to see him when I received a phone call to say we were too late and that he had passed away.

NATIONAL SERVICE

Due to a severe shortage of soldiers, the National Service was introduced in 1939 as Britain entered the Second World War. Single men aged between 20 and 22 were called up to one of the armed services, though, within a few months, the age range was extended to all men aged between 18 and 41. In 1942, women between 20 and 30 were added to the list, and the upper age range for men was extended to 51, all to support the war effort.

After the war, National Service remained. Men between 17 and 21 had to spend a year and a half in the armed forces to undergo training, and had to be on standby to fight, if needed, for four subsequent years. By the 1950s, National Service took men into training for two full years. Nearly two million went through it. "It served different purposes at different times," explained Richard Vinen, a historian at Kings College London, and author of a book on National Service in the post-war years. "Initially it was to train soldiers as a reserve force, and then it was to have them ready for immediate deployment, and then it was for colonial warfare." By 1957, as The Quarrymen were playing skiffle music for fun, the process was gradually winding down.

National Service was no longer needed, due to the post-war baby boom. After the atomic bomb, the whole nature of warfare was changing, and it was predicted

I don't know why they did not tell us he was so ill or we could have got up there sooner. He was only 58."

Norman Chapman was a quiet man and never wanted to talk much about his time with the group that would become The Beatles. "Dad was never jealous or bitter about his short time with the group and was also conscious of never wanting to cash-in on their fame for his own rewards. He was just happy with his life and got on with it." *(David Bedford Interview 2013)*

As Chapman recalled, "Being in music has cost me quite a lot actually, domestic-wise and otherwise, unfortunately, but I've also met some very nice people through being involved with music and also people who like to shoot The Beatles down. I don't know why, in their early stages, because they said they were semi-skilled and couldn't tune instruments or whatever, but who could at an early stage in their profession or starting off in music? Do I miss the fame, the fortune, whatever? Well, I don't. I'd like a few shekels from time to time but I wouldn't say I've missed it all that much, but people want me to have this down on everybody." *(Spencer Leigh Interview)*

When Norman died in July 1995, his sister Maria paid tribute to him when asked whether he was bitter because he had missed out on fame. "He was not that sort of person. His philosophy was 'what will be, will be'. He loved music and he loved the drums."

Would he have become The Beatles' permanent drummer? "He would probably have still been with them," observed Allan Williams, "as he got on well with them. Norman died young and I went to his funeral. I hardly knew him, but he was a nice man." *(The Man Who Gave The Beatles Away)*

What did The Beatles think of him? George Harrison was quoted as saying, "I remember him well, Norman Chapman. Big feller, did not talk much. In fact, I can't remember a word he ever said to me. He was a good drummer, though, and that's for sure." Ringo later commented on Norman, too: "The boys told me they had this drummer they heard rehearsing on his own. They thought a hell of a lot of him." *(Anthology)*

Was George's assessment a fair one? As Norman played on a 1974 EP record with Ernie Mack's Saturated Seven, we can analyse his drumming skills. For this release, the group recorded five songs "Down By The Old Mill Stream"/"Put Your Arms Around Me, Honey"/"Marjie", "St. Louis Blues" and "I'd Like To Teach The World To Sing".

The Saturated Seven consisted of band leader Ernie "Mack" McGrae (banjo and vocals), Joe Royal (Piano), Fred Harrison (Bass), Don Lydiatt (Clarinet), Bill Edwards (Trumpet), John Parkes (Trombone) and Norman Chapman on drums. The group had been going since the late 1950s and were based in the Broadway Club in Liverpool, not far from the New Clubmoor Hall where Paul McCartney made his paid debut with The Quarrymen. Joe Royle Senior passed away many years ago, but his son, Joe, who became a successful footballer with Everton, Manchester City and England, said how his father told him Norman was "his best ever drummer, and a great guy". *(David Bedford Interview 2015)*

In 1971, the Saturated Seven appeared in the film, *Gumshoe*, which was filmed in Liverpool and starred Albert Finney and Billy Whitelaw. The group was featured in a scene shot in the Broadway Club. They also appeared on the British television talent show, *Opportunity Knocks*, where they won in the studio and placed second in the postal vote. For many years, they were the resident band at the Broadway Club and were rated one of Liverpool's best jazz bands. Chapman took over from original drummer Fred Pettit in 1972.

Analysing Norman Chapman's Drumming

Mal Jefferson, Producer with Mastersound Studios, reviewed the EP recorded by Ernie Mack's Saturated Seven, with a particular mention of Norman Chapman's drumming:

"When doing record reviews, which I have done for many years for *Jazz Journal* and newspapers, the first thing I do is to start with the downside of the recording, then finish with some praise.

"I am having difficulty with this review; there is no downside – none at all. This is a 33 rpm microgroove EP, beautifully mastered with perfect compression (needed for vinyl) and the recording fidelity is wonderful. All of the instruments are clear and in tune, which is often a failing with Trad/ Dixieland bands.

"When I first heard it, I thought it was *(Chris)* Barber, *(Acker)* Bilk or *(Kenny)* Ball, the three leading British bands of this genre. If anything, it is better. It's a Liverpool band, well-rehearsed, playing with great verve and expertise. I only wish that it was a full-length album. It is an absolute joy.

"The drumming from Norman Chapman is an object lesson in controlled swing. His rolls and dynamics are terrific. The way he plays the 'St. Louis Blues' is a lesson in rhythm.

"How good is Joe Royle Senior on piano? Sensational! Fred Harrison on bass is note perfect, without getting in the way. Don Lydiatt on clarinet has never played better (had the pleasure of working with him at various times); John Parkes on slide trombone plays with a full rich tone and Bill Edwards on trumpet leads the horns better than Humph (Humphrey Littleton). Ernie Mack? Well he's no Mario Lanza, but he sings and plays in the exact humorous style needed for a romping, boozy jazz combo.

"I have played it to a number of musicians who are totally knocked out with it. Points? 10 out of 10 is hardly enough – a wonderful tribute to an entertaining band of players. I'm delighted to say that I'm flabbergasted."

Make It A Party with Ernie Mack's Saturated Seven - The Record

"Down By The Old Mill Stream"/ "Put Your Arms Around Me, Honey"/ Marjie"

This medley has close vocal harmonies, banjos and brass solos, but behind the songs is Norman Chapman's inventive beat, with a perfect tempo and feeling for the songs. He includes drum rolls, fills and excellent use of the cymbals, too.

"St. Louis Blues"

This song starts with several intricate drum rolls and solos from Chapman, which showcases his talent as a drummer and sets up this trad jazz classic perfectly. More than the other songs the group recorded, this one is the perfect vehicle for Chapman, and shows us what The Beatles could have missed.

Alex Cain and Terry McCusker, drummers with many years experience and authors of *Ringo Starr and the Beatles Beat*, critically analysed this track and Norman's drumming:

"Terrific playing in a heavily New Orleans jazz influenced style, Norman rips into 'St. Louis Blues' with gusto, the track being the perfect platform for him to exhibit his considerable 'marching band' drum chops. More than likely a rip-roaring live performance, he lays his intentions down from the get-go, with four

bars of military snare 'beefed up' with 'four on the floor' bass drum –
exactly what the bass drum player would be doing on the way back from a
'Naw-leans' funeral.

"However, it has to be said, Norman soon plays a little too busily as enthusiasm
gets the better of him and he overplays a little, with almost every trick in the
book on show. The track would have benefitted by being played at a slower
tempo, but as it goes on, Norman relaxes, giving the soloists plenty of room to
shine by going over to ride cymbal – and boy does he swing!"

"Ultimately, we have to remove ourselves from our present-day perspective, and
look at the time when it was recorded. From a local 1970's Jazzer's viewpoint,
this is as good as it gets."

"I'd Like To Teach The World To Sing"

"Another great version of a popular song done in their Dixieland Jazz style again
showcases Chapman's drumming technique and style, showing his control and
versatility behind the drum kit."

Norman Chapman The Fourth Beatle?

Chapman was certainly talented enough, and, with Tommy Moore, possibly the
most technically-gifted drummer who ever played with The Beatles.
Unlike other drummers, he fitted in well with John, Paul and George. Who knows
what would have happened if he hadn't been called up for National Service?
Would we have been talking about a Fab Four of John, Paul, George and
Norman? Out of those drummers who sat in with The Beatles, Norman Chapman
is probably the one who had the greatest potential to become the Fourth
Beatle – at least until fate stepped in the way.

It did mean that The Beatles were in need of a drummer for Hamburg, and they
would finally gain one who, for the next two years, would initially be the fifth
Beatle, and then the Fourth Beatle: Pete Best.

Best at the Star Club

August 1960

TERRY HYMANS: THE UNKNOWN DRUMMER

With Norman Chapman having been called up to do National Service, and Hamburg on the horizon, it was crisis time for the newly-named Beatles: they needed a drummer. This was one of those pivotal moments in Beatles history where their paths met a fork in the road. One way would lead to failure and the other to success.

On or around the 8th August 1960, they were saved by the bell – the bell of the telephone that rang in the Jacaranda. It was Bruno Koschmider, owner of the Kaiserkeller who, after successfully bringing Derry and the Seniors to Hamburg, was in need of another five-piece Liverpool group. Allan Williams promised to bring another group to Hamburg to play at the Indra Club in only one week's time.

To fill the spot, Williams approached the top groups in Liverpool. Gerry and the Pacemakers said no, as they had jobs, were a four-piece and were staying that way. Cass and the Cassanovas, with Johnny Hutch on drums, were also a four-piece and off to Scotland. Rory Storm and the Hurricanes, with Ringo behind the drum kit, were playing their summer season at Butlin's. What other option did he have? The group that he was managing: The Beatles. Their only problem was that they had no drummer, even though Paul had ably performed the task in the interim. But Paul couldn't do the job anyway as the group Koschmider needed for Hamburg had to be a five-piece. If they wanted the job, they needed to find a drummer, and fast.

The group invited Pete Best to audition, but another young drummer would also be briefly considered. On 10th August 1960, an advert appeared in the *Liverpool Echo*. The listing read: "Drummer. Young. Free KP 60."
(The 'KP60' was a private post-box number at the newspaper, designed to protect the identity of the advertiser.)

On 12th August, the same day that The Beatles invited Pete Best to audition, Paul McCartney responded to the unknown drummer's advertisement.

Remarkably, this letter first surfaced in 2011 when it was discovered inside a cheap book purchased at a car boot sale (flea market) in Bootle, Merseyside. Despite the pending Best audition, it's apparent that The Beatles wanted to keep their options open. Paul wrote:

Dear Sir,

In reply to your advertisement in Echo, Wed. night, we would like to offer you an audition for the position of drummer in the group.
You will, however, need to be free soon for a trip to Hamburg (expenses paid £18 per week (approx.) for 2 months.)
If interested, ring Jacaranda Club, Slater St.
(ROYAL 6544) and ask for either a member of the 'BEATLES', Alan Williams , or else leave a message, stating when you will be available.

Yours sincerely
Paul McCartney of THE BEATLES.

On August 12th, when Pete Best received that all-important phone call from Paul asking him to audition for The Beatles the following day, Pete agreed. Accompanied by his brother Rory, he went to Allan Williams' Wyvern Social Club and was offered the position with the group. He immediately packed his bags for Germany.

The Beatles never did receive a reply from the unknown drummer.

Who Was This Mysterious Drummer?

The mystery drummer revealed his identity on 17th December 1964 in the *Liverpool Weekly Star* in a special feature headlined: "MEET TERRY - THE NEAR-MISS MILLIONAIRE". Though most newspaper headlines can be misleading, this one had unmasked the "mystery drummer".

Terry Hymans was revealed as the drummer who had turned The Beatles down and, ignoring the fact that Pete Best played with the band for two years, the journalist posed the question: "Why does he want to kick himself every time he sees the beaming smile of Ringo Starr behind his drums?"

The writer revealed the story of the letter that Terry had received, how he was "a part-time drummer at the time with various beat groups in the city" and had placed an advertisement in the local paper, the *Liverpool Echo*, "offering his services to any group that might be short of a drummer".

Hymans admitted that he did receive a reply, "from a city group" and that the "money offered wasn't bad" but after thinking about it, "he decided against the offer" which, of course, was from Paul McCartney and The Beatles. The reason Terry gave was that "I'd never heard of the group and I couldn't see much of a future with them."

The newspaper finished the piece by saying that "if you see a young man, aged about 22, kicking himself and turning green every time he hears a Beatles record, you'll know it's Terry Hymans..............who didn't bother to answer a letter". *(Liverpool Weekly Star)*

No Reply

Hymans later admitted that he did phone the Jacaranda to follow up the letter, but was too late; he was told the group called The Beatles had gone abroad with someone else. *(TuneIn)*

Could He Have Been The Fourth Beatle?

To be fair to Hymans, the letter from Paul was dated 12th August 1960, and The Beatles were due to leave for Hamburg on the morning of the 16th. If the letter was posted on 12th August, it would have gone to the *Liverpool Echo* post box, and then the Echo would have had to contact him to come and collect it. Hymans might have been able to collect it on Saturday 13th August, but probably wouldn't have picked it up until Monday 15th August, the day before The Beatles were due to depart. This left precious little time to arrange an audition and a passport, let alone time to prepare for the trip.
Panic had clearly beset the group with Norman Chapman's call-up; they needed a drummer desperately. It was pointless to wait for a reply from a nameless drummer they didn't know when they had already contacted someone they did know – Pete Best – and offered him an audition and the chance to go to Hamburg.

What does the evidence say?

In every account of the transition from Norman Chapman to their next drummer, John, Paul, George, and manager Allan Williams have only ever mentioned one drummer they approached, and that was Pete Best.

Just a few months earlier, when they needed a drummer, The Beatles had turned to their new manager Allan Williams, who helped them acquire Tommy Moore. When Tommy Moore quit, and the group stood outside the Jacaranda and heard distant drumming, Williams dispatched Paul McCartney to offer Norman Chapman an audition. After Chapman had to quit, they sought advice once more from Williams, who says he went to the Casbah to check out Pete Best, and recommended him. Though this story hasn't been corroborated, The Beatles relied heavily on Williams, the man who gave them their bookings and had organised the trip to Hamburg. It only makes sense that they would have consulted him about Best.

Williams' account does support what the other Beatles said – that Pete Best was the only drummer they asked. And after Williams checked him out, it was Paul, who had previously approached Chapman, who made the phone call to Pete.

In reality, this letter to Hymans was nothing more than desperation on their part: a Plan B. There was no time, realistically, for Hymans to have received the letter and then audition before The Beatles headed to Hamburg.

So Terry, please don't kick yourself any more.

18

12th August 1960

GERARD "GERRY" WINSTANLEY: ANOTHER UNKNOWN

Gerry Winstanley was the drummer with Liverpool group The Black Velvets, and if not for a hasty decision, he could quite possibly have been The Beatles' drummer on their first trip to Hamburg.

The Black Velvets

The Black Velvets were formed in 1960 and initially consisted of Kenny Reece on guitar and vocals, Dave O'Neill on lead guitar, Stan Alexander on rhythm guitar and Gerry on drums.

Gerry's brother-in-law, Paul Stromberg, worked at the Cotton Exchange in Liverpool with Jim McCartney, Paul's father. The two men used to discuss music, especially on their regular job-related trips to Manchester.

Hamburg

Jim mentioned to Stromberg that his son's group, The Beatles, were heading to Hamburg, but, at the last moment, had lost their drummer, Norman Chapman. Stromberg told Jim that Gerry was a drummer in a local band, so Jim arranged an audition for Gerry with The Beatles. In all likelihood, this would have taken place on the same day that Pete Best was auditioning: Saturday 12th August 1960.

Out of the Picture

What did Gerry do? Instead of taking up an offer that may have resulted in the opportunity of a lifetime, he decided not to turn up because the name "Beatles" sounded silly. He'd never heard of them anyway, so he took his girlfriend to the pictures instead.

It was not long before Winstanley left The Black Velvets and was replaced by John Ryan. He spent most of his life as a professional drummer and drum tutor, working in Guernsey for a while before settling in Thailand, where he currently lives with his third wife.

John, Paul, George, Stuart and Gerry? Another drummer who missed out on famE.

Original painting by Paul Skellett

the beatles for theirians

At The Cavern
7-30 pm Thursday
5th April 1962   Tickets

Purchas
will rec
FREE p
and ma
free me
the Fan

Ticket
from |
White
Gt Ch
and at
Clh

12th August 1960

PETE BEST: THE RISE AND FALL OF A QUIET MAN

Call of Duty

When the telephone rang in Mona Best's sprawling town mansion in Haymans Green, West Derby, on 12th August 1960, it wasn't from the usual teenager enquiring about the Casbah Coffee Bar downstairs in her cellar. Much to her surprise the caller was Paul McCartney.

He knew Mona – and the club – very well. After all, he'd been one of the volunteers who helped to paint the club's interior and was a member of its first resident act, The Quarrymen. This time he wanted to speak to her son, Pete Best, the drummer with the club's former house band, The Blackjacks.

The last time Paul had had any contact with Mona was when he, John Lennon and George Harrison quit the Casbah Coffee Club in October 1959 in a petty dispute over money. Since then, The Quarrymen had been on a long, wandering road, morphing through several name changes and lineups, and Paul was hoping today might be another leap forward. He was phoning today because the group, now called The Beatles, had lost yet another drummer and needed a replacement in a hurry. Having recently worked their way through Tommy Moore and even Ronnie 'the Ted', they relied upon Paul to do the job with a drum set cobbled together with bits and pieces from his brother Mike's kit and one or two items 'accidentally left' at The Jacaranda Club by the rapidly departed Tommy. A short time later, they enlisted and quickly lost another drummer, Norman Chapman.

The lack of a drummer was a thorny issue for Paul during this period. He'd invested so much in his new Solid 7 guitar and in his developing relationship with John front of stage. Now he found himself hidden at the back behind Stuart Sutcliffe, whom he regarded as a rival, not only for Lennon's favour, but also the creative bond he'd worked so hard to build with John. If there was tension, Paul was always careful not to let it show, preferring a patient, long-term approach.

Many years later, he confessed to his frustration: "I was drumming with my hands, playing the hi-hat and bass drum with my feet and I had a broomstick stuck between my thighs on the end of which was a little microphone, and I'm singing 'Tell me what'd I say'. It wasn't easy!"

(McCartney quote to Mark Lewisohn. 1996)

As late July rolled into August 1960, the problem took on a serious note.

On 24th July 1960, The Silver Beatles' de facto manager, Allan Williams, clinched a contract to send Liverpool acts to a club run by Bruno Koschmider in Hamburg. The deal rested on the new act having five members to replace the last five-piece act, The Jets. Koschmider was fixated on five members and Williams obliged by sending Derry and The Seniors to launch what he hoped would be a money-making venture. However, they came unstuck when he tried recruiting more. Despite the number of groups in Liverpool at the time, few were available at short notice or willing to jeopardise their daytime jobs by travelling far from home. Worse still, very few had five members, including his troublesome ex-student act, The Silver Beatles.

The act Williams wanted to send was 'Mr. Showmanship', Rory Storm and The Hurricanes, whose drummer was the bearded Richard 'Ringo' Starr. Unfortunately, they were tied up with a summer season at Billy Butlin's Holiday

Camp in Pwllheli, North Wales. Allan's second choice was either Gerry and his Pacemakers or Cass and The Casanovas, but both turned him down, leaving him with a huge dilemma; no-one else was queuing for the job, except The Silver Beatles, who were nagging him for the chance.

According to Millie Sutcliffe, "Stuart and John got together with Allan Williams and said, 'We hear you're taking groups to Hamburg. What about us... Why can't we go?'" Williams' reply was typically blunt: "You haven't got a drummer. You can't go professional until you have a drummer." *(The Beatles. An Oral History)*

Williams' relationship with the young scroungers, who were forever using his Jacaranda café as a free student drop-in centre, can be summed up from start to finish as love and hate. So it remains uncertain whether or not his short, sharp response was intended to get them off his back or was a subtle hint for them to grow up and get their act together. Williams had got them out of a mess before. In that summer of 1960, he'd secured a dozen or more gigs for them to play, and when there was no one else available, he'd let them play in the cellar of the Jacaranda. He'd also found them a good drummer in the form of Tommy Moore. This time, though, Allan hedged his bets, partly because of what had happened to Tommy. "Nobody rated The Beatles at all early on," he said. "They were known as a rubbish group, and they had difficulty finding a drummer. Also, John was a very difficult person to get on with... Poor Tommy Moore… was ten years older than John and stood no chance at all." *(Drummed Out – The Sacking of Pete Best)*

If nothing else, The Silver Beatles certainly had charisma – as Williams conceded – along with the less palatable truth that other Liverpool artists regarded them as a 'crappy act' with a troublesome leader. It was a fact that Williams remembered in the weeks and years ahead, starting when he received a shocking reply to a pleasant letter he'd sent to the first Liverpool act he'd shipped to Hamburg, Derry and The Seniors. They were doing very well, but the idea to send The Silver Beatles set alarm bells ringing, as author Mark Lewisohn pointed out in *The Complete Beatles Chronicles*:

"Williams wrote Derry and the Seniors a courtesy letter informing them of the Silver Beatles impending arrival, and Howie Casey – with the signatures of all the Seniors except Derry Wilkie – wasted no time replying with a howl of protest, adding it would spoil the scene for everyone if he sent over such a bum group."

This wasn't unusual; The Beatles were regarded as out-of-towners.
Upstarts! No decent drummer was going to risk what he had going just to join a bunch of kids fresh out of college, with no residency, no regular gigs and no visible prospects. To make matters worse, Her Majesty's army decided to put the boot in on The Silver Beatles' newly-recruited sticks man, Norman Chapman. He certainly impressed, but after only a few gigs with the band he, too, received the dread letter. He was conscripted for National Service in Kenya and Kuwait, thus achieving the distinction of being the first and only Beatle ever to play in Africa and the Middle East.

When Herr Koshmider telephoned the Jacaranda out of the blue on Monday 8th August to give him some good news, Williams' heart must have missed a beat. Business was booming according to Bruno. So good that he wanted the second act Williams had promised to be in Hamburg by the 17th August to open at another of his clubs, The Indra. But he wanted a five-piece band and, with less

than a week to go, Williams realised he didn't have a band. The Silver Beatles hadn't found a replacement stickman either. Suddenly the situation became critical and, for two entirely different reasons, both parties found themselves racing against the clock. Strangely, despite Williams' veiled challenge to stand up and be counted, John Lennon had proved short of leadership skills at the crucial moment. Heads must have got together to discuss the problem, but it was left to Paul McCartney to step into the breach. But Paul's options were very thin on the ground and it must have dawned on him and George Harrison that it was fast becoming a matter of any drummer will do.

With barely seven days left before 15th August – the date that Williams' old wagon was due to roll out of Liverpool – the situation was becoming critical; no drummer, no Hamburg – and possibly nowhere else for the band to go if they could not deliver. Not that Paul was going to admit his desperation to Mona, or Pete, when he rang them on the 12th August. Being a smooth operator, Paul cleverly set up his pitching his offer as a golden opportunity with great benefits for the new boy.

As Pete recalled in his autobiography: "There was a call waiting for me at the house one afternoon. 'How'd you like to come to Hamburg with The Beatles?' an excited voice asked at the other end of the line. It belonged to Paul McCartney (surprisingly, I often thought later, because John had always struck me as being the boss). It was an extremely tempting and exciting offer." *(Beatle! The Pete Best Story)*

So, an overseas adventure! A steady job with good pay – and an established club! More importantly, local fixer, Allan Williams, had personally organised everything – the contract, the travel arrangements and good money. £18 pound a week! More than the average take-home pay in Liverpool in those days! The Beatles were ready to go and they wanted Pete to join them. All he had to do was bring his drum kit to an audition at Williams' Wyvern Club (later to become the Blue Angel). Pete elaborated: "He (Paul McCartney) said, 'Pete, we've got the offer to go to Germany. Would you be interested in going?' So I said, 'Yeah, sounds good.' He said, 'Check it over with your family.' I had a word with Mo (my mother) and she said, 'My boy, if that's what you want to do, do it.' So Paul said, 'Okay, come down and audition.' We went off to a little club, which was later to become the Blue Angel, and we blasted off about six numbers. All standard stuff, cover versions, 12 bar blues..." *(The Beatles. An Oral History)*

As Allan Williams recalled, "They remembered Pete from the Casbah and he was now playing on his new set of drums, which sealed it. They did not ask anyone else. Therefore I acted like a manager should and said he needed an audition, so Pete came down and played a few songs, but he had the job anyway." *(The Fab One Hundred and Four)*

The audition was a foregone conclusion. Of course he had the job. They did not ask anyone else because, more accurately (and honestly), they couldn't get anyone else in time.

Pete's younger brother Rory Best helped him get the drums down to the Wyvern Club that evening and stayed to watch the proceedings. "I don't know why they did an audition because they weren't trying other drummers out," Rory recalled. "They played about a dozen songs through, and I have to say they weren't that

Allan and Beryl Williams, Lord Woodbine, Stu Sutcliffe, Paul, George and Pete at the Arnhem War Memorial   *George, John and Paul on the roof of the Top Ten Club*

Although it has been suggested that Allan Williams was in charge of the audition, he wasn't, and anyone who knew Williams would smirk at that claim. The flamboyant Welshman was well-known for self-promotion, but here he confounds the claim in another interview. "I didn't know what made a good drummer, so I just asked him to do a drum roll and said, 'Okay, you're in.'" *(Tune In)*

good, but I did not tell our Pete because I did not want to put him off." *(The Fab One Hundred and Four)*

So that was it, short and sweet! Or was it? Pete Best remembers things very differently. "John Lennon was the only one there when I arrived. He played a couple of bars of 'Ramrod' while I beat the skins, until George and Stu turned up… Paul was the last, as usual, but once there they all joined in such numbers as 'Shakin' All Over'. We played for about twenty minutes in all and at the end they all reached the same conclusion: 'Yeh! You're in, Pete!' Allan Williams popped in toward the finale but heard little of the audition." *(Beatle! The Pete Best Story)*

So much for Williams being in charge! Nevertheless, what Pete didn't realise at the time was that the audition was nothing more than a deception – clever but irrelevant. As Williams was to admit, the real motive was to avoid giving Pete the impression they were more desperate than he could ever have imagined and knowing their desperation might have given Pete a bargaining chip by playing hard to get – or so Williams thought. Williams confirmed much later that the audition was indeed a smoke screen aimed at preventing Pete from asking for more money. He needn't have bothered. The drummer was already keen to join the others on their trip to Hamburg, and he'd already decided to go even before Paul's telephone call had ended.

If there was any benefit at all to a try out, it lay in the opportunity for everyone to join in a casual jam session as each arrived. Once that was out of the way, the

'quickie' marriage of convenience was pronounced official with, "Okay, you're in!" Williams did turn up if only to give his blessing at the end of the ceremony, but none of it really mattered anyway because the boys had seen Pete play at the Casbah only a week earlier and knew what he had to offer well in advance of his mock audition. It just so happened that, a few weeks earlier, Peter Harrison had also seen Pete Best drumming with his own house band, The Blackjacks, at the Casbah, and reported favourably to his young brother George Harrison. That led to the 6th August visit to the club by John, Paul and George during a night off. But was it really a casual night out – or was it a serious talent scouting mission? They gave nothing away but quickly learned two vital things. The golden boy had a new blue mother-of-pearl drum kit with genuine calf skins instead of the cheaper plastic versions. Secondly, The Blackjacks were disbanding. Three of the members were leaving in September to go to university, which meant that Pete would have had no alternative but to make a fresh start. Very handy to know if The Silver Beatles couldn't find anyone else in the meantime! In the end, time did run out and short of any reply from the previously anonymous advertiser in the *Liverpool Echo*, they had reached the end of the line. The advertiser never followed up, leaving Paul with no other choice but to make that call. Of course he wanted Pete. They ALL needed Pete. After all, this was business, not friendship, and besides, who else was there?

Fifteen years later, John Lennon summed it up in a scathing admission: "The reason he got in the group was because the only way we could get to Hamburg… we had to have a drummer. We knew of this guy who was living at his mother's house, who had a club in it, and he had a drum kit and we just grabbed him – auditioned him… and he could keep one beat going for long enough, so we took him to Germany." *(Paul Drew Interview. US Radio. 1975)*

In all fairness, Pete Best wasn't the only musician on the receiving end of John's caustic comments over the years. He had a low opinion of drummers generally, made clear in another interview. "People who owned drum-kits were few and far between," he said, "because it was an expensive item and they were usually idiots, you know. We got Pete Best just because we needed a drummer for Hamburg." *(Anthology)*

Presumably, John's harsh opinion applied to Ringo and Paul as well. Both could play the drums, and surely he remembered playing them himself during the making of *The White Album*. One wonders how much John really valued his other band mate, Stuart Sutcliffe, who was conned into buying a bass guitar with the money he had received from selling a painting. Admittedly, it took a little while to get up to speed with the others, but Stuart became an accomplished rock 'n' roll bass player.

Ticket to Ride

Having decided recently that they would be forever known afterwards as The Beatles, the boys finally got their fifth Beatle, Pete Best. They'd had a rehearsal at the Jacaranda on the Sunday evening, the first official appearance of The Beatles. Pete got a passport, as had everyone else - except for the band's figurehead, John Lennon. With the band due to depart on Tuesday morning, the first Beatle was very close to becoming the missing fifth Beatle. Without Lennon, the group would still be minus the obligatory fifth member, and therefore back to square one. The importance of John's predicament at this moment seems to escape some authors in their rush to get to the next little bit of history.

Yet here was another looming crisis which could have ended The Beatles story there and then.

A desperate John had badgered his Aunt Mimi for several days, but so far she was unable to produce the crucial birth certificate he needed to obtain his passport. Some writers suggest that John talked his way around the problem and persuaded the local passport office to give him the passport anyway.

Utter nonsense! Anyone with the slightest knowledge of officialdom and the red tape pervading government offices in those days can testify that getting anything without the right paperwork was near impossible. It therefore beggars belief that a teenage John would appear out of the blue at the passport office without any proof of identity and sweet talk his way to getting a passport over the counter. What we do know is that John's passport was dated and collected this day.

It's claimed that Mimi insisted she couldn't find the birth certificate. This is remarkable for someone who prided herself on being well-organised. Having once been a nurse and then a personal secretary, she was a strict disciplinarian when it came to order and efficiency and it would be astonishing if she didn't store important family documents safely in the house she famously called the 'House of Correction'.

Yet another nefarious claim is that she was stalling in an attempt to prevent John from going to Germany. Possibly, but as a student of a certain age, he'd already left home and was living with Rod Murray in his rented student flat, which he eventually left, owing Rod £15 in unpaid rent, a sizeable sum in those days. Besides, Mimi knew that John wasn't emigrating forever. It was a paid engagement that would last just a few months – a well-paid holiday!

Could it be that Mimi never had the birth certificate at all? The last time anyone had a serious need for it was when John was 5 years old – some 15 years earlier. Under her father's instruction, Mimi conspired with the local social services to make her John's legal ward to stop Julia from regaining possession of her son. Then, John's father, Alf duped Mimi into giving him permission to take John on holiday to Blackpool even though his real intention was to eventually migrate to New Zealand with his son. At this point the birth certificate would have been essential to obtain a family passport, but Alf's dream of a better life in the sun with John came to an abrupt end after Mimi panicked when they failed to return home. Alarmed, she alerted her sister, Julia, who being pricked by sudden mother-love, dashed to Blackpool with her lover, Bobby Dykins, and snatched John back. But on returning to Liverpool, she was forced to hand him over to Mimi yet again. It's a very sad saga, but the question must linger as to whether Mimi received John's birth certificate during that time, or whether it was kept by Julia – or even Alf.

Regardless of the dark family issues that dogged John's life, it's almost immaterial whether Aunt Mimi hid his birth certificate or not, because there was a very simple solution available to him all along. Even at short notice that the Hamburg trip was 'on', Lennon would certainly have made some passport enquiries earlier than Monday, 15th August, either at the local office or from others on the trip. He would have been told he could get a shortened version of his birth certificate simply by going to the local registrar's office, paying a small fee, and getting a Certified Copy of an Entry Pursuant to the Births and Deaths Registration Act 1953. But, even armed with this, Monday, 15th August was the earliest day the paperwork could be rubber stamped by the authorities.

For John it must have been an anxious wait overnight before he returned to the office on Tuesday morning to collect it. Any last-minute hitch would have ruined everything, and a refusal could have ended his days as Beatle No.1.

Meanwhile, Allan Williams was fully committed to the trip. Too much was at stake with Koschmider not to turn up. Paul and George were stuck between a rock and a hard place, too. Without Hamburg, their only prospect was to get a job, or worse still, wait for the dreaded National Service telegram. Looking back in 1997, Paul made a very telling observation: "I don't think there would have been The Beatles. I think we would have been a little group in Liverpool, and if we'd been very lucky we'd have had some small success in the local clubs. But then, just when we were getting somewhere, Ringo and John, being the eldest two, would have had to go into National Service, followed shortly by me and then a year later by George, and that would have split any chance of being a group." *(Many Years From Now)*

It seems improbable that John Lennon hadn't also weighed up his own situation. He'd already contemplated joining the merchant navy, or even running away to Eire *(Republic of Ireland)* to avoid conscription, so Hamburg was a very real make-or-break situation. If he didn't get the passport in time, it might be dream over. What then? He could try to follow on later when the paperwork was sorted, but how long would that take, and where would the money come from? He was broke and heavily overdrawn with the few friends he had.

To compound the problem, Herr Koschmider's demands were specific and inflexible. The band must have five members and they were scheduled to play on the 17th August. There was no room to manoeuvre, as Johnny Guitar from Rory Storm and The Hurricanes later confirmed: "When they give you a contract in Germany, you've got to stick to it. If Koschmider says that a five-piece group is to appear on stage, then a five-piece must appear. It doesn't matter that one might be a singer and doesn't sing all night. Koschmider would rush up and say, 'Where is the fifth man?' The singer might have gone to the toilet, but he'd tell us to get him back!" *(The Beatles in Hamburg)*

Which begs the question: If John couldn't have gone right away, would the others have simply gone home to face their parents and an uncertain future? Or would Paul, George and Pete have felt so bloody-minded they'd have gone anyway? It wouldn't have been the first time they'd gone separate ways.

The difference this time was that Williams was bankrolling them. All three could sing, they had a new drummer, and there was a good chance Williams could get them work of one kind or another. Knowing this, it would be surprising if George and Paul in particular hadn't privately considered their options while they waited for John. One thing is certain: the entire Beatles story might have been so different if they'd abandoned the trip, or gone without John!

The day of departure finally arrived. Tuesday, 16th August was the latest date they could leave for the long journey. That morning, 10:00 came and went as everyone waited nervously outside the Jacaranda in Slater Street. John was still nowhere to be seen.

Then, at the last minute, after a mad dash from HM Passport Office in windy Water Street on the riverfront, a breathless Lennon appeared, waving a new dark blue passport in his hand. The last man was in! Crisis over, Allan Williams shoe-horned his motley ensemble of travellers and their luggage into his battered Austin Commer van: himself, his wife Beryl, brother-in-law Barry Chang, the legendary Lord Woodbine, John, Paul, George and Stu. And Pete! What wouldn't fit inside was stacked high on a luggage rack on the roof – so high that Williams' van wobbled precariously out of Liverpool at 35 miles per hour and headed south. The occupants must have felt like sardines in a tin.

They still had to collect a tenth passenger on their way – a Koschmider associate by the name of George Steiner, who would serve as interpreter. Tight squeeze or not, nothing could dim the excitement inside Allan's old banger as they journeyed into the unknown. Much like rowdy schoolboys on a school trip, there was a mixture of laughter and noise, relief and hope. In spite of all the dangers, somehow they'd pulled it off!

The Beatles were leaving home for the first time on a mystery tour that would eventually lead to the world and beyond. The trip would also prove to be a rites-of-passage into the earthly delights awaiting them in sin city, for apart from Indian-born Pete Best, the lads had no real experience of the wider world at all.

They were leaving as boys. They would return as men.

August plays a curious role in Pete Best's story. A year earlier, on Saturday 29th August 1959, the Fab 3 plus Ken Brown played their first residency at Mona Best's Casbah Coffee Bar where Pete first saw them in their last incarnation as The Quarrymen. A year later, they returned as The Beatles to watch Pete show off his talent as a drummer before adding him to the lineup on Saturday, 13th August 1960.

They went to Hamburg mid-morning on Tuesday, 16th August, and exactly two years later to the day and at the same time – on Thursday morning, 16th August 1962 – Pete became the unwitting victim of a shameful act of self-interest when Brian Epstein and the Fab 3 conspired to ditch him.

And all because the naive Epstein misunderstood a careless remark by an equally careless producer George Martin – something about using a session drummer!

In Britain, August is associated with the onset of autumn, the season when trees drop their leaves. In America, the season is known rather more prophetically as The Fall.

The shop where John stole the harmonica

Before Hamburg. Blackpool Daytrippers, Yeah!

In the early 1960s, the idea of mass travel and tourism abroad was still in its infancy. For the great majority, holidays were symbolized by a deckchair, a paddle in the sea and boozy nights at resorts such as Margate, Clacton, Southend, Bournemouth and Skegness in the south and east. In the north-west of England, Liverpool was spoilt for choice with leisure spots at New Brighton, West Kirby, Southport, Rhyl, Llandudno and sprawling holiday camps at outposts such as Middleton Towers at Morecombe Bay and Billy Butlin's Camp at Pwhellhi. The holiday camps were highly-prized venues where Liverpool acts such as Ringo Starr's band, Rory Storm and the Hurricanes, played their summer seasons at Pwhellhi and Skegness – not to mention the dance halls at New Brighton. Then there was the jewel in the little felt cowboy hat: Blackpool.

For many teenagers at the time, Blackpool was as exotic and as far as it got, with its golden mile lined by millions of street illuminations, rickety trams, guest houses, pubs, Wimpy burger bars and a giant fun fair. Blackpool wasn't just for the holidays. It was for day trippers, too! A regular feature of Liverpool life was the annual bus or charabanc (coach) trip, a sort of magical mystery tour to Blackpool run by workmates, social clubs or neighbours.

Coaches were fully-booked for weeks in advance with any remaining space reserved for crates of beer for the outward journey which entailed the obligatory stop at the Halfway House pub for more beer, a ciggy and a hasty comfort break before the main event.

A day trip to Blackpool was about buying kiss-me-quick cowboy hats, saucy postcards and sticks of rock (candy), eating fish and chips in force-ten gales on the promenade and sizing up the fairer sex before going on a mile-long pub crawl. Nightfall signalled another piss-up, before heading to the fair and the big dipper with the ritual call to 'Rolf' before involuntarily vomiting on the crowd below. Waltzer rides came with the best rock and 'n' roll music for miles, and the obligatory leather-clad hunk to spin the ride. He'd spin and girls vomited, usually into the crowd again. Yes, it was horrid, but we loved it. Of course, the pinnacle of every young man's dreams at the end of the night was to get a cuddle or a 'leg over' from any young lady before heading home in a happy stupor.

Ah, those were the daze, my friends. Who needed 'abroad', wherever it was?

Tuesday 16th August 1960. Roll up! Roll up! For the Magical Mystery Tour

The idea of working overseas was a strange concept for ordinary folk in the late '50s and early '60s, unless you happened to be a sailor on military service in a far-flung colony or a squaddie in the British-occupied zone of partitioned Germany. Not so for The Beatles. At the first mention of Hamburg, they desperately wanted 'abroad'. It was the dream escape route to happiness.

Allan Williams, Lord Woodbine and Pete Best described the journey.

Williams: "We set off for Hamburg with all the equipment on the roof…"

Lord Woodbine: "Allan and I shared the driving so we had good seats. I don't know how comfortable it was for the ones in the back seat. (He laughed) I was fine while I was driving and the time went quickly. When I wasn't driving I was resting." *(The Beatles. An Oral History and The Beatles. An Aural History. Vol One.)*

Williams: "We had trouble getting (the van) on the ship as the famous photo shows… Dockers did not want to load it on to the ship, so I had to plead with them." *(David Bedford Interview 2008)*

At a time when roll-on, roll-off ferry ships were rare, hoisting a vehicle on a ship was done by teams of dockers aided by the ship's hoist. In this case, the dockers were concerned that Williams' top-heavy vehicle was far too unwieldy for the crane to cope with and the fear was that the load could collapse mid-air and crash onto the deck. Fortunately, with a lot of arm-waving and crossed fingers, the hoist eased the van slowly on board to the relief of all concerned. Another hurdle had been overcome.

Williams continued. "We landed at the Hook of Holland and took a wrong turn somewhere and we were lost. We arrived about 7am and of course, we were driving on the wrong side of the road. I remember it was like a sea of bikes. Lennon was telling them all to 'fuck off' and to stop leaning on the van. We arrived at the Arnhem War Memorial and that famous photograph was taken by my
brother-in-law, Barry Chang, which was a bit prophetic: 'THEIR NAME LIVETH FOREVER MORE'. John was not in it, as he did not want to be involved. I don't know if he was just being miserable."

Pete Best: "After Arnhem… John indulged in one of his light-fingered exercises. He had told me about his addiction to shoplifting during the time I had got to know him at the Casbah… The five of us made our first exploration. We watched him as he lifted a couple of things and were amazed at how expert he was. He seemed to have a flair for it. The rest of us did not join him…" *(Beatle! The Pete Best Story)*

Lord Woodbine: "We were all looking for fruit and vegetables and stuff, but John found a mouth organ – and stole it." *(The Beatles. An Oral History)*

Williams added: "They went into a music shop (Bergmann Muzik still exists) and all came out laughing. I asked them why, they laughed again, and John produced a mouth organ he had stolen from the shop. I thought we aren't going to get to Hamburg at this rate. What if he'd been caught?" *(Interview with David Bedford 2008)*

Best: "When we re-joined the rest of the party, John, as blasé as ever, began to empty out his spoils. The haul amazed even those of us who had been with him on the spree: two pieces of jewelry, a guitar string or two, handkerchiefs – and a harmonica! Allan Williams was appalled. 'You're nuts – the lot of you!' he berated us. 'The sooner we let you loose on the Germans, the better!'" *(Beatle! The Pete Best Story)*

Woodbine: "Allan (Williams) got really upset, because if we'd gotten caught we would have been deported immediately." *(The Beatles. An Oral History)*

Williams: "We had a real job getting through customs. We had to say we were all students on holiday and we were going to play in a café bar… The lads were messing around and in the end, the customs just said to go." *(Interview David Bedford 2008)*

What a journey. It was more than just driving from Liverpool to Hamburg.

This was a journey from obscurity to more fame than they could ever have imagined – their name in lights, playing the best clubs in Hamburg, as international superstars. Well, not yet.

Reality was far more of a shock than they had counted on.

We played for about twenty minutes in all and at the end they all reached the same conclusion: 'Yeh! You're in, Pete!'

EXCLUSIVE!

INTIMATE!

The Heartbreak Life of EX-BEATLE Peter Best

PETE BEST:
The Betrayed Beat

Unless you were living in Hamburg, Germany, or Liverpool between... early 1962, you wouldn't seen the Beatles' original drummer, Pete Best. By the the group had captured the attention of the media, Ringo Starr had taken over the... however, the two that Best spent as part of... Four helped cre... final Beatles...

and daughter. For the past 20 years he has worked for the British government.

Thanks to a couple of early Beatles singles and several bootleg albums, such as the three-record set, *Silver Beatles: Like Dreamers Do*—a collection of their Decca Records audition tapes—Pete Best's affiliation with the world's most famous rock 'n' roll group has at least

The funny... looked d...

SH-BOOM:

PETE: I sup... were infer... didn't hav... there, pla... seemed an... we disapp...

Original painting by Paul Skellett

"ICH BIN EIN HAMBURGER"

Call of Duty

"When they first arrived in Hamburg, they had very pointed shoes in grey crocodile, mauve jackets, black shirts and pants. The length of their hair caused a great stir around the area – it was thick at the back, almost coming down to their collars." Howie Casey

Having never ventured beyond the south coast before, and knowing next to nothing at all about Germany other than what they'd picked up from school books or family during the war years, The Beatles were totally naïve about where they were heading. To them, Hamburg was going to be something like Liverpool and Blackpool rolled into one. Mona Best knew otherwise. She was a woman of the world and hinted at the dangers when she counselled Pete about looking after himself. "Hamburg's a wild town," she warned. "Watch your step, Pete. You'll probably come back educated – a further education of a different type!" *(Beatle! The Pete Best Story)*

Since when did teenagers ever take advice from parents? Allan Williams and Lord Woodbine were different. Being men of the world, they knew exactly what lay ahead and Williams must have secretly smiled at the idea of seeing his cocky young protégés being brought down to earth soon enough. But not too soon! He wasn't going to spoil the surprise before he got them to their intended destination, as their contract specified.

Pete Best: "We were 17 and 18 and we had never been away from England. We didn't expect anything at all and we didn't know what Hamburg was like. Of course, when we got there and found it was sin city, we were just blown away."

(The Beatles. An Oral History)

Hamburg was a port city like Liverpool. Both suffered heavily from several years of concentrated bombing during WWII but, unlike Liverpool, Hamburg got substantial help under the American Marshall Aid Plan to rebuild its infrastructure, so that the suburbs became pleasant places to live once more. The older area around the St. Pauli district was different. A hundred years earlier, its own pop star, Johannes Brahms, had tickled his ivory keyboard in the same bawdy neighbourhood. But now in post-war Germany, St. Pauli was known better for its bars, strip clubs and brothels lit by bright neon signs – a bustling and frequently dangerous frontier town noted for laissez-faire attitudes to morality and sexual freedom that made it a honey pot populated by pimps, prostitutes, gangsters, sailors and pleasure seekers alike. It was in this rabbit warren of side streets just off the Reeperbahn that Bruno Koschmider's dream of building a clubland empire was growing and into which the young Beatles entered, eyes wide shut.

The Beatles Great Freedom

The venues that The Beatles would play in Hamburg over the next few months were all located in a little street called Grosse Freiheit (translation: Great Freedom), which was named after the religious freedom granted in the 17th Century to non-Lutherans such as Mennonites and Roman Catholics. Although the church of St. Joseph's is still located on the Grosse Freiheit, The Beatles certainly wouldn't be practising religious freedom here, though they could have needed confession! At the bottom of Grosse Freiheit was the Bambi Kino, a cinema where the group was expected to live. As they came out of the door, they only had to walk 100 yards to the Indra Club, situated at Grosse Freiheit 64. Just 200 yards further along the road was the Kaiserkeller, at Grosse Freiheit 36. And around the corner on The Reeperbahn was the Top Ten Club, a venue that would soon be the source of trouble for the band. By the spring of 1962, the Star Club at Grosse Freiheit 39 would join the roster of city nightspots that would become indelibly linked to the four lads. In a city the size of Hamburg, most of The Beatles' experience of Europe's largest port would be concentrated around this small red-light area. And what an experience it was.

"Any one of us could have been beaten up or killed in Hamburg," Tony Sheridan said, reflecting on his time there. "Fortunately, the gangsters and pimps loved the musicians." He forgot to mention the working girls liked them too, as The Beatles discovered. Pete Best takes up the story: "We could only gape in sheer wonder when we hit the Reeperbahn, a jungle of neon and sex, where every other door seemed to lead to a place where girls were taking their clothes off or otherwise providing entertainment… 'Here come the Scousers!' we yelled at each other as we cruised past this massive array of glitter." *(Beatle! The Pete Best Story)*

Allan Williams: "We finally arrived in Hamburg and pulled up outside the Kaiserkeller and saw Derry and the Seniors. They all thought this was great."
(David Bedford Interview 2008)

Pete Best: "Our bus pulled into the kerbside almost with a sigh of relief alongside the Kaiserkeller and we scrambled out and stretched our legs… Inside, the club was bright and lively and throbbing to the music of Derry and the Seniors. 'This is a bit of all right, lads,' Lennon said cheerfully. 'I think we're going to like it here,' said Paul." *(Beatle! The Pete Best Story)*

Welcome to the Pits

According to Williams, the initial euphoria was short-lived when "Herr Koschmider came over and said, 'You don't play here, you play at the Indra. We went over there and they had a striptease artist on. They *(The Beatles)* said, 'We've not come to Hamburg to back a stripper.' Remember, they had already done that in Liverpool."

Pete: "Bruno Koschmider was a heavy-set man, broad-shouldered with scarcely any neck, bushy eyebrows and an eye-catcher of a quiff that hung in rolls on his wide forehead. It was a face to be reckoned with." No arguments there, then! "Our excitement began to ebb away when Bruno showed us the club. It was about as lively as a cemetery chapel."

There was an ominous silence as The Beatles looked around. A small dingy place with the focus on a higher-than-usual stage so that punters could see the strippers better. Not that there were many people in tonight, only one or two at most, prompting Pete to ask a question in German. "'Is it open?' I asked Bruno, light-heartedly." To which Koschmider replied with what sounded suspiciously like an order from the Fuhrer. "Bruno treated us to what for him was a smile. 'You boys will make the Indra into another Kaiserkeller,' he instructed. 'No one comes to this place… But you will make it go when you Mach Schau!'"

(Beatle! The Pete Best Story)

Pete Best in Hamburg

Original painting by Paul Skellett (www.skellett.com)

"Any one of us could have
been beaten up
or killed in Hamburg,"

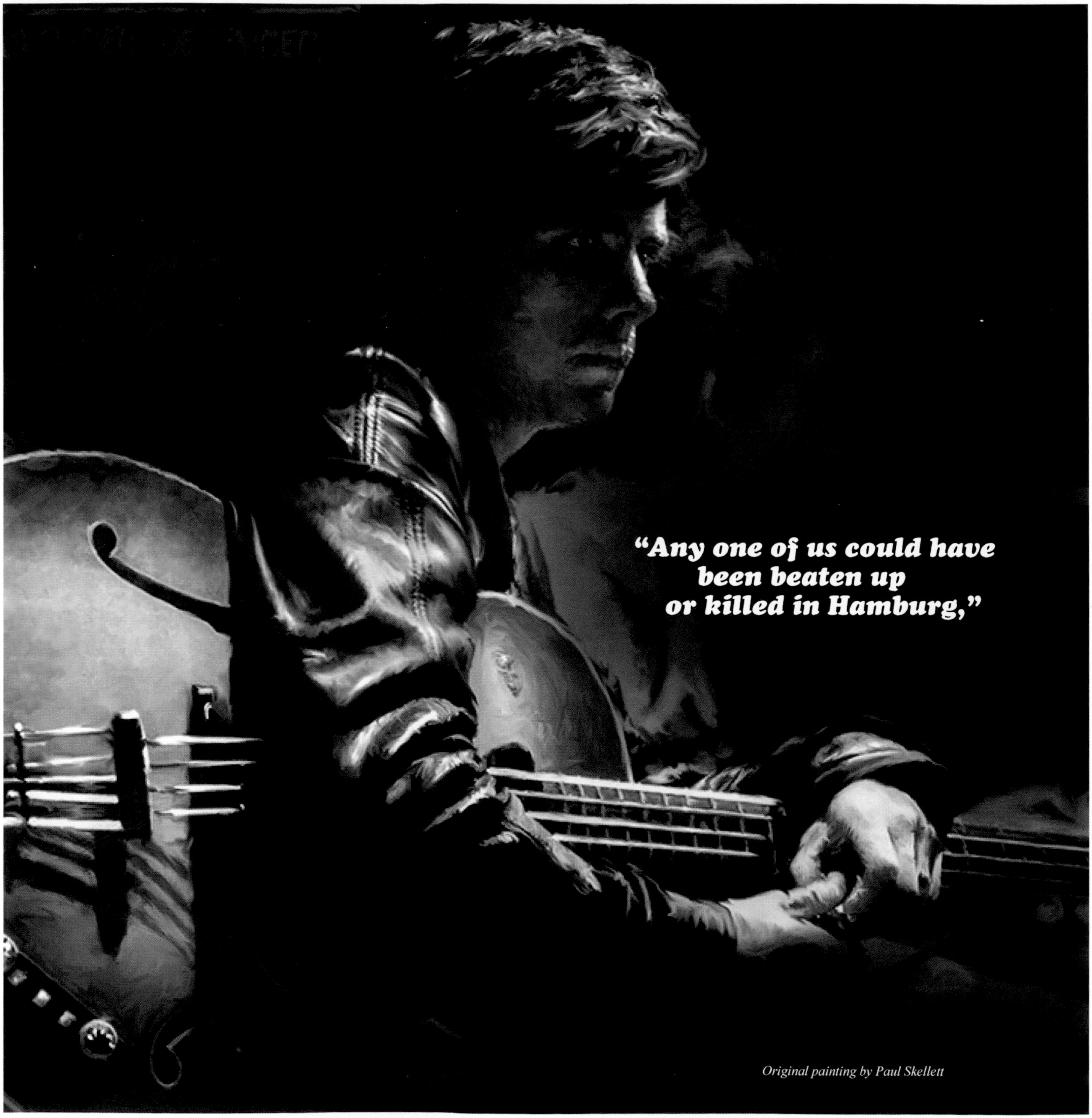

Original painting by Paul Skellett

Schau Time!

Make Show? Surely not tonight Bruno! But a contract is a contract and, more to the point, Herr Koschmider had stipulated the new five-piece act had to perform that night. A gangster, and probably a former SS man, rumour has it that he'd had his testicles demolished in the war (according to Spencer Leigh), he was not a man anyone wanted to argue with, so although they were tired, hungry and deflated, The Beatles went about their business.

Pete: "We took to the stage in the depths of depression. Bruno, very much in evidence, yelled at us that we must 'make show' (with Williams exhorting them to liven things up, he was shouting, 'Come on lads, make a show') which we did, more as a release for our mounting anger rather than to please him." Lennon cursed at their sorry plight, too. "All the way from Liverpool to leap around like a lot of idiots," he fumed as they began jumping around like performing monkeys. Pete concurred: "None of us had ever acted the fool like this on stage before. But this was the start and we had a lot to learn… so we did. Like five bloody lunatics."

By the end of the night, the sound of rock 'n' roll blasting out of the Indra had pulled in another half dozen late night drinkers and an unexpected visit by some old rivals from Liverpool – Derry and the Seniors.

Howie Casey: "The Beatles arrived, and we went to see them on the opening night as they started earlier than us. They kicked off, and my jaw went to the floor. There was such a difference from what we had seen in Liverpool and we were buddies from that moment on." Although the Seniors were safely established at the much bigger Kaiserkeller club, they immediately recognised the impact The Beatles would make at the Indra. No longer were they the ramshackle bunch of lads they'd last seen at the audition run by Allan Williams and London impresario, Larry Parnes for a backing group to accompany Billy Fury. This time things were very different. "There was something there, a spark, that extra little bit. We did a bit of harmony singing, but they were marvellous at it. They were stunning." *(Interview with Spencer Leigh)*

When Howie Casey returned to Liverpool a few weeks later, he repeated his praise to Mona Best and word spread quickly on the local grapevine – The Beatles were on the up and making a name for themselves in Hamburg. Several bands took note. It seemed like a good place to be.

For The Beatles, the opening night at the Indra was the first of many a successful hard daze nights. It was from this moment onward that their old lives and lifestyles changed forever as long working nights soon became the routine day, and every day was made night. Many more would follow for the rest of their careers but right now all that mattered was getting some sleep in the accommodation Koschmider had promised for them. As if the long journey and long night hadn't tested them enough, suddenly they were confronted by another nightmare at the Bambi Kino where they were to stay. Lord Woodbine explained: "We were tired and just wanted to get our accommodation together. They turned out to be a couple of rooms in an attic. It was really poor, but at the same time it was fun because we didn't know what to expect and it was exciting!" *(The Beatles. An Oral History)*

It was an understatement if ever there was one. John Lennon took one look and exploded, "What the fucking hell?" he cursed in his best Anglo-Saxon, and the others echoed a four-part harmony. "Fuck me!" they sighed, while trying to take in the rooms from hell. At home, Pete Best's lifestyle was a fifteen-room Indian-themed mansion set in one and a half acres of private grounds, complete with its own nightclub in the cellar. John Lennon and Stuart Sutcliffe had roughed it before as students, but otherwise they were both from good middle-class homes with all-mod-cons, while Paul and George had basic, but good, working-class homes on council estates. In Liverpool, they all lived in relative luxury compared to what they would endure here: two old camp beds and a rickety bunk bed without sheets or blankets, and a worn sofa in two squalid cells in the back of a run-down cinema. The Beatles renamed the Bambi Kino 'the pit' – a flea pit! No wonder Tony Sheridan and the Jets ran away from Koschmider's hospitality earlier in the year. The culture shock was enormous – even for Allan Williams. "Their accommodation was appalling," Williams said. "They were in a filthy dump in the Bambi Kino. The only water was in the toilet block of the cinema, so they had to wait until it was closed to get any. The place was disgusting, the filth was thick on the walls, but they were young enough to cope." They were and they did – all except for Allan Williams, Beryl, Barry and Lord Woodbine who were booked into a hotel elsewhere.

The short saga of The Beatles' first trip to Hamburg was an utter farce, ending abruptly amid bitter dispute when The Beatles attempted to better themselves with a move to the rival Top Ten Club. Herr Koschmider was furious, and in what was a vengeful act, had the underage George Harrison deported, followed by the arrest and deportation of Paul and Pete on the pretext of trying to burn down the Bambi Kino. Quite how a burning condom would ignite bricks and concrete is a mystery, but The Beatles deserve a medal for trying to erase a shabby, stinking blot from the landscape.

Their departure was followed a few days later by a crestfallen John, who arrived back in Liverpool, alone and penniless, and promptly went into a sulk for a week at Aunt Mimi's. Only Stuart survived the debacle, having moved out earlier to take up a fresh life with newfound love, Astrid Kirchherr. The Bambi Kino didn't burn down, more's the pity, but the pit of gloom was left in a worse state than ever before. As for The Beatles, they returned home to ponder their futures. Mona eventually got their kit back in one piece, probably after much nagging of the Hamburg police. It was a sorry saga, but good fun while it lasted. On the bright side, The Beatles' time at the Indra was short-lived, clocking up 48 nights before local police closed the strip club down.

Allan Williams: "They played for a couple of weeks and then there was trouble. A woman who lived above the club did not mind the strip music, but when the loud rock 'n' roll started, she complained about the noise, so they had to stop." Koschmider closed the Indra on 4th October 1960. Despite the setback, he knew The Beatles had pulling power, the kind that attracted thirsty punters. His much-larger Kaiserkeller club could profit from the misfortune, while he would also be honouring his contract with The Beatles at the same time.

As for The Beatles themselves, they still had to live in the appalling conditions at the Bambi Kino. At least they were on the move to a bigger club next time around. By contrast, the Indra served them well. Playing up to eight hours a day, six days a week had given them a crash course into what life and long hours was going to be about in future. Better still, they had become a powerhouse of sound unlike any other act and everyone in the local neighbourhood knew it. They could hear the pounding beat of Pete Best's atomic bass drum all the way down the street, and so could the punters who were drawn to the club like bees to honey.

The spell at the Indra also bought them something more precious than praise. It bought them time! Away from the pressures of a bigger venue, the little strip club was like a rehearsal for bigger and better things – the lull before the storm. They got to gel as a band, and they rapidly acquired a bigger repertoire to fill the long hours each night. It also allowed them to sow the seeds of a wild cabaret act whose effects would soon be unleashed on unsuspecting customers and management alike at the Kaiserkeller.

The 'Crazy' Beatles – Birth of the Punk Band

When The Beatles finally let rip, their act was something never seen or heard before. Nor was it seen again by the world after 1962 when new manager Brian Epstein decided to erase their real identities under a pile of schmaltz. Ironically, The Rolling Stones did the reverse with a lukewarm version of what they thought was 'wild', but it was to be another ten years before anyone else copied The Beatles' outrageous live performances. Then, the Ramones, the Stranglers and the Sex Pistols hit the stage in the 1970's, believing they were a new anti-establishment rock genre. Sorry guys, Punk Rock was born in Hamburg with a young band from Liverpool – better known by the Germans as the 'VERRUCKT BEATLES' – The 'Crazy' Beatles.

"If you never saw us in Hamburg or Liverpool, you never saw the real Beatles."

John Lennon.

Before Hamburg, The Beatles had only a hazy idea of what, how and where they wanted to be. 'To the toppermost of the poppermost' was their imagined destination, wherever that was, and they clung to the belief like a warm duvet, since it covered everything, for lack of a clearer plan. However, as most music historians would agree, Hamburg was a turning point – a red hot furnace where The Beatles' skills were forged in every way.

To understand this, one has to ask why they were in Hamburg at all – their raison d'etre? For The Beatles, it might have been to escape the norm, a day job, conscription or whatever. But for club owners in the St. Pauli district, there was only one reason to employ a musician. Pulling power! Attraction wasn't merely a desirable trait, it was the essential requirement, and The Beatles' chief role was to provide it by whatever means necessary. As Paul McCartney conceded many years later, "Our role in Hamburg was to make people buy more beer." Which led to the question of how? How on earth were five newly-formed professional musicians expected to pull customers off the street and downstairs into a dingy basement club?

As the old saying goes, 'necessity is the mother of invention'. To be more specific, necessity was the key. Having to cope with their grim surroundings

quickly became the mother of all Mach Schau! After a slow start, the act started to get better – and worse. Driven as it was by the frustration of having to play in a dive, exist in a pit, and still listen to the same demands of Herr Koschmider every night was like waiving a red rag to a Scouser. The intoxication of life in sin city didn't help either. Freed from the strict social and moral codes of Liverpool, it was John who led the rebellion, as always. One way or another, he was determined to show Koschmider and the Hamburgers a "schau" to remember. According to Pete, "John and Paul were the looniest. John did his best to imitate Gene Vincent (limping and lurching to mimic Vincent's obvious leg disability)… grabbing the microphone as if he were going to lay into the audience with it… leaping about with it like a maniac. Paul roared and screamed like Little Richard… Stu behaved like a puppet and managed to hold on to the sort of James Dean image he had fostered. There was not much I could do from behind the drums, other than stand up and hop around the kit… George paid serious attention to his guitar!"

Meanwhile Lennon tested his German audience with his acid Scouse wit before finally launching a torrent of foul mouthed abuse for good measure. It was all meaningless to them. They roared with laughter and shouted for more, egging Lennon on to new heights. "It'd be a far-out show now," mused John many years later, "eating and smoking and swearing and going to sleep onstage when you're tired." And that was only the edited highlights of what went on during their nightly routine! Far from putting customers off, their crazy antics provided the magic mix to attract the free-spending punters and rowdy sailors into the club. They loved it. They loved the crazy Beatles, and so did the gangsters, the club's heavies, the pimps and the girls in the district.

As Lennon admitted later, a continuous diet of sex, drugs and rock 'n' roll were to come at a high price. His stay in Hamburg left him hooked on 'prellies' – an appetite suppressant known as Preludin – and other illegal substances for years to come.

15th October 1960

JOHN, PAUL, GEORGE and RINGO - COME TOGETHER FOR THE FIRST TIME

Following the success of Derry and the Seniors and The Beatles in Hamburg, Rory Storm and the Hurricanes joined their fellow Liverpudlians on the Reeperbahn at the beginning of October 1960.

For the first time, The Beatles were sharing a stage with Ringo and his group, as equals. It was here that the friendship between Ringo and The Beatles originated, as they spent countless hours alternating on stage at the Kaiserkeller, and off-stage wherever they could find recreation.

It was the antics of the two groups on the Kaiserkeller stage that would attract the attention of club owner Bruno Koschmider. Together, The Beatles and The Hurricanes plotted to see who could put their foot through and break the fragile stage first. It was Rory Storm who achieved the dubious honour; he was eventually fired by Koschmider, who didn't see the funny side of it. In the musicians' minds, they were simply following the owner's command to "Mach Schau" by jumping and stomping on the stage. If it happened to break in the process, then the joke was on Koschmider!

Lou Walters

Allan Williams, The Beatles' manager, had followed his groups to Hamburg. While there, he decided to pay for Lou Walters to make a record, and hired the Akustik Studio on the seventh floor of 57, Kirchenallee (The Klockmann-House). Walters, The Hurricanes' bass player, was also an accomplished ballad singer with a fine voice, so it made sense to record him.

The studio was booked for 15th October 1960, and Walters was accompanied there by Williams as well as his bandmates Ty Brien, Johnny Guitar and Ringo Starr. Williams and Walters also invited John, Paul and George to the session. Stuart was with Astrid and, since he wouldn't be needed, Pete Best went shopping for drumsticks. Rory Storm turned up later in the day.

There has been much confusion over the years around this session, as there are no surviving tapes or records of the day. Lou Walters remembered that three songs were recorded: "Fever", "September Song" and "Summertime".

(From A Storm to a Hurricane)

Walters recalled that Williams "heard me sing and liked my voice, so he asked me if I would record while being backed by the Hurricanes." For "Fever" and "September Song", the lineup was Walters on bass and vocals, Ty Brien on guitar, Johnny Guitar on lead guitar and Ringo on drums. For "Summertime", John Lennon, Paul McCartney, George Harrison and Ringo Starr backed him – the first time that the future Fab Four appeared together on a record. Walters said that "The Beatles tagged along and we let them stand in to back me on 'Summertime'." *(From A Storm to a Hurricane)*

The only evidence is a photograph in Allan Williams' book, *The Man Who Gave The Beatles Away*, which shows a 78 rpm record with the words "Beatles and

Lou Walters (second from right) with Rory Storm and the Hurricanes

Wally Demo" and "Summertime" appearing across the label.

The B-side of the acetate would have contained no music, but rather a commercial for goods sold by the Klockmann Company which had a leather bag store in the bottom floor of the building. *(From Cavern to Star Club)*

The date has been verified as Johnny Guitar, who kept a brief day-to-day diary, simply wrote on 14th October 1960: "Wally and Beatles going to make a test recording tomorrow." Sadly, he didn't note anything in his diary for the following day, and nobody has a copy of the disc.

There is little doubt that this is the most sought-after record in Beatles history.

Spring 1961

ALAN LEYLAND: FOR ONE NIGHT ONLY

For one night only, a local teenager became The Beatles drummer.

One evening during the spring or summer of 1961, Johnnie Paul and the Dee Jays had played their set at the Aintree Institute and, as usual, remained at the venue to see their favourite local group, The Beatles. Time was marching on, and compere Bob Wooler became worried when only three Beatles walked in – John, Paul and George.

The group had already played earlier that same evening, possibly at the Cavern, but Pete had been taken ill and couldn't attend this second appearance of the night.

Wooler, ever the professional, was determined that the show go on; he couldn't let the audience down. Wooler turned to Alan Leyland, the 16-year-old drummer from the Dee Jays, and asked him to do what so many musicians wished they could have done: play with The Beatles. "We had been been hanging around, waiting to watch The Beatles, when Bob Wooler approached me," explained Leyland. "Thankfully, at that time, The Beatles weren't doing their own songs, just the rock 'n' roll standards, though I knew they were playing a lot of the American records that we couldn't get hold of. We played for about 20 minutes, just a short set, though I can't remember what we played, but it was fun.

I remember just playing a simple groove, and it all went well. They probably won't even remember it!" *(David Bedford Interview 2015)*

Although that was the only time he played with the group, they crossed paths on several occasions. "We ended up playing a few times on the same bill as The Beatles, at the Cavern, Aintree Institute and Litherland Town Hall," he recalled.

When it came to dating this event, Leyland recalled that "The Beatles had been to Hamburg, and Stu was not with them." The Beatles played for promoter Brian Kelly at the Aintree Institute more than thirty times, making their debut on 7th January 1961. Their next two appearances at the venue took place on 21st and 28th January. Each was preceded the same evening by a show at Lathom Hall, which made sense as both venues were promoted by Kelly. Alan Leyland thinks that The Beatles could have been at the Cavern earlier, which would tie in with 8th March, 21st July, 4th August or 18th August 1961.

Leyland had been playing drums from the age of 13, and had been part of Johnnie Paul and The Dee Jays for a while. "We were called the Dee Jays, not because of the latter name given to people who played records, but because of David James who was in the group. We stayed together until around 1970 when we morphed into Candlewick Green. We appeared on television and had a hit in 1974 with 'Who Do You Think You Are?'." Candlewick Green won the television talent show *Opportunity Knocks* and was subsequently signed to Decca records.

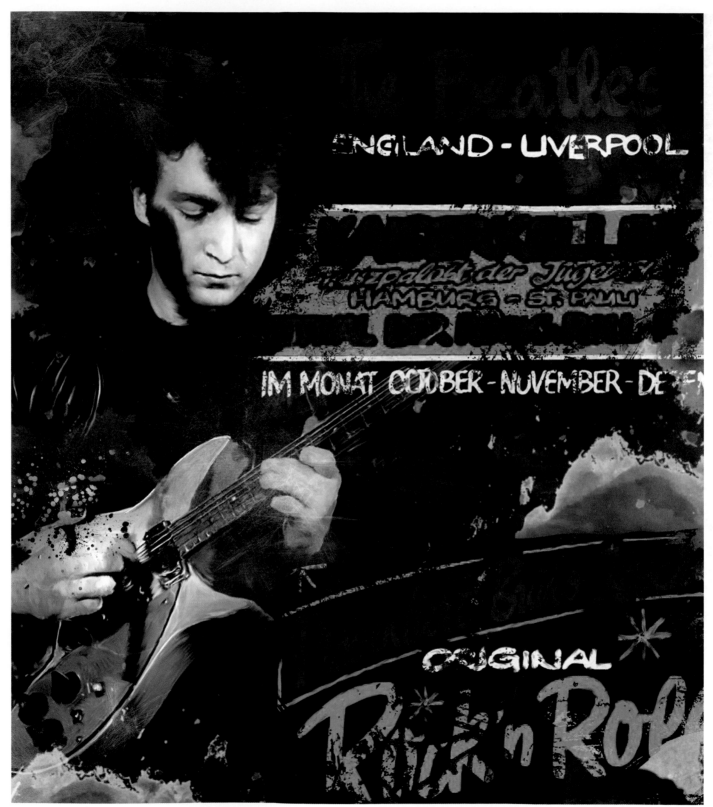

Original painting by Paul Skellett (www.skellett.com)

Alan Leyland drumming in Liverpool, 2018

"We then decided to do more cabaret and comedy, a bit like the Fourmost did, doing impressions and comedy as much as the pop songs. I spent almost as much time in costume on stage than behind my drums! Eventually, as the variety clubs started to close, we decided to give it all up, and I didn't play for a few years. But then, for my 65th birthday, my wife bought me another drum kit and have been playing again every week for the fun of it." *(David Bedford Interview 2015)*

The Candlewick Green single Alan drummed on

Original painting by Paul Skellett (www.skellett.com)

April 1961

DAS BEAT BROTHERS

"My Bonnie"

On 1st April 1961, The Beatles returned to Hamburg for a three-month engagement at the Top Ten Club, a popular spot run by Peter Eckhorn.

With Eckhorn's help, they had successfully appealed to the German authorities to allow their return after the ignominious deportation of George, Paul and Pete at the end of 1960. But unlike the first trip, this Hamburg residency would prove far more productive. This time, they would fulfil their dream of making a professional record.

John, Paul and George had experienced Percy Phillips' backroom studio in Liverpool in July 1958 when they recorded "That'll Be The Day" and "In Spite of All The Danger". But back then, the recording equipment was rudimentary at best; microphone hung from the ceiling as they recorded straight to disk on a portable machine. Their only other visit to a studio was when John, Paul and George backed Lou Walters with a drummer called Ringo Starr the previous October in Hamburg.

Their second recording session in Hamburg was to be completely different because internationally-renowned record producer Bert Kaempfert would be involved and he wanted to record British rock 'n' roller Tony "The Teacher" Sheridan. When Kaempfert asked Sheridan to choose some musicians to back him, he went with his Liverpool "pupils" The Beatles. After all, the group had been sharing a stage with Sheridan, and Kaempfert himself had seen the two acts performing together.

Berthold "Bert" Heinrich Kaempfert, known as 'Fips', was born in Hamburg. At the age of 37, he was the leader of a famous easy-listening orchestra and had achieved worldwide acclaim with his recent hit, "Wonderland By Night"

(Wunderland Bei Nacht), an instrumental that was also the title song of a best-selling LP. As it couldn't be released in Germany, he took it to Decca in America where it became a chart-topper in 1961, earning him accolades not only for the quality of the music but for an arrangement that combined melody with lush strings and brass. As well as orchestral and jazz-oriented records, Kaempfert wrote the music for "Strangers In The Night" (recorded by Frank Sinatra) and "Wooden Heart" (recorded by Elvis Presley) as well as hits for Nat King Cole and Al Martino. Kaempfert holds the distinction of being perhaps the only producer to have worked with Elvis, Sinatra and The Beatles. It therefore seems slightly incongruous for a man with a track record in orchestral arrangement and light music to want to record a rock 'n' roll star like Tony Sheridan. How and why did it happen?

A friend of Kaempfert's, Guntram Kuhbeck, who sometimes used the stage name Tommy Kent, went to the Top Ten Club one evening while he was in Hamburg for a recording session. "Every time I was in Hamburg to record for about five or six weeks, I stayed with the Kaempferts in the Inselstrasse," he said. One evening, he got a visit from Ivo Robic who "suggested I should go and kill some time on the Reeperbahn. I went into the Top Ten and there Tony Sheridan was performing with The Beatles. I was totally captivated by them."

(The Beatles Fact and Fiction)

When Kuhbeck returned to Kaempfert's home, the producer was entertaining Alfred Schact of the Aberbach Music publishing company. Schact had also seen

The Beatles i Hamburg

Sheridan and The Beatles, so Kaempfert decided to check them out for himself, visiting the Top Ten first with Kuhbeck and later with Schact. Pete Best remembers Kaempfert visiting, because it was "Peter (Eckhorn) who tipped us off that Bert Kaempfert was in the audience" and how he was "watching the band, seemed interested and had come back again to have another look." Kaempfert even took to requesting "certain songs, such as '*My Bonnie*', 'The Saints' and 'Take Out Some Insurance'", the tracks he was later to record.
(The Beatles Fact and Fiction)

Sheridan remembered the night "five or six people sat down in front of the stage". They later approached the band and asked, "how would you like to go into a studio?" *(The Beatles Fact and Fiction)*

The song that attracted Kaempfert to The Beatles was their instrumental, "Cry For A Shadow", which he also requested on his visits to the club.

Kaempfert saw something in Sheridan that made him want to record the band leader, singer and guitarist for the German label Polydor. But instead of recording the latest rock 'n' roll songs, Kaempfert wanted to produce an arrangement of the traditional Scottish folk song, "*My Bonnie* Lies Over The Ocean" and a variation of the well-known American Gospel song, "When The Saints Go Marching In". At the time, both were popular in the clubs and suited his penchant for middle-of-the-road, easy-listening music. What wasn't clear was his plan for a heavy rock 'n' roll group like The Beatles.

For the sessions, Kaempfert chose the stage of a school hall in Harburg, over twenty kilometres outside of Hamburg. While it was a step up from Percy Phillips' backroom, it still wasn't a "proper recording studio".

The Friedrich-Ebert-Halle, often used by Phillips and Polydor for recording, was more suited for assembling an orchestra to record than a five-piece rock 'n' roll group. However, Kaempfert was a bona fide record producer who had topped the charts in America. This could be their first, but certainly not their last, big opportunity.

Who Were The Beat Brothers?

Over the next few years, Kaempfert would use a number of session musicians on recordings, so it made sense to give The Beatles a generic name: The Beat Brothers. There has been some confusion as to which Beatles made up The Beat Brothers on these recordings, particularly since Stuart Sutcliffe had recently decided it was time to concentrate on his art and officially hand over the bass playing duties to Paul McCartney. On this day, Stuart came along solely for moral support. The Beatles were now officially a four-piece: John, Paul, George and Pete.

The Contract

The contract was signed at Kaempfert's house. He arrived home late and his housekeeper told him that some young men had arrived to see him. She said that she didn't like the look of them. According to the producer, "She wouldn't allow them into the living room and had stuck them out on the patio with some Cokes!" *(Beatles Appreciation Society Magazine September 1980)* Rather than sign The Beatles to the record company, Polydor, Kaempfert signed them to his independent company, Bert Kaempfert Produktion. Although the contract was in German, it was duly signed by John Lennon, Paul McCartney, George Harrison and Peter Best, which confirms that Stu Sutcliffe did not participate in these recordings. Only Sheridan signed a recording contract in Germany – and that was with Deutsche Grammophon in September 1961 through Kaempfert's considerable influence.

Kaempfert agreed to pay The Beatles 300 DM (Deutsche Marks) per person, with no provision for royalties. In effect, they were to be paid as session musicians. They had no contract directly with the record company, as Kaempfert would introduce the recordings to Polydor himself. According to the contract, any remuneration from Kaempfert would be paid to John Lennon as leader of the group, for him to disperse to the others. *(From Cavern to the Star Club)*

The contract, however, wasn't signed at the time of the recording, and only became effective on 1st July 1961, to run until 30th June 1962. It is not known why the agreement didn't cover these first recordings. Unfortunately, most of Kaempfert's paperwork was lost in a house fire in the 1970s.

The Kaempfert-Beatles contract would later have important implications for Brian Epstein. Though he could sign a management contract with The Beatles, he could not negotiate a new record deal while this contract was valid unless an agreement was made with Bert Kaempfert first.

22nd and 23rd June 1961 - Friedrich-Ebert-Halle, Harburg

With only four hours of sleep, The Beatles left Hamburg at 8am, unaccustomed to such an early rise. Fortified by the previous night's alcohol and preludin intake, the five musicians entered the school hall, not knowing what was about to happen.

Pete Best remembers walking into the 'studio'. "We had been expecting a recording set-up on the grand scale," recalled Best. "Instead, we found ourselves in an unexciting school hall with a massive stage and lots of drapes."
(Beatle! The Pete Best Story)

The stage and theatre where Tony Sheridan and the Beat Brothers recorded "My Bonnie"

Kaempfert arranged them on the wooden stage, facing an empty hall. "The recording equipment was backstage; we were expected to play behind Tony on the stage – as if the whole thing was an outside broadcast." *(Beatle! The Pete Best Story)* Thankfully, the 'dodgy' amplifiers that would later create problems at Decca and EMI would not be an issue here. Rather than use their own amps, known for emitting a horrible hum at the most inappropriate moments, the boys plugged into amps supplied to them by Kaempfert.

Pete's recollection of an "unexciting school hall" is a bit of an understatement, as the Friedrich-Ebert-Halle housed a huge theatre, with seating up in the balcony as well as in the stalls. Although there is an area above the stage where a recording could be controlled remotely, this day's session was recorded in the basement, below the stage. Once you see the size of the room, and the fact that a single voice echoes in the empty cavernous theatre, it is no wonder the engineer had problems recording the group. Pete's bass drum must have sounded like a thunderstorm as the noise bounced off the walls.

It is not known what songs were recorded, or in what order, as there is little paperwork from the sessions. It is generally accepted that seven songs were recorded with Kaempfert. On the 22nd June, and possibly on the 23rd June 1961, four songs were committed to tape: "My Bonnie", plus a German vocal titled "Mein Herz Ist Bei Dir"; "The Saints (When The Saints Go Marching In)";

"Why", written by Sheridan; and "Cry For A Shadow", George Harrison's skit on The Shadows, with a virtuoso solo performance, credited to Harrison/ Lennon. *(The Beatles Fact and Fiction)*

The Beatles were also invited to perform another song, and John chose "Ain't She Sweet", one of his favourites. It was a fitting choice as it satisfied Kaempfert's desire to record easy listening, old-time songs with which German listeners could identify. However, John's vocals were done in a harder, rockier-sounding style, just as he would have sung it on stage.

The song didn't really do him or the group justice because the vocal harmonies that would later become their trademark were nowhere to be found.

It is also thought that they recorded "Take Out Some Insurance On Me, Baby (If You Love Me, Baby)" at the same sessions, but there isn't any documentation to confirm this. Sheridan, ably assisted by Paul on bass and Pete on drums, also recorded "Nobody's Child". *(The Beatles Fact and Fiction)*

These were exciting times for the boys, as they were being recorded for the first time as a group, in a "studio", with a bona fide producer.

Tony Sheridan and The Beatles

It Was Loud!

The songs would have to be recorded live, without the option of multi-tracking r overdubbing. This posed a number of problems when it came to recording musicians, especially when it was a rock 'n' roll group. One of the biggest issues in a studio is the "bleed" that occurs when a guitar, voice or especially drums, are picked up on the open microphones, adversely affecting the quality and balance of the recording. Recording studios would later set up the drums behind a sound baffle that would isolate them from the rest of the group, but on this day in 1961, it would be the whole group, side-by-side on the stage. As we have seen, in this huge, grand theatre, the noise must have been almost uncontrollable.

Sound technician Karl Hinze worked on the session for Kaempfert. He confirmed in an interview with Ulf Kruger that they frequently used the Friedrich Ebert Halle, and the stage was "like a drawing room and there was some echo", with their portable studio equipment placed in a dressing room nearby. With the group set up on the stage, Hinze remembers the chief of production remarking on their appearance: "He said, 'you can't show them on TV. They look terrible.' He was the show-stopper who destroyed everything." The Beatles, to Hinze, looked "pretty wild". They weren't able to communicate to any extent, due to the language differences, so they just made music.

The song forever associated with these sessions was "My Bonnie", and that is what Hinze remembers most fondly: "(The noise was) loud, loud, loud. Loud was okay. When the people were on stage, they promote themselves with their 5000 watts...so loud is always good. I thought the recording of '*My Bonnie*' – I

still listen to it sometimes – was well, the drummer, for instance, was lousy. There is a passage where everything is a mess, but, well, the record sold."

(From Cavern to Star Club)

Pete Best's Drumming

Hinze's assessment was that Pete's drumming was "lousy", though it is more accurately translated as "just bloody (damned) awful". According to Tony Sheridan, Kaempfert suggested that Pete should "not play his bass drum, because he used to get too fast....the tempo was a problem." *(The Beatles Fact and Fiction)* Unfortunately, Tony Sheridan has never been the most reliable of eyewitnesses. It has even been suggested that Kaempfert took Best's bass drum and toms away *(TuneIn)*. Much like a lot of the information surrounding these sessions, there is an element of myth. Pete Best confirmed that his bass drum was not taken away; he was just asked by Kaempfert not to play the bass drum, as Sheridan had suggested. *(David Bedford Interview 2008)*

Can it be supported by evidence?

Hinze's interview was from 1996 – 35 years after the event – and he admitted he didn't remember a lot of the detail, understandably. But there's little need to rely on memory when we have the recording of Pete's drumming from this session to analyse. Were Hinze's and Sheridan's comments accurate, or not?

It has been suggested that Kaempfert removed Best's bass drum so he wouldn't play it. However, since there is no evidence to suggest that any of Pete's drums were taken away, this was probably some mischief from Tony Sheridan, the only person to make that suggestion. None of the other Beatles, or Kaempfert, has ever alluded to it. In all likelihood, Pete was allowed to keep his bass drum, but asked by Kaempfert not to play it. Pete would have been left with just his snare drum, hi-hat and a crash cymbal to play.

WAS THIS BECAUSE OF BEST'S DRUMMING?

Schlager Louts

Given Kaempfert's signature orchestral sound, it is no surprise that he didn't want to use the bass drum; it would have been much too dominant on the record. It is also quite likely that neither Kaempfert nor his engineer had ever recorded a rock 'n' roll group before, certainly not one with such a powerful sound. They simply wouldn't have known what to do with Pete's drumming, which as Hinze observed, was "loud". Most importantly, Kaempfert, throughout his career, only saw drummers in an orchestral sense, to provide a percussive element behind the song. Most Beat Brothers recordings were "percussively limited and he clearly didn't care for bass drum on his sound". *(TuneIn)*

Drummer Alex Cain explained what this means. "Kaempfert's music is 'Easy Listening'. The role of his drummer is to keep time. Notice how prominent the high-hat and snare are; the bass drum is used to punctuate the song. It is perhaps not surprising Bert Kaempfert didn't want Pete to use his bass drum if his usual 'Easy Listening' style was to downplay the instrument, something Pete's style was built upon, i.e. the 'Atom Beat'. However, he would have been aware he was recording rock 'n' roll, a genre a world away from his own. This is where

I think we have to acknowledge the engineer, Hinze, who said they didn't want Pete to play his bass drum due to his erratic playing. To me, it doesn't make sense to remove the bass drum from a rock 'n' roll session, even at such an early time in the development of the music. I suspect it was another case of a performer being unable to translate his style from a sweaty underground club to a recording environment. Don't forget, it wasn't a studio but a big, open hall. A guitarist can simply turn down his amp, it's very difficult for a drummer to do the same when even a deft touch will bounce back from the walls and hit your ears a few beats after you have struck the drum. I suspect this is why the bass drum was not used: to lessen the natural reverb created by the hall, which may have been causing Pete problems with his time-keeping. Coupled with Pete's inexperience and heavy bass drum style, it must have been a nightmare to record."

(David Bedford Interview 2017)

It seems that, regardless of the drummer, Kaempfert would probably not have wanted them to use their bass drum. Any examination of Kaempfert's discography will demonstrate that he was the king of what in Germany was called Schlager music, which became popular in Germany in the 1950s, partly as a backlash against American rock 'n' roll, so what Tony Sheridan and The Beatles were playing was the antithesis of Kaempfert's preferred sound. Schlager music was considered light entertainment, with bright and sentimental lyrics with an emphasis on the instrumental element of the song. That is why Kaempfert chose "My Bonnie", a Scottish folk song dating back to the middle of the 19th Century, "The Saints", better known as "When the Saints Go Marching In", an old American Gospel hymn made popular by jazz artists like Louis Armstrong, and why he allowed John to choose "Ain't She Sweet", a 1920s hit. Not exactly rock 'n' roll, was it? That is why Pete wasn't playing his full drum kit.

Lousy Drumming?

How did Pete cope with such a limited kit? Remarkably well. We asked three drummers to make an objective assessment of his drumming on "My Bonnie" and "Ain't She Sweet".

They were asked to comment on everything from tempo to accuracy, and also to respond to Hinze's comments that Pete was a "lousy drummer". Is there evidence to support either of these comments?

"My Bonnie"

"As Pete Best is not using his bass drum or floor tom, he does a really good job. Maybe Pete at that stage wasn't experienced or talented enough maybe to play quieter? That is great drumming and a really good, high-speed drum roll in perfect time. How could anyone criticise that?" – Mike Rice

"Very tight drum rolls at speed which is hard to do and keep in time. Especially as he didn't use his full kit, he is very inventive in the use of the snare, with good flicks on the hi-hat, using it like a crash cymbal. A very technical piece of drumming, expertly executed." – Derek and Andrew Hinton

"Ain't She Sweet"

"That sounds good, perfectly in time. No problem." – Mike Rice
"Again, with a limited kit, makes good use of it and delivers another great performance, driving the song and using his kit imaginatively."
– Derek and Andrew Hinton

Conclusion?

Based on these recordings, there is no evidence to support Hinze's statement or Sheridan's recollection of a problem with tempo. Because we don't know how many takes or rehearsals there may have been, we can only judge the finished songs.

Banging Away In The Background?

"My Bonnie" is a fantastic recording and a genuinely great early example of rock 'n' roll at its best, with Sheridan providing a powerful, polished vocal and guitar performance, ably assisted by The Beatles. Paul, despite having just taken over on the bass guitar, gives us a glimpse of the melodic bass lines that would underpin so many Beatles hits later on. While John and George don't really stand out as rhythm guitarists on the recording, they support Tony Sheridan perfectly. Pete provides a driving rhythm on his drum which belies the fact that he had such a limited kit.

"Ain't She Sweet", though a popular choice, doesn't showcase the talents of The Beatles that well. John's throat is raspy – the well-known Hamburg throat – and doesn't quite fit with the arrangement. Paul's bass playing is admirable, but George's guitar work is forgettable, especially during the solo.

"My Bonnie"

Although The Beatles expected a single to be released – "Ain't She Sweet" backed with "Cry For A Shadow" – it never materialized. It seems clear that Kaempfert, though happy with Sheridan's performance, was less than impressed with The Beatles. It defies logic that Kaempfert, who died in 1980, never went into any depth about his time recording the early Beatles, so we have very few details about the sessions and how they were conducted. It seems that everyone wanted to forget about it, especially The Beatles and their producer.

How did The Beatles remember their recording experience with Kaempfert? "It's just Tony Sheridan singing," said Lennon, "with us banging away in the background. It's terrible. It could be anybody." *(Anthology)*

Could be, but it wasn't.

"My Bonnie" wasn't released until October 1961, and though it reached number five in the German charts, it is still not regarded as a classic by many, including The Beatles themselves. However, it was this record that piqued Brian Epstein's interest when Beatles fans like Raymond Jones asked for it at the NEMS record counter, thus becoming the catalyst that brought Brian and The Beatles together. Not bad for a song recorded on a school stage in Germany with a drummer who only had half a kit.

LANE
L CLUB
rs. Ada Taylor
OF CLUBLAND

WELCOME FOR
AND FRIENDS

5 Social Club
D, LIVERPOOL
Mr. J. Guigan

PPY CLUB
BEST IS GOOD
FOR OUR
AND FRIENDS

IDE CLUBS
CIATION

uarters:
e Social Club

BEST
N SERVICE
ON MERSEYSIDE

OPEN TO ALL BONA FIDE
CLUB REPRESENTATIVES

Original painting by Paul Skellett

28th October 1961

ENTER MR. EPSTEIN: LIFTING THE FOG OF SMOKE AND MIRRORS

From start to finish, The Beatles' story is permeated with myths and misinformation.

The roots of these inaccuracies can be traced back to events that occurred between 1961 and 1962 when their newly-installed manager and disciple, Brian Epstein, took control of their destiny. Those were truly defining years for him and his boys, and it's important to understand why Brian felt it necessary to reinvent them. Since his very first immersion into the subterranean world of Liverpool's teenage beat scene in November 1961, Epstein was hooked by four rough-and-ready foul-mouthed punk-rocking scallywags. The Beatles stage act at the Cavern Club hit him like a tidal wave.

Here was an unknown culture – at least unknown to him, until Bill Harry strolled into his record store in July 1961 with a bundle of freshly printed music newspapers under his arm, with a mission to get Brian to stock a dozen or more every fortnight. Mersey Beat? What was this? Epstein had never heard of it before, nor should he. It was hot off the press, so underground, and so new, as were the people and venues suddenly popping out of its pages.

As a man whose business depended on knowing about national and international music trends, Brian prided himself on being ahead of the game. But the fact that a new music scene was happening in the basement of an old fruit and vegetable warehouse in Mathew Street, a back alleyway barely a few hundred yards from his NEMS office in Whitechapel, was nothing short of an epiphany for him.

Brian's surprise soon gave way to curiosity and Bill seized his opportunity. As the new scene's leading evangelist and a close friend and fellow traveler of The Beatles, he was only too happy to begin enlightening Brian's narrow cultural view.

The inaugural issue of Mersey Beat inaugural featured an article about The Beatles on page 2 – one that describes a group with 'dubious origins'! Assuming that Epstein even saw the article, the very word dubious would surely have raised his attention sharply, since it resonated with his own private life.

The article itself was penned by the group's leader, John Winston Lennon, who certainly had to contend with his own dubious origins. That aside, no one knew better than John did about how true this description fitted his band at the time.

Far from being the cute, mop-haired lads that Epstein wanted to portray to the world later on, The Beatles' entire act up until then had been shaped and sharpened by the worst excesses that Hamburg's seedy red light district could offer a bunch of Scouse teenagers. Here, sex, drugs, squalor and violence personified the endless hard days and nights of raw rock 'n' roll at its best.

The Beatles first left Liverpool's soot black scenery for the bright neon lights of Hamburg in August 1960 and made their second trip there in March 1961. They returned home from their first residency as rough cut diamonds, hardened, more rebellious and more anarchic on stage than ever.

They also brought back an electric powerhouse of sound never heard before and a presence that positively oozed sex appeal – long hair, leather and attitude!

27TH DECEMBER 1960 - LITHERLAND TOWN HALL

The Beatles' homecoming performance at Litherland Town Hall on 27th December 1960 was billed as "direct from Hamburg", leading most of the teenagers who crammed into the dance hall to assume they were a German band. The Litherland gig has entered Beatles and Merseybeat consciousness as a defining moment where the entire female audience suddenly surged forward like a tsunami. Boyfriends were ignored or abandoned as the first stirrings of hysteria began. A few rival promoters who were there sensed the impact The Beatles were making and lined up for an opportunity to slip backstage to do business. It was an eighteen-year-old junior promoter, Dave Forshaw, who got there first and signed the group for a series of bookings at £6.10 shillings, rising to £7.10 shillings per gig (all in). Only a few months earlier, The Beatles had been dismissed as mediocre no-hopers, but now, in the space of one night, they led the pack as the most sought-after band on Merseyside.

Fiction claims that Brian Epstein was there that night. He wasn't. Neither was his assistant, Alistair Taylor, despite the claim. It wasn't their scene.

The first brushfire of "Beatlemania" witnessed at the Litherland Town Hall quickly spread to other clubs and, over the coming months, the band's potent mix began attracting legions of fans. The same mysterious power of attraction also proved too much for Brian Epstein when he ventured down the steps of The Cavern nearly a year later. Lured by curiosity about the thriving underground club scene painted by Sam Leach and Bill Harry, Brian finally succumbed to Harry's offer to arrange a VIP visit to the Cavern. Here was his chance to experience the savage young Beatles in the flesh.

9th November 1961. The Invitation not to be Refused

At lunchtime on this day, Brian Epstein and assistant Alistair Taylor were met at the club entrance in Mathew Street by doorman Paddy Delaney, who ushered them down the stone steps to be met by the heat and stink of teenage nirvana. Positioning themselves discreetly (they thought) behind the crowd at the back of the club's main cellar, the two men must have been in a state of culture shock, but nothing like the one they experienced when The Beatles took to the stage.

Watching the rebel princes perform was an awakening for Brian. The full frontal assault on his senses ran much deeper than mere appreciation of the music alone, as friends and associates have since recalled. From that first moment, Brian was visibly mesmerized, and the impact was to last the rest of his life. Cavern DJ Bob Wooler noted the effect in a 1996 interview with reporter Gillian Gaar: "When I got to know Brian, I asked him what was his impression of the Cavern and The Beatles, and he said, 'Well, I thought the Cavern was a terrible place. I didn't really like the playing in such a fearful surrounding.'"

If Brian wasn't taken by the Cavern that day, it was obvious he was smitten by the four leather-clad lads on stage. They became an instant obsession, far more than a special music act. They were constantly on his mind and in his thoughts, and it was apparent. Not that his assistant Alistair Taylor noticed immediately.

A jazz and classical music fan like Epstein, Taylor was only there under

Alistair Taylor, Brian Epstein's P.A.

Original painting by Paul Skellett

sufferance because his boss had insisted on his company. Taylor's real opinion slipped out later when he remarked, "... these four horrible young men on stage, dressed in black leather trousers, black jackets, smoking, drinking and making a noise…" And then, as if sensing he'd just trashed Brian's officially-sanctioned version of events, Taylor backtracked again with, "... they (The Beatles) were charismatic and exciting… I thought they were sensational." Hmm! We can almost hear Epstein hissing like a cat before Taylor's embarrassing climb down!

How much we can actually rely on Alistair Taylor's view of history is open to question because he changed his story over the years. In other interviews, he claimed to be the chief instigator of the Cavern visit, supposedly inspired by a customer named Raymond Jones who'd visited NEMS store in Whitechapel and asked him personally for a record called "My Bonnie" by The Beatles – or, to be more accurate, by an obscure band called Tony Sheridan and the Beat Brothers. In effect, Taylor claimed the request led him and Epstein to the Cavern.

In an interview with David Bedford, Taylor was asked to clarify the story. "I was Raymond Jones. Kids were coming into the shop and asking for this record 'My Bonnie' by The Beatles. We didn't have it and until somebody put in an actual order, Brian wouldn't do anything. You see, Brian had this claim that if you ordered a record by anyone, anywhere, he would find it. However, no matter how many people asked for it, nobody had ordered it by paying a deposit. Particularly as this was a German import, this was even more important.

"I knew we would sell lots of copies, so I made out the order form and paid the deposit from my own pocket in the name of Raymond Jones, one of our regular customers. Now that we had an order, Brian and I set about tracking it down. Of course, it was recorded in Germany and was recorded under the name of Tony Sheridan and The Beat Brothers. Brian ordered the first batch and they sold out in no time at all. So, a few years ago, I announced that I was the real Raymond Jones. And that is it – it was me". *(DB Interview Liddypool 2008)*

Local writer and BBC radio broadcaster Spencer Leigh went in search of Raymond Jones and found him very much alive and well, confirmed by no less than Cavern DJ Bob Wooler, who also met him. Raymond Jones was a Cavern regular, and was in NEMS every Saturday morning. "I had never heard anything like them *(Hunter Davies. The Beatles)*." Jones had heard that The Beatles had released a record, so he went to NEMS as usual to order it. "Brian Epstein asked me, 'Who are they?' and I said 'They are the most fantastic group you will ever hear." *(The Beatles: 10 Years That Shook The World)*

Another fan, Bob Garroch, claims to have requested the record before Raymond Jones. "I was 17 years of age and a student at a Merchant Navy Radio School in Liverpool." Garroch also observed that, at the time, The Beatles didn't perform their own songs. "They were very laid back and would talk to all of us and play our requests. I was chatting to The Beatles during a break and Paul told me about the record they had made in Germany. I popped round to NEMS which was just round the corner from the Cavern. The ground floor was Classical Music only and there was a staircase on the left of the shop going down to the basement. Brian was behind the counter and I asked him to trace 'My Bonnie'. He asked me who The Beatles were. I told him they were playing at the Cavern." *(David Bedford Interview with Bill Harry)*

Brian duly ordered the record for Garroch.

Who it was and who made the request first is irrelevant because when so many fans requested copies, Brian was determined to track down the record. He eventually found it in Germany, and discovered that it wasn't "My Bonnie" by The Beatles, but "My Bonnie" by Tony Sheridan and The Beat Brothers, on Polydor Records. Brian made a note: "'My Bonnie'. The Beatles. Check Monday." *(Cellarful of Noise)*

Not to be outdone by Taylor's story, Epstein (being a master of spin) implied he was the person who served Raymond Jones and personally took his order enquiry. According to Epstein, it was his conversation with Jones that inspired him to visit the Cavern and 'discover' The Beatles single-handed. Someone was telling porkies, but who was it? Were they both reinventing history? What we can prove is that Raymond Jones and other Beatles fans were at NEMS asking for "My Bonnie", which was ordered and sold out very quickly. It piqued Epstein's interest.

Brian's typically narcissistic character would have the world believe he was entirely unaided by Bill Harry and the influence of his Beatles articles in *Mersey Beat* (of which Epstein was now a regular reader, advertiser and guest writer). Nor was he made curious by promoter Sam Leach's concert posters (featuring "The Beatles" writ large) displayed in his own shop windows or by the interest shown by Beatle fans who visited the store. In reality, the help offered by Bill, Sam and Bob Wooler was crucial to Epstein's success, until they were no longer needed and, one by one, they were ruthlessly jettisoned from his inner circle.

The sudden leap from the group's No.1 fan to making a serious business commitment to manage (exploit) their potential took a little longer, but not much. As always, Brian started his new project by carefully sounding out several friends and colleagues, not through direct questions or proposals, but by more subtle probing over drinks and business lunches. It was really an academic pursuit, because his mind was already made up, probably after being reinforced by the fan's all-consuming emotions expressed day after day, night after night. If The Beatles could do that in Liverpool, imagine the impact they would have elsewhere.

All it needed was a spark to inspire a great journey, and The Beatles certainly ignited Brian's fire. At last, here was Brian's ticket out of the stifling obscurity of retail shop management, out from under the scrutiny of Jewish parents, and out of Liverpool to new horizons and a lifestyle he felt he deserved. But exactly how he was going to achieve this was to be the trickiest part.

Bob Wooler's sage advice to all upcoming acts was that success all came down to A.I.M. – attitude, image, music! It was this wise observation that he passed to Brian Epstein, too. Epstein understood its message only too well. Whereas the pursuit of a recording contract may have been central to The Beatles' goals, as was the pursuit of money for Lennon, Epstein's knowledge of retail marketing and the music industry told him that artists came and went very quickly without clearly defined marketing plan and an acceptable image. And while he was already sold on their music, his main preoccupation was how to turn The Beatles into a saleable brand. With that in mind, he realised important changes had to be made, both in their professional approach and personal behaviour. The casual attitude in their performance and their timekeeping had to go, as did many of their unacceptable habits. And so did the leather gear! This had to be understood, and managed with a firm hand. But would they go along with the changes? Epstein would eventually map out his vision to The Beatles individually and collectively while taking the time to meet their respective parents and guardians

and explain his management proposals to them. After all, three of the four group members were under the legal age of consent. In due course, he was politely met by all of them, but their private responses were somewhat more guarded. Jim McCartney was not at all sold on Epstein, and Mona Best had her own reservations as well as a vested interest in The Beatles to consider. Brian was also very aware others were watching and waiting on the sidelines. He was still keen to manage them, but being a shrewd and observant businessman, he knew the dangers very well. One way or another, any distractions to his long-term plans had to be overcome – or neutralized – and the sooner the better if he was going to secure a deal with a record company. All he needed was a contract that gave him some authority.

It's a matter of record that during the initial verbal agreement to team up with Brian Epstein, The Beatles – or rather John Lennon – had laid down their own ground rules, too. Music was their domain with no interference from Brian, while his role would be to manage them all the way to the top. The challenge became a double-edged sword because, as Brian would have explained, getting to the top was not enough to secure a record label in London or sell records to local fans like Raymond Jones. They had to win over a mass audience in what was still a morally conservative, class-obsessed British society where Victorian attitudes still held sway. America would be an even bigger hurdle.

Meanwhile, for these rough teenage leathernecks to become chartbusters, they needed to clean up their act. Brian would have to fashion them into his image of a successful act, and that would require changing their look and their behavior. In short, they had to accept his rules. As if that was not enough, their backstory also had to be carefully scripted to avoid embarrassing skeletons falling out of the cupboard. No doubt Lennon smirked at the irony of Brian's suggestion and told him to do the same thing himself. In fact, both hid their private lives from the public for several years. But it was from this time, early in 1962, that the official Beatle myth machine went into operation. A veil was about to descend over the past and the legend of four cuddly mop tops would soon begin.

From Liverpool With Love

Within weeks of meeting The Beatles for the first time in November 1961, Brian Epstein was writing to record companies in the hope of securing a record deal for them. In Britain, the record market was controlled by four big companies – EMI, Decca, Pye and Philips – with contact usually made through the recording managers, a difficult task at best. These managers – the producers and A&R men (known as Artists & Repertoire) – held the power, and unless a prospective artist or their manager had a go-between or an established relationship with them, it took luck to even get an audition. Bear in mind that of the hundreds of would-be rising stars, only a select few were granted auditions by the labels and even fewer of those auditioned were able to secure a recording contract.

It was, therefore, a daunting task that lay in front of Epstein. Brian was a gentleman in every sense of the word. Reasonably well-educated, he had been shuffled around a half-dozen schools by his parents and had developed good tastes and exceptional manners along the way. He had an undoubted natural charisma that made him attractive to women, who were equally drawn by his cultural tastes and the fact that he was a snappy dresser with a preference for wearing tailor-made suits. It was a style that certainly elevated him above the

Brian Epstein

average Liverpool retailer. He was also well-versed in store management and a stickler for detail. But perhaps most important, he had something his ambitious rivals for the role of Beatles manager – such as Sam Leach and Mona Best – didn't have: reliable inside contacts at London's record labels.

Despite these assets, better men than him had tried and failed to break into the world of artist management and record production. Here he was handicapped from the start. He had little knowledge about managing a group, or club management, or event promotion, let alone any serious insight into the exacting technical demands of recording studios. And it would soon become apparent that he was even less aware of the fickle nature of the men who ran the record labels.

In reality, before life as a retailer, the nearest Brian Epstein had got to the world of entertainment was a failed love affair with the theatre. He'd dabbled briefly as a would-be actor, attending RADA's drama school in London. He also dallied with the idea of becoming a fashion designer, but as with most dreams he had up to this point, both came to nothing.

In 1957, his civilian life was interrupted when he was conscripted for national service in the army. 'Join the army and see the world', said the military blurb, but all Brian got was a deskbound job as a clerk in the Royal Army Service Corp. Perhaps it was the boredom of army routine, but it was here that his overdeveloped sense of self-importance got him into trouble when he took to wearing the kind of Savile Row suits worn by commissioned officers when off duty. There's no harm in looking well-dressed, except that one evening he was arrested while trying to solicit a bit of rough trade in London and charged with impersonating an officer. While homosexual practices were still a punishable offence in the 1950s, the idea of passing himself off as an officer to pull other gay men was something the army wouldn't tolerate. His defence was that the episode was a misunderstanding, his style of clothing being a matter of good taste, nothing more. Hard to prove or disprove, but nevertheless he was severely reprimanded and dismissed from the service on 'health grounds', whatever that may mean.

Embarrassed by his failed attempts at social climbing, the prodigal son slunk back to Liverpool in disgrace where he was welcomed by long-suffering parents. Far from giving up on Brian, they offered him a career in the family business, beginning with an apprenticeship at Clarendon Furnishings on the Wirral, followed by a management role in the city's first family-owned music and electrical store (NEMS in Charlotte Street) and, later, manager of the brand new NEMS store on Whitechapel. And there he stayed, locked in a frustrating world of retail management under the watchful eyes of his father and brother, his unfulfilled dreams still screaming to break out one day. As we know, that day finally arrived in 1961 when he ventured into the lunchtime gig at the Cavern Club.

Rather surprisingly, when he first met The Beatles, Epstein insisted he had no knowledge about the local underground music scene other than what he'd gleaned from a new local music sheet called *Mersey Beat*. In fairness, his own cultural tastes were poles apart from The Beatles. Jazz, the classics, theatre, opera and a natural attraction to the underground gay scene filled his private life.

Even so, it must seem extraordinary that a teenage music revolution was happening barely a few hundred yards from his Whitechapel store, and he was oblivious to it! Perhaps it comes down to the fact that the only revolution filling his head was a long overdue desire to do more with his life than what Liverpool and its local distractions had to offer. In short, he craved recognition. His overwhelming desire was to be someone.

So it was that the arrival of The Beatles in Epstein's life had reignited his hidden passions. The initial meeting he had with The Beatles at NEMS on the 29th November 1961 served to spur him on even more. Although it was only a tentative sounding to test their interest in his proposition to manage them, Brian was astute enough to get their measure; their ambitions were as keen as his own. Like him, they wanted to climb to the very top, wherever that may be. Perhaps inspired by this, Brian took the initiative and headed for the bright lights of London. He'd already taken a gamble by setting up two record label appointments.But what the hell, he was a risk taker.

Nothing ventured nothing gained.

9th November 1961

BRIAN EPSTEIN AND THE UNBREAKABLE, BROKEN CONTRACT

Brian was becoming ever more aware of The Beatles, especially in the pages of Mersey Beat, to which he contributed a column.

Brian decided to visit The Cavern to see The Beatles perform and, with Bill Harry's assistance, attended a lunchtime show with Alistair Taylor. The date was Thursday, 9th November 1961, one that would change the lives of both Brian and The Beatles.

Taylor remembered the day well. "Brian wanted to go and see The Beatles who were so popular. Everyone was talking about them and we had sold so many copies of the record. Brian didn't know where The Cavern was, which of course I did as I had been there when it was a jazz club. He was amazed to realize how close it was.

"We went down into the cellar, and that smell of rotting fruit and vegetables never left The Cavern. It was smelly and horrible, and Brian and I looked out of place in our smart suits. We sat at the back and watched while the place went mad for these scruffy musicians. The noise was terrible. They were loud, awful, unprofessional, scruffy and frankly not that good. But we both couldn't help tapping our feet to the rhythm. They had something. Don't ask me what it was, because I don't know. If I did I would have been a rich man. I call it ingredient 'X'.

"They played five songs I think, but the one that made us stop and take notice was when they introduced a song of their own called 'Hello Little Girl', which The Fourmost later recorded. It wasn't just that they were prepared to play their own song but that it went down well." *(David Bedford Interview 2004)* As Alistair observed, Brian, the record retailer who could spot a hit record from a mile away, took notice of the fact that The Beatles performed one of their own songs, which went down well with the crowd. He obviously saw the potential.

Brian recalled the visit in his autobiography, *A Cellarful of Noise*: "Inside, the club was as black as a deep grave, dank and damp and smelly and I regretted my decision to come. There were some 200 young people there jiving, chatting or eating." The Beatles appeared on stage, and Brian was transfixed for some reason. "I had never seen anything like The Beatles on any stage. They smoked as they played and they ate and talked and pretended to hit each other. They turned their backs on the audience and shouted at them and laughed at private jokes. But they gave a captivating and honest show and they had considerable magnetism. I was fascinated by this, to me, new music with its pounding bass beat and its vast engulfing sound." Brian approached the stage and spoke first to George, who asked "What brings Mr. Epstein here?" and then went to find the other three. Brian's main aim was to find out more about "My Bonnie". Brian recalled that "George got a DJ called Bob Wooler to play it for me."

Bob Wooler always said that Brian, a homosexual, was physically attracted to The Beatles, and that may have been the case. But this was more than just an infatuation or attraction; this was fate. Brian decided that he was going into pop management, and he and The Beatles were looking for each other at the right time.

What would you say to me managing The Beatles?

Brian and Alistair left the Cavern and went to the Peacock Restaurant, where Brian dropped the bombshell on his assistant. He asked Alistair; "Who do you work for? Me or NEMS? What would you say to me managing The Beatles?" Alistair was visibly shocked and lost for words. "Brian was a man who was

119

Brian in pensive mood

bored easily," said Alistair, "and The Beatles came along at the right time. He then made me the offer, which could have made me a wealthy man. He offered me a percentage of The Beatles, there and then. I couldn't contribute anything financially, so I said I couldn't accept his offer. Brian understood but asked me if I would work for him in managing The Beatles. Of course I would. I would have done anything for him. And so that is where it all began. It was the biggest financial mistake of my life, but you can't change things".

(David Bedford Interview 2004)

"This is me Dad"

The first meeting with Epstein happened towards the end of November, probably on the 29th, at NEMS in Whitechapel. At this stage, The Beatles were still unsure about Brian, so they took along their trusted confidant Bob Wooler, who John introduced as "me dad". *(Spencer Leigh, The Independent obituary)* (It is a Liverpool colloquialism to replace my with me, so John was meaning 'my dad'.) As Pete recalled, Brian chose his words carefully. *(Best Years of The Beatles)*

He outlined the idea of managing them, but wanted to know their current arrangements, if any. The Beatles told Brian that Allan Williams had been their manager, and that they had signed a contract with Bert Kaempfert in Hamburg a few months earlier.

Brian had already, on the strength of his initial discussions, started making enquiries at record companies and had meetings scheduled in London at the end of the week. He asked for a copy of the Kaempfert contract, which he wanted the next day. Brian was honest with them: "I've never been engaged in this kind of thing before." Pete said that John asked him what he thought, and Pete's response was: "We'll have to talk it over." John, as the group's leader, spoke for them all: "We'll let you know." Best agreed that Epstein could be their last chance if they "were ever to escape the Liverpool-Hamburg shuttle service. Eppy was in the record business; he would know people and he had promised to help." *(Beatle! The Pete Best Story)*

Epstein arranged a further meeting for the following week. For now, he had meetings in London to attend.

From EMI to Decca to EMI - On The Record

Within days of meeting The Beatles for the first time, Brian started contacting the record companies to get a deal. In Britain, the record market was controlled by the big four companies: EMI, Decca, Pye and Philips. The recording managers within these companies were the ones you had to contact, which was not easy. These managers, producers and A&R (Artists & Repertoire) men held the power, and unless you had a go-between or good relationship with them, you were lucky to even get an audition. Hundreds of singers and groups applied weekly to these companies, so it was not a simple task that lay ahead of Brian, especially with no background in the music recording business. Of the hundreds of groups that applied for auditions, only a select few were granted them, and only a limited number of those auditioned were given recording contracts.

It was therefore a daunting task that lay in front of Brian. Better men had tried and failed to break into the music business, but he was handicapped from the start. Although he was well versed in the business of retail management and had the usual trade contacts at London record labels, he knew next to nothing about artist representation, club management or event promotion. He knew even less about the exacting technical demands of recording studios and the fickle nature of the record industry generally.

Rather surprisingly, when he first met The Beatles, Epstein insisted he had no knowledge about the local underground music scene other than what he'd gleaned from a new local music sheet called *Mersey Beat*. In fairness, his own cultural tastes were poles apart from The Beatles. Jazz, the classics, theatre, opera and a natural attraction to the underground gay scene filled his private life. Even so, it must seem extraordinary that a teenage music revolution was happening barely a hundred yards from his NEMS store in Whitechapel and he was oblivious to it! Perhaps it comes down to the fact that the only revolution filling his head was a long overdue desire to do more with his life than what Liverpool and its local distractions had to offer. In short, his overwhelming desire was to be someone. He craved recognition.

The Beatles' arrival in Brian's life reignited his passions. And this time, it was their ambitions as much as his own that would drive him once again to the bright lights of London.

Mr. Epstein Goes to London

On 1st December, Brian headed to London for not one, but two appointments: first at EMI, and then with Decca in the afternoon. At EMI, he met Ron White, a marketing executive who Brian knew well from record company functions in London. He seemed to be the obvious man to start with, as White already knew Brian's credentials and reputation. The meeting with White well went, or so Epstein thought, and White promised to pass a copy of "My Bonnie" to his A & R men, which should have included George Martin. White also took the Kaempfert contract from Epstein and promised to review it and have it translated.

A letter from White soon followed on 18th December 1961 saying:

> "I'm sorry that I have been so long in giving you a decision but I have now had an opportunity of playing the record to each of our Artistes Managers. Whilst we appreciate the talents of this group, we feel that we have sufficient groups of this type at the present time under contract and that it would not be advisable for us to sign any further contracts of this nature at present."

(The Complete Beatles Chronicles)

This letter was to prove embarrassing for White when George Martin then signed

The Beatles to Parlophone, a division of EMI. Paramor, Ridley and Newell certainly turned down the chance to audition the group, but as Ron White clearly implied to Epstein in his letter, George Martin, as an A & R man for EMI, also heard the sampler and turned them down.

However, in stark contradiction to Ron White's claim at the time, George Martin asserted he did not hear the tape at all because he was not even available at the time, having taken a 'vacation' in December. There have been suggestions that his absence was either an attempt to repair a strained marriage, or an opportunity to spend some private time with an EMI employee, Judy Lockhart Smith. No matter which version is correct, it still leaves the earlier question unresolved: Why would Ron White imply that Martin had heard Epstein's sampler of The Beatles music and then had also 'passed' on the audition?

We will never know for sure because White has since passed on, but we suspect the reason is very simple. Epstein was pushing him relentlessly for an urgent response, and rather than hold on until January when George Martin could hear the tape upon his return White may have assumed that Martin's response would be the same as the others. As a consequence, Epstein received a 'unanimous' rejection to add to his other refusals.

Although White's letter to Epstein was to have embarrassing repercussions later on, the matter didn't end there. Far from being off the hook, EMI and George Martin would once again come under even more pressure from Epstein in January 1962, when Brian adopted a far more Machiavellian tactic to achieve his objective.

Plan B

After the EMI appointment, Brian headed to his meeting at Decca, probably unaware of the changes that had recently occurred at the company after a review in America. Decca Records began as a British record label established in 1929 by Edward Lewis. Its U.S. label was established in late 1934 by Lewis along with American Decca's first president Jack Kapp and later American Decca president Milton Rackmil. In 1947, dissatisfied with American Decca's promotion of British Decca recordings, and because American Decca held the rights to the name Decca in the U.S. and Canada, British Decca began to sell its records in North America under the London Records label. American Decca bought Universal-International in 1952, and eventually merged with MCA in 1962, becoming a subsidiary company under MCA.

The December 1961 issue of the American music trade publication Cash Box discussed the internal changes: "One of the most constructive moves to be made by Decca for many months is the formation of a new production team to handle the company's pop single output. Spearheaded by A&R manager, Dick Rowe, who will be directly responsible to the chairman, Sir Edward Lewis, the team is completed by Dick Rowe, Rowe's assistant and co-producer Mike Smith, Peter Attwood, recording engineer of three years standing and Tony Meehan, former drummer for The Shadows. Rowe, who will act in an advisory capacity, feels that this youthful team with their fingers on the teenage pulse, will be more than capable of producing the kind of sound that makes for chart success."

(How They Became The Beatles)

GEORGE HARRISON

JOHN WINSTON LENNON

JAMES PAUL McCARTNEY

PETE BEST

Brian had a contract drawn up which John, Paul, George and Pete signed................but Brian didn't

Ultimately, it would be Dick Rowe who would play a major part in the course of The Beatles' recording career. Brian was more successful at his second meeting with Decca when he secured an audition for the group at the company, thanks to two men: Mike Smith and Tony Barrow.

Barrow wrote for the *Liverpool Echo* as a record reviewer under the nom-du-plume of "Disker" in a weekly column called "Off The Record". At the same time, he was employed by Decca to write record-sleeve notes. Just after Brian had become The Beatles' manager, he wrote to "Disker" to ask him to feature his boys the column. Tony Barrow recalled it well:

"He wanted me to write about his group in 'Off The Record'. To his surprise, instead of getting a reply from a staff writer at the Liverpool Echo offices, he received my letter from London. As the column consisted entirely of record reviews, I wouldn't be able to write about The Beatles until they had released something, either an album or a single. I suggested that he should contact a feature writer on the full-time staff of the Echo, a flamboyant guy named, coincidentally, George Harrison, who had a daily "people" column called 'Over The Mersey Wall' and was always on the look-out for local stories. This wasn't good enough for Epstein, who arranged to come and see me at Decca in my tiny office hidden away in the backwater that was the Sleeve Department."

(John, Paul, George, Ringo and Me)

While still at Decca for the meeting, Brian went to find Tony Barrow as arranged. "Brian asked if he might play me a demo disc, an acetate recorded at the Cavern during a performance by The Beatles. He put it on the turntable and I tried to look interested, but all I could hear was a great deal of wild screaming and a back beat. I didn't even identify the tune that was being played. He excused the sound quality saying the recording was taken from soundtrack of a Granada TV documentary."

This was obviously a 'creative lie', as Granada did not film at the Cavern until August 1962. In fact, Epstein had simply used a handheld microphone and tape recorder in a packed Cavern. No wonder it sounded terrible. The original tape was likely transferred to acetate by Percy Phillips in his Kensington studio where, back in July 1958, The Quarrymen had made their first record. Epstein was a frequent visitor to Phillips' studio over the years because no other place in Liverpool provided this service.

Despite its poor quality, Barrow didn't leave it there, thankfully. "Against the advice of my proofreader, I called our Marketing Department. I approached them rather than the producers in A & R because I knew that Brian Epstein was a well-respected Liverpool record retailer. Marketing hadn't heard of Epstein but asked if his record shops bore his name. 'No', I said, his family has a chain of outlets in the city but they trade as NEMS, North End Music Stores. At this point, Marketing jumped to attention, telling me that NEMS was one of Decca's best customers in the north-west of England and any band they were connected with must be given the courtesy of an audition." *(John, Paul, George, Ringo and Me)*

Such were Brian Epstein's covert tactics to ensure that even if he had been promised an audition, his gambit here was to get the whole of Decca onside. It worked. Decca's A & R man, Mike Smith, promptly took it upon himself visit Liverpool on 13th December 1961 specifically to see The Beatles live on stage at the Cavern Club.

Just For A Chat

After his successful trip to London, Brian met up again with The Beatles at NEMS on 3rd December, at 4.30pm, for "a chat" though, in his mind, Brian was very keen to become their manager. Three Beatles turned up, with Paul famously 'still in the bath'. When an exasperated Epstein, a stickler for punctuality, demanded to know where Paul was, George informed Brian that his bandmate was still bathing. Brian exclaimed, "This is disgraceful, he's very late!" "And very clean", Harrison, the wonder of one-liners, retorted with "his slow, lop-sided smile". *(A Cellarful of Noise)*

Brian didn't know if "they were very respectful to me because I had money, a car, and a record shop," but it was a positive chat. It was decided to take things further, with discussions in "vague terms, contracts and their futures". John again voiced the feeling of the group: "Right then Brian, manage us now. Where's the contract, I'll sign it." *(A Cellarful of Noise)* Brian must have felt a rush of adrenalin as the news sank in that he was now the manager of The Beatles.

The Confusing Contracts

It is from here that nothing is as straightforward as it seems, with draft contracts, agreements, solicitors and confusion surrounding The Beatles' agreement with Brian Epstein.

Brian spoke to the group's accountant, Keith Smith, who worked for Bailey, Page & Co. in Liverpool to establish their financial information and what he was taking on. Most importantly, Brian needed a draft contract. On 6th December, Brian met with his neighbour E. Rex Makin, one of Liverpool's leading solicitors. Having been told by Allan Williams that "The Beatles will let you down" and that he wouldn't "touch them with a f**king bargepole", Brian, according to Makin, requested "an unbreakable contract" *(Drummed Out)*, which of course didn't exist. Makin knew Brian and his passing fads well, so probably didn't take him too seriously.

Brian's next meeting that afternoon, which proved far more productive, was with Keith Smith. "We drew up a sketchy Heads of Agreement" said Smith, though Brian wasn't keen on this first document. "I thought it an inhuman document," Brian would write, "providing simply for the enslavement of any artist." *(A Cellarful of Noise)*

However, it was a template and somewhere to start, and something to present to his new group at their next meeting, which took place, according to Brian, "the following Sunday at The Casbah". *(A Cellarful of Noise)* This would have been the 10th December, immediately after The Beatles had returned from their disastrous trip to Aldershot, near London, with Sam Leach. Because of the mix-up over the promotion, only 18 people turned up at their first performance "down south". However, it is unlikely that the meeting took place on this day, as The Beatles didn't arrive home until noon. They promptly headed for bed for a bit of rest before turning up late for their evening performance at Hambleton Hall.

Pete Best recalled them all happily signing the skimpy two-page "contract" at The Casbah. This document was most likely based on the "Heads of Agreement" and did not contain any of the parents' details, which would make it unenforceable in law, though The Beatles would have been unaware of this fact. A discussion took place, which outlined Brian's proposals to manage them, but he still needed to talk to a solicitor to get a formal contract drawn up. With their audition at Decca rapidly approaching, he wanted this done as soon as possible, but still hadn't found a solicitor to act for him. It seems clear that, with the Decca audition, and other potential managers still around, Epstein needed something, anything, in writing saying that he and The Beatles were joined together. After all, if they passed the Decca audition, which he arranged, and he had no agreement with them, they could proceed without him. Brian couldn't let this happen. This agreement would have to do until he could arrange for a solicitor to draw up a formal contract. Epstein resolved this by approaching another friend of the family, David Harris.

The First Management Contract

"I was a very young solicitor," said Harris. "I joined the firm in December 1957 and became a Junior Partner in 1960 and stayed until I left in 1988. Brian came to me, out of the blue, as I'd never done anything for him before," recalled Harris, "and he said to me he wanted to manage a group called The Beatles, of whom I had never heard, and I laughed. What sort of a name is Beatles? I knew him already, though I knew his brother better, but I knew him. Brian was known as being a dilettante, he never actually settled into anything. Until he found his metier with this, his life was going nowhere, and this made him, and indeed it killed him, too." *(David Bedford Interview 2015)*

Harris had never done anything like it before. "I was doing run of the mill criminal law, magistrates law, matrimonial law, contract law, road traffic accidents, so no previous experience in this area. At that time, there wouldn't have been anyone else in Liverpool doing show business contracts like this so far as I was aware."

The contract that Harris was asked to draw up was a management contract between Brian and The Beatles. "For every new artist, they had to have their own draft of the contract for themselves. If they wanted to take their own legal advice, they could, because I was acting for Brian, not the group." Such was The Beatles' confidence, or naiveté. They "didn't have their own representation, though at every stage we said to them, please take it away and get your own legal advice but they never did. As well as Brian wanting to be fair with them, I wanted it to be fair, too. He was very fair in everything he did." As he was representing Epstein, he met The Beatles "in his (Brian's) office, though possibly on only one occasion, as there was no need to, as I was representing Brian, not them."

(David Bedford Interview 2015)

The initial draft was drawn up between Brian Epstein and John Winston Lennon, George Harrison, James Paul McCartney, and Peter Randolph Best (accidentally reversing Best's first and middle names) who were "desirous of performing as a group of musicians to be known as 'The Beatles'". An interesting additional clause specified that "the manager may at any time, if he so desires, split up the Artistes with whom this Agreement is made so that they shall perform as separate individual performers". (TuneIn) This would have ramifications for Pete Best in the future.

Harris drew up the contract, leaving it with Brian to mull it over during the Christmas break. It wouldn't be ready by the Decca audition on 1st January. Brian would take a red pen to the draft, and in so doing, create a new contract that everyone but Brian would sign, and leave more questions than it answered; it certainly wouldn't be legally binding.

In the meantime, at Brian's behest, Decca was sending their A&R man to Liverpool.

Machiavelli

The term "Machiavellian" is derived from a book called The Prince by Niccolo Machiavelli (1469-1527), a political philosopher and author. He wrote: "A wise ruler ought never to keep faith when by doing so it would be against his interests" and "A prince never lacks good reasons to break his promise." To be likened to Machiavelli is to hold traits like honesty to be expendable if deceit, treachery, and force would be more expedient.

What he argues is that people in positions of power should choose to be "Machiavellian", even if that is not their natural leadership style. In psychology, to be Machiavellian is to be a master manipulator, and most successful leaders, whether political or other, will demonstrate some traits of a "Machiavellian" personality on their way to the top.

THE BEATLES' PARTNERSHIP AGREEMENT

While Brian had decided to get a formal management contract drawn up, it seems that The Beatles themselves decided to take legal advice, though not to discuss the contract, but to make their partnership as a group of musicians a legal entity. Eric Goldrein, Senior Partner at Silverman Livermore, the firm where Brian's solicitor David Harris also worked, received a visit from John, Paul, George and Pete, probably in December 1961. Because David Harris was already helping Brian with his management contract, the four Beatles were advised by Harris to seek out their own independent legal advice, so they decided it would be to their advantage to employ the same firm of solicitors, though they dealt with a different solicitor to avoid a conflict of interest.

"These four lads came to my office wanting a Partnership Agreement for their group," recalled Eric. "I remember thinking at the time; 'what a stupid name for a band: The Beatles', and spelled like that, too. And what a scruffy bunch of lads they were! Of course, they weren't famous then. There was nothing remarkable about them." *(David Bedford Interview 2015)* The Beatles visited Eric's Silverman Livermore office, which at the time was at 159, Dale Street, Liverpool, opposite the Mersey Tunnel entrance.

"They were just ordinary customers, and I never thought they'd achieve anything," Eric continued. "There was nothing to make you think they would be worldwide stars, just ordinary Liverpool lads." Eric didn't realise at the time that The Beatles' manager was also dealing with the firm. "David Harris was a junior partner at the time and he was articled to me." But since these were just straightforward cases, there was no reason for it to come up in conversation. For Eric, it was just all good clean fun.

These "scruffy Beatles wanted a partnership agreement", which was quite simple to prepare. "I took a draft partnership agreement from the Encyclopaedia of Forms and Precedents, which is a standard Partnership Agreement, and I would have simply added their names and addresses, and maybe a paragraph about them." All it took was a bit of editing, checking the relevant clauses. "All you have to do is put the names and addresses in and then get them to sign it," he said. "There was nothing special about it. The partnership agreement was probably about six or seven pages long. All they had to do was sign it once over the postage stamp. I doubtless witnessed it." *(David Bedford Interview 2015)*

The agreement was between The Beatles themselves as partners. "They needed a legal partnership, and they wanted some form of agreement, so I took the basic one and put in their names and it was typed out. Didn't think any more of it. Just another contract." Obviously, at the time, Eric didn't realise that he would be part of Beatles history, and hasn't told his story until now.

According to Eric: "Partnership agreements are similar whether you're a group of musicians, or doctors or whatever, it's a standard document. There are different paragraphs for different things, relevant to their trade. You don't start from scratch, you just take the template and give it to the girl to type." Eric met the four Beatles maybe only once or twice while he put the agreement together. "When the agreement was ready, they came to my office and all signed it."

Of course, this contract would have implications for the new partners when one of them became surplus to requirements the following summer.

The agreement shows conclusively that at the end of 1961, John, Paul and George

Eric, centre, who drew up The Beatles' partnership agreement

were happy to commit their group's future to their partnership with Pete Best, contrary to what many had thought. Legal advice would have told The Beatles that, as David Harris observed, a legal partnership already existed between them as they were working together as a group. But for Lennon, McCartney, Harrison and Best, this was not enough; they wanted to commit to a formal, legally-prepared, partnership agreement.

What does a typical partnership agreement seek to clarify?

- That the agreement is between the signed partners, in this case John, Paul, George and Pete.
- Their business and how it was conducted, i.e. as performing musicians
- Financial arrangements, e.g. How profits would be shared which, in the case of The Beatles, was equally.
- Bank accounts and accountant
- Obligations to each other
- Management and decisions
- Any restrictions on other activities
- How a partnership could be terminated

Being so closely tied to each other, getting rid of an "unwanted" partner was not easy, whether they had a legal agreement in writing or not. "To dissolve the partnership, if one leaves," observed Eric, "then there is a simple form for them to complete, which you get typed up and ask the partner who is leaving to sign and that is it. Routine stuff. Only the other partners could get rid of another partner. If any partner leaves, the agreement is broken and they could sue for breach of contract. There would have to be a new partnership agreement with the new partner, in this case, the drummer." *(David Bedford Interview 2015)*

Asked about it in 2016, some 55 years later, Pete Best couldn't remember signing a partnership agreement. This doesn't affect the legal status of the partnership; even without a signed agreement, the four Beatles were still partners, at least in the eyes of the law.

The Evidence?

Unfortunately, apart from Eric's testimony, we have no evidence to support it as no copies of this agreement have survived office relocations, even though Eric has tried to find it in the archives. Back then, it simply wasn't considered important enough to preserve. Is he a reliable eyewitness? As a World War 2 hero, a law graduate of Cambridge University, retired barrister and former Lord Mayor of Hale, near Speke, he is a reliable eyewitness. There is no reason for Eric to have made this up. He has never sought publicity nor felt he had anything to gain from revealing this story.

Eric's time with the pre-Fab Beatles was short-lived, as he left the firm to become a barrister in June 1962, just before the lineup of The Beatles, and the configuration of this historic partnership, changed.

"They needed a legal partnership, and they wanted some form of agreement, so I took the basic one and put in their names and it was typed out.

"Operation Big Beat I" (last Friday, Nov. 10th) was such a phenomenal success, that by public demand we now present

"OPERATION BIG BEAT II"

at the **TOWER BALLROOM,**
NEW BRIGHTON

on **FRIDAY, 24th NOVEMBER 1961**
7-30 p.m. to 2-00 a.m.

THE "BIGGEST BEAT" LINE UP EVER

The Beatles — Rory Storm and The Hurricanes
Gerry and The Pacemakers — The Remo Four
Earl Preston and the Tempest Tornadoes
Faron and The Flamingoes

Three Licensed Bars (until 12-45 a.m.) **Buffet**

TICKET 6/-

TRANSPORT ARRANGEMENTS:-
Excursions (to Tower and Return) from St. John's Lane,
(Lime Street) 7-0 p.m. to 9-0 p.m. Friday 24th November
(*Ring Crown Coachways CENtral 6107*)
ALSO LATE TRANSPORT
From Tower Ballroom to the following:-
To LIVERPOOL *Circular Trip to All Areas.*
To WIRRAL, *Wallasey, Seacombe, Birkenhead, Hoylake,*
W. Kirby, Leasowe, Moreton, Heswall, Bidston,
Ellesmere Port, ETC.

Operation 'Big Beat', run by promoter Sam Leach

9th December 1961

TERRY McCANN: ALDERSHOT TO PIECES

On 24th November 1961, after "Operation Big Beat 2", Sam Leach had a meal with John and Paul in Joe's Cafe, on Duke Street, and told them how he wanted to help them. "I said, 'I'm going to go to London and have all the agents come and see you'. At the time I had a gig lined up in East London at Leyton Swimming Baths," which had a dance floor covered a swimming pool, "so I said, 'I'll put you on there and promote you, but I want to be your manager. John said, 'OK, let's shake hands on that', so I shook hands with John, and shook hands with Paul.

"On the Monday after the handshake with John and Paul, George came down on his own, because he was working, and he didn't just shake my hand, he grabbed both hands over mine and said, 'you're sure we can do this? If anyone can do it, it's you.' Then Pete came down later and we shook hands. 'I hope you make it for us, Sam', but obviously he still wanted his mother still to be the manager.

"Then I found out that next weekend that my friend Terry McCann couldn't get Leyton Baths, because they had a swimming gala on the Friday before, and they couldn't get it ready in time for the next day. But he said, 'I've got you a place in Aldershot, just 30 miles away from London, through a mate of mine'. So I had no choice, because I had already secured the dates; I knew it was a bit of a race."

Was Aldershot a poor choice? It may not be as well-known as some other places in London, but if you lived within the city's commuter belt, you could be in the capital in less than an hour. Aldershot had a population of over 36,000, and a local area of nearly a quarter of a million people. It also had a lively music scene and, as the home of the British Army, many off-duty soldiers looking for entertainment.

If Sam Leach wanted to take The Beatles to a place that Brian Epstein wouldn't know – one that would be out of his clutches – then he miscalculated. In 1952, Brian had begun his National Service in the army in Aldershot.

But Aldershot it was, and Sam set off with big plans. "On the Saturday, I went with Dave Johnson, my driver, and hired a car. It was a Ford Classic in blue, with white-walled tyres and a white roof. It was the best-looking car in Liverpool at the time. I told The Beatles I'd see them on the Monday before going to London. I was doing it to show the car off, to show them I meant business. I remember Paul, John and Gerry (Marsden) wanted to drive around, so Dave drove them around town trying to chat up the girls!

"When they came back, Gerry said, 'can I have a word with you Sam? How come we did a record with you, but you're going to manage The Beatles?' I said it's The Beatles first, and then you, because they're more likely to do it right now. Okay? He said 'fair enough'. There was no handshake. I'd already told Kingsize the same thing. Ann Barton, a friend of Cilla, said to me, 'The trouble is that we won't see The Beatles again if you take them to London'. And I said. 'I will run coach trips like I used to do for The Blue Diamonds, so that was alright. Everyone knew about me taking them to London - that's what a manager does." Sam felt he had shown The Beatles that he could be their manager. All he had to do was make the Aldershot gig a success.

One of Sam's closest friends and allies was Terry McCann, who acted as bouncer, driver and, at Aldershot on 9th December 1961, drummer with The Beatles. According to McCann: "I started working for Sam after going to

Samson and Barlow's one night. I went up the stairs and there was Sam being threatened by these two men, and one of them had Sam by the throat. Well, crash, bang, wallop and one of them tumbled down the stairs, so Sam offered me the job as a bodyguard." *(David Bedford Interview 2015)* It was through his contacts that Terry arranged the gig at Aldershot's Palais Ballroom for Sam and The Beatles. Sam needed it to work out well but, as history has recorded, it was anything but a success.

The Palais Ballroom, Aldershot

The Beatles' Aldershot disaster is the stuff of legend. The Palais Ballroom was situated on the corner of Queens Road and Perowne Street. The original venue had burned down and a new building was erected on the site. Sam Leach had billed the event as a "Battle of the Bands":

Terry McCann (bottom left) Original painting by Paul Skellett

Liverpool V London

Liverpool's No. "1" Rock Outfit

Direct From Their German Tour

The Beatles

Versus

One of London's Top "Beat" Groups

Ivor Jay & the Jaywalkers

Plus Two Other Star Groups

Although two other bands were also billed to appear, this was a bit of advertising bluff as no groups other than the two headliners had been booked. Featuring a bar and a buffet, entrance was only five shillings. It all sounded so good.

Unfortunately, as history records, only around 18 people turned up to see The Beatles. Not even The Jaywalkers showed. According to Sam, "If you believe everyone who said they were there for The Beatles, we would have had 500 people!" The failure has been blamed on Sam's "bad cheque" not clearing with the newspaper which led to the lack of advertising, but Sam denies that. There was no problem with the cheque, other than Sam being a new customer, so the newspaper didn't run the advert.

A new twist in the story occurred in 2013. Sam explained: "Alan Hope from Screaming Lord Sutch's band told me that they had a gig the same night near ours in Aldershot, and they played regularly in the same venue we were playing in. So he went round tearing my posters down, and rang the local paper and said the gig had been cancelled. That's why the other band didn't turn up. He was boasting to my mate Terry McCann, and I saw him here recently, and he admitted it to me in front of my cousin; then of course he tried to backtrack."

Terry concurred that there was a deliberate attempt to sabotage the performance. "Sam went out and found that the posters I had put up a few days before had been torn down. They unloaded the equipment, and set up the gear, waiting for the crowds to flock through the doors. And they waited, and waited. Sam Leach's answer was to head over the road to the pub and invited people to come over. He brought them bottles of beer that can be seen in Dick Matthews' historic photographs. Leach also stopped people in the streets to come in and see what was happening, to try and make the numbers up. It didn't work."

To add to the merriment, Terry McCann had a brief stint as the Fourth Beatle. "Terry got up and played drums," recalled Sam. "It might have been in the interval, because The Beatles played for three hours with only a quarter-of-an-hour break, and they were all messing around." *(David Bedford Interview 2015)*

McCann laughed when he started retelling the stories surrounding that famous event. "That was a debacle," he exclaimed. "We left Liverpool at 6am, and of course there were no motorways back then. We went through a small village on way down, and saw a traditional tea room with the 'old dears' (old people) in there. We went in, the lads in their leather jackets and jeans, and we got chased out! But John had a pin on him, so he scratched 'The Beatles were here. John.' That could be worth a few bob if that was still there!"

Shall We Dance?

Pete Best, like the other Beatles, remembered the night with some fondness due to the fun they had: "Halfway through one number, George and Paul put on their overcoats and took to the floor to dance a foxtrot together, while the rest of us struggled along, making enough music for them and the handful of spectators. We clowned our way through the whole of the second half. John and Paul deliberately played wrong chords and notes and added words to the songs that were never in the original lyrics." *(Beatle! The Pete Best Story)*

But then Pete decided it was time to sing, which meant they needed a drummer. Usually this was Paul, but not on this occasion. Terry McCann had very clear memories of the night: "Everything had gone stupidly wrong, but the lads did their usual stuff. Anyway, Pete Best had got up to sing a couple of songs, so I got on the drums and played for a couple of numbers and we just messed about a bit. That was a night to remember. I can't remember what songs we did, just the usual chart songs from the set."

This wasn't the first time that Terry had sat in as a drummer, though he never considered himself a drummer or played in a group. "I lived in the Isle Of Man with my auntie when I was evacuated," Terry said. "I got stuck in the Scout Cubs, and they had a full kit there, so I played drums. When I was in the army, I used to box for the Battalion. Upstairs, over the gym, was where the band practiced, so I was shown how to play drums; four to the bar with the right hand, one with the left, and so I used to go up and play there.

"I knew how to keep a simple beat, but I wouldn't class myself as a drummer. When the drums were set up and the place was empty, I would get behind the kit and have a good old bash. I could do a great solo and could give it some stick when I was on my own! I played at a couple of weddings, but never regularly in a group. I got the nod to sit in for the odd 20 minutes or something, like with Rory Storm and the Hurricanes. I played at the Tower Ballroom when Ringo was the drummer. His girlfriend was there and he fancied a break, so I jumped up and

drummed for around 20 minutes or so to give him a break."

After the gig and Terry's brief appearance as The Beatles' drummer, there was a football match with ping-pong balls. "Lennon kept kicking me," said Sam, "and I was on his side! One girl said to me 'I've never seen a band like this before'. I think word got out for the next week."

The Crowd

There were a few locals who turned up and were less than impressed. Irene Stoker was a regular at The Palais in those days, but didn't stay for long that night. "It was probably quite early and there weren't many people there," she recalled. "The Beatles were sort of strumming on their guitars. They were on the edge of the stage and one of them even got off at one point. One of them called The Palais a village hall and we said it's not a village hall and that we had some good groups up here. We stayed for two or three dances, but got fed up with them and left. We didn't think they were very good. I just thought they were showing off. So we went to the nearby Havelock pub for a drink and then on to the Central Club and ended up having a good night."

That was the last she expected to ever hear of The Beatles, but of course they would soon appear in the national and international media. "The next time I heard about The Beatles was when I saw a magazine or newspaper article about them," she said. "I suppose it must have been 1963. At first I thought it can't be that group that played up The Palais, but I recognised them from the picture." She did notice that there had been some changes from the group that had played at the Palais. "Paul McCartney had hardly changed," she observed. "I remember thinking, well they won't last very long!" Obviously not a good judge, because she walked out of the concert in Aldershot, and then wrote them off in 1963. However, at least, along with only a few people, she could claim to have been there. "It's a funny thing, whenever I've told people that I saw The Beatles play in Aldershot before they were famous, they have always looked at me as if to say The Beatles wouldn't have played here." They did, but maybe they shouldn't have played there. *(Get Hampshire 9th December 2016)*

The Last Throw

But Lennon wasn't finished and wanted to leave his mark on Aldershot. Sam recalled: "John was going to throw a brick through the window and I stopped him, and I said, 'I'll do it', and took the brick off him, but then Paul stopped me from throwing it!" By anyone's standards, it was a disaster and they were rightly frustrated. However, as a testament to their professional attitude, The Beatles played their whole set and entertained the few people who had turned up.

The Blue Gardenia?

Terry McCann had made friends in London, one being Liverpool star Brian "Cass" Casser (also known as Casey Jones), who now lived in the capital city. "We went on to see Cass," said Terry, "and I got us all some fish and chips from a van, then we went to Casser's club." Casser, who had left Liverpool under a cloud of "woman troubles", had started running rock 'n' roll nights at the Blue Gardenia club, which became the All-Nighter after midnight. Although it has been claimed that all of The Beatles got up on stage that night, Terry remembers it clearly: "George was the only one who got up and jammed that night, because he was a talented guitarist who could play with anyone."

After a long night, it was time to head back to Liverpool. "Sam had hired this car with a driver, and I had the rented van," recalled Terry. "John and Paul sat up front with me, with George in the back and poor Pete on the floor of the van! Then we ran out of petrol; it sort of 'filled up again on its own' at 3 o'clock in the morning!" It wasn't quite a miracle, though, as Terry explained. "In the old petrol pumps, there was a little round piece of tin with one screw in it at the front of the pump. If the electrics went wrong, you could loosen the screw, and then, using the winding handle from car, you could manually get the petrol. So John Lennon got the handle and we filled the van again. I said that I had a fiver left and put it through the door; at least that is how I tell it!" It was an eventful day. *(David Bedford Interview 2015)*

Sam - Beatles Manager?

Sam knew he had blown his chances. He recalled: "On the way back to Liverpool after the gig, The Beatles decided they wouldn't go with me and go with Eppy. They asked to see me on the Tuesday in the Grapes, and when I walked in, John looked sheepish and I gave them the money I owed them. That trip cost me £500 with the van, car and all wages! John spoke up: 'I know we have a handshake with you Sam, but we've got a chance to be signed by a millionaire', and Paul said 'a millionaire Sam!' John said, 'Will you go and have a word with him and tell us what you think of him. And we will listen to what you say'.

"I went to see Epstein the next day and had a chat and he had the money, he had the shop and I think he would make it for them. On the walk back to the Grapes, I thought, 'why should I tell the truth because I'll lose them? First time I saw them and I booked them, I told them they were going to be as big as Elvis. John said, 'Oh he's a nutter!' and Paul said, 'But you've bookings for us, haven't you, Mr. Leach?' I was going to lie to them, but then I looked at them and had to tell them the truth. I said, 'I think he will be good for you and you will make it with him. Remember me when you're famous'." *(David Bedford Interview 2015)*

What did Terry think about Sam or Brian for manager of The Beatles? The first time Terry met Brian Epstein was on 24th November 1961, and it didn't go well. "Sam had booked Emile Ford for the Tower Ballroom," recalled Terry, "and then afterwards he arranged a party at the Iron Door. It was filled with young lads and girls, and then there was a smartly-dressed chap with a navy coat and blue polka dot scarf, who was looking especially at Pete Best in his leather trousers. He was sweating there in his posh clothes, really standing out from the crowd, so I threw him out! After all, why was an older man standing there looking at these young men in leather!

"Eppy turned up at the right time, and he was perfect for them. He was from a well-known family in Liverpool. Sam couldn't have agreed a contract with them as they were under 21 so he would have needed to see the families, and only Brian could have done that and got the families on board." Terry should know. He grew up very close to Cilla Black and her family, and was best friends with her brother George. For the first six months of her fledgling career, Terry acted as manager, driving her to the clubs and promising her mother to keep her daughter safe. He drew up a contract to manage her. "Cilla's father, 'Shiner', would never

have signed it with me. I was just a friend of the family, whereas Epstein had the respect and financial backing from a well-respected family in Liverpool."

Having deputised for both Ringo Starr and Pete Best, how did Terry rate the two drummers? "Pete Best wasn't a patch on Ringo. The Beatles used Pete, as his family had the Casbah club and they stored the gear and gave them somewhere to play. He had the money. Pete wasn't a bad drummer – he was alright – and got by when they needed him. But Ringo, for me, was a better drummer."

(David Bedford Interview 2015)

Aldershot, Again

This wouldn't be the last time Sam took a band to Aldershot. As he recalled: "I booked the ballroom for three weeks, so the next week Rory Storm with Ringo went down and played. I was due to go but I decided to stay and take Joan (my future wife) out the following day as it was my birthday. Two weeks later I asked her to marry me!

"Rory had 300 people there that night, because word had got out about The Beatles' performance the week before and how good they were. Nobody had seen anything like them before. But obviously the ones who were there enjoyed it and told everyone else.

"The advert ran the following week as planned. It hadn't been run before because of the phone call to say it was cancelled, but that wasn't me. The paper said there was a problem with the cheque to cover their backs because they had cancelled it by phone, which they shouldn't have done. There wasn't a problem with the cheque, because they never tried to cash it. It was fine the week after. If it had been a bounced cheque, they wouldn't have allowed me to put the advert in the second week.

"The third week would have been for Gerry. Terry McCann brought back a load of money from the Rory gig, but I couldn't be bothered doing a third one all that way down there." *(David Bedford Interview 2015)*

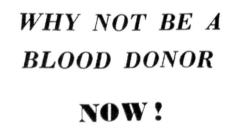

WHY NOT BE A BLOOD DONOR NOW!

10th December 1961. Hambleton Hall

With his dream of managing The Beatles in tatters, Sam Leach and his tired entourage returned to Liverpool. Heading home to their beds, they slept well into the afternoon of Sunday 10th December before meeting up again to play at Hambleton Hall in Huyton on the eastern edge of Liverpool. Still hung over, they arrived so late for the gig, they missed their allotted slot, which went down badly with everyone there, including Brian Epstein, who was by now a dedicated Beatle groupie.

Brian was visibly rattled by their late arrival. It wasn't what he expected of a group who wanted to get to the top and he said so without holding back, perhaps because the word had got out; Aldershot was a flop, Sam was out in the cold, and they'd had *A Hard Day's Night*. No sympathy there, then!

The late, late show may have been bad timing for them but it was a blessing in disguise for Brian because their recent bad run of events had effectively cleared the way for him to make his big move. He'd made his opening gambit at two earlier meetings with The Beatles but things hadn't been made final and it was this uncertainty that had allowed Sam Leach enough time to make his bid with Aldershot. Now fate had intervened. Not only that, but in the intervening period Brian had been given a winning ace to put on the table – the prospect of an audition!

HILLMAN MINX DE LUXE SALOON

Styled and built for years of up-to-date ownership! The Hillman Minx gives you economy hand-in-glove with exciting performance— together with 'see-everything' visibility ... big brakes ... and unshakeable stability—for your greater safety on today's roads.

12th December 1961. The Grapes of Wrath

As you might expect, the show had to go on for Sam Leach, too. For him and for The Beatles it was now a case of one door closing and another door opening up. "They asked to see me on the Tuesday in the Grapes, and when I walked in, John looked sheepish and I gave them the money I owed them. Then John spoke up; 'I know we have a handshake with you Sam, but we've got a chance to be signed by a millionaire', and Paul said 'a millionaire Sam!'

"John said, 'Will you go and have a word with him and tell us what you think of him. And we will listen to what you say'. I went to see Epstein the next day and had a chat and he had the money, he had the shop and I think he would make it for them.

"On the walk back to the Grapes, I thought, why should I tell the truth because I'll lose them? First time I saw them and I booked them I told them they were going to be as big as Elvis. John said, 'Oh he's a nutter!' and Paul said, 'But you've bookings for us, haven't you, Mr. Leach?' So I was going to lie to them, but then I looked at them and had to tell them the truth. I said, 'I think he *(Epstein)* will be good for you and you will make it with him. Remember me when you're famous'."

Sam Leach's dream of taking The Beatles to London and managing them didn't work out. But within days, Brian Epstein had set up an audition at Decca Records for The Beatles and would soon be confirmed as their manager.

Paul, Pete, George and John in The Grapes

13th December 1961

LONDON COMES TO LIVERPOOL

Brian Epstein's covert tactics were devised to ensure that he would get the whole of Decca onside, despite only having been promised an audition. It worked. Decca's A & R man, Mike Smith, promptly took it upon himself to visit Liverpool on 13th December 1961 specifically to see The Beatles live on stage at the Cavern Club. It appeared that Epstein, wielding his considerable business acumen and contacts in the record industry, was producing results at last because A & R men seldom left the comfort of egocentric London in those days. For Brian Epstein, it must have felt like a visit from royalty.

When Smith arrived at the Cavern Club, it was because he was determined to be at the heart of what would happen to The Beatles. Only 26 at the time, he was one of a new breed of A & R men and, between 1963 and 1970, Smith would go on to produce six No. 1 records for acts that included Brian Poole and the Tremeloes, Georgie Fame, Marmalade, Love Affair and Christie. He also produced many other hit records, but his missing out on The Beatles would overshadow an otherwise successful legacy.

"Somebody had to show some interest in The Beatles," said Smith, "because Brian Epstein's shop, NEMS, was an important account for our sales people. I went to the Cavern and I should have trusted my instincts, as I thought they were wonderful on stage." *(Spencer Leigh, Independent, Saturday 31st December 2011)*

Smith also echoed Paul's fear that Gerry and The Pacemakers would be of more interest to Decca. "There were other groups there. I remember Gerry and The Pacemakers having done an act. But I was there for The Beatles. And I must say, they put on a fine performance. I was taken by their visual impact as well as their

sound. They all had individual approaches and certainly very different personalities. I felt they just needed a little guidance and then they could go ahead and do well." *(True Story of The Beatles)*

Smith therefore arranged for an audition in London on New Year's Day, 1962.

1961: Epstein's Toppermost of the Poppermost

In the meantime, Brian was getting to grips with the record market and hit parade. Writing in Mersey Beat at the end of 1961, he reviewed the year under the title "My Top Pops", commenting from a commercial point of view that it had been a poor year, pop-wise. "Most of the discs in the earlier part of the year were very run of the mill," he noted. Not wishing to miss the chance to give his new group a good plug, he then mentioned "three very important records" for the beginning of 1962. First came Elvis Presley's release of "Can't Help Falling In Love", which was doing well in the U.S. Then came Cliff Richard's soundtrack to his film, The Young Ones; doing well, the title track was due for release. Finally, it was to The Beatles that he turned for his third choice. "And thirdly, of great interest to Mersey beaters, the fabulous record on which The Beatles back Tony Sheridan will be issued on January 6th. This could be the big one for The Beatles whose records I look forward to seeing in the charts in 1962." *(How They Became The Beatles)*

"My Bonnie"

"The Saints" was released on Polydor in the UK on 5th January 1962. It marked the first time the name 'Beatles' had appeared on a record, at Brian's suggestion, under the name of Tony Sheridan and The Beatles. Sadly, the record did very little at all, and certainly didn't trouble the charts.

The day before, the *South Liverpool Weekly News* carried an article on the record with the headline:

THEY'RE HOPING FOR A HIT RECORD

It predicted that the local boys who had been "full-time musicians, ever since they left school" could have a successful year. "Who knows," the piece proclaimed. "It might not be long before they achieve nationwide acclaim." *(How They Became The Beatles)*

The Beatles and local fans on Merseyside were delighted, but the record failed to make a mark at all in the national charts. Despite this, it served Brian well. He may have overstocked the record, but he knew it would be worth the investment and besides, he'd registered the first big step in achieving his and The Beatles' goals by raising them up another level; the first time their name had appeared in its own right on a record. It made a good impression on their families, too, helping to allay some of their doubts about Brian as well as creating momentum and publicity at local clubs via *Mersey Beat*. Just as important, he'd sent a signal to any doubters and potential predators; he was in charge.

18th December 1961: The Unwelcome Christmas Gift

Following his meeting at EMI on 1st December 1961, Brian's common sense seemed to desert him and he started besieging Ron White's office with telephone calls, pushing for a quick response. It was a rash move that led White to make an equally hasty decision. On 18th December 1961, Brian's naive attempt to push White backfired spectacularly when he finally received a letter.

"I'm sorry that I have been so long in giving you a decision but I have now had an opportunity of playing the record to each of our Artistes Managers. Whilst we appreciate the talents of this group, we feel that we have sufficient groups of this type at the present time under contract and that it would not be advisable for us to sign any further contracts of this nature at present." *(The Complete Beatles Chronicles)*

Paramor, Ridley and Newell turned down The Beatles outright, but for some reason, Ron White clearly suggested that George Martin also heard the sampler and also declined to audition The Beatles. In stark contradiction, Martin always firmly refuted the claim, stating that he did not hear the tape. Why? Because he'd been on vacation in December! There are suggestions that Martin's absence was due to the fact that he was spending private time trying to repair a rocky marriage. Another version is that he'd taken a break to be with his secretary, Judy Lockhart-Smith. Both versions have some truth, because George's first marriage broke up and Judy became his lifelong second wife and helpmate.

He died on 9th March 2016 at the age of 90.

No matter why George Martin was absent, it still leaves the big 'White lie' unsolved. Why did Ron White imply that Martin heard The Beatles' tape and, like the other three A&R men, had turned them down, too? We will never know for sure because White has also passed on. But we suspect the real reason is very simple. After returning home to Liverpool, Epstein started pushing him with endless telephone calls to get a response. To settle the matter, White sent the letter, probably gambling that Martin's eventual response on his return in January would be the same as the other A&R men. The timing was lousy and there can't have been many jingle bells in Epstein's life when he didn't get the Christmas present he wanted from Santa Claus.

That wasn't the end of White's headache, however, because his letter boomeranged even more spectacularly in 1962 when, far from being put off by the first refusal, Brian decided to apply yet more pressure on EMI (and indirectly on George Martin) using the kind of tactics worthy of the famous political strategist, Machiavelli.

1st January 1962

THE BEATLES & DECCA RECORDS: A GUITAR GROUP WAS ON THE WAY IN

Their resume hyped three lead singers who could also deliver a perfect three-part harmony – by far the most popular, crowd-attracting local guitar band. Founded as a skiffle group by schoolmates in 1956, they were inspired by Buddy Holly and The Crickets and turned professional in 1960. What record company wouldn't want to sign a band like this? Brian Poole and The Tremeloes were exactly what Decca sought. They lived locally in London and were already known on the *Saturday Club* BBC radio show, hosted by Brian Matthew.

The *Saturday Club* was an influential BBC radio programme in Britain, first broadcast on the Light Programme and then from 1957 until 1969 on Radio 1. It was one of the only pop music radio programmes in the country, presented for most of its duration by Brian Matthew, whose shows with The Beatles in the '60s are among their finest. A meeting with Decca recording manager Mike Smith at a local coffee bar frequented by musicians led to an audition for Brian Poole and The Tremeloes and, soon after, their signing by the label.

Since The Beatles' history closely paralleled Brian Poole and The Tremeloes in many ways, the question is why Decca chose them over The Beatles. Yes, they were Londoners and known to Decca's A & R man Mike Smith, but was there more to it? Lead singer Brian Poole wore Buddy Holly-style horn-rims and a large part of their act was devoted to Buddy Holly songs. Decca knew what they were getting with The Tremeloes, whereas big question marks still surrounded The Beatles.

Were guitar groups really on the way out as Decca producer and executive Dick Rowe supposedly told Brian Epstein? Mike Smith had raved about The Beatles

when he visited the Cavern just a couple of weeks earlier, so why would Rowe not like their sound? "When Mike came back," said Rowe, "I said, 'Well, what are they like?' I wasn't excited, but I was very interested because there was a lot of underground talk about them. Mike said, 'Oh, they're great!' I said, 'Well, you better bring them down and give them an audition." *(The Beatles: An Oral History)*

Surely, if The Beatles were a three-part harmony, guitar-based group like Brian Poole and The Tremeloes, the sound was comparable, so was it simply a case of the two bands being too similar? On the surface, the answer is yes. However, when you dig a bit deeper, you can see why Dick Rowe didn't sign The Beatles which, thankfully, meant that they were paired with George Martin and not Rowe. So why has Dick Rowe been blamed for turning down The Beatles? Is the criticism justified? Was it simply a north-south divide problem? Was he biased against Liverpool artists? History shows that Rowe was responsible for the first no. 1 record by a Liverpool artist, even if it was "(How Much Is That) Doggie In The Window" by Lita Roza in March 1953. He also recorded "Halfway To Paradise" and "Jealousy", two hits by Merseyside's first rock 'n' roll star Billy Fury. The handsome singer-songwriter hailed from Liverpool. Wouldn't that work in The Beatles' favour?

So what was it? Did Dick Rowe make the decision, or did The Beatles make the decision for Dick Rowe? Put yourself in Rowe's place; whom would you have signed? As you will see, it wasn't a straight comparison between the two groups after all.

1st January 1962:
Crying, Waiting, Hoping - The Story of The Audition

Let's examine The Beatles' Decca audition in more detail, song-by-song. Bear in mind that they performed these fifteen numbers in less than an hour, probably getting only one shot at each. Mike Smith has said that he expected them to reproduce the great performance he'd seen at the Cavern, and encouraged them to "play the whole spectrum of music" he'd heard.

Even though the songs were regularly performed in their act, they weren't really representative of The Beatles' sound. Brian was keen to demonstrate their wide range of talents, both individually and as a group, and to show their musical versatility. In hindsight, it was probably a mistake. But Brian didn't impose the songs on them. As George recalled: "In those days a lot of the rock 'n' roll songs were actually old tunes from the '40s, '50s or whenever, which people had rocked up. That was the thing to do if you didn't have a tune; just rock up an oldie. Joe Brown had recorded a rock 'n' roll version of 'The Sheik of Araby'. He was really popular on the Saturday TV show Six-Five Special and *Oh Boy!* I did the Joe Brown records, so I did 'Sheik of Araby'. Paul sang 'September in the Rain'. We each chose a number we wanted to do." *(Anthology)*

Pete thought that, in hindsight, they shouldn't have allowed Brian to have as much say in the songs they performed: "It was a strange dish to set before the recording kings, with the emphasis on standards which, I remember, was mainly at Brian's insistence. Really, we were doing little that was different." *(Beatle! The Pete Best Story)* John later said that the group "should have rocked like mad in there and shown what we're like when we're roused." *(The Beatles: The Biography)*

Snow White - Liverpool Comes to London

By far the bigger mistake occurred following The Beatles' long drive down to London in blizzard conditions, some of the worst on record, with torrential rain and snow. Pete Best recounted what happened on that 31st December 1961: "Neil drove us down by van and the journey took up most of the day. In the Midlands, he lost his way in the snow, and the revellers were already about in London's West End by the time we booked into the Royal Hotel near Russell Square." That was only the beginning. "Brian Epstein read the riot act to us before we went down – you know, be good little boys, you mustn't be out after ten o'clock, you know." But rather than follow Brian's orders, The Beatles chose to ignore him. After several beers in a Charing Cross pub, they decided to usher in the New Year with the revellers in Trafalgar Square. Pete continued: "We joined in the singing of 'Auld Lang Syne', kissed a few willing lips but we didn't exactly let ourselves rip, and we didn't even dip as much as a finger into the icy waters of the fountain. At last the big time was beckoning." *(Beatle! The Pete Best Story)* Later the same night, The Beatles encountered two men who were stoned. "They had some pot," said Neil Aspinall, "but I'd never seen that. We were too green. When they heard we had a van they asked if they could smoke it there. We said, 'no, no, no'! We were dead scared." *(The Beatles Hunter Davies)*

Dead scared? Gosh! Horror! Maybe Neil (or Hunter Davies, or both) had conveniently overlooked the fact that these were the same leather clad tear-aways who'd indulged in some pretty fast living with booze and drugs just a year earlier in sin city – Hamburg!

Paul is dead?

The Audition

Morning arrived all too soon – but not that early, as Brian Epstein noted: "At 11 am…we arrived at Decca in a thin bleak wind, with snow and ice afoot," he said rather poetically, carefully omitting the detail. *(A Cellarful of Noise)*

Pete recalled Brian's wrath after he'd warned them about staying out past ten: "When we got to the Decca studios the next day, we were late. Seems to be our history, being late, and Brian of course, was there before us. He was absolutely livid. He tore a strip off us left, right and centre. John just basically turned round and said, 'Brian, shut up. We're here for the audition, right.'" *(Beatles at The BBC 2012)*

For some unexplained reason, The Beatles had taken their own amplifiers, as if they were turning up for a live gig. That was the first problem. Their cheap amps may have been passable for performing in clubs, but the hum the amplifiers emitted in the recording studio was an issue. When the hum proved far too audible to the sound engineers, they had to be changed for Decca's own studio amps. "They didn't want our tackle," said Neil. "We had to use theirs. We needn't have dragged our amps all the way from Liverpool." *(The Beatles. Hunter Davies)* True! This clearly shows how ill-prepared and ill-informed they had been. Adding more headaches to their groggy condition, they also had to cope with a huge, open, icy-cold studio. Decca had been closed for the Christmas period and, consequently, there was little or no room heat.

The boys were accustomed to close interaction in their live performances, but the recording studio was quite another story. The unfamiliar layout meant they could not communicate in the usual way. To avoid sound bleeding into other microphones from the drums, Pete was situated behind a studio 'baffle', an isolation screen. This made direct eye contact with the others almost impossible for Pete as all four struggled to keep cue off each other. Don Dorsey, an engineer who has worked at Abbey Road, explained why this would be a problem: "A recording studio environment is quite different to a live environment. In a live hall, all band members are relatively close together and all their sound output mixes in the environment – the drummer hears everything. In a recording studio, it would be customary for the drummer to be separated from the rest of the band with a large wall-like sound baffle. The purpose of baffles is to keep sounds from one player intruding too much into the microphones of the others. As a result, to hear other band members well, headphones must be used and the sound would be nothing like a live appearance." *(David Bedford Interview 2007)*

The physical separation was new to The Beatles; the setup at the Hamburg recording sessions had been completely different. They also noticed for perhaps the first time the vast difference between playing to a control booth and performing in front of a live audience. As the top group in Liverpool and Hamburg, they had learnt to "mach shau" – to "work" the audience. This time around, the chance to recreate the magic of the Cavern, which Mike Smith had enjoyed so much, was impossible. On top of everything else, they had a classic case of audition nerves which affected their delivery of even the most familiar songs. No assessment of the Decca audition can be done without taking into consideration all these factors, both external and internal.

Seeing Red –
Songs in the Key of Fraught Nerves and Temper Tantrums

Tensions had simmered from the moment The Beatles arrived, gathering even more momentum when the ever-punctual Brian became angered by the late arrival of the Decca staff. Culprit-in-chief was Mike Smith who, like the four lads, was also hung over from the night before. Brian took it personally. "Mike Smith was late and we were pretty annoyed about the delay. Not only because we were anxious to tape some songs but because we felt we were being treated as people who didn't matter." *(A Cellarful of Noise)* Here, Epstein reveals his inner insecurity by letting slip his overblown sense of grievance about being treated as someone of importance.

In reality, The Beatles were no doubt relieved that they weren't the only ones to arrive late, or the only ones to rattle Epstein's code of behaviour. Dick Rowe avoided the flack this time. The man responsible for the final decision wasn't at the session. That was left to Smith, who would report the feedback to Rowe later. In the meantime, with everyone finally in place, studio equipment was set up, levels were taken by the engineers in the control booth, and they were off. The scary red light came on, and in the silence and isolation of the Decca studio, the audition began.

Although the use of the red light was customary to let everyone know that they were ready to record, it was a distraction. "They were pretty frightened," said Neil. "Paul couldn't sing one song. He was too nervous and his voice started cracking up. They were all worried about the red light. I asked if it could be put off, but we were told people might come in if it was off. 'You what?' we said. We didn't know what all that meant." *(The Beatles. Hunter Davies)* To add to the confusion, the group knew very little about all the microphones, booms and controls. The boys were truly in uncharted territory.

They had already played some of the "rave-up" songs first as warm-up numbers before recording began. But despite this, the recording process continued to overwhelm and intimidate them while heightening their apprehensiveness. "People nipped in and changed round microphone positions and had us standing in all different places," George Harrison recalled. Commands weren't delivered in person; "shouted orders came over the inter-com bit," George continued. "As they shouted, we jumped. In the end, we decided the best bet was to remember that we were at least all together and that we could stand up to anything they chucked at us." George admitted that they were "very nervous."

Even though they knew it was one of the most important dates of their lives, they still thought they could clown around as if they were in the Cavern. According to Harrison, they even "put on heavy, thicker-than-usual Liverpool accents to try and fool the Londoners. It was a bit of a defence mechanism." *(True Story of The Beatles)* John Lennon would later say that "somehow this helped get our spirits up again." Still, despite their best efforts, they were unable to recreate the energy and atmosphere of their Liverpool and Hamburg shows. As John recalled: "Remember that we had at the back of our minds that Brian Eppie had spent a lot of time already trying to get record companies interested in us, but without having any luck. I guess that was weighing on our minds."

(True Story of The Beatles)

As if all these pressures were not bad enough, tensions soon rose to the breaking point when Epstein's sense of self-importance tripped him up once again.

Dismissing normal studio protocol, he interrupted he proceedings and immediately got into an open altercation with John Lennon. Oops! The red mist descended over Lennon faster than a rainstorm. Pete Best: "...Brian began to voice some criticism either of John's singing or his guitar playing. I'm not sure which. Lennon burst into one of his bouts of violent, uncontrollable temper, during which his face would alternate from white to red. 'You've got nothing to do with the music!' he raged. 'You go back and count your money, you Jewish git!'" The sudden chill in the studio was far icier than the weather outside. "Brian looked like he had cracked down the middle. Mike Smith, the sound engineers and the rest of us all looked at each other in amazement." *(Beatle! The Pete Best Story)*

Brian wisely walked away from the confrontation. This was likely the first time he experienced a very public tongue-lashing from the often cruel tongue of John Lennon. It wouldn't be the last, and the fact that it happened at a crucial audition at Decca studios of all places shocked everyone watching. Not the best way to sell yourself.

The final order of the songs performed at the session is not known, but by the end they had managed to record 15 numbers, all live, with little or no opportunity to correct mistakes. Time was up.

Now, decades later, we ask you to put yourself in Dick Rowe's position. After all the feedback on the day's events, having listened to the session tapes, and knowing the comparisons and options concerning Brian Poole and the Tremeloes, Rowe had to make a straightforward commercial business decision whether to sign The Beatles or not. There was no crystal ball where he could gaze into the future; nor did he have the luxury of looking back in hindsight. With that in mind, and based on the known facts, what would you have decided? Would you have signed The Beatles?

Blame it on the Drummer – A Convenient Scapegoat?

These Decca auditions have been cited over the years as proof of Pete Best's poor drumming and one of the reasons why he had to go. "Worst of all was Pete's drumming," and "At Decca, Pete had the full kit at his disposal and did little with it." *(Tune In)*. But is there any basis in this assessment?

Examining Third Party Opinions: Is Criticism Valid as Evidence?

Writing for Ultimate Classic Rock, Dave Lifton also condemns Best's drumming. "The tapes prove George Martin's assertion that Pete Best was the wrong drummer for the group. For years, Best had said he was fired in favour of Ringo Starr because the band were jealous of his success with their female fans. But after one listen, it's obvious that Best was a limited drummer with a poor sense of timekeeping." *(The Story of The Beatles' Failed Audition for Decca Records)*

"I thought Pete Best was very average, and didn't keep good time. You could pick up a better drummer in any pub in London," recalled Decca session engineer Mike Savage in a 2007 interview. *(TuneIn)*

Very average and didn't keep good time? A better drummer in any pub in London? These emotive words condemn Best as a drummer; Savage's words are savage. In context, Mike Savage was the 20-year-old junior assistant to producer Mike Smith back in 1962. "If you've got a quarter of a group being very average, that isn't good," *(Tune In)* he continued. Granted, this is a fair comment. However, an analysis of the songs will demonstrate that the whole audition was average at best. Applying the scholastic tests, the Savage quote, the first by him was given 45 years after the original session, goes against the testimony by many '60s-era Liverpool musicians who describe Pete as a very good drummer. There is also no independent corroboration of these comments, and nobody else from Decca, including Mike Smith, commented on Pete's drumming. We will examine Best's drumming ability track by track to see if Savage's assessment holds up.

For our analysis of the Decca session, we invited three drummers to listen to the audition songs, each for the first time ever.

Each participant was played the song once, and was then asked for his immediate feedback on Pete's drumming as if they were at the session:

1. "Money (That's What I Want)"

John launched into a rocking version of "Money (That's What I Want)", a 1960 hit for Barrett Strong on the Tamla label. Written by Tamla founder Berry Gordy and Janie Bradford, it became the first hit record for Gordy's Motown label, whose roster included all the great American pop-soul artists The Beatles worshipped. John seems to be almost croaking, or trying too hard to sound like a rock 'n' roller, and overdoes the vocals. Though John's voice is too raspy, Pete's atom beat is strong and Paul's solid bass-playing augments the strong drum rhythm. This song was later recorded for EMI and issued on their second LP, with The Beatles.

Pete's drumming?

Mike: "Couldn't hear Pete enough because the balance isn't too good between the instruments. Pete's timing is good and he is playing the correct rhythm for the song, using his bass and floor tom well. Nothing wrong with his drumming."

Derek and Andrew: "Very good use of the full kit. Very tight and a good tempo all the way through. Drumming is fast and at a good pace with good syncopation."

2. "Till There Was You"

The Beatles switched the mood by performing "Till There Was You", a song written by Meredith Willson for his 1957 musical play *The Music Man*, and which also appeared in the 1962 movie version. It became a hit for Anita Bryant in 1959. Paul's singing is weak and too high-pitched – a poor vocal performance. Pete's hi-hat is very tinny and repetitive, but there is no sense of rhythm from any of the guitars, the bass or the drums. Who is in charge of rhythm? Paul is also singing a bit behind the instruments, and out of time. He then tries too hard to enunciate "music" with a heavy "ckkkkk", and though he corrects it by the end, it's too late. George plays a nice guitar solo. The Beatles recorded this song for EMI and it was issued on their second LP, with The Beatles.

The Savage Young Beatles

Pete's drumming?

Mike: "The whole song is terrible. All you can hear is Pete's hi-hat. I'm not keen on the drumming here and it is just a constant tapping on the hi-hat. He could have added the toms or more of a standard cha-cha-cha, but it is not great."

Derek and Andrew: "Pete's using the hi-hat like a guide track when recording. When playing live, guitarists can't hear the bass drum so they need to follow the hi-hat and the snare. This works very well here, but he doesn't just use the hi-hat, because as he is doing that he is using the rest of the kit as well. It is very difficult to keep that going for a whole song, and on this recording it is a bit loud, but that is down to the balance engineer, which wouldn't affect it in the recording process. As they approach the big ending and Pete introduces the snare, there is a slight increase in tempo, but that is hard to notice. The others don't seem to be working well together or know what they are doing, but the drummer is laying the foundation of the song down behind them."

3. "To Know Her Is to Love Her"

"To Know Him Is to Love Him" was written by Phil Spector, inspired by words on his father's tombstone, "To Know Him Was To Love Him". It was first recorded by Spector's group, the Teddy Bears, and it went to #1 on the Billboard Hot 100 singles chart in 1958. The Beatles' version was not officially released until 1994, when it appeared on their *Live At The BBC* compilation album. The song is in 12/8 time. John's lead vocal is good, though lacking in the quality we would expect, while the backing harmonies from Paul and George are perfect. Guitars, bass and drums all work together. This is possibly one of the best tracks of the day.

Never recorded by The Beatles with EMI, the song was performed for the BBC and a version was released on *Live At The BBC*.

Pete's drumming?

Mike: "I would have added something slightly different, personally, when they go in to 'Why can't she see.......', but that is still good, and the beat is good and regular, and he makes a good transition back into 'To know, know, know her...', so I've no real criticisms."

Derek and Andrew: "The timing on the hi-hat is like a metronome, it is that good and regular. He is playing almost freestyle, playing to the song – not just sticking to a set rhythm. He emphasises the melody and song, and doesn't have a set part to play which is very creative. Maybe needs a little variation with his use of the snare and the ride cymbal."

4. "Take Good Care of My Baby"

One of the best songs in the day's repertoire, "Take Good Care of My Baby" came from the famous songwriting team of Carole King and Gerry Goffin. Bobby Vee's hit version was released in America July 1961 and by September, it had reached #1 on the Billboard Hot 100. In The Beatles' version, George's vocal is superb, with John and Paul harmonising with him brilliantly; the group sounds tight.

Not recorded by The Beatles for EMI, the song was performed for the BBC and appeared on *Live At The BBC*.

Pete's drumming?

Mike: "Clean and clear sound, Pete's rhythm is the right one and nicely in time. Good performance."

Derek and Andrew: "The drumming is very tight, and has a good, consistent tempo. He uses a simpler pattern and rhythm, appropriate for the song. He stops perfectly in time with the rest of the group; the whole group performs this song perfectly. The drumming is holding the group together, and leading from the back. He is very inventive, using a different rhythm for each song, whereas most drummers would just do the same for each song."

5. "Memphis, Tennessee"

A good rocker, "Memphis, Tennessee" was composed by one of The Beatles' favourite songwriters, Chuck Berry, who released it in 1959. It is sometimes shortened to "Memphis". In the UK, the song charted at #6 in 1963 at the same time Decca Records issued a cover version by Dave Berry and the Cruisers, which also became a UK Top 20 single. Chuck Berry later composed a sequel, "Little Marie", which appeared in 1964 as a single and on the album St. Louis to Liverpool. Even The Beatles' idol acknowledged the importance of Liverpool to the music scene – and in the same year the lads conquered America.

This is easily John's best vocal performance. When he is not trying too hard, his great rock 'n' roll voice comes across really well, even if he gets a little lost in the middle. Nice chunky rhythm from Paul's bass, Pete's atom beat drums and John and George's guitars. Nice performance of the song in harmony with the original. George's solo comes in a bit quick, but still sounds good.
Another of the songs that first appeared on the *Live At The BBC* album.

Pete's drumming?

Mike: "That's nice, and you can just about hear it, but with the balance and production you can hear that driving beat. We used to do that one years ago, too, and that sounded good." Derek and Andrew: "He uses the floor tom all the way through which is very difficult to do, and very inventive. It fits the song perfectly, and his drumming really stands out. Very tight again and sounds good."

6. "Sure to Fall (In Love with You)"

"Sure to Fall (in Love with You)" was a 1955 song written by another of The Beatles' musical heroes, Carl Perkins, with joint credit alongside Bill Cantrell and Quinton Claunch. It was recorded for Sun Records by Perkins in December 1955 and was planned for release as the follow-up to "Blue Suede Shoes". However, the record wasn't released as a single by Sun, but appeared on the 1957 Sun LP *Dance Album of Carl Perkins*, re-released as *Teen Beat: The Best of Carl Perkins* in 1961. This album was also issued in the UK on London Records and this is where The Beatles heard the song.

As they perform a country song, Paul puts on a phoney American accent, supported by John and George, especially on the word "thang", imitating Elvis and/or Carl Perkins. The boys' attempt to adopt an American accent sounds terrible and too corny. Musically it works quite well, and George's solo is nice.

This song also remained unreleased by The Beatles until the *Live At The BBC* LP came out.

Pete's drumming?

Mike: "It sounded very tinny and overpowering on the hi-hat, and it was a boring song, which puts you off, too. The rhythm is right and regular, but I wouldn't have used the hi-hat as much. Too many beats on the cymbal to the bar. The song is horrible. It would have been better at a different tempo, maybe slower and too rushed. That could have sounded better."

Derek and Andrew: "This is lead drumming, driving the song from the front and excellent use of the full kit, with his use of the ride cymbal at the right time. He also uses what seems to be his signature move, his drum rolls, which are technically very good, precise and leading the rhythm section through the song. Pete seems to be showing them up. Again, great variety of drum patterns he plays."

7. "Crying, Waiting, Hoping"

There had to be a Buddy Holly composition included, and they chose "Crying, Waiting, Hoping" a song released in 1959 as the B-side to "Peggy Sue Got Married". There are actually three versions of Holly's song: the 1959 release, the 1964 reissue with different orchestration, and Holly's original home recording.

The Beatles' Decca version featured George Harrison on lead vocal whilst replicating studio guitarist Donald Arnone's instrumental bridge note for note. Everything about the song is great. George's vocal is once again the pick of the session, and the balance of the group's rhythm is very good.

The number was never an official EMI release by The Beatles, until it appeared on *Live At The BBC*.

Pete's drumming?

Mike: "Nice rhythm, good drum rolls at the right place, and variation in the chorus, too. A good performance and sounded great."
Derek and Andrew: "Again, Pete's drum rolls are excellent.
More variety in his choice of rhythm, with good variation on the snare drum. He is playing a standard 4/4 time signature but with a samba variation.

This is where he is listening to the group and playing the song well.
It is inventive and precise, with perfect patterns. Stunning performance by Pete, and this is probably the best the whole group has sounded together.
They all know what they are doing."

8. "Love of the Loved"

"Love of the Loved" was an original song, written mainly by Paul McCartney. It is one of his earliest compositions and was a mainstay in The Beatles' early live act, but never issued on any of their official releases. Instead, they gave it to Cilla Black as her debut single, produced by George Martin. It only reached #35 on the UK singles chart. For reasons unknown, The Beatles' audition version was left off *Anthology 1*, even though "Hello Little Girl" and "Like Dreamers Do" were included.

Paul's vocal is nervous and shaky and hits another heavy "ckkk" in singing "look", but he gets more confident as the song progresses and the boys sound good together. Any producer should have recognised a good song with hit potential, and realised Paul was nervous.

The only version of this song ever released is the one from the Decca session.

Pete's drumming?

Mike: "As it goes into the chorus, Pete stops in the right place, but maybe could have varied the beat a bit. But he was still in perfect timing and sounded good."

Derek and Andrew: "Pete's hi-hat is again like a metronome. They all start and stop exactly at the right time, and you can imagine the emphasis when playing live when they all come to a halt, and the snare goes "boom". He varies nicely between verse and chorus, dropping back in perfectly at each occasion very naturally. This has the sound of some of the early Motown and Soul drummers, who were trying to do something different, and Pete is using that and developing his own sound on top of it."

9. "September in the Rain"

One of the strangest choices for the day was "September in the Rain", a song by Harry Warren and Al Dubin, published as far back as 1937. The song was introduced by James Melton in the film *Melody for Two*.

Not a good song choice and they don't sound good together. Paul's jitters once again show in his vocal, and he is trying too hard to get it right. His phoney American accent doesn't help. In retrospect, the song shouldn't have been in the list. It might be good fun in the Cavern, but not in a studio.

The Decca version is thankfully the only recording of this song by The Beatles.

Pete's drumming?

Mike: "It's a nice song, but the arrangement is wrong. The vocalist (Paul) is too harsh and sounding like a Sergeant Major shouting at his troops. You have to feel the song, and I don't think any of them get it right. You can't blame the drummer, but it was all too harsh. Pete's drumming was ruled by the fact that he was following the shouting of the vocalist and was going along with that. If they had a smoother feel to the song, it could have been better, but Pete played the appropriate rhythm for the song, and in time."

Derek and Andrew: "He is using a shuffle/swing rhythm reminiscent of the jazz era, keeping the solid backbeat going, playing right up to the stops, then working up to the bluesy ending together. His timing is perfect, and this is not overplayed. He obviously knows a variety of music and styles and is confident to try using a variety of rhythms depending on the song."

10. "Bésame Mucho"

One of the favourites from The Beatles' live performances, "Bésame Mucho (Kiss Me Generously)" was a song written in 1940 by Consuelo Velázquez, a then-15-year-old Mexican songwriter. Written in the "bolero" style, it was recognized in 1999 as the most sung and recorded Mexican and Latin American song in the world. The song was inducted into the Latin Grammy Hall of Fame in 2001. The English-language version of the song was written by Sunny Skylar, and the lyrics are different from the direct English translation of the original, but retain the Spanish "Bésame Mucho". The song is also known by translated names such as "Kiss Me Much", "Kiss Me a Lot", "Kiss Me Again and Again", "Embrasse-moi fort", "Stale Ma Bozkavaj", "Suutele minua", "Szeretlek én" and "Mara beboos".

Paul McCartney is still not vocally confident, and he is probably holding back, but the group sounds good. Pete provides a good samba beat and Paul's bass works well with the drums, supported by solid rhythm guitars and good fun, evidenced by their "cha-cha-booms". The song shows they can entertain.

One of The Beatles' favourite songs, they also included it in the EMI audition in June 1962, and it is available on *Anthology 1*.

Pete's drumming?

Mike: "You can't hear the drums very well, which is down to the balance. Sounded good in the background, using bass drum and floor tom. That was fine, no problem."

Derek and Andrew: "You can tell that the drums have been moved further away from the microphones as they seem quieter here. You can hear his use of the floor tom and bass drum driving this song, and then he changes the emphasis in the chorus in the right place. His timing is perfect, and his drumming is perfect for the song."

11. "Searchin'"

"Searchin'" was on of two songs of the Decca audition written by the legendary songwriters Jerry Leiber and Mike Stoller. It was composed specifically for The Coasters and released as a single on Atco Records in March 1957. It topped the Rhythm and Blues Chart for twelve weeks, and also reached #3 on the national pop singles chart. "Searchin'" and its B-side, "Young Blood", triggered The Coasters' fame in the realm of rock 'n' roll.

Paul chose "Searchin'" as one of his *Desert Island Discs* in 1982. It was one of The Beatles' favourite songs by one of their favourite groups, and it shows. It features a solid vocal performance – possibly Paul's best of the day. John and George chipping in with the lyrics "searchin'" and "gonna find her" complement Paul's lead vocal. John's high-pitched "warble" even works well here. George provides a slightly clunky guitar solo but sounds good. We even get a glimpse of Paul's "whooo", which would become a vocal hallmark of "She Loves You".

The only recording of this song was from the Decca audition.

Pete's drumming?

Mike: "The drumming was good, and nice variation, too right for the song. Good tempo and rhythm."

Derek and Andrew: "His drum rolls again are perfect and he plays a good constant rhythm, good tempo – the right tempo – and he is again driving the song. Ideal drumming."

12. "Like Dreamers Do"

"Like Dreamers Do" was a song written by Paul McCartney in 1959. One of the earliest written songs credited to Lennon–McCartney, Paul has commented that he was not fond of it and considered it a throwaway. "I think the first original song we ever did was a really bad one of mine called 'Like Dreamers Do'". *(Anthology)* Whilst this was a bold move for the group – showcasing their songwriting talents – it may have been the wrong Lennon-McCartney song to perform. The guitars and drums serve the group well, but Paul's voice sounds unconvincing, especially when it goes high. The song has potential, but only for another artist.

"Like Dreamers Do" was never recorded by The Beatles with EMI, but it was recorded by The Applejacks in 1964, ironically produced by Decca's Mike Smith. The Beatles' version wasn't officially released until *Anthology 1*.

Pete's drumming?

Mike: "Pete did very well on that. Good use of the snare, and plenty of variety, in line with the singer, and didn't try to put too much in, like some drummers do."

Derek and Andrew: "Excellent drumming. It is quite a basic song for the guitars and vocals, so he uses a nice variety of styles and rhythms in the song to make it more interesting. You can tell it is Pete drumming, and he is using a standard 4/4 time signature, but then adding a beat on the snare drum on the offbeat between the 2nd and 3rd beat in the bar. It is almost too much, and too good for the studio, but live would be ideal. Technically very good, but maybe need to be simplified for the studio, but they were only used to playing live, so that is where a producer could advise them."

13. "The Sheik of Araby"

As if to show their "fun" side, the boys performed "The Sheik of Araby", a song written in 1921 by Harry B. Smith and Francis Wheeler, with music by Ted Snyder. It was composed in response to the popularity of the Rudolph Valentino feature film The Sheik. "The Sheik of Araby" was a Tin Pan Alley hit that also became a jazz standard after being adopted by early jazz bands, especially in New Orleans. It was a well-recognized part of popular culture. The "Araby" in the title refers to Arabia or the Arabian Peninsula.

The Beatles play the song well, and George's vocal again is good. But the overall song is played just for fun, with comical vocals from the others. Whilst it would be great performed live, it's not appropriate for a rock 'n' roll or pop group that wants to be taken seriously. This version was released on *Anthology 1*.

Pete's drumming?

Mike: "I think Pete did well on that, and his stop-start was spot on. I like that, though not the song."

Derek and Andrew: "Although a silly song, Pete uses drum rolls, his floor tom and hi-hat with good speed and timing."

14. "Three Cool Cats"

"Three Cool Cats" was a 1958 song written by Leiber and Stoller. It was originally recorded by The Coasters and released as the B-side of their hit single, "Charlie Brown". The Beatles performed this song several times during the infamous *Get Back / Let It Be* sessions in January 1969.

Another fine vocal performance from George with supporting harmonies from John and Paul, whose interludes are characterized by very dodgy foreign accents. These odd dialects, though well-suited for a live Cavern show, spoil an otherwise impressive group performance with tight vocals, guitars and drums.

First released on *Anthology 1*, this is The Beatles' only recording of a great song.

Pete's drumming?

Mike: "He varied the beat at the right time – better variation – and kept a good tempo. No problem with his drumming there."

Derek and Andrew: "Again, Pete adds his signature drum roll to perfection, and sounds really good. He uses great variety in the chorus with his use of the snare. Good variety in the lead guitar solo to back up what George is doing. Again, drumming is very tight with the group."

15. "Hello Little Girl"

The first song written by John, "Hello Little Girl" was always a first-rate song. According to Lennon, he was inspired by an old 1930s or '40s song that his mother, Julia, sang to him. Written in 1957, it was recorded in 1960 as a home demo, with Stuart Sutcliffe on bass a version only available on bootleg. It was the only original song in the set that The Beatles performed on the day Brian Epstein first saw them at The Cavern, and which helped Epstein see their potential as songwriters.

In 1963, The Beatles gave the song to another Liverpool group, The Fourmost. Their version reached #9 in the United Kingdom. The Beatles' version, which features John on lead vocal and would have made a great single, can be found on *Anthology 1*.

Pete's drumming?

Mike: "That's good, no criticism. Nice tempo, rhythm and variation, too."

Derek and Andrew: "Pete is more restrained and is holding back, like a session drummer would do. Not as flamboyant or trying to show off, he is playing the song well with a simple beat. The whole group sounds very tight and knows what they are doing."

And In The End? Conclusions from The Decca Audition

The Studio:

Steve Levine has been a successful record producer for many years, and was a good friend of George Martin. He has a unique insight into the recording environment and technology The Beatles would have used in 1962. For him, the whole process of stepping into a recording studio for the first time was a significant factor.

"Decca Studios and Abbey Road were designed for the recording of classical music. Abbey Road was created for English composer Edward Elgar to record orchestras. EMI originally recorded in Covent Garden, and of course everything was recorded live; 100% acoustic, with no electrical equipment. So for recording the piano, there would be a huge horn erected behind it to capture the sound, which would then go straight to disc. With the noise level in Covent Garden becoming greater, they felt they had to move.

"That is how they ended up in Abbey Road, because that was an old house considered to be on the outskirts of London, so it was much quieter. By the time the studio opened, they were moving towards the first electric recording. Decca was exactly the same. They were built for the composers of the day, requiring silence and a big empty room to put the orchestras in. We didn't have the understanding we have today of acoustics, so there would just be one microphone to capture the performance, and then create the balance there in the room. It was only as recording started to become what we know it after the second world war, but still at this point, in the UK, there was only direct to disc recording; no magnetic tape yet, which was captured from the Germans during the war.

"Everything then changed with magnetic tape, we could get into multi-track recording. So The Beatles were at the cusp of this change to our recording practices and to a different way of working. Now we were looking at recording small groups in a large empty room. Once The Beatles got into Abbey Road, they introduced baffles to break up the room, and added some element of overdubbing. Then you have the ability to use overdubbing, that really opens up the possibility of more control over the backing track and the vocals.

"They would have been recorded live, direct to mono, from which they would make acetates to listen back to their performance. Very few people, even in the record business, used reel-to-reel tapes, but they did have record players, and rather than leave it on tape, they would cut it on acetates, so if you wanted four copies, you would have to cut it four times. In the case of Decca, they would have recorded straight to tape, from which acetates could be cut for the various executives to listen to. The same would have happened with the EMI audition for George Martin. George would have listened to them on a record player later."

"As a producer; when you listen to it, you can understand why they were turned down. It was awful. It was badly recorded for a start, which probably means that on unimportant auditions, they put the tape operators and junior engineers who were learning their craft on to the task, so it is very likely that they were the new inexperienced younger engineers who were tried out.

"Secondly, it sounds like a feed off the PA desk. Therefore, had the executives come up and seen The Beatles live at the Cavern; they would have seen the real Beatles. What they ended up with from the studio was the audio without the physical. Had they had the two together, it might have been different.
I often record a concert live, and it is great at the time, but when you play it back, in the cold light of day, it is terrible. Because part of it is being there, and what the Decca session shows was that it was not very important for Decca, and only done as a favour to Brian's record shops. It was the Z-list team put on to record them.

"They didn't have particularly good gear to use, and they weren't studio match-fit, as they had not gained that experience in the studio. It still happens today; playing live and playing in the studio needs totally different techniques. You don't need to play the drums so loud and again, back to the times, very rarely were the drums mic'd up or even the guitar amps mic'd up. The term is P.A. (Public Address) so all that was coming through the speakers. The Reslo mic's were no good for live acts; they weren't fit for purpose. What the audience is hearing is a volume of the band at whatever settings they had. That is no way to record. The amps would have been too loud; the drums too loud. What you get is a live capture, which is very poor. One of the things that they probably didn't do at Decca was go into the control room and listen to what had been recorded, review it, because then the drummer can change the dynamic, or whatever they needed

to do, and analyse it. You need to have that first experience in the studio.

"At least by the time they get to Abbey Road, they have the experience of Decca. It was six months later, but at their age, they were learning and learning all the time. George Martin got them at a better time. What George was able to do was show them the potential of using the studio and equipment, and then they were off and running, but that took a little while. *(David Bedford Interview 2017)*

The Drummer?

Did our expert drummers agree with Savage's comments about Pete's drumming being "very average, and didn't keep good time. You could pick up a better drummer in any pub in London"?

"I don't know who these people are who criticise Pete's drumming because he was a great drummer," said Mike Rice. "He was fantastic to see live with The Beatles and his sound drove the group forward." *(David Bedford Interview 2015)*

As Derek observed: "Pete's timekeeping was like a metronome, and at times, it came across as if it was the drummer who was the leader of the group, like a Buddy Rich. In fact, Pete's drumming reminds me of 'Wipeout' by the Ventures, with that great use of the floor tom and that pounding rhythm that drives the song." It's noteworthy that both The Ventures' and Safaris' versions of "Wipeout" didn't come out until 1963, a year later.

Andrew notes: "Considering Pete had no training, he is very creative and he was creating sounds and rhythms for the first time. He knows what he is doing, is confident in his ability, and isn't simply copying the records or original version."

Derek concluded that Pete "is doing something different on virtually every song, and almost playing like the "Prog Rock" drummers were doing in the 1970s."

"We Wouldn't Have Used Pete Best"

Junior Engineer Mike Savage commented further on Pete's drumming: "If Decca was going to sign The Beatles, we wouldn't have used Pete Best on the records."
(Tune In)

Interestingly, the only comments we have from Savage pertain to Pete's drumming. But what did he think about John, Paul and George? Why do we not have those comments? Neither session producer Mike Smith nor Dick Rowe singled out Pete for particular criticism – the recordings reveal that, at various times, they were all culpable. However, as we will see in a later chapter on the use of session drummers, it wouldn't have mattered how well Pete Best did that day, because you could virtually guarantee that Decca or Parlophone were going to use a session drummer. That was no insult to Pete, or later, to Ringo.

When asked about the Decca audition in the February 2002 issue of The Beatles Monthly, Smith said: "Maybe I should have trusted my instincts and signed them on the strength of their stage show. In the studio they were not good and their personalities didn't come across. Maybe they were in awe of the situation. Of course I kicked a lot of furniture in the year or two afterwards when The Beatles started to happen for George Martin over at EMI. I would like to have auditioned the group when they had a better range of songs to offer, but NOT after they fired Pete Best. In my humble opinion he was a better drummer than Ringo."

Smith added that "the one that played the most bum notes was McCartney. I was very unimpressed with what was happening with the bassline." But he also wanted to qualify that observation, reminding us that "we are talking about four young men in a very strange environment, probably a very overpowering environment." *(Best of The Beatles)*

This is a fair comment to make about four young men entering a professional recording studio for the first time. It should come as no surprise that they were all affected by nerves. It is only natural.

Upon close examination of the songs, there is no reason to single out Pete Best for criticism. He could have added more variety to his drumming in a couple of the songs, but it was the producer's role to address the issue, just as George Martin did with John, Paul and George from 6th June onwards, and Ringo from September 1962. On the majority of songs, Pete kept a regular beat and certainly didn't overpower the others, showing good technique on a number of the songs. None of The Beatles came out of this audition covered in glory, but the day proved to be a valuable learning experience for the boys collectively – one that would eventually stand them in good stead. With an accomplished producer at their side, they would succeed. And they did. Unfortunately, Pete wouldn't have that chance, at least not with The Beatles.

Mike Savage: "If Decca was going to sign The Beatles, we wouldn't have used Pete Best on the records." *(Tune In)* How ironic that, just over a year later, Decca signed the second-most popular group in Liverpool, Lee Curtis and the All-Stars, whose drummer was, of course, Pete Best. Did they use a session drummer? No. It is also clear from what Smith has said that he was happy with Pete Best, and so he would not support the comments by Savage.

Decca released two singles, "Little Girl" and "Let's Stomp" but, unfortunately, neither made the charts. In mid-1963, the rest of the band decided to split from Curtis to form The Original All-Stars. That group became The Pete Best Four, who were also signed by Decca and produced by none other than Mike Smith. And again, no session drummer was used. The Pete Best Four and Pete Best Combo released several singles and albums. But despite Pete's profile and the songwriting talents of Wayne Bickerton and Tony Wadsworth, success eluded them.

As a former member of Pete's group, Bickerton was asked about his drumming. "Pete was a good drummer," Bickerton said. "All the stories of him not being able to play properly are grossly exaggerated.

The problem he fought against was being an ex-Beatle, which worked against us. The talent was in the band, but it was secondary to the Beatle-obsessed media and public." *(Let's Go Down To The Cavern)*

The Beatles failed the Decca audition as a group, with no single member to blame, be it Pete Best, John Lennon, Paul McCartney or George Harrison. This failed audition could have been the end of the road for The Beatles, not just for Pete. Brian, however, was not prepared to give up just yet. He took the boys out for a meal and tried to cheer them up. "The boys performed like real troopers when I stressed that this was only the beginning, not the end," Brian said. "I knew how disappointed and fed up they were." He felt he had let his boys down, but it was a learning experience for them all.

Take 2: Guitar Group Was On The Way Out

Mike Smith was clearly pleased with the audition – at least initially – because he had seen the group in the Cavern and enjoyed their performance. Smith also spoke positively to Tony Barrow who was just as eager to get the story out to their fans in Liverpool. Barrow recalled: "Mike Smith told me there was every chance that Decca would sign The Beatles and I printed this good-news story in my *Liverpool Echo* column. I wrote: 'Latest episode in the success story of Liverpool's Beatles: Commenting upon the outfit's recording test, Decca disc producer, Mike Smith, tells me that he thinks The Beatles are great. He has a continuous tape of their audition performances which runs for over 30 minutes, and he is convinced that his label will be able to put The Beatles to good use. I will keep you posted .' If I had heard the tapes before writing my copy, I would have been less keen to jump the gun." Was Barrow's conclusion fair?

(John Paul George Ringo and Me)

Smith had indeed jumped too soon and given The Beatles hope that a record deal was in the can. "When I saw The Beatles on stage, I was knocked out," said Smith. "I was entranced, I thought they were fantastic. It was only when they came into the studio that I discovered they weren't very good." *(Yesterday Came Suddenly)* This latter remark was added in hindsight, as Smith was keen to sign the group on audition day.

Silence Was Golden

Much has been made of Decca's choice between The Beatles and Brian Poole and the Tremeloes. When asked about it, Poole explained how he had approached Mike Smith in a coffee bar they both frequented. It was then that he learned that Smith was a Decca A&R man. They started talking and realised they had their glasses made by the same optician. "We became good friends with Mike," Poole recounted, "and went to parties together, and I got to know him. He said 'I will try and get you a recording deal at Decca and at least give you an audition, but lose the glasses!' and so I had to stop wearing them, and had no contact lenses. So we went and did the Decca audition, but we didn't get to record with Decca for a long time. Eventually, we pestered him and said, 'Isn't it time you recorded one of our songs?' so we eventually started making records."

(Pete Best of The Beatles DVD)

According to Dick Rowe: "The young man I had deal with The Beatles, Mike Smith, also auditioned Brian Poole. They came into London on New Year's Day. Both auditions were done on the same day, and Mike picked Brian Poole." *(The Beatles : An Oral History)* However, when Poole was asked about their audition, he said that they were recording "with Decca and EMI before The Beatles' January 1962 audition. We had already auditioned for Dick Rowe and Mike Smith months before that because we had the big hits with our 1962 record, so were obviously signed before the New Year's Day. We weren't there the same day that's for sure." *(Pete Best of The Beatles DVD)*

We know that Brian Poole and The Tremeloes did not audition on 1st January 1962, which is consistent with Poole's recollection, and not Rowe's version. Even though the two bands didn't audition the same day, it was, according to Rowe, left to Smith to make the final choice between the two groups. Dick Rowe said that "in fairness to Mike, he would have liked both of them, but you see, this isn't meant to blame anybody. I mean, it was my responsibility. Young people aren't too inclined to worry about money – the cost of things. They don't put that first. It's enthusiasm that comes first. So when Mike said to me that he'd like to sign both acts, I said to him, 'No, Mike, it's impossible. They can't both be sensational. You choose the one that you think is right. So he chose Brian Poole, and I can understand that because I heard the auditions. The auditions by Brian Poole were better than The Beatles." *(The Beatles: An Oral History)*

There is an inconsistency between the recollections of Brian Poole and those of Dick Rowe. If Poole had already been signed, which seems convincing, why did Rowe say that it was a choice between the two groups? If you were Dick Rowe, and had made possibly the biggest business mistake in history in turning down the cash cow that was The Beatles, wouldn't you attempt to rewrite history to make yourself look less of a fool? There are many inconsistencies in Rowe's story that make it seem like he was trying to preserve his reputation.

The evidence says that The Beatles were the only group auditioning at Decca that day, and it was more likely a simple choice of signing The Beatles, or not.

Maybe, in Rowe's defence, he was asking Mike Smith why he should sign another guitar-based group when he had just signed Brian Poole and The Tremeloes, as they were similar. That is a much more believable hypothesis.

The only guitar group in the charts at the time was The Shadows, so signing two new guitar groups would have been foolish, and risky. All Rowe had to go on was the audition tapes of both groups and Smith's recommendations, and he felt he could only have one guitar group, and The Beatles had nothing tangible to suggest they were a better investment than Brian Poole's group. The likelihood was, with Poole and his group already signed, and as Tony Barrow made clear, The Beatles were only being auditioned because of the importance of Brian's shop NEMS to Decca. Was there ever an intention from Decca to sign them?

Reflecting on the songs from the audition, Rowe elaborated on how he arrived at his decision, with some logical justification. "When I heard the audition tapes and I heard their renditions of tunes like 'Money' and 'Twist and Shout'," Rowe said, "to me, they were the same as a number of English artists like Terry Dean and even Billy Fury. They were adequate, they were making adequate covers, but there was nothing really that startling about them." *(The Beatles: An Oral History)* (It should be noted that, despite Rowe's recollection, The Beatles didn't perform "Twist and Shout" at the session.)

"Mike (Smith) brought the tapes from both tests to me," Rowe said, "and The Beatles weren't very good. They sounded completely different from a record Brian Epstein left me earlier that featured guitarist Tony Sheridan. I thought, 'What's this guy up to?' because I saw no connection between what they'd done at their audition and on the record he'd left me." *(Yesterday Came Suddenly)* Rowe had obviously been impressed by "My Bonnie" which The Beatles had recorded with Sheridan in Hamburg in 1961. "And, of course," added Rowe, "for perhaps a year, everybody, particularly in the United States, confirmed this back to me, saying, 'Well, they're never going to make it here.' Brian Epstein couldn't even get Capitol to release Beatles records." *(The Beatles : An Oral History)*

The mystery deepens here because Dick Rowe went on to claim he didn't dismiss The Beatles out of hand. Maybe because of Mike Smith's enthusiasm for the group, and partly because Brian Epstein believed in the group so much, Rowe claims he also made the decision to travel north himself to check the group out. "I went up to Liverpool to see The Beatles. I didn't even tell Mike Smith. I went there and it was – there's no other way of putting it – it was pissing with rain. It was falling down in buckets, and I went out to the Cavern and the place was crowded. You couldn't get in, and what with the rain outside, I was getting drenched. I thought, 'Oh sod it', and I walked away. How could I have been so stupid? The very fact that I couldn't get in because it was so full should have struck me. But it didn't. I think the rain, and the fact that I was getting soaked, made me walk away from it. And that's how we made that cock up." *(The Beatles : An Oral History)*

So, according to Rowe, seeing The Beatles live on stage would have made all the difference after all. At first glance, Rowe's reflections on his decision, and his trip to Liverpool, seem authentic – until we probe deeper.

What extra special reason did Decca's top man have to leave his London office on a whim, and suddenly venture north to see an obscure act in the middle of winter, when the man he paid to do such things, A&R Mike Smith, had already done just that? And why keep his visit so secret from Mike Smith anyway? More than that, why didn't he pay a courtesy visit to NEMS and Brian Epstein while he was there, at least to relax before the show after a long journey? Why was he then put off so quickly by a queue at the Cavern (rain or no rain) when all he had to do was walk up to Cavern doorman, Paddy Delaney, and establish his credentials? The Cavern management would have walked a mile over broken beer bottles to give the London boss of Decca Records instant VIP access. The honour, the honour! And how did Rowe know to go to the Cavern at that particular time on that particular day? And why the sudden haste to jump back on a train for what would then have been another long, slow journey home through the night, this time in soaking wet clothes? Exactly who was going to shout at him for being late next morning? Answer: nobody! It is only when these questions are raised (and without any plausible counter-response, we add) do we see through Rowe. As they say, you couldn't make such things up. Or could you?

In Mike Smith's experience, he was obviously disappointed in all four Beatles, having had high expectations after seeing the group at the Cavern. "In the studio they weren't very good. I think that we got to them too early, but it was probably just as well as I couldn't have worked with them the way that George Martin did at EMI. I would have got too involved in their bad parts and not enough in their good." *(Spencer Leigh, The Independent, Saturday 31 December 2011)*

In the meantime, The Beatles headed back to Liverpool in good spirits, confident that a record deal with Decca would soon follow.

History records that it didn't.

THE BEATLES' MANAGEMENT CONTRACT: NO SIGN OF BRIAN

On 24th January 1962, The Beatles finally signed the contract to appoint Brian Epstein as their manager. The initial contract that had been discussed was different to the final draft and, if The Beatles had taken David Harris' advice and employed their own solicitor, things would have been very different.

The contract was effective from 1st February 1962 for five years, with termination an option by either side giving three months' notice once twelve months had elapsed. It seems clear that when Brian asked David Harris to draw up the contract, he neglected to inform him of the ages of the individual group members. Harris was obviously concerned about possible future repercussions from this first contract. "After the first one was rushed through and then signed – when I realised the age of the boys – I realised that they had no signatures of the parents, so I said to Brian we are going to have to create another one which the parents would have to sign." *(David Bedford Interview 2015)* This, however, didn't happen until 1st October 1962.

Since he was 21, John Lennon was the only Beatle legally able to sign the contract. In the eyes of the law, anyone under 21 was unable to sign a contract without having it countersigned by one of their parents. This didn't stop all four Beatles from signing the contract, which was witnessed by Brian's assistant Alistair Taylor but not signed by Brian. This has been the subject of much debate ever since.

Did the absence of the parents' details make the contract illegal? No. "It was a contract that was unenforceable," said Harris, confirming it was not illegal or invalid. "As long as everyone did what they agreed to do, there was no problem, because both sides were happy." *(David Bedford Interview 2015)*

The very first, legally binding, enforceable contract was signed by Brian on 1st October 1962, though this time by John, Paul, George and Ringo. As Brian said when asked why he didn't sign the contract: "I abided by the terms and no one worried. I believe it was because even though I knew I would keep the contract in every clause, I had not 100 per cent faith in myself to help The Beatles adequately. In other words, I wanted to free The Beatles of their obligations if I felt they would be better off." *(A Cellarful of Noise)*

Why would Brian deliberately take out the necessity for the parents of three of the four Beatles to sign the contract? If Brian intended not to sign it, why would he go the extra mile to create an unenforceable contract? Was this the "Macchiavellian" side to Brian's business dealings? Was he not quite as innocent as he would have had us believe? Of course, it worked out in the end, but his motives must be questioned at this point. Why, after meetings in December, and drawing up the first unenforceable contract which The Beatles signed in December at the Casbah, did Brian insist on a contract being drawn up which was clearly going to be invalid, and virtually worthless? After all, as Pete Best has said, "Brian kept putting pieces of paper in front of us and we just signed them, because we trusted him."

Why did Brian not sign?

Why go the extra step and not sign a contract he already knew was unenforceable? Because if Brian had signed it, the contract could have been

John, Paul and George on the roof of the Top Ten Club, Hamburg

Rehearsing at The Cavern

enforced by the leader of the group, John Lennon, who was able to sign it without the need for a parental signature. To put it simply, Brian couldn't afford to sign. What if the arrangement didn't work out? What if there was backlash from one or more of the group members?

Maybe Brian acted as he did after receiving advice from his father, who was against him having anything to do with The Beatles. He didn't want his son, the manager of his NEMS Whitechapel store, wasting time with a pop group, or going off chasing another pipe-dream, like his earlier wish to be an actor. Harry Epstein was opposed to Brian's suggestion of managing a group, and didn't want any of the NEMS' money being spent, or most likely wasted, on a pop group. The manager who made The Beatles famous, and tragically died young, wanted to give The Beatles a way out if it didn't work out, remembering that this was a five-year contract.

The Beatles were happy to sign anything if it meant getting a record deal, and if Brian could do it for them, then they were happy to agree to it. They trusted Brian and believed in him, so they signed. We will never know Brian's true motivation, but The Beatles were unlikely to challenge the contract and so it became irrelevant.

How did Harris view the contract and the fact that Brian didn't sign it? "That I don't know," he said. "I've heard that (Brian didn't sign). Because they didn't sign it in my presence, I gave it to him (Brian) and gave him instructions on how to have it signed. That he forgot to sign it does not surprise me," he said, giving an alternative viewpoint. "Irrespective of that, it didn't matter whether he signed it or not because that was a contract without the parents.

It made it unenforceable, not invalid or illegal. He couldn't enforce the terms against anyone under 21, which is why we did another one with the parents to validate it." *(David Bedford Interview 2015)*

It does however confirm that, had Brian signed the contract, then John, the only 21-year-old in the group, could have enforced it.

The Beatles Management Contract with Brian

The contract stated:

This agreement is made the 1st day of February 1962 BETWEEN **BRIAN EPSTEIN** *of 197 Queens Drive in the City of Liverpool (hereinafter called "the Manager") of the first part* **JOHN WINSTON LENNON** *of 251 Menlove Avenue* **GEORGE HARRISON** *of 25 Upton Green* **JAMES PAUL MCCARTNEY** *of 20 Forthlin Road and* **PETER RANDOLPH BEST** *of 8 Haymans Green all of Liverpool aforesaid (hereinafter called "the artists") of the other part.*

A. The Artists are desirous of performing as a group of musicians to be known as "THE BEATLES" and pursuant thereto of taking engagements in the following branches of the entertainment industry.

This clearly establishes not only the appointment of Brian Epstein as manager of The Beatles, but also confirms the legal bond among the four individual Beatles for the next five years, renewable each year, with the proviso that "after 1st February 1963, either party to this agreement may by giving at least 3 months written notice to the other parties by registered post at their last known address" terminate the contract. The contract effectively gave Brian control over every aspect of their lives as Beatles, though this wasn't Brian signing The Beatles; it was The Beatles signing Brian. They employed him as manager and agent "throughout the world" and to perform the following services:

- **To undertake all necessary advertising and publicity**
- **To advise the Artists on all matters concerning clothes makeup and the presentation of the Artist's sets**
- **To use all reasonable efforts to procure employment for the Artists....and advise them in all matters concerning their professional interests**
- **To arrange recording sessions for the Artists**
- **To negotiate all enquiries and offers for employment of the Artists**
- **By written Agreement with the Artists to employ sub-agents in any part of the world**
- **To perform all the above-mentioned services in all parts of the world**

It has been suggested that Paul was the reticent one within The Beatles when it came to agreeing to let Brian manage the band. John, the group's impulsive leader, was clear: "Right then Brian, manage us." Paul was more cautious by nature, and said: "My dad was quite pleased when we went with Brian because he thought Jewish people had a flair with money, which I think is probably true." *(TuneIn)* However, Larry Kane, the respected American journalist who accompanied The Beatles on their American tours in the '60s, said that three separate sources "have quoted Jim McCartney telling his older son about his concern for doing business with a Jewish businessman." *(When They Were Boys)*

Is there any evidence to support either position? Paul's actions over meeting with Brian and discussing terms with him certainly suggest a reticence on his behalf; he famously turned up late for their first meeting with Brian because he had been in the bath. When Brian told George that Paul was "going to be late," George cleverly countered with "yes, but very clean." Turning up late to a meeting where they could acquire a new manager was not a good start.

Before signing the contract, Paul argued over one clause – the one related to Jim

McCartney's comment about having a Jewish manager. The young McCartney disputed the amount of commission Brian would earn. "He asked for 20 per cent and I argued with him. I said, 'Twenty, man? I thought managers only took 10 per cent.' He said, 'No, it's 20 these days.' I said, 'OK, maybe I'm not very modern.'" *(TuneIn)* Was Paul not as sure as John was that Brian was the right man, and maybe wanted to test Brian's resolve? It possibly says more about the characters of Lennon and McCartney than anything else: John was impulsive and would agree to anything. Maybe Paul was thinking that John, as leader of the group, should have been challenging Brian and not just saying yes to anything. Lennon wasn't that interested in the numbers, just in making records.

Brian conceded Paul's point about the percentage quite quickly, with no need to think about it. This either showed Brian's desperation, or proved that he wasn't in it for the money. He amended the clause, reducing his maximum commission from 20% to 15%. However, this change was not initialled on the contract by both sides so it could have been contended on that issue alone if challenged. Brian was determined to be fair; he never seemed to pay much attention to the percentages, a criticism that was levelled against him during The Beatles' career and dealings, especially with regard to merchandise and other revenue streams. What Brian knew was that he had a signed agreement, and maybe it is fairer to call it a "memorandum of understanding" between himself and The Beatles. Both sides were happy.

Brian was determined to land them a record contract and, after Decca, he was convinced he had already achieved this. He was going to take The Beatles to the toppermost of the poppermost, and, most importantly, the boys believed in him, trusted him, and didn't need a piece of paper to tell them that. Maybe both parties were a bit naive at that point. If it all worked out later on, the drafting of a proper agreement would certainly needed to be addressed.

Conflict of Contracts?

There was, as The Beatles had mentioned, an agreement in place already with Bert Kaempfert Produktion (BKP), effective from 1st July 1961, which was running until 30th June 1962. What he could establish was that the contract was between The Beatles and BKP, and not a recording contract, so he could still negotiate for a recording contract on their behalf. However, The Beatles could not be signed to a new recording contract while the BKP contract was still valid. Epstein would, as a priority, have to enforce the three months notice clause to terminate the Kaempfert contract, and ensure it would not be renewed. After all, Kaempfert was only interested in Tony Sheridan. With a twist of irony, as none of the parents of The Beatles had signed the BKP contract, there was even a possible case for challenging its legality. This could even had been the template that helped Brian shape his management contract, with 3 months notice and no parents included on the form common to both.

This management contract between The Beatles, jointly and individually, and Brian Epstein, effective from 1st February 1962, would become the basis for an intimate business relationship between them. It would also prove to be a formidable hurdle to getting rid of Pete Best in a few months time.

February 1962

RETURN TO DECCA: FROM DECCA TO PARLOPHONE

Arriving back in Liverpool following their London audition, The Beatles began 1962 assured that their future was bright. They had signed a Partnership Agreement together, were waiting to sign a Management Contract with Brian Epstein and then, just before "My Bonnie" was released in the UK, the latest *Mersey Beat* had proclaimed "Beatles Top Poll". This was going to be their year. All they had to do was wait for the call from Decca. And they waited, and waited. As the days turned to weeks, there was no response from Decca.

Groups of Guitarists Were On The Way Out!

Much to Brian's consternation, Decca's Dick Rowe took a long time to communicate his decision to The Beatles and him. "I returned to Decca again in March, on invitation for a lunch appointment," Brian recalled, though history shows the date to be mid-February. "I felt pessimistic, but tried not to show it when I met Beecher Stevens and Dick Rowe, two important executives. We had coffee, and Mr. Rowe, a short plump man said to me, 'Not to mince words, Mr. Epstein, we don't like your boys' sound. Groups of guitarists are on the way out.'"

Brian also showed the Decca executives the copy of *Mersey Beat* with the "Beatles Top Poll" headline and told them that "My Bonnie" had also been released in the UK, but Rowe and Stevens were unmoved. Brian threw down the gauntlet with his final argument: "I am confident that one day they will be bigger than Elvis Presley." *(A Cellarful of Noise)*

Not only was this a comparison with the world's leading pop star, this was the

Studio Two, Abbey Road

world's leading pop star that Decca was marketing and distributing in the UK on the RCA label – a point which wouldn't have been lost on Brian's audience of two. Elvis was doing for Decca what The Beatles would eventually do for the label's greatest rival, EMI. For Brian, there was no "Love Me Tender" from Decca, just "Return to Sender". They can't say he didn't give them the opportunity.

As Brian remembered, "Mr. Rowe and Mr. Stevens pursued their point. 'The boys won't go, Mr. Epstein. We know these things. You have a good record business in Liverpool. Stick to that." *(A Cellarful of Noise)* Brian must have felt terrible, but being the polite, professional businessman, he didn't give up. Good job Lennon wasn't there, as his response might have been different from his manager's!

Out of The Shadows

It wasn't quite over. Rowe, trying to be as helpful as possible in view of Brian's importance to the company, made a suggestion to him. "I have an idea that something might be done. You know who might help you? Tony Meehan." The former Shadows musician, still only 18 years old, was now an A & R man at Decca. "It was explained that I would be given the benefit of his experience," explained Brian, "and the use of a studio on payment of something approaching £100. This annoyed me because I couldn't see why I should have to pay £100 to make one recording of a group who were going to conquer the entire record world."

Brian agreed to meet Meehan the following day. Accompanied by Dick Rowe, Meehan was very blunt, as Brian recalled: "The A&R man who, two years later, I was to book as a drummer on one of my Prince of Wales bills, looked me straight between the eyes without enthusiasm and said: 'Mr. Epstein, Mr. Rowe and I are very busy men. We know roughly what you require so will you fix a date for tapes to be made of these Beatles, phone my secretary and make sure that when you want the session, I am available.' The date was arranged, but later abandoned because I felt that no useful purpose was served. I realized that there was nothing doing with Decca." *(A Cellarful of Noise)*

There was also one other possible deal that Epstein and Rowe could have made. "I heard afterwards that he'd (Brian) guaranteed to buy 3,000 copies of any single we let The Beatles make," Rowe said. "I was never told about that at the time. The way economics were in the record business then, if we'd been sure of selling 3,000 copies, we'd have been forced to record them, whatever sort of group they were."

Alistair Taylor, who worked so closely with Brian, was very gracious in his support for Rowe. "Dick Rowe has taken so much (flak) by the media as 'the idiot' who turned down The Beatles. But Dick Rowe listened. He was the one guy who sat down and listened, and he said no. There are people in the business turning down successful groups every day of the week. Okay, he made a mistake. Brian had his failures too." Taylor pointed out that some of Brian's acts weren't successful, like Tommy Quickly, The Rustiks, The Fourmost and others.

As Taylor rightly pointed out, at least Rowe took the time and trouble to listen to them before coming up with his decision. *(The Beatles : An Oral History)* But what did Dick Rowe mean by his two oft-quoted opinions to Brian? Was his

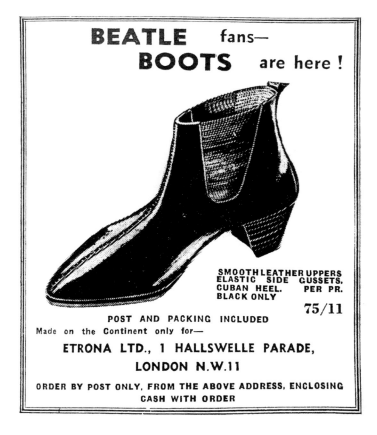

assertion that "groups of guitarists are on the way out" a polite way of letting Brian down? After all, Rowe signed Brian Poole and the Tremeloes, a guitar-based group. Maybe signing two similar groups would have been overkill? However, it is the second part that, after examining the session, makes more sense: "....we don't like your boys' sound."

An Identity Crisis? The Three Cool Cats

By saying "we don't like your boys' sound", what did Dick Rowe really mean? Could it have been that Epstein's meddling in the song choices performed at the session led Rowe to question their entire set-up? Was there confusion about their music style, their real strength, and and the identity of their lead singer? Was it John Lennon and The Beatles? Paul McCartney and The Beatles? George Harrison and The Beatles? Were they a pop group? Rock 'n' roll group? Country and western group? Covers group? Variety performers? A solo singer and a backing group?

For the audition, Brian and The Beatles had chosen a random medley of covers to show their versatility, thus abandoning the style of music that had first attracted Smith, earned them legions of fans and showed their true potential. Admittedly, the songs selected were from the extended repertoire the group needed to fill long hours on stage in the clubs of Hamburg and Liverpool. But surely Brian would have been aware of one of the fundamental rules of any pitch: to put forward the best of the best, leave out the so-so and, above all, highlight the burgeoning songwriting talent of Lennon & McCartney. It couldn't have been only Epstein's choices that were played. After all, nobody knew The Beatles' repertoire better than the boys themselves.

To Rowe's ears, they must have seemed like the Greek mythological beast Cerberus, the dog with many heads. Here was a 'beatle' with three heads, and just as puzzling – a riddle, wrapped in a mystery inside an enigma. Rowe couldn't see who or what they were, especially compared to Brian Poole and the Tremeloes. In his eyes, the latter represented what a group should be in the 'normal' world of pop music. In contrast, The Beatles were a muddle with no obvious leader. If only he'd realized that the "Three Cool Cats" standing in front of him were the real deal – three musicians, three singers sharing three-part harmonies, three frontmen who would take over the world.

Producer Steve Levine concurs with this opinion. "As a producer, you don't really know what you've got," he said. "They were coming from Hamburg and Liverpool, where they were mainly a covers band. I have it with bands that come to me. You have to find their sound; at that point, The Beatles didn't know what their sound was. They were just like a watch-seller with a lot of watches saying; which one do you fancy? Or how about these other ones? They didn't know what they were selling, so they gave Decca everything. When bands say to me; 'I've got 50 songs,' I tell them I don't want to hear 50 songs; I want to hear one really good one, because if they have one great song, you can work with that, and then you can find five or ten good ones.

"If they had a modern hat on, they would have selected one song each to show that they could all sing, but they'd have probably done three rock 'n' roll songs. However, rock 'n' roll wasn't defined as exactly as it is now, and they were also desperate for a deal. If Decca had been looking for a country and western band, they would have chosen those songs; they were so desperate. That's the other thing people forget; The Beatles aren't virtuoso musicians, but they worked so well together, which I think is more important. Virtuoso musicians make their own type of records. For pop music, you need people who are really good at what they do, and they became a great recording group.

"They hadn't defined their roles; they hadn't defined what they were doing. However, what was great about The Beatles was that they knew how to maximise what they had. They were gifted with three good singers and two great songwriters, and eventually a third great songwriter; the sum of the parts was important. I've seen other groups like that with talent, but they lack the drive. What The Beatles had was a drive to succeed. That's the one thing, particularly with McCartney, who had drive and ambition, and every group needs one person like that. If EMI had said they needed a backing band for someone, they would have done it. They wanted to be signed. Whatever they were offered; they would have taken. They found George Martin and pop/rock 'n' roll changed."

(David Bedford Interview 2017)

In the end, it must have seemed an easy choice for Rowe. Brian Poole and the Tremeloes had an established identity and leader, radio experience, and were a local London act with a loyal fan base. They were tailor-made for Decca whereas The Beatles lived 300 miles away and posed an enormous gamble. It was too much for Rowe and Decca to take on. If, like Epstein and Mike Smith, he had witnessed The Beatles in their own environment, experienced their humour and truly understood them, things might have turned out differently. But he didn't. It was going to take someone with greater vision and a sense of humour to help The Beatles break through.

Forgive Dick Rowe?

So should we forgive Dick Rowe after all these years? Not completely, no. If he had seen through the nerves, and listened closely enough, he would have recognized a talented group with original songs that could translate into hit records. There were three talented singers who blended together well. Putting it in the simplest terms, he should have listened to Mike Smith, who had seen them in the Cavern and knew what they could do in front of an audience. That was where they were comfortable; trying to perform in a proper studio for the first time was far more nerve-wracking.

Dick Rowe would be haunted for the rest of his life by his decision. "More people know me for that reason rather than for any successes I have had – because of Brian Epstein's vindictiveness," Rowe would recall. "I wasn't even present when The Beatles auditioned for Decca. I heard only the tapes they recorded. They sounded out of tune to me, but I had been told they were very nervous. They played mostly old standard tunes." *(Doncaster, Daily Mirror, 1980)*

It also seemed clear that Rowe didn't like Epstein, which would have made the decision to go with Brian Poole and the Tremeloes easier. "I don't like people, who – I guess because he was wealthy – don't wait to be asked to come into an office," Rowe said indignantly. "He'd open the door and walk in. I'm really not that kind of person, but he was so much like that, that I really didn't take to him. So when Mike said he wanted Brian Poole and the Tremeloes, the decision didn't mean that much to me. If The Beatles had done a great audition, I would have said, 'Mike, you're out of your mind! This group's fabulous!' My eyes and ears were open, and I was very conscious they were copying American records. So I put it all together and said, 'Go on and sign the Tremeloes." *(Yesterday Came Suddenly)* More than a hint of bitterness there.

Geography, personality and quality all played a role in the final decision. The economics of taking a chance with a London-based group like Brian Poole and the Tremeloes were far more favourable than a long-distant partnership with a group based in Liverpool. "Liverpool could have been in Greenland to us then," Rowe said. *(The Beatles. The Biography)* Maybe he should have listened, because when asked how The Beatles found America, John retorted: "Turn left at Greenland."

George Martin said that Dick Rowe shouldn't be singled out for blame: "(The EMI manager who had originally turned Brian down) Ron White says that two of the four EMI heads of label heard Beatles tapes before I did. The other three were Norman Newell, Walter Ridley and Norrie Paramor. Two out of those three must have been at least as guilty as poor old Dick Rowe of Decca, who got all the public 'stick'." *(All You Need Is Ears)*

The London Music Scene

Was the music scene in London part of the problem? Back in Liverpool, The Beatles were the kings of a rapidly-growing rock 'n' roll scene, with numerous groups, clubs and promoters, scattered around Liverpool and Merseyside. During their time in Liverpool, The Beatles in their various incarnations played at over one hundred different venues. There was a healthy competition among groups; The Beatles, Rory Storm and the Hurricanes, The Big Three, Kingsize Taylor and the Dominoes, The Remo Four and Gerry and the Pacemakers were among the countless acts that battled it out to reach the top of the musical heap in Merseyside. Sam Leach had just staged Operation Big Beat at the Tower Ballroom with one of the most sensational lineups of groups ever seen in front of thousands of fans. They were also rocking at clubs like the Cavern, the Casbah, the Iron Door, Lathom Town Hall, Litherland Town Hall and Aintree Institute.

In comparison, what was the London music scene like? Just as it had been in the days of skiffle, you had to visit Soho and the 2i's Coffee Bar to see a rock 'n' roll group. While the Cavern had introduced beat music into a jazz club back in May 1960, it was two more years before London's famous Marquee jazz club, now run by Cavern Club founder Alan Sytner, welcomed R&B there in May 1962. Liverpool's music scene was still years ahead of London, yet virtually no one from London knew it. Mike Smith witnessed some of that excitement at the Cavern, and Dick Rowe almost did, but what was happening in Liverpool was unique. Is it any wonder that London-based producers like Rowe had no idea of the talent that Liverpool had to offer? His assertion that groups with guitars were passé was based on the London music scene, not Liverpool where hundreds of guitar groups were active. London was still about the solo singers, backed by a group, performing songs written in 'tin-pan alley' for artists to perform.

Where in this London scene was a place for a guitar-based group who wrote and performed their own songs? Being 'Kings of Liverpool' meant nothing in

London, but that was hardly The Beatles' fault.

Dick Rowe was probably trying to do what George Martin contemplated. They were both looking for their own Cliff Richard and The Shadows. They were looking for their lead singer and a backing group, and didn't have the vision to realise that something genuinely original was right in front of their faces – a group that could not only play any type of music, but could also write songs that were commercially viable and had the potential to be hits. Dick Rowe took the easy way out and went for the "safe" option, and so missed out on one of the biggest paydays in the history of show business. Admittedly, The Beatles weren't at their best, but if you paid close enough attention, you could see that the right ingredients were there, waiting for a producer with artistic vision to bring out their best. John felt the same. "They should have seen our potential," he observed. "When you consider what was going on was The Shadows – especially in England. But they were so dumb, when they listened to these audition tapes, they were listening for The Shadows. So they were not listening to it at all – they're listening like they do now – you know how these people are – for what's already gone down. They can't hear anything new." *(Anthology)*

Were Groups of Guitarists Ever On The Way In?

One look at the latest charts for the period 28th December 1961 to 3rd January 1962 demonstrates why Decca was nervous about signing one group, let alone two. In the current Top 40 chart, Dick Rowe could quickly see that there were only eight groups. The Temperance Seven, Terry Lightfoot and His New Orleans Jazz Men and Kenny Ball and his Jazzmen all performed jazz; The Harry Simeone Chorale performed the hymn "Onward Christian Soldiers"; The Springfields, with a powerful lead vocalist in Dusty Springfield, played folk/pop; and the only "pop" groups were The Shadows (a group of guitarists) and the American Doo-Wop group, the G-Clefs.

In contrast, there were 25 solo male singers, like Americans Bobby Vee, Ray Charles and Dion and the UK's Cliff Richard and Billy Fury. These singers included the only Parlophone "pop" star, Adam Faith, who was produced by Ron Richards. There were also seven solo female singers, like Shirley Bassey and Connie Francis. Billy Fury was Decca's only entry in the Top 40 singles chart, which was obviously a concern; thus the reason why they were looking for their own Cliff Richard, not a group. Their London American label boasted Bobby Vee, Pat Boone and Sandy Nelson, the latter having an instrumental called "Let There Be Drums". Adam Faith was Parlophone's only pop star, with George Martin producing The Temperance Seven, who specialised in 1920s and '30s jazz. The label's stable also included Mrs. Mills, who performed sing-along classics made popular in the "music hall" style.

Decca had major hits with Lonnie Donegan, whose "Rock Island Line" inspired John's Quarrymen skiffle group; Bill Haley and his Comets', who hit it big with "Rock Around The Clock", plus legends like Buddy Holly, Little Richard and The Everly Brothers. However, by the end of 1961, its only entries in the U.S. Top 20 were Bing Crosby's "White Christmas" and Burl Ives' "Little Bitty Bear". The U.S. charts featured Chubby Checker's hit, "The Twist" at #2 and "Peppermint Twist (Part 1)" at #4. There were 23 solo male singers, three solo female singers and 13 "groups", though these included an orchestra, a choir, a country and western group and the Chipmunks. As in the UK, there was an absence of guitar-based groups. In the realm of American and British hit records, why was there no place for a guitar-based group from Liverpool, but room for a guitar-based group from London? Or was Decca too frightened to take on two guitar groups at the same time, when there was no retail evidence suggesting they would succeed?

Brian Poole and the Tremeloes

What did Decca do with the group it signed? The majority of their records were covers. Their first LP, *Big Hits of '62*, featured 22 cover versions of popular songs from 1962. They weren't just cover versions, but songs grouped together in medleys of either three or four songs. What the group showed to Decca was the ability to perform any currently-charted song, with no attempt to perform anything original.

In contrast, The Beatles performed a variety of songs from previous years while desperately trying to promote their own songwriting talents. If Decca was looking for a covers group to compete with those recording for Woolworths' Embassy label – the label that John Lennon joked would sign them – then costs had to be at a minimum because the profit margins would not be great. Signing a versatile group whose members lived locally was the obvious solution.

They could also act as a backing group, as they did for Jimmy Savile and The Vernons Girls. Decca worked in tandem with its sister label, London American, who released the original recordings by U.S. artists followed by Decca's release of a copy by its British artists. Brian Poole and the Tremeloes were the perfect, versatile, local group for the job.

The Beatles, who couldn't even do good covers of the songs in their repertoire, didn't stand a chance when it came to a straight choice between the two groups. Thankfully, Decca turned them down. Otherwise, it's likely they would have ended up just doing cover versions much as they had done in the clubs of Liverpool and Hamburg for years, while their own compositions languished.

What Could The Beatles Have Done Differently?

For starters, they could have rehearsed more prior to their London trip. They could also have followed Brian's advice and gone to bed early. Their new manager was not being a kill-joy; he simply felt that a good night's sleep after a nightmare journey was important, especially when they were mere hours away from auditioning to secure a recording contract with one of the biggest companies, Decca. This was their chance at the big time, and they were partying in Trafalgar Square at 2am! Not a great preparation.

However, their Decca experience proved invaluable as they prepared for Parlophone in June 1962; they realized that they needed to trim their audition down to six songs. If they had only chosen the best of the fifteen songs they performed for Decca, it could have been an entirely different story.

Had they selected "To Know Her Is To Love Her", "Take Good Care of My Baby", "Memphis Tennessee", "Hello Little Girl", "Crying, Waiting, Hoping" and "Love of The Loved", they would have showcased their singing talents, their three-part harmonies and their original songs. There would have been plenty for Dick Rowe to consider. Unfortunately, their solid performances were lost among the distractions of below-par songs. With a smaller selection, history might have been different.

What Did The Beatles Think of The Audition?

History would show that The Beatles' rejection by Decca was a lucky escape. But at the time, it was obviously a major disappointment to them. "I think we felt desperate more than anything else," recalled Pete. "We thought that we had Decca's contract in the bag. The final words from Mike Smith as we left were, 'Don't worry, lads'. We even went out and celebrated in St. John's Wood, a big lavish dinner, on Brian of course. The wine was flowing, and we all came back in high spirits." *(DVD Beatles Magical History Tour 2007)*

"We went back and we waited and waited, and then we found out that they hadn't accepted it," said John. It was as if their final chance had gone, and John was ready to give up. "It was only Brian telling us we were going to make it, and George. Brian Epstein and George Harrison." The Beatles had the opportunity to hear the recording, and Paul felt they were treated unfairly: "Listening to the tapes I can understand why we failed the Decca audition. We weren't that good, though there were some quite interesting and original things. There were good elements, and the producers should have picked up on them." *(Anthology)*

When John heard the recording, he was more pragmatic. "I listened to it," John would recall. "I wouldn't have turned us down on that. When you hear the tape, it's pretty good. I think it sounded okay. Especially the last half of it, for the period it was. There weren't many people playing music like that then. I think Decca expected us to be all polished; we were just doing a demo." *(Anthology)* On reflection, Paul was candid. "To be honest, we realised that we weren't at peak form. The nerves had shown through, even though we had enjoyed the session. But the boys in the studio seemed pretty impressed." *(True Story of The Beatles)* They missed the yells and feedback from an audience. Before going to Decca, they felt certain that if they could only get the record industry to give them a chance, it would be okay. But then it all went wrong. All four shared George's sentiment, wondering if there was "much point in trying to get away on a national level. Maybe, we reckoned, it was only Liverpudlians and Germans who could see anything in our sound. Silly way of thinking, sure – but we'd been batting our heads against a brick wall for a long time, remember." *(True Story of The Beatles)*

When John, Paul and George got together to discuss Dick Rowe, they were all clear how they felt. As George said, "The head of Decca, Dick Rowe, made a canny prediction: 'Guitar groups are on the way out, Mr. Epstein.'" "He must be kicking himself now," Paul added, before John made his feelings unambiguous: "I hope he kicks himself to death!" Pete, maybe with a foretaste of what was to come, was not told of the decision initially but found out a few days later. The Beatles was always about John, Paul, George and a drummer, as Neil Aspinall had said. Many had tried, and failed, to break into the threesome.

Did the Decca debacle signal the end of the road for The Beatles? As John had said: "We really thought that was it then; that was the end." *(Anthology)* Thankfully, it wasn't the end of the story.

8th February 1962

TEENAGERS TURN TO THE BBC

Seeking new exposure for The Beatles, newly-christened manager Brian Epstein applied to the BBC for a spot on a local radio show. Most of the BBC Radio's output was considered what the broadcaster titled 'light entertainment', almost assuring that very few teenagers would listen to pop music on the only national radio service in the UK. However, specialty radio shows were available for the teenage market, so it made sense to take every opportunity to gain exposure for the group beyond Liverpool. Epstein picked up an application form on 10th January and quickly dispatched it to the BBC.

The application arrived at the desk of the Light Entertainment producer Peter Pilbeam, who said that Epstein's application stood out because it was typed on his personal letterhead. Pilbeam scheduled an audition for 8th February 1962 and, if they passed, they would make their national radio debut on the BBC. They had auditioned for Decca, were under a record contract with Bert Kaempfert, had released "My Bonnie" in the UK in January and were hopefully now going to be stars of national radio.

But first, they would have to pass an audition with Pilbeam, who wasn't a pop music fan, but more of a big band music man. "In 1962," recalled Pilbeam, "I was the junior of three producers at the BBC in Manchester. It was my responsibility as the junior to arrange the auditions. The show was called Here We Go with the NDO (Northern Dance Orchestra), a very catchy title, which went out on the BBC Light programme every Friday as part of a series of broadcasts called Teenagers Turn. We did two shows each week, one on Monday and the other on Friday, and the two programs were recorded back-to-back on the same evening. There was a regular guest spot for an up-and-coming group of guitars

Peter Pilbeam at the Playhouse Theatre

The
Beatles

Best with John Lennon
George Harrison
Best wishes Pete Best
from Paul McCartney

Original painting by Paul Skellett

and drums. The most famous one, of course, was The Beatles, whose audition was on 8th February 1962." *(David Bedford Interview 2016)*

BBC Audition: 8th February 1962, Playhouse Theatre, Manchester

The Beatles arrived at the Playhouse Theatre and, though Brian had requested the opportunity for all three vocalists to be heard, Pilbeam only wanted to listen to John and Paul. He decided to assess them both to see if they would be suitable, and gave them the opportunity to perform four songs.

The Beatles performed two Lennon/McCartney songs, "Like Dreamers Do" and "Hello Little Girl", plus "Memphis Tennessee" and "Till There Was You".
They had played all of these songs at Decca just a few weeks earlier, and it was surprising that they included "Till There Was You", which had been an unmitigated disaster for McCartney at the audition.

History was about to repeat itself. Just as he had done at the Decca audition, Paul showed his nerves again. However, this time the boys passed the audition, making Pilbeam the first BBC producer to book The Beatles. He remembered that they stood out among the many other groups that had auditioned, recalling that there was a "load of rubbish – masses of rubbish – and then out of the blue this group turned up at the Playhouse at one of our audition sessions – called The Beatles." As with most places The Beatles went, their name was perceived as slightly odd. It was a "weird name and everybody said 'Yuk!'", Pilbeam said, "but I was impressed with them at the time." *(David Bedford Interview 2016)*

Pilbeam remembered the comments he made on their audition report form: "I wrote that they were 'an unusual group not as rocky as most, more country and western with a tendency to play music'. This probably sounds awfully crude, but it was praise indeed," he said. "Many groups just relied on noise to get them through the audition." It is interesting to note that Pilbeam saw them as a country and western group. First at Decca and now at the BBC, producers didn't know quite how to label the group. Pilbeam remembers most clearly his assessment of the singers: "John Lennon, yes. Paul McCartney, no. Paul seemed to overcome the setback," Pilbeam joked. *(David Bedford Interview 2016)*

Mike Smith of Decca had criticised McCartney's bass playing; now he was under scrutiny again, this time for his singing.

Conversely, Pilbeam was pleased with Pete's drumming as he noted that there was "good solid backing" on "Memphis Tennessee". Bert Kaempfert felt it was too risky to record Best's full kit, but Pilbeam was quite happy with the drummer. "I had no issue with recording Pete Best or with his drumming," he said, "and I thought he was very good." He also liked the John and Paul duet on "Hello Little Girl" and was surprised that The Beatles hadn't played any instrumentals.
Overall, he was delighted with the audition, which he felt deserved "high praise". His final notation read:
"Booked for TT's 7th March 1962." ("TT's" was Teenagers Turn.) *(David Bedford Interview 2016)*

Part one accomplished; they had passed the audition. Pilbeam arranged a date for them to return to Manchester to record their debut performance: 7th March. The programme would be broadcast the following day. Although the BBC wasn't the first place that teenagers turned for pop music, they regularly had audiences of around two million. This would be the first real opportunity for the British public to hear The Beatles. "I am proud to have been instrumental in introducing The Beatles to the Great British public on radio." *(David Bedford Interview 2016)*

Radio Recording Session: 7th March 1962, Playhouse Theatre, Manchester

When The Beatles arrived at the Playhouse Theatre to record in a "studio" for the first time in two months, they were glad to be performing in front of an audience rather than in a cold, empty, soulless setting like the one at Decca. Peter Pilbeam was again the producer, and they impressed him. "A first broadcast is quite something," he said, "no matter who you are and how brash you may appear normally, but they worked well. We used to get some terrific audiences down at the Playhouse for the teenage shows that we did, and we'd have the Northern Dance Orchestra on stage trying to look like teenagers with their chunky jumpers on." *(The Beatles At The BBC)*

The programme, which ran for 30 minutes, had a group, a guest singer and a presenter. "The Beatles came on and did a very good show," Pilbeam said. "I was very impressed with them and I booked them straight away for another date after that first show." *(The Beatles at the Beeb 62-65)*

The Beatles' first proper recording experience had been in a school hall in Hamburg, the second in an empty Decca studio, and now in a theatre in front of around 250 people. For their radio debut, they were wearing their new blue mohair suits for the very first time. Unfortunately, the two million listeners couldn't see them.

The songs were introduced by the announcer, Ray Peters, who also introduced the singer so that listeners would know it was a different vocalist. At the time, it was unusual to have more than one singer. The Beatles performed "Hello Little Girl" – which wasn't broadcast – then "Memphis Tennessee" *(both sung by John)*, "Dream Baby" (sung by Paul), then "Please Mr. Postman" *(another John vocal)*. Although Pilbeam had said a big 'NO' to Paul, Brian had convinced him to let Paul sing. It is interesting to note that although George's vocals were the best at Decca, Brian felt that he should only showcase the singing talents of John and Paul.

Pete Best's Drumming

Analysing the drumming on the songs is difficult, as the only surviving versions were recorded directly from the radio by a fan. On "Memphis Tennessee", you can hear that the arrangement is close to the original, and The Beatles sound very tight as a group, with a good driving rhythm. Pete's drumming has a perfect tempo and fits nicely with the song. On "Dream Baby", again the drumming sounds good and appropriate for the song. Paul mimics Roy Orbison's original vocal, tossing his nerves aside and giving an accomplished performance. On "Please Mr. Postman", the tempo is spot on. It is also very technically-proficient and Pete's style suits the song well. A good all-round performance.

With the recording session complete, the programme was broadcast the following day, and Pete Best remembers them sitting in the Casbah, waiting for it to start and that amazing feeling of hearing themselves on the radio for the first time, but certainly not the last.

Here We Go Again to the BBC
Recording Session: 11th June 1962, Playhouse Theatre, Manchester

The Beatles returned to the BBC in Manchester for a second recording session on 11th June, just days after their audition at EMI with George Martin. Although Pete didn't realise it, his days with The Beatles were coming to an end.

Once again, while introducing each song, the announcer also identified the vocalist. This time, John, Paul and George sang a song each, demonstrating their ability and versatility. Although the Lennon/McCartney song "Hello Little Girl" had been recorded in March for the first BBC broadcast, it was not aired. Consequently, the first Lennon/McCartney original to be heard on BBC Radio was "Ask Me Why", which was recorded by the group for Parlophone five months later and released in January 1963 as the B-side of their single, "Please Please Me". John took the lead vocal and, for the first time, we hear those three-part harmonies that became one of The Beatles' hallmarks. Pete uses the same rim shot rhythm on the snare drum that Andy White would use on "P.S. I Love You" in September.

It is interesting, but not surprising, that when they selected an original song, they didn't choose "Love Me Do" which had been a disaster the week before at EMI. It was obviously still a work in progress. What would have happened had they chosen "Ask Me Why" instead of "Love Me Do" to perform for George Martin? As the June BBC recording session continued, they performed "Besame Mucho", a song recorded at Decca and also played for George Martin just a few days earlier.

That version from EMI Studios was nowhere near as bright as the Decca version, but here, with an audience of their staunchest Liverpool fans present, it sounds vibrant and bounces along, with the vocal performance easily the best of the recorded versions from 1962. Pete's "atom beat" is evident here and you can hear his floor tom and bass drum driving the song perfectly behind them.

They have reinstated the "cha-cha-boom" that was evident at the Decca session, and that spark of life missing from both Decca and Parlophone is here in abundance. The audience obviously enjoyed it.

The final song, "A Picture of You", was sung by George and was another of the Joe Brown songs in The Beatles' set. It was a recent hit, and showed the BBC that they could perform a variety of songs, including an original, a classic and a chart song. Pete executes in this last song the perfect ending with a drum roll and a skipping beat, in time with the rest of the group – all part of a well-rehearsed finale.

You can hear in all of The Beatles' performances the difference a live audience made. Paul sounds confident for the first time and, as a group, they are performing at their very best. Pete's drumming is tight, shows a good variety and works well with the rest of the group. In spite of the poor recording quality of the BBC tracks, you can hear a group that excites an audience, eliciting wild clapping and occasional screaming, too.

Recording Session: 26th October 1962,
Playhouse Theatre, Manchester

The next time they returned to the BBC studios, on 26th October 1962, it would be to promote their new single, "Love Me Do", with Ringo Starr on drums. On that third programme produced by Peter Pilbeam, The Beatles performed "Sheila" (a Tommy Roe song that wasn't broadcast), "Love Me Do", "A Taste of Honey" and their B-side, "P.S. I Love You", which had featured session drummer Andy White on the record.

Sadly, no recording of this performance exists.

The Beatles at the BBC

Between March 1962 and June 1965, The Beatles recorded over fifty radio shows for the BBC. During that time, they performed 88 different songs, with 32 of them being Lennon/McCartney compositions. The others were covers of mainly American records. Of those songs, 36 were never issued on a record by the group.

These radio shows helped establish The Beatles as the top group in the UK, because they had more freedom to be themselves, having grown up listening to the radio, especially to the Goons.

33

21st February 1962

MR. "BERNARD" EPSTEIN MEETS GEORGE MARTIN

(Or How Decca Helped The Beatles Record With EMI)

Although Decca had rejected The Beatles, they actually helped them gain a record deal with their rivals, EMI. As it turned out, The Beatles' road to fame was just beginning. Brian had asked Decca to record the audition on tape and give him a copy, so he was able to walk out of Decca with something tangible in hand. Though not the usual practice, the handing over of this tape was key in Brian's ability to secure an audition with Parlophone.

He now had professional recordings of The Beatles, on reel-to-reel, to play to prospective London-based labels instead of the awful recording he had initially demonstrated to Tony Barrow. Epstein had met a man called Bob Boast in Hamburg in 1961 and the two struck up a friendship there, as they shared the same taste in music and also ran large record stores. Brian ran NEMS in Liverpool, the largest in the area, and Boast managed the HMV Record Store in Oxford Street, London, reputed to be the largest in the world.

His Master's Voice

After the rejection by Decca, and subsequent rejections by the remaining labels, Brian ended up in the HMV store in Oxford Street where a sequence of events took him to the doors of EMI.

There are two versions of the story. In the first version, Brian decided to look to his friend Bob Boast as a last ditch attempt to get something for his boys. The second version involves a fellow Liverpudlian.

Paul Murphy. In early 1957, Murphy (born in 1943) had recorded at the Kensington studio of Percy Phillips with Johnny Guitar from Rory Storm and the Hurricanes. For a time, he had been one of the Hurricanes. Spotted in Liverpool, Murphy was signed to EMI by Walter Ridley – one of the A&R men who later rejected The Beatles. His debut record was "Four & Twenty Thousand Kisses". Murphy left Liverpool for London to pursue his career singing with the Cyril Stapleton Orchestra. One day, he dropped into a hotel in Half Moon Street, London, to have a drink at the bar, and spotted Brian Epstein, whom he knew as the manager of NEMS in Liverpool. Brian appeared rather dejected, so Murphy approached him.

When Brian explained his difficulty getting A & R men to listen to his reel-to-reel tapes, Murphy told him that no one would listen to reel-to-reel tapes. He advised Brian to have an acetate made at the HMV store in Oxford Street where he had his own acetates cut. Accompanied by Murphy, Brian met up again with Bob Boast who helped him get the tapes transferred.

Murphy eventually made his way to Hamburg, where he worked as a record producer for Bert Kaempfert, making records with Tony Sheridan, Kingsize Taylor and the Dominoes and The Tremeloes. He later acquired the famous Star Club Tapes, the Kingsize Taylor recording of The Beatles performing live at the club at the end of 1962. Murphy's life and career seemed to cross paths with The Beatles on many occasions.

Something to Boast About

There is no way of knowing for certain which version is correct, as both are

Acetates

It wasn't a simple task making acetate discs, or test acetates as they were also known. They were not vinyl records made to be played hundreds of times, but rather designed as the transition between a master tape, which Brian had, and a vinyl record. A machine was manually operated to cut the audio-signal-modulated grooves into the surface of a special lacquer-coated disc on a lathe – a very skilled operation to say the least.

Most discs were 10, 12, or 14 inches in diameter and consisted of an aluminum core disc coated with black nitrocellulose lacquer, commonly, but incorrectly, called an "acetate". The term "acetate" is derived from the material used in examples cut before 1934, when the substrate was "cellulose acetate". Cellulose acetate was only in use for a short while, but the name "acetate" for these discs persisted. They would, in most cases, only contain one song per disc.

The acetate was normally used to assess whether the recorded music had been successfully transferred to disc, so it would be checked by the sound engineer and producer. While there may be only one copy made of a particular recording, sometimes more are cut and sent to the studio and band members for approval.

An acetate usually looks like a vinyl record, and was often one-sided, with no grooves on the reverse, and were much heavier than a vinyl record. They ring with a metallic sound when tapped, usually have a second, off-centre hole near the middle, and will invariably have handwritten labels. Acetates from the 1950s were only designed to be played between five and ten times at most and the sound quality would not be as good as vinyl. It could be played on a standard record player, though the wear would be more severe than a normal vinyl record.

Most of Brian's collection of Beatles acetates were sold for between £1,000 and £10,000 each at auction.

The acetates that Brian had cut in London, which he took to George Martin. Brian wrote:"Hullo (sic) Little Girl, John Lennon and The Beatles" and "Til There Was You, Paul McCartney and The Beatles" credible. However it happened, Brian ended up at HMV and a reunion with Bob Boast. Boast was happy to see his friend, though wasn't too impressed with the Decca audition tape of the As Tony Barrow commented years later, the other record labels didn't turn The Beatles down; they turned down The Beatles' audition at Decca. *(The Beatles Up Close And Personal)*

Although Boast sold records, he had no direct contact with record labels that could help Brian obtain an audition. Instead, he took The Beatles' manager to the first floor studio, where pop star hopefuls could cut a disc in the hope of being discovered. There, Brian was introduced to disc-cutter Jim Foy, who suggested transferring the best of the recordings from reel-to-reel to acetate discs, which would enable them to be more easily played by the record companies. This was no simple task, as Brian had fifteen songs on tape from Decca. This meant that, if all of the songs were transferred to acetates, he would have a number of very heavy discs to carry round with him. The impracticality forced Brian into a decision that wasn't necessarily the best one.

Foy and Epstein chatted during the process, and Foy was impressed with the recordings, especially when Brian told him that three of the songs they had recorded were original Lennon/McCartney compositions. Brian selected "Hello Little Girl", the Lennon song that had caught Brian's attention the first time he had seen The Beatles at the Cavern. He also chose "Till There Was You", which, even with McCartney's lead vocals, wasn't among their best from the audition. With his acetate (and likely a spare copy) in hand, Brian felt a renewed sense of optimism that he could still score that elusive record deal.

Armed with his acetates, Brian was happy. 'At last', he thought, someone was taking The Beatles seriously. Foy told him that the office of Ardmore and Beechwood, one of EMI's music publishing companies, was on the top floor of the shop, and asked if he should introduce him to the general manager, Sid Colman? Brian, naturally, said yes.

How Brian Epstein Obtained an Audition at Parlophone:
Version 1

After the disc was cut, Epstein accompanied Colman to his office. First Jim Foy, then Sid Colman and his assistant Kim Bennett heard something that Dick Rowe didn't: the quality of the original Lennon/McCartney song. Ardmore and Beechwood, they said, would be interested in publishing original songs. However, as Brian's priority was to get The Beatles signed to a recording deal, Colman explained to him how HMV and his own company, Ardmore and Beechwood, shared the same parent company: EMI.

Kim Bennett was interviewed for *Beatles Book Monthly* in 1969, and explained what happened. Bennett remembered that "Colman said, 'Now who hasn't got a group in EMI? Let me see, Norrie's got the Shadows', and then he ran through the list of A&R managers until he came to George Martin." Norrie, was George Martin's rival at EMI: Norrie Paramor, who looked after Cliff Richard and The Shadows, two of Britain's biggest ever pop icons.

None of the producers would want to take on a group similar to one they already had, so Colman had to find an A&R man who could give this group the attention they required. There was only one producer who fit the bill, and that was a producer who didn't really have any pop groups, or pop stars, but concentrated mainly on comedy and acts the other producers wouldn't touch. Would this man take them seriously? Colman made his decision; this was the only producer worth contacting, a man Colman knew well – the A&R head at Parlophone, George Martin. He rang Martin who, according to Bennett, was only "mildly interested". Bennett also recalled that "Colman had quite a job to persuade George Martin to see The Beatles." *(Beatles Book Monthly #70 May '69)*

Brian Epstein told Beatles biographer Hunter Davies a similar story. "The technician who recorded the tape told me it wasn't at all bad. He said he'd have a word with a music publisher upstairs, Syd Coleman (sic). Coleman was very excited and said he'd like to publish them and that he would speak to a friend of his at Parlophone, George Martin." An appointment was made to meet George Martin next day at EMI. *(The Beatles. Hunter Davies)*

How Brian Epstein Obtained an Audition at Parlophone:
Version 2

When interviewed in 2003, shortly before his death, Bennett contradicted his earlier version of events, denying the phone call had been made, saying that George Martin was the last person Colman would have called because he strongly disliked him. *(TuneIn)*

Bennett says that sometime after the initial meeting with Brian, Colman walked over to EMI with the acetate and tried to get one of the A&R men to sign the group. No one was interested. Then, Bennett says that he had a conversation with Colman and suggested that his boss should "go across to Len Wood and say that if EMI gives us a record, we will pay for its cost. Because it's a group, it'll be a straightforward studio production, no orchestra; we'll have got two copyrights for the next fifty years plus maybe a royalty on the record." *(TuneIn)*

In this second version, Kim Bennett suggests that George Martin had no say in signing The Beatles. He alleges that EMI Director Len Wood selected, and then ordered, George Martin to sign The Beatles, having uncovered news of Martin's affair with his secretary Judy Lockhart-Smith. Bennett says that Coman told him: "I've just been talking to Len Wood on the phone (and) we're going to get our record made after all." When Bennett asked who was going to do it, Colman replied, "George Martin". As Bennett added, "The Beatles record was going to be made as a gesture to Sid, to give Sid Colman a sop. Len was going to bow to our wishes at last." *(TuneIn)* In this latter telling of the story, Bennett, one of the best
record-pluggers in the business, and his boss Sid Colman, who wanted The Beatles signed to EMI for their songwriting skills, are responsible for the contract, and for The Beatles being signed to Parlophone.

Examining The Evidence

As this presents an entirely different take on the accepted history of Brian's first encounter with George Martin, we need to examine the old and the new evidence from the key eyewitnesses.

Kim Bennett

Bennett's original testimony from 1969 concurred with the original story, but then he has contradicted himself. Why? In the '60s, nobody would have criticised the established Beatles story, so you can understand if he followed the party line back then. The main problem is that there is no evidence to substantiate the story he told in 2003. This doesn't mean it's inaccurate, but certainly doubts are cast. The biggest issue is with the evidence from everybody else in the story, and the facts surrounding the meeting held the day after Brian met with Colman and Bennett.

In his second version, Bennett claimed that Colman made two separate trips to EMI in the days that followed, though no dates are mentioned. This doesn't give enough time for a meeting to be scheduled the next day between Brian and George Martin, unless that meeting never happened. Could Bennett be biased? He was partly responsible for getting The Beatles a record deal, and worked tirelessly to plug "Love Me Do", believing in the group when few others did. However, just when he thought that he and Colman were on to a great publishing deal, George Martin, with Dick James, took the publishing rights away from Ardmore and Beechwood, which could be seen as a stab in the back, so you could understand some ill-feeling towards Martin in particular. There is no evidence to support this second version of events.

George Martin

As you would expect, George Martin stuck to the original version of the story, but is that to protect him, or because it is true? Martin stated that he remembered receiving Colman's phone call, and that Colman told him that he had a "chap who's come in with a tape of a group he runs. They haven't got a recording contract, and I wonder if you'd like to see him and listen to what he's got?" Martin admitted that he was "willing to listen to anything" and agreed to allow Brian to come and see him. *(All You Need Is Ears)*

Although George Martin had made his mark by establishing Parlophone as a successful comedy record label, he was looking "with something close to desperation for an act from the pop world." For him, it was a matter of jealousy between the EMI producers, especially as his rival, Norrie Paramor, had signed one of the biggest pop stars Britain had ever seen – Cliff Richard – to the Columbia label, another division of EMI. Brian Epstein, in gratitude for Colman's generous act, offered Ardmore and Beechwood the first opportunity to publish the songs, if a recording deal could be agreed. If.

"Bernard" Epstein

George Martin recalled that first meeting with Brian. "It was on the 21st (February 1962) that I met Brian," he said, with his secretary Judy confirming it. "And I put 'Bernard' in the diary," she said, slightly embarrassed, having got Brian's name wrong. *(Arena: Produced by George Martin)* As this was the day after Brian's visit to HMV, it is difficult to see how else this could have been arranged in so short a time without the phone call from Colman to George Martin.

Brian Epstein

Brian Epstein remembered that when he was in Colman's office, the music publisher became "quite excited and said 'I like these. I would be quite willing to publish them'." Epstein also recalled Colman saying he would speak to a friend of his at Parlophone, a man named George Martin, and that he would like George to hear these and how he thought he might be "very interested". "Colman arranged for me to meet George's delightful and gracious secretary and assistant, Judy Lockhart-Smith. She arranged for me to come to EMI the following day." Brian walked into George Martin's office to begin discussions over a possible deal. He remembered how Martin listened to the acetate. He said that "he liked Paul's voice and George's guitar playing. Those were the two things he particularly said. John was singing 'Hello Little Girl' which he liked very much and Paul sang 'Till There Was You'." *(The Beatles. Hunter Davies)* However, George Martin remembered a slightly different view of that meeting: "What I said to Brian was if you want me to judge them on what you are playing me, then sorry I have to turn you down. He was terribly disappointed and I felt really sorry for him as he was such an earnest young man. I did like him. So I gave him a lifeline and said, 'I tell you what, if you want to bring them down from Liverpool, I'll give them an hour in the studio. Okay?'" *(Arena: Produced by George Martin)*

In February 2016, this acetate turned up unexpectedly when Les Maguire, keyboardist with Gerry and the Pacemakers, revealed that he had found the disc in his attic more than 50 years after Brian Epstein had given it to him (in 1963). Brian had received it from George Martin. The disc is very interesting in that it clearly shows the details of HMV's "Personal Recording Department, 363, Oxford Street, London, W.1." On one side of the 78rpm disc, Brian has written in pen "Hullo Little Girl", with a spelling mistake. Underneath, he has added "John Lennon & The Beatles", and, at the bottom, "(Lennon, McCartney)". On the other side, he has written "Til There Was You" with another spelling mistake and, to once again identify the singer, he has added "Paul McCartney & The Beatles". With Brian having written "John Lennon & The Beatles", and "Paul McCartney & The Beatles", it is easy to understand how George Martin would have been confused; was John the leader, or Paul? Most group names back in the day consisted of the leader's name followed by the group name. So was it John Lennon and The Beatles or Paul McCartney and The Beatles? Thankfully, Martin realised they were a group which he couldn't split.

This acetate, so recently unearthed, is a rare gem. Did the acetate make an impression with George Martin? No, not really. He wasn't knocked out by the songs, but he did agree to an audition; he must have heard something. The meeting between the successful entrepreneur Brian Epstein and the talented, school-masterly producer George Martin was the first of many that established a friendship and mutual admiration that would serve The Beatles well through the years. As Brian wrote in his autobiography, "George Martin was very helpful and discussed the difficulties of the record business, and the problems I would meet if I was going to be persistent, and said, 'I like your discs and I would like to see your artists'. We fixed a provisional date there and then." *(A Cellarful of Noise)*

Brian and George Martin, though from different parts of the country, were cut from the same cloth, and found in each other an instant rapport and mutual respect. Brian wasn't your average pop group manager, which must have been refreshing for Martin. As John would say, Brian was good at that "smarming and charming".

Tony Barrow

The Beatles' future PR guru Tony Barrow, who had helped Brian get the Decca audition, remembered Brian telling him about his success. "Brian was over the moon when he phoned me that day from 1, Manchester Square (EMI House) to say he had found an open door at last," Barrow recalled. "The truth was that George didn't have a full studio workload and The Beatles were useful time-fillers for him and the label." *(John, Paul, George, Ringo and Me)* As Ron Richards, one of the producers who would shortly be working with The Beatles, reflected, "George was desperate to get something off the ground in the pop department. It 'humiliated him' the way Parlophone got upstaged by its sister labels." Richards was proud of what would happen to Parlophone: "We had gone from being known as a sad little company to making a mint of money." *(The Beatles. The Biography)*

Len Wood

In December 1963, EMI Director L. G. "Len" Wood was asked to confirm how The Beatles came to Parlophone/ EMI. He stated that after Brian had The Beatles' demo put onto disc:

- The engineer at Oxford Street was quite impressed with some of the compositions and referred them (Brian and The Beatles) to Sid Colman (Ardmore and Beechwood).
- Colman then phoned George Martin, and he thought he ought to hear the tape and Martin agreed.
- Brian Epstein then took the tape to Martin, who agreed to give The Beatles a recording test. The producer, who conducted the test himself, was impressed with what he heard, signed them to a contract and the rest is public knowledge. *(The Beatles Complete Chronicles)*

Conclusion

There is no doubt that without Kim Bennett and Sid Colman, The Beatles wouldn't have had a chance – likely their very last chance – to secure a recording contract. Was George Martin instructed to sign this unknown group from Liverpool, or did he have more of a say in the contract negotiations? What Bennett suggested was that the phone call between Colman and George Martin never took place, and therefore that the meeting the following day never took place, despite evidence to the contrary. It would make sense that Bennett, a hard-working and dedicated plugger, pursued the publication of those original songs by putting pressure on EMI, as Epstein had promised to offer any published songs to Ardmore and Beechwood. pressure from Len Wood might have happened after the audition.

As is often the case, especially in the 1962 dealings with EMI, there seems to be more nebulous, ambiguous and conflicting evidence than at any time in the well-documented Beatles story. However it happened, Brian went to HMV with the Decca audition tape and destiny paired him with Sid Colman and Kim Bennett who wanted to publish the original Lennon-McCartney songs. This, in turn, resulted in Colman contacting George Martin, who met with Brian, offered The Beatles an audition, and eventually, a contract. It was that simple.

A group of guitarists was on the way out, but only from Decca to Parlophone, via HMV and Ardmore and Beechwood.

FOR THE CRITICAL EAR . . .
the new **G.B. 65** model
SEMI ACOUSTIC GUITAR

TODAY'S MOST SENSATIONAL GUITAR SOUND

Burns

Rickenbacker

LISTEN TO 'BEATLES' JOHN AND GEORGE THAT'S THE GREAT RICKENBACKER SOUND

In every important category—sound, appearance, ease of playing and dependability—Rickenbacker guitars lead the field.
They are made in America by the people with the longest experience in the manufacture of professional quality electronic guitars. Every Rickenbacker feature is an outstanding achievement in engineering and structural crafts-manship—a better instrument—to produce better sound.
Professional guitarists interpret the Rickenbacker playing accomplishment. It is a partnership of technology offering horizons of unlimited accomplishment.

Rose, Morris
SPONSORED INSTRUMENTS

Original painting by Paul Skellett

24th May 1962

BRIAN AND BERT IN CONTRACT CONTACT

(Just one more time - with feeling)

Once Brian Epstein had become The Beatles' manager, one of his first jobs was securing their release from the Kaempfert contract they had signed the previous year in Hamburg. When Brian visited EMI in early December 1961 to try to obtain a recording contract for The Beatles, he discussed the contents of the Kaempfert contract with Ron White, the company's General Marketing Manager. Epstein left the contract, which was written entirely in German, with White and in a letter the EMI executive wrote to Epstein on 7th December, he enclosed the "original of the contract you gave to me in confidence a few days ago and thought you might like to have a little translation to save you the bother of having it done." *(The Beatles Complete Chronicles)*

White was trying to do Epstein a favour as a valued client, possibly in the knowledge that although he would "ask our Artistes Managers if they are interested in the group", EMI would likely turn The Beatles down. White did advise Epstein that the Kaempfert contract would need "three months notice of termination before the 30th June 1962 if you are to obtain their services."

(The Complete Beatles Chronicles)

Epstein wrote to Kaempfert on 20th February 1962 to discuss terminating the contract. Kaempfert replied on 3rd March, saying that he was "in principle willing to release this group from their agreement before the official expiration of their contract."

Although Kaempfert had signed The Beatles personally, he had to approach Polydor on the matter. The German producer asked for one more recording session "for the Polydor label during their stay in Hamburg during April or May."

After this, he would release them, because he didn't want to "spoil the chance of the group to get recording contracts elsewhere." *(The Complete Beatles Chronicles)*

Recording Session - 24th May 1962

The session took place on 24th May 1962 at Studio Rahlstedt, Wandsbek, one of the boroughs of Hamburg. They recorded the instrumental backing on two more old songs, "Sweet Georgia Brown" and "Swanee River". It was an odd request by Kaempfert, who gave no real reason for it. Sheridan and Kaempfert had already recorded the songs, and released them on an album, called *My Bonnie*, including the title track and "The Saints" recorded the previous year.

For this session, John, Paul, George and Pete were not accompanied by Tony Sheridan, but by their new friend from the Star Club, Roy Young, a boogie-woogie piano player who was known as Britain's answer to Little Richard. They enjoyed their time on stage with Young, who had turned down Brian Epstein's invitation to join The Beatles. George didn't play, but provided backing vocals. Pete provided his snare drum rhythm, Paul played bass, John played rhythm and Roy was on piano. The result is competent, though it clearly lacks soul, and was only released on a limited basis in Germany and Greece.

The session signalled the end of Bert Kaempfert's time with The Beatles. He became yet another producer who failed to spot The Beatles' potential and missed the chance to sign them permanently. That would be left to George Martin.

Original painting by Paul Skellett

6th June 1962

THE BEATLES AT EMI: THE CONTRACT

(Dispatched telegrams)

This day has gone down in history as the day George Martin assessed and offered The Beatles a contract. Having been turned down by every record label, including EMI, Brian's last hope had been his 5th May 1962 meeting with George Martin, after which he received the contract by post, signed it, and immediately dispatched telegrams to "the boys" and to Bill Harry of *Mersey Beat*. But is this what really happened?

The telegram sent to Bill Harry, for publication in *Mersey Beat*, read:
"Have secured contract for Beatles to recorded (sic) for EMI on Parlophone Label 1st recording date set for June 6th. Brian Epstein."

Two others were sent to The Beatles at the Star Club, Hamburg:
"Congratulations Boys EMI request recording session please rehearse new material"

"EMI contract signed, sealed. Tremendous importance to all of us. Wonderful." *(A Cellarful of Noise)*

John, Paul and George reportedly sent telegrams back to Brian:

"When are we going to be millionaires?" – John

"Please order four new guitars" – *George*

"Please wire ten thousand pound advance royalties" – Paul

of the various types of sessions that could be held, i.e. an Artist Test, a Commercial Test, and a contractual Recording Session, with only the latter containing "contract terms" such as royalty rates and Musician's Union (MU) fees for the artists.

Since the still-existing forms associated with The Beatles' 6th June session contain the latter, including contractual information, Lewisohn opines that the red form document's entries are clear and irrefutable proof that the session was not either of the two types of Tests, but a contractually-based recording session.

Many authors propose that, despite the seemingly definitive appearance of that single document, a plethora of other evidence exists to the contrary; that the session was a Test of one form or another, and that a formal contract was dependent on the outcome of that Test.

We believe the contract status has a huge bearing on what happened next to the group, particularly with respect to the drumming situation, which is the principal subject matter of this book. It is therefore imperative that we examine all of the available evidence to see if The Beatles truly were performing under a contract when they visited EMI on 6th June, or whether such a contract was still looming, conditional on their satisfying the musical sensibilities of the Parlophone record label head, George Martin.

Just a few days after returning from Hamburg, excited by Brian's news about their recording session, John, Paul, George and Pete walked through the "tradesman's entrance" of EMI's Abbey Road studios for the first time. Over the

One of the biggest debates involving this day is whether **The Beatles** were already under contract to Parlophone or if this was merely an audition or test?

next several years, they would regularly cross the threshold of EMI's front entrance, though with a different drummer – for this day would be the beginning of the end for Pete Best in The Beatles. However, on 6th June, 1962, they entered as a group who, according to George Martin, were "…certainly a team. You got the impression that they'd have stood together and fought the whole darned world if anything upset them." *(True Story of The Beatles)*

Unfortunately, one of them was to be sacrificed, and without too much of a fight.

Were The Beatles under contract on 6th June 1962?

In the majority of Beatles books, including the two "authorised" bios – *The Beatles: The Authorised Biography by Hunter Davies (1968) and Anthology (2000)* – along with *The Beatles Recording Sessions by Mark Lewisohn (1988)*, it has been reported by several who were present at the 6th June session that this was an audition, carrying with it only the potential for a contract. And further, that the issuance of that contract would be chiefly dependent on whether they could sufficiently impress George Martin with their studio recording ability.

However, in his 2013 volume *Tune In*, the author has reversed course, and is now leading the side that claims that:

"…the crucial documents are clear beyond doubt and can dispel any misleading information for whatever reason it existed: this was no audition at all – The Beatles were at EMI because they already had a contract." *(Tune In)*

The crucial document he cites is EMI's "red form", typically filled out for each for each of the various types of sessions that could be held, i.e. an Artist Test, a Commercial Test, and a contractual Recording Session, with only the latter containing "contract terms" such as royalty rates and Musician's Union (MU) fees for the artists.

Studio Two at Abbey Road

AN AGREEMENT made the 4th day of June 1962 BETWEEN THE PARLOPHONE COMPANY LIMITED of Hayes in the County of Middlesex (hereinafter called "the Company") of the one part and BRIAN EPSTEIN, c/o N.E.M.S. Ltd., 12-14, Whitechapel, Liverpool 1., (hereinafter called "the Manager") of the other part:

WHEREAS the Manager:-

    i. has under his control a group of Instrumentalists professionally known as THE BEATLES (hereinafter called "the Artists").

    ii. Acts herein on behalf of the Artists.

    iii. has represented to the Company that he is in a position to ensure the carrying into effect of the terms and conditions of the Agreement following:-

NOW IT IS HEREBY AGREED as follows:-

1. FOR the purpose of this Agreement the word "record" shall mean a gramophone record, magnetic tape or any other sound-bearing contrivance or appliance reproducing a performance by the Artists under this Agreement.

2. THE MANAGER shall procure that

    i. the Artists shall during a period of 1 (One) year computed from the 6th day of June 1962 attend at such places and times reasonably convenient to the Artists as the Company shall require and shall render such performances (whether alone or together with one or more other Artists) as the Company shall elect for reproduction in by or on any record. The minimum number of performances shall be sufficient to comprise not less than the equivalent of 6 (six) sides of a gramophone record manufactured to play at seventy-eight revolutions per minute (hereinafter referred to as "78 r.p.m.").

    ii. The Artists shall at the request of the Company repeat any performance for the purpose of producing in the opinion of the Company a perfect record.

3. THE MANAGER undertakes that Artists shall not:-

    (a) during the currency of this Agreement render any performance whatsoever, and

Page 1 of the Parlophone Contract

The Paperwork Trail

Application for Artists' Contract submitted by George Martin to Miss Evelyn P Harwood (Administration) within EMI, commencing on 6th June 1962 for 1 year

Contract was sent from Miss Harwood to George Martin to be forwarded to Brian Epstein for him to sign

Mr. G. Martin

The Beattles/Parlophone (Manager Mr. Brian Epstein)

Enclosed please find copy of this contract for despatch to Mr. Epstein so that he can sign and return it to us.
Brian Epstein is getting a royalty and I asked especially whether any provision was to be made for payment of M.U. Rates to musicians at the recording sessions, but I was told no, they would not get any such payment. I hope this is correct!

Evelyn F. Harwood, Administration, EMI Records Ltd.

Inter-departmental Memo from George Martin to Miss Harwood confirming he would pay The Beatles 'Musicians Union' fees

Miss E. Harwood
Administration, Hayes

Re: The Beattles/Parlophone

Thank you for your memo' of May 24th, enclosing the Contract for the Beattles.

In point of fact, I will pay the musicians the ordinary M.U. Fee but I did not think that it was necessary to include this in the Contract.

G.H. Martin
E.M.I. Records Ltd.

Judy Lockhart-Smith, on behalf of George Martin, sends the contract Brian had signed to Miss Harwood

Miss E. Harwood
Administration, Hayes

Re: The Beatles

I am returning herewith contract for the above artist duly signed.

G. H. Martin.
E.M.I. Records Ltd.

18th June 1962
Memo from Miss Harwood to George Martin enclosing the contract which has been "signed by the Secretary and witnessed"

Brian Epstein / The Beatles

Herewith agreement between the above parties. This has been signed by the Secretary and witnessed,
and is for the artists retention.

Miss E. Harwood
Administration, Hayes

26th June 1962
Letter from EMI's General Marketing Manager Ron White to Brian Epstein

Brian Epstein, Esq.,
NEMS Limited, 12-14 Whitechapel, Liverpool, 1.

Dear Mr. Epstein,

I was nonplussed and somewhat embarrassed to see details of a contract going through for "The Beatles" especially in view of my letter to you of the 18th December, 1961 when I told you that our Artiste Managers did not feel that we could use them.
I hasten to say that I am very pleased that a contract is now being negotiated as I felt that they were very good but our Artiste Managers who heard the record felt at that time that they had the greatest difficulty in judging their quality from the record.

George Martin tells me that he has been suitably impressed with them and has made certain suggestions to you which in his view may improve them still further and it is for this reason that he has offered a contract.
My only reason for writing is to endeavour to explain what must appear to you to be an anomaly in our Organisation. I can assure you that the Artiste Managers did hear the record but I know you will appreciate that even Artistes Managers are human can change their minds!
With best wishes,

Yours sincerely,

R.N. WHITE
General Marketing Manager

29th June 1962
Brian Epstein replies to Ron White's letter

Dear Mr. White,

Thank you very much for your letter of the 26th instant regarding The Beatles. In the circumstances your attitude and remarks are greatly appreciated. As you will probably realise it is a great pleasure for me to be associated with EMI in this manner. I am very much looking forward to the issue of the groups' first disc which I expect should be towards the end of August - although I have not heard from George Martin recently.

Thank you again, kindest regards.

Yours sincerely,
Brian Epstein

The Contract - The Key Clauses
(The relevant contract clauses are spelled out on the following page.)

Whereas the Manager:-

i. Has under his control a group of Instrumentalists professionally known as **THE BEATTLES** *(hereinafter called "the Artists")*.
ii. Acts herein on behalf of the Artists
iii. Has represented to the Company that he is in a position to ensure the carrying into effect of the terms and conditions of the Agreement following:-

2.THE MANAGER shall procure that i. The Artists shall during a period of 1 (One) year computed from the 6th day of June 1962 attend at such places and times reasonably convenient to the Artists as the Company shall require and shall render such performances. *(whether alone or together with one or more other Artists) as the Company shall elect for reproduction in by or on any record. The minimum number of performances shall be sufficient to comprise not less than the equivalent of 6 (six) sides of a gramophone record manufactured to play at seventy-eight revolutions per minute (hereinafter referred to as "78 r.p.m.")*

ii. The Artists shall at the request of the Company repeat any performance for the purpose of producing in the opinion of the Company a perfect record.

3.THE MANAGER undertakes that Artists shall not:-
(a) during the currency of this agreement render any performance whatsoever, and (b)For the period of ten years immediately following the termination of this Agreement or any extension thereof perform any work recorded by the Company under this Agreement.

For any person firm or corporation other than the Company whereby their performance might be recorded in any form from which any gramophone record magnetic tape or any other sound-bearing contrivance or appliance may be offered to the public.

Royalties -

4. SUBJECT as hereinafter mentioned the Manager shall be entitled to a royalty in respect of each record sold by the Company and any person firm or corporation authorised by it after deducting fifteen per cent *(to cover records returned and/ or damaged in transit and/or used for demonstration or advertising purposes)*

as follows:-

(a) On a gramophone record manufactured to play at 78 r.p.m.
Reproducing -
(i) On both sides performance by the Artists alone
1d (one penny) **per record**
(ii) On both sides performance by the Artists together with other Artists a proportion of 1d (one penny) **per record according to the number of other Artists.**

In the case of such a gramophone record only one side of which reproduces the Artists' performance as aforesaid, the amount of royalty shall be one-half of the amounts set forth above.

Worldwide Agreement

9. THE company shall be entitled to the sole right of production, reproduction, sale (under such trademarks as it may select), use and performance (including broadcasting throughout the world by any and every means whatsoever) of records manufactured in pursuance of this Agreement.

10. THE Company shall at all times have the right at its discretion to decide whether and/or when to commence or discontinue or re-commence the said production, reproduction, sale, use and performance of records manufactured in pursuance of this Agreement, and the irrevocable right and licence to use and publish the Artists' names and photographs for labelling cataloguing and exploiting the said records AND to authorise any other person firm or corporation to do any or all such acts and things.

Extension

11. THE Company shall be entitled to continue this Agreement for 3 *(three)* successive periods of 1 (one) year each upon giving notice in writing to the Manager...................... Should this Agreement be extended for a further first period of one year then in respect of records reproducing performances recorded by the Artists during such first extended period the royalty referred to on Cl. 4(a) hereof shall be increased to 1 1/4 (one penny farthing). In case of any further extension then in respect of records reproducing performances recorded by the Artists during such further extension the said royalty shall be increased to 1 1/2d (three half pence).

Contract Law

Even though both authors of this book have experience in dealing with contracts, and contract law, we felt that we needed to obtain independent legal advice. Enter Peter Bounds CBE, former Chief Executive of Liverpool City Council and solicitor. He examined the contract, the correspondence, and the quotes from George Martin and the EMI staff, Brian Epstein, and The Beatles, before reaching his conclusions in an interview with David Bedford.

"In law, for there to be a valid contract," said Bounds, "there are three elements that need to be present:

1.   A valid offer and acceptance of that offer;
2.   Consideration provided by both parties; (both parties must bring something to the bargain/contract)
3.   An intention to create legal relations on the part of both parties

Certainty of terms is also important, although not a required element, but if other elements are in place, any uncertainty needs to be resolved by the parties."

(David Bedford Interview 2017)

Examining The Contract

The main question around the session is: when does it appear that the parties intended a legal contractual relationship to exist? "The contract may have been sent by the company as 'an invitation to treat' (i.e. to do business), with Epstein returning the signed copy as the 'offer' and EMI signing and returning it as the 'acceptance'," advised Bounds.

It is clear from the basis of the session on 6th June that neither side felt that the contract existed on 6th June, and that neither side intended to create legal relations until after the audition and the company had decided to go ahead. Further, by examining the clauses within the contract, especially Clauses 10 and 3, it probably served The Beatles better on 6th June for the contract not to have been in place. Why? Because this was a contract which heavily favoured the record company, and had it been in effect on 6th June, it could have had a detrimental effect on the group. The Beatles would have been tied to Parlophone, who had no obligation to release a record, but it would have stopped them from pursuing any other deals relating to their songs.

This is because under the contract terms of Clause 10, it is very clear that EMI's only duties were to record six songs, and then, at their discretion, decide whether to release them as records, or not.

Clause 10.
THE Company shall at all times have the right at its discretion to decide whether and/or when to commence or discontinue or re-commence the said production, reproduction, sale, use and performance of records manufactured in pursuance of this Agreement, and the irrevocable right and licence to use and publish the Artists' names and photographs for labelling cataloguing and exploiting the said records AND to authorise any other person firm or corporation to do any or all such acts and things.

This, too, was a reason why it would not have suited The Beatles being under contract yet on 6th June. The contract imposes no duties on the company, but significantly limits The Beatles' ability to do business elsewhere: so The Beatles would have no benefit claiming the contract existed at or before the audition.

How Does This Limit The Beatles ability to do business elsewhere?

Clause 3 prohibits The Beatles making recordings with anyone else, even if the company doesn't issue, or stops releasing, their records. If this had happened, it might have been regarded as oppressive.

Clause 3.
THE MANAGER undertakes that Artists shall not:-

(a)during the currency of this agreement render any performance whatsoever,

and

(b)For the period of ten years immediately following the termination of this Agreement or any extension thereof perform any work recorded by the Company under this Agreement for any person firm or corporation other than the Company whereby their performance might be recorded in any form from which any gramophone record magnetic tape or any other sound-bearing contrivance or appliance may be offered to the public.

In other words, if there were a contract in effect on 6th June, a day on which EMI recorded four of the group's songs, The Beatles would not have been able to record those same four songs with anyone else for at least 11 years (the current year of the contract plus the ten years following the end of that initial one-year term), even if EMI refused to release any of them as an actual record! The Beatles lucked out, at least as far as "Love Me Do", "Ask Me Why", "P.S. I Love You" and "Besame Mucho" were concerned. And, as we came to know, well beyond that.

Intention to Create Legal Relations

Peter Bounds further clarified the position of the two parties at the time of the session on 6th June, and how we can't determine that there was an "intention to create legal relations by both parties at that date."

"The way a court operates is to look at what happened and say; 'if the parties had described what they did at the time in legal phraseology, what would they have said they were doing at each point?" In this case, when the company sent the draft agreement out, they were most likely saying: 'if we take you on, we propose it will be on these terms'. But the crucial word is 'if'. Everything hinges on the audition. Hence the notion that the contract did not come into effect until after the audition and the company decision to go ahead, i.e. it was subject to a prior condition, or , in lawyer-speak, a condition precedent.

This would mean that the action of sending the contract to Brian Epstein was not seen as an offer, but an "invitation to treat", a phrase that has developed to represent the pre-offer stage.

What evidence do we have regarding the intention to create legal relations? We have to examine the conversation that took place between George Martin and Brian Epstein upon their first meeting. George Martin made it clear what would happen next:

"What I said to Brian was; 'if you want me to judge them on what you are playing me, then sorry I have to turn you down'. He was terribly disappointed and I felt really sorry for him as he was such an earnest young man. I did like him. So I gave him a lifeline and said, 'I tell you what, if you want to bring them down from Liverpool, I'll give them an hour in the studio. Okay?'" *(Arena: Produced by George Martin/ BBC Television)*

Brian, naturally, agreed to whatever terms were being offered to him from Martin, which was to give them an audition. In return, Martin agreed to pay them for the session. There was, therefore, no intention on George Martin's part to enter into a legally binding contract before seeing the group. This would have been standard industry practice. With the audition approaching, Martin sent the contract to Brian on the basis that, if the audition went well, Parlophone would give them the contract. George Martin was very clear about this:
"Why on earth would I have signed a group before I saw them? I would never have done that, it's preposterous." *(Mojo "The Beatles, Ten Years That Shook The World)*
The Beatles were also knew exactly why they were there, and in what capacity.

When Paul McCartney was asked about this momentous day, he stated: "We were told that it was an audition for George Martin." *(The Complete Beatles Recording Sessions)*

In *Anthology*, he said that George Martin "agreed to audition us, and we had a not-very-powerful audition in which he was not very pleased with Pete Best." George, also in *Anthology*, remembered the day and its purpose clearly: "The Parlophone audition was in June 1962. It went not too badly. I think George Martin felt we were raw and rough but that we had some quality that was interesting." *(Anthology)*

The Beatles, Brian Epstein and George Martin no doubt saw this session as an audition – and the day the draft contract that Brian had signed would go into effect, if they passed the test. There was therefore no intention to create legal relations, and so no valid contract at that date.

Timing

The evidence that has led some to believe that a signed contract already existed on 6th June appears at the top of the contract: "An Agreement Made the 4th June 1962", to be effective from "6th June 1962". At the bottom, it also states:

"**IN WITNESS** whereof **THOMAS HUMPHREY TILLING** on behalf of the Company and **BRIAN EPSTEIN** have hereunto set their hands the day and year first above mentioned."

This refers to the 4th June 1962 mentioned at the top of the contract. We know this didn't happen, as Brian had likely signed it earlier than 4th June, and George Martin had only sent it back to Miss Harwood on 5th June, as yet unsigned by EMI's authorised representative (Thomas Humphrey Tilling).

So, on its face, (prima facie in legalese), it may seem that the contract was bilaterally signed on 4th June and therefore was a completed contract. However, this was more likely the day that Martin received the contract from Epstein bearing the manager's signature, as George Martin sent it to Miss Harwood the following day (5th June). This was because, even though Martin had requested the contract to be drawn up, it was still to be agreed, subject to the audition. It does not mean that Martin, or the designated EMI signatories, had signed it that day. You can select any effective date for a contract as long as both parties agree to it. But a contract can still be agreed, even unsigned.

There was no logical reason to backdate the contract to 4th June. For the session on 6th June to count within the contract, it had to be effective from 6th June, and agreed before that date.

When was it signed?

It is difficult to be certain what the legal relationship was in the period from 4th June to whenever it was decided after the audition that the company wanted to go ahead with the deal, but it was probably a conditional contract – the contract would come into being, on the agreed terms, if the company agreed after the audition to go ahead. There is no evidence to show that it was signed on behalf of Parlophone immediately after George Martin received it back from Epstein.

Final page of the contract

Surviving paperwork indicates only that the contract (which had been "duly signed" by Epstein, but never by George Martin) was forwarded on 5th June from Martin's office to Evelyn Harwood in EMI Administration at their Head Office in Hayes, whence it originated. George Martin was not authorised to sign for EMI, so his signature was never placed on the contract.

A key piece of evidence can be found when Miss Harwood wrote to George Martin on 18th June, and returned the contract:

"between the above parties. This has been signed by the Secretary (Thomas Tilling) and witnessed (by E. Pearce) and is for the artists retention."

(The Complete Beatles Chronicles)

This clearly shows that sometime between 5th June and 18th June, the contract had been signed by EMI and the copy was to be forwarded to Brian Epstein.

Could it have been signed on or before 6th June?

If it had been signed anytime before the session on 6th June, then why would this letter have needed to be written and sent on 18th June, saying that it had been signed and witnessed? Wouldn't it have been prudent for EMI to have informed George Martin prior to the 6th June session that the contract had, by then, been bilaterally agreed to, and that he was operating under contract? Miss Harwood obviously was aware of the 6th June effective date of the contract, yet it was not until 18th June that she informed Martin (formally, at least) that the contract had now been signed by EMI.

So, while possible, it is highly doubtful that the contract was signed by EMI before the 6th of June. In all probability, this is what happened:

The twelve days that transpired between the audition (6th June) and the day Martin received the signed contract to forward to Epstein (18th June) probably involved the bureaucratic process at EMI. Ken Townsend, the Technical Engineer from the session, recalled fellow engineer Norman Smith sending a copy of the tape from the session to EMI's Manchester Square offices "about a week after the recording date. The likely scenario here would seem that Martin made his fateful decision in advance of one of the regular EMI recording manager staff meetings to consider potential artists, on or about 15th June. Even if the other managers thought that the group with the funny name, 'The Beatles', might be another of his comedy records, Martin had concluded that they had potential; potential that he needed to tweak in the studio if they were to be successful."
(Please Please Me: Sixties British Pop Inside Out)

The Eyewitnesses: "No, It's Not Signed"

In Billy Shepherd's *The True Story of The Beatles*, published in 1964, just two years after these events happened, The Beatles remembered hearing from Brian about the status of the Parlophone contract after their 6th June visit, but were quite certain it was still not a "done deal". John wanted to know more: "Yeah, it sounds great, but has the contract actually been signed? Is it absolutely definite?" Brian was honest with them. "No, it's not signed. Not yet. But I can only say that George Martin was most impressed and has told me that he wants to go ahead and get on with some releases." George Harrison, though happy, was not reassured, as it "wasn't water-tight enough to make us feel confident." *(True Story*

of The Beatles)

Brian and The Beatles told biographer Hunter Davies that they had attended "their audition before George Martin", and that, after they left, the producer "listened carefully to everything and said very nice. He liked them. He'd let them know. They'd expected a more definite reaction." *(The Beatles. Hunter Davies)* As Brian also recalled in his autobiography, *A Cellarful of Noise*, he was still concerned after the session because "there was still no contract and The Beatles and I left EMI full of hope but without money or security." That frustration must have been worrying for all of them, as this was the last throw of the dice.

The Artist Test/Audition

George Martin did not produce the session, which also suggests that this was a test, and why he delegated Producer Ron Richards to oversee it.

"Some sessions, I'd say, 'right Ron, you take that because I'm doing such-and-such'. When it came to doing artist tests, which this was – this was just looking at four berks from Liverpool – it didn't mean anything in our lives at all. I said, OK Ron, get it organised, I'll pop in and see what they're like. It's as simple as that." *(Mojo "The Beatles, Ten Years that Shook the World.)*

Norman Smith, the balance engineer, also recalled that it was an artist test after Martin had been fetched during "Love Me Do".

"The control room door opened and in walked George Martin himself.
And I thought to myself, 'This must be some kind of special artist test for him to show up.' Because producers didn't normally attend artist tests. It was always their assistants. And, of course, up to that time, George was not involved at all with any guitar groups. He did a lot of comedy records, like Peter Sellers and stuff like that." *(Recording The Beatles)*

One of the most significant indicators in determining the nature of the session was the fact that EMI "recorded The Beatles 'live', as they had done at Decca, and not recording the instruments first and then dubbing on the vocals." Malcolm Addey, a former EMI balance engineer, confirmed that the session probably constituted an artist test.

"The comparison I make to the EMI test is the motion picture industry screen test. They want to know how you sound on mic!" In short, the 6th June session could have functioned as a review to help the production team appraise the strengths and weaknesses of the musicians, their equipment, and their material." *(Please Please Me: Sixties British Pop Inside Out)*

What seems clear is that, although slightly different terms are used for the name of this session, this was not a recording session that would lead to a record being issued. This was an artist test that would enable George Martin and his team to witness what The Beatles were like in a studio, assess their strengths and weaknesses, and learn more about each member of the group.

The usual practice from here would be for Martin to head to Tin Pan Alley to find the right song to release, if he was going to sign them. However, with Ardmore & Beechwood keen to publish Lennon & McCartney songs, this would not be a straightforward group to record, if he was going to sign them.

Conclusions

The documentation within EMI shows that the bilaterally signed contract was only returned from EMI's Head Office on 18th June. All of the eyewitnesses have said that there was no signed contract when The Beatles left EMI Studios on 6th June. Many of the other EMI staff involved, like the studio engineers, were also certain it was a test. It is therefore self-evident that there was likely no contract in place on 6th June. If EMI didn't want to take The Beatles on after the audition, the pre-condition to the contract would not have been fulfilled, so the contract would not have come into being.

Although the contract wasn't agreed to or signed yet by EMI, George Martin had sat down with Brian in London on 9th May 1962 to discuss a proposed agreement. Martin described it as a standard EMI contract, effective over four years, which obligated the company to record only six songs, though EMI was only committed to the first year and could renew it if they so chose. At only 1d *(1 old penny)* per double-sided record, it was never expected that they were going to be rich from record sales alone.

What George Martin did was have EMI draw up the contract, get Brian to sign it and then audition The Beatles. If they were good enough, he would have the contract signed by EMI after the test, backdating it to include the 6th June session.

We contend that the presence of "contract information" on the red form could merely have been due to the fact that the preparer of the form had seen or was aware of the existence of a contract-like document, but was unaware that it hadn't been signed yet by both parties. The possibility also exists that the preparer, being unaware or ill-informed of its legal status, misconstrued it as a "done deal" and dutifully, but erroneously, included the non-enforceable document's detail onto the red form for the session.

George Martin saw this as an artist test, meaning that if he didn't want to sign them, he could simply tear up the document – which had only been signed by Brian – and walk away. As it turned out, he decided to recommend that EMI sign them and include the 6th June session. This was a clever move on Martin's part because even though they were unlikely to release a single from the session, four of the six obligatory songs under the terms of the contract had already been recorded. What George Martin had done was leave all possibilities open – rehearse them and assess them, sign them or don't sign them – but in the unlikely event they did record something worthwhile, they could still release it. But even that wasn't guaranteed. As the norm has always been in the music industry, the record company held all the aces.

EMI Director Len Wood summed it up well when he said that George Martin "agreed to give The Beatles a recording test, was impressed with what he heard, signed them to a contract and the rest is public knowledge."

(The Complete Beatles Chronicles)

The final piece of evidence comes in a letter to Brian from EMI's Ron White, dated 26th June 1962. White admitted to being "somewhat embarrassed to see details of a contract going through for The Beatles" because he had turned the group down in December 1961. As White said, the contract was "going through", though in fact it had already been completed. He also said that he was pleased that "a contract is now being negotiated" and that George Martin had been "suitably impressed with them and has made certain suggestions to you which in his view will improve them still further and it is for this reason that he has offered a contract."

This clearly shows that George Martin only recommended that a contract be offered after seeing and hearing them in the studio, and "making certain suggestions". Brian was obviously pleased to have an apology from a senior executive at EMI, though in his reply of 29th June, Brian is clearly frustrated that "I have not heard from George Martin recently." *(The Complete Beatles Chronicles)*

The evidence suggests that Martin had the contract drawn up in May, at which point it was sent to Brian for his consideration as a draft of the type of contract that could be on offer. Without consulting his solicitor, Brian agreed with the terms, signed and returned the agreement, "the offer", to George Martin, who then had it forwarded to the company's Head Office on 5th June. Then, around 17th /18th June, the company signed their part of the contract, "the acceptance", backdated to 4th June and effective from 6th June, the date of the session, "the consideration". From then on, The Beatles were under contract to Parlophone and EMI, and the most important musical collaboration between a group and a producer began in earnest, with "legal relations" and "certainty of terms" all agreed.

The deal was finally signed, sealed and delivered.

When did Brian, on behalf of The Beatles, Have A Legal Contract with Parlophone?

As we know, Brian Epstein signed the contract that George Martin sent to him in May 1962. EMI received it from Brian by 5th June 1962.

However, as Brian Epstein didn't sign the management contract with The Beatles in January – and we know it wasn't enforceable by him – then, in the eyes of the law, no formal agreement was in place when Brian signed EMI's contract. After all, the opening sentences of the contract clearly state:

An agreement made the 4th day of June 1962

BETWEEN THE PARLOPHONE COMPANY LIMITED of Hayes in the County of Middlesex *(hereinafter called "the Company")* of the one part and **BRIAN EPSTEIN, c/o N.E.M.S.** Ltd., 12-14, Whitechapel, Liverpool 1., *(hereinafter called "the Manager")* of the other part:

WHEREAS the Manager:-

1. Has under his control a group of Instrumentalists professionally known as THE BEATLES *(hereinafter called "the Artists")*.

2. Acts herein on behalf of the Artists

3. Has represented to the company that he is in a position to ensure the carrying into effect of the terms and conditions of the Agreement

following:-

The contract presumes and affirms that Brian Epstein, **"the Manager"**, "has under his control....The Beatles" and "acts herein on behalf of the Artists" and that he is "in a position....."
But he wasn't, because the management contract was unenforceable by him.

(Interview with David Harris by David Bedford 2016)

However, this was a situation that needed to be rectified, and something David Harris, Brian's solicitor who drew up the management contract, had spotted. He had realised that three of The Beatles were underage, so a new contract was required anyway. But of even greater irony was that the recording contract they had been chasing for so long was also unenforceable.

This probably explains why the new management contract became important, and had to be signed before the first record came out, so that it was valid.
Brian's desire to have the contract "open", unsigned and unenforceable could have seriously backfired on The Beatles' recording career. Thankfully, it didn't, and a new, valid Management contract was signed by Brian and The Beatles on 1st October 1962 – thereby finally putting in place the three numbered points set out in the **'WHEREAS'** clause in the contract – though there would be a new drummer by then.

And in the end

Whether they called it an artist test, recording test or commercial test, a test it was, and not a recording session from which a record would be produced.
They also weren't under contract yet, and it hung in the balance. It seems that the EMI staff knew this, but The Beatles and Brian weren't clear.

At the end of the day, this naivety of the process would have a disastrous consequence for Pete Best. However, they still had an audition to perform, and it could have gone so much better than they hoped.

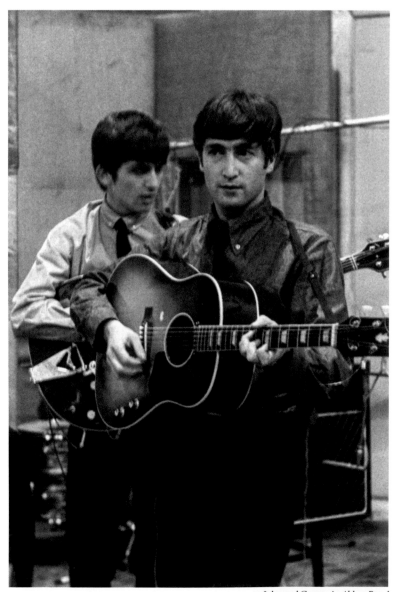

John and George in Abbey Road

6th June 1962

THE BEATLES AT EMI
(THE AUDITION)

Frustrated at the success of his fellow A&R men, especially Norrie Paramour, George Martin admitted that "I desperately wanted my own Cliff. I was so hidebound by Cliff Richard and the Shadows." What Martin wanted was a lead singer and a backing group. Who could blame him? After The Beatles' session, he pondered who should be the group's leader, his "Cliff". George and his team were the kings of skiffle and comedy, but nothing more. What The Beatles offered was Rhythm and Blues and hard rock 'n' roll, which was popular in Liverpool, but not London, or indeed the charts.

A quick look at the hit parade on 10th May 1962 shows what the record-buying public was purchasing:

1.   "Wonderful Land" by The Shadows, *(11 weeks on the charts)*

2.   "Nut Rocker" by B. Bumble and the Stingers, *(4 weeks on the charts)*

3.   "Speak to Me Pretty" by Brenda Lee *(5 weeks on the charts)*

4.   "Hey Baby" by Bruce Channel *(8 weeks on the charts)*

5.   "Hey! Little Girl" by Del Shannon *(8 weeks on the charts)*

The song that would most influence the upcoming session was "Hey Baby" by Bruce Channel. The song had made the harmonica popular again, and The Beatles took notice. At around 130 BPM (Beats Per Minute), it was quite slow compared to many pop songs, and this is reflected in the original version of "Love Me Do" which is just over 130BPM. However, it wasn't going to be that easy.

The Test Session - 6th June 1962

The first test for The Beatles was finding the studio. After driving down from Liverpool, which took several hours, Neil Aspinall drove the van around St. John's Wood looking for EMI, expecting it to look like Decca Studios, which of course it didn't. EMI Studios at 3, Abbey Road looked just like a mansion because it was originally built as a private residence. But the address was correct, so they started to unload the van and were greeted by a smiling Brian Epstein. Thankfully, they were in the right place and, unlike at Decca, they arrived on time and without hangovers.

They were ushered into Studio 2, a huge, empty studio, which must have been overwhelming, in spite of their Decca experience. To the staff, they must have looked confident, but Pete Best admitted they were "very nervous" and that they were "feeling the old butterflies". *(The Beatles Biography)* Ron Richards remembered The Beatles walking in, and was obviously fooled. "Most groups come in very nervous understandably. They've all got their heads down and frightened to say boo to a goose. But not The Beatles; they didn't care. They were a happy-go-lucky lot." *(Pete Best of The Beatles)*

Studio Protocols

EMI had their own way of doing things, with different roles carried out by several tiers of technicians, which must have been confusing for them. "You had the technicians making sure the gear worked, and the balance engineers, like Geoff Emerick and Norman Smith," said record producer Steve Levine.

John, Paul and George performing for George Martin at Abbey Road

"Then you had the producers, who were A&R men who had a musical background, like George Martin. The lines got blurred a little later in the '60s, but George Martin had very little to do with the actual recording, as he would ask whoever was running the session, like Ron Richards, to do certain things that he wanted. And then further down the chain you had the tape operators – which is how I started – who had a very important role as punching in, which was all done manually in time with the engineer. On classical music recording, you would also have an editor who would follow the score and make notes with the producer about which take was best. A solo could be overdubbed later, and then all mixed together.

"The four-track machines they used at Abbey Road were designed for Opera, which is why The Beatles were not using the from day one. They were available to George Martin but not for them. The only pop star to use the four-track at Abbey Road was Cliff Richard, who was a huge name then. Other than that, it was always classical music and especially opera. The Beatles wouldn't have known what to do with them at that stage. Maybe as they did with a bit of vocal overdubbing, but that would have been it." *(David Bedford Interview 2017)*

The Session

If they, and Brian Epstein were expecting George Martin, they were to be disappointed. With Martin not present, it was left to Richards to run through the basics with the group as they set up. As soon as they started to play, there were problems with their equipment.

Norman Smith explained how The Beatles' equipment was the first problem the group encountered, just as it had been at Decca. It seems that they still hadn't learned from their mistakes. "They had such duff equipment," Smith recalled. "Ugly unpainted wooden amplifiers, extremely noisy, with earth loops and goodness knows what." The noise coming from the amplifier, specifically the bass amp built for Paul by Adrian Barber in Liverpool, "was particularly bad." *(Mojo: The Beatles, Ten Years that Shook the World)* Smith and fellow engineer Townsend decided to go to the basement and fetch one of the large Tannoy speakers up for The Beatles to use. "I soldered a jack socket onto the input stage of a Leak TL12 amplifier," said Townsend. "We were soon back in business." *(Mojo: The Beatles, Ten Years that Shook the World)* They also had to "tie string around John Lennon's guitar amplifier to stop the rattling" and had a problem with Pete Best's cymbals. *(Recording The Beatles)* Thankfully, they got the equipment sorted out.

And so The Beatles were finally ready to record. Paul was again overcome with nerves, with memories of the Decca audition flooding back. Studio 2 was a cavernous room and, as McCartney recalled, it had this "endless stairway" up to the control room. "It was heaven, where the great gods lived, and we were down below. Oh God, the nerves!" *(Mojo: The Beatles, Ten Years that Shook the World)*

After some rehearsal time, they ran through several numbers. George Martin had asked Brian to draw up a list of songs so he could assess the vocalists separately. Would the group be renamed "John Lennon and The Beatles" or "Paul McCartney and The Beatles", as Brian had written on the Decca acetate labels to identify the lead singer? Brian decided to use the formula that he had established for Decca – a list of songs for John, Paul and George to perform.

The Beatles likely worked their way through some or all of the songs; no records were kept, and the exact order is unknown.

"The four-track machines they used at Abbey Road were designed for Opera ..."

Congratulations to The Beatles

on winning the poll for the second year running and for the great charts success with their first record **'Love me do'**

45-R4949

PARLOPHONE RECORDS

The suggested opening medley was:

* "Besame Mucho" - Paul McCartney
* "Will You Love Me Tomorrow" - John Lennon
* "Open (Your Lovin' Arms)" - George Harrison

There were then individual numbers, listed with the relevant singer:

Paul McCartney

"P.S. I Love You"

"Love Me Do"

"Like Dreamers Do"

"Love of the Loved"

"Pinwheel Twist"
These songs are noted as "original compositions".

It is interesting that Brian has listed "Love Me Do" under Paul, as it was usually sung by John.

"If You've Gotta Make a Fool of Somebody"

"Till There Was You"

"Over The Rainbow"

"Your Feets Too Big"

"Hey Baby"

"Dream Baby"

"September in The Rain"

"Honeymoon Song"

John Lennon

"Ask Me Why"

"Hello Little Girl"

"Baby It's You"
Noted as original compositions.

"Please Mister Postman"

"To Know Her Is To Love Her"

"You Don't Understand (or I Just Don't Understand)"

"Memphis, Tennessee"

"Shot of Rhythm and Blues"

"Shimmy Like My Sister Kate"

"Lonesome Tears in My Eyes"

George Harrison

"A Picture of You"

"Sheik of Araby"

"What a Crazy World We Live In"

"Three Cool Cats"

"Dream"

"Take Good Care of My Baby"

"Glad All Over"

- From this list, ten of the songs were hangovers from the Decca audition.
- Only seven are Lennon/McCartney originals, of which four were never released by The Beatles
- Paul had fourteen songs, John ten and George seven.

From the songs the boys had performed, Ron Richards selected four to record: "Besame Mucho", "Love Me Do", "P.S. I Love You" and "Ask Me Why". It is worth noting that three of the four selected songs were Lennon/McCartney originals, perhaps reflecting the influence of Ardmore and Beechwood who wanted to publish The Beatles' own songs. When Sid Colman from Ardmore and Beechwood contacted George Martin, it was on the strength of "Like Dreamers Do", though this wasn't one of the songs selected, which is a little strange.

The only two songs that were preserved from this day were "Besame Mucho" and "Love Me Do", which were recorded onto sample lacquer acetate discs to be evaluated later by George Martin. The songs themselves were thought lost, only to be discovered by George Martin's wife Judy at the back of a closet at their home, meaning they could appear on *Anthology*.

Considering how poor the version of "Love Me Do" was, the question remains why it was selected for recording over their better, more developed original songs?

Analysing The Songs

"Besame Mucho"

A permanent fixture in The Beatles' repertoire, this often-covered song written in 1940 was one that had proved disastrous for them at Decca, but was played with more success for the BBC in Manchester. When they performed it on the radio, they reinstated the "cha-cha-booms" and the audience participation made it a triumph. Although they didn't have an audience this time, they produced a creditable version. The song was also in the charts at the time, recorded by Jet Harris on Decca Records. The song appears again on *The Beatles At The Star Club recording*, with Ringo on drums.

Examining Pete Best's Drumming:

While the surviving recording is of dubious quality, drummer Mike Rice was able to analyse Pete's drumming. "You can't always hear what he is playing, but it was slightly different to the January recording (at Decca). Whatever it was, Pete started well, and came in when he needed to, so he did well. The balance on the tracks isn't good so how could the producers make a decision on this? You couldn't criticize Pete Best."

"Pete is playing quite similar as he did for Decca," said drummer Andrew Hinton, "but here you can hear what he is doing on the snare and hi-hat much better, and his drum rolls are excellent, and then back to the floor tom. It is exact, and precise. I couldn't fault it."

According to Andrew's father, guitarist and drummer Derek Hinton, "It has been recorded slightly differently to the Decca session and is very technical and precise."

"Love Me Do"

Chris Neal was also working on the session and, like Smith and Townsend, he was unimpressed with the songs they were performing – until they played "Love Me Do" and heard John's harmonica. "All of a sudden there was this raunchy noise which struck a chord in our heads. Norman (Smith) said to me, 'Oi, go down and pick up George from the canteen and see what he thinks of this'." *(TuneIn)* It was "Love Me Do" that brought George Martin to the studio. The Lennon/McCartney original that had the sound of "Hey Baby" caught their attention; had they found their hit record?

Unfortunately, it was this rendition of "Love Me Do" that would ultimately be Pete's downfall. This wasn't the version that would be released in October as The Beatles' first single, but a new version they had resurrected and adapted in Hamburg. Pete commented on this take of "Love Me Do", and how it is unfair to compare the two versions: "We had been doing it in Hamburg for the German fans, and we tried a few variations, and it went down well." It was a song they had only just revived, with a few minor changes. Pete continued: "What you have to remember is that it was only done a couple of times for the edification of George Martin and the sound engineers to let them know what the song was like. To let them think about it for next time we came back and have a better idea of what the arrangement was. You have to listen to it and realise it's not a finished recording, more like a glorified demo. The song changed a lot under George Martin from the way The Beatles – not me, but the group – had performed it. We did it slower and the change of beat was put in because it was fascinating to the audience." *(The Beatles Up Close And Personal DVD)*

This is a valid point, as the version that was released with Ringo playing was recorded at the end of at least fifteen run-throughs, after George Martin had suggested changes over the summer and during the session in September, which, of course, was an opportunity Pete Best never had. Although Best has been singled out for criticism, the arrangement must have been agreed upon by the whole group, because John and Paul, all through The Beatles' recording career, would tell Ringo how they wanted him to play on their songs.

Horst Fascher, The Beatles' trusted bouncer and Hamburg friend, had his reservations about "Love Me Do" as well. "One day Paul came to me and asked me, 'Horst, we wrote a new song, do you mind to listen to it?' I said, 'Yes, I don't mind to listen to it,' and Paul took his acoustic guitar and sat down on a backstage chair somewhere and was playing 'Love, Love Me Do. . . .' I interrupted him before the song was finished and said, 'Paul, it's better you stay to rock 'n' roll; I don't like that.' And he was disappointed. I saw his face, never again like that. It was all too soft." McCartney looked devastated. "'Love Me Do' wasn't the best song we ever wrote. But it really put us out front," McCartney

told journalist Larry Kane on the 1965 Beatles tour. *(When They Were Boys)*

George Martin also detected a problem with the new arrangement. With John singing lead and playing harmonica, it was impossible for him to sing when it came to the most important three words, the title of the song. He would sing 'Love Me...' and then start playing harmonica, which meant losing the word 'Do'. George Martin had a solution: ask Paul to sing that last line.

At Decca and the BBC Radio session, Paul had been overcome with nerves. It was no different at EMI. "God, I got the screaming heebegeebies," he said. "I mean he (George Martin) suddenly changed this whole arrangement that we'd been doing forever, and John was to miss out that line: he'd sing 'Pleeeeease', put his mouth-organ to his mouth, I'd sing 'Love Me Do' and John would come in 'Waahhh wahhhhh wahhhhhh'. We were doing it live, there was no real overdubbing, so I was suddenly given this massive moment, on our first record, no backing, where everything stopped, the spotlight was on me and I went, in a shaky singing voice, 'Love me doooo'. And I can still hear the shake in my voice when I listen to that record! I was terrified. When we went back up to Liverpool, I remember talking to Johnny Gustafson of the Big Three and he said 'You should have let John sing that line!' John did sing it better than me; he had a lower voice and was a little more bluesy at singing that line."

(Complete Recording Sessions)

We have to remember that Paul was approaching his 20th birthday, and we sometimes forget how young they all were.

Examining Pete Best's drumming:

Mike Rice: "The sound balance on this song is totally different to 'Besame Mucho', and his drums don't sound too good. That is not a great arrangement. I don't like that skip beat in the middle, but the whole sound is terrible, like it was recorded in a shed! But you can't get away from the terrible beat, and he

185

"**God,**
I got the screaming
heebegeebies,"
"**Waahh,**"

was wrong on the variation. If they had wanted Pete out, they would have played them that song. But you can't judge him just on that one song. If that was the arrangement the whole group decided on, then they are all to blame.

Nothing in the song was good. The final version was very different wasn't it, which was down to George Martin suggesting changes to the song. So why wasn't Pete given the same chance as the others to work with George Martin and improve the song, because the difference between June and September is huge."

Andrew Hinton: "Pete is using a nice rim shot on the snare and it is progressing well. They all lost the song in the middle eight and the drum part is lost completely, as was the bass at the start of this section. They obviously haven't rehearsed this song much because none of them sound confident, and Pete's drumming, compared to everything else we have heard, is confusing. I actually like the change of rhythm as it brings something different to what is quite a dull song. Obviously it is a work in progress and none of them know what they are doing, but with work and practice, I think it could have worked."

Derek Hinton: "The whole song seems wrong for them as it is. During the verse, everything works well, so you would expect a producer to tell them to try it again without that strange rhythm change. It was foolish, especially as they had so many problems at Decca, to elect to do a new song or arrangement on such an important day; it was crazy. Because of the arrangement, and the obvious change of rhythm, it is the drummer you notice the most."

If this was a recording session, then The Beatles would have been asked to do "Love Me Do" again, as surely this wouldn't have made it on to record. This was just a quick run-through to see what songs they had. They could have chosen a better song to do, and preferably one that they were confident with.

Love Me Don't

There's little denying that this was a horror show of a song arrangement, and the fact that The Beatles were signed after this was either down to luck or the fact that George Martin saw something in them that was more than the music. Although Pete's drumming on "Love Me Do" was not good, the other Beatles were no better, messing up at the start of that middle eight change of rhythm. It was foolish to have selected the song in the first place. But if this was the evidence from that day, and the only time the Parlophone production team witnessed Best playing, you can see why question marks were raised against Pete.

After the session was completed, everyone retreated to the control room where a now-legendary conversation took place. George Martin was telling them all about the technical aspects of the recording process, with Norman Smith and Ken Townsend looking on. The Beatles didn't say a word, until George Martin asked if there was anything they didn't like. After a dramatic pause, it was George Harrison, not the usually fast-mouthed Lennon, who spoke up first: "Well, for starters, I don't like your tie". There was another pause, before everyone laughed and the ice was broken. What the music couldn't do, the sense of humour could. As Norman Smith remembered, "for the next fifteen to twenty minutes The Beatles were pure entertainment. I had tears running down my face." George Martin observed that "it wasn't their music, it was their charisma. The music was almost incidental." *(The Beatles: The Biography)* Maybe in John Lennon, Paul McCartney and George Harrison, George Martin could see Peter Sellers, Spike

Milligan and Harry Secombe, better known as the Goons, for whom Martin had worked. According to all eyewitnesses, Pete was silent.

Norman Smith remembered that "Pete Best didn't say one word. I got the feeling something wasn't right between them; it wasn't only that George and Ron found fault with him as a drummer." *(TuneIn)*

Sadly, while the other three Beatles "gooned" around with George Martin, Pete didn't. Martin admitted that he was drawn to The Beatles' personalities more than their music, so this could have affected them, too. As Martin later observed: "They had this wonderful charisma – it made you feel good to be with them. I thought their music was rubbish." It must also have been a surprise to The Beatles to receive a contract offer by the comedy label within EMI. "We wondered why we had the comedy guy, not the music guy," said Paul. "But we loved the comedy; there was good music, 'Right Said Fred', you (George Martin) did good music at those times." Paul also admitted that they were already aware of George Martin. He had Peter Sellers' album Songs For Swingin' Sellers, which Martin had produced. "We had that record in Liverpool before we knew you, and I wore this record out!" *(Arena: Produced by George Martin)* It seems that The Beatles knew more about George Martin than he realised, even if Martin knew nothing about them.

Richards also recalled that, though he liked them as personalities, he was not terribly impressed; their songs didn't inspire him and he rated their musicianship as merely adequate. His conclusion: "I probably wouldn't have signed The Beatles." Norman Smith said they "didn't impress me at all" and George Martin, on listening to the playback, said "they were rotten composers" and "their own stuff wasn't any good." *(The Beatles: The Biography)*

The music Martin had considered almost incidental – which hadn't grabbed him – signalled the beginning of the end of Pete's career with The Beatles. However, it was Ron Richards, not George Martin, who had the biggest problem with the drumming. "It probably was me that had the problem because I had a thing about drummers," Richards admitted. "Drums were a big thing with me and I think I was asking him to play a certain beat and he couldn't cope – he couldn't do it – what I wanted. And I got a bit, 'Oh God, yeah, where do we go from here?' Come to think of it, if I'd asked Ringo to do it, he couldn't have either." *(Pete Best of The Beatles)* So Richards took responsibility for the decision, and seemed a bit harsh on Best.

One interested observer, who also happened to be a drummer, was engineer Norman Smith. "It wasn't how he was playing it, but what he was playing," said Smith. "I had my own jazz quintet and was used to arranging, but I was only the sound engineer, and it was nothing to do with production at that time, so I didn't say anything." *(The Beatles Up Close And Personal)* Ken Townsend also didn't see a problem with Pete. "I personally didn't see a reason for any session drummer to be brought in." *(Pete Best of The Beatles)*

All that mattered was that Ron Richards and George Martin had a problem with Pete's drumming and would be hiring a session drummer.

Further proof that this was only a test session is that George Martin and Ron Richards still had to decide who would be their "Cliff Richard", the lead singer

– John or Paul – if they were going to sign them. As Martin recalled in his autobiography, *All You Need Is Ears*: "I put them on test individually, getting them to sing numbers in turn, and my original feeling was that Paul had the sweeter voice, John's had more character, and George was generally not so good. I was thinking, on balance, that I should make Paul the leader. Then, after some thought, I realised that if I did so I would be changing the nature of the group. Why do that? Why not keep them as they were? It hadn't been done before – but then I'd made a lot of records that hadn't been 'done before'. Why not experiment in pop as I had in comedy?" *(All You Need Is Ears)*

Finally, a producer had seen the potential in The Beatles as a group with no leader. If only Decca had used the same logic, the label would have signed them. But they didn't. George Martin decided to take a chance where no other A&R man had the courage or vision to realise that here was a group on the brink of changing popular music forever.

After the session was over, Norman Smith voiced a clear opinion of what he had seen and heard. "They left, and George turned to me and said, 'Well, what do you think?' And I said, 'I've seen a lot of groups come in for artists tests, but this one – there is something special about them. I can't tell you what, but there is something there.' As I said, the test hadn't gone too well, and I wasn't impressed by their sound. But they had an appealing quality, a kind of charisma. And I told George, 'In my view, I think they should be signed.' And I'll never forget, his last words to me before he left were, "Okay. I'll think about it."'" *(Recording The Beatles)*

IF........

Martin decided that they wouldn't use Pete if The Beatles were brought back to make a record, and he confirmed this decision in a conversation with Brian. Over the years, Sir George gave slightly different versions of this conversation, not remembering exactly what he said, but in his accounts, he was always consistent.

"At the end of the test I took Brian to one side and said, 'I don't know what you're going to do with the group as such, but this drumming isn't good enough for what I want. It isn't regular enough. It doesn't give the right kind of sound. If we do make a record, I'd much prefer to have my own drummer – which won't make any difference to you, because no one will know who's on the record anyway." *(All You Need Is Ears)*

In a 1987 interview with Mark Lewisohn, Paul McCartney recalled that George Martin indeed made this admission, but not only to Brian. McCartney said that he, John and George were also present. Pete was out of the room, presumably packing up his drums with Neil. "George (Martin) took us aside and said 'I'm not happy about the drummer'. He said 'Can you change your drummer?' and we said 'Well, we're quite happy with him, and he works great in the clubs'. And George said 'Yes, but for recording he's got to be just a bit more accurate'." *(The Complete Beatles Recording Sessions)* Paul repeated this sentiment in *Anthology*. "George Martin was used to drummers being very 'in time', because all the big-band session drummers he used had a great sense of time.

Now, our Liverpool drummers had a sense of spirit, emotion, economy even, but not a deadly sense of time. This would bother producers making a record."

As McCartney explained: "We were used to hearing a bass drum in the right place, locking in with the bass guitar like it would now. We weren't really bothered with that. Ours was very four in the bar - boom, boom, boom, boom - we used to try and break stages with it. That's what eventually got called the *Mersey Beat*." *(The Complete Beatles Recording Sessions)* It was clear that The Beatles were happy with Pete as a drummer when playing live, but this was a whole new ball game, and George Martin was in charge. They had to listen to him.

George Martin was consistently clear that he would use a session drummer on any record they cut – a decision he felt would make little difference to the group. What is also significant is the wording that George Martin used: "if we do make a record". Martin still hadn't decided whether to sign the contract or not, and made sure that Brian knew this. Paul McCartney, when asked about this day, mentioned that they were already aware of the nature of the day, and that they had a chance, but nothing was guaranteed, because Brian had told them; "George Martin had agreed 'to think about it, possibly, maybe'." *(The Complete Beatles Recording Sessions)*

The Beatles already knew there was a big IF. Is it any wonder, with this being the last chance saloon, that the young Beatles panicked and saw Pete as the one who could stop them getting a contract if they didn't agree with Martin's decision? That must have been an awkward drive home from London.

It isn't clear whether it was just Brian alone or with John, Paul and George, that George Martin communicated his decision, but we can assume that the discussion centred around a few points:

1. **George Martin didn't like Pete's drumming enough, or didn't think he was good enough to drum on the record.**

2. **The Beatles still didn't have a signed contract and they had to do what ever George Martin said.**

3. **If they were going to make a record, then George Martin would use a session drummer.**

The three Beatles faced a dilemma about their drummer: could they get rid of him? Paul remembered it clearly. "No. We can't!' It was one of those terrible things you go through as kids. Can we betray him? No. But our career was on the line. Maybe they were going to cancel our contract." *(Anthology)*

Of all the theories about the ending of Pete Best's time with The Beatles, the most logical conclusion, based on the evidence, is that the decision was made by John, Paul and George based on the conversation that George Martin had with Brian, and possibly them, following the Abbey Road session. As we know from comments George Martin made in subsequent years, his intention was only to bring in a session drummer for the record, and saw no reason for Pete to leave the group.

This was standard practice within the music industry, but Brian Epstein was a record store owner, and neither he nor The Beatles, had any knowledge of record company procedures.

The Last Chance Saloon

Unfortunately for Pete, Brian, John, Paul and George misunderstood George Martin's comment. Therefore, when they discussed it, the boys likely took it as meaning that Martin didn't think Pete was a good enough drummer. What could the remaining Beatles do? Put yourself in the shoes of John, Paul and George, aged 21, 19 and 18 respectively, who were in the last chance saloon. Parlophone was their last hope of ever obtaining a recording contract, having been rejected by every other label. If the only barrier to gaining that elusive record contract was getting rid of Pete Best, then so be it. As Paul said, "Our career was on the line." *(Anthology)*

Can we prove that George Martin's comments were misunderstood? When Pete sat in Brian's office on the day the bad news was delivered, Pete recalled asking for an explanation. Brian told him: "George Martin doesn't think you're a good enough drummer." That isn't what George Martin said, or implied. But it is clear that it was what Brian, John, Paul and George understood from those comments.

What would you have done? You couldn't blame John, Paul and George for panicking and making the decision to get rid of their drummer in exchange for a recording contract. Pete Best had spent nearly two years as The Beatles' drummer. But now, The Fab Three were about to start looking for a new Fourth Beatle.

After The Session

As The Beatles returned to Liverpool, I wonder if they recalled their journey home after the Decca audition. This time, they were even closer to a record deal, with Brian having signed his part of the contract. Yet they knew that the fate of their contract – and their future – rested in the hands of George Martin, who was probably less enthusiastic than Mike Smith had been. But, with a contract already drawn up, surely they couldn't miss out again? Brian later said that he was hopeful of their first record being released soon after, but surely than conversation in the control room would have made it clear that there was no recording of quality from that day that could be released. George Martin was clear in his mind: if they were going to make a record, he had to find a song from Tin Pan Alley for the group to record, because nothing they showed this day was worthy of being issued as a single.

It seems clear that George Martin had yet to decide whether or not to sign The Beatles, and this is reinforced by what happened with the tape from the session. Ken Townsend recalled that nothing moved quickly at EMI. "We did that test, and the tape went into the library. And about a week later, Norman says to me, 'Here, Ken, what's the name of that group we had in last week? I've got to send a tape down to Manchester Square.' I said, 'The Beatles'. I mean, he'd actually forgotten the name of the group!" (Recording The Beatles) What George Martin still hadn't decided was which song to record because he wasn't convinced by any of their original songs and was focused on finding a song from Tin Pan Alley. For that reason, he was not in a hurry to make a record, or even sign the contract. Martin may not have even listened to the recording for over a week.

Kim Bennett of Ardmore and Beechwood, whose general manager Sid Colman had been responsible for The Beatles being at EMI, didn't give up pushing for the group to be signed. He wanted his company, a division of EMI, to publish the Lennon/McCartney songs. After George Martin had met with Epstein, Bennett kept doing what he was best at – plugging – by applying pressure at EMI to sign The Beatles. He had suggested that EMI Director L.G. Wood demanded that George Martin sign The Beatles, as Wood didn't approve of Martin's affair

with his secretary. This was corroborated by Norman Smith who said; "L.G. Wood didn't approve of people having affairs, and he certainly didn't approve of George going off with his secretary. Not at all. I think it offended his moral standards. L.G. virtually ordered George to record The Beatles." *(TuneIn)*

When would this pressure have been applied by Wood? It is unlikely to have been before the session on 6th June. It more likely happened when George Martin attended the regular EMI recording manager staff meeting, somewhere around 15th June. Martin would have taken the tape from the session and discussed signing The Beatles. If he was of two minds at this point, you could imagine Wood making the final decision, if he so chose. After all, Ardmore and Beechwood, a division of EMI, were keen to have the songwriters on the books, even if the group wasn't that special. Bennett's version of the story removes George Martin's input from the decision-making process, though such a thing seems implausible. He saw something that made him want to find out more, and the contract would hardly cost EMI the earth. It had to be worth a gamble. And it was one that paid off.

The Best of Sellers

As if to reinforce his decision to sign The Beatles, George Martin and his secretary, Judy, went up to Liverpool to see them play at the Cavern Club. Martin recalled that the atmosphere was electric and that it was "very raucous, and the kids loved every minute of it. The rock 'n' roll gyrations of Tommy Steele and Cliff Richard were clinical, anaemic, even anaesthetic, compared with the total commitment of The Beatles." As Martin wrote in his autobiography: "A group they were, and a group they had to stay." *(All You Need Is Ears)* Pete Best's drumming that night at the Cavern didn't cause Martin a problem because a group they were, but that group was about to change, and nobody thought to ask George Martin for his advice.

The Contract Finally Arrives

With the signed contract finally in Brian's possession in July, this was the best possible news for Epstein and his group. But it also meant that John, Paul and George would have to sacrifice their drummer on the altar of success. George Martin, who had agreed to the recording contract, didn't want to use their drummer. So why pay that drummer when somebody else would be playing on the records? They thought it better to replace him and get a drummer who could play both in the studio and in the ballrooms.

The sad irony is that they didn't necessarily have to replace Pete. Although they didn't have a signed contract on 6th June, they passed the audition and were subsequently offered the signed contract they had been chasing, as John, Paul, George and Pete.

Original painting by Paul Skellett (www.skellett.com)

6th June 1962

THE ROLE OF THE SESSION DRUMMER

When George Martin told Brian Epstein that, for the purposes of making a record, he would be using a session drummer, his comment precipitated the exit of Pete Best from The Beatles. But was this a reflection of Best as a drummer – his specific performance on "Love Me Do" – or would this have happened anyway, regardless of the drummer?

EMI producer Ron Richards admitted that he had a thing about drummers, and he asked Pete to do something specific on his kit, which he couldn't do. Richards later conceded that Ringo probably couldn't have done it either. It seems evident that Ron Richards was determined to use a session drummer, no matter how Pete had performed on "Love Me Do". Pete's inability to play as requested didn't determine Richards' decision, but merely reaffirmed it. Why would studios use a session drummer?

No book on the role of the drummer in this period would be complete without a true appreciation of the importance of the session drummer. As we know, Ringo Starr was replaced by session drummer Andy White for the recording of The Beatles' first EMI record, "Love Me Do". To be fair to Ringo, would it have made any difference how he drummed on 4th September 1962? Would a session drummer have been hired anyway – no reflection on the abilities of Pete Best or Ringo Starr, but rather because of studio practice?

The Session Drummers You've Listened To - Without Realising

You may own several hits from the sixties, assuming that the group's drummer played on the record, but that was not always the case. Some session musicians eventually became almost as famous as the stars, especially in the U.S. where the "Wrecking Crew" became synonymous with the hits.

The American Session Musicians

Session drummer Hal Blaine conceived the name for a group of musicians who could be called upon by record companies to support their artists in the studio. The Wrecking Crew musicians included bassist and guitarist Carol Kaye (one of the few female session players of her era), guitarist Tommy Tedesco, and other musicians like Glen Campbell, James Burton, Leon Russell and Earl Palmer. They dominated American popular music in the '60s, originally chosen by Phil Spector for his "Wall of Sound", and then as the instrumentalists selected by Brian Wilson to create his sonic masterpieces with The Beach Boys.

Members of the Wrecking Crew were present on some of the most iconic records of the time: Jan and Dean's "Surf City", Simon and Garfunkel's "Bridge Over Troubled Water", The Mamas and The Papas' "California Dreamin' ", Frank Sinatra's "Strangers in the Night", The Monkees' "Last Train to Clarksville", and the themes for "Batman", "Mission: Impossible", "Hawaii Five-O" and "Born Free". When it comes to a listing of the hit records that utilized the Wrecking Crew, this is the very tip of the iceberg.

The Funk Brothers were the go-to session musicians on many of the Motown records from the 1950s to the 1970s while Booker T & The MGs backed some of the greatest names on Stax Records, like Otis Redding, Isaac Hayes and Sam and Dave. Billy Preston, who recorded with The Beatles in 1969, was a session keyboard player who first met the group in 1962 in Hamburg. At the time, the 16-year-old prodigy was the organist for Little Richard.

They merely had to accept that, for their first record, Parlophone would be using a session drummer, a practice more common than anyone realised at the time.

The British Session Musicians

In the UK, it was more about individual session musicians, than a collective like the Wrecking Crew. Jimmy Page and John Paul Jones, who would later form Led Zeppelin, were among the busiest session musicians, with Page regarded as the hardest-working session guitarist of the 1960s.

One session drummer could have been the Led Zeppelin drummer, but was too busy with studio work to audition. Clem Cattini, formerly of The Tornados, was on the short list for the job that eventually went to John Bonham. One of the most prolific drummers in UK recording history, he holds the record for the most appearances on UK #1 singles – nearly fifty.

In addition to his work on the Tornados' #1 hit "Telstar", Cattini was session drummer on the iconic Johnny Kidd and the Pirates hit "Shakin' All Over" and played on hits by Tom Jones, Cliff Richard, the Walker Brothers and even on Engelbert Humperdink's "Release Me", the song that famously kept "Penny Lane/Strawberry Fields Forever" from the #1 spot in the UK. He also drummed for Dusty Springfield and Liverpool's Billy Fury.

Cattini recalled what happened with Led Zeppelin: "I was very busy doing sessions. I had been on the road for nine years, and suddenly I was at home, getting into my own bed at night. Peter Grant (Led Zeppelin's manager-in-waiting) saw me at a session, phoned me and asked me to go to lunch to him to talk about a project. We never had that lunch. Not for any reason. I was just too busy. He called again, but again we didn't have that lunch." *(Mark Forster)*

He did share the drumming with John Bonham on the Rock 'n' Roll Highway album which also included Page and John Paul Jones. Cattini continued to drum at sessions throughout the 1960s and beyond, but you won't see his name credited.

Bobby Graham, who turned down Brian's invitation to join The Beatles in July 1962, and declined the opportunity to replace an ill Ringo on the group's 1964 world tour, was one of the decade's busiest session drummers. He even did a session with The Beatles for a radio broadcast. He played on an estimated 15,000 records, including Dusty Springfield's "You Don't Have to Say You Love Me", Billy Fury's "It's Only Make Believe" and the Kinks' #1 single, "You Really Got Me". Like Cattini, he played a number of sessions with Jimmy Page.

Another session drummer with a Beatles connection was Andy White, who would replace Ringo Starr for the recording session at Abbey Road on 11th September 1962. White had played on Billy Fury's debut album, *The Sound of Fury*, and joins Cattini and Graham as one of the most active drummers in the '60s. When it came to session work, he was Parlophone producer Ron Richards' first choice and the two men knew each other well.

Though many cite George Martin as the culprit, it was actually Richards who sealed Pete Best's fate as he was the first to consider The Beatles' drummer unsuitable for recording work, an opinion shared by Martin and which later led to the use of the more reliable Andy White.

As was proved in September, it took Ringo and The Beatles approximately 17 attempts to get a usable take of "Love Me Do". Andy White, who had no prior knowledge of the song, came in and, within two hours, had recorded it, along with "P.S. I Love You" and a few takes of "Please Please Me". That is what a session drummer delivered – adaptability and speed with the goal of completing a record in as little time as possible, and at minimum expense.

How and Why Studios Used Session Musicians

"The recording process of the late '50s/'60s was the first time you have multi-mic'ing," said record producer Steve Levine, "so it became easier for producers to record the session. However, first of all, producers had an arranger and a fixer. The arranger would arrange the music and the style, etc. and the producer and the A&R department would discuss what arrangement was wanted, and then the fixer would say; 'we need this kind of drummer, or this kind of bass player,' and the fixer would go off and find the people from their lists. Very soon, it was the same people on the records working with the same producers. Once you have not only someone who knows what you want, and is used to the way you work, both technically and financially, it saves you so much time.

"In those days of overdubbing, the backing track was created by the session players, and then the singer could come into the finished track, which would be in the right time and in key. They couldn't waste time with the singer's own band getting it right. There wasn't time, and they didn't have the forensic ability we have today, where you can get right in and fix things to any great degree – until the mid-1960s. They needed someone who could play a thousand takes, and they would all be the same. You can't get that from just anybody; it's a real skill. When you look at who George Martin and others used, then it was the same group of musicians. It was very much the norm to have session players play the backing track; very, very rare to have a session lead vocalist. You could have the same band behind several singers on the same genre of music.

"If you look at it now, it looks like a cheat to bring in someone, but with your 1960s head, it was the standard practice. It wasn't even a mark of disrespect to Pete or Ringo; it's just the way it was. It might have hurt their feelings at the time, but it was normal back then.

"In fairness to Andy White, Ringo's kit would have not been particularly good, and we're not in the era of multi-mic'ing of drums, so the sound a drummer makes is a gift to the producer; a drummer who knew Abbey Road, knew the acoustics, and aware of tuning his kit. Again, it is not just the playing, but the tuning itself in the studio. Ringo wouldn't have had his Ludwig kit yet, and the skins were probably paper-thin from playing with Rory Storm and the Hurricanes and were worn out.

By hiring Andy White, you're getting professional, playing and hiring a kit that is sonically tuned to the standard of the studio. Neither Pete Best nor Ringo would have had that ability or experience to do that.

"Studio recording to live performing is the same as the difference between cinema and theatre. If you're in a theatre, you have to be loud as possible so that the people in the back seats can hear you. In the cinema, the camera can get really close up, and all you need is the look into the camera, and it says it all. It is the same with the drum kit. The microphones are right there, so you don't have to whack the drums like you would at a gig, where you have to be bigger and bolder, especially given the limitation of P.A. in those days, plus you've got the audience there. It is the detail in the studio that makes the difference.

I don't think The Beatles really got to that stage until *Rubber Soul*. By then they understood the detail and nuance of using the recording studio, and what they could do. They could get into the detail then.

"Ringo started dampening the drums, and playing with the acoustics and detail. He got into the detail of getting the metal snare that gave him the sound that he wanted. His kit became the model for drummers to use. Therefore, someone like Andy White would have brought that expertise to the right equipment and experience. They would often have a number of drums they could choose from, and depending on what configuration the producer wanted. They would even have drummer roadies that would go into the studio and set up for whatever the producer asked for. The producer liked what he heard, and so knew what he was getting." *(David Bedford Interview 2017)*

You can understand now why producers used the session drummers, and didn't rely on whoever walked through the door carrying their own drum kit.

One common factor among session drummers like Cattini, Graham and White was that, unlike most band members, they could read music.

Johnny Hutchinson was one of the few Liverpool musicians who could read music, and it is no surprise that after he stopped recording with Decca, they used him as a session drummer.

It was customary in the London studios for engineers, producers and musicians to work in three-hour sessions. These would usually run from 10am to 1pm, 2.30pm to 5.30pm and 7pm to 10pm. In that time, they were expected to record four songs. A session drummer could therefore record with a pop group at EMI in the morning, a jazz ensemble at Decca in the afternoon and, if they were lucky, work in an evening session at a third studio. A close look at The Beatles' tortuous sessions with Pete on 6th June and with Ringo on 4th September reveals why Andy White was needed.

Once you were established, you could, as The Beatles did, spend as long in the studio as you wanted. With a small budget and the immense difficulties inherent in recording drums, it only made sense to hire a session drummer when recording a single. Even Dave Clark, drummer for his own hit-making group, The Dave Clark Five, chose to use session drummer Bobby Graham on singles like "Glad All Over" so that he could devote more time to producing them.

Billy Kinsley, member of The Merseybeats, worked as a recording artist and session musician too. "I have learnt a lot about recording in the studios in the '60s, as I was involved in that of course. Like with Dave Clark and Bobby Graham, that was kept quiet at the time. It was accepted. When we did our first record with Phillips on Fontana, we were confident; I was only 16.

We'd got the songs done quickly. We got set up, and I had my bass amp, and John Banks set his drum kit up, and then went to get a coffee.

In the cafe was Jack Bruce, a session bass player at the time, who was going to play if I couldn't cut the mustard, and the session drummer, Bobby Graham, who was there. They were just hanging around to see what happened in the studio. They were on stand-by if we couldn't do it." *(David Bedford Interview 2017)*

With these session drummers and others like them playing on thousands of records, it's safe to assume that scant few drummers actually played on their own group's records. This wasn't a criticism of them as drummers. In all likelihood, irrespective of how well Pete or Ringo played at the test sessions, George Martin was going to bring in a session drummer. This was standard operating procedure in the recording industry and, when faced with a new group and a tight budget, it was always the best option.

If Brian knew this and understood studio practice, would the outcome for Pete Best have been the same?

6th June 1962

THE BOYS WANT YOU OUT

(A VERY SHAMEFUL COUP)

After the EMI test finished around 10.30pm that night, it was left to Pete Best and Neil Aspinall to load up the van for the long journey home. Home was 250 miles north, straight up the M1 and M6 motorways – a relatively new concept of motoring in those days, but still a 6 to 7-hour non-stop journey from London to Liverpool.

It isn't clear whether George Martin only spoke to Brian, or whether John, Paul and George learned of Martin's opinion at the same time. Nevertheless, a discussion had to take place about what to do next and where better to do that than on the journey back home? It has since been suggested that The Beatles travelled home together in the van, but there is no proof of this. Far more plausible is the notion that Epstein invited the three Fabs to accompany him on the way back home. Whenever the conversation took place, it had to happen, and soon. Brian wasn't making the offer merely to kill time; the journey was the only occasion he could speak freely with the three Beatles about the Martin conversation without prying ears listening in. Brian was also a very polite person, and this was an interminably long journey to make in silence. Besides, he liked their company, so they readily obliged, knowing the van would be an uncomfortable squeeze, what with all the kit to consider. This left Pete to accompany Neil, neither of whom would suspect what was afoot.

They left EMI with two questions hanging in the air, neither of which had been answered satisfactorily by George Martin. Heartened by what appeared to be a promising test at EMI studios, they had set off in typically good spirits. But eventually the banter would have given way to serious probing by the three Beatles about what would happen next.

A Hypothesis Ventured

George Martin would only say 'if', not 'when', there would be a recording contract with EMI. It left Epstein with an agonizing wait to find out whether he could go ahead. Meanwhile, he would recall that Martin had carelessly added an aside that he didn't like Pete Best's drumming and would use another drummer at the recording session. This is something that Martin made strenuous efforts to clarify for the rest of his life. None carried serious conviction, but Martin's comment clearly left Epstein unprepared. Martin might have better qualified what he meant by adding that he would use a session drummer, and that Pete could sit it out, which was not an unusual practice in studios in those days. Unfortunately, for whatever reasons, he didn't do so.

More to the point, he should have mentioned that Ron Richards, who led the studio session that evening, was fixated on getting the drum sound just right and preferred to use a session drummer he could rely on rather than a hitherto unknown and untried source. He didn't do that either. He might also have admitted that the studio had never heard drumming like Pete's before, because not only did it define the emerging Merseybeat sound – one relatively unheard of outside Hamburg and Liverpool – but would have been very familiar to any fan in the underground scene at the Cavern – that Atomic Beat!!

If only Martin had ventured north like Decca's A & R man Mike Smith had done – to watch the group play live and uninhibited in the Cavern – he would have appreciated them and their music far more. If only. But he didn't, until much later on. Consequently, he entered the EMI studio completely unprepared for

Brian admiring his boys

anything out of the ordinary. With his mindset and his ears still attuned to the familiar sounds around Parlophone at the time – comedy recitals, soft jazz, easy listening – it's no surprise he didn't think much of the music! A cursory check of what The

Beatles later recorded with 'Love Me Do' suggests that Martin and his team were looking for a safe and reliable sound they could work with – something with a softer, regular beat to accompany the melodic voice of McCartney, rather than overpower it.

With further hindsight, although the language of recording studios was familiar to George Martin with its laboratory standard techno-jargon, he really should also have been more aware of the need for tact to guard against careless talk in front of Brian Epstein, who was 'new' to it all. Perhaps Martin was lulled by Epstein's easy charm and The Beatles' own brand of comedy. Nevertheless, he should have checked with Epstein to see if he fully understood the words being used, but this didn't happen either. Nor would Epstein's ego have admitted that he knew next to nothing about such things. So it was that a steady accumulation of errors by both men would lead to far-reaching consequences.

On the drive home from London, with John, Paul and George looking to their mentor for his feedback on the session, Epstein would have explained what went on at EMI, and it is probable that he would have begun cautiously testing with innocuous questions and answers before broaching Martin's comment on Best. The speculation is that it opened up a whole raft of genuine concern. In moments of stress, it is so easy for logic to give way to irrational thoughts and decisions and, given that a recording contract was at stake, it is natural to assume that any long-term ambitions were reaching crisis point. Yet again, the contract seemed to be so near, and yet so far, to obtain. Failure was not an option for anyone now. Epstein had already exhausted his list of recording companies. He had pulled every trick in the book to get The Beatles a deal and had spent a lot of time and money in the process. Worn down by the relentless grind, he had nowhere else to go was and on the brink of calling time. What would have happened then for The Beatles? For the time being, everything was on hold because the problem uppermost in everyone's mind was what to do about Pete.

No one will ever know the truth about that night, or indeed if any agreement was reached. There are no records, no confessions, and no witnesses to the event unless we count Paul, and he's remained tight-lipped about it. We know from his memoirs that Brian liked Pete and was reluctant to see him go. Given that this was a terrible situation, he took great care to work out the next step, if only for legal reasons. That said, we can only speculate on what happened next.

Later interviews with John, Paul and George and their confidantes are illuminating, too. Paul has always been very clear about the reason Pete was replaced: "It was a big issue at the time, how we 'dumped' Pete. And I do feel sorry for him, because of what he could have been on to, but as far as we were concerned, it was strictly a professional decision. If he wasn't up to the mark – slightly in our eyes, and definitely in the producer's eyes – then there was no choice. But it was still very difficult. It is one of the most difficult things we ever had to do." *(Anthology)*

Once they had accepted the inevitable logic of replacing Pete, they would have had to discuss among themselves if they really could, and should, do it. It was at this point that each of them, including Brian, put forward reasons for dumping their drummer. The Beatles sounded and looked like a very tight group, but John was ambivalent, as usual. Discarding musicians was not a problem to him. This left Paul and George. Both were always looking to improve the group musically, and this was their moment to act. George Martin, who was the expert in these things, had already declared that Pete didn't measure up. He didn't like Pete, or his drumming. As they journeyed home, there may have been general comments thrown in about the times Pete couldn't play – possibly exaggerating the number of times just to make a point – and how the guy who sat in on drums, Ringo Starr, was actually quite good.

As night follows day, it may have been said that he never went out with them after gigs, or just sat at the back, sultry and unsmiling. A conspiracy of rumours and myth accelerated. He never took "prellies" in Hamburg. He often went off on his own. Plus, as John said later, they got Pete because they needed a drummer to go to Hamburg! And you can bet that, at this moment, they reminded Brian that this would be the perfect time to get Mona Best off his back. This may well have been the convincing argument for Brian. Driven on by unfolding events, each man would have quietly reviewed his excuses, adding fuel to the fire with a fall-back position, in short – an alibi. For Brian, the business of saying goodbye, although emotional, would have suited him well. Mona Best's continuous interference had long been a thorn in his side. Getting rid of her would be a godsend, especially now that she was heavily pregnant by her lover, Beatles roadie Neil Aspinall, a circumstance which, in itself, would present an awkward conundrum.

Now pregnant, Mona was winding down and would soon be closing the Casbah. She had cut back on her dealings with The Beatles and was in no real position to do anything serious about it. Neither was Neil, who had given up his job as a trainee accountant and was increasingly more dependent on his wages as the band's road manager. Brian also held the ace card: George Martin! Mona could hardly question his assessment, could she? So, from Epstein's point of view, it followed that if Pete was out, so was she. It seemed like a very promising move which would strengthen his own hand while removing yet another rival.

It's apparent that what started out as an unstructured conversation rapidly turned into a business decision. Even so, Pete Best had been a fixture since Hamburg and would not have gone quietly into the night without an argument, something no one could stomach. Certainly they dreaded any direct confrontation or an acrimonious fall out, but with no other remedy immediately available, it had to be done. He had to go if they were to survive. In the end, it was a mercenary decision which, as John later admitted, may have been cowardly, but this was business. As hard as it was, friendship had nothing to do with it. Call it fate but they had reached a defining moment where the proverbial wheels began falling off Pete and Mona's bandwagon.

At the same time, John's tangled relationship with Cynthia Powell was entirely of his own making. While he was still playing fast and loose with the group's female fans, he would soon discover that Cynthia was pregnant. With so many potential repercussions in Liverpool and elsewhere, John decided to do the right thing and tie a secret knot, even if it meant more grief from Aunt Mimi and Brian Epstein.

From John's point of view, Pete's dismissal would be too much to handle – as most things were when the going got tough. It would have to be sorted out by Brian. After all, wasn't he the manager? Their manager! One can imagine Lennon closing down the discussion rather abruptly by saying; 'Right Brian. You're the man with a plan. You wanted to manage us. You sack him.'

Little did John know that Brian couldn't sack Pete! Although The Beatles had established a bona_fide partnership among themselves, the reality was that they employed Brian, and not the other way round. His quest for that unbreakable contract had finally rebounded on him.

The obvious question of finding a replacement for Pete would soon have followed, which was easier said than done. Although Liverpool was blessed with talent, drummers were not always available. The Beatles needed someone who was ready to go, had few technical limitations, could hold his own, and fit in well with the group. It was a tall order and the list of names was shrinking fast! The big question was who?

The Gathering Storm

Once Epstein had reached an understanding with The Beatles regarding Pete Best, an unstoppable momentum was triggered. There was no going back now. In the remaining weeks between mid-June and August, Brian conducted several secretive soundings at Peacocks restaurant in Hacking Hey and at the Old Dive, a rundown working man's pub in Williamson Square (now demolished). The meetings were with a small inner circle of trusted friends and allies which would have included Bob Wooler, Alistair Taylor and Brian's friend, promoter Joe Flannery. These meetings would result in Ringo Starr being invited to join The Beatles. But first, Brian had to work out how to get rid of Pete – if they obtained a recording contract from George Martin. It's ironic that if the contract didn't materialize, there would have been very little point in getting rid of their drummer because, in all likelihood, it would have been the end of the road for The Beatles.

However, it was only the beginning.

39

27th June 1962

REPLACING THE BEST

(John, Paul, George and ...)

Following the first EMI session on 6th June 1962, the die was cast for Pete Best after his fellow band members' interpretation of George Martin's decision to bring in a session drummer for their first record. It was this misunderstanding of the situation that led to John, Paul and George approaching Brian Epstein about replacing Pete as their drummer. However, it was a moot point unless George Martin agreed to a recording contract, which is why nothing happened initially, and they clearly waited until the contract arrived at the end of July. What would have happened if they were turned down by Parlophone? There is a strong possibility that this would have been the end of the road for The Beatles. They were close to breaking up at the end of 1960 after the disastrous end to their first Hamburg tour, and at the end of 1961 when, having conquered Liverpool and Hamburg, they couldn't see a future, until Brian Epstein offered to manage them. Epstein offered hope, but that hope was closely entwined with obtaining a recording contract. Parlophone was their last chance, and if they failed, then there was no future for the group.

With some criticism of Pete's kit at Abbey Road, he even ordered a new Ludwig kit. "I ordered the Ludwig kit just before I was kicked out (of the band) from Barratt's in Manchester. When I started making enquiries about Ludwig they were almost unheard of. I went to Barratt's and they ordered them in Sea Jade and I've still got them. They're not immaculate, they've been well played." *(Mike Dolbear)* Unfortunately for Best, it would be Ringo behind a Ludwig kit with The Beatles, not him.

Now that Pete's role in the group following the 6th June session was in question, Brian had asked his solicitor for advice about replacing the drummer, but nothing

had been decided yet and he was getting impatient waiting to hear from George Martin. But, at the end of July 1962, the signed contract finally arrived.

(A Cellarful of Noise)

Pete's career with the group was reaching its conclusion and the task of finding a replacement drummer would need to commence. The irony, of course, was that now they had a signed recording contract from Parlophone, they didn't need to get rid of their drummer. However, they had already decided to replace Pete.

At this point, with the contract confirmed, it does make you wonder why Brian didn't contact George Martin for his advice about replacing Pete, and what type of drummer they should look for. This could have been the opportunity for Epstein and Martin to discuss the merits of retaining or replacing Pete, to clarify what Martin had meant when he told him he wanted to bring in a session drummer. For whatever reason, that call never took place.

Although it has been suggested that it was as simple as offering the position to Ringo, he wasn't the first drummer to be approached. In fact, three other drummers were asked to replace Pete. By the time Ringo made his debut in August 1962, several other drummers had been considered, and three were asked to join The Beatles, especially with a recording date of 4th September quickly approaching. Each drummer had his own strengths and weaknesses as far as The Beatles were concerned; the search for the Fourth Beatle had begun.

27th July 1962: Almost the Fourth Beatle - Bobby Graham

On Friday 27th July 1962, The Beatles were playing on the same bill as Joe Brown and the Bruvvers at the Tower Ballroom, New Brighton, a show promoted by Bob Wooler. Bobby Graham was the first drummer to be approached to replace Pete and, in the estimation of John, Paul and George, ideally suited for The Beatles and more than adequate for George Martin's needs. After all, the producer's problem with Pete had nothing to do with his live performances, but rather his drumming in the studio. Graham had extensive studio experience and, as would be proved, was one of the top session drummers in the '60s. Unfortunately for Brian, Graham turned him down.

No Thanks

Joe Brown was one of the highest-rated recording artists in the early 1960s and, in late 1961, he was looking for a new drummer for his backing band, The Bruvvers. Graham joined the group and on 27th July 1962, when Brown and the Bruvvers were playing on the same bill as The Beatles at the Tower Ballroom across the Mersey in New Brighton, Brian Epstein approached him. As Graham recalled: "He said that they needed a change. I said, 'No thanks' as The Beatles hadn't had any hits and anyway, I had a wife and family in London. I don't think he had even discussed it with The Beatles, as surely they would have wanted someone from Liverpool."

In a further interview with Spencer Leigh, Graham elaborated further on the discussion. "Brian Epstein invited us back to the Blue Angel after the show. He called me to one side and said he was having trouble with Pete Best's mum and he wanted him out of The Beatles. He asked me if I would take his place. Although I liked The Beatles, I turned him down because I didn't want to come to Liverpool. Besides, I liked Joe Brown, who was having hit records.
I met George Harrison about five years ago and he had no idea that Brian had asked me." *(Drummed Out)* Bobby Graham's loyalty to Joe Brown was admirable, but by the following year, Graham had left The Bruvvers and joined Marty Wilde's group.

The fact that he remembers Brian discussing Pete's mother Mona is interesting, let alone George's claim that he didn't know what was going on at the time. Was this Brian being the manager and trying to make the first move on behalf of his group? Surely Brian would have discussed any impending job offer with John, Paul and George; or was it just John and Paul? Either way, it is highly unlikely that Brian would have acted alone.

It has been suggested that Bobby Graham wasn't offered the permanent job. According to Mark Lewisohn in *TuneIn*: "He (Brian) can't have been offering the position permanently – John, Paul and George were clear they wanted Ringo – but Ringo was at Butlin's until early September.... Brian wondered if Graham could bridge the gap between Pete's departure and Ringo's return." *(TuneIn)*

Does the evidence support this claim?

When Graham was offered a job with The Beatles as Ringo's temporary replacement in June 1964, it was only, as he clearly remembered, "for a few days". But in 1962, Brian was offering Graham a permanent position in The Beatles as Pete's replacement, as it involved a move to Liverpool, a notion he

swiftly rejected.

Also, when Brian and The Beatles decided on Ringo in August 1962, he was offered the job in the middle of the week, with his debut slated for that Saturday, during the peak of the Hurricanes' summer season, so finishing early didn't appear to be an issue. The evidence therefore suggests that Bobby Graham was offered a permanent position in The Beatles, but he turned it down. Graham said: "I turned him down because I didn't want to come to Liverpool", a comment which suggests a move north if he accepted the job. If it was only going to be for a few weeks, surely they would have just kept Pete in the group until Ringo was free? And why did nobody check with Ringo?

Why would a professional drummer with one of the top acts in the country want to give that up for a few weeks just to "fill in" for an unknown group from Liverpool while they waited for another drummer to join? It didn't even make sense to him to accept the permanent position in a group that hadn't even made a record. We can also tell that Graham was offered the permanent position, because the same offer was made to Ritchie Galvin and Johnny Hutchinson; the permanent drummering role in The Beatles. There is no evidence to suggest it was on a temporary basis.

Corroboration?

Can Graham's story be corroborated? David Barnes became friends with Bobby Graham later in Graham's life, and attended several events with him, and worked with him too. "Every time Bobby told this story," said Barnes, "and he told it many times at his shows, the story was always the same, and never embellished. Brian Epstein approached him and offered him the chance to become the drummer with The Beatles, replacing Pete Best. Bobby was old school; an honourable man. And he was one of the finest drummers of his era."

(David Bedford Interview 2017)

There is no evidence to suggest that John, Paul and George had told Brian they wanted Ringo at this point. But what seems certain is that Brian didn't want Ringo, which maybe explains why he may have approached Graham.

No Thanks, Again

Bobby Graham didn't turn The Beatles down once, but a second time as well. He did, however, play on one of their early sessions and sat in for Ringo on a BBC session in 1963. *(Drummed Out)* Graham had a second opportunity to join them, albeit on a temporary basis, in June 1964 when Ringo was taken ill. Just as in July 1962, he declined the offer. The job eventually went to Jimmie Nicol. How many musicians turned The Beatles down, not once, but twice?

August 1962: Almost the Fourth Beatle - Ritchie Galvin

Another of Liverpool's best drummers, Ritchie Galvin from Earl Preston and the TTs, was asked by Brian to replace Pete. Ritchie was born Ritchie Hughes, but adopted the name Galvin from the group he was fronting, The Galvinisers. Spencer Leigh spoke to Galvin's girlfriend, and later his wife, Ann Upton. "Brian Epstein asked Ritch about joining The Beatles and he went to see Ritch's dad as he was still under age," Upton said. "Bob Wooler was with him, too. Ritch said that he didn't agree with Pete being replaced and he didn't like John Lennon's sarcasm as he thought that they would fall out. Also, to his credit, he didn't want to be leaving me as they would be working away from Liverpool quite a lot. He never regretted it and he said, 'No, I wouldn't have you and I wouldn't have my kids and I wouldn't have this life.' I was quite surprised when they chose Ringo. He was little and skinny and weedy and had a joke of a moustache. I always thought he needed a good scrub, but it worked out OK." *(Spencer Leigh: The Cavern)*

Can this be substantiated? Phil Brady and his group, The Ranchers, were at the forefront of the country music scene in Liverpool from the early '60s. Brady recruited Ritchie Galvin for his group in the 1980s, and Galvin told him about being approached to join The Beatles. "Ritchie told me how he was asked to join The Beatles," Brady said, "because they needed a drummer who would be less of an attraction and sit at the back, doing what he was told." Ritchie, who turned down the job, was happy with his decision and never regretted it.

(David Bedford Interview with Phil Brady 2015)

Mike Kinney played bass with Galvin, and remembers him fondly, and was also told of the job offer to join The Beatles. "I have to admit that when he first told me the story," recalled Kinney, "I was a teenager and didn't understand the great significance of it. As I got older and was still working with him in different bands, I realised what a great honour it was for him. At the time he was still in his teens."

The band they were in for a time was called Harvey, and were a four-piece country outfit, and as bass player, Kinney worked closely with Galvin. "Ritchie produced a powerhouse of sound on the drums, and was nicknamed 'thunder foot'. He was a great friend with a fabulous sense of humour, and an incredible drummer. When he set the tempo, he never moved either way. As a bass player it's exactly what you need from your drummer. He was one of the most respected drummers on Merseyside right up until he died. I shed many a tear when he passed." *(David Bedford Interview 2017)*

Earl Preston (real name Joey Spruce) was the leader of the TTs, for whom Galvin played drums at the time, and he explained what happened when Ritchie was offered the job. "Ritchie was 19, and his girlfriend Ann, who became his wife, was 21. Ritchie recalled that it was Brian that came along to see him and his father at their house, because he was under 21. Brian offered him the job to replace Pete Best. Ritchie and Ann had just placed a deposit down on a house, and his uncle had got him a job.

"He was looking to settle down, and wasn't prepared to jeopardise all of that. Ritchie did not have any time for John Lennon. He found him arrogant and unnerving to be around. That was his main reason to decline the offer. Brian did have a soft spot for Ritchie and loved his style of drumming, and he bought Ritchie a Zildjian cymbal from Hessy's, at the time that was the most expensive one of the day." Even that didn't persuade him.

Kinney adds: "I really believe that it was Ringo's destiny to become one of The Beatles. On saying that, the likes of Ritchie Galvin as a drummer would have added a great deal to their already extremely tight sound, as he did with all the bands we worked in together." *(David Bedford Interview 2017)*

August 1962: Almost the Fourth Beatle? Freddie Marsden

Gerry and the Pacemakers had recently signed with Brian, and Gerry Marsden said that his brother Freddie, the group's drummer, had been considered as a replacement for Pete Best, though Freddie Marsden always denied it. *(Drummed Out)*

August 1962 - Ringo Nearly A Pacemaker

While Ringo was with Rory Storm and The Hurricanes, EMI granted The Beatles the audition which lead to their contract offer. While the band was heading for the toppermost at EMI on 6th June 1962, Ringo felt he was going nowhere. But then, three offers arrived at once. First, Gerry Marsden asked Ringo to join The Pacemakers, but not as a drummer. "Gerry wanted me to be his bass player!" Ringo said in the *Anthology*. "I hadn't played bass back then or to this day, but the idea of being up front was appealing. That you'd never played a particular instrument before wasn't important back then!" *(Anthology)* After that, he was offered and accepted the drummer's job in Kingsize Taylor and The Dominoes, but soon The Beatles came calling and he reversed his decision.

August 1962 - A King-sized Offer for Ringo

Ringo's second offer of the summer was from Kingsize Taylor, who promised him £20 per week to drum for his group, The Dominoes. "Ringo was a very rare commodity on Merseyside," said Taylor, "due to the fact that drummers at this time were very hard to come by. I only asked him to join The Dominoes out of desperation, as we knew that Dave Lovelady could not go back to Hamburg with us for our second contract." *(David Bedford Interview 2015)*

Some irony, with this being the reason The Beatles hastily offered Pete the position under the same circumstances in August 1960. "Yes," he continued, "I did, off the top of my head, offer him 20 quid (£20) a week, which he did accept in spite of the fact that he said that he had never liked Hamburg when he was last there. Then along came The Beatles, and the rest is history. Ringo was not a better drummer than Pete – too much of a swing in his rhythm, and liked himself more than his music." *(David Bedford Interview 2015)*

Why did Ringo initially accept Taylor's offer? Because at this point, he had no offer to join The Beatles, and there were no guarantees it would happen, even if it had been raised as a possibility. He knew he wanted to leave the Hurricanes, and joining Kingsize Taylor and the Dominoes, one the best groups in Liverpool, was a step up as far as he was concerned.

But just when it looked as though his future had been sorted out, and that he would be joining Taylor in September, along came the offer to join The Beatles. But first, The Beatles had to get rid of Pete Best, a job they delegated to Brian. Although there had been hints as far back as June, when somebody said to Pete; they're thinking of getting rid of you, you know," Pete laughed.., and Brian appeased him. And then, sometime in early August, Pete had his heart set on buying a new Ford Capri car, but, when he mentioned it to Paul, McCartney responded; "If you take my advice, don't buy it. You'd be better saving your money." *(Shout!)*

There was also one more drummer to be asked to replace Pete, on the same day that Pete was given the bad news, after Ringo had been offered the job. However, Brian first had to do what the other Beatles had asked, and get Pete out of the group.

Freddie Marsden drumming with Gerry and the Pacemakers

Pete Best singing while Paul drums

Ritchie Galvin playing drums with Earl Preston and the TTs

WHY PETE BEST WAS NOT SACKED/DISMISSED BY BRIAN EPSTEIN

Since 1962, one of the hottest debates has centred around Brian Epstein's dismissal of Pete Best from The Beatles. The controversy has inspired articles, chapters and even entire books, all speculating on the reasons why Pete was dismissed from the group on the cusp of stardom. However, we have been looking at this most well-known chapter in Beatles history the wrong way.

As we know, Brian Epstein summoned Pete Best to NEMS on 16th August 1962, for what Pete thought was a routine meeting, but finished up being the day that would define his life. Even though we will demonstrate that Pete was not dismissed by Brian, this does not mean that either Pete or Brian have ever lied about what went on that day. The accounts from both of them have been consistent through the years. After nervously exchanging some small talk, Brian then uttered those fateful words:

"I don't know how to tell you this, but the boys want you out and it has already been agreed that Ringo is joining on Saturday."

Pete recalled what happened next. "I was stunned and found words difficult. Only one echoed through my mind. Why, why why? 'They don't think you're a good enough drummer, Pete,' Brian went on. 'And George Martin doesn't think you're a good enough drummer.' 'I consider myself as good, if not better, than Ringo,' I could hear myself saying.

"Then I asked: 'Does Ringo knew about this yet?' 'He's joining on Saturday,'

Eppy said. So everything was all neatly packaged. A conspiracy had clearly been going on for some time behind my back, but not one of the other Beatles could find the courage to tell me. The stab in the back had been left to Brian, and it had been left until almost the last minute. Even Ringo had been a party to it, someone else I had considered to be a pal until this momentous day."

There was a phone call during the meeting, which most people assume to have been Paul McCartney, checking to see if the deed had been done.

It wasn't over yet.

The meeting continued. "Epstein went on to what for him was simply next business at this shattering meeting. 'There are still a couple of venues left before Ringo joins - will you play?' 'Yes,' I nodded, not really knowing what I was saying, for my mind was in a turmoil. How could this happen to me? Why had it taken two years for John Lennon, Paul McCartney and George Harrison to decide that my drumming was not of a high enough standard for them? Dazed, I made my way out of Brian's office. Downstairs, Neil was waiting for me. 'What's happened?' he asked as soon as he saw me, 'you look as if you've seen a ghost.'" Pete walked straight passed Billy Kinsley and Tony Crane of The Merseybeats, the group Brian was hoping Pete would join." *(Beatle! The Pete Best Story)*

Billy Kinsley remembered that day well. "When we arrived at NEMS, as we opened the gates of the lift downstairs, Pete just walked passed us and didn't say anything, which was unusual. As we got up to the top floor, Brian's secretary met us and said that Mr. Epstein can't see you today. He will be in touch soon."

Billy and Tony ended up walking to Mathew Street, still bemused.

"I then visited the Cavern," continued Billy, "and Brian O'Hara came over to me and asked me; 'have you heard the news? They've got rid of Pete from The Beatles.' I said; 'you are kidding, and he said it's true', but I didn't believe him. Absolutely no way. So Brian said; 'I'll bet you 10 bob' (shillings). He brought someone over, and he said; 'tell Billy about Pete', and he said that they've had kicked Pete out of The Beatles. So I had to give the ten bob to Brian, and in disgust, he took it. There was no hint or sign of what was happening to Pete." *(David Bedford Interview 2017)*

Neil Aspinall

Was Neil in the meeting with Pete? Although this is mentioned in one account, when Pete has recalled what happened that day, he is usually quite consistent that Neil dropped him off at the office, and waited for him. Certainly, when asked, Billy Kinsley only remembers Pete walking passed him in NEMS, and not Neil. So on the balance of evidence, it is most likely that Neil was not in the meeting. Although Brian had sought out John Booker as a potential replacement for Neil, John, Paul and George wanted their "Nell" to stay. Pete says that Neil offered to quit, but that he told Neil to stay with The Beatles because they were going places. However, Neil Aspinall gave a different version in a later interview. "When Pete was sacked he wanted to drink with me all through the afternoon, but I said, 'No, I have to drive the van tonight.' He said, 'But I've just been sacked!' and I said, 'You've been sacked, Pete, I haven't been sacked. I've still got a job to do." *(Tune In)*

If Pete's account is accurate, it is a magnanimous gesture by Pete to his friend, and in keeping with his character. If Neil's account is true, that shows a selfishness and disloyalty to his good friend, and by his relationship with Mona, the father of Pete's new half-brother Roag who was just a few weeks old. He certainly showed his loyalty over the years to John, Paul, George and Ringo, and maintained a relationship with the Best family too, which can't have been easy either.

Examining the Evidence

We have to carefully look at, and challenge, every piece of available evidence, and consider the following statements:

- Pete was sacked/ dismissed by Brian - the accepted truth since 1962

- "He (Pete) was hired so he could be fired" and "John, Paul and George could fire him" *(Tune In)*

Definition of Dismissal:

"Dismissal *(referred to informally as firing or sacking)* is the termination of employment by an employer against the will of an employee."

Pete Best wasn't employed by Brian (in fact, Pete with the other Beatles employed Brian), so Brian couldn't sack him. Pete wasn't employed by John, Paul

and George, so they couldn't sack him. In fact, Pete was a self-employed musician, a partner in The Beatles, so couldn't be sacked by anybody.

Now that we know he wasn't sacked, we have to examine what really happened. The reason Brian used those exact words, "the boys want you out and it has already been agreed that Ringo is joining on Saturday" was not accidental; they were carefully chosen. Brian, as we know, was terribly nervous about the meeting and was clearly agitated, as Pete Best observed. It was because Brian had to get the wording right, or it could have had dire consequences.

That is because Brian had to convince Pete that he was being sacked and replaced, without saying those words.

Why?

Getting rid of Pete Best was not an easy matter; he couldn't be "fired, because he had been hired" *(Tune In)*, because when he joined The Beatles, he wasn't hired as a paid employee; it was as an equal member, and therefore they became a partnership. As we have seen, The Beatles of John, Paul, George and Pete signed a Partnership Agreement. Further evidence is provided by the management contract that John, Paul, George and Pete signed as members of The Beatles, and that Brian failed to sign. If Pete Best was simply a "hired hand", then the contract would not have included him. The four Beatles were performing as a group, as a partnership. No member of that partnership could fire another member.

There needed to be a complex examination of the legal partnership among The Beatles and that management contract. Epstein needed the help of his solicitor, David Harris, to find a way to follow the instructions of John, Paul and George to get rid of Pete Best from The Beatles.

Following the Parlophone session of 6th June 1962, The Beatles decided that they had to replace Pete, and told Brian about it. However, Brian knew it wouldn't be easy. Even though the 1st February 1962 contract wasn't enforceable on Brian's side, it had the provision for either party to walk away, subject to three months notice. That, however, wouldn't come into play until 1st February 1963. They couldn't wait that long.

On the 18th June 1962, Paul McCartney's 20th birthday, two significant events took place. Firstly, George Martin was sent the signed copy of the Parlophone recording contract between EMI and The Beatles. Secondly, back in Liverpool, Brian contacted his solicitor, David Harris, to seek his advice on how to remove Pete Best from The Beatles. Without mentioning him by name, Harris referred to Best as the "undesirable member", an unfortunate term. He explained the difficulties and possible solutions. "George Martin said he didn't want Best in the group," said Harris. "I have a letter from him (George Martin) on AIR headed paper from 1965 after I wrote to him. (AIR Studios was the Independent Music Studios set up by George Martin.) I asked him if he would have recorded the group had Best remained a Beatle. He said that he 'would record The Beatles, but not Pete Best.' If they were to advance their careers, and this was the big opening in the door, he (Best) was a stumbling block. I don't think they fell out with him (Best) personally, but they needed to hurdle him, which is why they decided he had to go, and Brian had to carry out their wishes." *(David Bedford Interview 2015)*

But it wasn't as simple as Brian telling Pete he was sacked. Legally, Brian didn't have the authority, which is why Pete Best was not dismissed by Brian, even if that is how it appeared to everyone, but especially to Pete. Pete and The Beatles employed Brian as manager and agent; Brian did not employ them.

"Best wasn't employed by Brian," said Harris, "he was in partnership with the other three Beatles, and they had a partnership as a group known as 'The Beatles'. Their partnership didn't have to be in writing - not all contracts have to be in writing - but in general terms, a contract doesn't have to be in writing. It can be verbal, like buying something in a shop. Same with this informal partnership agreement where they would work together as a group and share their profits. They could have agreed among themselves that they could divide the profits between themselves in any way they wanted." What Harris didn't know at the time is that The Beatles most likely had a formal partnership agreement arranged in December 1961.

"The problem was," advised Harris, "that it was a Partnership; Brian had no authority to get rid of Pete. They (the other three Beatles) had to get rid of Pete, and they had to dissolve the partnership. Brian could say Pete was being replaced by Ringo. I wrote a letter saying Brian would happily place him (Pete) in another group, as that was in his character anyway. He couldn't sack him. The personal relationships didn't suggest it, but the legal relationship did, that Pete was engaging Brian to provide work for him." *(David Bedford Interview 2015)*

Brian Epstein was therefore employed by Pete and the other Beatles.

Put simply; for someone to be fired/sacked/dismissed, they have to be employed. Brian didn't employ Pete, just as John, Paul and George didn't employ Pete as they were a partnership. Pete was self-employed as a musician, and didn't work for anybody, therefore he could not be fired. We therefore need to look at what really happened.

Because Pete was a partner in The Beatles, Brian couldn't, and didn't, say that Pete was dismissed. Brian said: "The boys want you out...." This was Brian's way of informing Pete that his fellow partners wanted him to leave, without the partners telling him so. Legally, the other partners should have dissolved the partnership, but they didn't.

By Brian then saying: "and it has already been agreed that Ringo is joining on Saturday", he is telling Pete that his replacement has already been notified and has agreed to join; it's a done deal. However, this wasn't necessarily the case; appearances can be deceptive.

What options did Pete have and what would the consequences have been?

What Brian had to do was to convince Pete that he was dismissed and Ringo was replacing him, and that he had no choice in the matter. Most young men in Pete's position would have assumed he was being sacked, and no one could blame him for accepting the fact. However, if Pete had said: "OK, Brian, I understand what you are saying as my manager. I am going to consult my solicitor and take his advice about what to do next", what could Brian have said? Nothing. Pete could have walked out of Brian's office still a Beatle and turned up at the next booking. Until the situation was resolved, Ringo wouldn't have been able to join. Who knows what would have happened next? Stalemate? Could they have resolved their differences with Pete remaining with The Beatles?

More importantly, if Pete had sought legal advice and forced John, Paul and George to dissolve their partnership, this would have been a lengthy process of completing the necessary paperwork, drawing up accounts and dividing the proceeds, which would all have to be agreed. What if that took weeks?

They didn't have the time to go down that route, because the following week they were being filmed for television for the first time, and on 4th September, only a couple of weeks away, they were due back at EMI studios to begin making their debut record. The Beatles didn't have time; they had to get Brian to make the move, and quickly, so they could get Ringo in place. This was their only option, and it was essential that Brian got it right. No wonder Brian was anxious that day; he had been put in an awkward position, but had to carry out their instructions, wording it exactly right so that Pete felt that he was being dismissed, and had no choice in the matter.

David Harris answered some more questions to clarify the options available to Brian and Pete.

If Brian provided other work for Pete, would he be fulfilling his part of the contract?

"I hadn't thought of it that way," said Harris, "but yes, you would be right." As David Harris confirmed, Pete was offered other work, including some gigs detailed in a letter Harris wrote to the drummer.

The final part of the plan was for Brian to fulfil his legal obligation to provide work for Pete in another of his groups or get him to break his contract with Brian, even though it was unenforceable on Brian's part because neither Pete's parents nor Brian had signed it. Getting rid of Pete also meant getting rid of Mo, too, so Brian was sold on that part of the plan. In all fairness, though, we have to believe that Brian would have fulfilled his part of the bargain if he had to, even if it wasn't ideal.

Pete was offered the drummer's job in The Merseybeats, who were still at that embryonic stage, having been formed only a year earlier as The Mavericks. Founding members Tony Crane and Billy Kinsley were just 16 and 15, respectively, and although Pete was promised that the group would be built around him as the "new Beatles", this could not have been seen as a suitable alternative to The Beatles for Pete. The ideal situation for Brian was in convincing Pete to quit, he would get rid of Mo, who was always getting in the way and rid himself of the Pete Best problem.

How could he achieve both aims? Joe Flannery, Brian's closest friend and confidant, had already hinted to Pete Best several weeks earlier that his time with The Beatles was running out. "Brian was a public schoolboy, very nice and quietly spoken," said Flannery, "and he found it hard to answer Mrs. Best. 'She keeps telling me she put the band together,' said Brian, 'so what am I going to do?' When Brian told me George Martin was going to bring in a session drummer for their record, and it was put to Brian and to me that Pete should leave The Beatles, I said to Brian; why not let me approach Pete to join Lee Curtis and the All Stars? Brian said; 'let's see if it will work.' So I approached Pete, which was easy enough for me to do." *(David Bedford Interview 2014)*

Pete could join a new group Flannery was putting together around his brother Peter, better known as Lee Curtis. If Flannery could entice Pete with a position in Lee Curtis and the All Stars, then he would be helping his friend Brian solve his problems. "I spoke to Pete and told him that I had been approached to ask him to join this new group. I told him it was very sad, and it was nothing to do with his musical ability or his looks, because he was a lovely young man, but that was how it was put to me by Brian. Pete was all for it."*(David Bedford Interview 2014)*

Pete Best, one of the most popular people on the Liverpool music scene, would go straight from the most popular group, The Beatles, into the lineup of Flannery's new supergroup. Flannery was right in his assumption. At the end of 1962, a poll was conducted to determine the most popular group in Liverpool. Lee Curtis and the All-Stars were voted number 2 ahead of Gerry and the Pacemakers and The Searchers, due mainly to the acquisition of The Beatles' former drummer. The perfect solution – for everyone except for Pete.

If Pete stayed under Brian's management, though not with The Beatles, would Ringo become part of the new partnership?

"He *(Ringo)* did! He became a Beatle, didn't he? And he signed a contract and officially became a partner with the new contract on 1st October and entered into a contract with the boys and NEMS Enterprises Ltd with Paul and George's parents signing for them as they were under 21. Ringo signed the contract and joined the group and the partnership."

Between Pete going and the new contract: If Pete decided not to accept work from Brian and accepted work from another group, would that take him out of the partnership?

"He did and that was his choice. I wrote a letter that Brian could offer him other work and he chose not to take it, or didn't take up the offer. He takes himself out of the partnership of The Beatles, but it doesn't stop him making a claim for compensation against The Beatles, for dissolving the partnership as far as he was concerned."

This was the ideal solution for The Beatles. Firstly, when Brian asked Pete to play for the gigs in between that day and Ringo joining on Saturday, Pete initially said 'Yes'. However, when Pete failed to show up, he was in breach of his agreement as a member of The Beatles to turn up and play. Here, Brian was offering him work, and Pete decided not to accept it. Secondly, Pete effectively took himself out of the partnership by joining another group. Pete took legal counsel, but was ill-advised. He tried to sue Brian, which he couldn't, and the solicitor neglected to correctly sue Pete's partners, John, Paul and George.

Was The Beatles' Partnership dissolved?

"It must have been," affirmed Harris, "because he (Pete) left. I wasn't involved in that, so I don't know. The partnership was dissolved because he left and the other three continued as The Beatles with Ringo. There are all sorts of ramifications that I can think of. It could have led to bitter partnership disputes, but it didn't. The only thing that happened was the letter from Pete's solicitors where he stated: 'He became a member of a group and had been a member until his summary dismissal in August *(1962)*'.

Well I suppose you could see it as being dismissed, but partnerships can always

be dissolved."

How Do You Legally Dissolve a Partnership?

Surely bands changed members all the time, so why was this different, if at all? "You have to give notice that you are dissolving the partnership. You can't just do it, and partnerships can always result in claims for compensation having been dismissed. I didn't formally do anything *(to dissolve the partnership)*." Eric Goldrein, who drew up The Beatles Partnership agreement, was also not requested to dissolve the partnership legally.

Dissolution of the Partnership

"There was an informal agreement *(partnership)*, so as far as I am aware, there was no formal dissolving of the partnership, no written dissolution of the partnership. There was clearly a verbal dissolution of the partnership because the partnership was dissolved as they went their separate ways."

This was communicated by Brian at the meeting with Pete, when he was told that his partners, John, Paul and George, wanted him out. "Usually when that happens, a partnership account is taken. Whether that happened here or not I don't know because I wasn't involved. I wasn't an accountant. I wasn't asked to consider it, or deal with it."

The partnership of The Beatles between John, Paul, George and Pete had to be dissolved for any three partners to remove the other from that partnership. "If you dissolve it in a split second, there can be consequences if people want to pursue them," advised Harris. "It was all very informal."

Mersey Beat - By Mutual Agreement

It was so informal, that it lead to one of the most contentious actions tied to Pete's departure from The Beatles, which occurred when Bill Harry reproduced Brian's press release in *Mersey Beat*, stating that "Pete left the group by mutual agreement. There were no arguments or difficulties and this has been an entirely amicable decision."

Although this has been questioned for many years, most of it is actually accurate. Pete had accepted Brian's comments that "the boys" wanted him out, and that "Ringo was joining on Saturday". By refusing Brian's offer to join another of his groups, Pete left Epstein's office and effectively walked out of The Beatles by mutual agreement, without difficulty or argument. However, what is not accurate is the comment that it was an "entirely amicable decision". Pete may not have fought or argued at that meeting, but it was anything but amicable. This changed Pete Best's life forever. He was tricked into believing that he was being dismissed, even if those words were never said. He was never sacked.

That edition of Bill Harry's *Mersey Beat* was published on 23rd August 1962 without fuss or fanfare, which is surprising, given that in Liverpool, the "dismissal of Pete Best" caused much rumour and speculation among the music fans which has never gone way. The news of his dismissal was buried away on page eight and ran to a very short statement saying that Pete had in effect left The Beatles by mutual agreement; nothing to report here then.

Ringo was about to become the Fourth Beatle

It was all old news, so move along, move along. And with that, the matter was given the last rights. Only it wasn't quite like that at all.

Bill Harry, chief editor and general factotum of *Mersey Beat* has stated later on that he received and published Epstein's message verbatim. It was accepted without question and with no reason to question its veracity, which is an almost implausible position to take, given that The Beatles were very special in the life of the *Mersey Beat* paper. Hadn't they figured large in its overall success and development? Not only that, but until they exited Liverpool for London in 1964, they'd topped Harry's list of personal friends anyway. Hadn't they contributed articles to pad out the paper in the early days? Suddenly they were going places now, and were a hot story? Hot enough to know that any rumblings of a coup were going to be of particular interest to Harry as a reporter.

At the time, Liverpool groups changed their line up with regularity as members came and went, but it is no excuse to suppose a member who'd been a regular feature with The Beatles for two years would have left when they were on the brink of success. Surely Harry would have picked up on it beforehand and if not, why didn't he run an investigative piece in the next issue to get at the truth? It would have made big headlines for him, and yet he did absolutely nothing, at least publicly.

As author Spencer Leigh said; Harry's version is 'far from the truth and must cast doubt on his integrity as an editor.' In his defence, Bill says the lead-time for the paper was very short and had to be ready to go to Swales printers on a quick turnaround, but this does not explain why the article should only have appeared on page eight. Why not the front page? The argument he put forward some years later was that it was the only page he could break into without disrupting everything else. Given its importance, we disagree. Here was a big news scoop that warranted pulling the front page and rewriting the headline. BIG!

Having worked on many papers and books assemblies, our view is that it wouldn't have taken too much effort to change this, remembering also that an exclusive story would have sold out on any news stand, which is the central purpose. Instead, it was tucked away, almost as an afterthought on page eight. For Epstein, it may have seemed a case of job done. The great manipulator had struck again, and spun a plausible story. Bill Harry had fallen for it, and seemingly gone along with it without too much fuss and so the news was killed off, leaving Harry's reporting instincts burning his ears off and his editing integrity in question. To this day the question remains; was he sat on, and by whom? Such was Harry's ire that he had been treated like this by Brian and The Beatles, he sought to rectify his error by co-writing a book with Pete Best, in an attempt to get to the truth.

Legal Action From Pete Best

Pete's legal advisers decided that it was constructive dismissal. By definition, constructive dismissal occurs when an employer has committed a serious breach of contract, entitling the employee to resign in response to the employer's conduct. The employee is entitled to treat himself or herself as having been "dismissed" and the employer's conduct is often referred to as a "repudiatory breach". The advisers mistakenly assumed that Brian was the employer and that he had been dismissed, when actually this was a partnership dispute, and his legal recourse was against his partners.

Brian Epstein's solicitor, David Harris

According to David Harris, Pete's solicitor sued Brian for breach of contract.

"Pete was saying that he had been dismissed," observed Harris, "and was seeking compensation. All we (on behalf of our client Brian) were saying was, 'We didn't employ you'. If he had wanted to sue, he would have had to sue The Beatles. You can't sue us. That was the line we took. If they had taken a different line of approach with us, we might have taken a different line back. I just don't know, I'm just speculating. They said 'our client has suffered a financial loss and tried to look to the group for compensation. Well that was right; they did. But not to Brian for compensation. The Beatles engaged Brian; he didn't employ them. That's my view. I just carried on negotiating with the solicitors less and less as time went on. It never went to litigation. We are just speculating as to what might have happened. Nothing fundamental happened in the UK. Pete got a settlement in England for a trivial amount as he didn't have much of a case. They (his solicitors) were bowling the balls, and I was simply responding to them, sitting back and dealing with them as they arose. It wasn't settled until the end of 1968, when Clive (Epstein) decided just to settle it and be done with it, get rid of it. It wasn't going anywhere so he decided to buy it off." *(David Bedford Interview 2015)*

In 1999, one of the biggest bands on the planet was Oasis. They had sacked their drummer Tony McCarroll for his "poor drumming skills", even though he had played on their 1994 debut album, *Definitely Maybe*, as well as number 1 hits, and had toured with the band. McCarroll approached solicitor Jens Hills to sue the drummer's former bandmates for loss of earnings, and this was resolved on the steps of the court before the trial started. McCarroll received approximately £550,000 from Oasis. Hills had also, by coincidence, represented Pete Best in his action for royalties for playing on ten tracks on *Anthology*.

A further example comes from one of the greatest bands of all time: The Eagles. When founding members Glenn Frey and Don Henley decided they didn't want guitarist Don Felder in the group any longer, they asked manager Irving Azoff to fire him, which Azoff did by letter. Although no longer able to play with The Eagles, Felder was still a partner, and so there were numerous lawsuits that followed, where Felder claimed wrongful termination, and breach of contract and fiduciary duty. It took them six years, but eventually it was settled out of court, with a non-disclosure agreement in place so that the details cannot be disclosed. That is what can happen when a group wants to fire a partner, and finds out they can't, even when they ask their manager to do so. In contrast, former members Randy Meisner and Bernie Leadon quit the group, and so there was no recourse for any legal action by them. Getting a member to quit the group is a much simpler method than trying to dismiss a partner.

Was Ringo a partner right away or not until the management contract was signed?

"He could have become a partner of The Beatles straight away as that was between them and they were acting as The Beatles. That was between the four of them," said Harris. "As a group they entered into a new agreement on the terms agreed, and then they all entered a new agreement to engage Brian as their agent and manager from 1st October."

This new Beatles partnership was established on new terms, and, according to Brian's close aide Peter Brown *(The Love You Make and David Bedford Interview 2015)*, Ringo was "hired on a probationary basis on a fixed £25 per week", which was different to the other three Beatles who were paid at least £50 per week.

This was the case until 1st October when, as an equal partner legally, Ringo signed the newly-drafted, first fully-legal management contract between The Beatles and Brian Epstein, though it isn't known when Ringo's pay increased. However, Brown's statement cannot be corroborated, though no evidence has been provided to disprove it either.

And in The End?

The Beatles partnership was never legally dissolved, even though it should have been. Pete Best was never sacked, even though he thought he had been. Pete turned down an offer from his manager, Brian, for alternative employment with The Merseybeats, even though that was never a suitable alternative for where he currently was with The Beatles. And, with the 'help' of Joe Flannery, Pete quit The Beatles and joined Lee Curtis and the All Stars. Pete then tried to sue Brian for wrongful dismissal, which he couldn't, as he hadn't been dismissed. And ever since, everyone, including Pete, has talked about how he was sacked: and he wasn't.

It's no wonder that Brian didn't want to do this. He was on edge having to carry out another political "Machiavellian" manoeuvre so it didn't leave him or The Beatles open to legal action.

Brian and The Beatles had got away with it – but only just. Brian didn't sack Pete. The Beatles couldn't fire him because they hadn't "hired him"; he was invited to join the band and was an equal partner. The management contract wasn't voided by Pete leaving; it just meant that Brian was only representing John, Paul and George now.

Pete Best would be forever asked why he was sacked. Now he can say that he wasn't, not that it will be much consolation. As most Beatles fans will agree, this was the grubbiest of episodes in Beatles history – and it may have just become a little grubbier.

By hook, or by crook, Brian had successfully carried out his task by convincing Pete that he had been dismissed, and allowed him to walk out on The Beatles, untold millions, and the fame and celebrity that came with being in the most famous pop group of all time. However, as John, Paul and George were intent on getting Pete out of the group, even if they had followed the legal process correctly in dissolving the partnership, Pete would still have been out of the group. For Pete, he was not to be the Fourth Beatle who made it big; Ringo was about to take his place behind the drums and help carry The Beatles into music immortality.

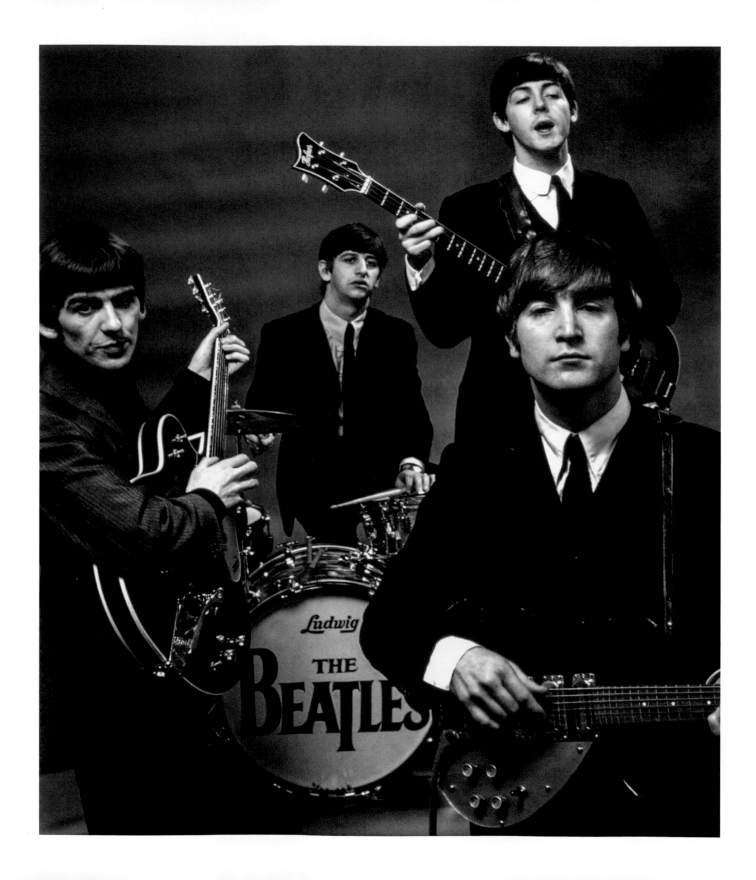

WHY DID THEY WANT TO GET RID OF PETE BEST?

("Pete Best was a great drummer, but Ringo was a great Beatle.")

Go to Facebook and mention Pete Best and the arguments rage about the reasons for his dismissal. As we all know, Ringo is a better drummer than Pete, any day! Alternatively, Pete is so much better than Ringo. Which do you believe?

As we have seen, the the impetus for this argument was the comment by George Martin at the end of their 6th June session that he would be using a session drummer. John, Paul and George, along with Brian, offered their own reasons and decided he had to go.

Some authors claim that John, Paul and George were emphatic in their reasons for getting rid of Pete. End of discussion...or is it? One quote out of context can be misleading, so we have reproduced a balance of quotes provided over the years.

John Lennon

Q.   "How come you suddenly threw Pete Best out of the group?"
A.   "Because he couldn't play very well."
Q.   "Is that why?"
A.   "Why else?"

John Lennon, 1971 NY phone in *(Tune In)*

John to Tony Barrow, their trusted Press Officer: "Pete Best was a great drummer, but Ringo was a great Beatle." *(John, Paul, George, Ringo and Me)*

"This myth built up over the years that he was great and Paul was jealous of him because he was pretty and all that crap. They didn't get on that much together, but it was partly because Pete was a bit slow. He was a harmless guy, but he was not quick. All of us had quick minds, but he never picked that up."

John Lennon, 1974 *(Anthology)*

However, did John also take a dig at Pete in a poem published in *In His Own Write* in 1964? Called "Randolph's Party", there are several lines that allude to Pete Best.

The first is in the title - Randolph. Pete's full name is Randolph Peter Best, and, just as Lennon hated being called "Winnie", Pete disliked being called Randolph. Within the text, there are several clues:

"Randolf looged saggly at his only Chrispbut cart from his dad who did not live there." A reference to the fact that Johnny Best had left the family home.

Lennon then mentions his "friends" turning up.
"then they all jumbed on him and did smite him with mighty blows about his head crying. We never liked you all the years, we've known you. You were never really one of us, soft head."

Maybe that was Lennon's first chance to say what happened, with the "mighty blows" being the way they got rid of him, but the last line maybe ties in with other quotes, especially from John and Paul, about Pete not fitting in: "you were never really one of us." And, in line with John's quote from *Anthology* that Pete wasn't quick-minded: "soft head". *(In His Own Write)* Typically cruel Lennon.

However, in one of his most in-depth interviews, John reflected on his favourite time with The Beatles, which was when Pete Best was the drummer:

"I thought we were the best f**king group in the goddamn world, and believing that is what made us what we were, whether you call it the best pop group or the best rock 'n' roll group or whatever. As far as we were concerned, we were the best, but we thought we were the best before anybody else had even heard of us, back in Hamburg and Liverpool. So in that respect I think The Beatles are the best thing that ever happened in pop music, but you play me those tracks and I want to remake every damn one of them." *(Playboy Interviews)*

"Our best work was never recorded. Because we were performers in Liverpool, Hamburg, and around the dance halls and what we generated was fantastic when we played straight rock. And there was nobody to touch us in Britain. As soon as we made it, we made it. But the edges were knocked off. Brian put us in suits and all that and we made it very big but we sold out. Our music was dead before we even went on the theatre tour of Britain (in 1963). We were feeling shit already, because we had to alter two hours playing, which we were glad in one way, to 20 minutes, and go on and repeat the same 20 minutes every night. The Beatles died then as musicians; that's why we never improved as musicians. We killed ourselves then to make it.... George and I are more inclined to say that because we missed the club days when we were playing music." *(Rolling Stone)*

Paul McCartney

"George Martin took us to one side and said, 'I'm really unhappy with the drummer. Would you consider changing him' We said, 'No, we can't!' It was one of those terrible things you go through as kids. Can we betray him? No. But our career was on the line. Maybe they were going to cancel our contract. It was a big issue at the time, how we 'dumped' Pete. And I do feel sorry for him, because of what he could have been on to; but as far as we were concerned, it was strictly a professional decision. If he wasn't up to the mark – slightly in our eyes, and definitely in the producer's eyes – then there was no choice. But it was still very difficult. It is one of the most difficult things we ever had to do." *(Anthology)*

"Pete Best's mother Mona – a very nice woman, an Anglo-Indian – ran the Casbah in a part of Liverpool, West Derby. We'd started to go round there and we'd ended up painting the place. It was great to be involved in the birth of a coffee bar – they were such important places then. The concrete and wood in the basement had been stripped and we painted each part a different colour. All of us lent a hand – John and George and all the others. And after we'd painted it up, it was our club – The Beatles used to play there. Pete had a drum kit so he would sometimes sit in with us. He was a good drummer, and when Hamburg came up he joined us. He was a very good-looking guy, and out of all the people in our group, the girls used to go for Pete." *(Anthology)*

Paul stated in an interview in the *Wingspan* documentary that "we had Pete Best who was a really good drummer, but there was just something; he wasn't quite like the rest of us. We kind of had a sense of humour in common, and he was nearly in with it all, and it's a fine line between what is nearly in and what is exactly in." *(Wingspan)*

"What's the truth about why Pete Best was sacked? Because George Martin wouldn't have him, is one good reason. And Ringo was better, was the other prime reason." *(Tune In)*

George Harrison

Letter to Arthur Kelly in 1960 from Hamburg: "We have Pete Best Mrs Bests little lad with us from Kasbah fame and he is drumming good."

"Historically, it may look like we did something nasty to Pete, and it may have been that we could have done it better, but the thing was – as history also shows – Ringo was the member of the band. It's just that he didn't enter the film until that particular scene." *(Best of The Beatles: The Sacking of Pete Best)*

"We weren't very good at telling Pete he had to go. But when it comes down to it, how do you tell somebody? Although Pete had not been with us all that long – two years in terms of a lifetime isn't very long – when you're young it's not a nice thing to be kicked out of a band and there's no nice way of doing it. Brian Epstein was the manager so it was his job, but I don't think he could do it very well either. But that's the way it was and the way it is."*(Anthology)*

"To me it was apparent. Pete kept being sick and not showing up for gigs, so we would get Ringo to sit in with the band instead, and every time Ringo sat in, it seemed like 'this is it'. Eventually, we realized, 'We should get Ringo in the band full time.' I was quite responsible for stirring things up. I conspired to get Ringo in for good. I talked to Paul and John until they came round to the idea."

(Anthology)

George Martin

(in a phone conversation with Mona Best)

"I never suggested that Pete must go. All I said was that for the purposes of The Beatles' first record I would rather use a session man. I never thought that Brian Epstein would let him go. He seemed to be the most saleable commodity as far as looks went. It was a surprise when I learned that they had dropped Pete.
The drums were important to me for a record, but they didn't matter much otherwise. Fans don't pay particular attention to the quality of the drumming."

(The Beatles Encyclopedia)

Pete Best also recalled that phone call:
"Mrs. Best, I never said that. I wasn't instrumental in getting rid of Pete. What I said was: 'What I hear isn't what I hear on the record in the present moment of time.' He mentioned the fact to Brian, but said, 'Don't break up the physical content of the band, because Pete is such an integral part of that.' He was 'of course surprised' when he was told that I had left the band and said it was as much of a shock to him as to everyone else." *(The Best Years of The Beatles)*

Bob Wooler

"Brian Epstein told me that Pete Best was going to be sacked. I could imagine it with someone who was constantly late or giving him problems, but Pete Best was not awkward and he didn't step out of line. I was most indignant and I said, 'Why are you doing this?' but I didn't get an answer." *(The Cavern)*

Allan Williams

"There wouldn't have been The Beatles without Pete". That's a big statement to make. Why do you say that? "There wouldn't have been The Beatles, as there wouldn't have been Hamburg without a drummer. I couldn't work it out. If he had been a bad drummer I could have understood, but he was with them six and seven hours a night, seven nights a week in Hamburg. It was as if they smelt the whiff of success and they didn't want him on the trip with them.

"And then of course they knew that Ringo and George got on very well together. I used to think Pete was too good looking, and as for not getting his haircut, that was just nonsense.

"I just think socially he didn't fit in, and as they had to live in each other's pockets, maybe they thought with Ringo they could have a better time."

(David Bedford Interview 2007)

Other Reasons?

Over the years, many reasons for Pete's "sacking" have circulated among scholars and fans – some more absurd that others.

Below, we suggest a few of the points that have been debated and the rationale behind some of these myths and truths:

Pete refused to grow his hair mop top style.
Take a good look at the photos of Pete after he left The Beatles and ask yourself, how long do you want? Pete says he was never asked to change it.

The other Beatles were jealous of his good looks.
Maybe Paul was, but was this really all about his position in the group and his youthful uncertainty. There is plenty of evidence to support this.

They were jealous of the attention he was getting from girls.
He definitely had a strong girl fan base, although it wasn't courted. Paul's father's irritating comment at the Manchester gig probably didn't help either, but then Paul and John could boast of their own conquests, probably far more than we will ever know. After appearing in Manchester, all but Pete made it back onto the coach, with Pete finally arriving, having been mobbed by girls.

Jim McCartney tore into Pete: "When I finally escaped he came up to me and said sourly; 'Why did you have to attract all the attention? Why didn't you call the other lads back?' I told him there was nothing I could have done. I was trapped and had to literally fight for my life to get out. His comment was: 'I think that was very selfish of you.' Later I reported the conversation to Eppy and he promised to talk to Jim McCartney about the incident. I don't know if he ever did." *(Beatle! The Pete Best Story)*

He didn't mix in or smile as much with the others.
Pete could scrap as good as the others when the situation called for it.
(The Hamburg street fight and Lathom Hall are just two examples).
He was a very good boxer and could hold his own in a fight. He could drink like a sailor, and he was no stranger to laughter, or to partying and socializing.
He also liked the girls and they liked him, but was careful how far he went because he was the only one in the group who was in a serious long-term relationship.
(At the time, Pete was dating his childhood sweetheart, Kathy. He later

married her, and they are still together.) The other Beatles were either free, or took chances with the females wherever they arose. As for the moody look? Yes it was cultivated. Pete took to it naturally, although is normally a quiet man who leads a settled family life. He was probably the most mature of The Beatles and treated the silly antics of the other three with some disdain. Admittedly, his ability to join in the banter and the general clowning while seated behind a drum kit was certainly restrictive, as Pete has himself said.

He was often missing for bookings.
There are four known absences in two years. This is still subject to speculation and could merely be the black art of disinformation at work. Remember, there had to be excuses of some sort. The truth is, drummers often exerted a lot more energy than guitarists during a performance and would often succumb to minor ailments. There are one or two quotable times when Pete was ill, although there is no evidence to suggest that he suffered prolonged bouts of sickness.

This was more than proved when Pete sued Ringo for alleging he deliberately made himself ill. Equally, there is no other evidence to suggest he was prone to illness any more than the next man. The other three were not immune to ill health either. Ringo was hospitalised and replaced by Jimmie Nicol for two weeks during The Beatles' 1964 world tour, and George fell ill in New York City, leaving Neil Aspinall to stand in for him at the group's rehearsals for *The Ed Sullivan Show*. John missed an important gig in February 1962 when he got laryngitis, and Rory Storm had to step in to sing. They all got over it.

He didn't blend in / didn't gel, with the group.
Looking at the quotes from John and Paul in particular, this is quite likely. Is that a crime worth a dismissal? How did Charlie Watts get on as a lifelong member of the Rolling Stones, I wonder? Most musicians who have been in groups will tell you how important it is to get along with your fellow members, even if musically you are talented.

The Beatles always wanted Ringo.
If they always wanted Ringo, why did it take them 2 years to decide they didn't want Pete? And they were friendly with Ringo, particularly at the end of 1961 onwards, when he first sat in with them. Ringo quit Rory Storm to go to Hamburg at the end of '61, so he was available then. When he quit Hamburg and returned to Liverpool in early '62, he was available, but they didn't ask him then. There is no evidence to suggest this was the reason. And why wasn't he the first drummer to be asked, until waiting for others to turn The Beatles down?

On their own, very few of these can be seen as the reason to get rid of the drummer who had been with them for two years. In the end, they did get rid of Pete Best, and he missed out on the biggest roller coaster ride in the history of pop music.

AFTER THE BEATLES

(The Pete beat goes on)

After Pete Best left The Beatles, he was asked to join Rory Storm & The Hurricanes as Ringo's replacement, but said no. Having also turned down Brian's offer to join The Merseybeats, Pete joined Lee Curtis and the All-Stars. With his the most high-profile change of personnel in a Liverpool group, Pete's decision to join the All-Stars meant that this new group gained a huge following in Liverpool and Hamburg. In 1963, with Pete on board, the All-Stars only just lost out to his old group, The Beatles, for best group in *Mersey Beat*.

I've Just Seen a Face

Soon after Pete joined the All-Stars, they twice ended up on the same bill as The Beatles, as Pete recalled: "We did two gigs (with the All-Stars) where I was on stage with them. Ringo was with them but there was no communication. But from that day to this, there's been no verbal communication – they've gone their way, and I've gone mine." *(Mike Dolbear)*

The All-Stars signed a record deal with Decca in 1963, but after their two singles failed to chart, Pete and the rest of the band broke away from Curtis and renamed themselves the Original All-Stars. In a strange twist of fate, producer Mike Smith from Decca, who had been partly responsible for turning The Beatles down in January 1962, signed the former Beatles drummer. Smith decided that they should change their name to The Pete Best Four. The newly-christened group released a number of records and made appearances on several TV programs, including *Ready Steady Go!* the top music programme in Britain.

Neither Decca nor Mike Smith had problems recording Pete's drumming this time around. Even more interesting, there was no suggestion of using a session drummer despite what junior engineer Savage had intimated following The Beatles' Decca audition when he said that "if Decca was going to sign The Beatles, we wouldn't have used Pete Best on the records." *(Tune In)*.

His timing is also precise. When you listen to the songs now, you can hear some of that great rock 'n' roll beat Pete became known for back in Liverpool and Hamburg.

New York

Through 1964 and 1965, the band changed its name again, this time to The Pete Best Combo, and completed a successful European tour before visiting the USA. Arriving in New York, they did interviews, recorded with famous producer Bob Gallo, and were signed to the Cameo label.

While in New York, Pete gave an interview to *Teen Life Magazine* about The Beatles and his trip to the States, including the revelation that he was hoping to move to America. He looked back on his time with The Beatles.

"I was particularly close to John", he said. "We hit it off almost immediately. I admired John for his wit, talent and brilliance. His Aunt Mimi liked me. She knew my grandfather. I never dreamed the day would come when The Beatles would want to get rid of me and replace me with another drummer." In another interview, this time with *FLIP Magazine*, he was a bit more philosophical.

"A little resentful of the way I was treated," he admitted, "but they are all good guys in the group. I've no gripe against the boys."

After their recording sessions, Pete and his band set off on a tour of the U.S.

and Canada. Though they were a popular live act, the records failed to sell in any great numbers, and it finally looked like success had eluded Pete for the last time. In 1968, he put down his drumsticks, and wouldn't pick them up again for another twenty years. He concentrated on being the breadwinner in his family, working at a bakery before joining the Civil Service as an unemployment counsellor working at Liverpool's Garston Job Centre. How ironic that one of the most famous unemployed drummers would find work helping others find jobs.

It was in 1988 when Cavern City Tours asked Pete to play a one-off gig at the Adelphi Hotel in Liverpool. He asked his younger brother Roag to play drums with him, and it was so successful that The Pete Best Band was born. Pete has been touring the world with his band ever since.

When The Beatles' *Anthology 1* was released on CD in 1995, ten of its tracks featured Pete on drums, earning him a sizable royalty cheque. Thirty-three years after he was booted out of the band, he finally received some long overdue payback. Beatles fans were ecstatic for him.

Come With Me, to Haymans Green

In 2008, The Pete Best Band released the critically-acclaimed *Haymans Green* album, which told some of Pete's story through song. He is playing less now, and enjoying his family more, but he still makes appearances around the world at Beatles conventions and events. In 2004, along with his brothers Rory and Roag, Pete reopened the Casbah Coffee Club as a tourist attraction – one which has become a "Mecca" for fans on their Beatles pilgrimage to Liverpool.

Pete v Ringo

Although Pete's lawsuit against Brian was eventually settled, there had to be a second lawsuit, this time against Ringo for a comment he made in an interview with The Beatles that appeared in the February 1965 issue of Playboy. In it, Ringo claimed that Pete would take pills to make himself ill just so that he would miss Beatles gigs. The libel suit was settled out of court in 1969. As records showed, Pete missed only four appearances in his two years with The Beatles, and it was not a recurring problem.

Pete Best is not a bitter man, though he attempted suicide in 1965 during a bout of depression. Thankfully, he was found by his mother and brother Rory and survived. He quickly realised that family was more important than anything, and he has never looked back. He is happy and does what he wants, when he wants, and has a wonderful family. That is all that he needs. *(David Bedford Interview 2007)*

Discography

Singles:

- "I'm Gonna Knock on Your Door" b/w
  "Why Did I Fall in Love with You" (Decca F 11929, Released: 1964)
- "Don't Play With Me (Little Girl)" b/w "If You Can't Get Her"
  (Happening 405, Released: 1965)
- "If You Can't Get Her" b/w "The Way I Feel About You"
  (Happening HA1117, Released: 1965)
- "Kansas City" b/w "Boys" (Cameo 391, Released: 1965)

- "(I'll Try) Anyway" b/w "I Wanna Be There"
  (Original Beatles Drummer 800, Released: 1965)
- "I Can't Do Without You Now" b/w "Keys To My Heart"
  (Mr. Maestro Records 711, Released: 1965)

Albums:

- *Best of The Beatles* (Savage BM 71, Released: 1965)
  Includes: "I Need Your Lovin'"; "Just Wait and See"; "Casting My Spell"; "Keys To My Heart"; "Why Did You Leave Me Baby?"; "Like My Sister Kate"; "I Can't Do Without You Now"; "I'm Blue"; "Some Other Guy"; "She's Alright"; "Nobody But You"; "Last Night"
- *The Beatle That Time Forgot* [Original Version]
  (Phoenix PB-Released: 1981)
  Includes:
  "I'm Checking Out Now Baby"; "I'll Try Anyway"; "I Don't Know Why (I Just Do)"; "How'd You Get To Know Her Name"; "She's Not the Only Girl in Town"; "If You Can't Get Her"; "More Than I Need Myself"; "I'll Have Everything Too"; "The Way I Feel About You"; "Don't Play With Me (Little Girl)"; "Rock and Roll Music"; "All Aboard"

- *Rebirth* (Phoenix PB-44, Released: 1981)

  Includes:

  "I Can't Do Without You Now"; "Off the Hook"; "She's Alright"; "I Need Your Lovin'"; "Why Did You Leave Me Baby"; "High School Shimmy"; "I Wanna Be There"; "Everybody"; "Pete's Theme"; "Keys To My Heart"
- *The Beatle That Time Forgot* [Reissue]
  (Phoenix PHX 340, Released: 1982)

  Includes:
  "I'll Try Anyway"; "I Don't Know Why I Do (I Just Do)"; "She's Not the Only Girl in Town"; "More Than I Need Myself"; "I'll Have Everything Too"; "I'm Checking Out Now Baby"; "How'd You Get to Know Her Name"; "If You Can't Get Her"; "Rock and Roll Music"
- *Back to the Beat* – (1995)
- *The Pete Best Combo: Beyond The Beatles* 1964–1966
  (1st February 1996)
- *Live at the Adelphi Liverpool 1988* – (23 September 1996)
- *Best* (18 August 1998)
- *Casbah Coffee Club 40th Anniversary Limited Edition (1999)*
- *The Savage Young Beatles (10 May 2004)*
- *Haymans Green* – Released 16 September 2008 (U.S.),

  August 2008 (UK) (The Pete Best Band)

RINGO BECOMES THE FOURTH BEATLE

(How It Happened - Examining The Evidence)

Over the years, in many interviews and books, the story of how Ringo came to join The Beatles has been told in so many different ways, it has become a real confabulation. The story has taken on mythical proportions and so created an amalgam of scenarios that somewhere among it, if you look hard enough, is the truth. There are many incidents recalled, though frustratingly without precise dates. Consequently, we have to investigate and piece the events together as best we can with exact times and dates. It seems that as more "facts" emerge, more versions of the events are retold, confusing the story even further.

George claimed to be the main instigator in getting Ringo into The Beatles. "To me it was apparent. Pete kept being sick and not showing up for gigs," he said, slightly exaggerating, as Pete only missed four gigs with The Beatles, "so we would get Ringo to sit in with the band instead, and every time Ringo sat in, it seemed like 'this is it'. Eventually, we realized, 'We should get Ringo in the band full time.' I was quite responsible for stirring things up. I conspired to get Ringo in for good. I talked to Paul and John until they came round to the idea." *(Anthology)* It certainly appears that George was convinced that Ringo was the right drummer, even if he had to persuade John and Paul.

George was obviously keen, even if his bandmates and his manager weren't. Although no evidence exists to show that Ringo was offered the drumming job in The Beatles before August 1962, it is clear that on the few occasions when Pete Best couldn't make it, Ringo was their go-to drummer, and so they got to know each other a little better, musically. Apart from making that record together in Hamburg back in October 1960, the first recorded time Ringo had sat in with The Beatles at their Christmas Party on 27th December 1961, when Best had asked him to play in his place. Ringo was also there on 5th February at the Cavern, plus

26th March at The Cavern at lunchtime, and the Kingsway Club in Southport in the evening, so they knew what he was like to play with, and obviously enjoyed playing with him in the group. This must have been a significant factor. The 26th March bookings did nothing to foster any relationship between Ringo and Brian Esptein, because when Brian was dispatched to collect Ringo, there was a problem. As the fans gathered at The Cavern, Brian was knocking on the door at 10, Admiral Grove. Ringo came downstairs to speak to Brian, still stood outside the house. Ringo, for some reason, decided that he would only accompany Brian to play with The Beatles after putting on his trousers, which was a reasonable request, and had a cup of tea; the latter one must have made the waiting Epstein want to explode. Brian had no choice, so he waited, and waited. Eventually, the two were speeding down towards The Cavern, and Ringo was on stage once again with John, Paul and George. This was becoming a regular occurrence. However, Brian wasn't impressed, and might have led to Epstein's resistance in choosing Ringo to replace Pete.

However, it wasn't as if they didn't know Ringo already. "We met in Germany when Rory played there and so did The Beatles," recalled Ringo, "but we didn't play with each other. There was heavy competition because we used to play weekends, twelve hours a night between the two bands, and we'd try to get the audience in the club, so there was a lot of competition. And then, at the four or five-in-the-morning set, if The Beatles were left on, I'd usually still hang around because I was drunk, asking them to play some sort of soft sentimental songs, which they did. So basically, they were at one club and we were at another club, and we ended up at the same club. That's how we sort of said hello." *(Modern Drummer December 1981)*

While Ringo was making a name for himself with Rory Storm and the Hurricanes, he and The Beatles rarely met up. When Ringo turned 21 on 7th July 1961, he had a party at 10, Admiral Grove, where many of the local bands turned up, including Gerry and the Pacemakers, The Big Three and Cilla Black. He told Hunter Davies that The Beatles didn't come, because he didn't know them, as they were from another part of Liverpool and just another struggling group. *(The Beatles, Hunter Davies)* As Ringo said; "we never played with each other, but then out of the blue, Brian came and asked me to play." *(Modern Drummer December 1981)*

We also know that, as Ringo alluded to, The Beatles were often playing on the same bill as Rory Storm and the Hurricanes, and were hanging out at Rory Storm's house, "Hurricaneville", where Vi "Ma Storm" Caldwell's open house policy made her one of the unsung heroes of the Merseybeat scene. There are several photographs taken where John, Paul, George and Pete are hanging out with The Hurricanes, including Ringo. However, as we have seen, three other drummers; Bobby Graham, Ritchie Galvin and Johnny Hutchinson were also asked to replace Pete. All of them turned The Beatles down. The pressure was building.

It's A Date

It was now into the second week of August. With a firm date of 22nd August set for Granada TV to film The Beatles at the Cavern, plus a recording date at EMI for 4th September, the search for the fourth Beatle intensified. For the recording session, EMI had booked a well-known London photographer who predominantly worked for *Record Mirror*. Dezider "Dezo" Hoffmann entered EMI Studios and took those first, professional photographs of the new Beatles lineup, capturing George Harrison's recently-dealt black eye.

The Hungarian-born Hoffmann was there to take the publicity stills for EMI, with Brian also negotiating an option on them. He would, of course, become The Beatles' favourite photographer. It was therefore imperative for Brian to have the new drummer in place for those photos, even if there was no plan for him to play on the record.

This certainly explains why Brian approached Bobby Graham, a man with studio experience. The problem in Liverpool was that the only drummer with any experience in the recording studio was Pete Best, and they were getting rid of him. They would, therefore, have to lower their aim to good, experienced drummers. Enter Johnny Hutchinson, recognised as the best drummer in Liverpool at the time, as well as the other aforementioned drummers Brian approached – all accomplished musicians.

Examining The Evidence

Although it has been suggested by some that it was always going to be Ringo, the evidence says otherwise. Regardless of what transpired before Ringo was recruited into The Beatles, the fact remains that he was the right choice – the perfect foil for the musical triumvirate of John, Paul, and George.

How did it happen? How did Ringo become the Fourth Beatle?

There are countless stories and multiple, often conflicting, versions of events.

Beatlemania was coming soon!

What does the evidence tell us?

In November 1962, Ringo told music journalist Chris Hutchins of the *New Musical Express* how he joined The Beatles. Keep in mind that this interview, complete with relevant times, dates and locations, took place just three months after Ringo had joined the group. As we know, for scholars and historians, the closer in time the eyewitness account is to the original event, the more reliable it is, and the less chance there is for embellishment.

Even though Ringo had sat in with The Beatles on four occasions over the previous year, with possible conversations about him joining the group, there is no evidence to support the fact that Ringo was offered the job before the weekend of 10th August 1962. In the interview, Ringo made no allusions to this, even a short time after joining them. The evidence only supports Ringo's version.

Wednesday, 8th August 1962: Craft Tailoring, Liverpool

with The Beatles appearing on television soon, Brian decided his boys needed new suits. On 8th August, he took John, Paul, George, and Pete for a fitting at his favourite tailor, whose shop was located in Queens Arcade, off Castle Street in Liverpool. The clothier, Walter Smith, laughingly remembered the group with a name he thought "was pretty stupid and unlikely to get them anywhere. Being wrong about something like that certainly teaches you humility." Brian and his brother Clive were regulars there and, according to Smith, Brian would come in "on a Wednesday, on his half-day off from the shop." When The Beatles dropped in for a measuring and fitting of the blue wool and silk mix suit – a thin-lapel box jacket with drop shoulders and drainpipe trousers – Walter had two requests: the first, "to leave their stinking, sweaty boots outside and the second, to watch their language." *(Liverpool Echo 23rd July 2013)* Smith confirmed that the suits were made in two weeks, just in time for the Granada Television performance at the Cavern.

This is proof positive that, as things stood, Pete Best was still a Beatle and was still being considered for the Granada performance. However, even though his suit was fitted, the following week would be Pete's last with the group.

Friday, 10th August 1962: 10, Admiral Grove

Unaware that Ringo was still at Butlin's in Skegness with Rory Storm and The Hurricanes, George was asked to contact the drummer to invite him to join The Beatles.

In an interview with *Mersey Beat*, Ringo's mother Elsie recalled this as the first time she had met George Harrison. She explained why he had called. "Ringo was at Butlin's when George came up to the house – I hadn't met him before – and asked if Ritchie was home," she said. "I told him he wasn't and he said, 'Tell him we're trying to get him to join us.'" *(Mersey Beat)* George corroborated this. "I went round to Ringo's house when he was playing at Butlin's, sat and had some tea with his mother and said, 'Next time, tell your Ringo to call me up because I want him to be in our group.'" *(TuneIn)*

George and Ringo had become friendlier in 1962, so it is no surprise that he made the first contact. Elsie's comments also confirm that she hadn't met George

before, so there is no evidence of a close friendship between George and Ringo at that point. Ringo seems to verify this: "I found it harder to get close to George Harrison. As the youngest Beatle, he tended to back off rather than try to compete for the limelight with the extrovert John and Paul. George was the original Little Boy Lost." *(Elvis Meets The Beatles)* Maybe they were simply friendly, and not close friends yet.

Saturday, 11th August 1962:
The Odd Spot Club and The Blue Angel

Ringo had returned to Liverpool from Butlin's and later recalled how he was asked to join The Beatles on this day. "One Saturday morning," Ringo said, "Elsie said that George Harrison had called and would I go down to see them at the Hot Spot (sic)?" This was actually The Odd Spot in Bold Street, Liverpool. "It was my night off and I couldn't think of a better way to spend it. During the break, John, Paul, and George invited me to join them at the Blue Angel later on. Pete Best wasn't coming, they said. At the Blue Angel, I was introduced to Brian Epstein. We shook hands and he seemed a bit surprised by my appearance. I had a beard and a gray streak in my hair then." *(Elvis Meets The Beatles)* Ringo, as he always did, discussed the offer with his best friend, Roy Trafford. "When Ringo was asked to join The Beatles, it was a surprise to him and he didn't know which way to go," Roy related, "so he asked me, 'What do you think?' I told him 'what have you got to lose? Have a go. I don't know whether I made a difference to his decision, but it definitely worked out for the best." *(David Bedford Interview 2015)*

The key phrase is that 'it was a surprise' to Ringo, clearly showing that he had no expectation of joining The Beatles.

Tuesday, 14th August 1962:
The Drive To Butlin's?

Did Paul and John drive to Butlin's to see Ringo? It is possible, but it was a long way – around 180 miles each way, and before there were motorways – with very little time to spare. We simply can't be sure if they made the trip. It certainly couldn't have happened around this weekend as they were fully booked.

There are eyewitnesses though as Johnny Guitar from the Hurricanes remembers seeing them there. "John and Paul knocked on the door to our caravan about ten o'clock one morning, and I was very surprised because John hated Butlin's. Paul said, 'We've come to ask Ringo to join us.' We went into the camp and Rory said, 'What are we going to do because this is mid-season and we can't work without a drummer?' Paul said, 'Mr. Epstein would like Pete Best to play with you.' We couldn't stand in Ringo's way 'cause we knew The Beatles were going to be big. We went back to Liverpool and saw Pete, but he was so upset that he didn't want to play with anybody." Spencer Leigh verified with Johnny Guitar that John and Paul did indeed visit Butlin's, Skegness. "Yes, Rory got a big shock when Ringo said he was going to leave, and so did I," Johnny said. "It is possible that Ringo had been tipped the wink on his last visit to Liverpool, but we had no inkling of what was going on." *(Drummed Out)* This would fit with the visit to Liverpool the previous weekend, as Ringo described. However, Ringo denied seeing them at Butlin's. "I don't remember John coming over, which was in somebody's book." *(Anthology)*

John hasn't mentioned it, and Paul doesn't have any clear recollection of it either. Neil Aspinall told author Mark Lewisohn that Paul once borrowed The Beatles' van to see Ringo at Butlin's, Skegness, though this was yet another report that couldn't be verified. *(TuneIn)*

If it did happen, then this may well have been a follow-up to the conversation that John, Paul, and George had with Ringo on Saturday 11th August when they took him to meet Brian. If this was the case, then the only possible day for this drive was 14th August when they were not playing during the day.

With Brian planning to phone Ringo why would they drive all the way to Butlin's? The likely reason was their pressing itinerary. Several drummers had already turned Brian down and two very important dates were quickly approaching – the Granada TV filming set for 22nd August and the recording date scheduled for 4th September. It was imperative to get Ringo on board before Brian's phone call and before Ringo agreed to join Kingsize Taylor. John, as leader of the group, perhaps felt that a personal visit, no matter the distance, was critical. It would certainly explain the need for the trip, but this one may have to remain apocryphal.

If this visit – assuming it was made at all – took place much earlier than this date, the word would surely have got out about Pete's dismissal from The Beatles and Ringo's departure from the Hurricanes. We also know that Vi Caldwell, Rory Storm's mother, telephoned Brian Epstein late on the evening of 15th August to ask Brian to persuade Pete to join the Hurricanes when he left The Beatles. *(TuneIn)*

This suggests that Vi and Rory had only just found out. Vi's daughter, Iris Caldwell, remembered clearly what happened, and why Vi and Rory were concerned, possibly sparking the trip. "John and Paul might have come down to Butlins, but the first contact was Brian Epstein telephoning Rory, and saying that The Beatles wanted Ringo to join them. Of course, Rory was concerned about the summer season where they were, and asked Brian if it would be alright if Ringo stayed for the last three weeks of the season. Brian said it would be alright."

This is possibly where the visit by John and Paul comes into the story, as quite suddenly, Ringo decided he wasn't going to stay for the three weeks, and was leaving almost immediately.

"It was Ringo's decision to say that he wanted to leave straight away, which left Rory in a difficult position, so he had to get a replacement drummer quickly. Rory understood, but he was disappointed that Ringo left straight away, after all he had done for him." *(David Bedford Interview 2012)*

This certainly demonstrates the problems facing Brian and The Beatles, though it is interesting to recognise that Brian was prepared to let Ringo stay for a further three weeks, missing the Granada TV date. According to Vi Caldwell, Brian's stipulation was that Ringo be free by the date of their first recording date of 4th September 1962. *(TuneIn)*

Does this suggest that John, Paul and George were accepting that Ringo would not be playing on the first record, as George Martin had said?

Ringo says he was approached by John, Paul, and George on 11th August 1962 and formally introduced to Brian for the first time. They had, of course, met briefly in March when Brian picked Ringo up from his house to drive to the Cavern. At the time, Brian was suitably unimpressed with Ringo, which explains why he looked elsewhere for Pete's replacement. However, he was convinced by John, Paul, and George to offer him the job. "They liked Ringo," Brian would write in his autobiography, "and I trusted the boys' judgment. If they were happy, so was I." *(A Cellarful of Noise)*

Tuesday, 14th August 1962: The Phone Call

Ringo confirmed that he received a phone call. "I thought no more about the meeting (on the previous Saturday) until the following Tuesday when, early in the afternoon, I received a message asking me to phone Mr. Epstein at midnight." *(Elvis Meets The Beatles)*

Ringo has confirmed this in several interviews over the years. By this time, Ringo was back at Butlin's with Rory Storm and the Hurricanes, and he phoned Brian as he was asked. "He (Brian) said, 'Would you like to join The Beatles?' I said I would and he asked me if I could make it the next day as Pete Best had left, so I said no, but I would join them on the following Saturday afternoon. I turned up that afternoon in a black corduroy jacket and trousers and a black polo-neck sweater. John said I looked like Billy the Kid." *(Elvis Meets The Beatles)*

If one accepts Ringo's version, then he did receive a phone call at Butlin's to confirm the offer to join the group – and before Pete was called into Brian's office to be dismissed. However, Ringo has also said that he was offered the job on the basis that Pete had left, but at this point, Pete hadn't been dismissed. Brian needed to know with some degree of certainty that they had a replacement before they got rid of Pete. They had too many bookings in the coming days, weeks and months to be without a drummer.

Based on the evidence, Brian offered Ringo the job probably late on 14th August or just after midnight on 15th August. Pete was then given the bad news on 16th August. It is also evident that when the offer came, it was out of the blue, which confirms why Ringo had accepted the job with Kingsize Taylor. Ringo said in a recent interview: "I was as surprised as anyone when the phone call came – 'do you want to join?' – and I said sure because I loved the band. It was not a difficult decision because I just loved to play with those three, not knowing where it was going to go, of course." *(Todayzaman April 2015)* This doesn't sound like he was waiting for weeks, or even months, for an offer to join The Beatles.

Wednesday, 15th August 1962: See You In The Morning

Pete assumed it was just another day and another two performances at the Cavern. Nothing out of the ordinary about that. They played their usual high energy set and, at the end of the night, as often happened, Brian asked Pete to see him in the morning. Before that meeting with Pete, Brian decided to approach Bob Wooler, and tell him of the plans to replace Pete. The meeting didn't go well. Wooler knew every band and every musician, and was crucial to the Merseybeat scene. Wooler recalled the meeting in a *Record Collector* interview in July 1998.

"I learnt that Pete Best was going to be sacked the night before it happened," he said. "I could imagine it with someone who was constantly late or giving problems, but Pete Best was not awkward and he did not step out of line. I was most indignant, and I said, 'Why are you doing this?', but I didn't get an answer." He also said, in an interview with Gillian Gaar; "I went along to this pub - the Old Dive - and knocked three times and was admitted into one of the back rooms. There was Brian and a couple of Beatles and they announced Pete Best was going. And I blew my top. I said, 'Why?'....'Because' they said, 'he wasn't such a brilliant drummer.' And I said, 'If he wasn't a brilliant drummer, it must've been apparent from the word go.' he went to Hamburg a couple of times with The Beatles and they did all these shows in Liverpool and now you want to give him the boot." *(Goldmine 8th November 1996)*

In *Anthology*, it is suggested that Best was not reliable, but Wooler refuted that. "It is absolute rubbish to say that. The most unreliable Beatle was Paul McCartney, who had the worst punctuality record, although he was not consistently late for engagements. I saw him on TV saying that Stevie Wonder was a bit unreliable, he turned up late, and I thought, 'Look who's talking.' I would say to Paul at Aintree Institute, 'You've missed the middle spot and you'll have to go on last', which is the going home time. He'd say, 'Sorry, I was busy writing a song.' That didn't impress me at all at the time as I had a show to put on. John, surprisingly, was quite dutiful. Maybe Aunt Mimi was the one behind him, telling him to get out of the house?"

Wooler was obviously angry about what was happening to Best. "I was annoyed about what happened to Pete Best, because I couldn't see any reason why he should have to leave the group. People said he wasn't a very good drummer - well, it makes you wonder who is a good drummer, because Ringo wasn't on the first record. But I was an outsider looking in. I was going to write an article called 'Odd Man - Out', but it never materialised, and I regret that very much."

Wooler had singled out Best in an article for *Mersey Beat* the previous year where he was sure that The Beatles were destined for great things. "I closed the article by saying The Beatles were so fantastic that I didn't think anything like them would happen again. The only Beatle that I mentioned by name was Pete Best. The poster for Jane Russell in The Outlaw described her as 'mean, moody and magnificent'. I applied that to Pete Best, and it stuck. Sam Leach called him the 'Atom Beat Drummer', which seemed appropriate, although I've no idea what it meant." Why did he specifically mention Pete Best? "Well, he smouldered, but so did the front line in a way. Paul, John and George were the communicators, but the girls would be looking beyond the front line to this moody guy on the drums, so there was a charisma about him that I always found fascinating."
(Record Collector July 1998)

Wooler and Brian then went on to discuss several drummers as possibilities.

August 1962: Almost the Fourth Beatle - Trevor Morais

Trevor Morais, who had played with Faron's Flamingos, was one of the top drummers on Merseyside. Wooler confirmed that Morais was considered, "but he was a centre of attraction and they (The Beatles) didn't want all the showmanship." Morais went on to become a successful professional drummer with The Peddlers and backing percussionist for such artists as Elkie Brooks and Bjork.

August 1962: Almost the Fourth Beatle - Bill Buck

Wooler also recalled that Bill Buck from Dale Roberts and the Jaywalkers was also considered for the drumming spot. Buck was another talented Liverpool drummer who joined Dale Roberts and the Jaywalkers in 1958 when they were a skiffle group, and first performed at the famous Cavern Club in 1959. He left the Jaywalkers to join the Remo Four, later leaving them when they were signed by Brian Epstein to turn professional. He wanted no part of that. Although on the short list, he was never approached by Brian, and first learned that he had been a candidate for Pete's replacement by Bob Wooler at the 40th anniversary of the Cavern Club in 1997.

Although Wooler went on to dismiss the idea of Johnny Hutchinson being the replacement because "The Beatles didn't want a drummer who would be a force to be reckoned with," Hutchinson was also about to be approached. *(Record Collector 227 July 1998)* But, firstly, Brian had to have that meeting with Pete Best.

Thursday, 16th August 1962: The Meeting

Pete was called into Brian's office and told that he was being replaced by Ringo Starr. It was a gamble, and one they didn't know would come off, but they all felt that Ringo would be ideal for the group. Brian wrote to his solicitor on 16th August to draw up the new contract, substituting Richard Starkey for Peter Best. But until the new management contract was signed with Brian on 1st October, Ringo would be on the wage roll as a temporary employee. He would be, in effect, on probation.

The evidence?

Peter Brown confirmed this in The Love You Make, a book written with the full cooperation of Ringo Starr and other key Beatle people. "Brian's most pressing problem, however, wasn't Pete Best, but that the group was in desperate need of a replacement drummer. Naturally, they would have preferred to hire the best drummer possible, but any drummer would do as long as he was good enough to record." At first glance, this could be seen as a derogatory statement by Brown, but he does qualify it, explaining why Ringo was a good fit for The Beatles. "The Beatles knew Ringo well, not only from the Liverpool circuit but from Hamburg as well. He was fun-loving and uncomplicated and got along well with everyone in the group - much better than Pete Best supposedly had. He (Ringo) would be on salary first, £25 a week, during a probationary period. Then if things worked out, he would be made a fully-fledged member."

Brown confirmed the accuracy of this statement in a 2015 interview with David Bedford that Ringo entered into the agreement with The Beatles on the full understanding that he was an employee on a weekly salary, on a trial basis, in the hope that he would be acceptable to George Martin, Brian, and the other Beatles. *(David Bedford Interview 2015)*

It was prudent, given the turmoil of the previous few weeks. Ringo has concurred with this account, claiming that he joined The Beatles at £25 a week. Even if this amount is not accurate, and he received a quarter share of the earnings, it is still the case that Ringo did not become a full member of the group until the new contract was signed on 1st October 1962, according to Brian's lawyer. Is there further evidence to back this up? We know Ringo didn't sign the contract with Brian until 1st October 1962, so it would seem that the probationary period ran from 16th August until 30th September 1962.

Additionally, Ringo told Hunter Davies that it was the money that convinced him to join the group. "I got another offer at the same time, from Kingsize Taylor and the Dominoes. He offered £20 a week. The Beatles offered £25, so I took them." Strange that he doesn't mention that The Beatles had a recording contract, but then it could be that they weren't expecting Ringo to drum on the record in light of George Martin's comments. Ringo's wage of £25 per week was half the amount the other Beatles were paid, as confirmed in Pete Best's legal deposition in 1965. According to Pete, "He (Brian) said that as long as I was under contract to him, he'd pay me the present wage that I was earning, which was about £50-£60 a week." In the *Anthology* book, Ringo also said, "I wasn't considered a real member at the beginning." *(Anthology)*

The driving force for him being on probation is that whichever drummer joined them, they would have to be acceptable to George Martin, or so they assumed.

16th August 1962: Almost the Fourth Beatle - Johnny Hutchinson

The last drummer to be offered the role of replacing Pete Best in The Beatles was an obvious choice, though the timing is more than interesting, as it happened after Ringo had been offered the job, and, maybe significantly, after Bob Wooler's meeting with Brian the previous evening.

On the afternoon of 16th August 1962, Brian had met with Pete Best and given him the news that he was being replaced in The Beatles. Pete initially agreed to fulfil The Beatles gigs until Ringo was due to arrive on Saturday. An obvious choice for drummer was Johnny "Hutch" Hutchinson. Hutch had sat in, albeit grudgingly, with The Silver Beatles at the Larry Parnes audition in May 1960. As the driving force behind The Big Three, Hutch was considered to be the very best drummer on the Liverpool music scene by most local musicians, including John Lennon. Considering that The Big Three had just signed a management contract with Brian on 1st July 1962, it made sense to approach him to help The Beatles out at short notice.

The Big Three had been playing in Hamburg for most of July before returning to Liverpool in time to appear at the Tower Ballroom on 27th July. After his arrival home, Johnny Hutch was asked to join The Beatles, and not just for the three upcoming appearances when Pete Best didn't show up. "I was playing with The Beatles in Chester.

With the Big Three playing on the same bill, Brian asked him to sit in with The Beatles. "I had to set up my drums and get dressed for our set with The Big Three, and then go and get changed and go back on stage with The Beatles." Brian was there and kept looking at me strange. I got off stage after the gig and had to zoom off. Brian said, 'I was looking at you to see how you'd fit with The Beatles'. I joked, 'I don't really.'" Little did he know what Brian was about to say to him.

"I don't remember dates, but I remember exactly where we were," Hutch recalled. "I was in the Grosvenor Hotel in Chester," after playing at the Riverpark Ballroom in Chester with The Beatles. "We sat down, and Brian Epstein and Bob Wooler were just looking at me. So I said, 'What the f##k do you two want?' And they looked at each other, and Brian said to Bob, 'What do you think?' Bob said, 'Well, Brian, I think John would suit The Beatles down to the ground.' Then Brian said, 'I do, too. John, I want you to be The Beatles' drummer.' I told him that 'I wouldn't join The Beatles for a big clock. The Beatles couldn't make as good a sound as the Big Three. My group is ten times better than The Beatles!' And Brian said, 'I know, but the Big Three are limited. The Beatles? The world is their oyster.' By that, I think he meant that I was the only one in the group who was grafting, really working hard. I was the drummer, doing the singing too, and with only three of us, there was only so much we could do. That's what I reckon he meant. Brian also said that he had been 'everywhere to get a drummer and that he couldn't get one.' And I said there must be another drummer out there, but Eppy said, 'there isn't anyone to suit The Beatles.' You see, it is often said that I hated The Beatles, but I didn't. I liked The Beatles, but hated the music. It wasn't for me, but it suited lots of people. That's why I wanted to stay with my band."

Johnny always said that he "wouldn't do the dirty on Pete, because he was a good friend of mine." One of the other reasons for turning The Beatles down was due to John Lennon. "Me and John were different people. I used to pick him up when he was drunk face down in his meal. I didn't drink. John made up with me — he always used to say, 'Johnny Hutch can sing better than you' to Paul. He wanted me to join." It has often been quoted that Hutch recommended Ringo to Brian, and he confirmed this. "Yes I did. I told him to go and get Ringo. He's a bum, he'll join anyone for a few bob." Johnny Hutch hasn't for one minute ever regretted his decision to turn down The Beatles. *(David Bedford Interviews 2015 and 2017)* He wasn't aware that Ringo had already been offered the job, or that they had got rid of Pete.

The Big Three had signed a management contract with Brian Epstein at the beginning of July, when Brian called Hutch to his flat at 36, Falkner Street. Epstein also secured an audition for the group with Decca. When, against the band members' wishes, Decca released their test recording of "Some Other Guy" as their first single, The Big Three never achieved the success their obvious talent deserved. Their partnership with Epstein ended in July 1963.

Still under contract with Decca, Johnny Hutch and Johnny "Gus" Gustafson started doing session work, a move which also proved unsuccessful. "I ended up as a session man to use up the contract," Hutch said. "They wanted me to go up and down to London and play with Johnny Gus, then get back here to Liverpool, and the phone would ring again and they'd want me to go back down to London again. And then there could be nothing for years. It was just sitting there in a studio and playing with musicians you don't know, and then you can't get it and end up there for fourteen hours trying to get a song working. So I gave that up and put my drums away." What did Hutch think of Ringo? "Critics would say he couldn't play, and was always in the background. The other Beatles just gave him the silly songs on albums." And The Beatles? "It could have been any group – it was the luck of the draw. It was all down to Eppy." *(David Bedford Interview 2015)*

What did other musicians think of Johnny Hutchinson? Spencer Leigh asked several leading names from the Merseybeat era. Fred Marsden, drummer with Gerry and the Pacemakers said: "The only person in Liverpool who did drum solos in Liverpool was Johnny Hutch from the Big Three. He was a very good drummer and even in 1962 he was into a heavy sort of rock 'n' roll music. Technically, he was the best in Liverpool – well, he was the only one who did solos so he must have been the best." *(Drummed Out)* Cilla Black sang regularly with The Big Three at the time Pete Best left The Beatles in August 1962. According to her, Hutchinson was first choice as his replacement.

But The Beatles had second thoughts because of Hutch's reputation for belligerency and felt they needed a drummer with a more subordinate personality. They chose Ringo Starr. *(Mersey Beat)*

Hutch pointed out a comment that Graham Nash from The Hollies – and later of Crosby, Stills, Nash and Young – made about him in his book. "He said that I was 'a great drummer, but had a short fuse'," Hutch said, laughing at the remark.
(David Bedford Interview 2017)

Most importantly, what did The Beatles think of Hutch? John Lennon said he was the best drummer in Liverpool, with Ringo second. *(TuneIn)*

Paul said he liked Hutch because he spoke in a mad hip lingo, saying things like "You drive me berdzerk, man." *(TuneIn)*

Johnny Hutch as the Fourth Beatle? Technically, he was an outstanding drummer – acknowledged as the best in Liverpool – admired and respected by his fellow musicians. He also became a successful session drummer at Decca and could read music, so would have been a perfect fit. He would have been, on paper, a great addition to the group. Would it have worked? Probably not. They were chalk and cheese, complete musical opposites, so it wasn't to be.

What are the implications of this revelation?

We know that Ringo was asked to join The Beatles the previous Saturday, 11th August, which was confirmed by a telephone call between Brian and Ringo on Tuesday 14th August. However, was the offer to Ringo only temporary?

Epstein's trusted aide at NEMS, Peter Brown, was clear that Ringo was placed on probation initially *(David Bedford Interview 2015)*, but would they have dismissed Ringo if Johnny Hutch had said yes? We cannot possibly speculate about that. Could Johnny have been confused? Not likely. His memory is very clear about the times and the places he played, and has never sought to make more of his part in the story, so he has always been a reliable witness. He is always clear: "What I tell you is the truth, and I don't make it up like others."
(David Bedford Interview 2017)

Is the date correct? Could he have been confused about when he had that conversation with Brian? No.

Although it is suggested in *Tune In* that the discussion with Brian and the offer to join The Beatles took place in July 1962, there is no corroboration for this, and Johnny denied that it took place then. The timing is all wrong. Bob Wooler wasn't made aware of the decision to replace Pete Best until the evening before that meeting with Brian on 16th August.

Crucially, Hutch is very precise in that Brian made the approach after Johnny had played drums with The Beatles, as well as with The Big Three, on the same evening. Apart from standing in for Tommy Moore back in 1960, Johnny never played with The Beatles again until 16th August, when Brian asked him to sit in for Pete. He also remembers the conversation being in Chester, which is where he and The Big Three played with The Beatles that night. Brian was accompanied by Bob Wooler, who we know was with The Beatles that evening in Chester, and had been told about getting rid of Pete the previous evening. Everything fits with his recollection of events, even if it adds an element of confusion. When asked in interview, Johnny has always given the same answers to every interviewer, including an interview with The Sun newspaper in 2015. *(The Sun, 21st August 2015)*

Can it be corroborated?

Sam Leach, friend of The Beatles and renowned promoter, remembered when Johnny told him what had happened, and confirmed the timing and place when the offer was made. Sam also said that Johnny, a very good friend of his, only ever told the truth, so he could be relied upon. *(David Bedford Interview 2016)*

What does it mean?

What the intentions were will probably never be known, but it is very intriguing indeed. Using abductive reasoning, the conclusion is that Hutch's recollection is accurate. Conan Doyle's Sherlock Holmes had a favourite phrase that he would often quote, which seems appropriate here. "When you have eliminated the impossible, whatever remains, however improbable, must be the truth."

One thing that is clear about the four drummers who were approached is that Bobby Graham, Ritchie Galvin and Johnny Hutchinson were all offered the permanent drummers job by Brian Epstein. It may have gone almost unnoticed, but the decision to approach Hutch included the opinion of Bob Wooler, one of the most respected men on the Merseybeat scene. The Beatles trusted him, and Brian trusted him. As we have seen, Brian and Bob discussed many drummers, including those asked to join The Beatles. Would this have been without the agreement of John, Paul and George? Highly unlikely, especially as Brian was neither a musician, nor had any in-depth knowledge of the Liverpool music scene. The remaining Beatles must have been in agreement with the choice of drummers being asked. Brian could not have chosen a new drummer on his own, so he needed the help of the other Beatles.

We know that it was John, Paul and George who took Ringo to meet with Brian, and made sure that Ringo was offered the job with them present. Does this show more of a reluctance on Brian's part to have Ringo in the group, after Ringo delayed Brian that time he picked him up from Admiral Grove to play with The Beatles? And does it show that Ringo really was the first choice of John, Paul and George? Possibly.

What we do know is that the first, second and fourth drummers turned Brian down, but the third drummer who was asked became the Fourth Beatle: Ringo Starr, and he would be making his debut two days later. It was a risk. There was little time to be ready to record, though George Martin had already told them he would be using a session drummer. Would he be acceptable to George Martin? Would his added experience help The Beatles? At such a crucial time in their career, recruiting Ringo was a gamble, though, thankfully, it paid off.

Saturday, 18th August 1962

The Fab Four were born when Ringo made his debut with The Beatles at Hulme Hall in Port Sunlight on the Wirral, and was obviously nervous. Ian Hackett, who had suggested that his father book The Beatles, remembered the night clearly: "There was a mass female chanting of 'We want Pete!' when they introduced their new drummer. There were more young people than locals. The problem was that the local people were angry as the young interlopers had only one thing on their minds: to show support for the sacked Pete Best. The Beatles never stood a chance. I was glad for this one that my dad took the flak, and not me!" Ian was impressed with the group. "I loved their treatments of 'Twist and Shout' and 'Besame Mucho' and John's harmonica in general, but especially on Bruce Chanel's 'Hey Baby'. At that stage, they weren't playing that many original songs." Ringo, however, was not enjoying his debut. "I ran into a miserable-looking Ringo in the gent's toilet during the break," Ian recalled, "and tried to cheer him up with a smile and an optimistic comment: 'Don't worry about tonight. Things can only get better.' And it was not long before they did."

(David Bedford Interview Fab104)

Sunday, 19th August 1962

Ringo's Cavern debut was not as bad as Hulme Hall but, unfortunately for him, there were still detractors in the audience shouting for Pete. The talk of the night would have been about Pete's dismissal, and the rumours circulating about why he was sacked. I doubt anybody bought the official line that had been printed in *Mersey Beat* – that the split had been "amicable". Brian had a bodyguard, and George ended up with a black eye. One common question, surprisingly, was 'who is Ringo?' Rory Storm and the Hurricanes had hardly been in Liverpool during the last twelve months, so it wasn't just about Pete having been replaced, but who The Beatles had hired to replace him. Ringo, wisely, kept his head down and just played the drums. After all, it wasn't his fault.

Ray Ennis from The Swinging Blue Jeans remembers that night at the Cavern well. He recalls seeing "George with a black eye and I asked him what happened and he said it was because of Pete." Ennis hadn't heard the news, so George told him that Pete had been kicked out of the group and replaced by Ringo. Ennis and his friends went down to the White Star pub for a pint and Ringo "came with us and he looked petrified, and he said to me, 'I think I've done the wrong thing. I'm not going to enjoy this at all.'" But Ringo went back to the Cavern because the other three were the ones being threatened. Ennis remembers the protests were not just the well-known chants of 'We want Pete' and 'Pete forever, Ringo never'. Some of the fans "waited for the bands to come on stage and then when they came on, a load of them all stood up and walked out." *(Pete Best of The Beatles)*

Wednesday, 22nd August 1962

The Beatles' first appearance on television – just four days after Ringo's debut – was quickly upon them, and it hastened Pete's exit that week. Paul remembered the first time they played together at the Cavern. "The first few minutes that Ringo is playing, I look to the left at George and the right to John, and we didn't say a word, but I remember thinking, 'Shit, this is amazing.' You could turn your back on Ringo and never have to worry. He both gave you security and you knew he was going to nail it." *(Rolling Stone April 9, 2015)*

The filming on 22nd August 1962 for Granada TV's *People And Places* programme had, in an awkward twist of fate, could have been initiated by Mona Best in a letter she sent to Granada in the summer of 1961. She received a reply dated 21st September 1961 confirming they might be interested in filming The Beatles at a later date. However, it wasn't until Leslie Woodhead from Granada visited The Cavern in July 1962 to watch The Beatles perform, that the possibility became a reality, and he made the arrangements for the filming, obviously happy with the lineup as it was, with Mona's boy Pete on drums.

Ringo was jeered by Pete's fans and he realized it would not be easy. "The birds loved Pete," he said. "Me, I was just a skinny, bearded scruff. Brian didn't really want me either. He thought I didn't have the personality. And why get a bad-looking cat when you can get a good-looking one?" *(The Beatles. Hunter Davies)*

Ringo has had the "lucky" tag thrown at him ever since he replaced Pete in The Beatles. How did he respond? "I'm sorry about Pete," he said, "but that's the way it goes. I was offered the job and I took it. But I was in right from the start of our discs so you can't really say I hopped on a bandwagon. It's just the way things go. I might have been 'Richard Starkey with his Four' and Pete might have been one of The Beatles now. That's life." *(FLIP Magazine 1964)*

The "bad-looking cat" had got the cream, perhaps fortunate that he had been in the right place at the right time. But as he said, that's life. How many times in the story of The Beatles that some things were just meant to be?

Ringo Starr was now a Beatle: the Fourth Beatle.

SENSATIONAL NEWS!!
THE BEATLES
(PARLOPHONE RECORDING GROUP)
will be playing a season of Thursday night engagements, starting
THURSDAY, 28th JUNE, 1962
at Merseyside's luxury ballroom
THE MAJESTIC, Conway Street, BIRKENHEAD
(only 10 minutes by train or boat from Liverpool)
TOP RANK DANCING   Manager: Bill Marsden

THE BEATLES ARE DEAD. LONG LIVE THE FAB FOUR.

(Rocked in: Popped Out)

Much has been made of the drumming skills of Pete Best and Ringo Starr, and opinions are often at odds. Each has been praised for his talent, or criticized for his lack of it.

As we have shown, Pete Best was removed from The Beatles because of George Martin's comments at the end of their June 1962 audition. Was it a clash of personalities, haircuts and the myriad other reasons given for Pete's "dismissal" – or was there something more fundamental going on which may have gone unnoticed? David Harris, Brian Epstein's lawyer, confirmed that when Pete Best left, The Beatles effectively disbanded and then re-formed with Ringo. Was this more than just a legal sleight of hand that happened in the blink of an eye?

There are certain crisis points in Beatles history where the evolution of the group required a personnel change and a new direction.

On 6th July 1957, Paul McCartney watched John Lennon's group, The Quarrymen, perform a mixture of country, rock 'n' roll and, for the most part, skiffle. Yet rock 'n' roll would always remain John's first love. However, at the time, The Quarrymen lacked the technical expertise to make that musical leap from a simple skiffle group to Lennon's beloved rock 'n' roll dream. John knew that if they were going to become a rock 'n' roll group, they needed more skilled musicians. Thankfully, Ivan Vaughan introduced him to his mutual friend Paul McCartney. All John had to decide was whether they would continue playing just for fun, or take themselves more seriously and bring in a musician who had the talent to improve them.

By inviting Paul to join The Quarrymen, John knew that most of his friends in

the group would soon be leaving. Rock 'n' roll bands didn't need a banjo, washboard or tea-chest bass and that reality hastened the departures of Rod Davis, Pete Shotton and Len Garry.

However, what John and Paul realised soon after Paul botched his solo on "Guitar Boogie" was that they needed a lead guitarist. Thankfully, Paul knew someone who could amply assume the role: George Harrison. Within the five months after John met Paul, George had replaced Eric Griffiths, and Rod, Pete and Len had departed, though not all by choice. Only Colin Hanton, the drummer, remained. The nucleus of The Beatles was in place; John, Paul and George were now together.

Although it had been their intention to evolve into a rock 'n' roll group, only John, Paul and George remained by the end of 1958, leaving them little choice but to disband. Not by design, they had lost their drummer that summer when Colin Hanton quit. In early 1959, after playing their last gig in Woolton, they had no further bookings. George joined the Les Stewart Quartet, and John and Paul met to play and write together. In a fortuitous twist of fate, George re-formed The Quarrymen to open the Casbah Coffee Club at the end of August 1959. Although Ken Brown played with them for a short time, it was John, Paul and George who would press on together.

The Quarrymen Are Dead:
Long Live The Silver Beatles/Silver Beats/The Beatals.

John, Paul and George were desperate to have their own rock 'n' roll group, so they offered a spot in the band to either Rod Murray or Stu Sutcliffe, depending on which man could get a bass guitar. Stu joined the group when he purchased a bass with the proceeds from the sale of one of his paintings. As they ditched the Quarrymen name, John, Paul, George and Stu needed a drummer. Their new manager, Allan Williams, recruited Tommy Moore, and, at long last, they were a rock 'n' roll group. Through Tommy first, then Norman Chapman, the boys were able to convince Williams to get them bookings and later, with new drummer Pete Best on board, to send them to Hamburg.

The Silver Beatles/Silver Beats/The Beatals Are Dead: Long Live The Beatles

With Pete now in the group, The Beatles became the greatest rock 'n' roll group Liverpool or Hamburg had ever seen. As Beatles promoter Sam Leach observed; "When The Beatles came back from Hamburg, in their black leathers, they were the greatest rock 'n' roll band anyone had ever seen, and only those of us on the scene then saw The Beatles at their best: they were pure rock. They lost some of that when Brian put them in suits, but it worked, and you can't argue with it. "

If The Beatles did their best work in Liverpool and Hamburg, then John is acknowledging that the group was at its best with Pete on drums – a point easily confirmed by any fan who saw the band perform in Liverpool or Hamburg. There was no one to touch them. However, John's comments need to be taken in context. He loved those early days playing rock 'n' roll, but his words shouldn't be viewed as a criticism of Ringo or what they went on to achieve.

This transitional period also saw a crucial change on bass guitar. Although Stu Sutcliffe was a decent rock 'n' roll bassist, it took Paul McCartney in that role for the group to make that next giant step forward in its musical evolution.

1962: Rocked in: Popped Out - The Beatles Are Dead: Long Live The Fab Four

What we witnessed during the summer of 1962 was the end of The Beatles, the great rock 'n' roll group that had conquered Liverpool and Hamburg through Pete Best's driving beat, Paul's thumping bass, John's fiery rhythm and George's infectious rock 'n' roll guitar licks. What we then witnessed, with the introduction of Ringo, was the birth of the commercially-viable, professional Fab Four – the pop group that would conquer the world. In 1962, they rocked in the year, but 'popped' it out in the charts with their new brand of music. They were at last achieving Brian Epstein's vision of a polished, theatrically-astute and aesthetic pop group.

When Brian first saw them on stage at the Cavern, they were scruffy rebels in black leather, rocking the joint while eating, drinking, smoking and clowning around. By the time they were presented to the music press less than a year later, they were four polite, cheeky, suit-and-tie-clad Liverpool lads with neat hair. Brian's vision of musical theatre was coming to fruition. His "boys" were now presentable in stage costumes with a rehearsed script and a set list.

They even bowed at the end of their performances, much like a curtain call for a play. Their shows became carefully-crafted pieces of musical theatre – a huge leap into the unknown for the band, but one fully-orchestrated by Brian, who was making up the rules as he went along. The Beatles had evolved into the Fab Four. We couldn't have both; one of them had to go, and the old style Beatles took the fall.

Things didn't quite work with Pete and his drumming, even though he was perfect for The Beatles were doing at the time – playing covers of other artists' songs. There were certainly no documented issues raised prior to George

Martin's comments at EMI in June 1962. Ringo wasn't even the first choice to replace Pete. What would The Beatles have been like had they hired Bobby Graham, Ritchie Galvin, Johnny Hutchinson or any of the other drummers they had considered? Whatever magic potion he possessed, Ringo fit in perfectly with John, Paul and George, and it worked; history confirms that. As with any team, The Beatles proved that the whole was greater than the sum of its parts. All that mattered was how they worked together. The group would always be greater than the individuals, regardless of talent. None of The Beatles was considered to be the best at his chosen instrument in Liverpool, but together they were greater than any musical team had even been, and likely will ever be.

"Pete Best was good, but a bit limited," said Paul. "You can hear the difference on the *Anthology* tapes. When Ringo joins us, we get a bit more kick, a few more imaginative breaks, and the band settles.

So the new combination was perfect: Ringo with his very solid beat, laconic wit and Buster Keaton-like charm; John with his sharp wit and his rock 'n' rolliness, but also his other, quite soft side; George, with his great instrumental ability and who could sing some good rock 'n' roll. And then I could do a bit of singing and playing some rock 'n' roll and some softer numbers." *(Anthology)*.

Was Pete Best a Good Drummer?

We have analysed Pete's drumming on the Tony Sheridan recordings from June 1961, as well as the Decca audition from January 1962, and have demonstrated that he was a more-than-capable player. Extensive research conducted with various Merseybeat drummers about Pete's drumming resulted in high praise from so many of them. For instance, Chris Curtis from The Searchers was clear on Pete's ability and attributes. "He was a genius," said Curtis. "You could put that man on a drum kit and ask him to play for 19 hours, and he'd put his head down and do it. He'd drum like a dream with real style and stamina all night long and that really was The Beatles' sound – forget the guitars and forget the faces – you couldn't avoid that insistent whack, whack, whack! The rhythm guitar went along with it, and the bass chucked in the two and four beats, and George was wonderful on the guitar. His little legs would kick out to the side when he did his own tunes. He'd go all posh and say, "I'd like to do a tune now from Carl Perkins, 'Everybody's Trying To Be My Baby', and it's in A." Who wanted to know what key it was in? However, he always said that."

Billy Kinsley, who later played with Pete in the Pete Best Band is adamant thatthey didn't get rid of Pete because he was a poor drummer. "You ask a lot of drummers who were around at the time," said Billy, "and they will all tell you that Pete was a great drummer. I never had a problem at all with Pete. He was great, absolutely superb. Nothing against Ringo, but there was nothing wrong with Pete. However, John, Paul and George knew nothing about the recording business, and nor did Brian. If you saw any of those gigs at the Cavern or whenever we played with them, all the girls were screaming for Pete and trying to get him to smile. That's what The Beatles was all about; those three crazy guys and the moody guy who didn't smile or was quiet, but it worked. Getting rid of him didn't make sense to us." *(David Bedford Interview 2017)*

Like many Merseybeat musicians, Curtis was speechless when The Beatles got rid of Pete. "I was amazed," he said. "When Pete left, I even thought of turning into a guitarist and getting him to drum in our band. The Beatles didn't hate Pete

Best, but they didn't want a star on the drums. Ringo was a good drummer, but he was more ordinary. At that Decca audition, I think they also realised that Pete had so much power that no one would know how to record him. That's why so many Merseyside discs are icky, all thin and weedy – except for The Searchers' (records). Our engineer knew what he was doing, but not always. "Love Potion No.9" was our biggest seller in America, and the drums are so thin on that record. It was right for their radio stations; they like that kind of sound." *(Spencer Leigh)*.

From You To Me

So if fellow musicians didn't see a problem with Pete, perhaps what we were witnessing was not just the influence of Brian but a change of influence within The Beatles from John to Paul. Paul's repertoire and more eclectic song choices would appeal to a wider variety of audiences, and were better suited to a group who wanted to make, and sell, records. When it came to covering some of the greatest rock 'n' roll and R&B songs, The Beatles with Pete were second to none. John admitted that.

However, for a group writing its own commercial pop songs, a change of direction was needed, and that meant a drummer who was used to playing a more varied song selection. They found that drummer in Ringo Starr, who had performed with Rory Storm and The Hurricanes at the Butlin's holiday camps, entertaining audiences other than those at the Cavern and the clubs of Liverpool. Brian Epstein was desperately trying to get The Beatles away from those clubs, and John, Paul and George knew that.

So, when Ringo joined the group, they went from being The Beatles, the rock 'n' roll kings, to the Fab Four, the greatest-ever pop group. It is possible that, by changing drummers, John was trying to suggest that The Beatles were dead; long live the Fab Four. Both were great bands in their own right, and each had a great drummer in his own right. Pete Best helped The Beatles conquer Liverpool and Hamburg, and also secure Brian Epstein, the manager who would make them famous and attain the record deal they craved. For his contributions, Pete Best should be celebrated and thanked.

Billy Kinsley of The Merseybeats concurs with this theory. "That's a good comment," Kinsley noted, "because they stopped doing just the rock 'n' roll covers and started doing more of their own songs. 'Falling in Love Again'; that was one of the songs that Macca used to do, and I loved that one. Also 'A Taste of Honey'. When The Beatles first performed 'A Taste of Honey' at one of their last lunchtime sessions at the Cavern, Macca came over to me and asked me if I liked it. I said it was great. So he said 'come with me'. He took me up to The Beatles' dressing room and said, 'tell them'. So I had to look Lennon in the eye and tell him I loved the song. Think about that song; that is what Macca was trying to do with his songwriting. However, it was a huge thing for The Beatles; a big change.

"Then you had 'Over the Rainbow', another one of Macca's big ones, and 'Til There Was You' and some of those other great songs The Beatles used to do. 'A Taste of Honey' flowed with those other new songs being introduced into their set. On the Bank Holiday, 3rd August 1963 at the Cavern, it was The Beatles' last appearance, and The Merseybeats were playing with them. The power went off, and it was very hot inside. There was only one bulb in the Cavern so that went off, and it was pitch black. John picked up his acoustic guitar, which thankfully he had with him, and said they were going to sing some songs. And then Macca started playing on the piano, and it was 'When I'm Sixty Four'. Of course, when

Sgt Pepper came out in 1967, we heard the song again. They used to do some great songs that they didn't record themselves, like 'Hello Little Girl', which was a fantastic song. It was superb live. Look at 'To Know Her Is To Love Her', 'Besame Mucho', 'Sure to Fall', 'September in the Rain'. That was what Macca was trying to write. Big songs; big ballads." However, Billy could see the benefits of having Ringo in the group. "He (Ringo) was totally original. There was no other drummer like him. Was it because of John and Paul's writing encouraging Ringo to stretch himself? However, he was superb. Very different to Pete." *(David Bedford Interview 2017)*

The Beatles were heading in a different direction from what had been a great rock 'n' roll band. This is further demonstrated by the fact that from September 1962, more and more original songs appeared in The Beatles' catalogue of songs. Over the next couple of months, they worked on "P.S. I Love You", "Tip of My Tongue", "Ask Me Why", "Please Please Me" and "Love Me Do". Very soon they would be working on "One After 909" and "I Saw Her Standing There", and even listened to a song penned by the new drummer; "Don't Pass Me By", though this latter song was laughed at by his fellow Beatles. However, what we do notice is that over those first few weeks with Ringo, they became a tighter unit.

Gary Astridge also agrees with this analogy. "I'm in a band, and we've been together five years and know each other well, so we know when someone is going to change, or stop. We just get a look, and we know where the song is going. I truly believe that is how it was with Ringo. I've been in bands that have a musician who might be good at what he does, but that musician isn't good enough to take the band to the next level, or do those extra songs that a different guy could do. Even if you have a band, and they have a rift, you eventually find the right musicians, the right chemistry, the right magic – and that worked. That's what happened with Ringo joining The Beatles. He was on their wavelength musically, and it worked to perfection. I've seen Pete Best play, and he's a great guy, but he didn't have that spark like Ringo.

"I've watched Ringo close up and seen him play on one of his Beatles kits, and he just sat there like a little kid, and was clearly enjoying himself. Everything he played just sounded good. You can't teach that." *(David Bedford Interview 2017)*.

It was never a case of kicking Pete out and letting Ringo in.

There was no Pete vs. Ringo debate, and it is tempting for Beatles fans to get entrenched in that argument. The problem is, we can only make that judgement based on the available evidence of the drumming abilities of Pete and Ringo as of August 1962, when the change was made. Unfortunately, we only have recordings of Pete, and not Ringo, so for most people this is a pointless exercise, as we weren't there. For those who were there, the general opinion is the same as Paul McCartney's previously-stated comment in *Anthology*: "Pete Best was good, but a bit limited. You can hear the difference on the *Anthology* tapes. When Ringo joins us, we get a bit more kick, a few more imaginative breaks, and the band settles." *(Anthology)*

Pete was a good drummer. However, for The Beatles to take that next step from a great live act to recording stars, Ringo would have to be the Fourth Beatle. He, too, should receive the acknowledgment of Beatles fans everywhere.

Therefore, in August 1962, we should say that "The Beatles were dead; long live the Fab Four".

THE FOURTH BEATLE
(How Richy became Billy Shears)

They said he was quiet, didn't seem to fit in and looked unhappy behind his drums. He also had a different haircut than the other three Beatles. Pete Best, you say? No, Ringo Starr.

In December 1964, *The Beatles Book Monthly* first used the term "Fourth Beatle". "Ringo is usually known as the 4th Beatle because he joined the group a mere two years ago. I think he is quieter than the others because of this fact." They also observed that Ringo "tended to be the 'odd man out' as the boys returned from their highly successful tour of Scotland with Helen Shapiro. He still felt he was a new boy." He rarely talked about the early days either. "Come off it, nobody's interested in all that. It's the other three who matter, not me."

(Beatles Book Monthly December 1964)

As for not looking happy, Ringo told Tony Barrow that "my face might not look too chuffed (happy), but the rest of me is." *(John Paul George Ringo and Me)*

They also observed that he was soon known as "the 'silent' Beatle", though Ringo said he didn't mind "not being drawn into the free-for-all discussion. It gives me that air of mystery, y'know. Sort of sets people wondering what is going on behind my bland, inexpressive, face." *(Beatles Book Monthly Jan 1965)*

So being quiet, not quite fitting in, looking unhappy behind his drums and having a different haircut had no more bearing on Ringo's presence in The Beatles than it did the dismissal of his predecessor.

In The Town Where I Was Born

Richard Starkey was born on 7th July 1940 and was the old man of the Fab Four, if only by three months. Restricted by ill health in his childhood, he missed more than a year of school when his appendix burst just before his seventh birthday. His Physical Training teacher from Dingle Vale Secondary Modern, Mr. Dawson, remembered one of his rare moments of sporting prowess: "He was always wanting to do the same things as the other boys," he said, "and I remember one incident which typifies this. It was during the middle of a P.T. lesson. All the class were jumping over the vaulting-horse in the centre of the gym. When it came to Ringo's turn, he was obviously pretty doubtful whether he would get over the obstacle because he had never done it before. He ran up to it, jumped, and just managed to clear it. When he found that he had succeeded and not fallen flat, his face burst into a really broad, satisfied grin." Sad to say, this may very well be his only achievement from eleven years at school.

In fact, when he returned from 18 months in hospital, the school couldn't find his records. However, Dawson observed what happened once Ringo had become famous: "Recently the school put an old desk of Ringo's up for sale. We had thousands of girls queuing up to try and buy it. He has certainly helped to make Dingle Vale School famous." *(Beatles Book Monthly 28)*

Drums weren't the first instrument he tried. "I tried everything else," Ringo remembered fondly. "Originally, my grandfather and grandmother were very musical and played mandolin and banjo, and we had a piano, which I used to walk on as a child. Being an only child and a spoiled brat, my mother would let

The cash price offer was £57 2 shillings and 6 pence, with a hire-purchase price of £68. After the deposit of £11, Richy would have to make payments of 16 shillings monthly until it was paid off.

Ringo with Rory Storm and the Hurricanes

me do most things, so I used to walk on the piano, but never actually learned it. Then when I was 7, my grandfather brought me a mouth organ, which I never got into either, and then they died and I sort of ended up with the banjos, but never got into that. Drums were just the ones I always felt an affinity with."

(Modern Drummer December 1981)

Another 18 months were spent in hospital when Richy contracted tuberculosis at age 13. It was during this extended convalescence that he ignited his passion for drumming. To keep the children happy, the nurse came round with a cart of musical instruments. As Ringo recalled: "We used to play on the little cupboard next to the bed, and then once a week, they had a band to keep us occupied since we were in there for a year. Because a lot of us stayed in bed a long time, they tried to keep us entertained. This woman came and she had a big board with yellow and red marks on it. If she hit the yellow, you'd hit the tambourine; if she hit the red, you'd hit the drum. That was when I got a drum for the first time, and then I wouldn't be in the hospital class band unless I was given the drum after that. We used to knit and do all stuff like that, anything to keep us occupied. "

(Modern Drummer December 1981 and Photograph, by Ringo)

His love of the drum was instant and it gripped him. "I knew immediately: 'I want to play the drums. I don't want to play piano, I don't want to play guitar.'" Like the other children, he would get bored easily, as the hospital was in Heswall, on the west coast of the Wirral peninsula, more than twelve miles from the family home in the Dingle. Richy's mum Elsie had to take two buses just to see her son once a week. *(Rolling Stone April 9 2015)*

His childhood friend Marie Maguire helped him cement this love for the drums. As she recalled, "Richy contracted tuberculosis (TB) which of course was serious. At the time, there was a terrible stigma attached to having TB, and so the family said it was pleurisy. He was at the convalescent home in Heswall on the Wirral. That is when I took him Eric Delaney's record, 'Bedtime for Drums', which he loved." *(David Bedford Interview 2009)*

Ringo, then known simply as Richy Starkey, remembered how he was obsessed with drumming. "Ever since I was 12, I've drummed around on anything handy. I used to play on tin cans – even played that way at a party once. There was a music shop I used to pass on the way to school, which had a tom-tom in the window. It cost six pounds. I used to look at it every morning, but we could never afford it. At 16, I bought a $3.00 bass drum, made a pair of sticks out of firewood, and used to pound that, much to the joy of all the neighbours. I couldn't really play; I used to just hit it. Then I made a kit out of tin cans, with little bits of metal on the snare. Flat tins were the cymbals, and a big biscuit tin with some depth in it was the tom, and a shallow biscuit tin was the snare drum, and so forth.

"But at Christmas 1957, Elsie and Harry bought me a full drum set, and I knew they couldn't spare the money. It was a great old kit—a great trap and all the wood blocks and everything, so I had that. I got that kit in January, 1958." It wasn't really a kit, though. "No, it was made up of all different pieces. There were two problems, though. One, I didn't have a car to carry it and, two, I wasn't in a band. But in February, one month later, I joined a band, although I couldn't play. Nobody knew, though, because they couldn't play that well either. We were all just starting out playing. It was the skiffle days in 1958 in England." *(Modern Drummer December 1981)*

Around the end of 1957, my best friend Roy Trafford and I started going to the Cavern Club. I used to admire the groups who played there and wished I could join one." *(Elvis Meets The Beatles)*

Roy Trafford lived at 7, Paulton Street, also in the Dingle, and his family had a small shop. Though the area has often been described as a poor, run-down neighbourhood, Roy disagrees. "It was a great place to live," he says. "It was such a great community. You could play out in the streets, and then go into your mate's house and his mother would look after you and then you'd go home. The houses were immaculate. Even though we had no toilets or bathrooms in our houses, the women had pride in their homes. The curtains were perfect, they would polish the window ledges and scrub the front step. Don't let anyone say it was a bad place to live because it wasn't." *(David Bedford Interview 2015)*

It was while working at H. Hunt & Son, a school equipment firm, that Richy and Roy, along with Richy's next door neighbour Eddie Myles, formed their first group. "One day, Eddie brought a guitar to work and we started playing in the cellar at lunchtime, among the sawdust, so Richy started banging a rhythm on anything he could find, like biscuit tins, chairs or boxes. I got a tea-chest bass and that is how we started. I used to have to carry it on the bus, and the conductor let me stand there in the aisle with it." *(David Bedford Interview 2015)*

Now that they had a group, Richy made the transition from tins to a small drum kit. "Richy started off with a basic kit," Roy recalled, "just a stand-up drum (floor tom), a snare and a cymbal. As he got better and better, his kit grew. Like all of us, we learned as we went along, and he became a great drummer with Rory Storm and the Hurricanes and then, of course, The Beatles. When we started to play, although Richy had a good sense of rhythm, I showed him how to make a noise like a train with his brushes on the snare because we were doing a lot of railroad songs. Of course, at the start, you couldn't tell what a great drummer he would become because we were just having fun." *(David Bedford Interview 2015)*

With drumming becoming Richy's life focus, his stepfather, Harry Graves, promised to buy him a better kit after he came out of hospital. And true to his word, Harry did just that. "When someone in Harry's family died," Ringo remembered, "he'd gone down to Romford and there was a drum kit for sale for £12. The whole family collected together and he brought this drum set to Liverpool. I was given it for Christmas." *(Anthology)* Harry remembered the trip well. "I brought them up from London in the guard's van," he said. "I was waiting for a taxi home at Lime Street when I saw Joe Loss walking over. I thought, if he asks me if I can play them, I'll have to say no. But he walked right past me." *(The Beatles. Hunter Davies)*

The new kit was Richy's greatest ever Christmas present, and although it was was a lot of money to the family, it was an investment in a career that would make him one of the most famous faces on the planet and one of the most respected drummers in the history of popular music. As he remembered: "I got the drum kit on Boxing Day and was in a group by February, so there wasn't a chance in hell that I could play by then. But neither could anyone else, except the guitarist, who knew a couple of chords." *(Anthology)*

Elsie also told Bill Harry about those early days. "When he was very, very young he always wanted to make a noise on something – empty boxes and suchlike. The first kit of drums he had we bought from some friends of ours. He used it for a little bit then went on to better things. He used to practice in the back room – but only for half an hour a night. That was all he was allowed because of the noise!" *(Mersey Beat)*

It wasn't long before Ringo decided it was time for a full drum kit, so he asked his Grandad Starkey to lend him the money for the deposit – £11 – which he would pay back at £1 per week. "If his grandad even refused him a shilling, he'd do a war dance," said Elsie. "This time his grandad came to see me. 'Hey, do you know what that bloody noddler of yours wants?' He always called him 'noddler'. But he gave him the money." Even though Richy was only 3 years old when his father left the family home, he had a very close relationship with his paternal grandfather.

His new kit – an "Ajax Edgware Drum Kit (Black Elegance)" – was obtained from Hessy's on 23rd April 1958, on Hire-Purchase. Although Grandad Starkey paid the deposit, it was good old stepfather Harry Graves who signed the hire-purchase agreement as witness Elsie stood by. The cash price offer was £57 2 shillings and 6 pence, with a hire-purchase price of £68. After the deposit of £11, Richy would have to make payments of 16 shillings monthly until it was paid off. Somehow, that young "noddler" had involved his whole family in the drum purchase.

According to Ringo, it was "amazing" and, for the first time, he had a complete drum kit comprised of a snare, bass drum, hi-hat, one small tom-tom, a top cymbal and a bass drum pedal, which meant he "didn't have to kick it anymore". He set it up in his bedroom, but then the shout would come from downstairs: "Keep the noise down, the neighbours are complaining!" *(The Beatles. Hunter Davies)*

He very quickly stopped and never practiced at home again. This first full kit stayed with him through the Eddie Clayton Skiffle Group and into his tenure with Rory Storm and the Hurricanes.

The Eddie Clayton Skiffle Group was founded by guitarist Eddie Myles, Richy's neighbour and workmate, a talented musician who was the driving force.

"We played at the Embassy Club in New Brighton, just the three of us," Roy Trafford recalled, "and the guy was good to us. He said, 'come back when you've built yourselves up'. So we then added Micky McGrellis who played washboard. He was a great washboard player and had a fantastic sense of rhythm. But, of course, Eddie was the star. He could play anything. As well as guitar, he could play the mandolin, banjo, piano and he even played the violin in a country group. He made the pick-ups for our guitars once we had moved on from the skiffle instruments. We both bought Hofner guitars, and he filed down the bridge on the guitar to make the strings closer to the neck of the guitar, so we had to apply less pressure on the strings. He then attached the pickups that he had made. I remember him playing 'Guitar Boogie' with the guitar behind his head. He was incredible. He even made his own steel guitar." *(David Bedford Interview 2015)*

By now, Richy had the drumming bug, and just as George Harrison was obsessed with guitars, Richy Starkey was obsessed with his drums. "He was always musically inclined you know, especially with drums," Elsie later said. "I think he's been drumming since he was about 17. He started in a skiffle group with two friends. There was Eddie Myles and Roy Trafford and Richard. Those were in the tea-chest days, of course. Then Eddie got married and they broke up. Richard

then joined the Dark Town Skiffle Group. He finished with them and joined Rory Storm and was with him for three or four years until he joined The Beatles." *(Liverpool Weekly News 1964)*

Richy was never one for playing on his own. "I'll play with any other musician all night, but I can't do it on my own. I don't find any joy sitting there by myself." Neither was he a fan of drummers in general. "I was never really into drummers. I loved seeing Gene Krupa in the movies, but I did not go out and buy his records. The one drum record I bought was 'Topsy Part Two' by Cozy Cole. I always loved country and western. A lot of it was around from the guys in the navy. I'd go to parties and they'd be putting on Hank Williams, Hank Snow and all those country acts. I still love country music. Skiffle was also coming through, and I was a big fan of Johnnie Ray. Frankie Laine was probably my biggest hero around 1956 – and I also liked Bill Haley." *(Rolling Stone April 9 2015)*

He had a few drum lessons from tutor Ernie "Red" Carter. "I had about three lessons. Once I got interested in drums I said, 'Right, I'll go read music and learn how to play' but I went to this little man in a house and he played drums and he got a manuscript and wrote it all down. I never went back – I just couldn't be bothered. It was too routine for me, y'know, all those paradiddles and that – I couldn't stand it." *(The Fab One Hundred and Four)*

The Eddie Clayton Skiffle Group

The Eddie Clayton Skiffle Group quickly became one of the best skiffle groups in Liverpool. "I don't know why," explained Roy, "but we just kept winning the cups. I remember us winning the cup for the best group in the area at the Locarno Ballroom. We played many places, some competitions, and if we got paid it was only 10 bob (50 pence), not much." They also played at a show at the Empire Theatre, the largest theatre in Liverpool. "I don't know where I got the bottle from to do that, to get up on stage in front of all those people. Where did we get the guts to do it? Maybe we had a couple of pints first? We were friends playing together, working together, having fun, so we probably helped each other. We were just having a laugh. We used to play for the men at lunch hour in the factory. It was mainly, if you had an instrument, you could join a band. It didn't matter if you could play. But my problem was I was always traveling on the bus, so I couldn't carry the kit.

"Then we started auditioning and we did every audition in the world, every free show we could do. We had no sense of time, so we'd start with the count of "one, two, three, four," and then it would be like an express train because we'd get faster and faster and faster. People were just dropping like flies on the dance floor because it was like, 'Can't you slow it down, can't you slow it down?' So we did a lot of free shows. In that band, I didn't really need the full kit, but I always wanted to play it. Anyway, I got the kit, and I set it up in the back bedroom like a professional, thinking, 'I'll practice and everything.' I only did that one night and we had all the neighbours yelling 'Shurup, get out of here,' because we were in very close proximity to everyone else. So I never practiced since that day, except with a band. I made all the mistakes on stage, as it were."

(Modern Drummer December 1981)

With so many skiffle groups in Liverpool, the competition was fierce. Each one had to stand out from the rest, and that usually achieved by selecting songs no one else was performing. "We were doing old folk songs and railroad songs from America," Roy said. "We listened to blues records, and went to watch people

like the blues duo Sonny Terry and Brownie McGhee. We sang 'Frankie and Johnny' and one of our favourites was 'The Titanic (It Was Sad When The Ship Went Down)'. It was one of our 'biggies' and not many others did it." The group played at as many venues as it could, with the hope of a small fee or winning a competition; they certainly weren't in it for more than the fun. "We played at various clubs, especially Wilson Hall in Garston a number of times, as well playing the Cavern ten times. We would play in the interval between the jazz groups. We also played at the '21 Club' in Croxteth Road," which was run by Cavern owner Alan Sytner, "and the Railway Club on Ullet Road."

(David Bedford Interview 2015)

Sometime in the spring of 1957, The Eddie Clayton Skiffle Group made its official playing debut at the Labour Club, Peel Hall, on the corner of Peel Street and Park Road in the Dingle. "We had no idea you had to keep the same tempo all the way through," Ringo recollected. "We used to start off performing 'Maggie May' at the right tempo and end up like an express train, we were all so excited. People had to dance to this." *(TuneIn)* When Eddie Myles quit music to get married, the group folded. For Roy, skiffle was just fun. He played a couple of times with Ringo in Rory Storm and the Hurricanes, but a music career wasn't for him. For Ringo, however, it was a springboard to becoming one of the greatest drummers in history.

The Darktown Skiffle Group

In 1958, Richy joined The Darktown Skiffle Group, widely regarded at the time as one of Liverpool's top groups. The ensemble boasted several members in its short history, including Dave McKew, bass player Keith Draper, guitarists Alan Robinson, Kenny Irwin and David Smith, and vocalist Gladys Jill Martin. They had other drummers, such as Brian Redman and Kenny Hardin, but for a brief period they had Richy Starkey in the drum seat. Soon, as was the case with most skiffle groups, the transition to rock 'n' roll also meant a name change.

The Cadillacs

The Darktown Skiffle Group became The Cadillacs. "I joined the Cadillacs in November of 1958," Ringo recalled in a November 1962 interview. "The leader had a car and used to pick me up, so for the first time I was able to take out the full kit. I still dressed like a Ted and I was going to dances and always getting into fights. So, when I got to join Rory Storm's group, I jumped at it. After all, I was fed up getting beaten up and it was a better way of meeting girls."

(Elvis Meets The Beatles)

From Texans to a Storm and Hurricanes

Somehow, Richy always ended up in Liverpool's top group. From the Cadillacs, he was recruited by Alan Caldwell to join his group, the Raving Texans, having auditioned in March 1959. After a couple of name changes, they settled on Rory Storm and the Hurricanes. Their love for cowboy films inspired each of them to assume a western alias.

Alan Caldwell became Rory Storm; Johnny Byrne took the name Johnny Guitar after the 1954 film of that name; Charles O'Brien, who was now on lead guitar, became Ty Brian after the star of the Bronco TV series; Wally Eymond, the group's bass player, was given the name Lou Walters and, as we know, Richy Starkey became Ringo Starr.

When the Gene Vincent show came to the Liverpool Stadium in May 1960, Rory Storm and the Hurricanes were on the stage, while John, Paul, George and Stuart could only look on from the audience with envy. When the Cavern Club held its first Beat Night in May 1960, Rory Storm and the Hurricanes was the first beat band to play there. With Rory celebrated as one of the top showmen in the city, the group's reputation was second to none. The Silver Beatles at that time didn't even have a regular drummer.

"I met Ringo during the old skiffle days," Lou Walters would recall in 1963. "He was appearing at the Mardi Gras with Rory Storm and was dressed in a long black Teddy Boy suit. Later, I joined the group which was then known as the Raving Texans and we played numerous dates around the Liverpool area. Ringo was not an exceptional drummer at the time, but as the group progressed he improved to such an extent that we realized he would be a very good drummer. We had some good times when we made our first appearance at Butlin's holiday camp. Ringo was the lazy one of the group. In the mornings he used to sleep late, and if woken would be very bad tempered. The first signs of him waking took the form of one open eye which was staring round the chalet. Then it would be between one hour and 1-1/2 hours before he'd stir properly. Then he wouldn't speak for an hour or so. After that, he'd revert to his normal self. He was the life and soul of any party we went to and was well liked because of his sense of humour. At that time, he started to show some of his exceptional talent on drums and he also started singing. One of the numbers was 'Alley Oop' and the girls started to scream their applause. Ringo was a born singer!" *(Mersey Beat in 1963)*

What did Rory Storm think of Ringo? In the January 1964 edition of *Mersey Beat* under the heading of "The Ghost of Ringo Haunts this Group", Rory revealed what it was like with, and without, Ringo. "Ringo was with us for more than four years. When the group started, only ourselves and The Blue Jeans were known on the Mersey Scene – we were the first rock group to do the rounds. During the four or five years Ringo was with us he really played drums – he drove them. He sweated and swung and sung. Ringo sang about five numbers a night, he even had his own spot – it was called 'Ringo Starr time'. Now he's only a backing drummer, The Beatles' front line is so good he doesn't have to do much. This is not the Ringo Starr who played with us." The Hurricanes went through several drummers and never really recovered from losing Ringo.

(Mersey Beat January 1964)

Iris Caldwell, Rory's sister, recalled when the boys were booked to appear at Butlin's Holiday Camp at Pwllheli and they "decided that they would look more professional if they wore makeup. All except Ringo. He refused point blank to 'put that muck on my face'. In the end, however, he gave in to stop the argument and smeared his face with a thin layer." Ringo was very popular with the girls at the camp, who loved "the grey streaks in his hair, even though Ringo hated them." She was clear that Rory "thought a lot of Ringo and gave him his own spot in the act calling it 'Ringo Starr Time'" where he regularly sang "Matchbox" and "Boys".

Then came the beard, which appeared during their "second session at the camp in Pwllheli. I think it was to try and draw attention away from the streaks in his hair," said Iris.

Back in Liverpool, after gigs, Ringo would often find himself at the Caldwell's house, and got to know the family well. Vi Caldwell, Iris' mother, remembered an incident when Ringo again tried some physical exercise – his first swimming lesson. "Rory found out that Ringo could not swim a stroke so he decided to try and teach him," recalled Vi. "It was fine at first, but then they became more ambitious and decided to go underwater swimming which almost caused a tragedy. Rory told me that suddenly a pair of hands appeared from beneath the waves, desperately searching for something to grab onto. Ringo's swimming obviously wasn't good enough for underwater yet. Luckily, Rory saw what was happening and pulled him out." *(Beatles Book Monthly 28)*

By 1960, and on the back of their success at Butlin's, it was time for Ringo to upgrade his drum kit again, and so, in September, he purchased a four-piece Premier "Mahogany Duroplastic" set. This new gear consisted of a 20x14-inch bass drum, a 16x16-inch floor tom, a shallow 14x4-inch Premier Royal Ace wood-shell snare drum, and an 8x12-inch rack tom, along with a non-standard Rogers Swiv-O-matic tom-tom holder. This would be the kit that Ringo used for the Hurricanes' first trip to Hamburg in October 1960, that he used on the first recording with John, Paul and George on 15th October 1960, and was still using when he joined The Beatles in August 1962. He nearly lost his kit on that first trip to Hamburg. "He travelled alone on the train and had to change in Paris," Iris Caldwell recounted. "During the usual scramble he lost track of his drum-kit." Unable to speak French, he did what most British people do abroad and tried to talk with his hands. "The French people thought he was mad and called the Gendarmes. Fortunately, one of them did understand English, and realized what had happened. He still had to stay in Paris overnight, but his drums were found by next morning." Not quite as bad as stealing a harmonica on the way to Hamburg as John Lennon had done.

By the end of 1961, Ringo was feeling frustrated at not progressing past holiday camp bookings. In December, with the promise of a good fee, an apartment and the use of a car, he left the Hurricanes to return to Hamburg as drummer for Tony Sheridan. On the surface, it sounded like a good deal, but with Sheridan's erratic performances on stage, Ringo decided he was better off with the Hurricanes. He returned to Liverpool and reclaimed the drummer's seat behind Rory Storm.

Ringo and The Beatles crossed paths many times over the years, in both Hamburg and Liverpool, until he was finally offered the drummer's seat in the group in August 1962. His future as the world's most famous drummer could have ended suddenly after a frightening incident on the way home from a Little Richard concert at the Tower Ballroom. Driving through the tunnel with Roy Trafford in the passenger seat, Ringo's car suddenly skidded on the wet pavement and spun around. Thankfully, he regained control and they arrived at home safely.

Maybe that was the only luck Ringo needed?

4th September 1962

EMI STUDIOS, ABBEY ROAD: HOW DID THEY DO IT?

Brian Epstein reported for Mersey Beat, and his story, carried anonymously at his request, told how they had met together at Liverpool Airport at 8.15am for their flight to London. Neil drove the equipment van on that long journey to the capital, though not in the midst of a snowstorm like the beginning of the year.

This time, it was just torrential rain, but still not for the faint-hearted. Brian even had his "boys" pose for a group photograph on the tarmac, but none of them looked impressed. Ringo sported his now-famous grey streak and George tried to appear oblivious to his black eye. The flight was not very smooth due to the weather, which did little to comfort George, who had an aversion to flying. They eventually arrived in London and checked into their hotel in Chelsea before heading to EMI Studios in Abbey Road, just as they had done in June.

No Session Drummer?

There is one major conundrum about that session on 4th September 1962. After the session in June, George Martin had told Brian he was going to use a session drummer if they made a record, but no session drummer was present on 4th September. Why? There are several possibilities to consider.

First, it has been suggested in *Tune In* that Brian telephoned Judy Lockhart-Smith, George Martin's secretary, to inform him that The Beatles had changed their drummer, although there is no evidence that the phone call ever took place. One of our researchers had asked author Mark Lewisohn in person (at the Chicago Fest for Beatles Fans in summer 2014), why there were no footnotes to support the narrative that Brian had called Judy to tell them about the new drummer, so our researcher asked for the footnotes to corroborate this important story. The author replied that "there's no evidence that the phone call happened, but it's safe to presume it did because it's the only way to explain everything that happened after". When asked by the author if she took a call from Brian regarding the

change of drummer, Judy, now Lady Martin, had no recollection of any call like that. No evidence exists that this call ever took place. *(David Bedford interview 2018)*

Second, Pete Best says that, following his dismissal, his mother Mona spoke to George Martin, as Brian had refused to see her or speak to her despite several phone calls and a visit to NEMS. When she rang Martin, Mo demanded to know why he wanted The Beatles to get rid of Pete. He assured her that "I never said that. I wasn't instrumental in getting rid of Pete. What I said was, 'What I hear isn't what I hear on the record in this present moment of time'." He said that he told Brian, "Don't break up the physical content of the band, because Pete is such an integral part of that." Martin also admitted surprise that Pete had left the band and said it was as much of a shock to him as it was to everyone else. *(The Best Years of The Beatles)*

However, as with the supposed telephone call to Judy Lockhart-Smith, there is no independent corroboration for this conversation, as it wasn't ever mentioned by George Martin. If this conversation had taken place soon after Pete left the group, which would be in Mona's nature, Martin could have learned of the change of drummer before the 4th September session from that phone call, but it cannot be proved.

Yes They Did

George Martin is also confused as to what happened. He has said in one account that he was informed, though not when or by whom. This would suggest that the informant wasn't Brian, or he would have said so. As several details around these early sessions remain confused, it is hard to be certain.

What George Martin did say was that "they had told me that they had found a great drummer from another group, whose name was Ringo Starr and who would be replacing Pete Best. I had said, 'Fine. Bring him along and let him see what we're doing and next time he'll have a go." *(All You Need Is Ears)* It isn't clear if this took place prior to the 4th September session, though this would suggest that George Martin was still intent on using a session drummer, whoever The Beatles brought with him.

No They Didn't

However, in a recent television documentary, George Martin was adamant that he hadn't been told. "That first occasion was Brian's fault," he said to Paul McCartney, "because nobody told me they had changed the drummer." McCartney didn't deny it. In this case, as in many others, the lack of supporting documentation makes it impossible to know exactly what transpired. Unfortunately, Martin then went on to say; "Then you (The Beatles) walked in with this little chap, and you said 'he's our drummer', and I said, 'no he's not, there's your drummer', because I've paid good money for that fellow (Andy White) and we had the best drummer you could get." *(Arena: Produced by George Martin)*

Unfortunately, on many occasions, George Martin has confused and conflated the two sessions from September, the 4th and 11th, which is understandable, and it adds to the nebulous nature of the summer of 1962 in Beatles history. Maybe, in Martin's mind, because 4th September was a catch up session, he only recalled the recording session on 11th September, which was the most important one for him as producer.

How Did You Do With It?

If Martin had been informed before their 4th September session that the group had changed its drummer, then it's only logical that he would want to assess the new recruit. If he hadn't been informed, it wouldn't have made much difference, as Martin was going to be using a session drummer on the record anyway. But there was an even more important aim for the day, and it wasn't to make a record. After the June session, it wasn't just Pete's drumming George Martin didn't like. He wasn't impressed with the songs or the arrangements, and the overall quality from the group was below-par. George Martin had told The Beatles to work over the summer on "How Do You Do It?", the Mitch Murray song he had sent them in late July, and "Love Me Do" – which was clearly not the finished product – and suggested some improvements.

Was This A Recording Session?

The normal practice was that a session drummer would only be hired when a song was ready to record, so that he could walk in, do a quick run-through with the musicians, and then record the song. On 4th September, The Beatles were nowhere near ready to record, and therefore it made no economic sense to pay for a session drummer to stand around all day when it was unlikely they would be making a record. Session drummers usually worked on three-hour sessions and, in that time, they could learn and record up to four songs. For producer Martin, there was still a lot of work to do with the group; they weren't ready to record the songs yet: they didn't even know which songs they were going to record, and whether any record would be released.

Possibly of more importance from the group's point of view was the fact that Dezo Hoffmann had been booked to photograph The Beatles for promotional purposes on 4th September. Irrespective of Ringo turning up, George Martin would still be hiring a session drummer for the record, and it wouldn't matter how well Ringo performed. The evidence therefore suggests that this was not a recording session from which a record would result.

How Should We Do It?

The Beatles walked into the studio and were met by their trusted roadie 'Nell', their 'headmaster' George Martin and producer Ron Richards, the latter two having contributed to Pete Best's downfall. The Beatles must have been nervous as they readied themselves for the session. "And so the moment came that so many aspirants long for, the moment when all was set to make a first disc. A first disc with the world's greatest recording organization," said a proud Brian Epstein. No pressure on the boys, then.

The afternoon session, a three-hour rehearsal slot which ran from 2pm to 5pm, would be followed by another three hours of recording between 7pm and 10pm. According to Brian, it wasn't an easy afternoon for The Beatles. "The rehearsal part of the session began," he recalled. "It was a long and hard afternoon's work. Six numbers were considered and eventually two were selected for the actual recording session in the evening." They definitely would have rehearsed "How Do You Do It?" and "Love Me Do", though the identity of the other four songs was not noted. They are thought to be "Ask Me Why", "P.S. I Love You", "Please Please Me" and a new original song in their repertoire, "Tip of My Tongue". All apart from the first song were Lennon/McCartney originals. Their mission was clear: record their own songs. And this is where the conflict arose.

George Martin wanted them to release the Mitch Murray song "How Do You Do It?", which the group had been working on over the summer. But they were equally intent on recording only their own songs and had been working on "Love Me Do" as Martin had asked them to do.

Ringo was now The Beatles' drummer. But that was just the start to his career with the group. All was going smoothly until the first EMI recording session on 4th September 1962, a little over two weeks after his debut. The new Fab Four headed to the EMI Studios in Abbey Road to record their first single.

They had taken "Love Me Do", which had been recorded in June as a bluesy dirge with a strange skip-beat, and increased the tempo. What resulted was a much brighter, more marketable song. But there were other songs in contention, too, which they wanted to perform for Martin before anyone decided which would be their debut single.

The June session had to be scrubbed as far as making a record was concerned, though George Martin still included those four songs in their total of six to record per the contract. This explains why no session drummer was present that day. They only had two songs left to fulfil the terms of the contract, and he wasn't going to squander money for a session drummer when they hadn't even decided which songs they were going to release.

George Martin knew he had to start again and Ringo seemed to confirm this.

"The response to us at EMI was okay, because we'd done the auditions and George Martin was willing to take a chance.

On my first visit in September, we just ran through some tracks for George Martin. We even did 'Please Please Me'." Norman 'John Lennon called me Normal' Smith, who had been involved in the June session, returned for this session and remembers that "it was really all John and George and Paul. Ringo had just joined and was put right at the back, being used rather like a puppet." What mattered at this session was having John, Paul and George up to speed on the songs, with George Martin still planning to hire a session drummer.

It seems incredible, despite numerous interviews and books, that nobody remembers with any clarity an important piece of information like telling George Martin about the change in drummers, especially as he was the one who had suggested to Brian that a session drummer be brought in. Ringo was also either confused, or was confusing the facts, when the subject of the session drummer came up. "I remember that, because while we were recording it, I was playing the bass drum with a maraca in one hand and a tambourine in the other. I think it's because of that that George Martin used Andy White, the 'professional', when we went down a week later to record 'Love Me Do'. The guy was previously booked anyway because of Pete Best. George didn't want to take any more chances and I was caught in the middle." *(Anthology)*

Was Andy White booked to replace Pete Best? No. White confirmed that he was only called in after the 4th September session, in the week before the second recording session *(David Bedford Interview 2012)*.

If we go on the basis that 4th September was a test session, then George Martin probably had a plan for a final recording date when the session drummer would be employed. That date became 11th September. In Martin's mind, the session drummer was still going to be brought in to replace Pete – but suddenly Ringo, not Pete, was there. As it turned out, Andy White was booked to replace Ringo, though just as Pete was kept in the dark about the Decca failure, nobody thought to inform Ringo when he was being replaced.

First Rehearsal Session: 2pm - 5pm

One of the interested onlookers this day was a new trainee engineer at EMI, Geoff Emerick, who would work with The Beatles throughout their recording career. Emerick knew nothing about George Martin or Ron Richards and asked fellow engineer Richard Langham about them. "They're both quite old, but they're good blokes once you get to know them," Langham said. "George is one of the producers on staff here, though. I've never known him to do a rock 'n' roll session before. I guess he's trying to get on the bandwagon. At least he's got the sense to use Norman on the session, who's a bloody good pop musician himself." (Here There and Everywhere) Parlophone's usual rock 'n' roll producer was Ron Richards, as George Martin tended to record comedians like Bernard Cribbins, Peter Sellers and Spike Milligan. Yet Martin was a surprisingly perceptive judge of good pop songs.

When The Beatles walked in, Emerick was bemused. "My first glimpse of The Beatles was not actually all that memorable." There were several people in the studio, but "their unorthodox haircuts" made The Beatles stand out, but not

much more. *(Here There and Everywhere)* He had been told to expect four leather-clad rockers, but they turned up in their new stage outfits, complete with ties, as captured on film by Dezo Hoffmann.

There was an interesting protocol in the studio which was confusing to the new boy Emerick. The balance engineers at EMI didn't dirty their hands setting up microphones and equipment. The staff in the white coats – the maintenance engineers – were told where to place them, and they took care of it. Any minor adjustments during the session could be carried out by the production crew, but only the men in white coats were allowed to change the cabling.

It was time for The Beatles to play. "After a brief period of tuning up," recalled Emerick, "I began hearing music filter through the control room loudspeakers, which drew me back to the window. The four Beatles were rehearsing, with George Martin sitting on a high stool between the two singers, Lennon and McCartney. The song they were playing was lightweight. Nothing out of the ordinary, but there was definitely an infectiousness to the beat. From behind a set of tall acoustic screens, I could see their drummer flailing away. He was a very small man with a very large nose, and he didn't seem to know the song as well as the others, who kept pausing to give him instructions." *(Here There and Everywhere)*

Ringo was obviously having trouble playing the original Lennon/McCartney songs, and the studio staff noticed it. But then, he had only just joined the group.

As the clock headed towards 2pm, they were ready to start rehearsing. The afternoon session of six songs included "How Do You Do It?" and "Love Me Do", plus "Please, Please Me" as Ringo had mentioned, "P.S. I Love You" and probably "Ask Me Why" and "Tip Of My Tongue". They were intent on winning over George Martin, especially with their own songs.

But despite their efforts, Martin was still not impressed with "Love Me Do", even with their changes. He didn't hold back in his judgment of "Please Please Me" either. "They played me 'Please Please Me' but it was very slow and rather dreary. I told them if they doubled the speed it might be interesting." And so George Martin's influential role with The Beatles had begun. "I told them what beginning and what ending to put on it," Martin added. *(TuneIn)*

John, Paul and George likely spoke to Martin and told him all about Ringo replacing Pete, and the producer agreed to take a look, but their new drummer didn't help his own cause. When it came to playing "Please Please Me", Ringo seemed to lose it. "I was playing the bass drum and the hi-hat, and I had a tambourine in one hand and a maraca in another, and I was hitting the cymbals as well, like some weird spastic leper, trying to play all these instruments at once." *(TuneIn)*.

Ringo did nothing to persuade George Martin that he could provide the solution in the studio. Martin and Ron Richards were clear: they needed a session drummer to get these songs recorded. This also adds to the confirmation that this was not a session where they were expecting a record to result.

How Did We Do It?

After the three hours of rehearsal, George Martin took The Beatles out for a meal. He got to know them better as people. More than their songs, he liked their personalities, and regaled them with tales about recording the Goons. But there was still work to be done on the four songs set to be recorded. However, Martin considered only two songs sufficiently progressed enough for recording: "How Do You Do It?" and "Love Me Do".

Recording Session - 7pm to 10pm

They returned to the studio to record the two songs. Norman Smith, not Ron Richards, was the engineer now and, with the red light on, the boys began recording "How Do You Do It?" on the studio's two-track recorder. "The lead singer, who also played rhythm guitar," recalled Geoff Emerick, "had a unique, nasally voice, and he sang on pitch, but without much enthusiasm, and the lead guitarist seemed to be somewhat fumble-fingered. Probably the most impressive thing about the performance was the powerful and melodic bass playing." Emerick wasn't too impressed with Ringo, either.
"In contrast, the drummer, who was indeed quite a bit shorter than the others, with an almost petite build, looked a bit dejected and didn't have much to say at all." *(Here, There and Everywhere)*

Emerick was almost echoing the complaints about Pete. But Ringo had never been in a real studio before, and he must have been nervous, just as Pete and The Beatles had been at Decca in January and at Abbey Road in June.

The recording of "How Do You Do It?" was completed quite quickly, in only a couple of takes, and though it was a good performance, it lacks enthusiasm and belief. There is no soul in the singing and playing, and they are clearly not interested in the song. "Love Me Do" was a different matter, Brian observed, as the song was "no simple matter. Everyone was anxious to attain a perfect sound, which would reproduce The Beatles' unique qualities exactly." As in June, this Lennon/McCartney original was causing problems for the recording engineers. Brian recalled it took around 15 takes to record, and that "John's mouth (on harmonica) was numb with playing and the atmosphere was tense." In fact, there were more than 15 takes for just the rhythm track, with the vocals added separately. With the vocals recorded, the session that should have finished at 10pm continued to nearly midnight, when "everyone was so dazed and tired that it wasn't really known how good or bad was the result." *(Mersey Beat)* After all this time, the second song was recorded to a reasonable enough standard to enable them to cut an acetate, which they would listen to the following day. Scheduled to record four songs, they had gone well beyond their allotted time and only managed two. The decision on which songs would be released was down to George Martin. In spite of their average performance, he clearly wanted "How Do You Do It?" as the A-side, with "Love Me Do" as the B-side, subject to reviewing the acetates. Not booking the session drummer was definitely a good idea.

Why Should We Do It?

Once they had completed several takes of "How Do You Do It?", there was a confrontation which has been remembered in different ways by those present. The fact of the matter was that The Beatles said that they did not want to release "How Do You Do It?". Considering how hard they had fought to get to this stage with a record deal, it does sound either courageous, or foolhardy, to approach George Martin with an ultimatum of this sort. They took a stand, declaring that they only wanted to record their own songs – a very brave move on their part. The standard practice was that the A & R man/producer would choose the song and tell the group what to record. A new group just signed to a record deal did not tell the producer what they would or would not record.

It was Lennon, as group leader, who confronted George Martin. "Look, George, I have to tell you, we really think that song is crap." Martin's face was obviously shocked, so John qualified his statement. "I mean, it may be all right, but it's just not the kind of thing we want to do." George Martin quickly responded. "Well, exactly what is it you want to do?" Lennon realised this was his chance. "We want to record our own material, not some soft bit of fluff written by someone else." Martin, who was obviously fond of the Liverpudlians, gave a wry smile. "I'll tell you what, John," he replied. "When you can write a song as good as that one, then I'll record it." *(Here There and Everywhere)*

What could Lennon say? Norman Smith was obviously amused by it all. "They've got some cheek, that lot," he said. "I reckon that's what got them this far, though?" *(Here There and Everywhere)*

Paul and John were later to tell US journalist Larry Kane, who accompanied The Beatles on their US tours, what they felt about their choice. "'Love Me Do,' Larry, wasn't the best song we ever wrote. But it really put us out front," McCartney told Kane on the 1965 Beatles tour. John was also emphatic. "In Hamburg we clicked. At the Cavern we clicked. But if you want to know when we knew we'd arrived," Lennon said, "it was getting in the charts with 'Love Me Do.' That was the one. It gave us somewhere to go." *(When They Were Boys)*

"Um, Without Ringo"

Norman Smith remembered the session, too. "They started to do 'Love Me Do' again, this time with George Martin." Smith looked back at the session from June, and the problem again was the drummer. "Ringo Starr's drumming did not impress. And so Ringo was taken off and replaced by a session drummer." *(DVD The Beatles UCAP - The Early Years, 2014)* This explained why it took more than 15 attempts to record "Love Me Do". Paul explained what happened:
"Horror of horrors! George Martin didn't like Ringo. Ringo at that point was not that steady on time." Were they in a better place than with Pete? "Now he (Ringo) is rock steady," Paul stated some thirty years later. "It's always been his greatest attribute. But, to George (Martin), he was not as pinpoint as a session guy would be. So, Ringo got blown off the first record." *(Anthology)*

Paul continued: "George (Martin) did the 'Can I see you for a moment, boys?' 'Yeah?' 'Um... without Ringo.' He said, 'I would like to bring another drummer in for this record.' George got his way and Ringo didn't drum on the first single." *(Anthology)* Norman Smith had another perspective: "I've a feeling that Paul wasn't too happy with Ringo's drumming, and felt that it could be better. He didn't make too good a job of it. I remember too that there was a fair bit of editing to be done." *(The Complete Beatles Recording Sessions)*

Geoff Emerick remembered the problems surrounding the recording of "Love Me Do". "The Beatles seemed to have a lot of trouble getting this one ("Love Me Do") right, though," he said, noting that they obviously hadn't rehearsed it as much as the other song. "Ringo was having difficulty maintaining a steady beat." More telling was the dissention in the group, as "Paul was starting get annoyed with him." They hoped that each take they finished would be good enough for George Martin. However, Emerick witnessed the conversations between Martin and Smith, where Martin criticized Ringo's "unsteady drumming."

When the session was finally over, George Martin appeared to be frustrated. He called a halt to the evening's activities, "not even bothering to invite the group up to the control room for a playback." The day wasn't over for Norman Smith, as there was still editing and mixing to be done. Even though The Beatles had played live, the instruments and vocals were recorded on separate tracks, which allowed Smith to balance the track and "also add echo and make minor changes to the tonal quality." *(Here There and Everywhere)* Smith then turned to Emerick to discuss the session. Smith said, "George has decided to bring in a session drummer when they come in again next week, so we shouldn't have those problems again."

How Did He Do It?

Why were they criticising Ringo? The Beatles recorded "How Do You Do It?" and did a good job of it, without looking to impress. Ringo's drumming is fine, and fits in well with the rest of the group. It seems that troublesome song "Love Me Do", which had already accounted for Pete, would now be finishing Ringo before he even got started. Naturally, we can only judge him on the finished song, which sounded good, but the struggle to get there, witnessed by the Parlophone engineers, and especially George Martin, seems to have left Martin duly frustrated.

As we know, "How Do You Do It?" was recorded in only a couple of takes, for a duration of no more than 20-30 minutes at most. EMI paperwork says they finished at 11.15pm, even though Brian said it was midnight (which was most likely the time they left the studio after packing up). No matter, it took nearly four hours to get a take of "Love Me Do" that was acceptable to Martin and Smith. As Brian observed, John's mouth was numb from constantly playing the harmonica part, and Paul was getting annoyed with Ringo, who was struggling to create a strict enough tempo for the record. No such opportunity was afforded to Pete Best. But the difference was that, with some patience, Ringo and The Beatles were able to craft a recording good enough to serve as their first single. It must have been an exhausting day for them all.

George Martin's opinion was based on what he had seen and heard. "I didn't rate Ringo very highly," he said. "He couldn't do a drum roll – and still can't – though he's improved a lot since. Andy was the kind of drummer I needed. Ringo was only used to ballrooms. It was obviously best to use someone with experience." *(The Beatles. Hunter Davies)*

Ron Richards and George Martin hadn't liked Pete Best's drumming in June, and now, three months later, Martin and Norman Smith cared little for Ringo's drumming. The Beatles knew there was one more recording session in which they could make their debut single, but it would be without Ringo on drums. Was this really due to Ringo's drumming quality or because it was record company practice to use session drummers at first? George Martin's mind was made that

he would be using a session drummer when the recording date was set, so we shouldn't be too harsh on Pete or Ringo, even if the producer had reservations about both drummers.

How Could We Do It?

George Martin's final decision after a long day in the studio was which songs to record. Now that he had a couple of recordings on acetate, he had to approach the publishers, discuss the merits of the songs, and obtain the copyright and permission. EMI's publishers Ardmore and Beechwood, who had introduced The Beatles to George Martin, were determined to have a Lennon/McCartney song on the A-side, so the pressure was on Martin to make this happen. Dick James said that Mitch Murray's song was too good for a B-side, so Martin knew what he had to do: put Lennon/McCartney songs on both sides of the record. The Beatles had got their way. *(TuneIn)*

After the 4th September session, there were two important decisions to address. First, a session drummer was still needed to make the record and, second, another Lennon/McCartney original was needed to replace "How Do You Do It?". They had a week to prepare for their final session, but nobody thought to inform Ringo of George Martin's decision. The fourth Beatle was in for a very big shock.

11th September 1962

ANDY WHITE

Andy White was born on 27th July 1930 in Glasgow, Scotland. He first played a side-drum at the age of 12 in the local Boy Scout band, parading around the local streets on the 'High days and Holy days'. "On VE Day, 8th May 1945," recalled White, "the band marched in the town for a parade, and enjoyed it so much that I decided that I liked it, and wanted to do this for the rest of my life."

But he would wait a few years before taking up the drums professionally. "From school, I joined an engineering firm, where I trained as an apprentice pattern maker," White recalled. "The pay wasn't great, and after five years as an apprentice, I was working 42 hours a week for £7 10 shillings. I got my first drum kit when I was about 21, and my professional debut was at a West Coast holiday resort. Some of the band were then offered a summer season on the Isle of Wight. It was while I was there that bandleader Vic Lewis contacted me and asked me to join his band. I then spent the next six years touring with Vic Lewis' orchestra, playing jazz and big band music.

"The Musicians' Union had got an agreement together so that if an American band came over to Britain, then a British band had to go on tour in America. And so, when one of the American bands came over here, the Vic Lewis orchestra went to the United States. So we got to spend three weeks in America on tour. This was my first taste of rock 'n' roll, because we were on tour with some of the rock 'n' roll stars of America, like Bill Haley, Chuck Berry, The Platters and many other stars. We were only doing about three numbers each, so I got to experience and watch rock 'n' roll in America before it came to Britain. We were doing big band songs, like those of Stan Kenton, but we were putting a backbeat into it to give it our own twist, and fit in with what was really a rock 'n' roll tour."

After the success of the American tour, White was given an opportunity that would establish him as one of the busiest and most successful session drummers in Britain. As he explained: "A friend of mine, Jackie Dougan, had the opportunity to appear on a television programme, *Boy Meets Girl*, but he didn't want the job, so he asked me if I wanted it. That was the start for me, and that

lead to a career in rock 'n' roll and a number of television appearances and shows, and I was in demand from then on. I gained a reputation as a rock 'n' roll drummer."

In 1960, White played on Billy Fury's album, *The Sound of Fury*, which is now regarded as Britain's first rock 'n' roll album. Billy Fury, born Ronnie Wycherley in the Dingle, Liverpool, attended St. Silas Primary School and Dingle Vale Secondary Modern with Richy Starkey, the soon-to-be world-famous Ringo Starr. Andy White would later play backup on Lulu's classic song "Shout" and Tom Jones' "It's Not Unusual" as well as accompany most of the era's top performers. In the mid-Sixties, he joined the orchestra supporting Marlene Dietrich for two weeks at the Queens Theatre in London and a week in Edinburgh and then toured the world for the next eleven years. "I applied for, and got a job working for BBC Scotland, but after a long strike by musicians, I lost my job, and that was the end of that! I met my second wife, who was American, and so, in about 1983, we decided to settle in New Jersey where we've been ever since. I returned to my first love, pipe bands, and have been training drummers for many years now, which I love." *(David Bedford Interview 2012)*

On 9th November 2015, Andy White died at age 85. His accomplishments with the many stars behind whom he played a steady beat would forever take a back seat to the one day he spent with The Beatles – 11th September 1962.

Would Andy White have become the Fourth Beatle permanently?
NO. But for a very important day, Andy White was the Fourth Beatle, and the man he was replacing was in for a shock.

Andy White, session drummer for a day

11th September 1962

GET BACK TO EMI STUDIOS, ABBEY ROAD

In his various books and interviews, George Martin has often confused, or confabulated, the 4th September session with the 11th September session and his first meeting with Ringo, again possibly confirming that the 4th September session was not expected to produce a record.

As Martin once stated: "On 11th September 1962, we finally got together to make their first record.

The boys meantime had brought along a guy, and they said 'we're going to get Ringo to play with us', and I said 'we just spent good money and booked the best drummer in London. I'm not having your bloke in. I'll find out about him later. Poor Ringo was mortified and I felt sorry for him, so I gave him the maracas." On the *Anthology DVD*, Martin reiterated this, saying that "when Ringo came to the session for the first time, nobody told me he was coming. I'd already booked Andy White and told Brian Epstein this."

George Martin had become so exasperated with getting The Beatles' first single recorded that he didn't attend the second recording session this day, leaving producer Ron Richards to oversee it.

For some reason, perhaps to protect Ringo's reputation, the 4th September session is rarely mentioned in the earliest Beatles books. Whilst Ringo has suggested that Andy White had been brought in by George Martin to replace Pete Best, it was better to suggest that White was hired because Martin was unfamiliar with The Beatles' new drummer.

What the evidence concludes is that following the 4th September session, George Martin decided that Ringo's drumming was not what he was looking for, so he booked Andy White to make the record. As Ringo later observed: "I went down to play; he didn't like me either, so he called a drummer named Andy White, a professional session man, to play the session" *(Modern Drummer 1981)*

That must have been devastating for Ringo. Was his career with The Beatles ending before it had begun? Ringo, unsurprisingly, was crestfallen. "I was devastated he (George Martin) had his doubts about me. I came down ready to roll and heard, 'We've got a professional drummer.' He has apologised several times since, had old George, but it was devastating – I hated the bugger for years" *(Anthology)*.

Ringo also told Beatles biographer Hunter Davies: "I found this other drummer sitting in my place. It was terrible. I'd been asked to join The Beatles, but now it looked as if I was only going to be good enough to do ballrooms with them, but not good enough for records. I thought; that was the end. They're doing a Pete Best on me. I was shattered. What a drag. How phoney the whole record business was; I thought. Just what I'd heard about. If I was going to be no use for records, I might as well leave. What could the others say, or me? We just did what we were told."

Much like the June session, John, Paul and George didn't mention the personnel change to their drummer; in June, it was Pete – in September, it was Ringo. You have to wonder why they failed to tell him earlier that week that he was not going to be playing on the next recording session. What kind of friends were they, not giving him advance notice that he was being replaced by a session drummer? It all came down to business. This was their last chance, and there was no room for sentiment.

Geoff Emerick was sitting in the control room when Ringo walked in. "Dejectedly, Ringo sank into a chair beside Ron, and the session got underway." After the prolonged recording session from 4th September 1962, George Matin was determined to call in session drummer Andy White to record with The Beatles. For the time White spent With the Beatles, he was paid £5 10 shillings, and though he would have long and distinguished career as a session drummer, it is for this day, 11th September 1962, that he would be best remembered.

The Session Drummer

"On 'Love Me Do', they were only recorded on mono at first," said producer Steve Levine. "And then they moved to mono on twin-track so they could record the backing tracks and then overdub the vocals on the other track." That is why it was crucial to have the session drummer at the beginning, because the whole rhythm track would be mixed and recorded on one track. It had to be right. You could not re-do the drums or guitars. As they moved to the "Please Please Me" album, he continued, "they were on one track, and the vocals added via speaker, so there was no mixing as such, just fine-tuning the balance of back-track to vocals. That way, you never had separation. That is why when you got the stereo from there, you had the backing track on one side and the vocals on the other. It was never intended to be like that." Drummers like Andy White were worth their weight in gold, and always in demand.

White was contacted by EMI for the job. "I received a call a few days before the session from the 'fixer' at EMI," said White. "Every record company had a guy, who often was a musician, who would contact the session musicians and book them for a particular gig. I received my call from EMI, and it was only when I walked in on the morning of 11th September that I realised it was Ron Richards producing the session" *(David Bedford Interview 2013)*

White remembered Ringo walking in on 11th September. "Ringo walked in with the others, and was obviously shocked to see me setting up my drums," he said. "It was clear that nobody had told him he was not going to be playing, and so we said a quick 'Hello', and that was it. He must have thought that I was going to replace him, but I was ten years older than him, and I'd have needed a wig after a year with them!" *(David Bedford Interview 2013)*

White had no prior knowledge of the group or the songs they would be recording, but that was the usual practice for session drummers. "As with any session, I had no knowing what I was going to be doing that day, so we sat down and discussed the songs. Most of the time I was talking with John and Paul, as they were the songwriters. Of course, they had no written music, but that was fine. They knew what they wanted to do, so we set to work. I was really impressed with them, and it was a nice change to be working on original songs, as a lot of my work was with artists covering American songs. We worked through the routines and started rehearsing. Most of what I was trying to do was work with Paul and match what he was doing with the bass guitar, to enhance the sound". *(David Bedford Interview 2013)*

Recording Session: 4.45pm-6.30pm

Andy White's presence in the studio demonstrated why George Martin's decision was such an important one. The studio was booked between 4.45pm and 6.30pm, which didn't leave them much time. In less than two hours, they managed to commit to tape excellent versions of "Love Me Do" and "P.S. I Love You", and also a couple of takes of "Please Please Me". The difference in studio time spent this day compared with the previous session was incredible. The Beatles had also now recorded three versions of "Love Me Do", each distinctive, and each with a different drummer.

P.S. You Love Me?

With Andy White on the kit, The Beatles first recorded "P.S. I Love You" and then "Please Please Me" to see which of the two would best serve as the B-side. Emerick remembers them playing "P.S. I Love You." After just a few run-throughs, and ten takes, he was amazed at how "White seemed to get the hang of it. I was amazed at how quickly he did so, and how well he fit in with three unfamiliar musicians – the mark of a great session player."

Ron Richards suggested to Ringo that he could go downstairs and join in with them, though only to play maracas. Emerick could "sense that he (Richards) was getting increasingly uncomfortable at having the sulking drummer sitting beside him, and this must have struck him as a good way of getting Ringo out of the control room." *(Here There and Everywhere)*.

A week after their first session at EMI's Abbey Road Studios, The Beatles wereonce again walking through its doors, something that would become routine to them over the next several years. That, however, was only a fantasy at this stage. They hadn't even managed to make their first record yet, and today would have to be the day they accomplished this, because there would be no more studio time.

The young Emerick was amazed at the turnaround in just a few days, noting that it was "considerably more polished than the previous week." The Beatles headed up to the control room for the playback, obviously happy with what they were hearing. According to Emerick, they "eagerly discussed making it the A-side, but Richards dismissed them imperiously. 'It's good, but it's no A-side,' he said. 'We'll use it as the B-side of your first single.'" *(Here There and Everywhere)*

One drawback Richards identified was the song title. "I was originally a music publishing man, a plugger," he said, "so I knew that someone had already done a song with that title." *(The Complete Beatles Recording Sessions)*.

Love Me, Do

After successfully recording "P.S. I Love You" and a run-through of "Please Please Me", they got down to the important matter of recording a third version of the song that would now become the A-side – "Love Me Do". Ron Richards called them back to their places quickly, aware of the passing time. "Now we need get back to work," he said. "George wants you to have another go at 'Love Me Do'". Geoff Emerick remembers Ringo looking expectantly at Richards, "but Ron shot him down again. 'I'd like you to play the tambourine on this,

Ringo; we'll stick with Andy on the drums.'" *(Here There and Everywhere)*

Again, it took White only a short time to familiarize himself with the song. "His timekeeping was definitely steadier than Ringo's had been the previous week," recalled Emerick. "The other three were playing a lot better, too, and Paul sang the lead vocal with much greater confidence." It was obvious to Richards and Emerick that The Beatles had done a lot of rehearsing during the week."

(Here There and Everywhere).

Norman Smith affirms the choice of Andy White, a drummer he knew well: "He started playing exactly as I thought the song should have been played, and how it should be done. Andy White was great, and so we created the master."

(The Beatles Up Close and Personal 2014).

Please Please Us

George Martin turned up towards the end to the session to see the group, and what progress had been made. Ron Richards could happily inform him that, in just under two hours, they had recorded both the A-side and B-side. Although "Please Please Me" was then run through and recorded with the modifications Martin had suggested the previous week, it still wasn't the finished article. Even so, it was vastly improved. Again, White played the drums, with no contribution from Ringo.
He gave the song an exciting rhythm, and his musical rapport with the other three Beatles was incredible. In less than two hours, they had taught him – and recorded! – three original songs.
That is the difference a session drummer can make. With the White version of the song now completed, Ringo was able to use it to create a similar drum pattern when the group re-recorded the song on 26th November 1962.

How do the two versions compare? "It's a strange one," said Alex Cain, "because on this occasion Ringo displays more solidity than the seasoned-pro. Ringo plays solid '8 in the bar' ride cymbal throughout, Andy offering a softer approach, playfully landing on his hi-hats around the snare beats, producing a stop-start feel. Andy's fills are somewhat hurried (1.00) and especially at (1.07), where he sounds as if he's thrown his drums down the stairs! Personally, I much prefer Ringo's performances, both in the studio and live, as it makes for a more energetic and youthful sound overall." Did Ringo's performance on 26th November convince George Martin to stick with Ringo, and not use a session drummer again? However, for the recording of "Love Me Do", everyone was happy; except for poor Ringo.

Love Me Do or Love Me Don't?

Comparing the Ringo and Andy White Versions

In his book *I Want To Tell You*, Anthony Robustelli examined the two September versions of "Love Me Do": "The second version of 'Love Me Do' (Andy White's version) is five BPM (Beats Per Minute) faster and therefore, rocks a little harder. The recording is far superior sonically to the other version with the kick and snare punchy and up-front in the mix. Furthermore, Andy White's kick drum pattern is much busier, and though it seems to lock in with the bass better, it's difficult to compare the kick's feel because of the drastic sonic differences.

On the original September 4th version with Ringo, the kick is barely audible. White's more swinging kick drum definitely propels the song forward more successfully, but the sonic punch and clarity undeniably helped, as did the addition of Ringo's tambourine and an additional five BPM." *(I Want To Tell You).*

The drum pattern between the versions doesn't vary at all, remaining virtually the same all the way through. The harmonica is better in September than in June, and is slightly brighter on Andy White's version, possibly because John's lips went numb through multiple takes the previous week. The White version reveals a bit of variation, with a good use of the crash cymbal before going back into the chorus after the harmonica solo. In contrast, Ringo uses a thud on the drum to bring it to a stop. White's snare drum is a bit lighter, due to the tuning styles of both drummers, but this doesn't affect the overall song. Ironically, one element that makes White's version stand out is the tambourine played by Ringo, which is quite loud, but makes the overall sound brighter. Finally, George uses his newly-acquired American Jumbo (J-160E) Gibson acoustic to further brighten the sound.

Drummers Alex Cain and Terry McCusker, authors of *Ringo Starr and The Beatles Beat* compared the two versions and concluded that Andy White's version "certainly has a punchier feel to it than Ringo's version. There is a more confident, professional presentation." They observed that "Andy White's bass drum is more precise, due to the more confident approach by the seasoned professional. Ringo's bass drum appears to have been equalised out of the mix in an attempt to hide the hesitant, lacklustre performance." They also maintained that the superior sound of White's version could be attributed in part to Ringo's tambourine.

Love Me Don't, Do, Don't, Do, Do

Comparing All Three Versions: Pete Best, Ringo Starr and Andy White

Drummer Mike Rice listened to all three versions of "Love Me Do".
"These latter two versions are a lot faster and much better than the version in June, which was horrible. There is not a lot of difference between Ringo's version and Andy White's. I don't mind either of them, and you couldn't really nitpick over them. They've had time to work it out and make it better, which is a bit unfair on Pete, but Andy White didn't do anything particularly different to Ringo." *(David Bedford Interview 2017).*

As mentioned earlier, the drum patterns played by Ringo and Andy White were virtually identical, and quite basic, with little variation in them. In fact, if you listen to the original June version, Pete Best is playing the same rhythm employed by Ringo and Andy White during the main part of the song, though much slower due to the arrangement. It was only when they tried that skip-beat variation in the middle-eight in June that it all went so horribly wrong. Interestingly, in early 1964, there would be a fourth version of "Love Me Do" recorded by a Beatles drummer when Jimmie Nicol laid down the track. He stuck to the simple rhythm, though did include a skip-beat similar to the one Pete Best had played in the June 1962 audition.

"Ringo Didn't Drum on the First Single"

Paul was convinced that Ringo didn't play drums on the group's first Parlophone single, "Love Me Do" – and Ringo agreed. *(Anthology)*

Yet history has shown that he was indeed on the UK single release.

Considering that Andy White was hired to drum on the recording, the question remains: Was Ringo's version mistakenly released on the UK single? After all, the White version of "Love Me Do" appeared on The Beatles' debut studio album "Please Please Me", the UK EP release *The Beatles' Hits*, and also on their U.S. single release.

Is there any evidence to support this?

If the Ringo version wasn't considered good enough after 4th September, necessitating a summons for a session drummer, why release that first version? Neither George Martin nor Ron Richards were sure if it was selected intentionally or not. *(TuneIn)*

The evidence reveals that releases of "Love Me Do", apart from the UK single, were White's. All versions issued after The Beatles' Hits on 21st September 1963 contained Andy White's version. Why? With the original master recording of Ringo's version of "Love Me Do" destroyed or recorded over, possibly as early as 1962, EMI only had Andy White's 11th September recording to use. It was the only remaining – and arguably the superior – version.

(The Complete Beatles Recording Sessions)

When "Love Me Do" was released in the U.S. in April 1964, it was Andy White's version that was used. As far as George Martin was concerned, Andy White's was the version he had faith in.

McArtney

A further mistake was made when 250 promo discs of "Love Me Do" were released, misspelling Paul's name as McArtney; something he was used to in *Mersey Beat*. One of these discs was sold in October 2017 for $14,757, the most expensive 7-inch single ever sold.

In a twist of fate – or was it an inside joke – when Apple decided to reissue "Love Me Do" on the 50th anniversary, they initially used Andy White's version. They then had to quickly recall those records, so that Ringo's version could be issued.

The final piece of evidence is one of omission. With the group's popularity starting to surge in late 1962, why did they not ask Ringo to re-record "Love Me Do" for the album, instead using Andy White's version? The conclusion is that Ringo' version was most likely released by accident, something that is not uncommon in the recording industry, even today. Nothing else really makes sense.

No More Session Drummers

Although George Martin wasn't initially impressed with Ringo's drumming, he grew to appreciate his style. They soon became good friends and the producer would replace him only one more time by a session drummer – Bobby Graham. "Ringo always got, and still gets, a unique sound out of his drums, a sound as distinctive as his voice," Martin said. "Ringo gets a looser deeper sound out of his drums that is unique. This detailed attention to the tone of his drums is one of the reasons for Ringo's brilliance. Another is that although Ringo does not keep time with a metronome accuracy, he has an unrivalled feel for a song. If his timing fluctuates, it invariably does so in the right place at the right time, keeping the right atmosphere going on the track and giving it a rock-solid foundation. This held true for every single Beatles number Richie played ... Ringo also was a great tom-tom player." Martin added: "Ringo has a tremendous feel for a song, and he always helped us hit the right tempo the first time. He was rock solid. This made the recording of all the Beatle songs so much easier." *(The Summer of Love in 1994)*

Ringo Starr - The Fourth Beatle, by Contract

In spite of being temporarily replaced by Andy White for one day, Ringo's position as the Fourth Beatle was cemented on 1st October 1962 when he, along with the other three Beatles, signed the new management contract with Brian Epstein. The Fab Three had found their drummer and the group, soon to be known as the Fab Four, was finally complete; after serving his probation, Ringo was now a full member of The Beatles. This was the first contract that Brian signed and the first time The Beatles were officially – and legally – tied to Brian. It contained a clause that Epstein had initially inserted to say that either party could walk away from The Beatles with three months' notice. By the beginning of 1963, Brian felt confident enough to have that clause removed as Ringo, the Fourth Beatle, was now part of the group.

Ringo Was The Right Angle

Paul McCartney aptly summed up Ringo's recruitment into The Beatles: "It was four corners of a square; it wouldn't have worked without one of the sides. Ringo was the right angle." It can't have been easy breaking into the Fab Three, as he would find out. They never mentioned to him John's August 23rd wedding, and when George Martin decided to replace him on "Love Me Do" with Andy White, the boys didn't bother telling him. As Ringo lamented: "They knew each other. They'd been through a lot in life; I still had to get into it with them."*(Anthology)* Ringo explained what he had to do to become The Beatles' drummer. "I was lucky to be on their wavelength when I joined the group," he said. "I had to be or I wouldn't have lasted. They all have strong personalities, and unless you can match it, you're in a bit of trouble. When I finally joined them, I had to join them as people as well as a drummer." *(Melody Maker 1964)*.

Growing up in the Dingle made you tough, and it was this determination and attitude that helped Ringo do what no other drummer had done over the years: break into the Fab Threesome. "I was in the band," Ringo would say, "but emotionally I had to earn my way in." *(Anthology)*.

He certainly earned his place in the group, and became an integral member, prepared to take on the world.

A Quite Brilliant Move

Brian had endured the rejection of the different drummers he had approached as Pete's replacement. Then, against his own better judgement, he blindly trusted John, Paul and George when they wanted to offer the position to Ringo. But by 1965, Brian knew that it had been the right decision. "Ringo's coming into the group was one of The Beatles' most brilliant doings," he said to Melody Maker in 1965. "It was something they wanted, and that I carried out. It was, for so many reasons, a quite brilliant move." *(Melody Maker, 1965)*.

So let me introduce to you, the one and only Billy Shears.

"Love Me Do" was released on 5th October 1962

Review of The Beatles' First Parlophone Single

Specially written for this Press Release By Tony Barrow, whose weekly column OFF THE RECORD by "DISKER" appears each Saturday in The Liverpool Echo and Evening Express

For many years the Tennessee town of Nashville has been known as the golden capital of America's Country & Western music industry. In its own way, I guess, Liverpool has become the British beat equivalent to Nashville for the city, deep in the heart of Z Cars country, boasts an almost incredible array of thriving rock 'n' roll beat groups.

WHINING HARMONICA

The most popular of these is The Beatles, a group which deserves the nationwide following which its Parlophone recordings will surely bring. On the evidence of "Love Me Do" nobody can claim that The Beatles are a carbon of The Everlys, The Brooks, The Allisons, The Shadows or any other existing outfit. Theirs is a thoroughly distinctive vocal sound backed by the semi-plaintive, semi-impatient rasp and whine of John Lennon's remarkably expressive harmonica plus a stout guitar and solid drum beat.

SIMPLY INFECTIOUS

The lyrics of this infectious, medium-paced ballad are simple and it is in this easy-to-remember simplicity that The Beatles can pin their well-founded hopes of hit parade headlines for their very first Parlophone outing.

ANOTHER PUNCHY VOCAL

The under-deck carries something much more than the traditional (albeit ungenerous) B side padding. "P.S. I LOVE YOU" is a bright, up-tempo ditty with another punchy John Lennon/Paul McCartney vocal and a smart, rhythmic backdrop which has a colourful Latin tint to it.

IF YOU CAN'T BEET 'EM.................

Beetles did you say, George? Course I've heard of them. Your Grandfather (may he rest in peace) used to put down some powdery stuff to stop them coming in the house."

"Hay? No, I'm sure it was powdery stuff. And who ever heard of beetles supping tea?"

"BEATLES, Grandma.
It's a group..., there are four of them... and they're on Parlophone".

"We haven't got a phone in the parlour, George. Anyway I don't to want hear any more about them.

They give me the creeps. Nasty big black things".

"But they're not black, Grandma...They're white ...

And they're British!....."

ANALYSING RINGO STARR

Is Ringo the Luckiest Man in the World - or a Great Drummer?

Ringo Starr's career with The Beatles started in difficult circumstances when, at the end of his first day in the studio, he was replaced for the next session by a session drummer. However, it is a testament to his character that it was one of the only occasions this occurred and it was his version of "Love Me Do" that was released as The Beatles' first single. It can't have been easy for him, breaking into the triumvirate of John, Paul, and George. "When we first started, they (Parlophone) basically went John and Paul's way because they were the writers, and they would say, 'This is the song', and I would play as creatively as I could. Sometimes I would have three people telling me how to do it. They were saying, 'play this like on that track'. I'm saying, 'For Christ's sake, there are two drummers there.' They could never hear that you know. You'd have to have four arms to do half the stuff they wanted me to do." *(Viva Magazine, 1978)*

Why Did They Choose Ringo?

For as long as The Beatles have been famous, this question has been asked, debated and discussed, precipitating endless arguments among Beatles fans. The majority of the squabbles end up with each protagonist claiming the moral high-ground because their ego is invested in the drummer in question.

It is Pete versus Ringo. Who will you choose?

Although, as we have seen, it was never the case that they got rid of Pete to get Ringo in, there was a change in the sound almost immediately, which the trained ear could notice. Mal Jefferson, whose band The Mastersounds took on the Cavern residency from The Beatles, is now a respected Musician/ Record Producer/ Studio owner, and he remembers that first time Ringo played at the Cavern with The Beatles. "It was fantastic," he recalled. "Paul spent the whole session looking at, and closely following, the timing of his bass drum. He smiled endlessly, suddenly released from the tedious four-four beat. The effect on the whole group was electric. Ringo's power and energy gave them a lift, which was seen by the excitement in the audience."

Mal feels that the big difference between Pete and Ringo was their use of the bass drum. "Pete always played four-to-the-bar. Ringo's bass drum beats included double-beats, off-beats and different patterns. This allowed the bass player to play different, and more melodic lines, which, of course, freed up and delighted Paul, a brilliant bassist. The syncopations also left rhythmic gaps, which could be filled with off-beats or riffs for the guitars. Lennon was very adept at these broken rhythms and was underestimated as a guitarist.

"This also helped vocal phrasing and made songs more 'jazzy' or 'rocky' giving better emphasis to key phrases and repeated riffs and figures."As an example," Jefferson continued, "listen to the two-bar drum break in 'A Picture of You', the Joe Brown hit. On Joe's record, Bobby Graham plays a double-beat, which Ringo played frequently in many songs. Playing the same song with The Beatles, Pete plays four-to-the-bar right the way through the solo. On 'Besame Mucho', Pete was excellent, because the rumba dictates an even four-four bass drum beat.

He played in the 'dance band' style, rather than the broken rhythms of the 'rock' style, which heralded the disco and jazz-funk syncopations. Ringo excelled in these styles and made his own 'figurative' patterns like in 'Come Together', which is highly praised by many heavy rock drummers. My favourite is *A Hard Day's Night*, because of his expert control and variation of his heavy hi-hats, which are the main driving force of the recording." *(David Bedford Interview 2017)*

In his autobiography, *Born To Run*, published in 2016, Bruce Springsteen made an interesting observation when giving advice to Jay Weinberg, son of E Street Band drummer, Max Weinberg. Jay sat in with the group, and Springsteen gave him some invaluable advice.

Jay had the power, the precision, the discipline. Still, something didn't feel quite right. When Jay initially started playing with us, my skin was moving right. Then, I realized with all his technique and power; he was playing on top of the band, riding over the surface of our arrangements.

We took a break; I walked over to him and quietly explained that drums were not part of the exoskeleton of these arrangements. The drums are the soul engine, buried down and breathing inside the band. You play not on top but immersed in the band.

You power everything from within. I said, take a breath, take it back down, and dig deep. When you hit that right position, when the beat is placed correctly, you'll drop inside the band naturally. That could be a pretty sophisticated idea for anyone to wrap their head around, much less an 18-year-old, who up to this point had mostly played to approximately 30 people at a local club. Jay brought fire, youth, intensity, and his own brand of showmanship to the band.

Perhaps when we look at the styles of Pete Best and Ringo Starr, could we apply the same logic? Much like Jay Weinberg's style, Pete Best's drumming technique was born in Hamburg, where his "atom beat" gave The Beatles the power and precision needed to draw the crowds into the clubs. The Beatles' driving rock beat, forged in Hamburg and Liverpool, made them what they were: the best rock 'n' roll band anyone saw.

However, as they made the transition from performing in clubs to making records, they no longer needed the power of Pete. What they needed was someone who could play within the song, not on top of it – within the arrangement and not outside of it. Jay Weinberg had Bruce Springsteen to help him make that transition; Pete Best had no such assistance. However, as George Martin later observed, Ringo possessed that ability Springsteen sought in his own drummer. He could play the song.

A Musician's Drummer

Speak to any musician who has been in a band for a while and they will tell you about something intangible. You can have a band comprised of the best individual musicians in their field, but if they don't have that extra instinct, a 'group think', then the band won't work at its best. When John wanted The Quarrymen to progress from skiffle to rock 'n' roll, he realized he couldn't do it with the musicians he had, so Paul McCartney was invited to join. Even with Paul in place, they needed a lead guitarist, so they recruited George Harrison. From the end of 1957, John, Paul and George had that 'group think' and, over the next few years, had several drummers. For two of those years, Pete Best served them well as a great rock 'n' roll drummer.

However, when they needed to evolve from a rock 'n' roll group to a recording pop group and were told by George Martin that a session drummer would be used on their records, John, Paul and George decided it was time for another change. They had to find a drummer who was musically on their wavelength.

Lucky guy or great drummer?

With Pete, that 'group think' wasn't there, despite his abilities as a drummer. When they recruited Ringo, they couldn't be sure if he was the one, so they put him on probation.

However, it became quickly apparent that Ringo possessed a certain synchronicity with the established trio of Lennon, McCartney and Harrison. It is something only musicians can understand, even if they can't quite explain it – that intuitive sense of where a song is going, and the ability to instinctively lead or follow the rest of the group. It can't be taught, and it can't be learned. It just happens, and when it does, the whole group knows. Paul McCartney said that when Ringo played with them, they all just felt like it was right.

Billy Kinsley's group, The Merseybeats, played alongside The Beatles with both Pete and with Ringo on drums. Kinsley rates both drummers very highly, but recognises their differences, too: "He (Ringo) was totally original. There was no other drummer like him. Was it because of John and Paul's writing encouraging Ringo to stretch himself? However, he was superb; very different to Pete."

(David Bedford Interview 2017)

Ringo's Unique Style

What made Ringo's sound so unique? A number of people, like George Martin, have commented that Ringo isn't technically a good drummer or even that accurate on time. "Although Ringo does not keep time with metronome accuracy," Martin said, "he has an unrivalled feel for a song. If his timing fluctuates, it invariably does so in the right place at the right time, keeping the right atmosphere going on the track and giving it a rock-solid foundation." *(With a Little Help from my Friends: The Making of Sgt. Pepper)* To a non-drummer, it may seem as if Ringo isn't a good drummer, but that isn't so. As George Martin observed, "He has a feel for a song."

Gary Astridge is the world's leading expert on Ringo's drum kits and works with Ringo as his curator. As he says, "I've been privileged to have my fascination with Ringo and his drum kits turn into a job that never existed, to work with him and for him on several projects. I feel blessed." Also a drummer, Gary is one of the few people who can offer a special insight into Ringo's drumming.

Like so many Beatles fans, Gary first saw the group on *The Ed Sullivan Show*. "I was seven, and I remember after watching them, the very next day I was starting to play on coffee tins and anything I could find. I'd never thought of playing the drums before. I got my first drum kit at eleven. My parents didn't have a lot of money, but I didn't realise it at the time. So I started with just a snare drum and built up from there. I think of what Harry Graves went through to get Ringo his first kit, going all the way to London, lugging the kit across London to the train station, changing trains and getting home – that's a lot of love."

So what makes Ringo's sound so unique? "I can't put it into words. You just know. When Ringo was inducted into the Rock 'n' Roll Hall of Fame, I helped with the interviews with all of those famous drummers. I saw those great drummers who were humbled and excited about giving their opinion about Ringo. It was obvious that they had spent a lot of time thinking beforehand about what to say about Ringo. They said things like 'he is the king of feel',' or that he has that 'magic touch'. Drummers just know." *(David Bedford Interview 2017)*.

Record producer Steve Levine, who has worked with some of the biggest names in popular music, including Ringo, offers an insight into what made Ringo stand out from other drummers. "Ringo didn't have a unique sound, but a distinctive sound, and a unique style of playing. A lot of the drummers from the '50s and '60s learnt to play in the old-fashioned way of holding the sticks, like in the big-band era. Ringo changed that, and it became the norm. Ringo's use of the hi-hat is quite distinctive and his use of the toms, too. Listen to 'Ticket To Ride'. Ringo was playing the floor tom like the hi-hat. Furthermore, when you watch him, he plays his fills with only two toms, unlike Keith Moon who had more toms. Look at their different setups. That makes you play differently. Max Weinberg (from Bruce Springsteen's E Street Band) plays like Ringo because that is how he learnt to play; his influence. So Max sits just like Ringo, though the style is different, because of the requirements of playing with Bruce Springsteen's band. However, it's a similar way of playing to Ringo.

"Ringo's style may not be as obvious to members of the public, but it is to a producer or artist. Ringo had a very distinctive way of playing the open hi-hat, too. Ringo's influences would have been the drummers of the time. With any drummer, you have to look at each generation and their influences, and who was around when they were learning their craft. For Ringo, there were only the show bands and the jazz bands to listen to. The drummers who were big in the late '60s and early '70s would have been influenced by Ringo.

"As a producer, I'd much sooner have someone who is brilliant at the bit they are good at than vague about what they can't do. The fact that The Beatles were very good at what they did within what they had available to them is a positive, not a negative. Ringo isn't Buddy Rich, which is actually his strength, and I really do mean that. He did what he did really, really well, and that's very important as a drummer and for a producer." *(David Bedford Interview 2017)*

Ringo "Plays The Song"

Levine continued: "Ringo would mimic the song and make a drumming phrase, or a melodic phrase or a feeling that he got from the track, and that is very important. You get a feel for that, and don't learn it, so it resonates with other musicians. The feel of the song is really important, which is why Motown was so successful.

The basic 4/4 feel is what most people can do when they tap along to a song. That's what Ringo could do. He would cut away all the fat, and in some ways that made him almost invisible in the record. But he didn't get in the way with unnecessary fills. He did great flams (one of three basic strokes on the snare drum comprised of two single strokes that are played at different heights), or play with rim shots (a drum stroke in which the stick strikes the rim, and the head of the snare drum simultaneously) instead of hitting the middle of the snare, which again became a trademark. Now whether that grew out of trying to be heard in The Cavern, I don't know.

"When I worked with Ringo, I was trying to get some samples for a Fairlight Digital Synthesizer, and he was just playing a cymbal and trying to get the right sound, and was so easy to work with. He simply came in, and started playing his kit and was just great. I even had him on timpani, and after we recorded it, I slowed the speed down so that they were in tune with the music. He gave me some samples to use and they were then sampled and used for the track 'California Calling' *(on the album, The Beach Boys)*. It vindicates what I said. Even though he is playing with The Beach Boys, it still sounds like Ringo." *(David Bedford Interview 2017)*.

Gary Astridge agrees with that assessment: "Ringo never rehearsed in the studio, and only played when recording with The Beatles. He just has an instinct. Paul and Ringo had a chemistry. Alternatively, John would say; 'try this, and Ringo just played. With some Lennon songs, there were so many strange timing structures and Ringo followed him every time. How did he do that? He makes it work. You can't teach that.

"You can listen to a Beatles record," Astridge added, "and hear a drum fill in a song. You'd learn it and assume it is the same through the whole song, but it isn't. If you listen carefully, there's always something different going on. Ringo makes it work. Every new Beatles record came out, and we were listening to the songs. I would study everything Ringo did, and I thought wow, what is he doing now? It was so exciting! I wouldn't listen for the bass line or the guitars, just the drums." *(David Bedford Interview 2017)*.

Ringo tried to explain further what he describes as playing the 'feel' of the song. "I play with emotion and feeling and that's what rock is," he said. "Rock is not reading (music), and I'm not putting reading down, although it's something that I don't do and something I never wanted to do. I did have one lesson in the old days and the guy wrote all those dots on the paper, but I felt it wasn't the way I wanted to play. I only wanted to play, and some days it's a real bummer for people, because if I'm on a downer, I still have to play and you only get what's in my soul at the time. But that's life. We all make a choice. A lot of session guys can go in and read and play five different sessions a day—totally different types of music. He just reads it and plays it, but that's a different musician to me."

(Modern Drummer December 1981)

But not everybody agrees. Lou Longobardi thinks it is more complicated. "Unfortunately, I think this phrase (Ringo plays the song) is too often used to admit to Ringo's, and George's, inability to be super-fast and flashy on their instruments, but defend them by saying that they didn't do that because the song didn't call for it. I think that term carries a very subtle, denigrating message. I can attach a different, and positive, meaning to that expression, but I don't think that is how it is generally meant." *(David Bedford Interview 2017)*

How can we further define Ringo's ability to "play the song?" One of the co-authors of this book, David Bedford, remembers his own experiences. "From a young age, I was playing in a church music group, mainly on guitar, accompanying a classically trained pianist. However, when it came to doing a rock 'n' roll version of a well-known hymn, the pianist would hand it over to me, and I would play the song on the piano. Unable to read music, and having only had two piano lessons when I was eight, I couldn't follow the music as the pianist did, so she was technically at a much higher level than me. However, she admitted to me that she couldn't play like I did, because of the way she had been trained.

Whenever I play piano in church, as I still do today, I play the song in the context of the church service that day, and how the song should be played at that moment. It will rarely be the same way twice, because I'm not following a manuscript, but following the feel of the song."
In the same way, when George Martin hired Andy White to replace Ringo on "Love Me Do", he knew he was getting a session drummer who would learn the part quickly and could replicate that part exactly, as often as needed.

What Martin and The Beatles found with Ringo was that he would create a drum part based on how the song should feel at that moment. Try it the following day and it would be different, depending on what he felt would work.

Ringo changed the way drummers contributed to songs. He evolved as a drummer by working closely with his fellow Beatles throughout the development of the song, as it was changing. This was part of a process that often took weeks, or even months, especially late in their career. You can't get that from a session drummer. Technically, session men like Andy White, Bobby Graham and Clem Cattini were at the top of their game, could read music and create an arrangement for a song that they would learn and recreate for the record. But it was just a job – something they would do three or four times each day with different groups. You can learn the guitar solo for a song recorded by a famous artist, but you will soon find that it is not enough to simply learn it. It is often impossible to recreate because guitarists like George Harrison or Lawrence Juber play what and how they feel. Most guitarists who attempt to recreate those solos will rarely capture the sound because Harrison and Juber they play the song in a unique way, as only they can.

A similar analogy can be made with singers. How many Beatles tribute bands can recreate the songs perfectly, yet you know the musicianship is not that of John, Paul, George or Ringo? Only they could sound like they did because they stamped their own personalities on the songs. Gone were the days when recordings were noted more for their technical proficiency than the musicianship of the artists. Groups could finally throw about the manuscript paper and express themselves through their songs. The best groups – the ones that lasted – had their own style and own music. The Beatles started a revolution that the rest of the world is still benefitting from today.

Ringo was at the vanguard of this new musical movement, paving the way for other drummers. While most drummers can learn Ringo's parts, few will be able to reproduce the feel of the song that Ringo created.

Backbeat, or Back of a Beat?

Mitch Kozera is another drummer inspired by Ringo to take up the kit, and has spent four decades playing in bands. "In 1994, the movie Backbeat was released," Kozera says. "It dramatizes the early days of The Beatles in Hamburg, nearly up to the point when they would add Ringo Starr to the band, completing the legendary lineup. The title was a premonition of times to come. The Beatles with Pete Best behind the kit were a fine straight-ahead rock band. Their early use of period R&B hits was the perfect material to hone their stage act, and the catalyst for what their own songwriting would become. But they knew then that something was missing. That something was swing. And as energetic as the band was at the time with Pete, they lacked that ingredient.

"Enter Ringo Starr. Ringo was an experienced, professional drummer. His timing was impeccable, and he could be counted on to play with control, and skillfully channel the feel of those R&B hits. In many cases, he improved upon the originals. His approach was to play as far back in the beat as possible, almost seemingly behind. This technique was jazzy in nature and introduced suspense and 'soul' into the music. It also is the intangible element that gets people tapping their feet and up out of their seats. It can be argued that it was the critical final component in elevating The Beatles to a great pop-rock band.

Kozera continues: "In order to accomplish this technique, Ringo would place 'lag' notes in the beat with his bass and snare drums. This propelled the music in a funky and indirect way. Slightly behind metronome time, it was by far more effective than the straight 'four-in-the-box' (boom-chick-boom-chick) technique to create an almost bluesy dance-ready rhythm. A great example can be heard in their cover of the Shirelles' 'Baby It's You' from the "Please Please Me" *album*. It uses punctuation snare hits on the second of four counts, combined with a stutter bass drum figure to form the resulting rhythm. Similarly, on Arthur Anderson's 'Anna (Go To Him)', Ringo utilizes high-hat strikes to seemingly delay the snare attack and add great anticipation to the beat. It should be noted that while the original versions of these songs employed similar techniques on the drums, Ringo's interpretations were more pronounced, with a funk that made The Beatles' versions more danceable.

"Ringo didn't invent this technique. It was and is in wide use to add swing and dramatic effect to ballads and emotional songs. What Ringo did was employ it with great success on harder rocking numbers. Combined with his internal clock, the swing of the drum beat fused with the other instruments to build a steady and powerful musical force – a juggernaut that would soon be making audiences scream all over the world. Some of the best examples exist, again, on the *Please Please Me album*. Both 'Twist and Shout' and 'Ask Me Why' use delayed snare and bass drum shots in the back beat to 'deepen the groove.' On 'Twist and Shout', Ringo's interpretation is so much more creative and complex than the Isley Brothers' original that The Beatles' version is the recognized standard of the song to fans everywhere. The style developed into a signature element of Ringo's playing on early Beatles recordings. 'All My Loving' (from with The Beatles*)* wouldn't have been nearly as catchy with a four-in-the-box beat. You hear immediately how John Lennon's rhythm guitar locks in with the drums to create a foundation of controlled chaos by which the Paul McCartney vocal and George Harrison lead guitar could safely ride.

"What's most remarkable about The Beatles early recordings, and the *Please Please Me album* in particular," Kozera concludes, "is that the band was recorded almost exclusively live, with only vocal and minimal instrumental overdubs. Ringo recorded the song 'Boys' while simultaneously playing his drums and singing the lead vocal on the track, all in one single take. Listen to the song. You get a strong sense of how well prepared Ringo was to rock and swing with his new band on that record. Even if they didn't realize it the time, this was the beginning of something very special." *(David Bedford Interview 2017)*

A Tricky Lefty on a Righty

Rob Shanahan knows as well as anybody what Ringo Starr is like as a drummer, having worked with him as his photographer for many years. "I was introduced to Ringo by Sheila E.," Shanahan says. "I had just finished shooting her record cover for Heaven when she was asked to do the All Starr tour. At the start of the tour, I met him in her dressing room, and my life has never been the same! Through the years, since 2001, I've been fortunate to get to know one of the most important drummers in rock history. I realize how lucky I've been and how far I've travelled from a small town in Minnesota." Shanahan is not only one of the top rock photographers, but is also an accomplished drummer, and a "lefty" like Ringo – a left-handed drummer playing a right-handed kit.

But what does being a "lefty" on a right-handed kit mean for Ringo? "Lefty on a righty, tricky indeed," Shanahan points out. "Leading with your left, and working around a righty kit can be challenging if you are trying to sound like a right-handed drummer. However, Ringo plays by feel, and never tried to sound like anyone else. He just played what he felt and sounded right for the song. This is why there are no big drum fills muddying up Beatles tracks. Also, a big advantage is that your dominant left hand plays the snare drum on the 2 + 4 of a drum beat, which is 'the back beat' that drives the song."

"He has a groove that just feels good," Shanahan observes. "When he first gets up on his kit at sound check and lays down a beat, you will usually find me, Gregg Bissonette and Ringo's long-time drum tech Jeff Chonis right behind the drum riser with our mouths agape! I just returned from a shoot in Nashville with Elvis' drummer D.J. Fontana, who played on all the early Elvis hits from the 50's and 60's. He is also the master of laying down a real simple drum beat that just feels so good. After all, people dance to the drummer, not the guitar player."

Ringo is certainly a drummer who doesn't like fills on the drums, which Shanahan says is a strength. "For Ringo, it goes back to laying down a simple drum beat groove that makes the song feel so good. Kick, snare, hi-hat, that's all you need. When you're busy playing a big tom fill, you're putting the heartbeat of the song on pause. His personality and humor come out in his drumming, and his drumming style is definitely unique." *(David Bedford Interview 2015)*.

Another strength that Ringo brought to The Beatles is versatility. "Yes, versatility is a strength for any musician," Shanahan notes. "With the All Starrs, Ringo plays many different styles. Even so, he always puts his signature Ringo stamp on anything he plays. A good example is how he plays on the Santana songs with Gregg Rollie in the band." *(David Bedford Interview 2015)*.

The naturally left-handed Ringo was forced by his superstitious grandmother to be right-handed, so he is ambidextrous. Like Paul with his guitar, Ringo never thought of having a left-handed drum kit, so he naturally developed this unique style, which made him stand out.

"Everyone used to sort of say, 'those silly fills he does'," Ringo said, and yet somehow, he inspired a generation of drummers. "But I didn't know that then. Everyone put me down—said that I couldn't play. They didn't realize that was my style and I wasn't playing like anyone else—that I couldn't play like anyone else." His style, particularly the use of the toms, became his signature.

"That was my style. Also, I can't do a roll to this day, and I hit with the left first, while most drummers do it with the right first. Mine might be strange in its way, but it was my style. I can't go around the kit, either. I can't go snare drum, top tom, middle tom, floor tom. I can go the other way. So all these things made up these so-called "funny fills," but it was the only way I could play. And then later on, after I was always put down as a drummer with "his silly fills and he can't play." *(Modern Drummer December 1981)*

Mitch Kozera concurs that Ringo's left-handed style was an important element in Ringo's sound. "Ringo assembled and played his kit in the conventional right-handed setup, based on what he'd seen others do. This means, generally, right hand over the high hat, and left hand over the snare drum. It's how we see most drummers play. With this arrangement, it's natural to begin beats and fills with the right hand. While Ringo did play his kit with his right hand over the high-hat, and left hand over the snare, interesting idiosyncrasies in his style would emerge. Fills started with his left hand would be a signature component of his style that added drama to the songs. The left hand lead allows for Ringo to have both hands free to finish the figure with a cymbal accent, and come back strong to the top of the beat, each time he plays it. Throughout The Beatles' career, Ringo would employ this technique with great precision.

Later, on *Rubber Soul*'s 'Drive My Car', Ringo uses it on the opening snare intro, which powerfully kicks the band into the track. Drummers, for decades, have been trying to master this fill, typically with a right hand lead. It's not at all easy. Not surprisingly," Kozera says, referring back to his earlier point, "that snare on 'Drive My Car' also comes in at the back of the beat." *(David Bedford Interview 2017)*

A Righty Trying to Emulate a Tricky Lefty on a Righty

"Certain drum fills that Ringo does are tricky because he will start a fill with his dominant hand," Gary Astridge commented, "going with his left. Then, being creative, he can do things in a unique way that, as a right-hander, you can find yourself in all kinds of trouble. Even if you learn the patterns and fills, you may technically know how to do it, but to do it with the feel of Ringo is totally different. It is so difficult to learn his parts. It is amazing what he has done. People say; 'Ringo wasn't technically proficient, but...' Why say that? He proved what a great drummer he is over the years. What else do you need? *(David Bedford Interview 2017)*

A Ringo Tribute

Another man who understands and appreciates Ringo's style is Phil Kelly, who has played drums in several groups, including Beatles tribute bands. Kelly grew up in a diverse musical household that was heavily influenced by the big band music his father loved, and the artists of his brother's generation – Elvis Presley, Buddy Holly and, of course, The Beatles.

"Like most kids who grew up in the early sixties, we all huddled together in the family room on Sunday nights at 8pm and turned on *The Ed Sullivan Show*. With only ten days before my eighth birthday, my life would change forever when the camera focused in on Ringo and his Ludwig Black Oyster Pearl kit; that was it. I knew right then and there that I wanted to be a drummer."

Since then, Kelly has never looked back, playing with a number of Boston-based '60s and '70s bands such as The Jammers, Sherman and the Waybacks, Mr. Peabody as well as the Beatle tribute bands Instant Karma, BeatleTracks, and Glass Onion.
"Seemingly, all became clear when the camera zoomed in above John, Paul and George in the middle of 'I Want To Hold Your Hand'," Kelly says. "I was immediately awestruck by how easily Ringo swayed to the music behind his Ludwig Black Oyster Pearl kit. So, without even knowing his impact upon the

world, Ringo has inspired millions of kids just like me to pick up a set of sticks and emulate every little nuance of his playing."

But for many drummers like Kelly, attempting to mimic Ringo's playing style wasn't as easy as it appeared. "The problem is that Ringo is a left-handed drummer playing a right-handed kit," said Phil, "and as a result, his drum fills are counter-intuitive and difficult to reproduce exactly."

Kelly explained what it is like for a drummer, especially one who has played in a Beatles tribute band, to recreate Ringo's drum patterns. "When a right-handed drummer like myself does a drum fill around the kit, we lead with our right hand. Ringo, being a left-handed drummer, leads with his dominant left hand. The end result of this unorthodox style of drumming produces a different sound because of the crossing of the left hand over the right. This nuance is inherently Ringo's playing style and, ironically, it is what makes his drumming style challenging.

"A practical example of this uniqueness can be found when Ringo plays the opening measures to 'Tell Me Why'. He leads with his left hand in the tumbling drum fill off the tom and snare. Later in that song, he plays a measure of triplets (again leading with his left hand) that leads nicely into the final refrain, and the tumbling drum fills to end the tune. The same can be said for Ringo's drumming on 'I Want To Hold Your Hand'. In this song, he attacks the snare and tom with powerful accents, again leading with his left hand that complements the phrasing by John and Paul on the song's title.

"Another nuance that was revolutionary and a very much a part of the early Beatle recording (and one that I learned early in my Beatle tribute band days) was to play the hi-hat in a slightly opened position, playing the time sequence (usually in quarter notes) in a figure eight pattern. When Ringo played this unique style, it produced a totally different sonic than playing straight up and down quarter notes. The result is a rhythmic pattern that gives the song a swing feel and, because of the slightly open positioning of the hi-hats, creates a sizzle or swishing sound. Ostensibly, Ringo's style of hi-hat play turned the hi-hat into what sounds like a ride cymbal. Evidence of this style of hi-hat playing can best be found in 'I Want To Hold Your Hand', 'It Won't Be Long' and 'All My Loving'.

Kelly commented further: "Ringo's drumming is not overly technical, but the strength of his drumming is his feel for the song. There are hundreds of technically superb drummers who are adept at sight reading from charts, but few have the feel for a song that Ringo possesses. Jim Keltner, the great studio drummer and longtime admirer of Ringo's playing said 'everything Ringo played had such great, deep natural feel. He's a song drummer – guys who sit down and they hear the song, and they play appropriately for that song.'

"Anyone can learn how to play quarter, eights and sixteenth notes but having a feel for a song is a very special skill. I realised early on in my playing career that to accurately reproduce Ringo's drumming style, I needed to master the use of my left hand in accentuating my fills around the kit, while focusing on that relaxed swing he brought to every note. The challenge for myself, even today, is to allow that feel to come through without rushing the tempo.

"One of the things that always amazed me about Ringo's drumming," Kelly continued, "is his ability to reproduce a nearly flawless tempo take after take. His drumming is consistently spot on; he never overplayed his part, and always provided exactly what the song needed. As a young drummer learning the craft, I try to model these tenets of playing into my own style. Ringo, for me, and I'm sure many others influenced by him, is the reference point used as to what a great drummer is and should be. I've always argued with my musical colleagues that The Beatles don't become The Beatles without Ringo's unique style of drumming.

"Ringo's drumming is as varied as The Beatles catalogue with a progression that is in lockstep with the other three lads' musical development. From my perspective," said Kelly, "I look at Ringo's drumming in terms of three categories: early, middle and later years."

Lou Longobardi suggests a fourth era too, and their views bring an incredible focus to the evolution of Ringo's drumming.

1. **Please Please Me** to **Help!**:

"His early drumming on 'Please Please Me', 'All My Loving', 'She Loves You', and maybe the quintessential one, 'Roll Over Beethoven', probably the most representative sound of Beatlemania. 'Tell Me Why' has that prominent swing feel, indicative of the Big Band sounds of the '40s that were a signature rhythm throughout these early recordings. Hallmark styles: Ringo swishing hi-hats; emphasis on the 2 and 4 upbeats.

But the swishing open hi-hat pretty much ended in '65 with 'The Night Before'. Emphasis on the 2nd and 4th upbeats *(i.e. the '2 and' and the '4 and')*. This is a hallmark of Ringo's early style, especially in the *Please Please Me* and *With The Beatles* albums."

Best examples:
"Twist & Shout"; "Boys"', "All My Loving" *(except he mixes it with heavy downbeats in the choruses, which is great)*, "Little Child", "Please Mr Postman" and "Money".

"In the same way his upbeat snare strike is louder than the downbeat strike, his 'machine gun rolls' always ended louder than their start. Eerily, this is a precursor to the backwards drum/cymbal sounds that will come in 1967, where the sound fades in and up to the louder attack point. Ringo's early rolls always faded in and upward."

Longobardi also considers 'repeated' styles:
#1 "Arthur Alexander beat"
What I call the "pop-boom; tsst-pop, boom boom" repeatedly. "And these also really emphasize the upbeat: 'Anna *(Go to Him)*' and 'All I've Gotta Do'. Then, not used for two years, until '65 on 'In My Life' and 'It's Only Love': the drums are barely audible, but it's in there.

"It could have fit on any of these, but wasn't used: 'If I Fell', 'And I Love Her', 'Every Little Thing', 'I'll Be Back' and 'You're Gonna Lose that Girl'.

#2 **Heavy 2 and 4 downbeats**:
'Can't Buy Me Love', 'I Should Have Known Better', 'Things We said Today', 'Eight Days A Week', 'Baby's in Black', 'Help!' and 'Another Girl'.

#3 **Heavy 1, 2, 3, and 4 downbeats:**
'All My Loving' *(Chorus)*, 'You Can't Do That', 'When I Get Home' and 'Dizzy Miss Lizzie'.

"All of the above are done with that 'swing' feel on the cymbal."

#4 **Country & Western Songs.**
Very fast 16th note shuffle on the closed hi-hat: 'Act Naturally', 'I Don't Want to Spoil the Party', 'What Goes On', 'You Like Me Too Much'.

As an aside, Longobardi observes that "Pete Best also showed he could do this fast hi-hat work on 'Sheik of Araby'. Pete's Decca drumming is the 'best', most spot on, most spirited, and most early Ringo-like *(emphasis on the 2 and 4 upbeats)* on a Lennon/McCartney composition, mostly, 'Like Dreamers Do', but even 'Hello Little Girl'. Maybe he could have done the same as Ringo did, having been given the chance to work on more Lennon/McCartney songs."

2. Rubber Soul and parts of **Revolver:**

"I like to think of this as Ringo as 'percussionist/drummer', says Longobardi, and Kelly considers it Ringo's "middle drumming years (1965-1967) on 'She Said, She Said', 'A Day In The Life' and 'Rain' give us a window into the experimental side of Ringo's drumming."

"His use of the drums is less of providing a backbeat, and more of providing "percussive sounds" to the songs," said Longobardi, "unlike the early period where he drives the songs; now the songs drive him. Despite my vociferous rejection of the 'plays the song' theory, this period would be the closest example of doing just that, but I think, in a manner different from what I think is usually meant by 'playing the song'. I look at it this way: he wasn't 'playing' the song. In my mind, he was composing/creating the song, and in the process, creating a new and unique drumming style, in concert with the new and unique musical styles being created by John, Paul and George in the studio. He was doing so because he had to e.g. there was no previous song like 'Wait' to mimic the drumming of. A new style had to be created, and Ringo had to be the one to create it, unless John or Paul thought of one first, like with 'Ticket to Ride'. Of course, this also continued into Period #3, with the likes of 'Lucy in the Sky', 'Strawberry Fields Forever' etc.

"So, in this creative milieu, he virtually abandoned the styles/beats of his past, except he never lost their 'feel', and created a new style of drumming. But they were not 'styles' in the typical sense of the word, i.e. that could be mimicked by others, or duplicated beat for beat, or fill for fill in other songs. They were part of the 'melody' of those specific musical compositions, and those compositions alone. In my opinion, I always thought George and Ringo should have gotten composing credits."

3. Sgt. Pepper to **Magical Mystery Tour**:

Longobardi starts with Sgt. Pepper, "but can probably start this period with 'Paperback Writer'/ 'Rain'/ 'She Said'/ 'Tomorrow Never Knows'." Kelly calls this the 'creative drumming' period, though Longobardi likes to call it "punctuation drumming, almost timpanic. A lot of 'funny fills' off the bass drum and closed hi-hat, punctuated by hesitative rests throughout the fills. The best examples are 'A Day in the Life', 'Hello Goodbye', 'Strawberry Fields Forever' and the Revolver tracks previously mentioned."

4. **The White Album** to **Let It Be**:

"His later drumming years on 'Happiness Is A Warm Gun', 'Here Comes The Sun', and the Abbey Road side two medley," says Kelly, "show Ringo's maturity as a drummer and his ability to handle complex time sequences. For example, in 'Here Comes The Sun', he moves effortlessly in the complex bridge sequence of 11/8, 4/4 and 7/8 time signatures.

"In total, Ringo was and continues to be an inspiration that is a part of my musical genetic make-up. He was more than a drummer…he was our hero."

(David Bedford Interview 2017).

The Swish of The Cymbal

As Kelly mentioned, one of the unique aspects of Ringo's drumming style was his use of the hi-hat cymbals. How many times have you watched footage of The Beatles playing on stage? Ringo perched on his raised platform, smiling as he drums, playing his hi-hat with his left foot almost motionless on the pedal as the drumstick crosses the top of the cymbal from side to side. Lou Longobardi concurs with that iconic image.

"Ringo swaying to the music was a very powerful image, and when I think of him playing 'Long Tall Sally' at the Washington D.C. Concert, it is just amazing and fun to watch." According to drummer Alex Cain, "The famous 'Ringo Swish' was something he perfected, which had the effect of filling out the sound of the band and making the kit sound bigger.

"Furthermore, he had a unique way of playing the open hi-hat where his right hand moved laterally left to right rather than up and down, something we hadn't seen a drummer do before. He achieved this by using his foot to keep the hi-hat cymbals ever so slightly apart, and striking the top cymbal so that it hit the bottom cymbal making an open 'swishing' sound. The hi-hats were only closed when the song determined it, for example, going into the bridge or possibly a chorus, at which point his foot would instinctively move up and down while he played the hi-hat in the 'normal' operating position. A fantastic example of this is 'It Won't Be Long'. Notice how the hi-hats are snapped shut at the onset of the middle 8." *(David Bedford Interview 2016)*

Mike Rice met Ringo not long after he had joined, when The Beatles were playing on one of the famous Mersey Ferry River Cruises. As Ringo was setting up his drums, Mike approached Ringo and they began talking drums, and especially the hi-hat. Mike was curious, and so he asked Ringo: "What height do you have your adjustment screw at?" he said, and was met with a blank stare from Ringo. "I looked at the hi-hat, and there was no adjustment screw." To the non-drummer, this means nothing, so Rice explained what this does. "The

adjustment screw sets the angle of the bottom of the two cymbals to make the right sound that you are looking for. With no screw there, this gave that open swish sound that he became famous for." *(David Bedford Interview 2017)*

Just as cymbals can be adjusted, drums, more importantly, need tuning. As producer Steve Levine observed: "Drums have a note; they can be tuned. An example from an orchestra: timpanis are tuned to different notes, which is why they have four or five drums, and the pedal allows them to vary the tuning. With Ringo's drum sound, it is very open on the hi-hat. Having the head on the bass drum was normal. Then as you look later on, not only has the drum head come off, but there are towels and tea-towels in there to dampen the sound, which mutes the note – like on 'Come Together' – making a more upfront sound. Even though he fundamentally stuck to the same kit, the sound changed as musical taste changed. They went from one mic over the drums to having multiple mics in the '60s, so The Beatles never worked in the 16-track world, but they did in their solo careers.

"Listen to 'A Day In The Life'. The drums are tuned in completely with the song, and that was achieved by changing the timing of the tape. If you listen to those tom-toms, it sounds like they were recorded at a slightly higher speed, and then slowed down to fit in with the song. Tuning the drums is a real skill, so that it is in tune with the song." *(David Bedford Interview 2017)*.

The Engineers

Longobardi raises an interesting point about the development of the drum sound that Ringo perfected with The Beatles, and that was the work of the engineers. As we have seen and heard when the albums were remastered, there was an opportunity to hear more of the drumming sound being created by Ringo. But it also allows us to hear what the engineers, like Norman Smith and Geoff Emerick, did to help create the right sound, and they should receive their credit.

Ringo on Solos

"I never did any drum solos, no," Ringo said adamantly. "Never have: never wanted to, even at the beginning. While we were still at this holiday camp *(Butlins),* we used to play in the Rockin' Calypso, but on Sunday, the big night, they had a big theater there and they'd have name acts, and the local people working there would be on the bill. So we were working with the Happy Wanderers, an English street band with a big walking bass drum, trumpet, clarinet, and they were like a walking jazz band. They used to walk around the streets of London playing songs, and then the guy would walk around with the hat. They became very well known. At the end of the show, it used to get to the solo and I used to let their drummer take the solo on the bass drum: 'boom, boom, boom, boom.' I would never do the solo, even then. Never liked them." Ringo told George Martin in a documentary how much he hated solos, and that if he was asked to recreate the famous solo on *"A Day In A Life"*, which they had to persuade him to do, he couldn't do it. He just played what he wanted at that moment.

"I think that the drums are an emotional instrument and there's no melody. It's not like you can sit in a room with a guitar or piano and play. It's only "boom, boom, boom" or "rata tat tat," and there's no real melody there. That's why I dislike solos. I don't care which drummer does a solo—it's not melodic and he just has an ego problem." *(Modern Drummer December 1981)*

The Creative Input?

With Ringo having such a unique style, the question is often asked as to whether he contributed to the song's development, or just told what to do by whoever had written the song, and how much input was there from George Martin." Well, at the beginning, George Martin dictated a certain amount," Ringo said, "and then it was John and Paul's writing to consider. See, what helped me a lot was that I had three frustrated drummers around, because everyone wants to be a drummer for some reason. John could play and Paul could play and George could play, but they each had one standard style. We all have one standard style, but they only had one sort of groove where I have two or three. John and I used to have, not arguments, but discussions, because we'd be playing all these records and he'd say, 'Like that,' and I'm saying, 'But John, there's two drummers on there,' and he could never hear there were two drummers. They'd play stuff with two drummers on it and the three of them each had their own idea of what the drummer should do and then I had my idea. So all I would do was combine my idea, their three ideas, and the ideas of two drummers on a record. They got what they were given and it worked.

"On the finished tunes, they'd sit at the piano and play them. Then we'd go through several different changes of how we all felt it should be done. Mainly, the writer had the definite idea, but if anyone did anything to change it and it was good and moved into a place they enjoyed, that's how it would be.
There was a lot of open-mindedness. There were very few tracks with, like, the definite idea—this is how it has to be. Mostly, if someone came up with anything that was different and worked, then everyone would go along with it.
I was allowed to create anything I could as long as it worked, and it was the same with the guitar or the bass or the piano. It was all the same, but the difference was that it had to fit around their song.

"But that helped me to play, and also, the long hours in Germany, you know, you soon get your act together. And the style was there from the beginning. It's the same style as I play now, although I can never do a fill in the same place at the same time, ever. I could never double a fill. Some of the fills I do today, I've done for 15 years, though if you listen to the record, the style has changed in its way. But there's still stuff coming out that I did before, that I still enjoy. It's not exactly the same, but it's similar. When in doubt, I half the speed of the track, where drummers will do a fill maybe twice as fast as I."
(Modern Drummer December 1981)

"The Rhythm's In The Guitar"

When the group consisted of just John, Paul and George, McCartney said that he used to tell potential promoters that, even though they didn't have a drummer, that "the rhythm's in the guitar." But did this affect the way that they thought about the rhythm in the group?

This was yet another way that Ringo developed a unique sound, contributing to a drumming style that stood out from all others, adding another magical component to The Beatles' music.

EXAMINING RINGO STARR'S DRUMMING
IN RECORDINGS

Once Ringo found his place in The Beatles, he produced some of the most memorable drumming performances to ever appear on a record. However, there are a couple of bootleg recordings of The Beatles with Ringo, including the famous "Star Club Recordings" made in Hamburg at the end of 1962.

The Cavern Club Rehearsal - October 1962

The first recording that came to light involves a rehearsal at the Cavern club, probably around October 1962. The surviving recording includes attempts at playing "One After 909" and "I Saw Her Standing There". In his book, *The Unreleased Beatles*, Richie Unterberger suggests that the reason for making the recording was possibly to show George Martin that they had a wider catalogue of original recordings that could be considered for a potential album. The recordings show the songs at an early stage, and certainly nowhere near as good as the finished songs. It is clear that Ringo is still getting used to playing with his new bandmates, and that the songs are at the beginning of the embryonic process.

Mike Rice, who watched both Pete Best and Ringo Starr play in Liverpool, listened to these tracks with interest. "With that first recording of 'I Saw Her Standing There', he is just playing a straight beat that any drummer could do, with almost no fills, a bit like a guide track. When they play 'One After 909', you can hear some more variation in the beat and he throws a few fills in there, which is better. But certainly nothing more than any other drummer could do. It's not the Ringo of a few years later, but he is obviously just learning to play with the band." *(David Bedford Interview 2017)*

The Star Club, Hamburg - December 1962

Some of the most famous unreleased recordings featuring The Beatles were recorded at the Star Club at the end of 1962, probably over more than one night. It is hard to judge any of The Beatles on these performances, those it is an interesting stop on the journey between the September '62 recording sessions, and the Please Please Me LP that would be issued just three months later. Notable absences are their current single, "Love Me Do" and "P.S. I Love You", and the song they had only just recorded, "Please Please Me". But it is a final glimpse of The Beatles leaving their rocking roots behind. What is interesting, is that the only original song in the list is "Ask Me Why". Where is their current single "Love Me Do", or "Please Please Me" or any other original compositions?

"I know it must be a rough recording, but all you can hear is the hissing of the hi-hat, and if you were to compare to Pete Best, where is the bass drum? You can bet Pete's bass drum would have been bouncing the sound off the walls! Again, this is not a recording you would use to showcase your talents, because Ringo is playing well, but it is virtually all covers of standard rock 'n' roll songs that any competent drummer could do." *(David Bedford Interview 2017)*

Studio Outtakes - 5th March 1963

As they worked towards making their debut album, The Beatles had decided to give "One After 909" another go, and this session possibly consigned the song to the "could do better" file. This was John's rock 'n' roll roots, which he was clearly clinging on to desperately.

However, his comments during the session show some of his frustrations with the swing style that Ringo had brought to the group, as he berated Ringo during Take 1: "What are you doing? Are you out of your mind? Do the boom-boom-boom-boom," *(The Unreleased Beatles)* which was, ironically, the style Pete Best was famous for. John was still a frustrated rock 'n' roller.

The Beatles On Record

To examine what Ringo brought to The Beatles, drummers Alex Cain and Terry McCusker, authors of *Ringo Starr and the Beatles Beat*, give their critical appraisal of his drumming on some of The Beatles' greatest songs. Having evaluated "Love Me Do" from their first LP, *Please Please Me*, released in March 1963, we see how Ringo's drumming evolved alongside the songwriting talents of John and Paul, and George as well, and took drumming to a new level.

As evidenced on each single and album, Ringo pushed the boundaries, not just on drums, but through the extensive use of percussive instruments like maracas, claves, bongo drums – and even hand claps. A bigger challenge to the drummer was the experimentation with the time signature of the songs, from the standard 4/4 rhythm that was the backbone of rock 'n' roll to changing the time signature mid-song, as on "Good Day Sunshine" which is in 4/4, 3/4 and 5/5, or the more obscure 12/8 signature on "Norwegian Wood" and "This Boy".

(Ringo Starr and the Beatles Beat)

At each stage, Ringo's drumming was up to the task, often under the direction of the songwriter, especially Paul, an accomplished drummer himself.

Their relationship was pushed to the limit during the recording of *The White Album*, leading to Ringo walking out, and Paul stepping in on drums until they persuaded the drummer to return.

For many, there would be no "Beatles sound" without the songwriting talents of Lennon and McCartney, or the guitar work of George Harrison. Ringo could be considered superfluous. However, what Cain and McCusker show is that Ringo's contribution to the group's hallmark sound was just as important.

Join us on a chronological journey through the highlights of Ringo's drumming career with The Beatles, as we examine his progress alongside the group's progress in the studio.

Recording "Please Please Me"
(Album released 10th March 1963 UK)

For The Beatles' first album, Ringo used his Premier Mahogany Duroplastic drum kit which served him well through the marathon recording session on 11th February 1963. Starting at 10am, The Beatles recorded the ten songs that, along with the four sides of their first two singles, would comprise the LP. Ten takes of "There's A Place" and nine takes of "I Saw Her Standing There" (then known as "Seventeen") were recorded. After three hours, it was time for a lunch break, but The Beatles wanted to continue rehearsing. Tape operator Richard Langham said, "When we came back, they'd been playing right through. We couldn'tbelieve it. We had never seen a group work right through their lunch break before."

(The Complete Beatles Recording Sessions)

RINGO STARR:
The Beat Behind the Beatles by Robyn Flans

Richard Starkey was born into a working-class home in the Dingle, a rough neighborhood in Liverpool, England, on July 7, 1940. A sickly boy, he spent several years in a children's hospital, and while there he was taught how to play drums by a percussion band that showed up regularly to entertain the kids. At 16 he bought a $3 bass drum and built a kit around it out of tin cans.

In 1959, Richard—now called Ringo—became popular around Liverpool drumming for Rory Storme & the Hurricanes, a skiffle group that would evolve into the city's top rock 'n' roll band...until another outfit called the Beatles started competing with them.

When Ringo joined the opposition in mid-August 1962, he hit the ground running, for the Beatles had just landed a contract with EMI and were beginning one of the most remarkable careers in music history. Within a year and a half, Ringo was an international celebrity.

Because of his sweet, placid nature—coupled with the fact that he rarely sang and didn't begin writing songs until late in the Beatles' career—Ringo's talented, often volatile mates overshadowed him. He was often perceived as the "dull" or "dumb" Beatle.

However, as John Lennon remarked to Tom Snyder on the *Tomorrow* show in 1974, "He ain't dumb."

After the 1970 breakup of the group, Ringo enjoyed a string of Top 40 charters, including two #1 hits, "Photograph" (which he wrote with his pal George Harrison) and "You're Sixteen," in 1973. He also starred in a dozen or so films, including *That'll Be the Day*.

Now closing in on 50, Ringo is married to his second wife, Barbara Bach, and has been a grandfather for five years. He returned to the limelight last year with a successful 30-city American tour. He also, in his own words, "returned to the land of the living" by entering a detox center and ending his alcohol dependency.

We spoke to Ringo in Beverly Hills.

Ringo was a Teddy Boy during his time with Rory Storme & the Hurricanes.

SH-BOOM: I understand you changed your name to Ringo Starr while you were with Rory Storme's band?
RINGO: We all thought we'd change our names because show biz means changing your name. [Laughs] So the guitarist called himself Johnny Guitar, and in the end, because we're all English, we all picked cowboy names like Ty Hardin, Lou O'Brien, Rory Storme and Ringo Starr—because of the rings, which I always wore then.
SH-BOOM: Did the West fascinate you?
RINGO: Yeah, cowboys. Your cowboys were great heroes to us. To an English

Ringo: The Beat Behind The Beatles

The afternoon recording session began at 2.30pm, continuing until 6pm.

They started with seven takes of "A Taste Of Honey", with Paul double-tracking his lead vocals. They also recorded eight takes of "Do You Want To Know A Secret", which George sang. John then began recording his harmonica overdub onto "There's A Place" (which took only three attempts), and handclaps – which were to become a feature of The Beatles' recordings – were added to "I Saw Her Standing There". The final song of the afternoon session was "Misery", another Lennon-McCartney original.

The third and final session of the day took place from 7.30pm-10.45pm, although it was scheduled to end at 10pm, the usual finishing time at EMI. The Beatles started off with 13 takes of "Hold Me Tight", which didn't make it onto the first album, but appeared on their second LP, with The Beatles. The group then recorded three takes of Arthur Alexander's "Anna (Go To Him)", followed by a single recording of "Boys", the latter featuring Ringo simultaneously on vocals and drums. This was Ringo's debut as a soloist, performing one of his favourites. Next, it was George's turn to take the lead on "Chains", written by Goffin and King, and made famous by The Cookies. The first of four takes made the final cut. The Beatles then performed The Shirelles' "Baby It's You" in only three takes, with John on lead vocal. Having started the day with ten takes of "There's A Place", they were able to get the best version of "Baby It's You" in only three.

By now, it was 10pm and EMI was set to close for the night. There was, however, one final song to record – "Twist And Shout", the Isley Brothers' number, with John taking the lead. By now, they had been recording for 12 hours, and their voices were shot, especially John's. "They only had one chance to do it right. John sucked a couple more Zubes (throat sweets), had a bit of a gargle with milk, and away we went," engineer Norman Smith recalled.

(The Complete Beatles Recording Sessions)

The Beatles channelled all of their energy from months of stage performances into one final dynamic, vocal-shredding performance, with John, by now, singing bare-chested. "The last song nearly killed me," Lennon said. "My voice wasn't the same for a long time after; every time I swallowed it was like sandpaper. I was always bitterly ashamed of it because I could sing it better than that, but now it doesn't bother me. You can hear that I'm just a frantic guy doing his best." *(Anthology)* They actually managed two takes of the song, the first one selected for the album.

The 11th February recordings, along with *Love Me Do* and *P.S. I Love You* *(The Andy White versions)* and *""Please Please Me""* and *"Ask Me Why"* *(both recorded with Ringo on 26th November 1962)*, comprised The Beatles' debut album, *"Please Please Me"*, released on 22nd March 1963. The rest, as they say, is history.

As Ringo's drum kits evolved, so did his drumming. We have selected some highlights from Ringo's tenure as The Beatles' drummer, though you may have your own candidates. Do you agree with our experts? Listen again to the tracks, and pay special attention to Ringo. You'll gain a new appreciation for his drumming and percussive prowess.

1. "I Feel Fine"
(Single released 27th November 1964 UK)

This tune was only intended as an album song, but the finished recording was so good, it became a single. Lennon recalled: "Going into the studio one morning, I said to Ringo, 'I've written this song, but it's lousy.' But we tried it, complete with riff, and it sounded like an A-side, so we decided to release it just like that."

(Anthology)

Analysis

"I Feel Fine" possesses the (in)famous and groundbreaking opening bars of guitar feedback – yet it's the prominence of the drum pattern that is arguably its most striking feature. By late 1964, The Beatles were afforded more time to develop their songs in the studio, and the drum parts were no different; they would evolve.

Utilizing his snare more freely than usual, Ringo developed his drum part throughout the early takes, feeling his way, and formulating the beat that was needed. By Take 6, however, it was clear that the drum part was not doing the song justice. Probably at McCartney's insistence, Ringo took a cue from Ray Charles' "What'd I Say", with movement from tom to cross-stick snare, and an interplay between drums and ride cymbal bell. This was not a massive shift from the earlier takes. Ringo is essentially playing the same arrangement, but with greater fluidity than the 'stuttering' pattern produced by staying on the snare. He instead allows time to trade off *(and be more inventive with)* the bell of the ride cymbal.

Perhaps to lengthen the song, the guitar solo is extended with a 4-bar guitar break, Ringo reintroducing the song with an offbeat feel between the snare and a combination of bass drum and floor tom.

The use here of the pattern from "What'd I Say" is particularly interesting, as it is Ringo's performance of this song while deputising for Pete Best that proved to be the defining moment of his career – the point at which John, Paul, and George instinctively knew he was the right man for the job.

Alex Cain and Terry McCusker

2. "Ticket to Ride"
(Single released 9th April 1965 UK and on LP Help!)

When "Ticket to Ride", the first song from the *Help!* soundtrack was released, the music press saw it as a new direction for the Fab Four. For a start, it was over three minutes long, their first single to achieve this feat. John saw it as "a new sound for the time. It was pretty f**king heavy for then if you go and look at the charts for what other music people were making." *(Anthology)*

It was also the first Beatles' song recorded in the now customary manner of laying down the rhythm track first, followed by other takes and overdubs, with the extra layers of the song built up on four-track machines. Paul also played lead guitar on a Beatles song for the first time.

Ringo's drumming was a particular feature that John admired. "It's a heavy record," he said, "and the drums are heavy, too. That's why I like it." *(Anthology)*

Analysis

Possibly one of Ringo's most lauded tracks, "Ticket To Ride" provides a feast of drumming invention and originality, sounding unlike any record yet released. At the heart of the song is Ringo's magnificent drum pattern, embellished with a refreshing variety of tom fills and no-nonsense tambourine. The drum pattern, apparently suggested by McCartney, sees the snare falling on the 2nd and '3 and' beats to the bar, with the tom on the '4 and' beat. Alongside the prominent placement of a tambourine from the off – on the 2nd and 4th beats – we have Harrison's Duane Eddy-style downward guitar strokes, providing a percussive constant while lending the song a stark syncopation.

The final verse sees added urgency and fluidity provided by a variation on the main pattern heard earlier, with the snare now falling alongside the tambourine on beats 2 and 4. Muted off-beat handclaps on the play-out mimic the main drum pattern of the song, the tambourine injecting urgency. Also worthy of mention, Ringo plays his snare and tom with both hands, adding another layer of depth to an already atmospheric soundscape. The Beatles often played the song live, and though it was a challenge to make the drums sound as full as the recording, Ringo drove the beat with strength, discipline, and confidence, carrying it off with ease. *Alex Cain and Terry McCusker*

3. "Rain"
(Single released 10th June 1966 UK)

One of the most underrated Beatles songs reveals Ringo at his best. "My favourite piece of me is what I did on 'Rain'", Ringo explained. "I think it was the first time I used this trick of starting a break by hitting the hi-hat first instead of going directly to a drum off the hi-hat. I think it's the best out of all the records I've ever made. 'Rain' blows me away." *(The Beatles: Off The Record)*

Although credited to John, Paul also contributed to the piece. "Songs have traditionally treated rain as a bad thing," McCartney said, "and what we got on to was that it's no bad thing." The Beatles were exploring a heightened consciousness through LSD. However, as McCartney observed, it wasn't the lyrics of the song or even the melody that made the song a gem, but the recording processes used to bring it to life. *(Many Years From Now)*

In 1966, The Beatles began experimenting with tempo. They would record a song at a fast tempo, and then slow it down, essentially transforming the song. On "Rain", Paul felt that nothing worked better than the marriage of his bass guitar and Ringo's drums. "The drums became a giant drum kit....we got a big, ponderous, thunderous backing and then we worked on top of that as normal so that it didn't sound like a slowed-down thing. It just had a big ominous noise to it." *(Many Years From Now)*

Ringo's performance here – and certainly one of his personal favourites – is quite unique and remarkable. He busily attacks his kit from the get-go, with fills every few bars as the pleasure takes. Of note is the empathy between bass and drums, enhanced with a "trippy" feel by way of tape/speed variation.

Analysis

A sharp, attention-grabbing sixteenth-note snare pattern introduces the song and sets the tone. Everything here is purely instinctive and bears all the hallmarks of his left-handed drumming on a right-hand kit. Of particular note throughout is the movement between hi-hat and snare, at [0.16], rather than moving from snare to tom as he had moments before. A prominent tambourine simultaneously overdubbed with the backing vocals plays on the 4 beats of the introduction, then on beats 2 and 4 until the final two verses, thus keeping a constant focal point around which the drums move. Towards the end of the second verse, we hear an isolated bar of 2/4 meter. This was more likely played by accident than by design, with all four Beatles "feeling" their way through the passage while frantically glancing back and forth at each other.

The interplay between bass guitar and drums at [2.24] below is truly innovative, as is the dramatically syncopated fill and melodious bass that bring it cascading back in.

With "Rain", Ringo sets a precedent for the expansive approach to his work on *Revolver* and Sgt. Pepper, and he carries it off with aplomb.

Alex Cain and Terry McCusker

4. "Tomorrow Never Knows"
(On LP Revolver released 5th August 1966 UK)

John, Paul and George called Ringo the greatest rock 'n' roll drummer, even as The Beatles' sound drifted east with George's love for Indian music and the sitar, in particular. At the same time, Lennon decided to open his mind and let it drift, embracing the psychedelic thoughts of Timothy Leary and Richard Alpert, especially their 1964 book, *The Psychedelic Experience: A Manual Based On The Tibetan Book Of The Dead*. Lennon and McCartney had purchased the book at the Indica bookshop, where John delved into the book. There, on page 14 of Leary's introduction were the words that would inspire the opening line of "Tomorrow Never Knows": "Whenever in doubt, turn off your mind, relax, float downstream". *(Many Years From Now)*

Paul and John were amazed that so many Indian songs were all played in just one chord. McCartney recalled a meeting with George Martin at Brian's house in Belgravia, London, where "John got his guitar out and started doing 'Tomorrow Never Knows' and it was all in one chord." Paul gives Martin credit for being open-minded. The producer was always willing to listen to what they had to say, whatever it was, and not just walk away, or say, "Bloody hell; it's terrible!".

(Many Years From Now)

Ringo is a minimalist drummer. When you listen to what he did with a small set, it is simply brilliant."

"Ringo started with a Premier kit, and the tone of the kit wasn't as good; it was a higher pitch," said Ringo's kit expert Gary Astridge. "He then had four Ludwig kits; two were called 'Downbeat', with smaller toms and bass drum. Next he had the Super Classic, which had a larger bass drum, and was easier to tune. It had a more tonal quality to the low or high tones. Ringo uses the same drum heads; he doesn't change them, as many drummers can change them all the time. There's a lot of miles on them!

"On Abbey Road, he was using the calf-skin heads which have a warmer feel, and then he would use tea-towels to dampen the sound. After that, it depends upon the material – how thick the weave is, or how he folds it up. Furthermore, whether it is on top of the head, or using tape – masking or duct tape – then where the microphones are positioned around the kit." "So we were playing and making these records," recalled Ringo, "and then we sort of got free formed rock in our own way, though it was a lot tighter than acid rock because we had songwriters and we did songs and didn't just jam. We went through a lot of changes on records. Then in '68, I got the kit with the calf skins and that changed everything. Then it really became tom-tom city because of the calf and wood. When you're touring, everyone thanks God that the plastic heads were invented because you're playing outside in the heat, or the wet, or whatever, and skins are very hard to handle. But since '66, we were in a controlled environment, in the studio, so the temperature was always the same and you could deal with calf. You can't deal with them outside, although drummers have for thousands of years, but if we had played Pasadena and Denver, one night the skins would be very taut and in Pasadena it's soggy, so they'd get real messy and you'd be tuning forever. So plastic heads were a God-send on the road, but then when we were just in the studio, I ordered this kit and I had calf skins put on." *(Modern Drummer December 1981)*

"George always wanted Ringo to try playing more drums. George went to do some recording with Jackie Lomax in L.A. where Hal Blaine had his own kit, with seven concert toms made from fibreglass. George asked Hal for a set, which he shipped over to the UK for Ringo, who sat down at his kit with the new toms, played them once, then said, 'get them out of here'. Ringo is a minimalist drummer. When you listen to what he did with a small set, it is simply brilliant."

Ringo took possession of his first Ludwig drum kit, an Oyster Black Pearl "Downbeat" drum kit, on 12th May 1963. This consisted of an 8" x 12" tom, 14" x 14" floor tom, 14" x 20" bass drum, and 5.5" x 14" snare drum with chrome-over-brass (COB) rims. This first Ludwig kit was purchased from Drum City in London and was delivered to Alpha Television Studios in Aston, Birmingham, Warwickshire, England where The Beatles were making their first appearance as headliners on Thank Your Lucky Stars. Ringo last used his Premier kit during the rehearsal of this show and used his new Ludwig kit for the performance. One of the most significant dates in Beatles history was 9th February 1964, when they appeared on The Ed Sullivan Show in New York. Ringo, with the help of Drum City in London, visited Manny's in New York, where he purchased a Ludwig Oyster Black Pearl Downbeat kit. Ringo had brought his Ludwig Oyster Black Pearl snare drum, cymbals, and a new Beatles drumhead with him from England. The day before the show, Manny's delivered a used Ludwig White Marine Pearl Super Classic kit, which Ringo used for Saturday's rehearsal.

His new Oyster Black Pearl kit, which would become the one most associated with him, was delivered for the Sunday morning dress rehearsal. Ringo drum expert Gary Astridge revealed that when the rack tom was mounted, it was mistakenly placed upside down and was used that way for all the performances.

However, on returning to the UK, Ringo opted for a new kit – the Ludwig Oyster Black Pearl "Super Classic" drum kit comprised of a 9" x 13" tom, 16" x 16" floor tom, 14" x 22" bass drum, and a 5.5" x 14" snare. This set was acquired on 31st May 1964 and became the most widely used by Ringo for both recording and touring. It also made numerous appearances in promotional photographs and films including "Hello Goodbye", "I Am The Walrus", "Hey Jude" and "Revolution". There was an exception, though. For the purposes of the 1965 U.S. tour, Ringo acquired a second Ludwig Oyster Black Pearl "Super Classic" drum kit, with specifications identical to the Ludwig kit he was using at the time. In 2015, the Jazz Festival snare drum from the Sullivan kit was sold at auction for $75,000, and the "Sullivan" bass drum head sold for a staggering $2,050,000.

The Golden Snare
The final drum has an air of mystery around it. On September 5, 1964, the Ludwig Drum Company presented Ringo with a Super–Sensitive snare, plated in gold. Pictures were taken of the official presentation, and then it seemed to disappear. Only five were made and the lucky recipients were Ringo Starr, Chicago percussionist Bobby Christian, Dave Brubek's drummer Joe Morello, Ludwig marketing director and Chicago Symphony Orchestra drummer Dick Schory, and Indiana University's George Gaber, who was the first-call percussionist of many famous conductors. Each owner's name wasengraved on a small, gold-plated name tag fastened to the outer shell.

On his 70th birthday in 2010 – almost 46 years later – Ringo's golden snare resurfaced at the Metropolitan Museum of Art in New York. Regrettably, it was in a sorry state, having been hammered by an unknown drummer's relentless play through the decades. Ringo certainly played it at some point, but it is not known who left it looking like it did when it turned up.

At the end of 1968, Ringo decided to change kits again, although he stuck with Ludwig. This time, he acquired a Ludwig Maple "Hollywood" drum kit, which consisted of an 8" x 12" tom, a 9" x 13" tom, 16" x 16" floor tom, 14" x 22" bass drum, and a 5.5" x 14" snare drum with chrome-over-brass (COB) rims. This kit was used on the Let It Be and Abbey Road albums as well as the famous rooftop concert on 30 January 1969. Ringo later used this kit when he performed with George Harrison at the "Concert For Bangladesh" and on the 1971 album, *B.B. King Live In London*.

Gary Astridge with Ringo

The title of the song was pure Ringo. As Lennon pointed out, "That's me in my Tibetan Book of the Dead period. I took one of Ringo's malapropisms as the title, to sort of take the edge off the heavy philosophical lyrics." *(All We Are Saying)*

Analysis

"Tomorrow Never Knows" pushes Ringo's drum kit and his idiosyncratic technique to the forefront of the mix, and as on "Ticket To Ride", he takes centre stage. The relentless, repetitive pattern, played with such feel and solidity by Starr, is taken to a different level by engineer Geoff Emerick's close-microphone technique and removal of the bottom drum heads.

Utilizing his ambidextrous ability to the full, Ringo maintains right-handed constant eighth notes on the ride cymbal, drawing powerful sixteenth note beats from the tom-tom with his left hand. With this approach, Ringo is able to draw more sound from his cymbal than he would otherwise have been able to if he had struck the tom-tom with each hand, keeping the track awash with sound.
With such a simple, repetitive drum track, creative use of the tambourine provides a variety throughout, weaving and snaking its way around Ringo's drum track to great effect. A truly mesmerizing sonic experience.

Alex Cain and Terry McCusker

5. "Strawberry Fields Forever"
(Single released 17th February 1967 UK)

One of The Beatles' greatest ever songs, Lennon's nostalgic look back to the Salvation Army orphanage behind his childhood home in Liverpool, had been conceived in Almeria, Spain during the quiet times between filming scenes for *How I Won The War*.

At the end of the summer of 1966, having ended their touring days for good, The Beatles began to spend more time in the studio. The weeks turned into months of groundbreaking work and, in February 1967, at Brian Epstein's insistence, *"Strawberry Fields Forever"* and *"Penny Lane"* were issued as a single. They would never make it onto the upcoming album for which they were intended: *Sgt. Pepper's Lonely Hearts Club Band*.

Whereas *Please Please Me* was largely recorded in one day, in straight takes, recording techniques had improved to such a degree that they could now use multi-tracked recorders. If we look at those who appeared on *"Strawberry Fields Forever"*, and the range of instruments used, we see how far the group had progressed in less than five years:

John Lennon: Vocals, acoustic guitar, piano, bongos, Mellotron
Paul McCartney: Mellotron, bass, electric guitar, timpani, bongos
George Harrison: Electric guitar, svarmandal, timpani, maracas
Ringo Starr: Drums, percussion
Mal Evans: Tambourine
Neil Aspinall: Güiro
Terry Doran: Maracas
Tony Fisher, Greg Bowen, Derek Watkins, Stanley Roderick: Trumpets
John Hall, Derek Simpson, Norman Jones: Cellos

When the engineers joined two versions of the song together, recorded at different speeds, they unknowingly created a masterpiece.

Analysis

In "Strawberry Fields Forever", we hear Ringo very much at the fore, and once again proving he's not just along for the ride. His display adds a weight and touch purely sympathetic to the song, and thankfully so, as Ringo (probably under instruction) declines to fill out the song with the usual steady beat. Hi-hats are entirely absent, relying on the bass and snare drums to keep time. Unusual for a Beatles recording (of any period), the tambourine is largely absent. Instead we have maracas, prominent in the mix from the start, also filling the gap usually reserved for hi-hats.

Drums enter the fray with a nice loose fill over two bars before moving into a solid snare, and bass drum beat. These rich, languid fills punctuate throughout, the interplay between toms and snare (0.14 and 1.43) particularly notable. As hinted at the song's introduction (below), just when you thought the song was settling into a straight 4/4 measure, the meter is dictated by the evocative lyrics:

4/4 -

    2/4 - "Nothing to get

       4/4 - hung about"…...

          3/4 - "Straw-be-rry Fields For…

            4/4 - ever…."

Ringo was a master of translating and conveying his bandmates' erratic use of meter (time) and, here, he achieves this with a simple combination of bass drum and snare.

The completed release of "Strawberry Fields Forever" is a composite of two versions differing in tempo, cleverly masked not only by engineer Geoff Emerick's quite brilliant edit at 0.59 – across "go-ing to" – but also Ringo's hurried drum fill. When coupled with a variation in tape speed, the change in tempo adds to the deceptive backwards cymbal.

Additionally for good measure, at 2.11, in the absence of drums or percussion, and providing the rhythm and purpose, George Martin introduces John's current 'flavour of the month' – the recording of a cymbal strike looped and played backward. At 2.32, we have the addition of overdubbed and accented snare, beefing up the already busy drum track.

Ringo's bass drum punctuation of the chorus (bars 13 and 14 above) is mirrored by a floor tom at the song's finale, preceding the lengthy instrumental coda. Ringo is clearly given license to add as much colour as possible, a task made all the easier by multiple overdubs by The Beatles and their entourage. With more than a little help from his friends, we hear a busy 16th note dampened bass drum (or over-turned floor tom) overdubbed during the choruses, and the fade in/out. The extraordinary play-out features tambourines, timpani, maracas, bongos, and backwards cymbal tapes. *Alex Cain and Terry McCusker*

6. "A Day In The Life"
(On Sgt. Pepper's Lonely Hearts Club Band LP released 1st June 1967 UK)

"The drum fills on 'A Day In The Life' are very complex things," Genesis drummer Phil Collins said in a 1992 interview. "You could take a great drummer today and say, 'I want it like that.' They wouldn't know what to do."

Analysis

While "A Day In The Life" is often regarded as Ringo's finest work, his performance is greatly enhanced by engineer Geoff Emerick's treatment of his drum kit. Having recently and similarly experimented with Ringo's drums on "Tomorrow Never Knows" from *Revolver*, Emerick slackly-tuned the top drum skins and removed the bottom skins and the front bass drum skin. Microphones were placed deep inside the drum shells while the snare drum was closely mic'd. With heavy compression added to the drum track, Ringo's drums possessed a deeper, "fatter", more open and powerful sound, lending a sense of drama and weight to the drums which would have been otherwise absent.

A great deal of Ringo's drumming on *Sgt. Pepper's Lonely Hearts Club Band* takes the form of simple timekeeping and while "A Day In The Life" is no exception, Ringo plays with an empathy and creativity that befits the song. Mimicking the rhythmical nature of the lyrics, he perfectly places his drums alongside the vocals of both Lennon and McCartney. With slight variation, his tom fills dominate, occasionally appearing unexpectedly from the shadows, punctuating and driving the song forward.

Following the simple and perhaps unusual combination of gentle "8 in the bar" maracas (played by Harrison) and subtle, low in the mix congas (Starr), Ringo introduces his drums in the second verse to great effect, subliminally referencing the sound of the car crash in the lyrics. Notice how, in this first interjection, Ringo also imitates the cadence of the lyric "He blew his mind out in a car", a device that continues to be employed throughout. From here on in, the snare is gradually introduced between the increasingly hurried and tumbling tom fills, providing power and purpose, building towards the climactic orchestral rush. As this "link" had yet to be decided upon when the drum track was recorded, Ringo knits the sections together by playing simple "4 in the bar" hi-hat beats, with occasional bass drum and cymbal crashes. While roadie Mal Evans also keeps time by counting aloud, the congas and maracas are swiftly removed from the mix.

Ringo's in a playful mood on McCartney's jaunty middle section, a heavy "4 in the bar" snare leading us through the change in tempo. Alongside a tambourine, swift bars of 2/4 are interjected to emphasize the hurried nature of the lyric. By slipping out of the 4 beats of snare into 2 beats per bar, Ringo leads us back into the main body of the song, as if we are indeed drifting off into a dream.

The final verse again sees Ringo engaging in a "call and response" with the vocal phrasing, sometimes almost matching Lennon consonant for consonant on "Now they know how many holes it takes to fill the Albert Hall", with busking fills to the orchestral finale. With the benefit of hindsight, "A Day In The Life" (and indeed the whole of *Sgt. Pepper's Lonely Hearts Club Band*) can be viewed as the pinnacle of The Beatles' creativity, with Ringo rising to the challenge magnificently. The other side of the coin is Ringo's recollection of recording the album as an opportunity to learn to play chess; he viewed his contribution as being nothing more than "another day in the office". *Alex Cain and Terry*

7. "Back in the U.S.S.R."

(On The Beatles LP, known as The White Album, released 22nd November 1968 UK)

Things came to a head for The Beatles, and Ringo in particular, during the recording of *The White Album*. At first, all was going well. As Ringo commented, "While we were recording *The White Album*, we ended up being more of a band again, and that's what I always love." However, it wasn't long before there was trouble because there were "moments of turmoil because I left the group for a while that summer." That day was 22nd August 1968, and Ringo couldn't carry on the way things were going.

He says he left "because I felt I wasn't playing great" but also because, as the last to join, he still felt like a newcomer. Ringo has often lamented that he "also felt the other three were really happy, and I was an outsider." Ringo went to see John, who was now living in Ringo's old flat in Montagu Square. He told Lennon that "I'm leaving the group because I feel unloved and out of it, and you three are really close." However, John obviously felt the same and replied, "I thought it was you three!"

Ringo then headed over to Paul's house and had the same conversation, with the same outcome. Paul assumed it was the other three. Ringo didn't even bother going to George's house. He packed his bags, grabbed the kids and went on holiday to Sardinia. *(Anthology)*

Had it been in the cards? Ken Scott, EMI engineer remembered Ringo "being uptight about something; I don't remember what, and the next thing I was told was that he'd quit the band." *(The Complete Beatles Recording Sessions)* The Beatles were going through another transition and, as George Martin observed, Ringo was probably "feeling a little bit odd because of the mental strangeness with John and Yoko, and Paul, and none of them having quite the buddiness they used to have." *(Anthology)*

For Ringo, walking away was the only option.

Was that the end of The Beatles? No. In fact, that evening, John, Paul and George entered Abbey Road to record "Back in the U.S.S.R.".

With a thoroughly despondent Ringo having left the group, it's no surprise McCartney saw fit to take up the drumming duties on this track and also Lennon's "Dear Prudence". How many of us instinctively believed it was Ringo playing on the first two tracks of *The White Album*?

Analysis

It was critical that they create a seamless percussive feel in Ringo's absence. To this end, McCartney's drum track was further enhanced with snare overdubs by both Harrison and Lennon on a separate channel. The layered effect of these multiple snare drums appears disjointed on the stereo mix, especially when joined by multiple handclaps. The effect of these dislocated overdubs is lessened on the mono mix; the overall impression is of a greater sense of solidity and continuity.

As for the main drum track, Paul lays down a forthright and powerful backing, creating a Ringo-esque performance by playing ever so slightly behind the beat. "Back In The U.S.S.R" also demonstrates McCartney's penchant for a hurried closed hi-hat timekeeping between lines and verse and chorus. Note the slightly

off-beat matched-stroke snare/tom fills at 2.14 and handclaps throughout, a percussive style which Paul would later use to great effect when drumming on his *McCartney* and *Band On The Run* solo albums. *Alex Cain and Terry McCusker*

Ringo's absence didn't last long. Suitably refreshed, having written "Octopus's Garden", and having received a telegram from John, Paul, and George, he rejoined the group. In the telegram, his bandmates wrote, "You're the best rock 'n' roll drummer in the world. Come on home, we love you." When Ringo walked back into the studio, he was touched to see it covered with flowers, thanks to George. "I felt good about myself again," Ringo said. "We'd got through that little crisis; it was great." *(Anthology)*

8. "Helter Skelter"

(On The Beatles LP, known as The White Album, released 22nd November 1968 UK)

Acknowledged by many as the first heavy rock song, Paul McCartney's "Helter Skelter" was The Beatles' most raucous composition to date, showcasing the versatility of the group that had sung "She Loves You" just a few years earlier. McCartney was obviously pleased with the outcome. "You can hear the voices cracking, and we played it so long and so often that by the end of it, you can hear Ringo saying, 'I've got blisters on my fingers.' We just tried to get it louder: 'Can't we make the drums sound louder?' That was all I really wanted to do." *(Anthology)*

Analysis

Attempting to outdo The Who's recent aural pyrotechnics on "I Can See For Miles", McCartney oddly opted for an annoyingly simple drum track, leaving the vocal, guitars and overly busy bass to do the damage. "Helter Skelter" is a great example of Ringo playing under instruction. He nails his colours to the mast with a snare/floor tom buildup before settling into a driving beat that utilizes sparse and heavy-handed '4 in the bar' strokes on the cymbal or half-open hi-hats. He keeps his fills simple with just small variations on a relatively unimaginative theme.

Disjointed on the inferior stereo version by being panned to the right channel, Ringo's playing appears more coherent and forceful in the mono mix, largely due to his kit (his snare in particular) being smothered in echo and (somewhat contradictory) buried deep in the mix. A real shame Ringo wasn't more expansive here, but it's likely that his remit was to play it straight and keep it simple. That's not to say Ringo doesn't play hard, he gives it all he's got; he does acquire those infamous blisters after all. *Alex Cain and Terry McCusker*

9. "Here Comes The Sun"

(On Abbey Road LP released 26th September 1969 UK)

Although Ringo had left and returned, the group's internal problems were coming to a head, especially with the nightmare that was Apple. Just as Ringo had been inspired to write "Octopus's Garden" on his sojourn in Sardinia, George was sitting with a guitar in the garden at Eric Clapton's house when he wrote one of his best songs, "Here Comes The Sun". As he noted: "It seems as if winter in England goes on forever; by the time spring comes you really deserve it."

Thinking he was back at school, he decided to "slag off Apple" and, in doing so, wrote this masterpiece.

John was absent on the recording, having recently been involved in a car accident. What George had devised was one of the most complex time signatures of any Beatles song.

Analysis

This proves to be an excellent example of Ringo's ability to cope with multiple time signatures, namely 4/4, 2/4, 3/8 and 5/8. "Here Comes The Sun" is also noted for its wonderfully laid-back feel. The opening bars set the tone with a delightful double-fill into the first verse before settling into that 4/4 groove. The numerous time changes within the song first make their appearance on the bridge. This section sees a bar of 2/4 ending the flow of the song, before alternating between 3/8, 5/8, 4/4, a 2/4, and finally 3/8 that returns to 4/4. For the song, Ringo instinctively draws upon his experience with Indian music timekeeping rather than the usual Western manner for counting out the time.

Used to great effect, multiple handclaps cleverly hasten the end of the bridge. The complexities and pitfalls of three people *(George, Ringo and Paul)* negotiating a minefield of shifting time signatures, is swept away with ease, as they clap their way through bars of 4/4, 2/4, 3/8, and 5/8.

Ringo's drums sound fantastic here, benefitting greatly from the brave new world of transistor technology in a newly-installed mixing desk. As a treat, brand new calf skins were employed. The snare and hi-hats sound crisp and tight, while the drums have a punch not previously heard on Beatles recordings.

Alex Cain and Terry McCusker

10. "The End"
(On Abbey Road LP released 26th September 1969 UK)

How fitting that the final song on the final Beatles album was titled *"The End"* (forgetting "Her Majesty"); the lyrics seemed to encapsulate everything that The Beatles had stood for.

In a 2015 interview for *Rolling Stone*, McCartney made an observation about Ringo: "I never met a drummer who more hated the drum solos. We had to beg him to do it. The point where 'Carry That Weight' goes into 'The End', I told him dramatic change in energy and tempo; we need just a few seconds. And he finally agreed to do it. And Ringo was great." *(Rolling Stone 2015)* Ringo, however, was very honest about that drum solo: "You know that fill I do on 'The End' on *Abbey Road*? I've got no idea how to do it. I could never do it again. Can't do it!" *(Rolling Stone 2015)*

Geoff Emerick remembered Ringo being talked into it. "The thing that always amused me was how much persuasion it took to get Ringo to play that solo. Usually, you have to talk drummers out of doing solos."

Analysis

The use of his drums – where 'space' is used as an instrument between fills – is

cleverly underscored with a powerful bass drum hammering 'eight in the bar' beats.

This device of maintaining a constant allows him to look ahead, take a very short break from the rest of his drums, and think of what he is going to do next. Once into his stride, Ringo opens his shoulders and lets loose with fluid and forthright tom fills which sit perfectly upon the bass drum and similarly drive the rhythm along. Of note is his movement around the drums, not only from left to right but from floor tom to his smallest mounted tom to his left, a Ringo 'trademark' due to his left-handed playing of a right-handed set-up. At 0.29, we hear a hint of a breath from Ringo, and an ever-so-slight increase in tempo on the bass drum prior to his last tom fill – perhaps a sign of relief at completing his solo. *Alex Cain and Terry McCusker*

A Drummer's Drummer

How will history record Ringo Starr's contribution to music history?

Do people like him just because he was a Beatle, or because he genuinely was a great drummer? As legendary jazz figure Buddy Rich once observed: "Ringo Starr was adequate. No more than that." However, Buddy Rich seldom had anything good to say about other drummers! Ringo did respond to the snide comment, describing Rich's style as sounding like a load of rats running over a drum. Touché, Ringo.

Max Weinberg, the drummer who has put the beat into Bruce Springsteen's E Street Band since the 1970s, wrote a book in which he interviewed and profiled some of rock's greatest drummers. Weinberg was very clear about how important Ringo Starr was to his life. "More than any other drummer, Ringo Starr changed my life," Weinberg said. "The impact and memory of that band on The Ed Sullivan Show in 1964 will never leave me. I can still see Ringo in the back moving that beat with his whole body, his right hand swinging off his sock cymbal while his left hand pounds the snare. He was fantastic, but I think what got to me the most was his smile. I knew he was having the time of his life." Weinberg also observed: "D. J. Fontana had introduced me to the power of *The Big Beat*. Ringo convinced me just how powerful that rhythm could be. Ringo's beat was heard around the world, and he drew the spotlight toward rock and roll drummers. From his matched-grip style to his pioneering use of staggered tom-tom fills, his influence in rock drumming was as important and widespread as Gene Krupa's had been in jazz." *(The Big Beat)*

D. J. Fontana remembered seeing Ringo. "I was playing maracas or something behind him, just listening to him," Elvis' drummer said. "I swear he never varied the tempo. He played that backbeat and never got off it. Man, you couldn't have moved him with a crane. It was amazing. He played a hell of a backbeat, man, and that's where it's at." *(The Big Beat)*

A Motivating Influence

The editor of Modern Drummer magazine, presenting the Editor's Achievement Award to Ringo, said: "What is beyond question is Ringo's impact on an entire generation of drummers who first became drummers as a direct result of seeing and hearing him play in the early days of The Beatles. Literally hundreds of thousands of players – including some of the greatest drummers playing today –

cite Ringo as their first motivating influence."

Kenny Aronoff, who has played drums with the likes of John Mellencamp, Bob Seger, Belinda Carlisle, Elton John, John Fogerty, Lynyrd Skynyrd and Meat Loaf, gave his opinion of Ringo: "I consider him one of the greatest innovators of rock drumming and believe that he has been one of the greatest influences on rock drumming today. Ringo has influenced drummers more than they will ever realize or admit. Ringo laid down the fundamental rock beat that drummers are playing today, and they probably don't even realize it. Ringo always approached the song more like a songwriter than a drummer. He always served the music."

(Modern Drummer, Dec. 1987)

One opinion that seems to be prevalent among drummers is that Ringo was a drummer who liked to play behind the song, not dominate it. Stewart Copeland, drummer with The Police, confirmed this. "Ringo is the leader in the education for all young drummers of style over flash," he said, "always playing the right things rather than a lot of things." *(The Big Beat)*

George on Ringo

George Harrison was always loyal to Ringo as The Beatles' drummer. He was the one who wanted Ringo in the group, more than John or Paul. George was also the one who refused at first to go on the world tour in June 1964 when Ringo fell ill, claiming that unless all four went, the tour couldn't proceed. In the end, he had no choice but to accept Jimmie Nicol as a temporary replacement.

However, in 2017, George's widow Olivia revealed that she had found a song, written by George, called "Hey Ringo". This clearly showed how Harrison felt about his good friend.

Hey Ringo, now I want you to know, that without you, my guitar plays far too slow. And Ringo, let me say this to you, I've heard no drummer who can play it quite like you. Hey Ringo, there's one thing I've not said, I'll play my guitar with you till I drop dead. *(I, Me Mine)*

Ringo on Ringo

How did Ringo view his career? "First and foremost, I am a drummer," he said. "After that, I'm other things. ...But I didn't play drums to make money. I played drums because I loved them. ...My soul is that of a drummer....It came to where I had to make a decision: I was going to be a drummer. Everything else goes now. I play drums. It was a conscious moment in my life when I said the rest of things were getting in the way. I didn't do it to become rich and famous; I did it because it was the love of my life." *(The Big Beat)*

Ringo Starr is a drummer's drummer – one who may never be considered the most technically-gifted drummer of all time. But does it really matter? He put the beat behind The Beatles and influenced generations of drummers and, for that, he deserves full credit.

After all, he was the drummer chosen by the Fab Three to be the permanent Fourth Beatle.

22nd February 1963

ASK ME WHY: LENNON AND MCCARTNEY'S PUBLISHING CONTRACT

From 1st October 1962, The Beatles finally had a valid, legally-signed management agreement with Brian, a recording contract with Parlophone and their first record due out in four days. So much of this success can be attributed to Ardmore & Beechwood's general manager Sid Colman and his assistant Kim Bennett, who set up the meeting between Brian and George Martin in May 1962. That meeting was the catalyst for The Beatles' recording contract. How did Brian thank Colman? Once Ardmore & Beechwood were awarded the publishing rights to "Love Me Do/P.S. I Love You", Brian, with a little help from George Martin, moved the publishing to Dick James Music. Not exactly a heartfelt thanks from Brian.

Colman and Bennett were instrumental in securing The Beatles' contract and it was assumed that, as a division of EMI, Ardmore & Beechwood would not only publish the group's first record, but all the records that followed. But as in life, there were never any guarantees.

Love Me Do

Although press agent Roger Stinton did some of the early publicity for The Beatles' first single, it was down to Kim Bennett, one of the best record pluggers in the business, to ensure that Ardmore & Beechwood's newest recruits had a successful debut single. This would be a double score for EMI, which would not only have winning record sales through Parlophone, but the publishing rights with Ardmore & Beechwood. Bennett realised that the BBC was ignoring "Love Me Do" and that Radio Luxembourg was paying little attention to it, especially since popular chart show host Jack Jackson was suitably unimpressed. "I've seen pictures of them," said Jackson, "and my first reaction was that there was

something wrong with my eyesight." *(Beatles Book Monthly 13 August 1964)*
It was fellow Radio Luxembourg deejay Ted King who led the way, thanks again to Kim Bennett. "We met one lunchtime in a Tin Pan Alley pub," recalled King. "I knew a little bit about The Beatles, of course, but wasn't mad about the disc. But Kim was so enthusiastic over it all that I decided if you can't beat 'em, then you have to join 'em. So I played it. And I must say now that I'm mighty glad I did so." *(Beatles Book Monthly 13 August 1964)*

It is no surprise that it took Bennett's efforts to create the buzz around this particular record because there was an average of thirty new record releases each week, and every record company made demands on radio stations to have its record played. That is why people like Kim Bennett deserve credit for helping cut through the clutter for the artists they believed in.

It's A Funny Business

The Beatles attended meetings with journalists, but they weren't necessarily successful at first. John wasn't impressed with the whole music business.
"It's a funny business, this," Lennon said. "It's one great big vicious circle, really. Nobody wants to know about you until you get in the charts: but how do you get in the charts if nobody wants to write about you in the first place?"
(Beatles Book Monthly 14 September 1964)

What we have to realise is that The Beatles were four Liverpudlians in a foreign land, with long hair and a funny, often unintelligible accent. One journalist who was a fan of Frank Sinatra and Ella Fitzgerald later admitted: "I couldn't see what these shy, awkward, gauche lads had to do with music."

He delegated the interview to a junior reporter who was baffled by the quartet. "I couldn't understand a word they were saying," he recalled. "I mean that. They mumbled, gabbled: that Liverpool accent was thicker than anything I'd heard from pop singers before."

That North/South divide was a bigger barrier than they ever realised, and they hated being dragged from journalist to journalist. Paul would always be the lively, jovial one, with John quickly becoming bored. Ringo sat to the back, as he was the new boy. "It wasn't much good for me," said Ringo, "because I sometimes felt I was simply being left out of the conversation." One observer said that Ringo "sat, rigidly upright, with rather a morose expression. Occasionally he smiled. He said little." (*Beatles Book Monthly* 14 September 1964)

The Beatles were downhearted, and likely voiced their concerns to Brian. "Our trouble was simply this," George said. "We'd usually gone down well in Liverpool and Hamburg. Deep down, I suppose we were a bit overconfident about our chances once the rest of the world had a chance of hearing us on radio or something. So we sulked a bit." (*Beatles Book Monthly* 13 August 1964)

The Publishing Rights

Despite Bennett's hard work, "Love Me Do" had only crept into the Top Twenty. But it was a start. It therefore is somewhat bewildering that Epstein was convinced to take the publishing rights elsewhere. After all, it was because of Colman and Bennett's interest in publishing The Beatles' songs that Brian had secured the recording contract. Why was it so important to have a separate publishing contract?

The recording contract covered The Beatles as performers only as well as the records they made. As we know, the contract gave them one penny per record sold, which had to be split between Brian and the Fab Four. They would have had to sell a million records to make £100,000 between them. However, when any record was sold, a royalty was also paid to the songwriter, and if the performer was the songwriter, then they got paid twice. At this stage, only Lennon and McCartney were composing, and George Martin was unimpressed with what they had demonstrated so far. Neither "Love Me Do" nor "P.S. I Love You" was going to set the world on fire. But everything changed on 26th November 1962.

Thank You, Please Please Me

The Beatles had put together a version of "Please Please Me" and, on 11th September, made a rough demo of it with drummer Andy White. George Martin wasn't too impressed with it and, making a few suggestions, told them to go away and work on it. They brought it back into the studio on 26th November, this time with Ringo on drums. This was probably the first time Martin saw the boys working together as a unit with a song he was happy with. As he said to them: "Gentlemen, you've just made your first number 1." (*All You Need Is Ears*)

Martin now saw a group that had gelled in the studio, recording a song with all the earmarks of a hit – and a songwriting partnership with the potential to produce even more hits. Suddenly, the idea of having Lennon and McCartney tied to a publishing contract became imperative. It was highly likely that John and Paul would make far more money from songwriting than performing if they could write more numbers like "Please Please Me". George Martin decided he had to act.

Epstein was said to be unimpressed with Ardmore & Beechwood's efforts to promote "Love Me Do", which seems a little unfair. After all, they were trying to promote an average song by an unknown group from Liverpool in a competitive market. When interviewed years later, Kim Bennett was understandably unimpressed with what had transpired. "When a song's been established in the charts," he said, "there's no reason to change the publishing setup unless you want to be spiteful. George was very naughty in getting them away from us." (*TuneIn*)

You could also understand it if George Martin had indeed been pressured into signing The Beatles by Len Wood, who had been pressed himself by Colman and Bennett. Maybe this was his revenge?

The fact is that George Martin did suggest going elsewhere, and Brian and The Beatles had several options. Brian liked the idea of approaching the American company Hill and Range, who published Elvis' records. An association with Elvis, however remote, must have been an exciting prospect. However, George Martin wanted to steer Brian in another direction. He suggested Dick James, David Platz and Alan Holmes who were all well-known in Tin Pan Alley, the home of music publishing in London and, by default, for the whole country. In fact, George Martin had personal experience with several offices who had published the producer's own compositions. Martin opted for Dick James, who, as well as publishing original George Martin compositions, had written a song with him – "If This Should Be A Dream". With lyrics by Dick James and music by George Martin, it would be released the following year on Parlophone by Christine Campbell. It is therefore no surprise that George Martin steered Brian, who was out of his depth anyway, towards Dick James.

So, on 27th November 1962, the day after "Please Please Me" and "Ask Me Why" had been recorded, Brian walked into Dick James' office. James, on the back of George Martin's recommendation, was eager to publish the songs. However, nothing could have prepared James for just how good The Beatles were.

"I just hit the ceiling," James would recall. "He (Brian) said, 'What do you think?' and I said, 'I think it must be number 1. If we get the breaks and can get the exposure on the record, it must be number 1.'"

Thank Your Lucky Stars

The first thing James did, to prove he was the right man for the job, was to telephone Philip Jones, producer of ITV's hit television show, Thank Your Lucky Stars. James placed the telephone receiver by the gramophone and played the song over the wires. Jones must have been impressed as The Beatles would record their debut appearance on *Thank Your Lucky Stars* on Sunday 13th January 1963. Kim Bennett had been plugging "Love Me Do" to Jones, and 600 signatures had been sent to the host Brian Matthew from Beatles fans in Liverpool. While it may have been inevitable that they would get on the program, Dick James made it happen. (*TuneIn*)

What else did Brian Epstein have to do to make all his dreams come true?

He duly signed the contract with Dick James Music on behalf of Lennon and McCartney, and all the money from their songwriting – sheet music, covers, airplay by other artists – would go into the account. James suggested that they would split everything 50-50 – 50% to Dick James, 20% to John, 20% to Paul, and 10% to Brian. Although this may have looked like a good deal, Brian negotiated a contract that gave no controlling majority rights to Lennon and McCartney and himself. When, in future years, Dick James Music wanted to sell up, it couldn't be stopped. All Brian had to do was negotiate a 51% share and they would have been alright. For the first time, and certainly not the last, Brian's business dealings left a lot to be desired. However, as with many of these early contracts, hindsight is a great thing. Even in the 21st Century, artists are still arguing with record companies over their publishing deals: artists rarely have any control over their work.

This was the start of the process that would lead to legal wranglings that still reverberate around the ownership of The Beatles' songs today. It also cut George and Ringo out of the mot lucrative side of the business at the very start. But then, it's "Only a Northern Song".

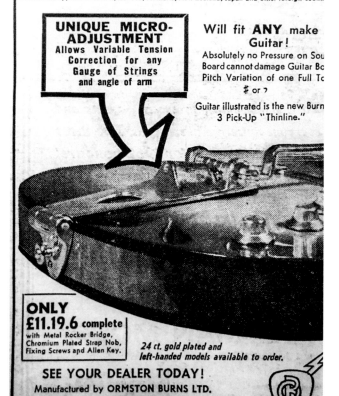

24TH MAY 1963

BOBBY GRAHAM
ALMOST THE FOURTH BEATLE, TWICE

In July 1962, Bobby Graham turned down Brian Epstein, who had hoped the drummer would accept the job as Pete Best's replacement. But, within months, Graham would cross paths with The Beatles again.

Bobby Graham - also known as Bobbie Graham - was born Robert Francis Neate in Edmonton, north London, on 11th March 1940, at the height of the London blitz. Like many drummers-in-waiting, he would bang knives and forks on tables. His father, fed up with the noise, created a drum kit for him out of biscuit tins and anything else he could find.

Despite the lack of formal musical training, Bobby was a natural. Like so many of the new breed of drummers, he didn't take a single lesson. Nor could he read a note of music. He got his first real kit and focused solely on his chosen craft, practicing up to eight hours a day to the exclusion of everything else. He became more proficient with time, as he emulated his drumming heroes like Ronnie Verrall from Ted Heath's band.

Bobby loved jazz and had no interest in getting a 'proper job'. He left school at the age of fifteen and wanted nothing else but to be a professional musician. Playing a bit of skiffle at first, he later scored a job drumming once a week at a north London coffee bar called The Witch's Cauldron. It was here, playing jazz, that he adopted his stage name of Bobby Graham. Then, in 1960, he got the opportunity to join a rock 'n' roll band when a school friend, Billy Gray, needed a drummer for a season at Butlin's in Yorkshire. He was prepared to give up jazz for a regular wage. The wine, women and song were tempting, too!

At Butlin's, the group caught the attention of producer Joe Meek with a repertoire of covers of popular artists like Cliff Richard and The Shadows. Billy Gray and the Stormers disbanded and re-formed with a new front man as Mike Berry and The Outlaws, with Bobby Graham on drums.

A technically brilliant drummer with a very distinctive style, Bobby was reliable and not prone to error and quickly established a reputation as one of the leading drummers in the business. After several arguments with the erratic Joe Meek, he quit the group and joined Joe Brown and The Bruvvers. It was on tour with Brown in Liverpool that Brian Epstein offered him the job of replacing Pete Best in The Beatles, an invitation he declined.

Another Beatles Session Drummer

Though he wouldn't become their permanent drummer, Bobby would play for them. "George Martin used me for session work and I did get involved in one of The Beatles' early sessions, although I've no idea which one." What he did remember was that he "did play with The Beatles on one of their *Pop Goes The Beatles* sessions from the Paris Theatre and that was because the BBC didn't think Ringo was adaptable enough for what they wanted at that time."
(Drummed Out)

Graham was indeed brought in to replace Ringo on that occasion, though there are no records to indicate which session it was. Regardless, this would mean that Ringo was not only replaced by session drummer Andy White, but by Bobby Graham as well.

The Beatles recorded 15 shows for the BBC under the title Pop Goes The Beatles, with the first episode recorded on 24th May 1963 and broadcast on 4th June. During the series, the group played many songs that they had performed in Hamburg and Liverpool, but never recorded for Parlophone.

In early 1963, around the time of his work with The Beatles, Bobby left the Bruvvers to do full-time studio work, further cementing his stature as one of Britain's best, and busiest, session drummers, playing on an estimated 15,000 records.

Bobby, or Jimmie?

Bobby had one final encounter with The Beatles in June 1964 when he was asked to join the group on a temporary basis when Ringo collapsed on the eve of their world tour. Graham once again turned them down, but recommended fellow session drummer and friend, Jimmie Nicol.

There is no doubt that Bobby Graham would have made an excellent Fourth Beatle, possessing both the talent and experience that would have served them well.

He died in September 2009.

Some of the records Bobby Graham played on during his long career.

The Animals – "We Gotta Get Out Of This Place"

The Bachelors – "I Believe"

Dave Berry – "The Crying Game"

Petula Clark – "Downtown"

Marianne Faithfull – "Come And Stay With Me"

The Fortunes – "Here It Comes Again"

Cilla Black – "You're My World"

Engelbert Humperdinck – "Release Me"

Tom Jones – "It's Not Unusual"

The Kinks – "You Really Got Me"

The Kinks – "All Day And All Of The Night"

The Kinks – "Tired Of Waiting For You"

Brian Poole and the Tremeloes – "Do You Love Me?"

P.J. Proby – "Hold Me"

Dusty Springfield – "I Only Want To Be With You"

Dusty Springfield – "You Don't Have To Say You Love Me"

Them – "Here Comes The Night"

The Walker Brothers – "The Sun Ain't Gonna Shine Anymore"

The Dave Clark Five – "Glad All Over"

The Dave Clark Five – "Bits And Pieces"

He also played on major hits by Peter and Gordon, The Animals, Herman's Hermits, Rod Stewart, Lulu, Joe Cocker and Van Morrison's group, Them.

"You don't stop drumming because you get old, You get old because you stop drumming."

Bobby Graham

16TH APRIL 1963

NORMAN SMITH
THE DRUMMING ENGINEER

Norman Smith, nicknamed "Normal" by John Lennon, had the distinction of being The Beatles' engineer from the day they auditioned for George Martin on 6th June 1962, through to the *Rubber Soul* album – nearly 100 songs. Smith also worked with Gerry & The Pacemakers, The Swinging Blue Jeans, Helen Shapiro, Billy J. Kramer and The Dakotas, Manfred Mann and Barclay James Harvest.

Born on 22nd February 1923, Smith started playing drums aged seven, before learning the trumpet and other brass instruments, as well as vibes. After leaving the RAF in 1947, he joined the BBC, producing jazz and music programs. He remained there until 1958, when he left for a position with EMI. He was of the opinion that "not enough was made of rhythm sections", a sentiment proven by his love of working with The Beatles. After moving on from The Beatles, he discovered Pink Floyd, signed them to EMI, and produced the group's first three albums between 1967 and 1969. In 1968, Smith even replaced Pink Floyd drummer Nick Mason on "Remember A Day", when Mason couldn't quite come up with the right drum part during the recording of *A Saucerful Of Secrets*.

Four years later, as Hurricane Smith, he would break the top ten with a hit of his own: the self-penned ode to his wife Eileen, "Oh Babe, What Would You Say?", which was featured on his 1972 debut LP. He also wrote "Don't Let It Die" when John Lennon joked that The Beatles were short a song while recording the soundtrack for *Help!*

Drumming With The Beatles?

Four years before he sat in for Nick Mason on drums, Norman performed similarly for The Beatles. On 16th April 1964, during the recording of "A Hard Day's Night", he stepped from behind the control desk and played the bongos. He also averted a mini crisis that occurred during the recording of "Can't Buy Me Love", which was recorded in Paris and London. It had been laid down in four takes on 29th January 1964 at EMI's Pathé Marconi Studios in Paris, after recording "Sie Liebt Dich" and "Komm, Gib Mir Deine Hand" the German-language versions of "She Loves You" and "I Want to Hold Your Hand", respectively.

There was a problem with the recording and, once back in London, Smith was called in to help. Beatles engineer Geoff Emerick recalled what happened: "It had the same level of excitement as previous Beatles singles and was quickly slated to be an A-side, but first there was a technical problem to be overcome, discovered when the tape was brought back and played at our studios. Perhaps because it had been spooled incorrectly, the tape had a ripple in it, resulting in the intermittent loss of treble on Ringo's hi-hat cymbal. There was tremendous time pressure to get the track mixed and delivered to the pressing plant, and due to touring commitments The Beatles themselves were unavailable, so George and Norman took it upon themselves to make a little adjustment.

"As I eagerly headed into the engineer's seat for the first time, Norman headed down into the studio to overdub a hastily set up hi-hat onto a few bars of the song while I recorded him, simultaneously doing a two-track to two-track dub. Thanks to Norman's considerable skills as a drummer, the repair was made quickly and seamlessly." *(Here, There and Everywhere)*.

For his handiwork, Smith was credited with the role of "drummer" on the track.

So take a bow Norman "Hurricane" Smith

– a man whose contributions were anything but "Normal".

Norman Smith behind his drum kit (By kind permission. From the Norman Smith memoirs)

54

4TH JUNE 1964

JIMMIE NICOL

THE FIRST FIFTH BEATLE IS THE FOURTH BEATLE FOR A FORTNIGHT

Since the breakup of The Beatles in 1970, few questions have fuelled as much debate, yet drawn as few conclusions as this one: Who was the Fifth Beatle? Was it Pete Best or maybe Stuart Sutcliffe? Maybe it was Brian Epstein or George Martin? However, the first candidate ever to be given that title by several newspapers was Jimmie Nicol. It was June 1964.

With one phone call, Nicol went from relative obscurity to playing drums in the most famous group in the world, The Beatles – even if only for a couple of weeks. That time with the Fab Four would affect him for the rest of his life. But how did he come to get the biggest gig in pop music?

On 3rd June 1964, on the eve of The Beatles' first world tour, Ringo was rushed to hospital after collapsing at a photo shoot. Suddenly, all those weeks and months spent planning and coordinating concerts in Denmark, the Netherlands, Hong Kong, Australia and New Zealand were up in the air. When Ringo was diagnosed with tonsillitis and pharyngitis, it was obvious that he would require an operation and be in hospital for at least a couple of weeks, putting the whole tour in jeopardy. Panic set in, and it was clear to George Harrison what that would mean: no Ringo, no tour.

However, with no escape clauses in their insurance, they had no alternative; the tour had to go ahead. They were left with only one option – a replacement drummer. Having spent years trying to find the perfect drummer for the group, who could they get to stand in for Ringo at such short notice? The Beatles faced the same predicament they were in just days before their first trip to Hamburg, when they called Pete Best. Back then, Norman Chapman had to enlist in the army, so Best, whom they knew well, was approached. This was different. Back in 1960, they were a relatively unknown Liverpool group, heading abroad for the first time, trying to make a name for themselves. This time, having recently returned from

their conquest of America, they were the biggest pop group on the planet.

Ringo Is Replaced

The Daily Mail covered the story on 4th June 1964. Under the banner "Ringo Is Replaced", they revealed the truth behind the headline. Nicol "told reporter Robert Bickford, 'I'm knocked out man. It's quite a laugh being one of The Beatles. I can handle the job okay. Ringo can swing all right, but I've got more range." The newspaper was keen to support Nicol's addition to the tour: "An expert drummer, he is highly regarded by the record industry and was at home in Barnes, Middlesex, when The Beatles' recording manager George Martin phoned and asked him to go straight to the EMI studios where the other three band members were recording. After a two-hour rehearsal, John Lennon told him: 'You're in. This should be worth a couple of quid to you.'" The journalist also spoke to Ringo in the hospital to see how he was feeling. "I'm not too bad really", he said. "I feel pretty groggy but I am sure I'll be well enough to go with the boys on Sunday to Hong Kong. It's pretty nice in here. I'm surrounded by hot water bottles but I am still shivering. It's a terrible drag not being able to go with the boys to Europe."

Ringo was down and out, but who was his replacement?

James George Nicol

James George Nicol was born on 3rd August 1939 at St. James Hospital in Battersea, London, to George and Edith Nicol of Silverthorne Road. Jimmie's first instrument was a piano, but drumming was always his ambition. "I was basically an all-round drummer," said Nicol. "I started with the Boys Brigade, which is similar to the Scouts. After that, I went into the Army Cadets' Military Band and played Gershwin and marches. I was their percussionist, played xylophone and timps. While I was at school, I formed a small band with two trumpets and a saxophone, a little dance band. We used to play church halls. Then, just before I left school, I sold my train set and my Dinky toys and I got a deposit to buy a drum kit."

After he joined the Army Cadet Force in 1950, he became a drummer/percussionist in the ACF Band, learning how to read music, which was more than The Beatles could do. He began performing with the band on marches, parade, church services and concerts, giving him great experience early on. Nicol knew what he wanted to do from a very young age. "I knew what I wanted to be when I was a child still at school," said Nicol proudly. "I wanted to be the country's top drummer, and I achieved my ambition. I just go out and get it, and nothing on earth will stop me. Only myself if I allow myself to be lazy." He was quite philosophical about life. "I can do anything I want, nothing is impossible. Man can move mountains. He may need 10,000 other men to do it, but one man has to I think it out. And once you've achieved the impossible, you find out you have more powers than you thought. And from mistakes you learn." *(Interview Evert Vermeer)*

At the age of fourteen, Nicol acquired his first drum kit from a local pawn shop. Initially inspired by jazz music, he soon found himself in the world of rock 'n' roll. The centre for the music scene in London was in the Soho area, specifically the now-legendary 2i's Coffee Bar at 59 Old Compton Street, which had opened in 1956. Many of the stars of the late '50s and early '60s were discovered there, like Tommy Steele, Joe Brown, Johnny Gentle, Billy Fury, Marty Wilde, Georgie Fame and Vince Eager. Some have gone so far as to proclaim it as the birthplace of British rock 'n' roll. This is where Nicol would end up playing, along with other coffee bars in the area.

He got his first job at the music store, Boosey & Hawkes, repairing and maintaining drums, which gave him a great technical knowledge of the instrument. "There I got in touch with all the top drummers in the country. I used to repair all their drums." *(Interview Evert Vermeer)* But it was playing as a professional drummer in a band that drove Nicol on. At 2i's, he began sitting in with any group that needed a drummer, and he would soon join his first group. When Tony Crombie, drummer with the Wee Willie Harris band, left to form his own group, Nicol happily filled the vacancy. Harris was a great showman and taught Nicol the art of putting on a show, not just playing the music.

The Blackjacks

After the Wee Willie gig, he joined a trio called The Blackjacks, led by drummer Rory Blackwell, one of Britain's first rock 'n' rollers. It's interesting to note that The Blackjacks was one of the early names that The Quarrymen used, and also the name of the first group Pete Best would join. When Blackwell left his drums

to take centre stage, Nicol would jump up and sit behind the kit, easily making the transition and becoming a better drummer every day. Guitarist Rick Hardy even commented that Nicol was "so good when he arrived that he must have had previous experience."

Jimmie Nicol became one of the most popular drummers at the 2i's club, sitting in with many bands and gaining more experience with every performance. But all the while, he wanted to join a group as a permanent member. He didn't have to wait long. Tommy Hicks, who took the Parnes-inspired stage name Tommy Steele was already an established star, but he wasn't the only talent in the family. His brother Colin had formed his own group and big things were expected of him. "Then a friend, Bobby Green, told me there was an audition for Tommy Steele's brother's band, Colin Hicks and the Cabin Boys," Nicol would recall. "I started professionally with them. They were handled by the Larry Parnes Organisation, who also handled Tommy Steele." *(Interview Evert Vermeer)*

Jimmie Nicol was on the ladder to success.

At the age of eighteen, on the back of his impending success as a professional drummer, Jimmie married his girlfriend Patricia. A recording contract soon followed, though Nicol and his fellow musicians were not to play on the record itself; the company would use session musicians – not the first time that had happened to a Beatles drummer. Their first single was "Empty Arm Blues", though regrettably for them, it flopped. However, they soon caught a break when at the last minute, singer Terry Dene had to drop out of a tour. Colin Hicks and His Cabin Boys took the spot and made their stage debut in December 1957, backing one of Parnes' most successful acts, Marty Wilde, at the Finsbury Park Empire.

European Nights

The group made its first appearance on television performing the song "Giddy-Up-A-Ding Dong" which had been a hit in 1957 for Freddy Bell and the Bellboys. Despite being on tour and receiving rave reviews, they lost their record deal. Having already gained experience in clubs, theatres and television, Nicol was about to broaden his horizons when the band was asked by Italian director Alessandro Blassetti to appear in his film European Nights as a typical rock 'n' roll band. They performed "Twenty Flight Rock", the song Paul McCartney played for John Lennon at the Woolton fete, and Jimmie played a drum solo on his all-white pearl Gretsch kit. They shot it in a theatre, and a tour of Italy followed the film's release. Colin Hicks and His Cabin Boys appeared at Genoa's own Cavern, La Grota ("The Cave"), supporting The Platters. Keyboard player Mike O'Neil became good friends with Nicol, and their mutual love of jazz would lead to a future connection for the drummer. O'Neil is credited with turning Georgie Fame onto jazz and when Fame needed a drummer later on, he recommended jazz fan Jimmie Nicol.

It was time for Nicol to gain valuable studio experience. David Matolon ran the Broadway International record label and signed Colin Hicks and His Cabin Boys to record cover versions of some of the biggest hits of 1958, like "Maybelene" and "Johnny B. Goode". Among these tunes was the one they had featured in the film: "Twenty Flight Rock". Against the norm of the day, their version featured a drum solo by Nicol which lasted almost a minute. Even early on, he had the confidence to carry a song with the drums alone. The records didn't bring them much success and the group fell apart at the end of 1958. Colin Hicks and Mike O'Neill chose to stay in Italy, while the rest of the band, Nicol included, returned home.

Once again, and not for the last time, Nicol had to move on from a group and start over. Each time, however, he gained a difference experience and, in the process, made an investment for his future. What he didn't expect on his return home was to learn that his wife was pregnant. Now there would be an extra mouth to feed. He would retain his position at Boosey & Hawkes, whilst drumming with any act that needed him at the 2i's and other coffee bars in Soho. Again, opportunity knocked for Nicol when he was offered the chance to drum with the band in the orchestra pit at London's Theatre Royal for the Lionel Bart musical, *Fings Aint Wot They Used to Be*. With his son Howie on the way, Nicol had to find a more

permanent job.

Parnes Is Eager

By far the most influential man in popular music at that time was Laurence Maurice "Larry" Parnes, the first real pop manager and a man Brian Epstein would later try to emulate with The Beatles. Parnes had a "stable" of stars, such as Johnny Gentle, Duffy Power, Marty Wilde and Liverpool's Billy Fury. Each of his clients was given a new, more attractive and marketable name. In 1960, Parnes would have a significant impact on the life of The Beatles when he brought Fury to Liverpool in search of a backing group. The Silver Beatles auditioned and Parnes offered them the gig backing Johnny Gentle, giving them their first taste of touring. However, it was another of Parnes' singers who would be the next stepping stone in Nicol's career.

Roy Taylor from Lincolnshire doesn't sound like a very rock 'n' roll name, but when Larry Parnes changed it to Vince Eager, the stage was set for minor stardom. Eager was one of the greats of the early British rock 'n' roll scene, a giant of a man with a great voice. While performing at the 2i's Coffee Bar, Parnes spotted him and signed him up. Initially contracted to Decca, Eager soon moved to an ill-conceived record label started by Parnes – a move that proved disastrous for both men.

Tony Sheridan

Although Eager was to recruit Nicol, the drummer was first employed by a man who would feature heavily in Beatles lore. Anthony Esmond Sheridan McGinnity, better known as Tony Sheridan, had a group called Tony Sheridan and the Wreckers, and quickly added the experienced Jimmie Nicol to the lineup. One of the bright lights of the fledgling British rock 'n' roll scene, Sheridan was destined for great things, and it's interesting to speculate what might have happened if Nicol had accompanied Sheridan to Hamburg, where he met The Beatles.

Sheridan was suitably impressed with Nicol. "It was impossible not to like him," he told author Jim Berkenstadt. "He had a warm personality and he was bright and had a great depth, too." Sheridan, not usually known for his praise of other musicians, did not hold back in his support of Nicol. "Jimmie was an exemplary drummer," he said, "one of those drummers appreciated by all other musicians, though they might not admit it! It was one of those things, really; right time, right place, right chemistry."

However, in early 1959, Parnes was about to intervene in Nicol's musical journey, by taking him from Sheridan's group and placing him on a permanent contract with Vince Eager to form his backing group, the Quiet Three.

By May 1960, Vince Eager and the Quiet Three, including Nicol, were about to depart on a Scottish tour at the exact same time that Johnny Gentle and The Silver Beatles were being dispatched to Scotland. Both tours took place under the watchful eye of promoter Duncan McKinnon. "With most of my TV appearances in the late 1950s being on the BBC," Eager said, "there was a brief period when my profile in Scotland was greater than that of both Marty Wilde and Cliff Richard. Apparently it was due to television transmissions and where they were, or were not, received." Apparently, many parts of Scotland couldn't

THE

CAVERN

10 MATHEW ST., LIVERPOOL
PRESENTS ITS
EVENING SESSIONS

FRIDAY, 27th JULY—
Billy Kramer with the Coasters : The Searchers

SATURDAY, 28th JULY—
Dee Fenton and the Silhouettes : **THE BEATLES** : The Red River Jazzmen

SUNDAY, 29th JULY—
The Saints Jazzband

TUESDAY, 31st JULY—
The Bluegenes, the Dennisons Ken Dallas & the Silhouettes

Wednesday, 1st August—
THE BEATLES : The Mersey Beats : Gerry and the Pacemakers

receive ITV, which had *Oh Boy!* featuring Wilde and Richard whereas the BBC had *Six Five Special* and *Drumbeat*, showcasing Eager. "My band, the Quiet Three, consisted of Kenny Packwood, guitar, Tex Makins, bass, and Jimmy *(sic)* Nicol, drums."

National DisService

In Liverpool in the summer of 1960, drummer Norman Chapman had to quit The Silver Beatles just before the Hamburg trip because he was called up for national service with the army. The same fate had nearly befallen Jimmie Nicol in 1959. He was called for a medical, but had no intention of passing it! Having stayed up all night, and being blind drunk, he was suitably unhealthy enough the following day to fail his medical and return to the group. Vince Eager and the Quiet Three headed out on tour in the summer of 1959, playing rock 'n' roll, plus show songs and jazz numbers a drummer of Nicol's technical ability could use to showcase his talent.

In 1960, Britain witnessed firsthand a joint tour by two of rock 'n' roll's most influential trailblazers – Eddie Cochran and Gene Vincent. The Parnes-promoted tour featured Vince Eager and the Quiet Three and, again, there was a brief intersection with Beatles history. The two megastars were scheduled to appear in Liverpool in May 1960, but before the show took place, tragedy struck when Eddie Cochran was killed and Vincent injured in a car crash on 16 April 1960. Parnes and Allan Williams managed to rearrange the schedule for the concert at Liverpool Stadium, and the show went on with Vincent as the solo headliner, bolstered by Liverpool groups like Rory Storm and the Hurricanes, featuring Ringo Starr on drums, and Gerry and the Pacemakers.

Vince Shoots Jimmie

It was after the success of the concert that Parnes returned to Liverpool and secured The Silver Beatles to back Johnny Gentle on that tour of Scotland while, at the same time, dispatching Vince Eager and the Quiet Three on their Scottish tour. One of Eager's ideas for this excursion involved Nicol. "In 1960 I bought a blanked-off .38 Smith & Wesson *Revolver* to use in my act," he said, "when I would pretend to shoot my drummer, Jimmy (sic) Nicol during a drum solo." This nearly backfired at one concert and got Eager into trouble; thankfully, Nicol wasn't shot! *(Vince Eager)*

Another summer Parnes tour signalled the end for Nicol as part of Vince Eager's backing group. From the end of the pier in the Norfolk seaside town of Great Yarmouth, it was the end of the road for Vince Eager and Larry Parnes, leaving Jimmie Nicol in search of another group. However, the relationship between Larry Parnes and Jimmie Nicol remained intact as the impresario offered the drummer another opportunity with television producer Jack Good, mastermind behind the hit music talent showcases Six-Five Special and *Oh Boy!* Parnes and Good teamed up to take Parnes' singers out on a different type of tour, this time mixing rock 'n' roll and trad jazz. Parnes needed a 15-piece big band to back his singers, and who better to lead that band than one of the finest drummers and trad jazz fans he had ever seen: Jimmie Nicol. Having been in the shadows, Nicol would now be the star for the first time, a role he would relish as leader of Jimmie Nicol and his 15 New Orleans Rockers.

The tour opened on 25th September 1960, not long after The Beatles began their first tour in Hamburg. Nicol was in his element, playing the music he loved, and finally leading a band. Also on the bill was Georgie Fame, who carefully observed Nicol's drumming for future reference.

Next, Nicol joined the Oscar Rabin Band, led by David Ede ever since bandleader Rabin's death in 1958. Crossing between jazz and rock 'n' roll, this band was ideal for the BBC radio shows *Go Man Go*, a live program, and *Saturday Club*. This meant that the band was required for two broadcasts every week, which gave Nicol the benefit of playing in yet another medium, helping him further develop into one of the most versatile drummers around. As if all this wasn't enough to keep him busy, he still sat in with groups at the 2i's in Soho to supplement his income.

"At 21, I decided to stop rock 'n' roll and go into big bands," said Nicol. "The big bands at that time were fading out, but I caught the last two. One was the Oscar Rabin Band, who had a weekly radio show called *Go Man Go*, and the other one was Cyril Stapleton. I stayed with Rabin for a year because my philosophy is that you should never stay with a job more than 18 months, otherwise you'll start getting stagnated. Then I went with Cyril Stapleton, a bigger band, more difficult to play with. And of course, the drummer being the most important person in the band, I had a ball." *(Interview Evert Vermeer)*

Top Six Records

With his battered Trixon drum set feeling its age, Nicol felt it was time for another upgrade: a shiny blue Trixon Luxus kit with a crocodile-style design. Nicol worked closely with Johnny Harris, trumpet player with the band, and the two became good friends. Their relationship would be especially important to Jimmie's career when Harris was offered the position of Producer/Arranger at Pye Records, where he developed a great reputation and came to the attention of an Australian executive from Top Six Records.

Bill Wellings had this idea to put out an EP of cover versions of the top six chart hits, offered at a cheap price so those music fans who wanted the latest songs, but couldn't afford the real artists, could have a version of six songs for the price of one. When Wellings approached Johnny Harris to arrange the songs, he knew which drummer was experienced and versatile enough to do the job: Jimmie Nicol. As well as being a great drummer, Nicol could also read music, which was a tremendous advantage to Harris who had to record lots of songs on a tight budget, and with a quick turnaround time. This was 1964, and which band was on top of the charts? The Beatles, of course. It was this twist of fate that would, within a few months, help to earn Nicol the biggest job on the planet.

A Taste of Fame

As always, Nicol didn't stick to one job. He was now playing regularly with Georgie Fame and the Blue Flames in the evenings. But it was for his drumming on the Top Six cover songs that would serve as a useful audition. In early 1964, he recorded covers of "From Me To You", "All My Loving", "She Loves You", "I Wanna Be Your Man", "Love Me Do" and "Please Please Me", plus covers of songs The Beatles hadn't written, but had included on their albums and in their live sets. The Top Six songs were also featured on Radio Luxembourg.

"Love Me Do" Again

Jimmie Nicol became the fourth Beatles drummer to record "Love Me Do" and it is an interesting version of the song. It doesn't sound the same without John's distinctive harmonica, but it is the drum track that makes it worth a listen. The song is recorded at a faster rate per minute than all of the previous versions and, on the whole, hand claps included, it doesn't vary greatly from the Ringo or Andy White recordings. However, in the instrumental passage it becomes of particular interest because Nicol, an accomplished musical arranger, decided to introduce a "skip-beat", the downfall of the Pete Best version from June 1962. This time it works well, and was obviously well-practiced, unlike the June 1962 attempt. There is no way that Nicol would have heard the song's original arrangement, so he obviously felt that, like The Beatles in May 1962, he had to tinker with the arrangement and add some variety.

Drummer Alex Cain analysed the track and compared it to the two versions from September 1962. "Nicol is playing the same beat, but is heavier on the snare, giving a stronger backbeat. The Ringo version has equal emphasis on bass and snare; the Andy White version emphasizes the bass drum with, of course, the added punch of Ringo's tambourine on top of the snare."

Jimmie Nicol and Beatle Mania

In January 1964, Top Six released an EP entitled "Beatle Mania Special" using the phrase coined in October 1963 to describe the fans' love of The Beatles. This record featured "She Loves You", "Twist and Shout", "Please Please Me", "I Wanna Hold Your Hand", "From Me To You" and "Love Me Do". Incredibly, this record sold 100,000 copies. Nicol was now a successful recording artist and session drummer whose skills would be required very soon. In February 1964, as The Beatles were heading off to conquer America on *The Ed Sullivan Show*, Nicol was asked to form his own band and release a single, arranged by Johnny Harris. Jimmie Nicol and the Shubdubs released a ska version of the old nursery rhyme "Humpty Dumpty" on Pye Records.

Nicol Records Quickly for Brian Epstein

Cyril Stapleton was brought in by Decca Records to make a ska record, to tap into the latest music trend. Stapleton immediately brought in Nicol to provide the drumming behind singer Chris Farlowe on the song, "Blue Beat", using the group name The Beazers. Although the record made no impression on the charts, it once again showcased Nicol's incredible versatility and brought him into contact with Beatles manager Brian Epstein. While Epstein was busy planning The Beatles' first world tour, he was also working tirelessly for his other artists, including Tommy Quigley who, with a nod to Larry Parnes and his artist name changes, soon became Tommy Quickly. Epstein had obtained a recording contract for Quickly at Pye, but without much subsequent success.

Epstein visited the studio to oversee the Quickly session and noticed that Pye's resident session drummer, Jimmie Nicol, was particularly impressive. Quite prophetic of his own career, Quickly sang "You Might As Well Forget Him (aka Walk The Streets)". The song failed to chart and within two years Quickly's career was over. But Epstein wouldn't soon forget the drummer.

McCartney sees Nicol

In May 1964, Nicol's friendship and work with Georgie Fame finally bore fruit when Fame's drummer, Red Reece, became too ill to tour. Who else would Fame ask to replace Reece but the only guy who had sat in for him, Jimmie Nicol. One of Georgie Fame's biggest fans was a fellow musician who would often go to see him perform at the Flamingo Club: Paul McCartney. He and Georgie Fame became good friends, and it wouldn't be long before that friendship would change Nicol's future forever.

Ringo Collapses

McCartney and his fellow Beatles were preparing to leave on their first world tour and attending a photo shoot on 3rd June 1964 when Ringo collapsed and was rushed to hospital. What could Epstein do? What should The Beatles do? They could cancel or postpone the tour, but breaking their commitments to promoters and venues would cost a fortune. Their first world tour had to proceed, so there was only one solution: bring in a replacement drummer until Ringo recovered.

Jimmie Nicol had been playing covers of Beatles songs, had drummed in the studio for one of Epstein's artists Tommy Quickly, and had played in one of Paul McCartney's favourite groups, Georgie Fame and the Blue Flames. Neil Aspinall was sent to speak to their first choice to replace Ringo, and it was not Jimmie Nicol.

Almost the Fifth Beatle - Raye Du-Val

Raye Du-Val was the first drummer approached by Neil Aspinall, but he turned the offer down. At the time, in June 1964, Du-Val was playing with the Blue

Born of Anglo-French parents, Raymonde Du-Val broke the world record for continuous drumming in October 1959 when he drummed non-stop for 82 hours, 35 minutes, 14 seconds.

Du-Val had been the drummer with Emile Ford and the Checkmates when they played a Sam Leach-promoted show at the Tower Ballroom, New Brighton on 6 April 1962, with The Beatles as their support group. The poster shows them billed as The Beetles. Du-Val had many hits with Emile Ford and had earned a gold disc for "What Do You Want To Make Those Eyes At Me For". Raye also played for Ricky Valance, Jerry Lee Lewis, Gene Vincent, Johnny Duncan and the Bluegrass Boys, and Jimmy Justice. He backed singers such as Frank Ifield, and did session work with Millie on "My Boy Lollipop" and Johnny Kidd and the Pirates on "Shakin' All Over".

Raye appeared on television programmes such as Oh Boy!, Six Five Special, and Sunday Night at the London Palladium.

Notes in London. So near, but yet so far. "This chap asked me to fill in for Ringo who was ill," he said. "It's not for me. I am doing just fine with my band The Blue Notes right now. There were so many bands like The Beatles in 1964, I thought, they are not going to make it." How wrong could he be? With Du-Val declining, did The Beatles then to Nicol? No!

Almost the Fourth Beatle and Almost the Fifth Beatle

In a strange repeat of history, Epstein turned again to a drummer he had approached in 1962 as a possible replacement for Pete Best: Bobby Graham. Back in July 1962, Graham was drumming with Joe Brown and wouldn't leave them to join an untried band like The Beatles. Two years later, he was one of the best session drummers around but, as in 1962, he turned the request down. Not many people are offered two bites of the cherry and reject them both!

"When Ringo had his tonsils out, I was asked to take his place on tour for a few days, but was getting so much session work that I couldn't do it and I recommended Jimmie Nicol instead. I did play with The Beatles on one of their Pop Go The Beatles sessions from the Paris Theatre and that was because the BBC didn't think Ringo was adaptable enough for what they wanted at that time." *(The Beatle Who Vanished)* Pop Go The Beatles was a radio series on the BBC which ran for 52 episodes from June 1963.

The First Fifth Beatle - Jimmie Nicol

Paul McCartney was asked by Brian to follow up on Graham's recommendation – Jimmie Nicol, a drummer they both knew well. Paul rang his good friend Fame and asked if The Beatles could borrow his drummer for a couple of weeks while Ringo was in hospital. Fame, always happy to help his friends, was only too glad to oblige. He telephoned Nicol, asked him if he had a passport *(which he didn't)* and told him the good news.

Ringo, naturally, was devastated. "It was strange, them going off without me. They'd taken Jimmy Nicol and I thought they didn't love me any more – all that stuff went through my head." *(Anthology)* George Harrison made it clear that he didn't want to go without Ringo. "Of course, with all respect to Jimmy *(sic)*," George said, "we shouldn't have done it. The point was, it was the Fabs. Can you imagine the Rolling Stones going on tour: 'Oh sorry, Mick can't come.' – 'All right, we'll just get somebody else to replace him for two weeks.' It was silly, and I couldn't understand it. I really despised the way we couldn't make a decision for ourselves then. It was just: 'Off you go' – 'But Ringo must come with us.' 'No, sorry, you'll get a new drummer.' As we grew older, I suppose, we would have turned round and said we wouldn't go, but in those days it was the blind leading the blind." *(Anthology)*

However, the decision was made. Nicol recalled the events: "I was actually making money as a drummer, something many were not doing. Brian called me and I went down to his office. I nearly shit in me pants when he told me he wanted me to play for The Beatles in place of Ringo, at least until he was well enough to rejoin the group somewhere in the tour. I was truly shocked by it all... Brian asked me if I had practiced with any of The Beatles hits and I said I had. It was 1964 and The Beatles had so many hits but they had a hell of a lot of good album songs as well.

Nicol continued: "Well, Brian had all of The Beatles, with the exception of Ringo who was already in the hospital getting the swelling down in his throat from his inflamed tonsils – in an outer office. In a passing motion, he waved them in to meet me. I was floored. The Beatles were actually there to meet me! My mind was blown. I would have played for free for as long as they needed me. I shook all their hands and blurted out tones of admiration that I think made them embarrassed. They were very nice." *(Austin Teutsch)*

The subject of how much he had been paid has been in dispute. As Nicol recalled, "When Brian talked of money in front of them, I got very, very nervous. They paid me 2,500 pounds per gig and a 2,500 pounds signing bonus. Now that floored me. When John spoke up in a protest by saying 'Good God, Brian, you'll make the chap crazy!', I thought it was over. But no sooner had he said that when he said, 'Give him 10,000!' Everyone laughed and I felt a hell of a lot better. That night I couldn't sleep a wink. I was a f**king Beatle!" *(Austin Teutsch)*

Nicol didn't even have to do an audition. "Just one rehearsal in the studio with George Martin," he said. Jimmie Nicol was now a Beatle, at least for the time being. As George Martin later recalled: "They nearly didn't do the Australian tour. George is a very loyal person and he said, 'If Ringo's not part of the group, it's not The Beatles. I don't see why we should do it, and I'm not going to.' It took all of Brian's and my persuasion to tell George that if he didn't do it he was letting everybody down." On Nicol, he was very complimentary. "Jimmy Nicol was a very good drummer, who came along and learnt Ringo's parts well.

Obviously, he had to rehearse with the guys. They came and worked through all the songs at Abbey Road so he got to know them. He did the job excellently, and faded into obscurity immediately afterwards." *(Anthology)*

The press gathered at Abbey Road Studios for a photocall with The Beatles' new drummer. The boys were seen joking together, with Nicol sitting behind Ringo's drum kit – a pose which must have been a gut punch for Ringo. They ran through six songs together: "I Want to Hold Your Hand", " She Loves You", "I Saw Her Standing There", "This Boy", "Can't Buy Me Love", and "Long Tall Sally". Due to his experience earlier that year with the Top Six label, he knew the songs well. After the session, Nicol was taken to meet Ringo. But first, although he had been developing a suitable haircut of late, he had to truly look like a Beatle. "A wardrobe lady came over to my flat and a hairdresser cut my hair in a mop-top. In the mirror, I cut a mean figure as the new Beatle. I was on top of the music world, for sure." Then on to meet Ringo, which was a bit surreal for him. "Ringo kidded me when they took me over to introduce me as his replacement. There were a lot of jokes over that scene. John was super nice as well as Paul and George, with George being about as nervous as I was of the tour." *(Austin Teutsch)*

The niceties done, Jimmie Nicol was about to embark on a whirlwind two weeks with the three most famous people on earth, and his newfound status wasn't lost on him. "The day before I was a Beatle, not one girl would even look me over. The day after, when I was suited up and riding in the back of a limo with John Lennon and Paul McCartney, they were dying just to get a touch of me. Strange and scary all at once. It's hard to describe the feeling but I can tell you it can go to your head. I see why so many famous people kill themselves. There is so little sanity to it all." *(Austin Teutsch)*

Did he think he was up to the task? "Without being conceited, at that time in England there were only two drummers who had this 'feeling'," said Nicol, describing his ability to play the song, and not just stick to the music. "One was Phil Seamen, who was my idol as a drummer," said Nicol. "And the other was myself. Phil at that time was very much into drugs and injecting, and they used to book the two of us for recording sessions, so that I could play in case he wasn't fit to play. That's why I can say I was one of the top drummers in the country. Not the greatest, because I don't put enough time into it, and technically I'm not as good as, say, Buddy Rich, but it's more that I'm competent." So, confidence was not a problem then. But how did he rate the man he was replacing? "Without being unkind, Ringo Starr isn't really a drummer. On some of the recordings he played really well – he's got a good feel when they get together. But The Beatles weren't the greatest band. In fact, as a group, they were pretty bad."

(Interview Evert Vermeer)

And so Nicol was off to start a world tour with this "pretty bad group", replacing a drummer who he said wasn't really a drummer. His life would never be the same again.

Denmark - Coping In Copenhagen: 4th June 1964

On Thursday, 4th June 1964, John, Paul, George and Jimmie headed to London Heathrow Airport with their chauffeur Bill at the wheel of their Austin Princess car. They were allowed to board the aircraft before the other passengers and, of course, were asked for autographs by the crew. The co-pilot, who had probably

The Beatles, with Jimmie Nicol, land in Denmark

281

been asked by his daughter to get their autographs, mistook Paul for Ringo – who wasn't even on the plane! George, spotting the chance for a laugh, urged Paul to sign. "Go on, Ringo", he told Paul, "Give him your signature".

With the other passengers on board, the plane took off for Denmark.

Almost The Fifth Beatle - Torben Sardorf

The Beatles' world tour had started, and it turned out they could have had yet another drummer – Torben Sardorf of the support group The Hitmakers. When Ringo was taken ill, panic spread in Denmark, especially when there was doubt the tour would proceed. Sardorf was offered to Brian by the group's manager Niels Wenkens for The Beatles' Copenhagen visit. Epstein thanked him for the offer, but told him he wanted someone he knew from England to accompany the group in Ringo's absence.

When they arrived at Copenhagen on June 4th, they were met by over 6,000 fans, though, unlike other receptions, it was the male Beatles fans who did the yelling, while the girls stayed quietly in the background. They even dressed like the British Mods and Rockers. The Beatles checked into the Royal Hotel in Copenhagen, opposite the Tivoli Gardens, where they were due to appear that evening. Interestingly, they discovered that they were staying in the same suite of rooms Russia's premier Khrushchev would occupy a mere two weeks later. George found out that he would be sleeping in the same bed, so he said, "Right, I'll be leaving a note for him under the pillow!" *(Beatles Book Monthly 12)*

The group attended its first press call at the hotel, and while John, Paul and George were used to the attention, Nicol was a bit like a deer caught in headlights. "A lot of drummer fans were disappointed, I'm sure, because they wanted to see Ringo," Nicol would later recall. "John would introduce me at some of the concerts and at some he wouldn't. Also, I think I was accepted by most of the fans 'cause I fit in. I wore the suit and hair and tried to play like Ringo in his nonchalant fashion. I also bowed when the rest of them did and that went over big." *(Austin Teutsch)*

Aside from trying to look like a Beatle, Nicol had to sit behind Ringo's Ludwig drumkit, a constant reminder that he was only Ringo's stand-in. He also had to wear Ringo's suit, which didn't quite fit. Paul apparently wrote a note to Ringo: "Hurry up and get well Ringo, Jimmy is wearing out all your suits."

(Beatles Book Monthly 12)

Understandably, Nicol found it hard to fit in. Leslie Bryce, photographer for *The Beatles Book Monthly*, witnessed Nicol's induction: "1 didn't realise how difficult it was to be a Beatle until you see a new man among them." The British Ambassador in Copenhagen visited The Beatles, though there were riots at the end of the second show, when one of the local boys threw a flower pot at the organisers because The Beatles wouldn't be on for another encore! An early taste of flower power? *(Beatles Book Monthly 12)*

Nicol was clearly nervous and and behind the beat at times, but John watched over him and brought him back up to speed. Part of the problem was hearing his fellow bandmates, which was a new experience for him. Just before their final song, "Twist and Shout", Paul introduced the group's newest member to the crowd: "Before we go, we would like to say that we are sorry that Ringo isn't here. But we'd like you all to clap and give a really big hand for our drummer, Ring...." deliberately almost saying Ringo's name, then announcing, "eh Jimmie!" The recorded audio of that concert reveals the audience's immediate response – an ovation lasting almost 20 seconds. As the final chord drifted off into the expanse of the K.B. Hallen, Jimmie and his fellow Beatles left the stage, the first stop on their world tour completed. *(The Beatles Interviews)*

After the gig, George observed: "Playing without Ringo is like driving a car on three wheels, but Jimmy (sic) has grasped our rhythm very quickly." This was high praise from George, who had been very vocal about not doing the tour without Ringo. First one down, plenty more to go. *(The Beatles Interviews)*

Jette - I Can Almost Remember the Funny Faces

One of the eyewitnesses to The Beatles' appearance in Copenhagen was Jette Gottrup, whose fiancé Niels Wenkens, helped arrange the concert. Henrik Enevoldsen spoke to Jette about her memories of that momentous concert. She was with Nicol and The Beatles during the evening of 4th June 1964. When they heard that Ringo wouldn't be appearing, there was a lot of concern about the concert. "Actually I think many people were sad because Ringo didn't come," Jette said, "because we all had our favourites and I had one too and it was Paul McCartney. Some felt deeply sad that Ringo didn't come, and I don't think Jimmie Nicol was feeling good, because I don't think – when I think back on that evening – that he was accepted into the group. In the end, he was a substitute." It was clear to Jette that Nicol was an outsider.

How much did she recall about Nicol's performance? "I don't remember at all that I noticed him (Jimmie). I did notice the three others, but I didn't notice him at all. I do have his autograph; he's on the paper with the three others. I don't recall at all that I had any conversations with him." Jette told Henrik about George using Jette's powder for his face (which she helped him apply) and he recalled a picture with Pattie Boyd doing the same thing. Maybe it was a Harrison subterfuge to get near the girls. In those days, Jette was blonde and attractive, the same type as Pattie.

Jette also remembered an embarrassing moment. "At the press conference, Jimmie Nicol stayed in the background. When the concert was over and the limousine brought The Beatles back to the hotel, they forgot Jimmie at the venue, K.B. Hallen." Whether accidental or intentional, this couldn't have given Jimmie's ego much of a boost.

Jette could have been partying with The Beatles, but her boyfriend wanted to take them to the Kakadu Bar, which was really little more than a strip club. Jette suggestion of a nicer club fell on deaf ears, so she went home. As prepared for bed, she received a phone call from Derek Taylor. They had gone to the club she suggested after all and he asked her to join them. But she was tired and said 'no!' "I could have danced with all The Beatles," she says, adding that she doesn't "cry over spilt milk."

Later, in May 1966 in London, Jette and Niels Wenkens met Brian Epstein and his boyfriend at the musical On The Level and drove with them to Savoy Theatre to meet Cilla Black backstage. *(Henrik Enevoldsen interview for David Bedford 2015)*

Roll Over Beethovens

On the bill with The Beatles that night was a group called The Beethovens, and John Gerwin, their bass player, recalled how Jimmie nearly destroyed The Beatles' reputation, but very quickly saved their tour. "I have thought about the day, 4th June 1964, and there are many pictures, but the sound I recall is mostly screaming and shouting. Jimmie Nicol appeared, as I remember him, very friendly and integrated with the group, and he came down from the stage with the three others, looking friendly, looking to the right and left with his drumsticks in his hands, which he taps the rhythm, nods his head. The Beatles were rather small on the stage. When they were going to play 'Roll Over Beethoven', Jimmie comes in too late. John opened his arms with a despairing look and shook his head but Jimmie looked in a friendly way at John. It's completely unimportant as you can't hear anything because of the girls' screams, but here two different kind of people appear. Jimmie continued as if nothing had happened, but who is it now who forgets to play? John Lennon!" Gerwin revealed the true professional: "It's not John, as you don't do that. You don't let your saviour (Nicol) look like a fool in the K.B. Hallen in front of over 4,000 fans and, at the same time, you are the fool yourself. Jimmie Nicol had saved their tour."

Gerwin also remembered another fascinating story. "When our drummer Carsten hit a beat on the little drum, there came the sound of a beat from the ceiling a little later – a sort of an echo – and it was rather disturbing, and I remember it, because Carsten said to me, 'John, listen'. Then he hit the little drum 'bang' and shortly after 'bang, bang' came from the ceiling. I noticed that poor Jimmie had a problem with that. K.B. Hallen was a rumblebox to play in – with very poor acoustics – but it gave many fantastic experiences."

Poul Fogde Christensen was also playing that night with The Beethovens. "It was an evening I remember reasonably clearly," he said, "though it's 51 years since The Fab Four went crazy and played with lots of energy in K.B. Hallen. Regarding Jimmie Nicol as stand-in for Ringo, I can't tell you much, though I found him to have a much better drum technique than Ringo. But at the concert it was unimportant because it was nearly impossible to hear anything due to the infernal noise the audience created. Jimmie Nicol was probably chosen for the job when he – besides his drum skills – fitted in to the 'family picture' with height, body look and haircut. A couple of things I clearly remember is the Fab Four's mega-use of makeup and hairspray. I remember the stir it brought backstage with The Beatles when the Hitmakers played a terrific cover of 'Long Tall Sally'. The Beatles went into a panic, because they had planned to play this as an extra number, which was going to be released as single shortly after."

(Henrik Enevoldsen interview for David Bedford 2015)

Photograph

Knud Ørsted was the photographer assigned to cover The Beatles' appearance in Denmark. He remembered how the tour came about, and the shock when it was revealed that Ringo would not be joining the tour for the opening concerts. "The English director (Steven Gottlieb) of Scandinavian Grammophon, owned by EMI, and the sales director (Kurt Hviid Mikkelsen) had a meeting with Brian Epstein in the summer of '63, where Brian Epstein came over (to Denmark) to meet Danish managers and promoters.

They were all invited for lunch with Brian Epstein, but nobody turned up, which

> The Hitmakers were a top Danish pop group established in Copenhagen in 1960 by Jørgen Wulff Krabbenhøft (guitar and vocals) and Benny Qvotrup (drums). By 1961, the band had added Steen Bergstrøm on guitar and Erik Grønfeldt Hansen on bass. The band was considered to be one of the pioneers of Danish pop/rock, creating a sound that was compared to Cliff Richard and The Shadows, and, of course, The Beatles. This made them the obvious choice as a support act for The Beatles when they began their world tour in June 1964.

meant that nobody of them was going to make a concert with The Beatles." This might explain why Brian went to Sweden instead in 1963. "Just think about what they missed. They were nothing special then, and were just beginning to be popular. The general opinion was that they were never going to be stars and that it was soon over."

"I'm not a real photographer," he continued, "but a photojournalist, and the difference to the real photographers working for the newspapers is that I was there from the moment they arrived in Denmark until they were put on the plane for Amsterdam. The real photographers were working on a schedule, for example from 8am to 2pm and another from 2pm to 8pm and so on. There were a lot of photographers and fans at the arrival, but nearly nobody at the departure. You can tell if The Beatles have flowers at the arrival, and, if they have papers *(New Musical Express)*, it's at the departure."

The Beatles, not The Beatles

Ørsted continued: "The story about Niels Wenkens (impresario) being called from London and told that Ringo was ill and he goes to Knud Thorbjørnsen (impresario/colleague) to tell him is true. Then he says to Knud Thorbjørnsen: 'Ringo is ill, so it's not the real Beatles we've got!' Knud replied, 'Yeah, that's fine, and George had got German measles, right!' He didn't believe Niels because they often had fun with each other."

Of course, as they would soon find out, it was true. Ørsted then talked about Nicol as Ringo's replacement. "It's very interesting that he (Jimmie) was with The Beatles in Copenhagen. It made it a different story than the normal stories about The Beatles. The concert was completed and what's special is that it was one of the few concerts in which it was accepted that The Beatles were not The Beatles, and yet it was The Beatles."

For Ørsted, the group without Ringo wasn't really The Beatles, and Jimmie could never be accepted as a Beatle. So, how was Jimmie Nicol received? "All four Beatles were worshipped," he said, "but Jimmie was nothing, so I will not sit here and say they (the fans) were crazy about him, because they weren't."

Jimmie said that before The Beatles, the girls didn't even want to look at him, but

Jimmie (top) looks startled at he faces his first interview as a Beatle

after he joined The Beatles, all the girls wanted to touch him. "Yes, that's true, very true. They would, in Copenhagen, too, but they were not crazy about the person Jimmie Nicol. They were crazy about a person who was IN The Beatles. That's the truth and it's sad. Today I read in *Politiken* (a newspaper) about CityBoyz (a Danish X-Factor band) where a girl said 'When I saw them, I would be their fan no matter what happens' and that means that girls attach to one person; some liked Ringo, some liked Paul, some liked John and some liked George. Some liked even the most ugly of the band, believing they then had him for themselves, and of course they didn't!" *(Henrik Enevoldsen interview for David Bedford 2015)*

Torben Sardoff was offered as a replacement for Ringo, but what did Ørsted know about it? "Well, offered in that way, it was not a real proposition. When Paul McCartney, John Lennon and George Harrison saw him in K.B. Hallen, they realized what an extraordinary drummer he was because he was an expert in exactly the type of songs The Beatles played, and which The Hitmakers had in their repertoire.

One of the reasons that Torben Sardorff was such a skilled drummer is, just like The Beatles, he played over 300 times in Hamburg, where they practiced and practiced in their rooms because they had nothing else do.

It was the same thing with The Hitmakers in Finland, where they toured several times for nearly half a year – at least 3-4 months or something like that. What should they do when they were not on stage? They practiced and they practiced and they practiced and they got better and better and better. If you have read books about management, you will read about musicians, that it's not enough to be talented, the last part is just as important: to practice. That's what brought The Hitmakes to such a high standard and what Torben Sardorff had in common with The Beatles and made him such an experienced and skilled drummer – that he could play everything."

Did John, Paul and George watch Sardorff? "They were standing watching the warm-up groups and especially when The Hitmakers played 'Long Tall Sally'. It went wrong, so The Beatles didn't play 'Long Tall Sally' in their first concert, but played it in their second concert, where The Hitmakers didn't play it. That was the deal. It was really chaotic and it is one of the good stories to tell."

And what did Ørsted think about Jimmie and The Beatles? "I can tell you about Jimmie Nicol, that he didn't feel comfortable and accepted. The Beatles didn't bring him into the group. He was forgotten at the K.B. Hallen. He was just left standing and staring there. No, it was not nice - he felt like an outsider from the very start. It's very important to know each other, and they didn't and they never did. In Australia, Ringo and Brian Epstein were back.

(Henrik Enevoldsen interview for David Bedford 2015)

The Weedons

Flemming Gyldstrand Jørgensen was with the group, The Weedons, who also appeared on the roster supporting The Beatles. "Our pass to be supporting band to The Beatles was our hit 'Shimmy Shimmy'," he said, "which reached the Top 20 in 1963 and 1964. Not quite the same style as The Beatles', but we were actually big fans of The Beatles and we had a couple of their numbers in our repertoire, amongst others 'She Loves You'. The problem to perform Beatles numbers was that you had to be pretty strong as vocalists, and we were absolutely not."

Jimmie with The Beatles on stage in Denmark

What did he remember about the concert? "We knew of course that Ringo was ill and was replaced by Jimmie. We didn't regard Ringo as a very good drummer, and rumours said that others were used during their recordings. I remember how impressed I was about Jimmie's performance. My opinion is that he didn't make one single mistake during the concerts. It was a secure and capable performance, maybe a little impersonal. If he had made mistakes, I'm sure we would have noticed it. Another thing I remember from the concerts is that we actually didn't see John before he, from the dressing room, went directly on stage. It was quite different with Paul and George. They came backstage before they went on stage and they looked over the hall to get a feeling of the atmosphere. That meant that you could easily talk to the two, and we, of course, made use of the opportunity and got their autographs. Paul and George seemed forthcoming, but John seemed a little shy and not interested. I don't think I can add more. It is, after all, 51 years I have to go back in my memory." *(Henrik Enevoldsen interview for David Bedford 2015)*

The concerts in Denmark were a baptism of fire for Jimmie Nicol and it is clear that he coped remarkably well, if only with the music. Breaking into the Fab Three was impossible, as so many others had discovered over the years.

The Beatles at Blokker

Netherlands - Going Dutch: 6th June 1964

After Denmark, The Beatles headed to Amsterdam in the Netherlands and, over the following two days, wreaked total chaos. A new city meant more photocalls and press interviews, but Jimmie was settling into the groove. The boys were presented with bunches of flowers and traditional Dutch hats, and then went straight to a television rehearsal at the Tres Long restaurant in Hillegram, 26 miles from Amsterdam. It was an incredible show and some audience members jumped up onto the stage and sang with the boys into the microphones. As in Denmark, mostly boys made the noise.

On the show, Nicol was asked about his debut. "I was very, very, nervous yesterday at the first appearance in Copenhagen," he recalled. "Sweat was rolling off my cheeks in buckets." At a second interview, Nicol was asked more questions, leading him to open up about his role in the group. First, the interviewer wanted to know if it was difficult to take over the role of Ringo. "Uh, no, not really, no. As far as Ringo, I could never make up for what Ringo is. I just try my best." A brilliant, diplomatic response which would satisfy any PR man. The interviewer proceeded with this line of questioning, asking if he was Ringo's understudy. "Yes I am," he said confidently. "Do you think it is a great break?" he was asked. "Oh yes, excellent," he replied. The final question was one he had to get right, and he even looked over at a smiling John and Paul when asked if the other Beatles were treating him well. "Yes, marvelous." Audition passed!

(The Beatles Interviews)

Jimmie back behind the drums, in 1984

As they were in Amsterdam, the four Beatles went on a well-photographed sightseeing tour around the canals in a glass-topped tourist boat. Crowds lined the banks, shouting and cheering for their heroes. Jimmie Nicol was enjoying the spotlight despite the presence of banners that read "Ringo, Quick Recover". Some fans even dived into the canal, and when the police manhandled them while dragging them out of the water, John got upset. "I've got to protest about this," he said about the unnecessary roughness with which the teens were treated.

(Beatles Book Monthly 12)

Then the group was driven in white Cadillacs some 36 miles to the Exhibition Hall at Blokker, where they would play two incredible concerts.

Tres Long 1984

Jimmie returned to Tres Long in 1984 for a Beatles convention, signing autographs and talking about his time with The Beatles, before being asked to join The Clarks on drums for a concert. At the time he was talking about writing a book, though he never did, sadly.

They Saw Them Standing There

Frits de Lange, aged 18, saw The Beatles in Blokker, but it wasn't easy.

"My parents didn't want me to go, because at that time I had to go to school every Saturday. But I was lucky. My parents had an excursion that day, so I decided to skip school. I travelled to Blokker, bought a ticket for the afternoon performance, because it wasn't sold out. It only cost 7 guilders and 50 cents, from money I had saved myself. I also had to pay for the train and the bus, a drink and the toilet, so you can imagine that my money-box was almost empty. I couldn't even buy a program, due to lack of money. And that's a pity, if you know the value of such a program nowadays!

Theaterproducties Dick van Gelder • N.V. Nederlands Theaterbureau

en **Ben Essing** presenteren onder auspiciën van maandblad

muziek expres

in de beroemde **Veilinghallen** te **Blokker** op **zaterdagavond 6 juni, 8 uur**

persoonlijk optreden van

THE BEATLES

Voor deze meest sensationele show van het jaar zijn kaarten via „MUZIEK EXPRES" te bestellen!! Vul nevenstaande bon DUIDELIJK en VOLLEDIG in en zend hem spoedig mogelijk (bij voorkeur geplakt op een briefkaart) naar: „Muziek Expres", Theresiastraat 11, Den Haag!

Rotterdam, Den Bosch, Arnhem, Utrecht, Hilversum, Amsterdam, Haarlem, Alkmaar, Groningen en Leeuwarden. De buskaarten worden per separate post (dus niet gelijk met de entréekaarten) onder rembours toegezonden, met opgave van tijd en plaats van vertrek.

ENTREEPRIJS

De entréeprijs voor dit wereldevenement bedraagt ƒ 10.— per persoon. De bonnen worden behandeld in volgorde van binnenkomst. De kaarten worden ná 20 mei onder rembours verzonden, de entréeprijs wordt derhalve met 50 cent per persoon

Pauze

21.00 - 21.20 uur

7. Kwintet Dominique
8. Wanda
9. THE BEATLES

Na afloop
ongeveer 22.30 uur

GROOT BAL

met Kwintet Dominique
en The Hotjumpers

Theaterproducties
DICK VAN GELDER
Amsterdam

BEN ESSING
Blokker

N.V. NED. THEATERBUREAU
's-Gravenhage

presenteren in
samenwerking met

STIBBE/PARLOPHONE

THE BEATLES

THE BEATLES UITSLUITEND
OP PARLOPHONE

met medewerking van

THE BEATLES

Wanda
Ciska Peters
Jack and Bill
The Torero's
Herman van Keeken
Don Mercedes and his Improvers
The Fancy Five
Karin Kent
Candy Kids
Hotjumpers
Kwintet Dominique
John Rassel and his Clan

programma
festival
blokker
1964

6 juni

aanvang:
middagvoorstelling 14.30 uur
avondvoorstelling 20.00 uur

prijs 50 ct.

7. The Torero's
8. Ciska Peters
9. THE BEATLES

Programma

AVONDVOORSTE
Aanvang 2

1. The Hotjumpers
2. Wanda
3. Candy Kids
4. John Rassel and his Clan
5. Karin Kent
6. Herman van Keeken

zie vervolg

THE BEATLES

exclusief op
Parlophone/Stibbe Grammofoonplaten

45 t. SINGLE	GEP 8883 — I SAW HER STANDING THERE / Misery / Anna / Chains
R5114 — CAN'T BUY ME LOVE You can't do that	
R5055 — SHE LOVES YOU I'll get you	30 cm LP
	PMC 1202 (stereo PCS 3042)
HHR125 — TWIST AND SHOUT	'PLEASE PLEASE ME'

koop hier een
BEATLE-SLIERT *

95 ct

* een strip met 20 unieke foto's, horoscopen en karakterschetsen van de Beatles.
Gevouwen als een harmonika, uitgetrokken één-meter-tweeëntwintig lang en dan zeer geschikt om aan ... ur te prikken.

287

"I was so impressed with the concert; it was quite a happening, but it took a long time before The Beatles arrived on stage, and then within half an hour, it was over. Jimmie Nicol was very nervous and got regular advice from the side. John Lennon would always turn around to help him play the songs and keep it going. I think he was a fine drummer."

After the concert, Frits returned home well in advance of his parents' arrival. "After an hour, my parents came back and asked me what I had done during the day. I said, 'Listening to music'. My father replied, 'I think The Beatles!' So I didn't need to lie. Twenty five years later, we saw a documentary about The Beatles in Blokker, and my father saw me in the public and I was forced to tell the whole truth after all those years!"

Frits became a fan of The Beatles when he first heard "She Loves You" on BBC Radio 2 on Allan Freeman's *Top of the Pops*. "It was so refreshing at that time," he said. "They made music which was so inventive. It was also a kind of protest against the music my parents liked." *(David Bedford Interview 2015)*

Corrie Rock-Korver was just 15 when she attended the Blokker concert. She had been a Beatles fan since the age of 13 when she "listened to the radio. It was said that there is a new craze in England. Everyone absolutely loved The Beatles," she remembered, though she had never heard of them. Unlike many young fans, she didn't jump on The Beatles bandwagon at first. But that all changed when she heard "She Loves You". "I was an instant fan. I did everything to hear it again." She immediately saved up the money to buy that record.

"All of my girlfriends were also Beatles fans," she continued. "I played my single with my girlfriends, sometimes as many as 30 times a day." However, like many parents at that time, hers weren't impressed. Still, Corrie's mother was soon singing along with the group.

"They also found it beautiful. Much later, 'Yesterday' was one of her favorite songs, and we played that song at her funeral."

Hearing the songs on the radio and the record player was one thing, but nothing could compare to seeing The Beatles in person. "I was very very excited when I heard that The Beatles were coming to The Netherlands. I did everything to get to that concert. My mother ordered a ticket for me, in that time via Radio Veronica, a music channel with popular music for the youth.

"Shortly before the concert, I was told that Ringo wouldn't be there because he was sick. Jimmie Nicol took his place." Did that make a difference to Corrie? "That Ringo wasn't there I found not very interesting. I was totally in love with Paul. Paul was the most beautiful Beatle. He had beautiful eyes and he was the man of my dreams."

Corrie journeyed to the concert with a bus full of teenagers, though she didn't know any of them. "On the bus we were singing Beatles songs. Everyone was so excited about the concert, though no one said anything about Jimmie or Ringo." The concert didn't disappoint her, even in Ringo's absence. "It was a magnificent concert. The first and best concert of my life. I was all the way at the front, right by Paul. Just like all the other girls, I screamed! Paul gave me a wink, and I think all the other girls also thought it was for them, but I was sure it was for me!" Corrie was so wrapped up in Paul that she "did not notice that Jimmie Nicol was drumming. I didn't see him, I only saw Paul and John. It made no difference that

Jimmie on stage with The Beatles at Blokker

Jimmie was there."

Corrie's parents came to take her home from the bus. "I was not allowed to go into Amsterdam to see The Beatles." Corrie was fortunate, though, because her girlfriends' parents didn't even allow them to go to the concert. "After years of searching, I found a video on YouTube where I saw myself, in my Beatles dress, walking to the entrance of the concert in Blokker."

Corrie was profoundly affected by the concert. "The Beatles have had a major influence on my life. I love music, but never has anyone been able to outperform The Beatles." In 2015, she attended McCartney's Amsterdam show with her brother Robbie and his 17-year-old daughter, also a great fan of The Beatles. "Between the songs, Robbie and I started to sing very loud 'Give Peace a Chance', and Paul responded by saying: 'Oh, there is another concert going on, let's listen to them.' He picked up a guitar and started to sing along. This was a highlight. Contact with Paul!!!! Who would ever have dreamed?"

Corrie became a painter 10 years ago, and has created many paintings of her favorite group. "There are still a lot of fans in The Netherlands, and that makes me very happy! The Beatles have the most fantastic music ever."

(David Bedford Interview 2015)

In between shows, the boys had to stay in their dressing room because of the crowds, so they tried to curl up and go to sleep, the screams still ringing in their ears. John pulled off their suit covers, made himself a little bed and quickly nodded off. Nicol slid under the table and also caught some sleep. George found himself a corner and closed his eyes, while Paul grabbed some golden slumbers.

No one told them before they got in their winks that they were supposed to be attending a civic reception at a local restaurant and visiting a traditional Dutch village. There were some stories in the local press saying that The Beatles had let them down. Luckily for them, it didn't end as disastrously as a similar situation did two years later in Manila, Philippines when, after an unintentional snub of First Lady Imelda Marcos, the band was denied police protection and roughed up by locals and military personnel upon their departure!

The British press covered the tour with even more interest, under the strange headline, "Bonk! To Paul, with love". *The Daily Mail* revealed how girls tried to storm the stage in Copenhagen, and were met by a dozen 'hefty ushers' who showed them back to their seats. They also explained the headline. "Paul McCartney was hit on the head by a piece of paper thrown by a girl who screamed, 'It was a love letter.' Outside the hall, police used dogs to help disperse fans who were unable to get into the hall." They were also keen to highlight how well the new drummer was received: "Inside the hall, the audience gave a special ovation to Jimmy (sic) Nicol, the stand-in for Ringo Starr." *(Daily Mail)*

They Never Saw Him Crawling There

Beatles fans never knew what happened after dark in Amsterdam. Being mischievous Beatles, they knew, as most people did, that Amsterdam had a notorious red-light district, which surely brought back memories of Hamburg. John Lennon was definitely involved in an incident, though it isn't clear how many of the others took part. With the assistance of the local police, they were taken into the red-light area. They spent part of the night in a brothel. "There's photographs of me groveling about," recalled Lennon, "crawling about Amsterdam on my knees, coming out of whore houses, and people saying 'Good morning John'. The police escorted me to these places because they never wanted a big scandal. When we hit town, we hit it – we were not pissing about. We had them (the women). They were great. We didn't call them groupies, then; I've forgotten what we called them, something like 'slags'." *(Anthology)*

Jimmie and Paul were also seen at a nightclub, the Femina, in Rembrandt Square. Carensa Maar helped arrange the visit. "It was about half past one at night, with a few people from the hotel and a couple of policemen having a cigarette. Suddenly, The Beatles said, 'We want go to the whores!' Well, what do you do?" She decided to keep an eye on them, so she used an undercover police car and they headed to the red-light area. They looked around and spotted a streetwalker, who recognised them. "She said, 'Here, look, what dirty guys! It seems to be The Beatles!' I said, 'I do have a nice nightclub for you.'" They avoided the streetwalker and headed to the Femina on Rembrandt Square. "There, they tried to talk to one of the ladies, which she found too dirty!" The Beatles were turned down. "Can you imagine," said Carensa, "while outside were 25,000 girls who would love to dive into bed with them!" *(www.onsamsterdam.nl)*

Hong Kong Calling: 9th June 1964

They had just found their feet in Holland when they were whisked away to that exotic Far East port, Hong Kong.

Tony Sheridan - Again

With John's Aunt Mimi and wife Cynthia having joined the entourage, it was time to cross to the other side of the world. Their flight proved interesting, as one of their fellow passengers was a former bandmate of both The Beatles and Jimmie Nicol: Tony Sheridan. Away from the cameras and journalists, The Beatles indulged in pillow fights, drinks, and another old "friend" from their days in Hamburg – preludin pills.

The group arrived in Hong Kong safely and, as Nicol was finding out, yet

DJ Ray Cordeiro

another series of press interviews was first on the agenda. It is worth noting that when press officer Derek Taylor introduced each group member, the three Beatles turned to Jimmie at the mention of his name, clapping and whistling in a very obvious show of support. Naturally, the journalists wanted to briefly speak to Nicol, and the line of questioning would be the same everywhere: "How do you feel being rushed into this vast world of publicity all at once?" Once again, he gave a stock reply: "It's a most exciting experience." *(The Beatles Interviews)*

During the interview, John, Paul and George tried to bring Jimmie into the discussion, but the interviewers insisted on talking to the "real" Beatles. Eventually, they got back around to the drummer, asking the obligatory question about what he would do after Ringo rejoined the group. "Then I go back to London," he replied, "and things seem to be jumping in London, so you know... I've got a couple of television shows and a band's being formed and everything. So it looks as though things might happen for me, you know." He was getting used to be asked the same question, just like his bandmates.

Q: "Gentlemen, you've had a chance to see something of Asia's beauty."

PAUL: "Lovely, yes."

Q: "What's your impression?"

PAUL: "Lovely. Marvelous. Beautiful. Very good, isn't it?"

JOHN: "Yeah."

PAUL: "Very great. Marvelous. Love it."

Q: "With all this traveling about, how do you get time to rehearse?"

JOHN: (giggling) "We don't!"

Q: "You don't rehearse?"

JOHN: "We do, a bit. We rehearse with Jimmy 'coz he's new."

Q: "One of the reports made here was that you'd chosen Hong Kong yourselves. You've been offered several places and that you, yourselves had chosen Hong Kong. Is that true?"

JOHN: "Yes."

Q: "Why was that?"

JOHN: "Cuz we wanted to see it."

In Hong Kong, they also met a man they had befriended in London.

Ray Cordeiro was the radio DJ who had sparked the birth of Hong Kong's pop music scene. He had managed to interview The Beatles three times in a matter of days – in the UK just before the tour started, and in Hong Kong. Ray noted the similarities between the Hong Kong and British music scenes before The Beatles arrived. "We were also influenced by the U.S. scene," he said, "with the Beach Boys, the Walker Brothers, Ricky Nelson, Paul Anka and the like. As you know, The Beatles' arrival changed the scene completely."*(David Bedford Interview 2015)*

In Hong Kong, radio was the only, and best, entertainment and Ray Cordeiro arrived at the right time, returning to Hong Kong from Macau during the Second World War. Nearly twenty years later, on joining Radio Hong Kong, Ray was sent by the station to the UK and enrolled onto the BBC for a three-month course. It was here that he first met The Beatles. "At the end of the course," he recalled, "I had two weeks' free time before flying back to Hong Kong. So I decided to do some interviews with the UK pop stars for my own radio shows in Hong Kong. I went up to the EMI office and met the senior man at the desk, whose name was Stan Stern, who offered to help. He asked who did I have in mind for the interviews and I replied, of course, at the top of my list was The Beatles who were red hot with a string of top hits."

Stern picked up the phone and called Brian Epstein, who said that the timing was perfect as The Beatles were due to have a press interview the next morning at his NEMS offices. By chance, on his way to the interview, Ray picked up a magazine featuring The Beatles on the cover, not realising that the whole magazine was dedicated to them. "When I approached this important venue," Ray said, "Paul McCartney was at the door to greet the press with a big happy 'Hi' and he asked me what was the magazine I was holding under my armpit. I said it's a Fab mag featuring The Beatles and he asked if he could have a look." Ray passed McCartney the magazine and asked him to autograph it; he gladly obliged. "I had no idea that as he went along and autographed every page with his photo on it, and even more, as he flicked the pages, he signed the entire magazine. As I approached John Lennon and he saw what Paul did, he followed suit. Then, of course, followed by George Harrison and Ringo Starr." *(David Bedford Interview 2015)*

Ray then interviewed the four Beatles, and he still has it "on an EMI tape and box, and this is worth a fortune." The following day, Ray noticed in the newspaper that The Beatles were holding a second interview, and this time only for foreign correspondents. "Since I'm from Hong Kong, I considered myself foreign, so I went along for the second interview, too. Again, Paul was at the door and when he saw me, he said 'Weren't you here yesterday? Where are you from?' I said 'Hong Kong'. He said, 'We are going there in a couple of days and we know nothing about Hong Kong. Can you offer some advice?' I did, and we became closer friends." Cordeiro then headed back to Hong Kong to await The Beatles' arrival. *(David Bedford Interview 2015)*

The Khaki Concert

In Hong Kong, the promoter priced the tickets at £2 – practically a king's ransom for the ordinary fans. "The concert was poorly attended," explained Cordeiro, "because the teenagers couldn't afford the price for the tickets and their parents didn't even know who The Beatles were! The sponsors had to invite members of the British army to fill up the hall. The Beatles were highly and loudly received and it was huge success, but not money-wise." *(David Bedford Interview 2015)*

Some of those who had to miss the concert did manage to greet the group at the airport, so at least they got to see them in person. As with most places they visited, The Beatles were confined to the hotel because it was too dangerous to venture out into the busy streets. Instead, they stayed sequestered in their rooms at the President Hotel in Kowloon. Paul attempted to "escape" but had to quickly head back to the hotel, while Jimmie was able to slip out and explore the city unnoticed.

On the first evening, they once again missed an engagement they were due to attend – the Miss Hong Kong pageant. Though it was held at the hotel, the boys were tired so they sent their apologies, which weren't well-received. John decided to make a brief appearance on behalf of the group, no doubt doing so as an excuse to check out the "local talent".

The Beatles gave two concerts at the Princess Theatre at 130, Nathan Road, Tsim Sha Tsui, in Kowloon. The support act, The Maori Hi-Five, was described as a showband that performed a mix of musical comedy and cabaret, tourist variety act, vaudeville show and rock and roll dance. They could perform soulful ballads followed by a satirical skit, laughing at their own Māori culture while also educating the audience. This was just the kind of group that would have suited George Martin and his comic roots, and they obviously did. In the December 1961 edition of Disc magazine, Martin is quoted as saying, "I have just signed an outfit that does sound different – the Maori Hi-Fives. I think they'll be a sensation." Unfortunately, nothing came of this, and Martin was soon diverted by the group The Maori Hi-Five were supporting – The Beatles.

During the visit, a photograph was taken of The Maori Hi-Five with The Beatles, but without Nicol. The lineup included Paul McCartney, Wes Epae, John Lennon, Paddy Te Tai, George Harrison, Robert Hemi Te Miha, Solly Pohatu, the local agent and a couple of unidentified people. The group became the only New Zealand band to support The Beatles. They were also the first Maori showband to play in Las Vegas, paving the way for other Maori groups. Though they released numerous singles and albums, they were far more popular overseas than in their native New Zealand.

Some audience members recalled being underwhelmed by the concert. Anders Nelsson, the teenaged lead singer of the band The Kontinentals, and Philip Chan Yan-kin of the Astro-Notes, clearly remembered throngs of screaming female fans. Nelsson couldn't even make out the music, which was obviously important to him. "The girls were screaming so loud and the PA system was so bad," he said, "that it was basically an experience, rather than a concert". Chan clearly enjoyed it: "From the first chord, we couldn't hear a thing because of the girls; they were screaming like in a horror flick. We'd seen that in the newsreels, but to be there and see these short little Chinese girls and Western girls – that made me want to be a pop singer." *(South China Morning Post)*

The Beatles showed Nelsson and his fellow musicians that the power of rock 'n' roll came from more than just the music. "(We realised) that if you grew your hair longer and you shook your head and went 'woo', the girls would scream," he says. This was a revelation to Nelsson. "Before, we just played and we were fairly serious about our playing. We hadn't realised that you could make girls faint." Like teenage boys in bands all over Hong Kong, he wanted to have that effect on girls, and now thanks to The Beatles they all knew how. "All of us started growing our hair and trying to do things to make the girls squeal." *(South China Morning Post)*

The local press was not impressed by Beatlemania or the Western influences that the commotion promoted. Following the concerts at the Princess Theatre, Hong Kong's Chinese language newspapers printed negative reviews that condemned the behavior of the fans, focusing more on the public reaction than on the group or their music. According to one newspaper account, "The Beatles fought a losing battle against the screams." John Lennon disagreed "Compared with other audiences," he said, "they were quiet." *(Anthology)*

The venue only held 1,700 seats, and with neither show sold out, it seems unlikely that the noise was an issue. Paul observed that "Hong Kong was a slightly flat performance in a smallish place. They behaved themselves, and it looked like a khaki audience," supporting what Cordeiro said about the audience being filled with British soldiers. "We played, but I don't think we enjoyed the show too much – although at least we could be heard." *(Anthology)*

It's Getting Better

In one Hong Kong radio interview, Nicol revealed more about his musical background and influences, and commented how different it was playing with The Beatles. He mentioned names like Dave Brubeck, Cannonball Adderley, Duke Ellington and Count Basie, observing that "I've played in big bands, and I've played arrangements by all these people." He even mentioned a fondness for Latin American music, an affinity that would serve him well later on.

With each concert, Nicol became increasingly more acclimated to the music and the mayhem. When asked how he was adjusting, he would always say, "It's getting better". According to Beatles biographer Hunter Davies, it was this oft-stated quote from Nicol that would inspire the title for a McCartney track on the Sgt. Pepper album – perhaps The Beatles' permanent tribute to him.

As for Uncle Ray Cordeiro, his timing was perfect. With the popularity of The Beatles at its peak in Hong Kong, he began establishing the pop scene with his radio show. Six days a week, he played the interviews he had conducted in the UK with The Searchers, The Dave Clark Five, The Hollies, and many others. "I started the pop scene here in Hong Kong in the '60s," Cordeiro declared proudly, "and I was named 'Uncle Ray' by the local press." *(David Bedford Interview 2015)*

Australia - Going Down Under

It was a chance meeting between Brian Epstein and Kenn Brodziak, a Melbourne promoter with years of theatrical experience, that took The Beatles to Australia. Brodziak had begun booking touring musicians back in the 1950s, and was responsible for bringing acts like Cliff Richard and the Shadows, Lonnie Donegan and the Dave Brubeck Quartet all the way Down Under.

On a trip to London in mid-1963, he first came across The Beatles by chance after being given a list of five bands by an agent who wanted him to book them for an Australian tour. Brodziak decided that he didn't want five groups, just the one, to see if it would work out. "The agent said, 'which one would you like?', and I said 'I'll take The Beatles'," Brodziak recalled. "That was all there was to the story. I didn't know anything about the group except that their name sounded familiar – I think because of their playing in Germany."

Because The Fab Four were still establishing themselves, Brodziak struck a verbal agreement Brian Epstein for a flat fee of only £1500 a week. It seemed like a reasonable deal all around, but as 1963 progressed, and Beatlemania was born, it became one of the shrewdest – and most lucrative – deals in Australian music history. In December 1963, the contract for the Australian tour was finally signed. Epstein decided he should renegotiate the fee on behalf of The Beatles, while remaining fair. The new fee, £2500 per week, was still quite the bargain.

Details of the deal to bring The Beatles to Australia had been shared with the group, as Brodziak recalled in an interview years later: "One of the first things that George (Harrison) said when the band arrived in Sydney was, 'You got us at the old price, didn't you?' I said 'Yes', but he didn't seem to mind." Brodziak, who received many notable honours in the entertainment industry, including an O.B.E. (Order of the British Empire) from the Queen, used to be frustrated that, for all he accomplished, people remembered him most for bringing The Beatles to Australia. "Now I realise," he said shortly before his death, "what a landmark moment that was. There will never be another group like them." *(James Wigney, news.com.au 24th May 2014)*

Sydney: 11th June 1964

On 11th June 1964, The Beatles headed to Sydney. After a brief stop in Darwin, they arrived at 6.30am at Sydney's Mascot International Airport. Although it would be their one and only tour Down Under, the country would never be the same again. They were greeted by a crowd of around 1,000, but not everyone was pleased to see them. One group of protestors held up a banner that read, "Go Home Bugs – NSW Anti-Trash Society." Nevertheless, the new independence of teenagers and various social changes assured that the tour was branded a cultural phenomenon. Despite a blustery cold wind and rain falling in sheets, the band was paraded on the back of an open-top truck. Suddenly, a woman ran to the moving vehicle and threw her six-year-old disabled child at The Beatles, shouting, 'Catch him, Paul'. Did she really believe that a pop musician could provide a cure for her child? McCartney caught him and the boy was passed back to his mother when the truck stopped, but incidents like this must have been disturbing for the group. *(The Beatles Down Under: 1964 Australia and New Zealand Tour)*

"When we arrived in Sydney, it was pissing down with rain," recalled Beatles roadie Neil Aspinall. "We got off the plane and they put The Beatles on the back of a flat-back truck so the crowd could see them. They were carrying umbrellas and wearing the capes made in Hong Kong. The driver was doing one mile an hour, and John kept leaning over and saying, 'Faster, faster!' but he wouldn't go any faster. I was saying, 'Go faster – it's pouring down,' and he said, 'these kids have been waiting here for twenty-four hours to see these guys.' Nothing was going to make this big Australian trucker go any faster. By the time they got to the hotel, everybody was blue because the dye in the capes had run and soaked right through; they all looked like old Celtic warriors covered in blue dye."

(Anthology)

The young people of Australia had followed the fortunes of The Beatles, especially the successful U.S. tour and their assault on the American charts. What the four musicians encountered here was even bigger and better than their reception in New York, with the largest crowds ever recorded on a Beatles tour. Even the weather must have reminded them of home, with torrential rain the order of the day!

Going Down, Under

Although the press covered the best parts of the tour, things went on behind the scenes which were kept under wraps. The tour manager, Lloyd Ravenscroft, later confessed what happened when the cameras stopped clicking. "They had girls in their room, yes. That was in the hand of their trusted Beatles roadie Mal Evans, who was very good at picking the right girls. It was all very discreet and well-organised. When they were getting involved in that sort of thing, I kept right out of the way." *(The Beatles Down Under: The 1964 Australia and New Zealand Tour)*

Journalist Jim Oram revealed the story in more detail, claiming that John and Paul especially "rooted themselves silly" with an "endless and inexhaustible stream of Australian girls". Bob Rogers, who accompanied The Beatles on their tour, witnessed "just so many women". They weren't particularly fussed if the girls were beautiful or plain, and had almost seemed "supremely indifferent to it all" as girl after girl lay themselves in front of, and beneath, The Beatles. One thing did surprise Rogers. "There was no pill in 1964 and with the amount of Beatle screwing that went on, I just can't believe that there wasn't an explosion of little Beatles all over Australia in 1965. Maybe there was." Maybe Rogers was right. Were there little Beatles running all over Australia in the mid-to-late Sixties? One girl from Queensland claimed to have been "screwed by all four Beatles in one night". Jimmie Nicol must have thought that all of his Christmasses had come at once. He was living in the eye of the hurricane, and must have wondered what was happening to him. *(The Beatles Down Under: The 1964 Australia and New Zealand Tour)*

Don't Throw Sweets

At the concert, Paul McCartney pleaded with the hysterical Sydney fans to do them a big favour: "Don't throw those sweets because they get in our eyes." One young fan, Pauline Bayliss, who had won two tickets in a limerick competition, decided not to throw sweets, but took the opportunity after the concert to sneak onto the stage to grab a sweet. "When the crowds had died down, we went down and picked up a jelly baby from the stage, thinking this is amazing, it might have hit one of The Beatles," she said. Thankfully, she had no intention of eating it, so she placed it in a matchbox, wrapped the box in paper and put it away in a drawer where she left it for years.

Did Pauline enjoy the music? Even though her seats were close to the stage, hundreds of screaming girls rushed to the front, blocking her view. But that didn't matter. "I can't hear a thing, I can't see a thing, but we are here," she remembered thinking.

Roslyn Forrest was also at the concert and, at age fourteen, she, like many young girls, was accompanied by a chaperone. In her case, it was her older brother who "kept telling me I couldn't scream," she said. "And after three songs, he said, 'You can scream'. And I screamed myself hoarse." *(The Sydney Morning Herald)*

There must have been a lot of sore throats across Sydney and the rest of Australia when The Beatles came to town. The Beatles, however, had no chance to rest their sore throats because everywhere they went, there was yet another interview to do. In Sydney, they met the press at the Sheraton Hotel. After first grilling John, Paul and George, the attending reporters, prompted by Lennon, turned to Nicol and asked the usual questions about replacing Ringo.

The Interview

Q: "How about you, Jim? You haven't said anything. How do you feel, Jimmie, being in with The Beatles, a new talent, standing-in for Ringo?"

JN: "It's a good experience, man."

Q: "How is Ringo?"

JN: "Umm, he's much better. He joins them on Sunday."

Q: "What do you do then?"

JN: "Umm, I go back to London and they're fixing up a band for me, and I do some television."

John jumped in with a joke: "And he's away!"

Q: "You're progressing well with your Beatle haircut."

        JN: "Yes, I've been growing it for about three months."

The conversation then veered away from Nicol, addressing that all-important issue – Beatles haircuts. Hardly cutting-edge journalism! After some time, the interviewers focused once again on Jimmie.

Q: "Have you got an agreement that Jimmie mustn't speak?"

George quickly responded. "Ask him a question." Jimmie replied to George's comment with some Beatlesque humour: "I can't answer questions that, umm, I don't know anything about."

Q: "What's the group you play with in England?"

JN: "Well, I've played with a lot of groups in England. Just before I left, I was playing with a rhythm and blues band."

Q: "You were in the Blue Flames for a while weren't you?"

JN: "Yeah, that's right. Well, only for a matter of days. I played on Friday. I didn't even know what I was doing just on Wednesday, you know."

Q: "Does Brian Epstein manage you?"

A good question which broke the flow of the interview;
Nicol thought before answering.

JN: "Nobody.... No he doesn't." The other Beatles laughed with him, before John added a comment.

John: "You'd know if he did!"

Q: "Jimmie, what was your first reaction when you were told that you were going to play with The Beatles?"

JN: "I couldn't believe it, really."

Q: "   Did you have to do much rehearsal with the boys to get their sound?"

JN: "No, we rehearsed about five or six numbers, which took about half an hour."

Q: "And away you went?"

JN: "Yeah."

Q: "Pretty frightening?"

JN: "The first show was very, pretty, frightening, yeah. But, uh, they reassured me."

Paul and John decided to show support for their drummer.
Paul: "He did grand."

John, in one of his funny accents: "He did grand job."

Jimmie had handled the questioning well, and, when needed, the other Beatles gave him moral support, which must have given him confidence. After the press conference, The Beatles entourage flew on to Adelaide to continue their short concert tour.

Adelaide: 12th June 1964

Originally, Adelaide was not going to be in the tour schedule, but the people of Adelaide were desperate to see The Beatles. Entrepreneur Ron Tremaine had won the support of John Martins Department Store to guarantee the financial success of the visit, and he also enlisted two popular radio DJs, Bob Francis and Jim Slade, to gather more than 80,000 signatures on a petition to persuade promoter Ken Brodziak to bring the group here. Four new shows were added to the tour, with the takings to go directly to the band's management. Adelaide showed its gratitude by the most amazing reception The Beatles would ever have, but not when they first arrived.

When they arrived in Adelaide, there was complete silence: no fans to greet them, which was strange. At the top of the steps as they disembarked from the plane, John Lennon said; "Why don't you let the kids into the airport?" George joined in too: "Yeah, we want to see the kids."

The four musicians walked down the steps whistling and singing a few bars of a song before greeting the photographers. In front of them was a white, open-top

JIMMY NICOL:
The Beatles Stand-In
by Austin Teutsch

Imagine yourself being asked to join the Beatles at the height of Beatlemania. Well, that's what happened to drummer Jimmy Nicol. When Ringo Starr came down with tonsillitis on June 3, 1964, at the beginning of a Beatles world tour, Nicol took over his duties in Denmark on the following day. For the next week-and-a-half Nicol filled in during the group's jaunt through Amsterdam, Hong Kong and Australia, until Ringo rejoined them in Melbourne on June 14th.

Nicol (pronounced like nickel) got his first drum kit at a Liverpool pawn shop when he was 14 and began playing "with some of the worst players" in town. Initially inspired by jazz drummer Gene Krupa, he found his calling when he attended a Chuck Berry rock 'n' roll concert in London. "Chuck let the drummer cut loose on

a particular song. Man, that was it for me. I loved it."

Jimmy Nicol, who now lives in South America, was working as a studio session drummer "for all the hundreds of Buddy Holly and Elvis Presley imitators bouncing around Liverpool" when manager Brian Epstein called him to join the world's most famous band.

SH-BOOM: What did you think of Ringo Starr when you first heard him?
JIMMY: I thought he was good—innovative and all. Ringo was making the drums an interesting instrument for all aspiring musicians. I liked his style of doing rimshots on the snare, then onto the tom-tom. In "Ticket to Ride" he used it as an accent of George's strumming chords, and in "She Loves You" he used it as a lead-in to the bridge. He was different. I loved how he used to attack the high hat.
SH-BOOM: How'd you meet Brian?
JIMMY: Brian helped in his father's furniture store after his father put in a record department and hi-fi section. He had a used hi-fi that I bought from him for about ten pounds, and he threw in an early Beatles record with it. He later told me that was the real reason why he chose me to play that '64 tour. I bought a player he couldn't get rid of. Anyway, Brian liked me. He had heard me and knew I was better than average.
SH-BOOM: When did you first learn of the tour and Ringo's illness?
JIMMY: My girlfriend at the time brought home a paper, and I saw an advertisement for the tour in it. Then I read in *Mersey Beat* or somewhere then (continued on page 68)

Jimmy Nicol (between John and Paul, below) joined the Beatles for a 1964 tour.

car with the four Beatles' names on it: "John, Paul, George and Ringo". Paul spotted the problem straight away. "What's that?" Paul asked, pointing at the car. "It's got Ringo's name on it but he's not coming." It didn't seem to matter to the girls when they finally emerged from the airport. *(Adelaide's THE NEWS on Friday 12th June 1964)*

A police car led the motorcade with the car carrying The Beatles into the city. Two police motorcycles flanked The Beatles' car and Brian Epstein rode in another car behind them, followed by two vans containing The Beatles' security guards. They were taking no chances.

The roads were packed, but with stationary traffic as there was nowhere for anyone to park. Lucky pupils at Plympton High School, whose school was close to Anzac Highway, were allowed to watch, and scream at, The Beatles as they drove by. It was becoming more and difficult for the police to control the crowds.

Everybody wanted to turn out and see The Beatles. Many school pupils "wagged school" to get tickets to the concerts. This was the biggest event in the city's history and nobody wanted to miss it. Some lied to their parents so they could see The Beatles. One girl, Maureen Hall tried to get away with it, but when she was spotted on the television news by her father, her trip was over. Others slept in the street just for the chance of seeing their heroes. As the cars carrying The Beatles drove down Anzac Highway, the crowd was ten-people deep.

However, when they got off the airport grounds, there the fans were, waving and screaming as usual. The journey of over 12 kilometres was packed with Beatles fans: the reception in Australia was incredible. This was, however, the calm before the storm, because as they reached the Town Hall in Adelaide, an estimated crowd of 300,000 people greeted them, the most they had ever seen, and Jimmie Nicol was part of the group - could it be any better? Nicol and The Beatles played four concerts over two nights before thousands of fans, but in the back of his mind, Nicol must have known that his time with the group was coming to a close. When interviewed years later by Austin Teutsch, he remembered Adelaide clearly. "I just thank God that I was there to live it with them. Needless to say, the 300,000 people screaming at me and tearing me coat off to the skin was a trip in itself."

The Beatles were interviewed in front of the crowd. George was asked what he thought about the reception in Adelaide. "It's marvelous," said George, before turning to the crowd. "Hello! Hello! It's the best reception ever!" The feeling was the same for the whole group, standing there in front of the most amazing sight of their lives; people just standing there, waving and cheering for them. As a group, this was possibly the highest point of their touring career.

They held another press meet at Adelaide's South Australian Hotel.

Although appearing at the press conferences, Nicol was still the invisible Beatle. Unlike his bandmates, he could go walkabout in Australia – which he gladly did – accompanied by Mal Evans. While in Sydney the night before, he had visited the well-known club, Chequers, where the resident singer was 51-year old American cabaret performer Frances Faye. When she recognized him, he was invited to play on stage with her.

At the Adelaide press conference, he was asked about it.

Q: "What happened with Frances Faye? You went to play the drums, didn't you, Jim?"

JN: "No, I went down to, you know, enjoy myself."

Q: "How did you get up on stage? Did she call you up?"

JN: "Well, as soon as I walked through the door, she was just finishing the latter part of her act. And she said, 'The Beatles are coming!' because everyone turned 'round. And she invited me back to her dressing room."

This was the perfect opportunity for a bit of Lennon innuendo.

John: "Oh, you never told us about that!"

Everybody laughed with John's comments. Nicol, not thrown by it, continued his story.

JN: "...Where we had a drink, you know. And then the second show, I did the whole lot."

Everybody continued laughing, and the laughter didn't end with the next question.

Q: "She gave you something in return, didn't she, Jim?"

Everybody laughed at the double entendre.

JN: "   She hasn't given me anything, but she is going to. She's going to give me all her albums, and also she's having a sweater made for me."

John couldn't resist a laugh, interjecting a comic "Huh hooo!"

Q: "Jimmie, having played with all these bands, what's it like being suddenly thrust in with The Beatles?"

JN: "It's the end, you know."

Q: "Do you have any trouble getting the same beat as Ringo?"

That was a question he had to answer carefully, because if he said it was easy, he could offend Beatles fans, or look big-headed. He decided on a diplomatic reply.

JN: "Well, I do my best."

This went down well, and John decided to give him sympathy with a comical "awwww", which brought more laughter. He was obviously getting more comfortable among The Beatles and was getting a lot of support from the others, especially John.

In June 2014, on the 50th anniversary of The Beatles' visit, *The Sydney Morning Herald* newspaper tracked down some of the musicians who had opened for The Beatles. Johnny Chester had one very clear memory. He had used creative lighting while performing the Peggy Lee song 'Fever'. "I just wanted to make it memorable," Chester recalled. "The house lights were turned off and I had ultraviolet lighting to pick out the white gloves of the bass player and drummer with a red spotlight shining on my face." "That was f**king great," John Lennon had told him.

The support acts for the tour were booked by venues manager Dick Lean. Melbourne-based instrumental group The Phantoms, styled on Britain's Shadows, were chosen as backing band for Chester and another artist, Johnny Devlin.

Noel Tresider was the keyboard player with The Phantoms, and he remembers being thrust into the limelight. "I was brought in especially for the tour," he recalled. "I was 23 years old and studying chemistry at Royal Melbourne Institute of Technology. My musical career was just part-time and the £50 a week contract was much more than the three guineas a week I was earning as an accompanist on radio 3DB in Melbourne." Tresider also remembered the crowds, with more than 250,000 people lining the route from Adelaide airport to the city.

The Beatles traveled in a convertible, the rest of the party in sedans. "The fans were all screaming as we went past. They had no idea who was in the cars."

There were two concerts a night, the first at 6pm and the second at 8:30pm. The first half would begin with British compere Alan Field performing several Frank Sinatra songs. He would then introduce Devlin, dressed in a black leather suit, who sang four numbers including the hit Eddie Cochran hit "C'mon Everybody". Chester followed with four numbers ranging from Elvis Presley's "(You're So Square) Baby, I Don't Care" to Little Richard's "Miss Ann". The 45-minute first half would conclude with the British instrumental group Sounds Incorporated, who were part of Brian Epstein's stable.

After the interval, The Beatles would perform a 30-minute set of just 11 songs from their first two albums, as well as "Can't Buy Me Love" from their soon-to-be released album, *A Hard Day's Night*. The support acts stayed to watch the proceedings. "You couldn't hear the music," Devlin recalled. "It was a mad screaming frenzy." Chester agreed:

"None of us were used to anything on this scale. Although the adulation wasn't directed at us, it was hard not to get caught up in all the excitement." Bob Rogers, a disc jockey for Sydney radio station 2SM, was with the group throughout the tour. "To be on tour with The Beatles meant living every minute upside-down and inside-out," he recalled. "It was mentally and physically exhausting. And everything The Beatles said or did was of momentous importance, even if they'd said or done it many times before. That was part of Beatlemania."

The musicians had the chance to hang out with The Beatles backstage, too. "Between shows, we would eat together and talk in the dressing rooms," Chester said. "I remember having a long talk with George Harrison backstage at Festival Hall in Melbourne. We shared a similar interest in cars – with one difference. He had just bought an E-type Jag while I was still driving my FE Holden."

Tresider swapped jokes with Lennon and talked with McCartney as he played his guitar backstage. He also remembered the crush to attend the after-show parties on tour. "These were mostly people who were well-connected or in society. And there were lots of girls who were very keen to party with anybody from the

tour." Was it worth it? Young fan Elizabeth Golding couldn't hear the concert for the noise. "There was so much screaming that you could only SEE the concert. But I didn't care". Two young Adelaide girls, Ann Domingo and Heni Noll, briefly met The Beatles. They had a feeling that the group would be staying at the South Australian Hotel, so Ann's mother agreed to book them a room. The girls checked in just before The Beatles arrived and waited in the corridor just along from the rooms in which the Fabs were staying. Press officer Derek Taylor noticed the girls and asked them if they'd like to see the press conference. "I had the chance to chat briefly with John," Ann says "and I literally hung onto his coat after the conference finished so we could stay with them and talk for a while. John asked Derek if Heni and I could stay on and we chatted with the guys about their music, other singers and fashion. I often reflect back on that day and think, wow, how lucky were we?" *(www.adelaidenow.com.au June 2014)*

The Fourth Beatle Joins The Fifth Beatle: 13th June 1964

On 13th June, DJ Bob Rodgers interviewed The Beatles and quizzed Nicol about his adventures with the band and the fact that his final appearance with them was that very evening.

BR: "Jimmie, you've got your final performances tonight and then Ringo arrives tomorrow."

JN: "Yes, that's right. I'm looking forward to meeting him."

BR: "And then it's all over for you. What's going to happen? I hear you may not be going back to England?"

JN: "Not for a little while, no. I fancy going back to Sydney."

Despite Nicol's wish to stay in Australia, that was not going to happen. Maybe Brian didn't want him stealing any of the attention from his well-planned tour schedule. He would have to return to England. When Austin Teutsch interviewed Nicol years later, he asked him to sum up his experience.

"I started on June 4th of '64 in Copenhagen, Denmark, our first gig of the tour. I played 10 shows in five cities until Ringo joined us in Melbourne, Australia. I was praying he would get well; at the same time I was hoping he would not want to come back. I was having a ball, truly." When Ringo arrived, and they all met up in the hotel, Ringo shook hands with Nicol, as if to say "thanks, but I'll take it from here."

Sunday 14th June 1964 was a strange day, because, with a recovered Ringo now in Australia, there were five Beatles to be interviewed in Sydney Airport.

However, the focus was now on Ringo, not Jimmie, as the interview bounced back and forth among the four of them. Eventually, Nicol was predictably asked about life after The Beatles. He confirmed that he wanted to remain in Australia, but with no firm offer, nothing was certain. As the questioning returned to the reunited quartet, the limelight was beginning to fade on Jimmie.

Melbourne: 14th June 1964

Chris Mannix was only six years old when The Beatles came to Melbourne. "Having never seen anything like the crowd that came to wave," recalled Chris, "the police were completely overrun and the army were called in to try and control the crowd, at least a little bit. The police force had no idea what was going to happen. In fact, none of us did.

I remember holding my brother's hand so tight because I was terrified that if I lost him, or mum or dad, I'd be trampled to death. I'd been to the MCG (Melbourne Cricket Ground) with a hundred thousand other football fanatics, and that, at my age then, was intimidating enough. But it did not hold a candle to the chaos and euphoria outside the Southern Cross Hotel. It was great to be there, but frightening, but once we got home and had a night's sleep, it was great to talk about it and to think we were part of it all. If mum and dad had known what was going to occur, there is no way they would have taken us, so on this occasion, ignorance was bliss.

I'm still chuffed that I can say I was there; a spectacular like Australia had never seen before, and will never see again. With my brother's enthusiasm about their music and the experience we had, I was converted, well and truly."

Chris' older brother Gary went to see the concert at the Festival Hall and, many years later, told his little brother that it was the worst concert he had ever attended. "He didn't like the support acts, who, in my opinion, were there to give the audience a couple of hours of music. The Beatles performed for 30 to 35 minutes; no encore, and before anyone realised they weren't coming back with another song, the boys were out the back entrance in a limo – GONE!"

(David Bedford Interview 2015)

Considering the country had long awaited this tour, it seems a shame that all they got was just over half an hour. Their set list was: "I Saw Her Standing There", "I Want to Hold Your Hand", "All My Loving", "She Loves You", "Till There Was You", "Roll Over Beethoven", "Can't Buy Me Love", "This Boy", "Twist and Shout" and perennial favourite "Long Tall Sally". Just ten songs, and four of those were covers of rock 'n' roll standards. You can understand the fans of the music, and even The Beatles themselves, feeling frustrated with the song selection. Is it any wonder that, even now, Paul McCartney gives a three-hour concert? Maybe he's trying to make up for those short shows. Then again, the band would never play longer shows than this, not even in America.

Even if some of the fans felt short-changed, the group's visit to Australia left a lasting impression, even on a six-year-old boy like Chris. "Once the tour and subsequent excitement was over, remembering that this was the biggest social phenomenon Australia had ever seen, not counting the stupidness of the two wars. Every place The Beatles had been, and not been, was reported, especially the concerts, the crowds, the excitement and so on. Afterwards, we all felt somewhat empty, and in many cases depressed. As quick as they arrived, they were off 'a few minutes later' to the next country. It was a nationwide downer, and it is said that some politician, full of his own importance, reported to Parliament that productivity had dropped to levels not seen in his parliamentary career. 'Sickies' were taken all over the country at a level never seen before, as we all realised they would never be back to such a small country. I remember at the dinner table there was very little talk; even mum and dad felt it. It took some time for things to get back to normal.

Normal became different to what it was before. It seemed that everybody, as well as my brothers and me, saved every penny we could round up to be prepared for the next single or LP.

The wait for the next song, I remember, was excruciating, even though they were prolific at having music out in singles, EPs and albums regularly. They were great days," he said reflecting on this momentous event, "probably just about the best we ever had." Local newspapers reported that offices with typing pools, made up by a predominantly female staff, were deserted. Productivity was down while The Beatles were there, and for a time afterwards. Chris' brother, who already owned all The Beatles albums, went on a hunt to buy more, but they were all sold out – everywhere. On the TV news, they reported that retailers could not keep up with demand, even though the record manufacturers were running 24/7. "It was the first time I had ever heard the term 'Black Market'", admitted Chris.

"Gary explained it all to me, supply and demand and price points." Albums were exchanging hands for large sums of money as Beatlemania retained its grip on the nation. *(David Bedford Interview 2015)*

It is incredible to think that a pop group from a small, provincial English town could affect a country the size of Australia in such a small time, and in such a big way.

The Invisible Beatle

The second interview of the day was held at the Southern Cross Hotel in Melbourne. Outside the hotel, the fans were chanting, so they headed to the balcony, with all five Beatles waving to the crowd. Although Jimmie was smiling and lapping it up, he knew it was the beginning of the end, so he made the most of it. The funniest moment occurred when Jimmie pointed out to Ringo that there was a camera trained on them. Ringo leapt into action, pretending to strangle Jimmie, so the now-ex-Beatle drummer jokingly grabbed Ringo's throat in return. Makes you wonder what was going through Jimmie's mind at that moment, doesn't it?

The five Beatles headed back inside for their next interview with the waiting journalists. As with the first interview, the banter between John, Paul, George and Ringo was as funny as ever, with Ringo prominent throughout. It was as if Nicol was the invisible Beatle; Ringo was back and all was good, except for Jimmie Nicol. At one point, a reporter asks him about his plans while the other Beatles are still being interviewed. He is quickly shut down.

In *The Beatle Who Vanished*, author Jim Berkenstadt reveals that Brian Epstein had a row with Nicol when they got back to their suite, because he had started talking while the press conference was focusing on the others, and under no circumstances should there be a side conversation. A blazing row followed between Epstein and Nicol, where Epstein made it clear that Nicol would not be staying in Australia and would be flown home immediately. It was an ignominious end to what, just a couple of days earlier, had been the highlight of his career, and his life.

On reflection, Nicol was asked about how he was treated and how he felt sitting in for Ringo in the biggest group on the planet. "After Ringo returned, they changed. It was like welcoming a close member of the family back. They treated me with nothing but respect as a musician. And I think they thought I was very good. John once told me I was better than Ringo but that I just missed the ship. When I was on the plane back to London, I felt like a bastard child being sent back home from a family that didn't want me. When you have had the best, you can't accept anything else." *(Austin Teutsch)*

Jimmie getting ready to rehearse

Under Curfew

The Beatles were under curfew, instigated by Brian, and overseen by Derek Taylor and Mal Evans. However, it was Nicol's last night in Australia, and he wasn't going to abide by any curfew. After all, he had sneaked out before and had fun, going mostly unrecognised. This time, it was different. He had only been out for a short time when Taylor and Evans turned up at the bar, grabbed Nicol and took him back to the hotel. After all, he was still a Beatle! Everything had changed, because not only had Ringo arrived, but Brian Epstein as well. Nicol's short career with The Beatles ended not in a blaze of glory, but a mild whimper.

Back Home - Hello, Goodbye

The following day, 15th June 1964, Brian took Jimmie to the airport before he could even say goodbye to the Fab Four, who were still in bed. If ever there was a photograph that needed no caption, it was the one of Jimmie sitting all alone in a near empty airport with nobody paying any attention to him. How things had changed in just a matter of days. When asked about that photograph, and if he felt lonely, Nicol said: "That's a beautiful picture. Well, if you look at that photograph, that answers your question." *(Evert Vermeer)*

No words were needed

However, a TV reporter spotted him, and Nicol gave his final interview as a Beatle, reflecting on his exploits in Australia. He was asked, in a different way, the same question about what he would do next. "Well I hope to do something that I want to do. Now there might be a possibility that I might be able to do something....maybe earn enough money to study in America. That is what I want to do, is study drums in America and American music. And learn to arrange."

(The Beatle Who Vanished)

With Brian sitting nearby, the television interviewer brings him into shot to say an awkward 'thank you' on camera to Nicol. "I'd just like to say to you Jimmie that The Beatles and I are very, very grateful for everything you have done. You carried out a fine job for us and we're very, very pleased. We hope you have a great trip back to London and every success to you in the future." Jimmie's response? "Thank you very much Brian." It looked and sounded staged, broadcasting an obvious lack of emotion between the two men. In front of the camera, they were both professional, but Nicol, like so many people who featured in the story of The Beatles, had his part to play and then retired to virtual anonymity.

It was at this point that Brian gave Jimmie a parting gift: a gold watch inscribed with the words, 'To Jimmy *(sic)*, with appreciation and gratitude – Brian Epstein and The Beatles'. He was also handed £500. Brian walked and talked amicably with Nicol as he headed for the plane, and, at the top of the steps, Nicol took one last turn and wave, and was on his way home and into obscurity; at least that is how many people saw it. *(Beatle Who Vanished)*

Days before, as Nicol had disembarked from the plane as one of The Beatles, there were thousands of cheering fans there to receive that wave. This time, it was his way of saying goodbye to the fame of being a Beatle and, although he didn't know it, to a career that would never scale those heights again, or even come close. What must he have been thinking on that long flight home? Was it the end? In truth, this was the beginning of a whole new adventure that would see him travel the world and create more music in strange and wonderful countries.

Jimmie Nicol wasn't finished yet.

In his interview with Teutsch, Nicol reflected on his time with The Beatles.

T: "Did you ever see them after the tour?"

JN: "I had a band (The Shubdubs) and Brian put us on the same bill *With The Beatles* and the Fourmost one night (12th July 1964 at the Hippodrome Theatre in Brighton). Backstage, we talked, but the wind had changed since we last saw each other. They were pleasant."

T: "Why do you think you were forgotten after all this?"

JN: "When the fans forget, they forget forever. After The Beatles thing was over for me, I played around for a few years then got away from the music scene. I mean, when you've played with the best, the rest is just, well, the rest."

T: "Any regrets?"

JN: "None. Oh, after the money ran low, I thought of cashing in in some way to other. But the timing wasn't right. And I didn't want to step on The Beatles' toes. They had been damn good for me and to me."

When Nicol said he "played around for a few years then got away from the music scene", it was an understatement. For two weeks, he was a Beatle; for the rest of his life, he was the guy who had been a Beatle – that drummer who stood in for Ringo. His life would never be the same again.

British paper *The Daily Mail* followed up their coverage of the tour by catching up with Nicol once he was back in London. "I nearly went potty," he said. "It was a marvellous experience but I wouldn't want to be a Beatle full time.

They live in boxes, in cars, aeroplanes, hotel rooms. They're all shut in.

I couldn't stand it. I like to walk about free. On my last night with them in Australia when Ringo came back, I just wanted to go out and walk about. I wasn't allowed to. Brian Epstein didn't think it was a good idea. I suppose he was right. He runs an infallable organisation. It's incredible. He says 'jump' and everybody jumps. But that night I nearly went potty. They said there had to be a security guard with me. I said, 'But I'm finished with them now.

It was ridiculous. But they insisted that I went to bed."

After The Beatles

Nicol returned to London a changed man. People recognised him on the street, and he had several career options. After all, he had been a Beatle. Should he return to Australia and hook up with Frances Faye? When he left England, he was on loan from Georgie Fame and the Blue Flames, so he could always rejoin that group. However, he chose not to go back, only forward, much to Georgie Fame's annoyance. While he was in Australia, MarMar Records had re-released Nicol's Pye record, "Humpty Dumpty", credited to 'Jimmy Nicol – Now with The Beatles.' Pye then released "Husky" which Jimmy and the Shubdubs had recorded earlier that year. The label suggested he form a touring band, but he was about to stand in for yet another sick drummer.

The Shubdubs

The Dave Clark Five, who were hitting the charts on both sides of the Atlantic, had a crisis. Drummer Dave Clark had been rushed to hospital with an ulcer. They had a summer season coming up, but instead of Nicol playing drums with the Dave Clark Five, it was Jimmie Nicol and the Shubdubs who secured the gig. One slight problem was that he hadn't re-formed the Shubdubs.

With media assistance, Nicol was able to get a group together. "After I was with The Beatles, I formed the Shubdubs. We had recorded before I went with The Beatles, and afterwards we actually started to perform as a band. That didn't last very long, I'd say about six months." *(Evert Vermeer)* With the Shubdubs back together, Jimmie Nicol was top of the bill.

Nicol in Liverpool

Nicol, with "Husky" now released, headed to The Beatles' hometown to do some publicity, where Bill Harry interviewed him for *Mersey Beat*. "I last visited Liverpool about five years ago," said Jimmie, who was stopping by local record shops in connection with promotion for 'Husky'. Bill asked him how he got on with The Beatles. "We're hardly friends," he said, "but I had a marvellous time touring with them, of course. They're great lads and soon made me feel at home."

Naturally, Bill wanted to know how much of a difference touring with The Beatles had made to his life. "It's great, naturally. I don't think the publicity 'made' me, but it certainly gave me a push in the right direction. I tried to form a group before I temporarily joined The Beatles and found it impossible to get work, but afterwards it was easy enough to form a group. I have only two of the original Shubdubs with me now, however."

Nicol put his recruitment down to being in the "right place at the right time. The tour was fabulous, of course," he told Harry. "I enjoyed every minute of it, especially Hong Kong," he added, making an interesting observation. "I found that the refugees there were very grateful to the British, and I visited one or two refugee colonies during the short time I was there." He also showed that he wanted to be more than just a drummer. "I want to go around the factories and see just how discs are manufactured," he said. The following week, they would be in the recording studios themselves, deciding on the next single. "After that, we do a series of one night stands."

Almost, Almost the Fourth Beatle

His first selection would have been Roy Dyke of the Remo Four who he felt was "an obvious choice, particularly as he is in the Epstein stable." His second choice was more obvious – Trevor Morais, the former Faron and the Flamingos drummer who Azurdia affirmed as "one of the finest drummers in the business." The third drummer was "Ringo's old mate Brian Redman of the Hillsiders, would have been delighted to team up with The Beatles for the tour."

Even so, Azurdia does credit Nicol with being a good choice. "Jimmy Nichol (sic) is not only a first class drummer, he was also lucky enough to be in London just when he was wanted – so he got the job. But it would be interesting to know who would have been picked if everyone had been available and had time to get to London and rehearse."

When Pete Best was asked if he had been considered for the role, he gave a typically diplomatic reply: "We were on tour anyway and I couldn't have joined The Beatles. In any case, I don't think I would really like to go back now." *(Mersey Beat 18th June 1964)*

Jimmy Nicol's post-Beatles single, "Husky"

At The Cavern

Despite Nicol's new high-profile summer season in Blackpool and the publicity push by Pye, the record "Husky" failed to be a hit. As their contract was for three records only, Nicol and the Shubdubs had one last chance with their record company and issued "Baby Please Don't Go"/ "Shubdubbery". Unfortunately, at the same time, "Baby Please Don't Go" was also released by Them, featuring Van Morrison and Jimmy Page. Nicol hit the road again, and came back to Liverpool to make a headlining appearance at The Cavern on 8th August 1964.

Still convinced that success was just around the corner, Nicol maintained an extravagant lifestyle that soon led to divorce and a move back home to his mother. Fan mail was still pouring in from Australia, and Larry Parnes offered him a 35-night UK tour. The release of "Baby Please Don't Go" coincided with this new tour, but it was Van Morrison's version, not Jimmie's, that made it into the Top 10. Success was still eluding him. Without any record success, Pye dropped Jimmie Nicol and the Shubdubs, even though the group was heading back to Denmark, supported by a local band called The Beatmakers. Still billed as the "Fifth Beatle", Nicol held out hope that the rewards would follow.

However, the crowds and venues were getting smaller, and the costs of running the band were escalating. At the end of 1964, the Shubdubs split.

The Sound of Jimmy Nicol

Over the years, Nicol maintained that Brian Epstein had held him back and even blacklisted him, though there is little evidence to support this theory. Probably the sensible thing would have been to return to his previous job as one of the best session drummers in London, which would have provided a steady income. However, he was still convinced his future lay as a bandleader. With a manager in Tommy Sanderson, he launched a new group, The Sound of Jimmy Nicol, and secured a record deal with Decca. Finally, four years after missing out on The Beatles, Decca had signed another Fifth Beatle; they already had Pete Best on their books. Nicol borrowed money to buy equipment, got a new group together and recorded "Sweet Clementine". But even an appearance on BBC television couldn't help him and in April 1965, after just four months, Decca dropped him. The band folded and his manager left. In just twelve months, Jimmie Nicol had gone from relative obscurity to being in the world's most famous group. Now he was divorced, had no record deal and, by the end of 1965, had filed for bankruptcy. What a year. *(The Beatle Who Vanished)*

However, one Beatle in particular hadn't forgotten him. Paul McCartney contacted Peter Asher and recommended that he hire Nicol. Even Georgie Fame decided to let him come back and play with his group for a short time. But none of it was permanent. He still had dreams.

The Spotnicks in Sweden and to Mexico

Scandinavia was then to pop up in his life again. "I joined the Spotnicks," said Nicol. "They came into a club I played in with the Shubdubs in Denmark. They were impressed by my playing, and when their drummer had to do something else, they rang me and offered me the job.

I made lots of records with the Spotnicks, and we did a world tour. We went to Japan as a number one group and got the same sort of reception The Beatles got. I was with them for 18 months." *(Evert Vermeer)*

They travelled to Mexico City and stayed there for a month. Nicol loved it, even when an earthquake disrupted one show. Next stop was Tokyo, where The Spotnicks were hugely popular, receiving an award for selling one million copies of "Karelia". While there, they were recorded, leading to the release of *The Spotnicks in Japan*. They also released *Christmas in Winterland* and *The Spotnicks Around The World*.

Nicol loved his time with the Spotnicks. They were an "arty" group that wore spacesuits and were the first to have transmitters on their guitars. "Bo Winberg, the actual brain behind the Spotnicks, is an absolute technical genius," Nicol said. *(Evert Vermeer)*

In 1966, they embarked on a second world tour, visiting Germany, Holland, Belgium, Switzerland and Austria. The Spotnicks gave Jimmie Nicol a place in a group celebrating worldwide success. They recorded the theme song for a TV drama in Paris, and their Christmas album came out at the end of 1966. Surely he was happy now. Jimmie's 18-month philosophy was about to rear its head again.

While in Mexico City, he started missing rehearsals, and his use of cannabis was progressing to heavier drugs, leaving him so stoned that he fell off his chair. This was the last straw, and he was removed from the group and replaced by a Swedish drummer. He says he left on good terms. "After I had left the Spotnicks, we kept up a good friendship. I didn't leave in any bad terms, because I don't believe in shutting doors. Winberg sent me a tape of their new recordings, and

Interestingly, in the Mersey Beat issue of 18th June 1964, Bob Azurdia posed the question: "Would They Have Had a Liverpool Drummer?" Azurdia opens with a thought-provoking comment for its local readers. "The fact the folk on Merseyside have been realising slowly over the last twelve months that The Beatles no longer belong to Liverpool was underlined by the events of the last few weeks."

Azurdia wonders if The Beatles really had to hire a "southerner" to replace Ringo. But as they were under the pressure of "time and distance", they really had to find someone quickly. It only made sense to get someone local to them in London. "Surely there are plenty of more-than-capable performers from Liverpool who would have done equally well – and who would have preserved the all-Merseyside flavour of the boys," said Azurdia.

Jimmie with The Spotnicks

that was very impressive. He asked me to promote them in England, but I'm a little too busy for that at the moment, and I need to work with them for a while."

(Evert Vermeer)

Nicol was once again out of a group, and becoming invisible. He decided to further remove himself from his Beatles connections, in his words, to "evolutionize; to gain wisdom and knowledge, and to travel." The change of country suited him, too. "I did all sorts of things in Mexico. I arranged jazz concerts in universities, I worked for the government in communications, composed music for movies, produced and directed TV programmes for Polytechnic Channel, and did publicity for a film I had written the music for, and I got that into the San Francisco, Edinburgh and Washington film festivals. All promotional things. And marketing. I introduced buttons (badges) into Mexico."

(Evert Vermeer)

He loved Mexico, and even began gigging. All was not over, and the president of RCA hired him as A&R man, knowing his reputation with The Spotnicks. Nicol hired Eddie Quinn and wrote and recorded an album with Los Nicolquinn, who he considered the next big thing. Sadly, like his previous efforts, the record failed. He then composed a film soundtrack for *El Mes Mas Cruel*, but the film flopped after one week and the music was never released. Full of ideas, he dreamt up this idea for a travelling show about the group he originally tried to distance himself from: The Beatles. He met a Swedish-born dancer and choreographer, Julia Villasenor, and they put the show together. Ironically, it would feature Nicol playing a medley of Beatles songs. The reviews were glowing, and so were Jimmie and Julia. They had fallen in love.

At this point, Nicol had the chance to finally make it big in Australia but, now in a relationship, he decided to stay in Mexico. Their marriage didn't last and they were divorced after one year. However, they were to work together again on a film, *Anticlimax*, for which Nicol composed the music. They even appeared regularly on television there, but were not making much money.

Working for Buttons

He tried teaching at a college, and even making button badges, which was quite successful. He even tried again with a new band, but it didn't work out.
He returned to London in the mid-1970s without telling anybody, and set up a company in the building trade. "I have a company that restores houses back to their original state," recalled Nicol in the 1980s. "The team of people that I have – I don't employ them, they're proprietors in their own right – are of different trades. There's people who do roofing, carpenters, joiners, plasterers, bricklayers, architects, civil engineers and so forth. And my company is an umbrella company which specializes in sales and the coordination of the work to be done. I can do wallpapering, or painting, or carpentry. I am a metal-worker, an inventor, designer. I'm not the greatest in any, but it's something which I recognize a talent for in myself, and I let that talent manifest itself. And I enjoy everything I'm doing. The suffering is for people to do something they don't really want to do. When I came back from Mexico after eight years, I found I couldn't really speak English anymore!" Nicol described himself as a "jack of all trades, master of none. I'm not a master of anything because I'm not prepared to devote my whole life to one particular thing. The only things I will be a master of are the things that I want to do. One passes through life only once."

(Evert Vermeer)

Nicol remained philosophical throughout every stage of his life.

Beatles Unlimited

In 1984, on the 20th anniversary of The Beatles' appearance in Holland, Jimmie Nicol appeared as a guest at a special Beatles event run by the Official Beatles Fan Club, later known as Beatles Unlimited. One of those who witnessed the appearance was Pete Nash, editor of the magazine for the British Beatles Fan Club. "I remember the one and only time I ever met Jimmie Nicol," he said. "It was at The Beatles Unlimited Convention in Treslong, Holland in June 1984, which was an event organised to celebrate the 20th anniversary of The Beatles' appearance on Vara TV. Incredible to think that it's now over 30 years since that 20th anniversary event! Jimmie was a good sport that day, even donning a Beatle jacket and playing drums with Beatles tribute band The Clarks. He was also interviewed and took questions from fans. However, the Q&A session was less than illuminating as Jimmie seemingly answered every question with 'you will have to wait for my book to come out to find that out!' Sadly, Jimmie's autobiography never did appear." *(David Bedford Interview 2015)*

The aforementioned book was going to be produced by him and his son Howie, but they disagreed on the format and it never happened. So it seemed that Jimmie Nicol had played for the last time. Rumours spread that he had died. Howie, strangely enough, became a sound engineer, and worked on The Beatles *Anthology*, winning a BAFTA award. Apparently, Paul McCartney asked Howie if Jimmie would appear in *Anthology*, but he declined. In 1996, Britain's *Daily Mail* newspaper carried an article on Nicol titled the "Penniless and Forgotten Beatle".

Jimmie at the 1984 in Holland at Beatles Unlimited

he proved to be.

Soon after *The Daily Mail* interview, Nicol disappeared again. He was reportedly last sighted in Utrecht, Holland, in 2011. Maybe Jimmie was right: "Standing in for Ringo was the worst thing that ever happened to me. Until then, I was quite happy earning thirty or forty pounds a week. After the headlines died, I began dying, too."

Jimmie Nicol came closer than many to being the Fourth Beatle, and was the first Fifth Beatle. He was technically a very good drummer, one of the best to have ever played with The Beatles, and he certainly exceeded all expectations while he was with them. However, it was clear that he was only ever going to be a stand-in for Ringo.

There was only one Fourth Beatle, and that was Ringo.

In 2004, under the headline "Life moves to a slower beat for Beatles' forgotten drummer", Jonathan Este wrote an article on Nicol for *The Weekend Australian*, and tracked him down to a flat in London. His conclusion? "Nicol, estranged from his family for years, has virtually made himself disappear.

These days he flatly refuses to talk on the subject of his fleeting fame. "I really don't want to talk about it – I can't remember anything," he said." The following year, *The Daily Mail* in London went on the hunt for Nicol again, and a photographer staked out his London home.

The Beatle Vanishes Again

When asked if it had been a fascinating experience to be part of the Beatle circus, he replied, "It was disappointing, not fascinating, because I had been used to it before. When rock 'n' roll first hit, I was touring with screaming kids. That was another reason why they chose me. They knew how I would act as a person coming into a pre-made image. They didn't want to admit it, even though it was written in black and white, that there was anybody else playing the drums except Ringo. They wanted to present The Beatles as a whole. Obviously, they were extremely afraid of a failure of the tour, of an outsider coming in." The biggest problem was that Nicol knew he was never going to be a permanent member of the group, and didn't even know how long he was going to be with them.

He could only live day to day. "Probably, that put a lot of pressure on me, this situation makes you uneasy, and I wasn't as mature as I am now." As for the fans, they had no choice to accept him or not. Many accepted him, whereas others just ignored the fact that Ringo wasn't there. "Basically, the fans had no choice. It was either The Beatles with me or no Beatles at all. But, of course, no one is indispensable. If I hadn't been the right person in the right place at the right time and with the right background, obviously someone else would have done the job." But Nicol was the right man, at the right place, at the right time, and will forever be remembered as Ringo's replacement – and a very able replacement

Jimmie back behind the drums, sitting in with The Clarks

11TH APRIL 1966

ANIL BHAGWAT
'LOVE YOU TO"

As George Harrison and The Beatles began to immerse themselves in Indian culture, it was inevitable that this would be reflected in their music. Although they had introduced the sitar in "Norwegian Wood (This Bird Has Flown)" on *Rubber Soul* in 1965, when George Harrison wrote and recorded "Love You Too", it was the first Beatles song to fully embrace Indian music. It was essential that the feel of the song was as authentic as it could be and so, with minimal help from the other Beatles, George enlisted the assistance of the Asian Music Circle in London, which included tabla player Anil Bhagwat.

The musicians on the song were:

George Harrison:	Lead and backing vocals, acoustic guitar, sitar, rhythm guitar, fuzz-tone lead guitar
Paul McCartney:	Backing vocal
Ringo Starr:	Tambourine
Anil Bhagwat:	Tabla

Unnamed musicians from the Asian Music Circle: Sitar, tambura

The guide track for "Love You To" was recorded at Abbey Road Studios on 11th April 1966. Harrison sang and played acoustic guitar, with Paul McCartney on backing vocals. By the end of the first session, they had recorded three takes of the song, with George introducing his sitar on the last of these takes. When they resumed at 8pm, Anil Bhagwat was introduced to the studio via Patricia Angadi. Bhagwat remembered what happened: "A chap called (Ayana) Angadi called me and asked if I was free that evening to work with George ... he didn't say it was Harrison. It was only when a Rolls-Royce came to pick me up that I realised I'd be playing on a Beatles session. When I arrived at Abbey Road, there were girls everywhere with Thermos flasks, cakes, sandwiches, waiting for The Beatles to come out." *(Complete Beatles Recording Sessions)*

Bhagwat recalled Harrison's musical direction: "George told me what he

wanted and I tuned the tabla with him. He suggested I play something in the Ravi Shankar style, 16-beats, though he agreed that I should improvise. Indian music is all improvisation." *(Complete Beatles Recording Sessions)*

After rehearsing the song together, Harrison and Bhagwat recorded the sitar and tabla parts onto the vocal and guitar performance taped earlier that day.

The Tabla

The tabla, deriving from tabl, a Persian and Arabic word for drum, consists of two single headed, barrel-shaped small drums of slightly different size and shapes: daya also called dahina, meaning right, and baya (also called bahina), meaning left. With its origins in the Indian subcontinent, it consists of a pair of drums used in traditional Indian classical, popular and folk music, and has been especially significant in Hindustani classical music since the 18th century. The tabla is still used in India, Pakistan, Afghanistan, Nepal, Bangladesh and Sri Lanka.

Each drum is made of hollowed-out wood or clay or brass, the daya drum laced with hoops, thongs and wooden dowels on its sides. The dowels and hoops are used to tighten the tension of the membrane. The musician uses the heel of his hand to change the pitch and tone colour of each drum during a performance. The playing technique is complex and involves extensive use of the fingers and palms in various configurations to create a wide variety of different sounds and rhythms, reflected in mnemonic syllables.

The *Revolver* LP was truly revolutionary – the harbinger of things to come for The Beatles. "Love You To" would prove to be a watershed moment for the LP, the band and western audiences as the Indian classical influence was introduced to rock music for the first time. Anil Bhagwat's role in this "new" sound cannot be underestimated.

1ST JUNE 1966

MAL EVANS

SUBMARINER

Liverpudlian Mal Evans had been with The Beatles from the early days and, along with Neil Aspinall, was a member of the band's "inner circle". During his time with the group, he went from being a telephone engineer in Liverpool to a bouncer at The Cavern, a roadie, personal assistant and record producer.

He contributed to some of The Beatles' songs, travelled with the group, and its individual members, and appeared in *A Hard Day's Night, Help!, Magical Mystery Tour* and *Let It Be.*

Along with Peter Asher, who was the A&R head of Apple Records, Mal went to see a Welsh group, The Iveys, perform at London's Marquee Club and knew that they had a great future. He pestered The Beatles until they agreed to sign them, and they became the first non-Beatle act on the Apple Records roster. A little more than a year later, at Neil Aspinall's suggestion, they changed their name to "Badfinger". Mal would produce the group's 1970 hit, "No Matter What" and most of their first two Apple albums.

During one particular conversation between Mal and Paul McCartney on a plane, the concept and name of Sgt. Pepper emerged. On 27th January 1967, Mal wrote in his diary: "Did a lot more of 'where the rain comes in' (i.e. "Fixing A Hole").

Hope people like it. Started *Sergeant Pepper*." On 1st February, he continued: "Sergeant Pepper sounds good. Paul tells me that I will get royalties on the song – great news, now perhaps a new home." Sadly, he never received any credit or royalties, but was one of the few people invited to McCartney's wedding to Linda Eastman on 12th March 1969.

While his primary function was as The Beatles' roadie, Mal would also play a part in their recording career, even if only as a footnote:

- He banged a hammer against an anvil for "Maxwell's Silver Hammer"
- Played single notes on the organ in "You Won't See Me"
- Controlled the alarm clock and carefully counted in the long 24-bar pause in "A Day in the Life". He also joined John, Paul and Ringo in playing the piano chord at the end of the same song
- He played tambourine on "Dear Prudence"
- Played trumpet on "Helter Skelter"
- He stirred a bucket of gravel on "You Know My Name (Look Up The Number)"
- Played harmonica on "Being for the Benefit of Mr. Kite!"

However, it is for his contribution to "Yellow Submarine" that he is included in this book.

Yellow Submariner

The recording of "Yellow Submarine" began on 26th May 1966, and as The Beatles had started to explore different recording techniques, they later enlisted the help of several people, including Mal. However, the first job was to get the rhythm track and vocals recorded.

Geoff Emerick was in charge that night, and it was a night he would not forget.

BEATLE BUYS

As he recounted in his book, *Here, There and Everywhere: My Life Recording The Beatles*: "As it happened, George Martin was out sick with food poisoning the night we began work on it; he sent his secretary *(and future wife)*, Judy, along to keep an eye on things…and I suppose to make sure we all behaved ourselves! She sat in George's place at the console making sure that The Beatles got everything they wanted…while I took the helm. George's absence clearly had a liberating effect on the four Beatles – they behaved like a bunch of schoolboys with a substitute teacher filling in. As a result, there was a lot of clowning around that evening – silliness that George Martin would not have tolerated – and so rehearsals took up a lot more time than the session itself."

The silliness included recording several sound effects to add to the ambience of a children's song. With George Martin now recovered, the group set about finishing the tune. Emerick continued: "Paul had conceived 'Yellow Submarine' as a sing-along, and so a few of the band's friends and significant others had been invited along for the evening session. Following a long dinner break *(during which we suspected more than food was being ingested)*, a raucous group began filtering in, including Mick Jagger and Brian Jones, along with Jagger's girlfriend Marianne Faithfull and George Harrison's wife, Pattie." They were soon back in the studio and ready to have some fun.

EMI employee John Skinner joined in: "There was a metal bath in the trap room – the type people used to bathe in in front of the fire. We filled it with water, got some old chains and swirled them around. It worked really well. I'm sure no one listening to the song realized what was making the noise. They also recruited Rolling Stones guitarist Brian Jones to tap drinking glasses, The Beatles' chauffeur Alf Bicknell rattling old chains, and roadie Mal Evans beat a bass drum as they all joined in singing the final chorus."

So Mal Evans can rightly claim to have played a drum with The Beatles. In fact, he enjoyed it so much that EMI recording engineer Ken Townsend remembered Mal marching around the studio after the session was concluded, wearing the big bass drum on his chest, leading a conga-style line of people as they sang the chorus of "we all live in a yellow submarine".

Evans was a larger than life character who was a trusted friend of The Beatles and played a significant part of their career throughout the '60s. Although his life ended tragically in Los Angeles in January 1976, he will be fondly remembered as part of The Beatles family.

Un Autre Batteur?

In the middle of the song, there is a short solo, and it was suggested that this should be performed by a brass band. However, instead of hiring a session band to record a brief solo, George Martin decided to use a snip of an existing recording to provide the brass band. They identified a suitable song, "Le Reve Passé", and in order to avoid breaking copyright laws, they chopped up the required section and reassembled it. And so within that recording is un autre batteur – another drummer – providing the marching beat to this historical French song.

For a few seconds, this unnamed musician was unknowingly included in a Beatles song.

15TH MARCH 1967

NATWAR SONI
"WITHIN YOU, WITHOUT YOU"

After the incredible response to *Revolver*, mostly favourable, it was clear that The Beatles were pressing ahead with their experimentation of Indian music. On *Sgt Pepper's Lonely Hearts Club Band*, this sound would be heard again on "Within You Without You".

Like "Love You To", the song was composed by George Harrison, who was inspired by his six-week stay in India (September-October 1966), studying with a musical mentor he revered: Ravi Shankar. The song didn't feature the other three Beatles at all. Instead, George returned to the Asian Music Circle for the musicians he would use on the song. "Within You Without You" would mark a transition from the group's typical lyric style into one that exemplified a new culture, tradition and religion. George was embracing Hinduism, and wanted to reflect this in his music.

Though the four Indian musicians used for the recording were not credited on the album, Liverpool academic Dr. Mike Jones tracked them down and celebrated their contributions in a June 2017 Liverpool concert. Jones told the *Liverpool Echo*: "John Ball and I were approached by Utkarsha Joshi, son of the late Anna Joshi, who played dilruba for George Harrison on the 'Within You, Without You' recording session. We discussed that the four Indian musicians have been 'unknown musicians' for 50 years."

Jones, who helped arrange the concert, was delighted that it was a "one-off opportunity to recognise and celebrate their contribution to what is arguably The Beatles' most famous album."

The musicians on the original recording of "Within You Without You" were:

George Harrison: Lead vocals, tambura, sitar, acoustic guitar

Anna Joshi: Dilruba

Amrit Gajjar: Dilruba

Natwar Son: Tabla

Buddhadev Kansara: Tambura

Uncredited: swarmandal

Erich Gruenberg, Alan Loveday, Julien Gaillard, Paul Scherman, Ralph Elman, David Wolfsthal, Jack Rothstein, Jack Greene: Violins

Reginald Kilbey, Allen Ford, Peter Halling: Cellos

Road manager Neil Aspinall also contributed by playing a tambura.

Using a tabla, as Anil Bhagwat had done on "Love You To", Natwar Soni provided the drumming behind Harrison's song.

Recording

The track was recorded on 15th March 1967 at Abbey Road Studio 2. Harrison wanted to create the right environment for the record and his guest musicians, so they all sat on a carpet in the studio. The walls were draped with Indian tapestries, the lights were turned low and incense was lit.

Although he wasn't performing on the song, the session was also attended by John Lennon. Artist Peter Blake was also present as was John Barham, an English classical pianist and student of Shankar who shared Harrison's desire to promote Indian music to Western audiences. Barham recalled that Harrison "had the entire structure of the song mapped out in his head" and sang the melody that he wanted the dilruba player to follow." *(While My Guitar Gently Weeps: The Music of George Harrison)*

Natwar Soni's twin hand-drums of the tabla were close-miked by recording engineer Geoff Emerick in order to capture what he later described as "the texture and the lovely low resonances" of the instrument.

Soni probably had no idea that the rhythm track that he was laying down that day would be so significant in modern popular music.

Imagine

Keith Moon drumming with The Beatles?

Keith Moon: legendary drummer with The Who

25th JUNE 1967

KEITH MOON

WHO?

Keith John Moon was born on 23rd August 1946, and tragically died at the young age of 32 on 7th September 1978. He made his name as much for his wild and destructive off-stage antics as he did for his undoubted prowess on stage as drummer for The Who, arguably one of the most dynamic and popular British groups. He was the original hard-living rock star, who delighted in mayhem and destruction on a grand scale. He lived the old adage of wine, women and song to excess, and was probably the first king of room-trash. Conservative estimates reckon he caused over £500,000 damage at 1970s prices, resulting in The Who being banned from many hotels around the world.

Moon spent 15 years as drummer with The Who, and became an integral part of the band's legacy. Whereas Ringo was the king of playing the song, Moon was best known for his unconventional, over-the-top, heavy drumming style. Although their playing techniques couldn't have been more different, the two drummers were great friends. Keith became godfather to Ringo's son, Zak Starkey, and gave his godson a drum kit for his 8th birthday. Many years later, Zak sat in the drummer's seat with The Who on several tours and albums, and recreated the sounds his "Uncle Keith" had made with some aplomb.

Drumming With The Beatles?

In 1967, when The Beatles were asked to perform on *Our World*, the global satellite broadcast, they not only wrote a new song, "All You Need Is Love", but invited their friends to the studio to join them during the broadcast. The group sent out word that they wanted to perform in front of a live audience that would also help with background vocals and hand claps during the recording.

Many answered that call, including members of The Rolling Stones and their wives or girlfriends, and other leading musicians of their generation, like Eric Clapton and Graham Nash. Naturally, one of those in attendance was Keith Moon.

Keith and his wife Kim spent the day singing backup and clapping to the beat. However, when you closely observe the Our World performance footage, you can see that Keith is seated right next to Ringo, using his brush sticks to play on the drum alongside his Beatle friend. Moon's use of brushes was probably a wise decision. Considering his reputation as the wild man of rock, he would have drowned out the entire studio!

At around 3 minutes and 33 seconds into the broadcast, Moon can be clearly seen next to Ringo, where he remains throughout the performance.

Imagine Keith Moon drumming with The Beatles?

All You Need Is A Drum Roll?

The Beatles began recording "All You Need Is Love" on 14th June 1967, at Olympic Sound Studios in Barnes, London. The group decided to use some unconventional instruments, as Lennon recalled. "We just put a track down. Because I knew the chords I played it on whatever it was; a harpsichord? George played a violin because we felt like doing it like that and Paul played a double bass. And they can't play them, so we got some nice little noises coming out. It sounded like an orchestra, but it's just them two playing the violin and that. So then we thought, 'Ah, well, we'll have some more orchestra around this little freaky orchestra that we've got.' But there was no perception of how it sounded at the end until they did it that day, until the rehearsal. It still sounded a bit strange then." *(Anthology)*

On 19th June 1967, the group overdubbed more drums, plus vocals, with piano played by George Martin and the banjo by Lennon. However, on 25th June, having gone through takes 48-58, with 58 being the live BBC broadcast, there was still some work to do in the studio. Although it is recorded that "we overdubbed a snare drum roll by Ringo for the song's intro", *(Complete Recording Sessions)* The song was recorded after the television broadcast, and not many people realise that the single was slightly different to the version broadcast around the world on television.

Did Ringo really do the opening drum roll? Very few drummers we have consulted during this project believe it was Ringo.

As George Martin has been quoted as saying, "Ringo couldn't do a drum roll - and he still can't", though it is hard to know when he found that out and how.

The opening drum roll on "All You Need Is Love" has a military drum roll as accompaniment to the "Marseillaise" (French National Anthem), which, when you listen to the song, has a totally different drum sound to the rest of the track. The drum roll is quite bright, as if played on a military snare or side drum, whereas the drumming in the song starts off as almost inaudible, but develops with quite a dull sounding beat behind the song, with more emphasis on the cymbal but sounding like it comes from a drum kit.

Did George Martin insert a recording of the "Marseillaise"? Another drummer, as we have seen, could easily have provided the drum roll for the song if Ringo couldn't, which would be no reflection on Ringo's ability.

Maybe there is another drummer out there?

13th JANUARY 1968

MAHAPURUSH MISRA
"THE INNER LIGHT"

The first George Harrison song to make it onto a single was "The Inner Light", issued in March 1968 as the flip side of "Lady Madonna". After the success of "Love You To" and "Within You Without You", George followed up with "The Inner Light". However, this was his last "Indian-inspired" song, as he had come to the realisation that he could never perfect the sitar.

The song was influenced by The Beatles' embrace of Transcendental Meditation, having studied under Maharishi Mahesh Yogi in Rishikesh at the time of the single's release.

In his autobiography, *I, Me, Mine*, George Harrison recalled that he was inspired to write the song by Juan Mascaró, who was a Sanskrit scholar at Cambridge University. Mascaró had taken part in a television debate on The Frost Programme on 4th October 1967, during which George Harrison and John Lennon discussed Transcendental Meditation with an audience of academics and religious leaders. Mascaró sent a letter to Harrison on 16th November, enclosing a copy of his book *Lamps of Fire*, which was an anthology of religious writings that included passages from Lao-Tzu's Tao Te Ching. Mascaró told Harrison how much he had admired the spiritual message in "Within You Without You", and wondered "might it not be interesting to put into your music a few words of Tao, for example no. 48, page 66 of Lamps?" *(I, Me, Mine)*

Not only was the song inspired in India, but it became the only Beatles song to be recorded outside of Europe, with the instrumentation of the song laid down in January 1968 at HMV Studios in Bombay, where George was already working on the soundtrack to the film *Wonderwall*. His lead vocal and the backing vocals of his fellow Beatles were recorded in London.

For the recording, George selected some of India's finest musicians:

Aashish Khan:	Sarod
Mahapurush Misra:	Pakhavaj
Hanuman Jadev:	Shehnai
Hariprasad Chaurasia:	Bansuri
Rijram Desad:	Harmonium

Pakhavaj

The Pakhavaj is a north Indian version of a mridangam, a barrel-shaped drum that is similar to the more popular tabla. The left head is similar to the tabla bayan, though there is a temporary application of flour and water instead of the black permanent spot. It is laced with rawhide and has tuning blocks placed between the straps and shell. Pakhavaj compositions are passed down through the generations and, like the tabla, they are taught by a series of mnemonic syllables known as bol. For a brief time in 1968, Misra was the drummer supporting George Harrison on a Beatles record.

Paul drummed with The Beatles on record

22nd AUGUST 1968

PAUL, JOHN AND GEORGE AS DRUMMERS

Once Ringo had joined, there was only going to be one drummer in The Beatles – at least until an argument during the making of the *White Album* proved otherwise. The recording of the album had already become a nightmare for the group, and when Ringo supposedly couldn't drum the way Paul had asked, it became the proverbial last straw. Ringo walked out and quit. Ringo remembered it slightly differently to the well-known story.

"I thought I just had to go away and straighten my head out because it was getting too silly," he said emphatically. "And while I was away, I got telegrams from John saying, 'The best rock and roll drummer in the world,' and when I came back, George had the whole studio decorated with flowers. So Paul may have been pissed off. I don't know - he never did anything. But he never actually said to me, 'That's not good,' or whatever, so I don't know where that rumour came from. He was never that critical." *(Modern Drummer December 1981)*

Paul recalled what happened: "I'm sure it pissed Ringo off when he couldn't quite get the drums to 'Back In The USSR', and I sat in. It's very weird to know that you can do a thing someone else is having trouble with. If you go down and do it, just bluff right through it, you think, 'What the hell, at least I'm helping'. Then the paranoia comes in - 'But I'm going to show him up!' I was very sensitive to that." *(Beatles Encyclopedia: Everything Fab Four)*

Record producer Steve Levine has listened to the track, and with his professional ear said; "Listen to 'Back in the USSR', when Ringo wasn't playing drums, and you can hear the joins of where the various bits of drumming were added. You can hear where McCartney is playing and where John and George added their parts. You can tell it isn't Ringo playing. And you can also tell it's not proper drumming, but made up of bits and pieces." *(David Bedford Interview 2017)*

Paul, John and George

But Paul wasn't the only one to play drums on "Back in the USSR". John and George played alongside Paul. Did it really take three Beatles to equal one Ringo? This song became the opening track on the *White Album*, with Paul also playing on the following track, "Dear Prudence".

The multi-instrumentalist McCartney, who had appeared on his own when he recorded "Yesterday", had his first "solo" recording session when he played every instrument on another *White Album* track, "Martha, My Dear", accompanied by an orchestra.

With Ringo away filming *The Magic Christian* and George on holiday, Paul also famously drummed on 1969's "The Ballad of John and Yoko" as John played guitar in a rare Lennon-McCartney studio collaboration.

Heather

A mention should be given to Heather McCartney too, who, during "Let it Be", hit one of Ringo's drums, and giggled after doing so as Ringo pretended to be shocked. Not quite the Fourth Beatle, but she was a smash hit!

Over the years, Paul mainly played guitar, piano and bass, but proved to be a more-than-capable Fourth Beatle when needed.

All you need is drums, John

WITH A LITTLE HELP FROM MY FRIENDS:

OTHER DRUMMERS WHO PLAYED WITH THE BEATLES

Although several drummers played as part of The Beatles for a day or more, there were others who drummed for one or more of them outside of The Quarrymen/Beatles or joined them onstage during their early days in Liverpool and Hamburg. Even though they may have shared the stage with various band members, they cannot be counted as one of the Fourth Beatle drummers.

July 1958 - Drummer Aneurin Thomas and the Men of Harlech

Although not a drummer behind the Fab Three, Thomas played with Paul and George. In the summer of 1958, the two Quarrymen decided to hitchhike to Wales. With their guitars in hand, and not much else, they looked for a town name that they could recognise. Some 85 miles from Liverpool, the pair spotted Harlech, made famous in the Welsh anthem, "Men of Harlech".

They found a local cafe, and listened to the jukebox in the corner. They soon hooked up with a local group called The Vikings, and played with them in the basement of a barbershop. McCartney and Harrison decided to pitch their tent in a field belonging to the family of Vikings member John Brierley and soon started discussing music. They were invited into the farmhouse and, in return for bed and breakfast, they agreed to play with the band. Brierley, drummer Aneurin Thomas and the rest of The Vikings were performing regularly at the Queens Hotel, which was run by Thomas' dad.

The group often played on Saturday nights, so for one evening, Paul and George stepped up and performed with John and Aneurin as a quartet in Harlech.

Aneurin Thomas remembers those days well. "As for the visits by Paul and George to Harlech where my parents ran a hotel," he said, "they remain indelible in my memory. Who would have thought! The Beatles? Whilst I have no photographs with Paul and George, the odd one of The Vikings survived, but roaming the globe does not seem to encourage the keeping of memorabilia from those days. Then again, that was a different marriage as well! I continued to play drums at different postings till I came to Dubai where being self-employed has been an excuse to work, work, work, but I carry a pair of brushes with me and very often accompany on a restaurant table!"

Thomas is now in his 70s and a resident of Dubai, where he has lived for nearly 40 years. He still has fond memories of those days with his fellow Vikings, as well as Paul and George, recalling "John Brierley, whose bungalow was our rendezvous, Polly the horse that Paul and I attempted to steal for an innocent ride, and so much more." *(David Bedford Interview 2015)*

February 1959 - The Les Stewart Quartet: Drummer Ray Skinner

With The Quarrymen running out of bookings, and just John, Paul and George as members, the group effectively disbanded. George, desperate to play music, joined The Les Stewart Quartet, who were playing regularly at Lowlands in West Derby.

The group consisted of Les Stewart on guitar and vocals, George and Ken Brown on guitars and Ray Skinner on drums. When George and Ken quit that band after an argument over opening the Casbah Club, George contacted John and Paul and

STORYVILLE
JAZZ CLUB
(Old " Iron Door " Premises)
13, TEMPLE STREET,
LIVERPOOL, 2.

Introducing on 17th January, 1962—

WEDNESDAY AFTERNOON SESSIONS
(Dancing 12-30 p.m. - 4 p.m.)
with

RORY STORM and the WILD ONE

plus GUEST ARTISTES.

ADMISSION FREE TO MEMBERS
(First two weeks only)

New Members Welcome (over 18 year

Coffee, Snacks, etc. available. - Luncheon Vouchers accept

ITS FREE AND TOO GOOD TO MISS ! !
SEE YOU THERE ON WEDNESD

'Swinging Lunch Time Rock Sessions'
AT THE
LIVERPOOL JAZZ SOCIETY,
13, TEMPLE STREET (off Dale Street and Victoria Street),
EVERY LUNCH TIME, 12-00 to 2-30
RESIDENT BANDS:
Gerry and the Pacemakers,
Rory Storm and the Wild Ones,
The Big Three.

Next Wednesday Afternoon, March 15th
12-00 to 5-00 Special
STARRING—
The Beatles,
Gerry and the Pacemakers
Rory Storm and the Wild Ones.

Admission—Members 1/-, Visitors 1/6

" Rocking at the L. J. S. "

The Victor Printing Co 230. West Derby Road. Liverpool. 6

re-formed The Quarrymen, with Ken Brown making up the numbers.

4th October 1960
Maching Schau: Drummers Pete Best and Jeff Wallington

With new drummer Pete Best in tow, The Beatles arrived in Hamburg and, on 18th August 1960, began playing at The Indra Club, just off the Reeperbahn. After their set had finished, they would head over to the Kaiserkeller to watch Derry and the Seniors, the first Merseybeat group to head to Hamburg. "The Beatles would always come over to see us," said Howie Casey of The Seniors, "and they would get up on stage with us and we'd jam, so they became recognised in the club." It was here that Jeff Wallington, drummer with the Seniors, played with The Beatles/ Seniors collective on stage. *(David Bedford Interview 2013)*

15th March 1961 and Other Probable Dates
The Wild Ones: Drummer Ringo Starr

Promoter Sam Leach ran regular shows at the Iron Door and the Cassanova Club in Liverpool, where he would book Rory Storm and the Hurricanes and The Beatles. Some of the Hurricanes still had jobs, so Rory Storm created a band called "The Wild Ones", comprised of whatever musicians were available at the time. Leach remembered it well: "There was a great one at the Cassanova Club in Dale Street, where they appeared at an afternoon session one Sunday – the launch of the club. The Beatles were playing regularly at The Cavern and Ray McFall, The Cavern's owner, told The Beatles they couldn't play at the Cassanova. I had promoted the concert but I was in a dilemma. Suddenly, The Beatles turned up.

"Apparently, someone had let off stink bombs in The Cavern," Leach recalled with a mischievous smile, "and they had to shut it down for the afternoon. So they turned up and played for me. The Beatles were threatened with being banned from The Cavern. What would have happened then? The Beatles never officially appeared again at the Cassanova, but billed as Rory Storm and The Wild Ones, John, Paul and George would come along and play. Whoever was free at the time got up on stage."

There was therefore on 15th March 1961 some combination of Rory Storm, Lou Walters, Johnny Guitar, Ty Brian and Ringo Starr appearing on stage with John, Paul and George as "The Wild Ones", though the exact combination of musicians is not recorded.

It is also reasonable to assume that various members of The Beatles played with The Wild Ones on other dates as a known handbill promoting the March 15th gig calls The Wild Ones a "resident band" of the Liverpool Jazz Society (Iron Door). This would mean that The Wild Ones played there regularly, and likely alongside a Beatle or two.

This unlikely grouping provided yet another opportunity for John, Paul and George to play a show with Ringo Starr.

19th October 1961 -
The Beatmakers: Drummers Pete Best and Freddie Marsden

One of the greatest ever Merseybeat lineups appeared on stage on 19th October 1961 when The Beatles and Gerry and the Pacemakers joined forces with popular singer Karl Terry at Litherland Town Hall. George was on lead guitar, Paul played rhythm, and the drumming duties were split between Pete Best and Freddie Marsden. Les Chadwick played bass guitar and John Lennon manned the piano, with Karl Terry joining in on vocals. Finally, Gerry Marsden played guitar and sang, while Les Maguire played the saxophone.

5th April 1962 - Beatles "Pinwheel" Twist:
Drummers Pete Best, Paul McCartney and Dave Lovelady

When The Beatles performed their composition, "Pinwheel Twist", they decided to swap instruments with their friends. Pete Best emerged from behind his drums and took to the dance floor, dancing with his girlfriend Kathy – the future Mrs. Best. Paul McCartney replaced Pete on drums, as he liked to do. They also decided to invite members of The Four Jays onto the stage.

Billy Hatton from The Four Jays, later The Fourmost, remembered it well: "This was one of the most fulfilling nights we had at The Cavern. We were chuffed about it; it was The Beatles Fan Club Night and the only bands were The Beatles and The Four Jays. Freda Kelly had asked who they wanted and they settled for us. I remember doing 'Mama Don't Allow' with The Beatles. Paul was on piano, John stayed on guitar, I played guitar, we had two drummers with Pete and Dave Lovelady, and Brian O'Hara brought out an old violin. George Harrison found an old trumpet and he was blowing that. It sounds good but it was ten minutes worth of crap." *(Spencer Leigh The Cavern)*

If you can't beat it, join them.

NOT THE FOURTH BEATLE

THOSE WHO CLAIMED TO HAVE DRUMMED WITH THE BEATLES, BUT DIDN'T

Two drummers claim to have played with The Beatles, but there is no evidence to support their story.

Bernard Purdie

One of the most outrageous claims of drumming with The Beatles has been made by Bernard Purdie.

As one of the leading jazz, pop and rock drummers of the twentieth century, Purdie has played with Aretha Franklin, B.B. King, Steely Dan, Miles Davis, the Rolling Stones, Dizzy Gillespie, Hall & Oates, James Brown, Paul Simon, Cat Stevens, Ray Charles, Jeff Beck and, so he claims, The Beatles. He is one of the most recorded and respected drummers in the world.

But what about The Beatles?

He not only claims to have drummed with them, but on no less than 21 Beatles tracks, either as an overdub, or as a substitute for Ringo. Max Weinberg, the legendary drummer with Bruce Springsteen's E Street Band, wrote a book called *The Big Beat* and interviewed Purdie. However, when he asked Purdie to name the tracks he played on, he refused to disclose the information.

Here's the strange exchange between the two drummers:

Weinberg: "You played on Beatles' tracks?"

Purdie: "Twenty-one of them."

Weinberg: "Do you remember which ones?"

Purdie: "Ummhmm."

Weinberg: "Which ones?"

Purdie: "That's information I don't disclose."

Weinberg: "Why won't you name the tracks?"

Purdie: "Because if I need that information to get me some money, then I'll have what's necessary. I also played on songs by The Animals, The Monkees."

Weinberg: "Everyone knows The Monkees were a fabricated band, but The Beatles?"

Purdie: "Ringo never played on anything."

Weinberg: "Ringo never played on anything?"

Purdie: "Not the early Beatles stuff."

So Purdie claims that Ringo never played on any of The Beatles' early recordings, and that he was brought in during the summer of 1963 to record with Capitol on the U.S. releases.

Purdie went into more detail in 1978 when interviewed by Gig magazine. "I had never heard of The Beatles," he said, "but their manager, Brian Epstein, called me and took me down to Capitol's 46th Street studio in New York.

I overdubbed the drumming on 21 tracks of the first three Beatle albums."

He didn't remember the exact tracks except for the one he called 'Yeah Yeah Yeah', an obvious reference to "She Loves You".

"I got paid in five figures," Purdie said, "and that was the largest amount of money I'd ever gotten in my life. I thought they were paying me all that money because they liked what I played. Then Epstein told me I was being paid to keep my mouth shut."

Although Purdie claimed that he signed a contract, he would only confirm that it was in "the check that I signed – and I cashed it! On the back of the check, it was spelled out what I did ... 'payment for services rendered'. It took up half the check. But I didn't think about making a photocopy. It didn't mean anything to me." Such a shame the evidence has gone.

Purdie said he worked on finished tapes only, and not with the group. By his account, since the early Beatles albums had already been released in England, the original English versions would feature Ringo while the American LPs would feature Purdie on some tracks, Ringo on others, and both of them on the rest. Yet Purdie can't – or won't – identify them.

"They had four track recorders," he continued, "and they put me on two separate tracks. I would listen to what Ringo had played and then overdub on top of it to keep it happening."

He also recalled that "the only people in the studio were me, the engineer, and Brian Epstein and a few of his people." Purdie also suggested that George Martin was unaware of what he did. George Martin always denied using another drummer, and no one at Capitol Records has ever commented on it.

Purdie says it was all down to Brian. "The manager did everything", he recalled. "Epstein instigated everything that had to be done. He was the one who told me to keep my mouth closed. He was the one."

Is there any evidence to support his claim?

Purdie published his memoirs, *Let The Drums Speak*, in October 2014. His Beatles 'experiences' are chronicled in the chapter "The Ringo Starr Controversy", but as expected, nothing is resolved. The topic becomes only more ambiguous, with no clarification of his role or the sessions.

Was his alleged work done on the Ringo Starr or Pete Best recordings?

The possibility exists that when the Hamburg recordings with Tony Sheridan were re-released in 1964, Purdie was working as a session drummer for Atco Records. The label had secured the rights to four of The Beatles' Hamburg recordings, but to achieve a more commercial sound for the American market, certain overdubs were required on "Ain't She Sweet", "Take Out Some Insurance On Me, Baby" and "Sweet Georgia Brown". Purdie claims to have added the drums heard on these U.S.-only mixes. This would make sense considering that the drumming on the early recordings with Pete Best lacked power and depth after Bert Kaempfert asked Pete to use only his snare drum. Purdie's claim, therefore, is plausible. A session guitarist, Cornell Dupree, was the likely guitarist who also contributed some overdubs.

This is the only time that Purdie would likely have drummed on any Beatles recordings, but again, we can't be certain, and he has failed to provide proof.

Hans Olof Gottfridsson wrote the booklet for the *The Beatles with Tony Sheridan: First Recordings - 50th Anniversary Time Life CD release* – and his essay goes some distance to clarify the controversy.

According to Gottfridsson, "Atco decided that the recordings they'd licensed needed to be enhanced. Session musicians were hired to overdub drums and guitar on 'Sweet Georgia Brown' and 'Take Out Some Insurance On Me, Baby'. On 'Ain't She Sweet', they only added drums. In the editing room, 'goddamn' was edited out of 'Take Out Some Insurance On Me, Baby', and 'Nobody's Child' was shortened by almost one minute. All this was done sometime in mid-January 1964 at the Atlantic Recording Studio in New York."

Purdie has apparently had death threats from irate fans and has hidden himself behind the "anonymity" of being a session drummer, saying less in his book than he had in interviews.

Purdie Drummed on Sgt. Pepper

His only twist of fate? When the 1978 film *Sgt. Pepper's Lonely Hearts Club Band* was released, fronted by the Bee Gees and Peter Frampton, the drummer in the band was no less than Bernard Purdie. In that instance, the evidence is abundant!

David Rowe

David Rowe claimed that he 'stood in' for Pete Best for a few weeks whilst the band awaited the arrival of Ringo Starr. The cracks in the story are already obvious.

Rowe was dating 18-year-old Linda Smith in 1962, and she asked him to get The Beatles' autographs. David, who played drums with Johnny Kidd and the Pirates, was able to obtain their signatures whilst having breakfast with the band at the Seaman's Mission, which was famous for English breakfasts.

The autographs clearly show the signatures of John, Paul, George and Ringo. The Seaman's Mission is most likely the one in Hamburg, where the British ex-pats would gather to get a proper English breakfast. This would place Rowe's encounter with The Beatles in Hamburg. However, the group only played two residencies there in 1962 – in April, four months before Pete was 'sacked', and in December, four months after Ringo had joined them.

Also, his girlfriend Linda says that Rowe told her that he stood in for Pete Best "for a few weeks". As we know, after Pete was dismissed, Johnny Hutchinson sat in with The Beatles for a couple of days until Ringo could join them.

Was he The Beatles' drummer? If you had an 18-year-old girlfriend and wanted to impress her, this would make a good story. But nothing about it makes sense, and there is no evidence to support any part of a story that only came to light when the autographs were put up for sale in 2014.

DRUM ROLL PLEASE!

WE FOUND THE FOURTH BEATLE!

What began as a book about the twenty three Beatles drummers has evolved into a re-examination of some of the critical points in Beatles history.

Despite countless books on The Beatles, from Hunter Davies' official biography, to The Beatles' *Anthology* and *Tune In*, we felt that there was a need to look again at those key events and test every account, every eyewitness testimony, and search for the evidence that would reveal the truth.

We found twenty three drummers and a few others who accompanied the Fab Three along the way. But, more importantly, our research revealed that most crisis points in The Beatles' storied career revolved around their search for the right drummer. As The Quarrymen, Colin Hanton was the perfect fit for playing skiffle music with his friends. After he quit in the summer of 1958, the group was without a drummer until May 1960. When John, Paul and George decided it was time to become a rock 'n' roll group, Allan Williams found their drummer in Tommy Moore.

As if to show what chaos there was in 1960, they played with nine different drummers, many of them just the once, though one of those was Ringo in October 1960. Although Moore was their first drummer, he arrived late for their first performance at the Larry Parnes audition. Johnny Hutchinson sat in with them until Tommy turned up. After their Scottish tour, during which they backed Johnny Gentle, Moore was so fed up with John Lennon that he quit the group. Despite the band's desperate pleas, he refused to play with them again.

They played with several drummers, including Ronnie "the Ted", and one 16-year-old, Jackie Lomax, who wasn't a trained drummer - who later recorded with Apple - until Norman Chapman came along. He appeared to be just the guy to fill the spot permanently – at least before he was called up to the army and another crisis ensued. Stability was found with Pete Best, and they headed off to Hamburg for a baptism of fire in the clubs in St. Pauli. It was here that The Beatles learned their stage craft, creativity and endurance, redefining rock 'n' roll as we knew it. They took Liverpool and Hamburg by storm, and were at their best in those days, according to John Lennon.

In June 1961, now a four-piece group with Paul taking over on bass from Stu Sutcliffe, they recorded for Bert Kaempfert, backing Tony Sheridan. Although The Beatles never liked the recordings, it was their first record – and the one which brought them to the attention of the man who changed everything, Brian Epstein. Brian always tried to do his best, even refusing to sign the first management contract so that his "boys" could walk away if he ever failed them. He didn't. He secured an audition at Decca, which The Beatles thought went well. But the record company would make up an excuse to get rid of Brian, and turned them down. Looking back with some perspective from our panel of drummers and record producer Steve Levine, it is clear that Brian and The Beatles made mistakes – lessons not altogether learned by the time they were invited to audition for George Martin.

As we have demonstrated, at their first visit to EMI Studios in June 1962, they were given an artist test which the group barely passed, though at the price of losing their drummer, Pete Best.

Although they didn't have to get rid of him, they felt they had no option as he stood between them and their holy grail: a record deal. Within days of receiving the contract, Brian began asking drummers to join The Beatles as Pete's replacement. Bobby Graham, Ritchie Galvin and Johnny Hutchinson all turned him down. Others were considered, too.

However, when John, Paul and George took Ringo Starr to meet with Brian Epstein on 11th August 1962, Brian offered Ringo the drummer spot, which was confirmed on the Tuesday. The following day, Pete was brought into Brian's office and, as the evidence reveals, Brian convinced Pete that he was being fired, even though he had no authority to do so.

Pete took it that he had been sacked and, through Brian's friend Joe Flannery, accepted the drummer's seat in Lee Curtis and the All-Stars. Ringo joined The Beatles. The old Beatles were dead; the Fab Four was born, and they had finally found the Fourth Beatle. But even Ringo's first session at EMI turned into a personal nightmare as he was promptly replaced by drummer Andy White on "Love Me Do" and "P.S. I Love You". However, Ringo soon adapted to studio life and became an integral part of the group that would dominate popular music and, in the process, define the '60s and change history.

Still, one final crisis loomed.

When Ringo collapsed on the eve of their first world tour, Brian and the boys turned to Jimmie Nicol as their drummer's last-minute replacement in the biggest show on earth. Two weeks later, Nicol went from hero to zero as Ringo rejoined his mates and continued to be The Beatles' drummer. Although other drummers appeared on record, Ringo was always the Fourth Beatle.

Elizabeth Reigns

For Ringo, 2017 ended with the news that he was to receive a knighthood from Her Majesty the Queen for services to music and charity, in spite of his song "Elizabeth Reigns" poking fun at the monarchy, with his final words being "there goes the Knighthood!" Thankfully, for Ringo, or Sir Richard Starkey, the Queen doesn't bear a grudge.

Sir Paul McCartney was quoted as saying; "Huge congrats Sir Ringo!
Sir Richard Starkey has a nice ring to it. Best drummer, best pal! X Paul."

Yoko also congratulated Ringo; "Dear Sir Ringo, I am very happy that you have received this honour from the Queen. It's about time! Huge congratulations!

I am delighted for you and your family. It is an honour for everyone in The Beatles family and I love you very much.
love, hugs and kisses,
Yoko x"

Ringo was naturally delighted.

"It's great! It's an honour and a pleasure to be considered and acknowledged for my music and my charity work, both of which I love.
Peace and love."

The Beatles' path was never a smooth one,
and the search for the right drummer,
the Fourth Beatle,
was one of the most difficult roads they travelled
in their long and winding story.

And that story deserves the drum roll
of all drum rolls!

BIBLIOGRAPHY/ SOURCE

Author
Book Title
Publisher

Badman, Keith
The Beatles: Off The Record
Omnibus Press

Cain and McCusker
Ringo Starr and the Beatles Beat
Matador

Baker, Glenn A
The Beatles Down Under: The 1964 Australia and New Zealand Tour
Glebe: Wild and Woolley

Cepican, Bob
Yesterday Came Suddenly
Arbor House

Barrow, Tony
John, Paul, George, Ringo and Me
Andre Deutsch Ltd

Davies, Hunter
The Beatles, The Authorised Biography
W. W. Norton & Co

Beatles, The
The Beatles Anthology
Chronicle Books

Davies, Hunter
The Quarrymen
Omnibus Press

Bedford, David
Liddypool: Birthplace of The Beatles
Dalton Watson Fine Books

Drew, Paul
John Lennon interview
U.S Radio Broadcast (station not known)

Bedford, David
The Fab One Hundred and Four
Dalton Watson Fine Books

Emerick, Geoff
Here, There and Everywhere: My Life Recording the Music of The Beatles
Non Basic Stock Line

Bedford, David
Allan Williams Interview with David Bedford
David Bedford

Epstein, Brian
Cellarful of Noise
New English Library Ltd

Bedford, David
Pete Best Interview with David Bedford
David Bedford

GBF Popper
Mersey Beat Groups and Artists list
GBF/Popper Collection

Berkenstadt, Jim
The Beatle Who Vanished
Createspace

GBF Popper
Post war clubs and venues
GBF/Popper Collection

Best and Doncaster
Beatle! The Pete Best Story
Plexus Publishing Ltd

GBF Popper
Pre WW1 Music halls list
GBF/Popper Collection

Best, Peter
Best Years of The Beatles
Headline

Gentle, Johnny
Johnny Gentle and The Beatles
Merseyrock Publications

Brown, Peter
The Love You Make
Penguin Classics/ Press

Gottfridsson, Hans Olaf
From The Cavern to Star Club
Premium Forlag AB

Harrison, George
I Me Mine
Genesis Publications

Leigh, Spencer
The Beatles in Hamburg
Omnibus Press

Harry, Bill
Mersey Beat
Harry, Bill

Leigh, Spencer
The Best of Fellas
Drivegreen Ltd

Hertsgaard, Mark
A Day in the Life: The Music and Artistry of The Beatles
Macmillan

Leigh, Spencer
The Cavern: The Most Famous Club in the World
SAF Publishing Ltd

Hogan, Anthony
From A Storm to a Hurricane
Amberley Publishing

Leng, Simon
While My Guitar Gently Weeps: The Music of George Harrison
Hal Leonard Corporation

Howlett, Kevin
Beatles at The BBC
BBC Books

Lewisohn, Mark
Beatles Live!
Harper Collins

Howlett, Kevin
The Beatles at the Beeb 62-65
BBC Books

Lewisohn, Mark
The Beatles: All These Years: Vol 1. Tune In
Little, Brown Group

Hutchins, Chris
Elvis Meets The Beatles
Neville Ness house

Lewisohn, Mark
The Complete Beatles Chronicles
Bounty Books

Kane, Larry
When They Were Boys
Running Press Adult

Lewisohn, Mark
The Complete Beatles Recording Sessions
Hamlyn

Kehew and Ryan
Recording The Beatles
Curvebender Publishing

Liverpool Reference Library
WW2 Statistics
GBF/Popper

Krasker, Eric
The Beatles: Fact and Fiction
Seguier

Martin, George with Jeremy Hornsby
All You Need Is Ears
St Martin's Griffin

Leigh, Spencer
Drummed Out: The Sacking of Pete Best
Northdown Publishing

Miles,Barry
Paul McCartney. Many Years From Now
Vintage

Leigh, Spencer
Howie Casey Interview with Spencer Leigh
Spencer Leigh

O'Mahoney, Sean
Beatles Appreciation Society Magazine
Beat Publications

Leigh, Spencer
Let's Go Down to The Cavern
Royal Life Insurance

O'Mahoney, Sean
The Beatles Book Monthly
Beat Publications

Pawlowski, Gareth
How They Became The Beatles
Penguin Books Ltd

Pritchard, David and Alan Lysaght
The Beatles. An Aural History. Part One
Amazon

Pritchard, David and Alan Lysaght
The Beatles. An Oral history
Stoddart Publishing, Ontario, Canada

Purdie, Bernard
Let The Drums Speak
Pretty Media LLC

Robustelli, Anthony
I Want To Tell You
Shady Bear Productions

Sheff, David
All We Are Saying
St Martin's Griffin

Shepherd, Billy
The True Story of The Beatles
Beat Books

Spitz, Bob
The Beatles: The Biography
Back Bay Books

Starr, Ringo
Photograph
Genesis Publications

Swearingen, Mark
The Beatles "Speaking Words of Wisdom"
Createspace

Teutsch, Austin
Sh-Boom Magazine
Dawson and Flynt

Thompson, Gordon
Please Please Me: Sixties British Pop Inside Out
Oxford University Press

Unterberger, Richie
The Unreleased Beatles
Backbeat UK

Various
The Beatles: 10 Years That Shook The World
Mojo Magazine

Vermeer, Evert
Beatles Unlimited
Beatles Unlimited

Weber, Erin Torkelson
The Beatles and the Historians: An Analysis of Writings About the Fab Four
McFarland & Co

Weinberg, Max
The Big Beat
Contemporary Books, Inc

Williams, Allan and William Marshall
The Man Who Gave The Beatles Away
Coronet Books

Womack, Ken
Beatles Encyclopedia: Everything Fab Four
Greenwood

IMAGE ACKNOWLEDGEMENTS

Where possible, we have endeavoured to track down the copyright owner of every photograph used in this book. However, the proliferation of Beatles images across thousands of websites on the internet, makes it almost impossible to determine who the owners are. If you are the owner of a photograph used in this book, and can prove ownership, we will be happy to credit you in future editions.

NAME	PAGE(S)
Astridge, Gary	9, 18, 261
Atherton, Mave	48
Bedford, David	8, 15, 16, 18, 40, 58, 70, 76, 103, 107, 113, 158, 163, 171, 176, 238, 244, 255, 278, 293
Cain, Alex	18
Cordeiro, Ray	289
Davis, Rod	41
Goldrein, Eric	126
Gunderson, Chuck	68
Harris, David	206
Hinton, Derek	18
Hutchinson, John	63
Jorgensen, Erik	286
Kelly, Phil	18
Kozera, Mitch	18
Leach, Sam	128
Longobardi, Lou	18
Naboshek, Mark	142, 316
Nash, Pete	56, 137, 299, 301, 302
Nugent, Geoff	72
Opone, Ann-Marie	76, 79
Orsted, Knud	281, 284
Popper, Garry	22, 23, 34
Rex Features	116, 118, 120, 122, 127, 139, 153, 163, 179, 181, 195, 205, 208, 215, 231, 242, 258, 260, 265, 277, 297, 308, 312, 314
Rice, Mike	18
Roberts, Charles	47
Roberts, David	200
Roland, Cheniston	53, 64
Roosenbrand, Hans	285, 286, 287
Shanahan, Rob	18
Skellett, Paul	7, 12, 19, 25, 35, 43, 50, 52, 74, 84, 92, 93, 96, 98, 102, 104, 108, 110, 112, 114, 130, 159, 166, 168, 184, 190
Smith, Norman	273
Taylor, Kingsize 'Ted'	66
Unknown	14, 80, 89,95, 100, 106, 134, 145, 151, 163, 183, 200, 226, 229, 246, 270
Williams, Allan	75, 87

FINDING THE FOURTH BEATLE - CD2

CD2

TRACK		ARTIST	DRUMMER
1. Memphis Tennessee	(BBC March 1962)	The Beatles	Pete Best
2. Dream Baby	(BBC March 1962)	The Beatles	Pete Best
3. Please Mr. Postman	(BBC March 1962)	The Beatles	Pete Best
4. Besame Mucho	(EMI June 1962)	The Beatles	Pete Best
5. Love Me Do	(EMI June 1962)	The Beatles	Pete Best
6. Ask Me Why	(BBC June 1962)	The Beatles	Pete Best
7. Besame Mucho	(BBC June 1962)	The Beatles	Pete Best
8. A Picture of You	(BBC June 1962)	The Beatles	Pete Best
9. Boys		The Pete Best Combo	Pete Best
10. A Picture Of You		Joe Brown and the Bruvvers	Bobby Graham
11. What'd I Say		The Big Three	Johnny Hutchinson
12. How Do You Do It	(EMI 4th September 1962)	The Beatles	Ringo Starr
13. Love Me Do	(EMI 4th September 1962)	The Beatles	Ringo Starr
14. Love Me Do	(EMI 11th September 1962)	The Beatles	Andy White
15. P.S. I Love You	(EMI 11th September 1962)	The Beatles	Andy White
16. Please Please Me	(EMI 11th September 1962)	The Beatles	Andy White
17. I Wanna Hold Your Hand		The Beatles	Jimmie Nicol
18. Twenty Flight Rock		Colin Hicks and his Cabin Boys	Jimmie Nicol
19. Love Me Do		Top Six	Jimmie Nicol
20. Back In The USSR		The Beatles	Paul McCartney